THE NEW
NAME
DICTIONARY

DATE DUE	
DEC 05 2002	
1-13-05 ILL	
12/10/13 ILL	

ALSO BY ALFRED J. KOLATCH

The Complete Dictionary of English and Hebrew First Names
The Concise Family Seder
The Family Seder
The Jewish Book of Why
Jewish Information Quiz Book
The Jonathan David Dictionary of First Names
The Name Dictionary
Our Religion: The Torah
The Second Jewish Book of Why
These Are the Names
This Is the Torah
Today's Best Baby Names
Who's Who in the Talmud

THE NEW
NAME
DICTIONARY

Modern English and
Hebrew Names

by
ALFRED J. KOLATCH

Jonathan David Publishers, Inc.
Middle Village, NY 11379

THE NEW NAME DICTIONARY:
Modern English and Hebrew Names

Jonathan David Publishers, Inc.
68-22 Eliot Avenue
Middle Village, New York 11379

4 6 8 9 7 5

Library of Congress Cataloging in Publication Data

Kolatch, Alfred J., 1916-
  The new name dictionary.

  Rev. and expanded ed. of: The name dictionary. 1967.
  Includes indexes.
  1. Names, Personal—Jewish.   2. Names, Personal—
English.   I. Kolatch, Alfred J., 1916-   Name
dictionary.   II. Title.
CS3010.K65   1989   929.4'089924   88-25826
ISBN 0-8246-0331-1
ISBN 0-8246-0376-1 paperback

Printed in the United States of America

Table of Contents

For
HELEN
and
ARTHUR

Preface

My interest in the subject of Hebrew and English names
grew out of a practical need to assign Hebrew names to the
children of our congregational school in Columbia, South Carolina. The vast majority of the children did not know the Hebrew names that had been given them at birth, and in many
cases their parents were unable to recall them as well.

I decided to follow a naming system that had been used
over the centuries in Jewish communities throughout the
world. This system involved choosing for each child a Hebrew
name that would correspond in meaning to his or her English
name. I found that the system worked very well, and my
research in the area led to the 1948 publication of my first
book, *These Are the Names*.

Over the years, my study of Hebrew and English names
and the linking of the two according to meaning continued,
and in 1967 I issued *The Name Dictionary: Modern English
and Hebrew Names*, an enlarged edition of the earlier work.

The current volume, *The New Name Dictionary*, is a totally
revised and expanded version of *The Name Dictionary*. Not
only have a great many English and Hebrew names been
added, but the system of transliteration has been changed.
All Hebrew names are transliterated in accordance with the
Sephardic (rather than the Ashkenazic) pronunciation, which
is now employed in Israel and in much of the Diaspora. In
addition, in order to facilitate usage, where an English name
is derived directly from a Hebrew root or source, the Hebrew
name associated with it is spelled out in Hebrew characters
immediately after the English entry.

A word should be said about how the Hebrew names in
this volume were assembled. The process began more than
forty-five years ago when, in 1942, I conducted the first of
three surveys. Questionnaires were mailed to the heads of for-
ty-nine Hebrew schools in thirteen states. The other two surveys were conducted in 1943 and 1945. The purpose was to
determine which Hebrew and English names were most commonly used by Jewish children and what type of correlation
existed between the two. From the 15,000 names that were

submitted, it was quickly evident that a minimal relationship in meaning existed between the Hebrew and English names given to children. (The details of these surveys may be found in the appendices to *The Name Dictionary*.)

In 1966, at my request, Hagai Lev, a member of the Institute of Contemporary Jewry at the Hebrew University in Jerusalem, combed through various lists of Hebrew names (totalling 100,000) and extracted from them several thousand preferred names, many of which have been incorporated into this work. His primary source was the Registry of Births in Israel, which is under the supervision of the Ministry of the Interior. Also consulted were lists of public school and high school students.

In 1983, Elinor Slater, of French Hill, Jerusalem, agreed to search out new and uncommon Hebrew names that had come into being during the previous twenty years. Her findings have also been used in preparing this volume.

In 1985, telephone books from all parts of Israel were scanned for first names, and a rich harvest of new names was uncovered in these sources.

Two other sources were used extensively in the preparation of this work. The first is a pamphlet issued by the Academy of the Hebrew Language in Israel, which proposes names for newborn children. The second is the list of masculine and feminine names included in Abraham ibn Shoshan's *Ha-milon He-Chadash*, undoubtedly the most useful Hebrew dictionary ever published.

The New Name Dictionary presents the more popular names in use today. Those particularly interested in names found in the Bible and Talmud should consult my *Complete Dictionary of English and Hebrew First Names*, published in 1984. This volume not only lists biblical and talmudic names, but also cites specific sources and identifies or characterizes the individuals whose names are listed.

In the back of this book the reader will find an exhaustive appendix of Hebrew names, written in Hebrew characters, which includes a great many names that do not appear in the body of the work. A second appendix contains a list of the most popular Yiddish names, transliterated into English. Also appended is a comprehensive listing of transliterated unisex Hebrew names. The Index contains all Hebrew names (transliterated) that appear in the body of this work.

ALFRED J. KOLATCH

January 1989
Wassaic, New York

GENERAL INTRODUCTION

I

Where Our Names Come From

Old Testament Names

The earliest personal names on record are found in the Bible. Many are still in use in their original form. For the most part, biblical names (which were often based on life experiences of the individual) are easy to understand because their roots are easily traced, usually to the Hebrew; in fact, many are explained in the Bible itself.

The Hebrew root of the name Cain, for example, is *kano*, meaning "to acquire, to buy." Genesis 4:1 explains: "And she [Eve] conceived and bore Cain, and said, 'I have *acquired* a man [Cain] with the help of the Lord.' "

Abraham and Sarah named their son Isaac. Abraham was 100 years old at the time, and when Sarah was told she was to bear a child, she said, "Everyone who hears about it will *laugh*." The Hebrew root of the name Isaac, *tzachok*, means "laughter."

Scores of such examples can be found in the pages of the Bible. Names sometimes describe a physical attribute (Korach, meaning "bald," or Charim, meaning "flat-nosed"), an inspiring or unusual experience (Moshe was so named because he was "drawn out of the water"), resemblance to or reminders of animal features or characteristics (Yona, meaning "dove," or Devora, meaning "bee") or affection or affinity to plants or flowers (Tamar, meaning "palm tree," or Tzemach, meaning "plant"). The Bible also contains many God-centered names (such as Yonatan, meaning "gift of God," or Yoel, meaning "God is willing") and names that express hope for a bright future or better conditions (Yosef, meaning "may God increase").

Christian Names

Christians of the first centuries used Old Testament Hebrew names. In time, however, these were abandoned by many New Testament figures as a form of protest against Judaism. Thus, the man once known as Simon bar Jonah came to be called Peter, and Saul of Tarsus became known as Paul.

During those early centuries many Christian parents followed the pattern of choosing names associated with mythology and idolatry, even though they abhorred both. Phoebe, Olympius, and Jovianus were commonly used. The seventh-century Bishop of Seville was outraged by the use of these names. In his *Etymologia* he wrote of the significance of biblical names, urging Christians to use them, but to no avail.

The Reformation

Not until the Reformation, in the 1500s, when as a rebellion against the Catholic Church and its authority Protestantism came into being, did biblical names—particularly Old Testament names—again become popular. In seventeenth-century Puritan England, where the Reformation turned into a crusade against all Church dogma and ceremonials, New Testament names in particular were renounced in favor of Old Testament names.

Many Puritan extremists, even those living as late as the eighteenth and nineteenth centuries, went so far as to use the most obscure and odd-sounding names they could find; they even took phrases from Scripture and used them—in their entirety—as names. Ernest Weekley, in his book *Jack and Jill*, reports that at the beginning of the twentieth century there was a family with the names Asenath Zaphnath Paaneah, Kezia Jemima Keren Happukh, and Maher Shalal Hashbaz. The average Puritan, however, was satisfied with Old Testament names as well as those derived from abstract virtues, such as Perseverance, Faith, Hope, Humility, Charity, and Repentance. A pair of twin girls born to the English Wycliffe family in 1710 were named Favour and Fortune.

Opposition to New Testament Names

The Quakers (Society of Friends), like the Puritans, preferred Old Testament names and despised the nomenclature of the New Testament, probably as part of their protest against the Church of England, with which they broke in 1648. The Quakers disapproved of the elaborate ceremonies of the established Church.

The life of John Bunyan (1628-1688), author of *Pilgrim's*

Progress, epitomizes the conflict between the Quakers and Puritans and their opponents. In his early years, Bunyan was an antagonist of the Quakers. For this reason he named his children Mary, John, Thomas, and Elizabeth—all but the last being New Testament names. By the time of Bunyan's second marriage his philosophy had changed. No longer an opponent of the Quakers, he had become intensely opposed to the established Church and its bishops. His children by his second wife were named Joseph and Sara, after Old Testament figures.

Current Use of Biblical Names

Although biblical names have fallen in and out of favor in the course of history, over the last two generations they have proven to be among the most popular names in use, irrespective of religion or race. In a study of 10,000 personal names appearing in the birth columns of *The New York Times* between 1943 and 1946 (as reported in the author's earlier book, *The Name Dictionary*), of the ten most popular masculine names six were biblical or of biblical origin—two (Michael and David) from the Jewish Bible and four (Stephen, Peter, Steven, Mark) from the Christian Bible. Among the female names, five of the ten most popular were biblical or of biblical origin: Jane, Ann, Joan, Nancy, Judith (Jane, Joan, and Nancy are variant forms of Ann). The 1948 New York City birth records reveal a striking similarity: among the ten most popular masculine names in that year were John, James, Michael, Joseph, Thomas, Stephen, and David—three Old Testament names and four New Testament names. The ten most popular feminine names included two names of biblical origin: Mary and Nancy.

Studies of the 1980 and 1981 birth rolls of New York City, Detroit (with a large black population), and the State of Pennsylvania reveal an amazing consistency in the selection of biblical names by parents.

The 1981 list of New York City births shows seven biblical names (Michael, David, Jason, Joseph, John, Daniel, James) to be among the ten most popular male names, and five biblical names (Jessica, Michelle, Elizabeth, Lisa, Danielle) to be among the ten most popular female names.

The Detroit 1981 birth records show five biblical names (Michael, Jason, James, David, Joseph) among the ten most popular male names, and three biblical names (Jessica, Sarah, Andrea) among the ten most popular female names.

The 1980 report from Pennsylvania includes seven biblical names (Michael, Jason, Matthew, David, John, James, Joseph) among the ten most popular male names of that year, and two biblical names (Jessica and Sarah) among the ten most popular feminine names, with the next four names on the list (Rebecca, Stephanie, Elizabeth, Lisa) also biblical or of biblical derivation.

The 1987 New York City birth records reveal that masculine biblical names continue to be popular. The ten most popular male names were Michael, Christopher, Jonathan, Daniel, David, Anthony, Joseph, Matthew, John, and Andrew. Of these, only Christopher, Anthony, and Andrew are not biblical. With regard to feminine names, of the ten most popular—Jessica, Jennifer, Stephanie, Melissa, Christine, Nicole, Amanda, Ashley, Tiffany, Samantha—only one name, Jessica, is of biblical origin.

Names from Places

Many first names, like surnames, have been borrowed from the names of places. The Bible, of course, has many such examples.

Efrat is the place where Rachel died and was buried; Efrata is the name of Caleb's wife in the Book of Chronicles. Ofra, the name of a city in the Book of Joshua, is also a masculine first name. Ur, a place-name in the Book of Genesis, is a masculine first name that appears in the Book of Chronicles.

In more recent times, Myrna Loy, the actress, was named after the whistle-stop Myrna, a name her father found intriguing. Portland Hoffa, the radio comedienne and wife of Fred Allen, was named after Portland, Oregon. Florida Edwards is the name of a radio actress. Actress Tallulah Bankhead was named after her grandmother, who in turn was named after Tallulah Falls, Georgia. Philadelphia Levy was the daughter of a Philadelphia family prominent at the end of the eighteenth century.

Calendar and Holiday Names

Among the Christian holidays, Easter and Christmas have long served as sources for forenames. Pentecostes was the name of a servant of Henry VIII. Easter is commonly used and can be found as a character in Lillian Smith's novel *Strange Fruit*, and Christ and Christmas are the backbone of names such as Chris, Christopher, Christina, Christine, Natalie, Noel, and Noelle.

Among Jews, too, many names now in use are derived from the calendar and holidays. In fact, the Hebrew term for holiday, *yom tov*, is sometimes used as a personal name. In the

Middle Ages, it was common to call boys who were circum-cised on Purim by the name Mordechai, in honor of the hero of the holiday. Those born on Tisha B'Av were often named Menachem, meaning "comforter," because the ninth (*tisha*) day of the month Av is a fast day commemorating the destruction of the Temple in Jerusalem, and in the Prophetic portion (Isaiah 40) read in the synagogue on the Sabbath following that fast day the Prophet *comforts* Israel. Among the Jews of Eastern Europe, a son born on Chanukah was usually called by the name of the holiday.

Particularly among Sephardic Jews, children born on Yom Kippur were often called Rachamim ("mercy") and those born on Passover were sometimes named Pesach. Shabbat and Shabetai were popular Sephardic names for boys born on the Sabbath. One rabbi, the father of twelve sons, is reported to have named each son after a different Hebrew month.

Among the general population in America and elsewhere, names associated with holidays as well as names of the days of the week and the months of the year are used: Noel, Tuesday, April, May, June, and so on.

Numeral Names

Numbers are another source for names that were used a great deal in the past and are used in some rare instances today. The Romans were the first to take numeral names. Among the more common are Quintus (5), Octavius (8), and Septimus (7). Among Tripolitan Jews in North Africa, Hmessa and Hammus, meaning "five," are used as feminine and masculine personal names respectively. Recently a Michigan family with the surname Stickaway named their three boys One, Two, and Three; and their three girls, First, Second, and Third.

One of the rare present-day examples of a number being used as a personal name made its appearance recently in the case of a young rabbi who, having difficulty finding a satis-factory Hebrew name for his first daughter, decided to name her Rishona (first).

It is interesting to note that the Puritans, and especially the Quakers, refrained from using the names of months and substituted numbers in their place. They believed that since most months had names of pagan origin, it would be best to avoid using them as personal names. For this reason we find, as we study some of the official records and tombstone engravings of the seventeenth century, that months are referred to by number rather than name—January referred to as 1, February as 2, and so on.

Occupational Names

Many occupational names have become first names, although the vast majority have come down to us as last names. Most fall into the category of the name Wright, which is an Old English name meaning "artisan, worker." It is used occasionally as a first name (e.g., Wright Morris, author), but for the most part it has remained a surname (e.g., the brothers Wright, Orville and Wilbur).

Middle English names were often occupational names. Bannister, meaning "one who draws a crossbow," and Brewster, meaning "one who brews beer," are used from time to time. Newly created names are rarely based on occupation.

Celebrity Names

Many names in use today have been adopted because they are the names of celebrities. In this category we include not only contemporary celebrities in the fields of entertainment, sports, music, and politics, but also the great figures of history, political as well as religious, whose charisma was so great that parents named children after them.

Alexander the Great entered Palestine in 333 B.C.E., and according to legend all Jewish boys born in that year were named Alexander in his honor. Although we do not have records indicating how popular that name became among the masses in the years immediately following Alexander's visit, we do know that one Jewish king (Alexander Janneus) and one queen (Salome Alexandra) did use the name. A bit later, in talmudic times, we find the name being used by the scholar Rabbi Alexandri (Yoma 53b).

Over the years many Jewish boys have been named Theodor Herzl, after the founder of modern Zionism, and more recently the names of Israel's popular prime ministers (Ben-Gurion and Golda) have been used. Inspired by the Israel-Egypt Peace Treaty, signed in Washington, D.C., in March 1979, Mr. and Mrs. Hotam El Kabassi named their triplets born on April 5, 1979, Carter, Begin, and Sadat—in honor of U.S. President Jimmy Carter, Israeli Prime Minister Menachem Begin, and Egyptian President Anwar Sadat, the three principals at the signing.

The custom of naming children after celebrities, however, has never been particularly popular among Jews. In fact, in scanning the Bible one finds that the names of heroes mentioned early in the Bible are not used again by anyone later in the biblical narrative. No one but the original Abraham, Sarah, Isaac, Rebecca, Jacob, Rachel, Leah, Joseph, Moses, Aaron, Miriam, Isaiah, and Jeremiah carry those names. The reason for this strange circumstance has not been explained. Nor has it been explained why at least a few of the Rabbis of the Talmud were not named after some of the most revered personalities in the Bible. Not one scholar in the Talmud is named Abraham, Israel, or David. Some of the names of Jacob's sons are used, but Dan, Gad, and Asher are not among them. Of the Prophets, Isaiah, Hosea, Joel, Amos, Obadiah, Micah, Habakkuk, Zephaniah, and Malachi are not used in the Talmud at all.

It is indeed difficult to explain why many Rabbis of the Talmud are named Ishmael, but not one is named Abraham and only one is named Moses. Attempts have been made to explain the use of the name Ishmael, but they are not satisfying. Rabbi Jose (Genesis Rabba 71:3) finds some justification in the explanation that Ishmael is an example of a person whose "name was beautiful but whose actions were ugly." The commentary (Tosafot) on Berachot 7b justifies the use of the name by observing that Ishmael, Abraham's son by his concubine Hagar, was a sinner who repented, and it was, therefore, quite proper to use his name.

Name Changes

Since early Bible times it has been customary to modify somewhat an individual's name, or change it entirely, when a change in the status of the individual was anticipated or had been achieved. Among the more prominent examples: Abraham (from Abram), Sarah (from Sarai), Jacob (to Israel), Joshua (from Hosea), Gideon (to Jerubaal), Zedekiah (from Mattaniah), and Jehoiakim (from Eliakim).

Though name-changing is no longer common, there is an old Jewish custom of changing a person's name in time of serious illness, which persists in certain circles. It is hoped that the change of name will cause the angel of death to question whether the person he is about to visit (who has a different name than expected) is the correct target. Sometimes, if the patient is young, the name Alter ("old one" in Yiddish) or Alterke (for a female) is added to or substituted for the original name. The thought is that the angel of death would be confused if, when he is assigned to take action against, say, Alter or Chayim Alter, and he finally finds him, the person turns out to be young rather than old as his name implies.

Masculine/Feminine Interchanges

Many names in contemporary usage have been "borrowed" from the opposite sex, sometimes without modification but more often with a slight change. The practice of interchang-

ing names between the sexes is an old one. The Bible contains
many examples of names common to both sexes. In II Kings
8:26 Athaliah is the daughter of Ahab and Jezebel, while in
I Chronicles 8:26 Athaliah is used as a masculine name. Efah,
the concubine of Caleb, is also used as a masculine name.
Shlomit appears in both a masculine and feminine form, as
do Tzivya, Bilga, Chuba, Noga, Chupa, Gover, Buna, Bina,
Aviya, Ofra, Rina, Chavila, and Simcha. (See Appendix I for
a listing of 188 unisex names.)

A number of outstanding contemporary male personalities
have been given names that are characteristically feminine:
polar explorer Richard Evelyn Byrd, noted author Evelyn
Waugh, Congressman Clare Hoffman of Michigan, among
others.

Among women's names we find a large number adopted
from the masculine forms. In many instances, the feminine
name is so long established and accepted that we no longer
realize that it had its origin in a masculine name. In this
group we find Alexandra and Alexandria from Alexander;
Charlotte and Charlene from Charles; Davi, Davida, and
Davita from David; Erica from Eric; Frederica from Frederic;
Georgia, Georgine, and Georgette from George; Harriet and
Harri from Harry; Henrietta, Henri, and Henria from Henry;
Herma and Hermine from Herman; Josepha and Josephine
from Joseph; Louise and Louisa from Louis; Roberta from
Robert; Stephanie from Stephan; and Willa and Willene from
Will or William.

Unconventional Spellings

For the past two or three decades many new first names
have come into being as a result of a desire on the part of
parents to be different or distinctive. They have increasingly
been taking popular names and spelling them differently.

The most common characteristic of this new fad is substi-
tuting a "y" for an "i" or adding an "e". Fannye was once
Fannie, and Mollye was formerly Mollie. Likewise, Sadie has
become Sadye, and Edith has become Edyth or Edythe. Shirley has become Shirlee, Shirlie, or Sherle. Similarly, the letter
"i" has been substituted for "y" and new spellings like Tobi,
Toni, and Ricki have become common.

Sometimes letters are dropped or added to old names to form
new ones. Consequently, names like Sarah and Hannah have
become Sara and Hanna. Esther can now be found as Ester
and sometimes as Esta or Estee.

Among the many feminine names that have, because of
a new spelling, made their appearance of late are Rosalin,

Rosaline, Rosalyn, Roselyn, Roslyn, Roslyne, and Rosylin from Rosalind; Debra and Dobra from Deborah; Karolyn and Carolyn from Caroline; Alyce and Alyse from Alice; Gale from Gail; Arlyne from Arline; Arleyne from Arlene; Lilyan from Lillian; Elane and Elayne from Elaine; Ilene and Iline from Eileen; Ethyl and Ethyle from Ethel; Janis from Janice; Jayne from Jane; Madeline, Madelon, Madelyn, Madelyne, and Madlyn from Madeleine; Marilin and Marylin from Marilyn; and Vyvyan and Vivien from Vivian.

Changes in spelling also account for a large number of new masculine names: Allan, Alyn, Allyn, and Allen from Alan; Frederic, Fredric, and Fredrick from Frederick; Irwin, Erwin, Irving, and Irvine from Irvin; Isidore, Isador, and Isadore from Isidor; Laurance, Laurence, Lawrance, and Lorence from Lawrence; Maury, Morey, and Morry from Morris; Murry from Murray; and Mervyn from Mervin.

Pet Forms (Diminutives)

Pet forms, often called diminutives, make up a large portion of our contemporary first names. This group grows larger and larger as the desire for self expression grows stronger. Often, the given first name of an individual is completely abandoned and the pet name becomes the real name. James Earl Carter, the thirty-ninth president of the United States, is a prime example. Although his original and legal name is James, Jimmy is the name he prefers and the name he used when signing official documents.

II

The Naming Process

Hebrew and Secular Names

Throughout most of Jewish history, Jews have used both secular, non-Jewish names and Hebrew names. In the Talmud (Gittin 11b) it is noted that "the majority of Jews in the Diaspora have Gentile names." This observation can be applied to every period in Jewish history, from the Babylonian Exile (586 B.C.E.) onward. Daniel (of lions' den fame) and his friends had Hebrew and Aramaic (Babylonian) names. Daniel's Aramaic name was Beltshatzar. His friends, popularly known as Shadrach, Meshach, and Abed-nego, were known also by their Hebrew names—Chananya, Mishael, and Azarya. (Biblical names ending in "a" or "ah" are generally Aramaic: Ezra, Nehemiah, etc.)

In the fourth century, with Alexander the Great's conquest of Palestine, Jews came into closer contact with Greek (Hellenistic) culture. As a result they soon began using Greek names. This practice spread, and some of the greatest among the Sages of the early talmudic period, as well as some of the most revered leaders of the Jewish people in the early centuries B.C.E., carried Greek names such as Antigonus, Avtalyon, Jason, Onias, and Alexander. Some used both a Hebrew and a Greek name; thus someone with the name Netanel or Yonatan would choose Dositheus or Theodotian as his Greek name, based on a similarity of meaning. In the same manner, Tobiah (Tuviya) also became known as Agathou, Uri as Phoebus, and Tzadok as Justus.

The practice of Jews using both Hebrew and secular names grew in popularity with the passage of time. Among Italian Jews in early times we find Diofatto used for Asael, and Tranquillo and Tranquillus for Manoach and Menachem. Among French Jews we find a great leader of the thirteenth century, Rabbi Yechiel of Paris, also known as Vivant. Frenchmen with the Hebrew name Matityahu also were known as Dieudonne, Chaim as Vive, Ovadya as Serfdieu, and Gamliel as Dieulecresse.

xviii

Jews living in the Arab world used Arabic names along with their Hebrew names. Thus, Abraham also was called Ibrahim, David was also known as Daoud, Eliezer as Mansur, Matzliach as Maimun.

Girls in Syria were often given an Arabic first name and no Hebrew name at all. In recent years, however, Syrians have added a Hebrew name to the Arabic, usually selecting a Hebrew name that corresponds in meaning to the Arabic name. Thus, a girl named Diamela, meaning "beautiful" in Arabic, was named Diamela-Yafa, Yafa meaning "beautiful" in Hebrew.

(The Jews of India, known as Bene Israel, modified their Hebrew names so they would have a Hindi sound. Thus, Benjamin became Benmanjee, Abraham became Abrajee, David became Dawoodjee, and Jacob became Akkoobjee.)

The practice of giving a child both a Hebrew (or Yiddish) and a secular name continues to this day. More often than not, the only association between the Hebrew and secular name is a similarity in sound, and the similarity is most often confined to the first letter or syllable.

Names to Be Avoided

Although there are no strict religious rules dictating which names may or may not be used, there are Jewish traditions suggesting the wisdom behind avoiding certain names. The Sages (Midrash Genesis Rabba 49:1) suggest, for example, that one avoid using the names of wicked people—including Pharaoh, Sisera, and Sennacherib. This practice seems to have been observed over the centuries.

Rabbi Chayim Azulai, an eighteenth-century scholar, author of an encyclopedia containing the biographies of 1,300 scholars and writers, suggested that Jews avoid using all names that appear in the Bible before the time of Abraham. He considered it improper to name a child after Adam or Noah or Shem or Ever—people who preceded Abraham. Azulai also condemned anyone who would select the name Yafet (Japheth), a name already belonging to the father of third-century Palestinian scholar Benjamin ben Yafet (Berachot 33a).

A noted contemporary of Azulai, Elazar Fleckeles, disagreed, asserting that it was quite proper to use pre-Abrahamitic names. Fleckeles calls attention to the talmudic scholars Benjamin ben Yafet and Akavya ben Mehalalel (both Yafet and Mehalalel are pre-Abrahamitic biblical names).

The cautions of Rabbi Azulai have been largely ignored, and for the past two centuries many illustrious persons have carried pre-Abrahamitic names.

Naming Children After Relatives

Ashkenazic Jews—the Jews of Germany, France, Russia, England, etc., and their descendants—adhere closely to an old Jewish belief that a man's name is the essence of his being; the name is his soul. When a child is given a relative's name, he is also being given the relative's soul. If the relative is still alive, the soul would have to be shared by two people—the older living relative and his namesake. For that reason, Ashkenazic Jews discourage naming a newborn after a living relative, for it might result in the shortening of the older person's life. While Ashkenazim refrain from naming their offspring after living relatives, they generally do name them after deceased relatives.

In the twelfth century, the noted mystic Judah ben Samuel of Regensburg (popularly known as Rabbi Yehuda Hechasid, meaning "Judah the Pious One") introduced a practice which forbade a man from marrying a woman with exactly the same name as his mother. Rabbi Yehuda was fearful that this might lead to the embarrassing situation of a man's mother answering when he is actually addressing his wife. This concern aside, Ashkenazic Jews in particular consider such marriages ill-advised, because if a man were to marry a woman with the same first name as that of his mother, and his mother were to die, the man would not be able to honor his deceased mother by naming a future daughter after her (because his wife—still living—carries that same name).

Generally, Yehuda Hechasid disapproved of naming any child after a living relative; but he also disapproved of naming a child after a deceased relative, out of fear that the soul of the deceased might be disturbed. In his will, the rabbi instructed that none of his descendants be called by his name or the name of his father, Samuel.

Sephardic Jews—from Spain, Portugal, Italy, North Africa, and the Middle East—do not share the Ashkenazic belief that a person's life will be shortened if a newborn is named after him. Sephardim therefore do not hesitate to name their offspring after living grandparents, and occasionally, though infrequently, even after themselves.

There is a longstanding tradition justifying the Sephardic practice. As far back as the fourth century B.C.E., at the height of Greek influence in Palestine, Jews used the names of living relatives. In the family of the High Priests, the names Onias and Simon were used alternately, between 332 and 165 B.C.E. In the early talmudic period (beginning with the first century B.C.E.), Hillel the Great's family repeated the names Gamaliel and Judah for several generations, with occasional use of the names Simon and Hillel.

The practice continued through the Middle Ages, and many examples can be cited. Generally, the eldest son in a family was named after the paternal (and sometimes maternal) grandfather. The grandson of the eminent eleventh- and twelfth-century philosopher and poet Yehuda Halevi was also named Yehuda (during the poet's lifetime). In the family of the twelfth-century philosopher Moses Maimonides, we find that the name of Maimonides' grandfather was Yosef son of Isaac, son of Yosef, son of Ovadya, son of Shlomo, son of Ovadya. And the same pattern of naming after living relatives can be seen in the family of the thirteenth-century Italian talmudist Rabbi Isaiah ben Elijah de Trani, whose maternal grandfather's name was Isaiah, and in the family of thirteenth-century Spanish-born Moses ben Nachman (Nachmanides), whose grandson had the same name as his maternal grandfather, Jonah (Girondi).

In most Sephardic communities today, the generally accepted rule is to name the first son in a family after the paternal grandfather, living or dead. (The Spanish-Portuguese Jews of Holland do not name a child after a living relative.) The second male child is named after the maternal grandfather. The first female child in a family is named after the paternal grandmother and the second after the maternal grandmother.

Naming Children After Non-Relatives

The Talmud cites instances where, for a variety of reasons, children were named after persons—living or dead—not within their own family. In one case (Shabbat 134a), the second-century scholar Nathan of Babylonia (Natan HaBavli), a contemporary of Judah the Prince, advised a mother who had lost two sons as a result of the circumcision procedure not to circumcise her third son. She followed the scholar's advice and her son survived. In gratitude she named him Nathan, meaning "He [God] gave [life]." In another case (Bava Metzia 84b), Rabbi Eliezer ben Hyrcanus, a first-century C.E. scholar and disciple of Yochanan ben Zakai, was considered so helpful by several women in answering their questions that the women later named their children after him.

As mentioned above, the idea of naming a child after a celebrated person did not take root in Jewish tradition. Aside from Chasidim who have occasionally named children after a deceased *rebbe* whom they adore, and Jews who have named their offspring after personal heroes (such as Herzl, Balfour, Ben-Gurion, Golda), the practice has never been widespread. Quite likely, the reason for this hesitancy is linked to the belief that a man's name is his person, that a man's name is his soul. Jews who may have wanted to name a child after a celebrity did not do so out of fear that the soul of that person would be acquired along with his name, that is, that it would occupy the body of the infant. This would place a very grave responsibility on the child, who would have to measure up to the life of the great soul now occupying his body.

When and Where Is a Boy Named?

Although there is a tradition that girls and boys are to be named in the synagogue on the first Sabbath after their birth, today it is established custom to name a boy at his *brit* (circumcision), which is held on the eighth day after birth. However, neither the Bible nor the Talmud mentions this fact. In the few instances in the Bible where the circumcision rite is mentioned (Genesis 17:24 for Abraham; Genesis 17:25 for Ishmael; Genesis 21:4 for Isaac; and Exodus 4:25, where Tzipora, wife of Moses, circumcises her son), no mention is made of naming the child. What appears to be the rule is that children in the Bible were named at the time of birth, not later: all of Jacob's sons were named at the time of birth (Genesis 29 and 30); Tzipora named her son Gershom at the time of birth (Exodus 2:22); Samson was named immediately after birth (Judges 13:4).

Only in the New Testament do we find references to people being named at the time of their circumcision. In Luke 1:59 Zacharias and Elizabeth have a son who is named John at the time of his circumcision, and in 2:21 Jesus is named at the time of his circumcision.

There are at least two references in talmudic literature that describe what transpires at a circumcision ceremony. In the Midrash (Ruth Rabba 6:6), a detailed description is given of the proceedings at the *brit* of Elisha ben Avuya. All segments of the population of Jerusalem—rich and poor—are invited. A banquet is prepared and much merrymaking ensues after the ceremony. Some stay on for hours and sing and dance and play games, while the more learned gather in a separate room to discuss Tora. But no mention is made of the naming of the child at the ceremony.

Similarly, another celebration of this kind was held about 100 years later in Sepphoris, a city in northern Palestine. Here again the Midrash (Kohelet Rabba 3:4) describes all the merriment that ensues, but no mention is made of naming the baby.

Scholars are of the opinion that the actual practice of naming a child formally at the *brit* began some time in the middle of the twelfth century, but no information is available to explain why the practice began precisely at that time. By the sixteenth century, the practice was commonplace, as indicated in the *Shulchan Aruch*. The *brit* being the first major religious event in the life of a male child, it is quite understandable that his naming should take place at that time.

When and Where Is a Girl Named?

Among Ashkenazim and most Sephardim a girl is named in the synagogue on the first Sabbath following birth, when a *minyan*—a quorum of worshippers—is assembled. On that occasion the father is honored with an *aliya* (called to the Tora), after which the baby girl is named. The naming can also take place at the morning service on a Monday, Thursday, or on Rosh Chodesh (New Moon), since the Tora is read on those occasions as well and the new father can therefore be given an *aliya*.

Jews from Morocco and countries such as Turkey, which were once part of the Ottoman Empire, name girls in a home ceremony called Zeved Ha-bat or Zebed Ha-bat ("gift of a daughter"). The ceremony is held as soon as the mother has recovered. If the girl is the mother's firstborn, she is generally named Bechora or Buchuretta, or by the diminutive form, Buzika. (Firstborn boys are named Bechor or Buki, a pet form.)

In naming boys and girls, the name of the newborn is mentioned in the blessing, together with the name of the father. Today, in many instances, the name of the mother is mentioned at the ceremony as well.

Naming an Adopted Child

The Talmud (Sanhedrin 19b) says: "Whoever raises an orphan may be considered to be his parent." From this statement later authorities concluded that if one adopts a child, and the child has not yet been named, he or she may be called by the name of the adoptive father. Thus, for example, a girl is to be called _____ *bat Moshe* (adoptive father's name) and a boy _____ *ben Moshe*. If the child was named before being given up for adoption, the name of the natural father is to be retained.

The Talmud also arrives at this conclusion from the biblical account of King Saul and his daughters Michal and Merav. Merav had several children, who were raised by her younger sister Michal; and the Bible refers to these children as Michal's children even though she was not their real mother. Based on this, it was concluded that it is proper for a child who has been adopted to be called by the name of his adoptive parents. It must be said, however, that in Jewish law the natural parents never lose their rights or status, and a child must mourn for them when they die. The child is also obligated to say *Kaddish* for adoptive parents when they die, because of the strong emotional ties that normally develop between children and those who have cared for them all or most of their lives.

Names for Converts

Although there is no legal requirement mandating that a convert use the name of Abraham or Ruth or Sarah as a first name, there is a longstanding tradition to this effect. In most cases, a male convert is named Avraham ben Avraham Avinu (Abraham the son of Abraham our father), and a female convert is named Sara bat Avraham Avinu (Sarah the daughter of Abraham our father) or Rut bat Avraham Avinu (Ruth daughter of Abraham our father). The use of "ben Avraham" and "bat Avraham" is generally insisted upon for purposes of identifying an individual as a proselyte (*Shulchan Aruch,* Even Haezer 129:20).

Two reasons are offered for naming converts Avraham. First, the Bible (Genesis 17:5) speaks of Abraham as being "the father of a multitude of nations"; and since proselytes come from diverse peoples and backgrounds, it is appropriate that they be called sons of Abraham.

A second explanation is offered in the Midrash: Since the Children of Israel are called God's "friends"—as it is written, "the seed of Abraham My [God's] friend" (Isaiah 41:8)—and since proselytes are called God's "friends"—as it is written, "God is the friend of the proselyte" (Deuteronomy 10:18)— it was concluded that Abraham has a special relationship to proselytes. In Jewish tradition, Abraham became known as "the father of proselytes," because once they have converted to Judaism, they have forsaken all previous family connections, and the family of Abraham becomes their family. The Talmud (Yevamot 22a) calls them "newborn babes."

Offering the convert the name of Abraham is explained by the Midrash to be an expression of deep love. The Midrash says: "God loves proselytes dearly. And we too should show our love for them because they left their father's house, and their people, and the Gentile community and have joined us" (Deuteronomy Rabba 8:2).

It is, of course, a matter of history that not all proselytes have taken the name Abraham. The scholar Onkelos was a proselyte. Flavius Clemens, nephew of the Roman Vespasian, was a proselyte. The Talmud (Berachot 28a) also refers to a proselyte named Judah the Ammonite.

Female converts take the name of Sarah because she was the First Lady of Israel, the wife of Abraham; and they take the name of Ruth because Ruth of the Bible is the epitome of loyalty to Judaism. Ruth is famous for swearing her eternal allegiance to her mother-in-law Naomi, which was expressed in these immortal words (Ruth 1:16):

> Whither thou goest, I will go,
> Where thou lodgest, I will lodge,
> Thy people shall be my people,
> And thy God my God.

Using the Matronymic Form
When Praying for Good Health

As a rule, in Jewish life a person is identified by his or her father's name; he or she is referred to as _____ *ben/bat* _____ (his/her father's name). This, for example, is the form used when writing a person's name in a Jewish marriage contract (*ketuba*) or a Jewish divorce document (*get*). There is, however, one notable exception: when a person is sick and a prayer for recovery is recited, the mother's name (matronymic) is used.

Apparently, the practice of using the matronymic form on this occasion developed quite early and was already in vogue in talmudic times. The fourth-century talmudic scholar Abaye said: "My mother told me that all incantations [prayers for recovery] which are repeated several times must contain the name of the mother . . . " (Shabbat 66b).

The Zohar (on the Bible portion "Lech Lecha") makes a similar point when it says that all appeals to supernatural beings, whether in prayers or on charms, must be made in the name of the mother.

To find biblical justification for the practice, the Sages pointed to the verse, "I am the servant, the son of Thy handmaid, Thou hast loosened my bonds [saved me]" (Psalms 116:16). From this verse the inference is drawn that in an emergency, when one prays to be saved, the matronymic rather than the patronymic form should be used.

Using the Matronymic Form
to Avoid Confusion

There are times when the matronymic form is used to identify a person simply to avoid confusion and misunderstanding. Thus we find, for example, that the talmudic scholar Mari, who was a proselyte, was named Mari ben Rachel (mother's name). His status as a proselyte was immediately known to all.

It is considered important that the individual's status as a Jew be readily known because that status in large part determine his or her legal rights. A proselyte, for example, may not marry a *Kohayn (Shulchan Aruch,* Even Haezer 6:8). Since the status of one named Mari ben Rachel, for example, would be immediately known to all, no one would introduce him to the daughter of a *Kohayn* with an eye towards marriage.

The noted eighteenth-century Polish scholar Ezekiel Landau made the point that when one writes a document of divorce *(get)* for a proselyte, the matronymic rather than the patronymic should be used because many proselytes are generally named _____ *ben Avraham,* and this could conceivably lead to some confusion at a future date (many *born* Jews are also named _____ *ben Avraham).* By using the matronymic form, a misunderstanding might be avoided. In fact, some scholars favor using the matronymic form in the divorce document in cases where, in general, the mother in the family is better known than the father.

In the same way, to avoid error and misunderstanding, the child of a Jewish mother and a non-Jewish father was called by the matronymic (_____*ben* _____ [the mother's first name]). Using the matronymic form at a *Pidyon Haben* (Redemption of the Firstborn), for example, makes it evident that the father is probably not Jewish and that as a non-Jew he should not be called upon to recite the prayers that a Jewish father normally recites.

Using a Grandfather's Name

Rabbi Moses Isserles, in his Notes on the *Shulchan Aruch* (Orach Chayim 139:3), suggests that one should assume his grandfather's name if his father has converted to another religion. When given an *aliya,* it is suggested that the convert's son be called to the Tora by the name of his maternal grandfather. By so doing, the son would be making a clear statement that he disapproves of his father's action. Isserles also indicates that when in the past the son has received many *aliyot* in that community and is well known by his father's name, he should continue to be called as he was in the past (before his father's conversion).

Naming a Child Born Out of Wedlock

If a child is born out of wedlock to a Jewish mother and the father's identity is unknown, the child should be named at the appropriate time and place (at the *brit* for a boy or in the synagogue for a girl), and he or she should be named after the mother—for example, _____ *ben Rachel* or _____ *bat Rachel.* According to Moses Isserles, in his Notes on the *Shulchan Aruch,* Orach Chayim 139:3, such a child (called a *shetuki* in Hebrew), when given an *aliya,* should be called to the Tora by the name of his maternal grandfather in order to avoid embarrassment that might be caused by those wondering why the individual was using his mother's name.

The Naming Ceremony for a Boy

Before commencing the actual circumcision, the *mohel,* who is the surrogate of the father, recites the following blessing in Hebrew: "Blessed art Thou, O Lord our God, King of the universe, Who has hallowed us by Thy commandments and commanded us to circumcise [our sons]". The father then recites: "Blessed art Thou, O Lord our God, King of the universe, Who has hallowed us by Thy commandments and commanded us to enter this child into the Covenant of Abraham our father."

Upon completing the operation, the *mohel* holds up a cup of wine and pronounces the blessing for wine. He then continues with a prayer for the welfare of the child and his parents, which includes the words, "And may he henceforth be known in Israel as _____ son of _____." This prayer, which includes verses from Proverbs 23:25, Ezekiel 16:6, Psalms 105:8-10 and 118:1, and Genesis 21:4, concludes with the words, "This little child named _____, may he grow to be great! Even as he now enters the Covenant [of Abraham], so may he enter the world of Tora study, a life of connubial bliss, and a life in which he will perform good deeds."

The *sandek* ("godfather"), who holds the baby during the circumcision, then drinks some of the wine and a few drops are dabbed on the lips of the infant.

The Naming Ceremony for a Girl

The naming ceremony for a girl is simpler. Among Ashkenazim and most Sephardim, on the Sabbath following the birth of the child, the father visits the synagogue and receives an *aliya* (a Tora honor). After his portion of the Tora is read, the father recites the final Tora blessing. The sexton or rabbi then recites a special prayer for the welfare of the mother, asking for her return to good health now that the delivery is over. This prayer is known as a *Mi Shebayrach,* which are the first two words of the prayer, meaning "May He who blessed." A second *Mi Shebayrach* is then recited, and as part of this prayer the baby is named. The general wording of the prayer is, "May he who blessed our forefathers Abraham, Isaac, and Jacob bless _____ and his daughter just born to him, and she shall henceforth be known in Israel by the name _____ daughter of _____. Guard and protect her father and mother. May they live to rear her to be a God-fearing person, and may they raise her to achieve connubial bliss and a life of meritorious deeds."

In some Reform congregations today, the child is named on the first Sabbath that the mother and child are well enough to visit the synagogue together. A similar custom seems to have been followed in some communities in medieval Germany.

Masculine Names

Masculine Names

Aaron (אַהֲרֹן) The Anglicized form of Aharon. *See* Aharon.

Abahu (אַבָּהוּ) From the Aramaic, meaning "God is my father." The exact Hebrew equivalent is Abahu. FEMININE HEBREW EQUIVALENTS: Avi, Avicha'yil, Aviem, Aviya, Avuya.

Aba'ye (אַבָּיֵי) From the Aramaic, meaning "little father." The exact Hebrew equivalent is Aba'ye. FEMININE HEBREW EQUIVALENTS: Aviela, Aviga'yil, Avishag, Aviya, Imma.

Abba (אַבָּא) From the Aramaic, meaning "father." The exact Hebrew equivalent is Abba. FEMININE HEBREW EQUIVALENTS: Avi, Avia, Avichen, Aviel, Avirama, Imma.

Abbe, Abbey From the Old French and Latin, meaning "the head of a monastery, an abbot." *See* Abbot.

Abbie A variant spelling of Abbey. *See* Abbey. Also, a pet form of Abba.

Abbot, Abbott Greek and Latin forms of the Aramaic Abba. *See* Abba.

Abe A pet form of Abraham. *See* Abraham.

Abel (הֶבֶל) From the Assyrian, meaning "meadow," or from the Hebrew, meaning "breath." The exact Hebrew equivalent is Hevel. FEMININE HEBREW EQUIVALENTS: Carmela, Gana, Nirel, Yardeniya, Zimra.

Abelard From the Anglo-Saxon, meaning "noble, nobly resolute." HEBREW EQUIVALENTS: Achiram, Aminadav, Ish-hod, Yehonadav, Yisrael. FEMININE HEBREW EQUIVALENTS: Nedira, Ne'edara, Sara, Yisr'ela.

Aberlin A Yiddish form of Abraham. *See* Abraham.

Abi A pet form of Abraham. *See* Abraham. Also, see variant spellings of Avi. *See* Avi.

Abida A variant spelling of Avida. *See* Avida.

Abie A short form of Abraham. *See* Abraham.

Abiezer A variant spelling of Aviezer. *See* Aviezer.

Abihu A variant spelling of Avihu. *See* Avihu.

Abimelech A variant spelling of Avimelech. *See* Avimelech.

Abimi A variant spelling of Avimi. *See* Avimi.

Abin A variant spelling of Avin. *See* Avin.

Abina A variant spelling of Avina. *See* Avina.

Abinadab A variant spelling of Avinadav. *See* Avinadav.

Abinoam A variant spelling of Avinoam. *See* Avinoam.

Abir (אַבִּיר) From the Hebrew, meaning "hero, strong." The exact Hebrew equivalent is Abir. The exact feminine Hebrew equivalent is Abira.

1

Abiram A variant spelling of Aviram. *See* Aviram.

Abiri (אֲבִירִי) From the Hebrew, meaning "my hero, gallant one." Used as a masculine and feminine name. The exact Hebrew equivalent is Abiri.

Able A variant spelling of Abel. *See* Abel.

Abner A variant spelling of Avner. *See* Avner.

Abraham The Anglicized spelling of Avraham. *See* Avraham.

Abram A variant spelling of Avram. *See* Avram.

Abrasha A variant form of Avraham. *See* Avraham.

Absalom A variant form of Avshalom. *See* Avshalom.

Adad A variant form of Hadad. *See* Hadad.

Adael (עֲדָאֵל) From the Hebrew, meaning "God is witness" or "adorned by God." The exact Hebrew equivalent is Ada'el. FEMININE HEBREW EQUIVALENTS: Ada, Ada'ya, Adi, Adiella.

Adair From the Celtic, meaning "food near the oak tree." HEBREW EQUIVALENTS: Ela, Oren, Rechov. FEMININE HEBREW EQUIVALENTS: Alona, Ela, Selila.

Adam (אָדָם) From the Hebrew, meaning "earth." Also attributed to a Phoenician and Babylonian origin, meaning "man, mankind." The exact Hebrew equivalent is Adam. The exact feminine Hebrew equivalent is Adama.

Adar (אָדָר) From the Babylonian *daru,* meaning "darkened," or from the Hebrew, meaning "noble, exalted." The exact Hebrew equivalent is Adar. The exact feminine equivalent is Adara.

Adelbert A variant form of the Old High German, meaning "noble" and "bright," hence "illustrious person." HEBREW EQUIVALENTS: Avihud, Avner, Nadav, Shimshon, Uri, Yisrael, Zerach. FEMININE HEBREW EQUIVALENTS: Behira, Me'ira, Nediva, Ora, Yisr'ela.

Aden A variant spelling of Adin. *See* Adin.

Adi, Addi, Addie (עֲדִי) From the Hebrew, meaning "my adornment" or "my witness." Used also as a feminine form. The exact Hebrew equivalent is Adi.

Adiel (עֲדִיאֵל) From the Hebrew, meaning "adorned by God" or "God is my witness." The exact Hebrew equivalent is Adiel. The exact feminine Hebrew equivalent is Adiela.

Adif (עָדִיף) From the Hebrew, meaning "excellent." The exact Hebrew equivalent is Adif. The exact feminine Hebrew equivalent is Adifa.

Adin (עָדִין) From the Hebrew, meaning "beautiful, pleasant, gentle." The exact Hebrew equivalent is Adin. The exact feminine Hebrew equivalent is Adina.

Adir (אַדִיר) From the Hebrew meaning "lord, noble, majestic." The exact Hebrew equivalent is Adir. The exact feminine equivalent is Adira.

Adiv (אָדִיב) From the Hebrew and Arabic, meaning "pleasant, gently-mannered." The exact Hebrew equivalent is Adiv. The exact feminine Hebrew equivalent is Adiva.

Adlai (עֲדְלָי) From the Aramaic, meaning "refuge of God" or "God is witness." Also, from the Arabic, meaning "to act justly." The exact Hebrew equivalent is Adlai. FEMININE HEBREW EQUIVALENTS: Avigdora, Chasya, Chosa, Magena, Shimriya, Ya'akova.

Adler From the German, meaning "eagle." The exact Hebrew equivalent is Nesher. FEMININE HEBREW EQUIVALENTS: A'ya, Da'ya, Efrona, Silit, Tzipora, Tzofit.

Admon (אַדְמוֹן) From the Hebrew *adom*, meaning "red." The exact Hebrew equivalent is Admon. FEMININE HEBREW EQUIVALENTS: Almoga, Odem, Tzachara.

Adna, Adnah (עַדְנָה) From the Aramaic, meaning "good fortune" or "adorned." The exact Hebrew equivalent is Adna. FEMININE HEBREW EQUIVALENTS: Ashera, Asherit, Ashrat, Gadiel, Gadit, Oshrat.

Adni (עַדְנִי) From the Hebrew, meaning "my delight." The exact Hebrew equivalent is Adni. FEMININE HEBREW EQUIVALENTS: Adina, Na'a, Na'ama.

Adolf, Adolfo Variant German forms of Adolph. *See* Adolph.

Adolph From the Old German, meaning "noble wolf" or "noble helper." HEBREW EQUIVALENTS: Elazar, Eliezer, Ezra, Nadav. FEMININE HEBREW EQUIVALENTS: Aleksandra, Milka, Nediva, Ne'edara.

Adolphe The French form of Adolph. *See* Adolph.

Adon (אָדוֹן) From the Hebrew and Phoenician, meaning "lord" or "master." The exact Hebrew equivalent is Adon. FEMININE HEBREW EQUIVALENTS: Adira, Malka, Yisr'ela.

Adoniya (אֲדוֹנִיָּה) From the Hebrew meaning "the Lord is my God." The exact masculine and feminine Hebrew equivalent is Adoniya.

Adoram (אֲדוֹרָם) A short form of Adoniram. From the Hebrew, meaning "God is exalted" or "my master is mighty." The exact Hebrew equivalent is Adoram. FEMININE HEBREW EQUIVALENTS: Ram, Rama, Rami, Ramit, Ramot, Romemiya.

Adrian A short form of the Latin name Hadrian. From the Greek, meaning "rich." Also, from the Latin, meaning "black, dark." HEBREW EQUIVALENTS: Adar, Hotir, Huna, Yishai, Yitro. FEMININE HEBREW EQUIVALENTS: Adara, Ashira, Shechora.

Adriel (אַדְרִיאֵל) From the Hebrew, meaning "God is my majesty." The exact Hebrew equivalent is Adriel. FEMININE HEBREW EQUIVALENTS: Adira, Ge'ona, Ge'onit.

Afek (אָפֵק) From the Hebrew, meaning "horizon" or "water channel." The exact Hebrew equivalent is Afek. The exact feminine Hebrew equivalent is Afeka.

Afik (אָפִיק) A variant form of Afek. The exact Hebrew equivalent is Afik. *See* Afek.

Afra A variant spelling of Ofra. *See* Ofra.

Afri A variant spelling of Ofri. *See* Ofri.

Agel (אָגֵל) From the Hebrew, meaning "I will rejoice." The exact Hebrew equivalent is Agel. FEMININE HEBREW EQUIVALENTS: Aliza, Avigal, Aviga'yil, Gil, Gila, Gilana, Gilit, Giliya.

Agil (אָגִיל) A variant form of Agel. The exact Hebrew equivalent is Agil. *See* Agel.

Agmon (אַגְמוֹן) From the Hebrew, meaning "reed." The exact Hebrew equivalent is Agmon. The feminine Hebrew equivalent is Kaniela.

Agnon A variant form of Ogen. *See* Ogen.

Agron (אַגְרוֹן) From the Hebrew, meaning "correspondence" or "vocabulary." The exact Hebrew equivalent is Agron. The feminine Hebrew equivalent is Soferet.

Agur (אָגוּר) From the Hebrew, meaning "knowledgeable, learned." The exact Hebrew equivalent is Agur. FEMININE HEBREW EQUIVALENTS: Chochma, Da'at, De'a, Tushiya.

Aharon (אַהֲרֹן) From the Hebrew, meaning "teaching" or "singing." Also, from the Hebrew, meaning "shining" or "mountain." Or from the Arabic, meaning "messenger." The exact Hebrew equivalent is Aharon. The exact feminine Hebrew equivalent is Aharona.

Ahava, Ahavah (אַהֲבָה) From the Hebrew, meaning "love." The exact masculine and feminine Hebrew equivalent is Ahava.

Ain From the Scottish, meaning "belonging to one." HEBREW EQUIVALENTS: Achuzat, Ka'yin, Kenam, Lihu, Mikneyahu. FEMININE HEBREW EQUIVALENTS: Achuza, Be'ula, Li, Liat.

Ainsley From the Scottish, meaning "one's own field." HEBREW EQUIVALENTS: Achuzat, Ka'yin, Kenan, Nir, Niram, Nirel, Yanir. FEMININE HEBREW EQUIVALENTS: Achuza, Be'ula, Nir, Nirit.

Akavel A variant form of Akiva. *See* Akiva.

Akavya The Aramaic form of Akiva. *See* Akiva.

Akevy The Hungarian form of Jacob. *See* Jacob.

Akiba A variant spelling of Akiva. *See* Akiva.

Akim A Russian short form of Yehoyakim. *See* Yehoyakim.

Akiva (עֲקִיבָא) A variant form of the Hebrew name Ya'akov (Jacob), meaning "to hold by the heel." The exact Hebrew equivalent is Akiva. FEMININE HEBREW EQUIVALENTS: Efrat, Magena, Ya'akova.

Aksel From the Old German, meaning "small oak tree." HEBREW EQUIVALENTS: Alon, Armon, Ela, Elon. FEMININE HEBREW EQUIVALENTS: Alona, Ela, Elona.

Al A pet name for many first names, including Alan, Albert, Alfred, and Alexander.

Alan Of doubtful origin, but usually taken from the Celtic, meaning "harmony, peace," or from the Gaelic, meaning "fair, handsome." HEBREW EQUIVALENTS: Avshalom, Lavan, Na'aman, Shalom, Shelomo. FEMININE HEBREW EQUIVALENTS: Achino'am, Na'ama, Na'omi, Shifra, Shulamit.

Alard From the Old German, meaning "of noble ancestry." HEBREW EQUIVALENTS: Achinadav, Adon, Chirom, Ish-Hod, Nadiv, Ne'etzal, Yisrael. FEMININE HEBREW EQUIVALENTS: Adina, Adira, Adoniya, Atzila, Sara, Yisr'ela.

Alastair From the Greek, meaning "the avenger." The Hebrew equivalent is Elnakam.

Alban From the Latin, meaning "white." HEBREW EQUIVALENTS: Lavan, Levanon, Livna, Livni. FEMININE HEBREW EQUIVALENTS: Livnat, Levona, Malbina.

Albert A French form of the Old High German Adelbrecht, meaning "noble, nobility." HEBREW EQUIVALENTS: Achinadav, Achiram, Adar, Adir, Adon, Nadiv, Yisrael, Yonadav. FEMININE HEBREW EQUIVALENTS: Adina, Adira, Adoniya, Nediva, Ne'ederet, Sara, Yisr'ela.

Albie A pet form of Albert. *See* Albert.

Albin A variant spelling of Alban. *See* Alban.

Albion A variant form of Alban. *See* Alban.

Albrecht An early German form of Albert. *See* Albert.

Aldan A variant spelling of Alden. *See* Alden.

Alden From the Middle English, meaning "antiquated, aged." HEBREW EQUIVALENTS: Kadmiel, Kedem, Saba, Yashish, Zaken. FEMININE HEBREW EQUIVALENTS: Bilha, Keshisha, Yeshana, Zekena.

Alder From the Old English, meaning "old." Also, from Middle English, meaning "tree [of the birch family]." HEBREW EQUIVALENTS: Alon, Amir, Arzi, Bar-Ilan, Kadmiel, Kedma, Yashish, Zaken. FEMININE HEBREW EQUIVALENTS: Alona, Ariza, Arzit, Bilha, Ela, Livnat, Zekena.

Aldo An Old German and Italian form of Alder. *See* Alder.

Aldon A variant spelling of Alden. *See* Alden.

Aldous A variant spelling of Aldus. *See* Aldus.

Aldred From the Old English name Ealdred, meaning "old, wise counsel." HEBREW EQUIVALENTS: Bina, Buna, De'uel, Ish-Sechel, Navon, Utz, Zaken. FEMININE HEBREW EQUIVALENTS: Berura, Beruriya, Nevona, Tushiya, Zekena.

Aldren Probably a variant form of Alder. *See* Alder.

Aldus A Latinized form of the Old German Aldo. *See* Aldo.

Aldwin From the Old English, meaning "old friend." HEBREW EQUIVALENTS: Amit, Amitai, Amitan, David, Dodi, Kadmiel, Kedem, Zaken, Ze'ira. FEMININE HEBREW EQUIVALENTS: Achava, Amit, Amita, Keshisha, Yeshisha, Zekena.

Alec, Aleck Short forms of Alexander, popular in Scotland. *See* Alexander.

Alef, Aleph (אָלֶף) From the Hebrew, meaning "number one" or "leader." The exact Hebrew equivalent is Alef. The exact feminine Hebrew equivalent is Alufa.

Alemet (עָלְמָת) From the Hebrew, meaning "concealed, hidden." The exact Hebrew equivalent is Alemet. FEMININE HEBREW EQUIVALENTS: Shemura, Tzofnat.

Alex A popular short form of Alexander. *See* Alexander.

Alexander From the Greek name Alexandros, meaning "protector of men." The exact Hebrew equivalent is Aleksander. The exact feminine Hebrew equivalent is Aleksandra.

Alexandri A variant form of Alexander. See Alexander.

Alexis A form of Alexander. See Alexander.

Alf, Alfeo, Alfie Pet forms of Alfred. See Alfred.

Alfonse, Alfonso, Alfonzo Variant spellings of Alphonso. See Alphonso.

Alfred From the Old English, meaning "old, wise counsel." HEBREW EQUIVALENTS: Avin, Bina, Buna, Chachmon, Chachmoni, De'uel, Ish-Sechel, Navon, Utz, Zaken. FEMININE HEBREW EQUIVALENTS: Berura, Beruriya, Ge'onit, Nevona, Tushiya, Zekena.

Alfredo The Spanish form of Alfred. See Alfred.

Alger From the Anglo-Saxon, meaning "noble spearman" or "warrior." HEBREW EQUIVALENTS: Avicha'yil, Ben-Cha'yil, Gad, Gibor, Ish-Cha'yil, Mordechai, Nimrod. FEMININE HEBREW EQUIVALENTS: Amtza, Gavriela, Gavrila, Gibora, Tigra.

Ali From the Arabic, meaning "exalted." HEBREW EQUIVALENTS: Achiram, Atalya, Atlai, Ram, Yigdal, Yoram. FEMININE HEBREW EQUIVALENTS: Ge'ona, Ge'onit, Rama, Roma, Romema, Sara.

Alis A short form of Alistair. See Alistair.

Alistair A variant spelling of Alastair. See Alastair. May also be derived from the Arabic, meaning "bird." HEBREW EQUIVALENTS: Deror, Efron, Gozal, Tzipor, Yarkon, Zamir. FEMININE HEBREW EQUIVALENTS: A'ya, Da'ya, Efrona, Gozala, Tzipora, Yarkona.

Alitz (עָלִיץ) From the Hebrew, meaning "joy." The exact Hebrew equivalent is Alitz. FEMININE HEBREW EQUIVALENTS: Alisa, Aliza, Aviga'yil, Gila, Gilana, Tzahala.

Alix A variant spelling of Alex. See Alex.

Aliz (עָלִיז) From the Hebrew, meaning "joy, joyful." The exact Hebrew equivalent is Aliz. The exact feminine Hebrew equivalent is Aliza.

Allan A variant spelling of Alan. See Alan.

Allard A variant spelling of Alard. See Alard.

Allen A popular variant spelling of Alan. See Alan.

Allison A masculine name derived from Alice, meaning "Alice's son." See Alice (feminine section).

Allistair A variant spelling of Alastair. See Alastair.

Allister A variant form of Alastair. See Alastair.

Allix A variant spelling of Alex. See Alex.

Allon A variant spelling of Alon. See Alon.

Allyn A variant spelling of Alan. See Alan.

Almagor (אַלְמָגוֹר) From the Hebrew, meaning "fearless." The exact Hebrew equivalent is Almagor. FEMININE HEBREW EQUIVALENTS: No'aza, Odeda.

Alman (אַלְמָן) A variant form of Almon. *See* Almon. The exact Hebrew equivalent is Alman.

Almog (אַלְמוֹג) From the Hebrew, meaning "coral," a reddish rock. The exact Hebrew equivalent is Almog. The exact feminine Hebrew equivalent is Almoga.

Almon (אַלְמוֹן) From the Hebrew, meaning, "forsaken" or "widower." The exact Hebrew equivalent is Almon. The exact feminine Hebrew equivalent is Almana.

Alon (אַלוֹן) From the Hebrew, meaning "oak tree." The exact Hebrew equivalent is Alon. The exact feminine Hebrew equivalent is Alona.

Alphonse The French form of Alphonso. *See* Alphonso.

Alphonso From the Old High German, meaning "of noble family." HE-BREW EQUIVALENTS: Achiram, Adoniya, Aminadav, Chirom, Nadav, Yisrael. FEMININE HEBREW EQUIVALENTS: Malka, Nediva, Ne'edara, Yisr'ela.

Alpin From the Latin name Alpes (Alps), meaning "high mountain." HE-BREW EQUIVALENTS: Aharon, Gal, Gali, Haran, Harel, Sinai. FEMININE HEBREW EQUIVALENTS: Aharona, Chermona, Harela, Horiya.

Alroy From the Latin and Old English, meaning "royalty, ruler." HEBREW EQUIVALENTS: Aluf, Avraham, Elrad, Sar, Yamlech, Yisrael. FEMININE HEBREW EQUIVALENTS: Alufa, Malka, Sara, Yisr'ela.

Alsie Probably a form of Alson. *See* Alson.

Alson From the Anglo-Saxon, meaning "noble stone" or "son of Al." HE-BREW EQUIVALENTS: Achitzur, Elitzur, Tzur, Tzuriel, Tzuriya. FEMININE HEBREW EQUIVALENTS: Avna, Avniela, Ritzpa, Silit, Tzurit, Tzuriya. *See also* Al.

Alta From the Latin and Spanish, meaning "tall, high." HEBREW EQUIVA-LENTS: Aharon, Alyan, Aram, Ramya, Romem. FEMININE HEBREW EQUIVA-LENTS: Aharona, Alya, Givat, Rama, Romemit, Romit, Siona.

Alter From the Old English and the Old High German, meaning "old one." Popular as a Yiddish name. The exact Yiddish form is Alter. HE-BREW EQUIVALENTS: Kadmiel, Yiftach, Kedem, Kedma, Yashish, Sava, Zaken. FEMININE HEBREW EQUIVALENTS: Bilha, Yeshana, Yeshisha, Zekena.

Altie A pet form of Alta or Alastair. *See* Alta *and* Alastair.

Alto A variant form of Alta. *See* Alta.

Alton From the Old English, meaning "old town." HEBREW EQUIVALENTS: Chetzron, Kadmiel, Kedem, Ma'on, Zevulun. FEMININE HEBREW EQUIVA-LENTS: Lina, Me'ona, Tira, Yeshisha, Zevula.

Altus A variant form of Alta. *See* Alta.

Aluf, Aluph (אַלוּף) From the Hebrew, meaning "master, prince, leader." The exact Hebrew equivalent is Aluf. The exact feminine Hebrew equivalent is Alufa.

Alva From the Latin, meaning "white, bright." HEBREW EQUIVALENTS: Lavan, Livni, Me'ir, Zerach, Ziv, Zivan. FEMININE HEBREW EQUIVALENTS: Behira, Me'ira, Levana, Levona, Tzahara.

Alvan From the Old English, meaning "beloved friend." HEBREW EQUIVA-
LENTS: Ahuv, Ahuv-Am, Ahuvya, Chaviv, Chaviv-Am, David, Yakir. FE-
MININE HEBREW EQUIVALENTS: Ahava, Ahuva, Ahuvya, Chaviva, Davida.

Alvin A variant form of Alvan. *See* Alvan.

Alvis From the Old Norse, meaning "wise." HEBREW EQUIVALENTS: Avida,
Bina, Chacham, Chachmon, Haskel, Navon. FEMININE HEBREW EQUIVA-
LENTS: Chanuka, Nevona, Tushiya.

Alwin, Alwyn From the Old English, meaning "old, noble friend." HE-
BREW EQUIVALENTS: Amitai, Amitan, Eldad, Elidad, Raya, Yadid, Yedid,
Yisrael. FEMININE HEBREW EQUIVALENTS: Achava, Amit, Rut, Sara, Yedi-
da, Yisr'ela.

Alyn A variant spelling of Alan. *See* Alan.

Amadore From the Greek and Italian, meaning "gift of love." HEBREW
EQUIVALENTS: Achiman, Ahud, Ahuv, Amizavad, Avishai, Doron, Matan,
Matityahu, Netanel, Netanya, Teruma. FEMININE HEBREW EQUIVALENTS:
Ahada, Ahava, Ahavat, Chiba, Dorona, Matana, Netanela, Zevuda.

Amal (עָמָל) From the Hebrew, meaning "work, toil." The exact masculine and feminine Hebrew equivalent is Amal.

Amali (עֲמָלִי) A variant form of Amal. From the Hebrew, meaning "my
work, my toil." *See* Amal.

Amand A French form of the Latin name Amandus, meaning "worthy of
love." HEBREW EQUIVALENTS: Ahuv, Ahud, Ahuvya, Bildad, David,
Eldad, Ohad, Ohev, Yadid, Yedidya. FEMININE HEBREW EQUIVALENTS:
Ahava, Ahuva, Chaviva, Davida, Doda, Dodi.

Amania A variant spelling of Amanya. *See* Amanya.

Amanya (אֲמַנְיָה) From the Hebrew, meaning "loyal to the Lord." The
exact masculine and feminine Hebrew equivalent is Amanya.

Ambler From the Old French, meaning "one who walks leisurely." HE-
BREW EQUIVALENTS: Darkon, Divon, Shuach. FEMININE HEBREW EQUIVA-
LENTS: Nacha, Nachat, Yanocha.

Ambrose From the Greek, meaning "divine" or "immortal." HEBREW
EQUIVALENTS: Amiad, Aviad, Chiel, Netzach, Perida, Peruda. FEMININE
HEBREW EQUIVALENTS: Cha'yuta, Chi'yuta, Nitzcha, Nitzchiya, Nitz-
chona.

Amel (עָמֵל) A variant form of Amal. *See* Amal. The exact Hebrew equivalent is Amel.

Amery A variant spelling of Emory. *See* Emory.

Ami (עַמִי) From the Hebrew, meaning "my people." The exact Hebrew
equivalent is Ami. FEMININE HEBREW EQUIVALENTS: Amiya, Bat-Ami,
Le'uma, Uma.

Amiaz (עֲמִיעַז) From the Hebrew, meaning "my nation is mighty." The
exact Hebrew equivalent is Amiaz. FEMININE HEBREW EQUIVALENTS:
Amiya, Amtza, Ariel, Gavrila, Gibora.

Amichai (עֲמִיחַי) From the Hebrew, meaning "my nation lives." The
exact Hebrew equivalent is Amichai. FEMININE HEBREW EQUIVALENTS:
Cha'ya, Cha'yuta, Le'uma, Uma, Yechiela.

Amidan (עֲמִידָן) From the Hebrew, meaning "my people [nation] is just, righteous." The exact Hebrew equivalent is Amidan. FEMININE HEBREW EQUIVALENTS: Amior, Amita, Chasida, Dana, Danit, Kedosha, Tamar.

Amidar (עֲמִידָר) From the Hebrew, meaning "my nation is alive." The exact Hebrew equivalent is Amidar. *See* Amichai for additional equivalents.

Amidor (עֲמִידוֹר) From the Hebrew, meaning "my generation of people." The exact Hebrew equivalent is Amidor. FEMININE HEBREW EQUIVALENTS: Dor, Dorit, Dorya, Le'uma, Uma.

Amidror (עֲמִידְרוֹר) From the Hebrew, meaning "my nation is free." The exact Hebrew equivalent is Amidror. FEMININE HEBREW EQUIVALENTS: Derora, Derorit, Deroriya, Li-Deror, Sera, Serach.

Amiel (עֲמִיאֵל) From the Hebrew, meaning "God of my people." The exact Hebrew equivalent is Amiel. FEMININE HEBREW EQUIVALENTS: Amior, Bat-Ami, Le'uma, Uma.

Amihud (עֲמִיהוּד) From the Hebrew, meaning "my nation is glorious." The exact Hebrew equivalent is Amihud. FEMININE HEBREW EQUIVALENTS: Amieta, Amiora, Amya.

Amin (אָמִין) From the Hebrew, meaning "trustworthy." The exact Hebrew equivalent is Amin. The exact feminine Hebrew equivalent is Amina.

Amior (עֲמִיאוֹר) From the Hebrew, meaning "my nation is a light, a beacon." The exact masculine and feminine Hebrew equivalent is Amior.

Amir (עָמִיר/אָמִיר) From the Hebrew, meaning "mighty, strong." Also, from the Hebrew, meaning "sheaf of corn" (when spelled with an *a'yin*). The exact Hebrew equivalent is Amir. The exact feminine Hebrew equivalent is Amira. *See also* Amira (*feminine section*).

Amiram (עֲמִירָם) From the Hebrew, meaning "my nation is mighty" or "my nation is exalted." The exact Hebrew equivalent is Amiram. FEMININE HEBREW EQUIVALENTS: Amira, Amitza, Amtza, Avirama, Etana, Me'uza, Odedya.

Amiran (עֲמִירָן) A variant form of Amiron. The exact Hebrew equivalent is Amiran. *See* Amiron for additional equivalents.

Amiron (עֲמִירֹן) From the Hebrew, meaning "my nation is a song" or "my people sings." The exact Hebrew equivalent is Amiron. FEMININE HEBREW EQUIVALENTS: Ariana, Bat-Shir, Negina, Shira, Zemira, Zimra.

Amit (עָמִית) From the Hebrew, meaning "friend." Akin to Amitai. The exact masculine and feminine Hebrew equivalent is Amit.

Amitai (אֲמִיתַי) From the Aramaic, meaning "true, faithful." The exact Hebrew equivalent is Amitai. FEMININE HEBREW EQUIVALENTS: Amit, Amita.

Amitan (אֲמִיתָן) From the Hebrew, meaning "true, faithful." The exact Hebrew equivalent is Amitan. FEMININE HEBREW EQUIVALENTS: Amit, Amita.

Amiti A variant form of Amit. *See* Amit.

Ammi A variant spelling of Ami. *See* Ami.

Ammiel A variant spelling of Amiel. *See* Amiel.

Ammos A variant spelling of Amos. *See* Amos.

Amnon (אַמְנוֹן) From the Hebrew, meaning "faithful." The exact equivalent is Amnon. FEMININE HEBREW EQUIVALENTS: Amana, Amanya, Amina, Emuna.

Amon (אָמוֹן) From the Hebrew meaning "hidden." The exact Hebrew equivalent is Amon. FEMININE HEBREW EQUIVALENTS: Eliraz, Razi, Raziela, Tzefuna, Tzofnat.

Amory A variant spelling of Emery. *See* Emery.

Amos (עָמוֹס) From the Hebrew, meaning "burdened, troubled." The exact Hebrew equivalent is Amos. FEMININE HEBREW EQUIVALENTS: Teruda, Tzara.

Amram (עַמְרָם) From the Hebrew, meaning "mighty nation." The exact Hebrew equivalent is Amram. FEMININE HEBREW EQUIVALENTS: Abira, Amitzya, Avirama, Bat-Ami, Chava, Cha'ya, Me'uza, Nili, Uza.

Anan (עָנָן) From the Hebrew, meaning "cloud" or "soothsayer." The exact Hebrew equivalent is Anan. FEMININE HEBREW EQUIVALENTS: Chazona, Nevia.

Anani (עֲנָנִי) A variant form of Anan. *See* Anan. The exact Hebrew equivalent is Anani.

Anatole From the Greek, meaning "rising of the sun" or "from the east." HEBREW EQUIVALENTS: Aharon, Kadmiel, Kedem, Kedma, Me'ir, Shimshon, Uriya, Zerach. FEMININE HEBREW EQUIVALENTS: Chamaniya, Kedma, Me'ira, Noga, Ora, Ye'ira.

Anatoly A Russian form of Anatole. *See* Anatole.

Anav (עָנָב) From the Hebrew, meaning "grape." The exact Hebrew equivalent is Anav. The exact feminine Hebrew equivalent is Anava.

Anavi (עֲנָבִי) From the Hebrew, meaning "my grape." The exact Hebrew equivalent is Anavi. FEMININE HEBREW EQUIVALENTS: Anava, Eshkola.

Ancel From the Old German name Ansi, meaning "god, godlike." HEBREW EQUIVALENTS: Adiel, Adon, Adoniya, Asael, Avdel, Azriel, Imanuel, Lemu'el, Yechiel. FEMININE HEBREW EQUIVALENTS: Bat-El, Betu'el, Imanuela, Micha'ela, Michal, Yo'ela.

Anchel, Anchelle Variant spellings of Anshel. *See* Anshel.

Anders A patronymic form of Andrew, meaning "son of Andrew." *See* Andrew.

Andor A variant form of Andrew. *See* Andrew. Akin to Anders.

André A French form of Andrew. *See* Andrew.

Andrew From the Greek, meaning "manly, strong, courageous." HEBREW EQUIVALENTS: Ariav, Arye, Avicha'yil, Ben-Azai, Ben-Gever, Gavriel, Gever, Gibor, On, Onan. FEMININE HEBREW EQUIVALENTS: Amtza, Ariel, Ariela, Atzma, Gavrila, Gibora, Nili, Odedya, Uzit.

Andy A pet form of Andrew. *See* Andrew.

Angel, Angell From the Greek, meaning "messenger" or "saintly person." HEBREW EQUIVALENTS: Arel, Devir, Kadosh, Malach, Malachi, Zakai. FEMININE HEBREW EQUIVALENTS: Arela, Devira, Erela, Kedosha, Malach, Serafina.

Angus From the Gaelic and Irish, meaning "exceptional, outstanding." HEBREW EQUIVALENTS: Adif, Aluf, Ben-Tziyon, Ila'i, Mehudar, Meshubach, Tziyon, Yitran, Yitro. FEMININE HEBREW EQUIVALENTS: Adifa, Alufa, Degula, Idit, Ila, Ilit.

Anschel A variant spelling of Anshel. *See* Anshel.

Ansel, Anselm From the Old German, meaning "divine helmet," symbolizing protection. HEBREW EQUIVALENTS: Avigdor, Betzalel, Bitzaron, Elitzafan, Lotan, Machseya, Shemarya, Shimron, Ya'akov. FEMININE HEBREW EQUIVALENTS: Avigdora, Magena, Megina, Shimra, Sitriya, Tzina, Ya'akova.

Anshel (אַנְשֶׁל/אַנְשֶׁעל) A Yiddish form of Asher. *See* Asher. Also, a Yiddish form of Anselm. *See* Anselm.

Anson, Ansonia From the Anglo-Saxon, meaning "the son of Ann" or "the son of Hans." *See* Hans and Ann (feminine section).

Antal A form of Anatole. *See* Anatole.

Anthony From the Greek, meaning "flourishing," and from the Latin, meaning "worthy of praise." HEBREW EQUIVALENTS: Admon, Efra'yim, Gedalya, Hillel, Nitzan, Pirchai, Savyon, Segal, Yehuda. FEMININE HEBREW EQUIVALENTS: Devora, Hila, Hillela, Nirit, Nitza, Yehudit.

Anton, Antone, Antonin Variant forms of Antony. *See* Antony.

Antony A variant form of Anthony. *See* Anthony.

Ara (אָרָא) From the Hebrew, meaning "to pluck, gather." The exact Hebrew equivalent is Ara. FEMININE HEBREW EQUIVALENTS: Asafa, Ketifa.

Arad (עֲרָד) From the Hebrew, meaning "wild ox." HEBREW EQUIVALENTS: Arad, Ard, Ardi. FEMININE HEBREW EQUIVALENTS: Arda, Ardona.

Aram (אֲרָם) From the Assyrian, meaning "high, heights." HEBREW EQUIVALENTS: Aram, Marom, Ram, Rami. FEMININE HEBREW EQUIVALENTS: Meroma, Rama, Ramit, Romema.

Aran (אֲרָן) From the Assyrian and Arabic, meaning "chest, sarcophagus." HEBREW EQUIVALENTS: Aran, Aron. The feminine Hebrew equivalent is Arona.

Arba (אַרְבַּע) From the Hebrew, meaning "four." The exact Hebrew equivalent is Arba. The exact feminine Hebrew equivalent is Arba'a.

Arbel (אַרְבֵּל) From the Hebrew, meaning "sieve." The exact Hebrew equivalent is Arbel. The exact feminine Hebrew equivalent is Arbela.

Arbie Probably from the Old French, meaning "crossbow." HEBREW EQUIVALENTS: Kashti, Kish, Kishoni. The feminine Hebrew equivalent is Keshet.

Arch A short form of Archibald. *See* Archibald.

Archibald From the Anglo-Saxon, meaning "bold" or "holy prince." HEBREW EQUIVALENTS: Arye, Avinadav, Chagiga, Devir, Gavriel, Kadish,

Kadosh, Yisrael. FEMININE HEBREW EQUIVALENTS: Ariel Ariela, Chagiga, Devira, Malka, Sara.

Ard (אַרְדְ) A variant form of Adar. *See* Adar. The exact Hebrew equivalent is Ard.

Arden From the Latin, meaning "to burn." HEBREW EQUIVALENTS: Aviur, Esh, Gacham, Lahav, Nur, Nuriya, Udi. FEMININE HEBREW EQUIVALENTS: Uriela, Urit.

Ardon (אַרְדוֹן) From the Hebrew, meaning "bronze." The exact Hebrew equivalent is Ardon. FEMININE HEBREW EQUIVALENTS: Arda, Ardona. Also, a variant form of Ard. *See* Ard.

Arel (אַרְאֵל) From the Hebrew, meaning "lion of God." The exact Hebrew equivalent is Arel. The exact feminine Hebrew equivalent is Arela.

Areli (אַרְאֵלִי) A variant form of Arel. The exact Hebrew equivalent is Areli. FEMININE HEBREW EQUIVALENTS: Arela, Ariel, Ariela.

Argus From the Greek, meaning "bright." HEBREW EQUIVALENTS: Avner, Bahir, Barak, Bezek, Me'ir, Zerach, Zerachya. FEMININE HEBREW EQUIVALENTS: Behira, Me'ira, Noga, Ora, Orit, Zakiya, Ziva, Zivit.

Ari (אַרִי) From the Hebrew, meaning "lion." The exact Hebrew equivalent is Ari. FEMININE HEBREW EQUIVALENTS: Ariel, Ariela, Kefira, Levia.

Aric, Arick Early German forms of Richard. *See* Richard.

Arie A variant spelling of Ari. *See* Ari.

Arieh A variant spelling of Aryeh. *See* Aryeh.

Ariel (אַרִיאֵל) From the Hebrew, meaning "lion of God." The exact masculine and feminine Hebrew equivalent is Ariel.

Arik A pet form of Ariel and Aryeh. *See* Ariel *and* Aryeh.

Ario A variant form of Ari. *See* Ari.

Arky A pet form of Archibald. *See* Archibald.

Arlando A variant form of Orlando. *See* Orlando.

Arlen The Celtic form of the name Arles, meaning "pledge." HEBREW EQUIVALENTS: Nidri, Sheva. FEMININE HEBREW EQUIVALENTS: Batsheva, Elisheva, Nedira, Nidra, Sheva, Yehosheva.

Arlin A variant spelling of Arlen. *See* Arlen.

Arlo Probably from the Old English, meaning "fortified hill." HEBREW EQUIVALENTS: Aharon, Bira, Biranit, Gal, Ma'on, Tel, Tilom. FEMININE HEBREW EQUIVALENTS: Aharona, Gal, Gali, Gilada, Givona, Talma.

Arlyn A variant spelling of Arlin. *See* Arlin.

Armand The French and Italian form of the Old German name Hermann, meaning "warrior." HEBREW EQUIVALENTS: Gad, Gadiel, Gavriel, Gevarya, Gidon, Gidoni, Mordechai, Nimrod. FEMININE HEBREW EQUIVALENTS: Gada, Gadit, Gavrila, Gibora, Merav, Tigra.

Armando The Spanish form of Armand. *See* Armand.

Armen, Armin Variant forms of Armand. *See* Armand.

Armon (עַרְמוֹן/אַרְמוֹן) From the Hebrew, meaning "castle, palace." When spelled with the Hebrew letter *a'yin*, rather than *alef*, the meaning is "tree in the oak family." The exact Hebrew equivalent is Armon. The exact feminine Hebrew equivalent is Armona.

Armond   A variant spelling of Armand. *See* Armand.

Armoni (עַרְמוֹנִי/אַרְמוֹנִי)   A variant form of Armon. Armoni is the exact Hebrew equivalent. *See* Armon.

Arnan (אַרְנָן)   From the Arabic, meaning "lotus fruit." Also, from the Hebrew, meaning "roaring stream." The exact Hebrew equivalent is Arnan. The exact feminine Hebrew equivalent is Arnona.

Arndt   A variant form of Arnold. *See* Arnold.

Arne   A variant form of Arnold. *See* Arnold.

Arni, Arnie   Pet forms of Arnold. *See* Arnold.

Arno   A pet form of Arnold. *See* Arnold.

Arnold   From the Old German, meaning either "honorable, honest ruler" or "the power of an eagle." HEBREW EQUIVALENTS: Amitai, Avicha'yil, Avraham, Melech, Nesher, Sar, Yisrael. FEMININE HEBREW EQUIVALENTS: Atara, Laya, Milka, Sara, Tamar, Yisr'ela.

Arnon (אַרְנוֹן)   From the Hebrew, meaning "roaring stream." The exact Hebrew equivalent is Arnon. The exact feminine Hebrew equivalent is Arnona.

Arnoni (אַרְנוֹנִי)   A variant form of Arnon. *See* Arnon. The exact Hebrew equivalent is Arnoni.

Arny   A pet form of Arnold. *See* Arnold.

Aron   A variant form of Aharon (Aaron). *See* Aharon.

Arsen   From the Greek, meaning "manly, strong." HEBREW EQUIVALENTS: Amiram, Aviaz, Avicha'yil, Aziel, Ben-Cha'yil, Ben-Gurion, Gad, Gadi, Gavriel, Gever, Gibor, Ish-Cha'yil, Yisrael. FEMININE HEBREW EQUIVALENTS: Abira, Aza, Azriela, Gavriela, Gavrila, Gibora, Yisr'ela.

Art   A pet form of Arthur. *See* Arthur.

Arthur   From the Gaelic, meaning "rock, rocky hill." Also, from the Celtic, meaning "bear." HEBREW EQUIVALENTS: Aharon, Avniel, Dov, Dubi, Haran, Mordechai, Tzur, Tzuriel. FEMININE HEBREW EQUIVALENTS: Avna, Avniela, Dova, Doveva, Sara, Tzurit, Yisr'ela.

Artie   A pet form of Arthur. *See* Arthur.

Arty   A pet form of Arthur. *See* Arthur.

Artza (אַרְצָא)   From the Hebrew, meaning "earth, land." The exact Hebrew equivalent is Artza. The exact feminine Hebrew equivalent is Eretz.

Artzi (אַרְצִי)   A variant form of Artza. *See* Artza. The exact Hebrew equivalent is Artzi.

Arvid   From the Anglo-Saxon, meaning "man of the people" or "friend of the people." HEBREW EQUIVALENTS: Aluf, Amit, Amitai, Raya, Regem, Re'uel, Yedid, Yedidya. FEMININE HEBREW EQUIVALENTS: Achva, Amit, Amita, Yedida.

Arvin   A variant form of Arvid. *See* Arvid.

Ary A variant spelling of Ari. *See* Ari.

Arye, Aryeh (אַרְיֵה) From the Hebrew, meaning "lion." The exact Hebrew equivalent is Arye. FEMININE HEBREW EQUIVALENTS: Ariel, Ariela.

Aryel, Aryell Variant spellings of Ariel. *See* Ariel.

Arzi (אַרְזִי) From the Hebrew, meaning "my cedar." The exact Hebrew equivalent is Arzi. FEMININE HEBREW EQUIVALENTS: Ariza, Arzit.

Arzon (אַרְזוֹן) A variant form of Arzi. *See* Arzi. The exact Hebrew equivalent is Arzon.

Asa (אָסָא) From the Aramaic and Arabic, meaning "create" or "heal." The exact Hebrew equivalent is Asa. FEMININE HEBREW EQUIVALENTS: Asaela, Refaela, Refua, Rofi.

Asael (עֲשָׂהאֵל) From the Hebrew, meaning "God created." The exact Hebrew equivalent is Asael. The exact feminine Hebrew equivalent is Asaela.

Asaf (אָסָף) From the Hebrew, meaning "gather." The exact Hebrew equivalent is Asaf. The exact feminine equivalent is Asafa.

Aser A variant spelling of Asser. *See* Asser.

Ash From the Old Norse and the Middle English, meaning "tree of the olive family." HEBREW EQUIVALENTS: Almog, Alon, Arza, Bar-Ilan, Eshel, Etzyoni, Ilan, Oren. FEMININE HEBREW EQUIVALENTS: Alona, Ariza, Ela, Etzyona.

Asher (אָשֵׁר) From the Hebrew, meaning "blessed, fortunate, happy." The exact Hebrew equivalent is Asher. The exact feminine Hebrew equivalent is Ashera.

Ashley From the Old English, meaning "field of ash trees." *See* Ash.

Asiel (עֲשִׂיאֵל) A variant form of Asael. The exact Hebrew equivalent is Asiel. *See also* Asael.

Asir (אָסִיר) From the Arabic, and Aramaic, meaning "bound up, imprisoned." The exact Hebrew equivalent is Asir. The exact feminine Hebrew equivalent is Asira.

Asis, Asiss (עָסִיס) From the Hebrew, meaning "juice." The exact Hebrew equivalent is Asis. The exact feminine Hebrew equivalent is Asisa.

Asriel (אַשְׂרִיאֵל) From the Hebrew, meaning "prince of God." The exact Hebrew equivalent is Asriel. The exact feminine Hebrew equivalent is Asriela.

Assa A variant spelling of Asa. *See* Asa.

Asser A variant form of Asher. *See* Asher.

Assi (אָסִי) From the Aramaic, meaning "doctor." The exact Hebrew equivalent is Assi. FEMININE HEBREW EQUIVALENTS: Asaela, Refa'ela, Refa'ya, Terufa.

Atar (עָתָר) From the Hebrew, meaning "to pray." The exact Hebrew equivalent is Atar. FEMININE HEBREW EQUIVALENTS: Ateret, Atira, Tehila.

Atid (עָתִיד) From the Hebrew, meaning "timely, prepared, ready" or "the future." The exact Hebrew equivalent is Atid. The exact feminine Hebrew equivalent is Atida.

Atir (עָתִיר) From the Hebrew, meaning "wreath, crown, ornament." The exact Hebrew equivalent is Atir. FEMININE HEBREW EQUIVALENTS: Atara, Ateret.

Atzmon (עַצְמוֹן) From the Hebrew, meaning "strength." The exact Hebrew equivalent is Atzmon. The exact feminine Hebrew equivalent is Atzmona.

Aubrey From the Anglo-Saxon, meaning "[elf] ruler." HEBREW EQUIVALENTS: Aluf, Avraham, Ba'al, Elrad, Moshel, Yisrael. FEMININE HEBREW EQUIVALENTS: Alufa, Sara, Sarit, Yisr'ela.

August A variant form of Augustus. See Augustus.

Augustus From the Latin, meaning "revered, exalted." HEBREW EQUIVALENTS: Atlai, Atalya, Avraham, Ram, Rami, Segev, Seguv, Yigdal, Zevulun. FEMININE HEBREW EQUIVALENTS: Ge'ona, Ge'onit, Ramit, Ramot, Sara, Sarit.

Aurel From the Latin and French, meaning "gold, golden." HEBREW EQUIVALENTS: Elifaz, Ofar, Ofir, Paz, Zahav, Zahavi. FEMININE HEBREW EQUIVALENTS: Ofira, Paz, Paza, Pazit, Tzehuva, Zehuva, Zehuvit.

Austen, Austin Variant Anglicized forms of Augustus. See Augustus.

Av (אַב) From the Hebrew, meaning "father." The exact Hebrew equivalent is Av. The exact feminine Hebrew equivalent is Imma.

Avdan (אַבְדָן) From the Hebrew, meaning "father is judge." The exact Hebrew equivalent is Avdan. See also Avidan.

Averel, Averell From the Anglo-Saxon, meaning "to open," connoting springtime. HEBREW EQUIVALENTS: Aviv, Pesach, Pesachya, Petachya, Yiftach, Yiftach-El. FEMININE HEBREW EQUIVALENTS: Aviva, Avivi, Avivit.

Averil, Averill Variant spellings of Averel. See Averel.

Avery A variant form of Aubrey. See Aubrey.

Avi (אָבִי) From the Hebrew, meaning "my father." The exact Hebrew equivalent is Avi. The feminine Hebrew equivalent is Immi.

Avia A variant spelling of Aviya. See Aviya.

Aviad (אֲבִיעַד) From the Hebrew, meaning "my father is witness" or "my father is eternal." The exact Hebrew equivalent is Aviad. FEMININE HEBREW EQUIVALENTS: Nitzcha, Nitzchiya, Nitzchona.

Aviah A variant spelling of Avia. See Avia.

Aviam (אֲבִיעָם) From the Hebrew, meaning "father of a nation." The exact Hebrew equivalent is Aviam. FEMININE HEBREW EQUIVALENTS: Le'uma, Le'umi, Uma.

Aviasaf (אֲבִיאָסָף) From the Hebrew, meaning "father of a multitude" or "my father has gathered." The exact Hebrew equivalent is Aviasaf. FEMININE HEBREW EQUIVALENTS: Asafa, Ketifa.

Aviav (אֲבִיאָב) From the Hebrew, meaning "grandfather." The exact Hebrew equivalent is Aviav. FEMININE HEBREW EQUIVALENTS: Aviem, Savta.

Aviaz (אֲבִיעַז) From the Hebrew, meaning "father of strength." The exact Hebrew equivalent is Aviaz. FEMININE HEBREW EQUIVALENTS: Aza, Aziaz, Aziza, Azriela, Me'uza, Uza, Uzit.

Avichai (אֲבִיחַי) From the Hebrew, meaning "my father lives" or "father of all living things." The exact Hebrew equivalent is Avichai. FEMININE HEBREW EQUIVALENTS: Achiya, Chava, Cha'ya, Cha'yuta, Yechiela.

Avicha'yil (אֲבִיחַיִל) From the Hebrew, meaning "father of strength" or "my father is strong." The exact masculine and feminine Hebrew equivalent is Avicha'yil.

Avichen (אֲבִיחֵן) From the Hebrew, meaning "father of grace." The exact Hebrew equivalent is Avichen. FEMININE HEBREW EQUIVALENTS: Adiva, Chana, Chanina, Chanita, Chanya, Chenya.

Avida (אֲבִידָע) From the Hebrew, meaning "my father knows." The exact Hebrew equivalent is Avida. FEMININE HEBREW EQUIVALENTS: Daat, Datiela, De'a, De'uela.

Avidan (אֲבִידָן) From the Hebrew, meaning "my father is judge [or judgment]." The exact Hebrew equivalent is Avidan. FEMININE HEBREW EQUIVALENTS: Dana, Daniela, Danit, Danita, Danya.

Avideror A variant spelling of Avidror. *See* Avidror.

Avidor (אֲבִידוֹר) From the Hebrew, meaning "father of a generation." The exact Hebrew equivalent is Avidor. FEMININE HEBREW EQUIVALENTS: Dor, Dorit, Dorya.

Avidror (אֲבִידְרוֹר) From the Hebrew, meaning "father of freedom." The exact Hebrew equivalent is Avidror. FEMININE HEBREW EQUIVALENTS: Derora, Derorit, Deroriya, Li-Dror.

Aviel (אֲבִיאֵל) From the Hebrew, meaning "my father is God." The exact Hebrew equivalent is Aviel. FEMININE HEBREW EQUIVALENTS: Avi, Aviela.

Aviem (אֲבִיאָם) From the Hebrew meaning "father of mother, grandfather." The exact masculine and feminine Hebrew equivalent is Aviem.

Aviezer (אֲבִיעֶזֶר) From the Hebrew, meaning "God is help, salvation." The exact Hebrew equivalent is Aviezer. FEMININE HEBREW EQUIVALENTS: Eliezra, Ezraela, Ezriela, Sa'ada.

Avigdor (אֲבִיגְדוֹר) From the Hebrew, meaning "father protector." The exact Hebrew equivalent is Avigdor. The exact feminine Hebrew equivalent is Avigdora.

Avihu (אֲבִיהוּ) From the Hebrew, meaning "he is my father." The exact Hebrew equivalent is Avihu. FEMININE HEBREW EQUIVALENTS: Avi, Avichen, Aviel, Avramit, Avuya.

Avimelech (אֲבִימֶלֶךְ) From the Hebrew, meaning "father of the king" or "my father is the king." The exact Hebrew equivalent is Avimelech. FEMININE HEBREW EQUIVALENTS: Avi, Avicha'yil, Aviel, Aviela, Avigal, Avramit.

Avimi (אֲבִימִי) A contraction of *avi immi,* meaning "grandfather." The exact Hebrew equivalent is Avimi. FEMININE HEBREW EQUIVALENTS: Aviem, Savta.

Avin (אֲבִין) The Aramaic form of Av, meaning "father." The exact Hebrew equivalent is Avin. FEMININE HEBREW EQUIVALENTS: Avi, Aviel, Avirama, Avramit, Imma.

Avina (אֲבִינָא) From the Aramaic, meaning "father." The exact Hebrew equivalent is Avina. *See* Avin *for additional equivalents.*

Avinadav (אֲבִינָדָב) From the Hebrew, meaning "my father is noble." The exact Hebrew equivalent is Avinadav. FEMININE HEBREW EQUIVALENTS: Nedava, Nediva.

Avinatan (אֲבִינָתָן) From the Hebrew, meaning "my father has given, father's [God's] gift." The exact Hebrew equivalent is Avinatan. FEMININE HEBREW EQUIVALENTS: Aviya, Matnat, Netana, Netaniela, Netanya, Netina.

Avinoam (אֲבִינֹעַם) From the Hebrew, meaning "father of delight." The exact Hebrew equivalent is Avinoam. FEMININE HEBREW EQUIVALENTS: Achinoam, Adina, Na'a, Na'ama, Ne'ima.

Avira (אֲוִירָא) From the Aramaic, meaning "air, atmosphere, spirit." The exact Hebrew equivalent is Avira. The exact feminine Hebrew equivalent is Avirit.

Aviram (אֲבִירָם) From the Hebrew, meaning "my father is mighty." The exact Hebrew equivalent is Aviram. The exact feminine Hebrew equivalent is Avirama.

Aviri (אֲוִירִי) From the Hebrew, meaning "air, atmosphere." The exact Hebrew equivalent is Aviri. The exact feminine Hebrew equivalent is Avirit.

Avital (אֲבִיטַל) From the Hebrew, meaning "father of dew." The exact masculine and feminine Hebrew equivalent is Avital.

Avitul (אֲבִיטוּל) A variant form of Avital. *See* Avital. The exact Hebrew equivalent is Avitul.

Avitus From the Latin, meaning "bird." HEBREW EQUIVALENTS: A'ya, Deror, Efron, Tavas, Tzipor. FEMININE HEBREW EQUIVALENTS: A'ya, Da'ya, Salit, Tzipora, Tziporit.

Avituv (אֲבִיטוּב) From the Hebrew, meaning "father of goodness." The exact Hebrew equivalent is Avituv. FEMININE HEBREW EQUIVALENTS: Tova, Tovat, Tovit, Yatva.

Aviv (אָבִיב) From the Hebrew, meaning "spring, springtime." The exact Hebrew equivalent is Aviv. The exact feminine Hebrew equivalent is Aviva.

Avivi (אֲבִיבִי) From the Hebrew, meaning "springlike, springtime." The exact Hebrew equivalent is Avivi. FEMININE HEBREW EQUIVALENTS: Aviva, Avivit.

Aviya (אֲבִיָּה) From the Hebrew, meaning "God is my father." The exact masculine and feminine Hebrew equivalent is Aviya.

Avner (אַבְנֵר) From the Hebrew, meaning "father of light" or "father's candle," connoting strength and inspiration. The exact Hebrew equivalent is Avner. FEMININE HEBREW EQUIVALENTS: Me'ira, Me'irit, Menora, Ne'ira, Nera, Ner-Li, Orit, Ornina, Uriela, Zohar.

Avniel (אַבְנִיאֵל) From the Hebrew, meaning "God is my rock," signifying strength. The exact Hebrew equivalent is Avniel. The exact feminine Hebrew equivalent is Avniela.

Avraham (אַבְרָהָם) From the Hebrew, meaning "father of a mighty nation" or "father of a multitude." The exact Hebrew equivalent is Avraham. FEMININE HEBREW EQUIVALENTS: Avirama, Avrahamit, Avramit.

Avram (אַבְרָם) In the Bible (Genesis 17:5), Avraham's original name. The exact Hebrew equivalent is Avram. *See also* Avraham.

Avrom A variant Yiddish form of Avraham. *See* Avraham.

Avron (אַבְרוֹן) From the Hebrew, meaning "father of song." The exact Hebrew equivalent is Avron. FEMININE HEBREW EQUIVALENTS: Anat, Arni, Arninit, Ronela, Ronit, Shira, Shirel.

Avrum A variant Yiddish form of Avraham. *See* Avraham.

Avshalom (אַבְשָׁלוֹם) From the Hebrew, meaning "father of peace." The exact Hebrew equivalent is Avshalom. FEMININE HEBREW EQUIVALENTS: Meshulemet, Shelomit, Shulamit.

Axel, Axtel Swedish names of Germanic origin, meaning "divine source of life." HEBREW EQUIVALENTS: Amichai, Amram, Bachya, Bar-Yocha'i, Cha'yim, Yechiel, Yocha'i. FEMININE HEBREW EQUIVALENTS: Achiya, Chava, Cha'ya, Cha'yuta, Techiya.

Ayal (אַיָל) From the Hebrew, meaning "deer" or "ram." The exact Hebrew equivalent is A'yal. The exact feminine Hebrew equivalent is A'yala.

Ayali (אַיָלִי) From the Hebrew, meaning "my deer" or "my ram." The exact Hebrew equivalent is A'yali. The exact feminine Hebrew equivalent is A'yala.

Az (עַז) From the Hebrew, meaning "strong." The exact Hebrew equivalent is Az. The exact feminine Hebrew equivalent is Aza.

Azan (עֲזָן) From the Hebrew, meaning "strength." The exact Hebrew equivalent is Azan. FEMININE HEBREW EQUIVALENTS: Aza, Aziaz, Azriela, Uza, Uziela, Uzit.

Azarya, Azaryahu (עֲזַרְיָהוּ/עֲזַרְיָה) From the Hebrew, meaning "the help of God." The exact Hebrew equivalent is Azarya. FEMININE HEBREW EQUIVALENTS: Azriela, Eliezra, Ezr'ela, Ezriela, Ozera.

Azaz (עֲזָז) From the Hebrew, meaning "strength." The exact Hebrew equivalent is Azaz. FEMININE HEBREW EQUIVALENTS: Aza, Aziaz, Azriela, Uza, Uziela.

Azi (עֲזִי) From the Hebrew, meaning "strength." The exact Hebrew equivalent is Azi. FEMININE HEBREW EQUIVALENTS: Aza, Aziaz, Aziza, Azriela, Me'uza, Odeda, Uza.

Aziel (עֲזִיאֵל) From the Hebrew, meaning "God is my strength." The exact Hebrew equivalent is Aziel. The exact feminine Hebrew equivalent is Aziela.

Aziz (עֲזִיז) From the Hebrew, meaning "strength." The exact Hebrew equivalent is Aziz. The exact feminine Hebrew equivalent is Aziza.

Azriel (עֲזְרִיאֵל) From the Hebrew, meaning "God is my help." The exact Hebrew equivalent is Azriel. The exact feminine Hebrew equivalent is Azriela.

Azzy A pet form of Azarya or Azriel. *See* Azarya *and* Azriel.

Baba A variant spelling of Bava. *See* Bava.

Baldwin From the Middle High German, meaning "bold friend." HEBREW EQUIVALENTS: Bildad, Binyamin, David, Rayi. FEMININE HEBREW EQUIVALENTS: Chaviva, Davida, Hadasa, Rut, Yedida.

Balfor A variant spelling of Balfour. *See* Balfour.

Balfour (בַּלְפוּר) From the Old English, meaning "hill along the way." The exact Hebrew equivalent is Balfur. The exact feminine Hebrew equivalents are Balfura and Balfuriya.

Banet A short form of Barnett and Benedict. *See* Barnet *and* Benedict.

Bani (בָּנִי) From the Aramaic, meaning "son" or "build." HEBREW EQUIVALENTS: Bani, Ben, Bena'ya, Bena'yahu, Buni. FEMININE HEBREW EQUIVALENTS: Bat, Bat-El, Batya, Bona, Yavn'ela.

Barak (בָּרָק) From the Hebrew, meaning "flash of light." The exact Hebrew equivalent is Barak. FEMININE HEBREW EQUIVALENTS: Bareket, Behira, Me'ira, Ne'ora, Ora.

Baram (בַּרְעָם) From the Aramaic, meaning "son of the nation." The exact Hebrew equivalent is Baram. FEMININE HEBREW EQUIVALENTS: Bat-Ami, Bat-Tziyon, Le'uma, Le'umi, Uma.

Bard From the Gaelic and Irish, meaning "minstrel" or "poet." HEBREW EQUIVALENTS: Amiron, Ami-Shar, Liron, Ron, Ronen, Shiron, Yoran, Zimri. FEMININE HEBREW EQUIVALENTS: Oda, Odiya, Ronit, Piuta.

Bari A variant spelling of Barrie. *See* Barrie.

Barker From the Old English, meaning "logger of birch trees." HEBREW EQUIVALENTS: Almog, Alon, Bar-Ilan, Bros, Ilan, Oren. FEMININE HEBREW EQUIVALENTS: Alona, Ariza, Arna, Ilana, Livnat, Shikma.

Barnaby From the Aramaic, meaning "speech." HEBREW EQUIVALENTS: Amarya, Divri, Imri. FEMININE HEBREW EQUIVALENTS: Amira, Devora, Niva.

Barnard The French form of Bernard. *See* Bernard.

Barnet, Barnett Variant forms of Bernard. *See* Bernard.

Barney A pet form of Bernard or Barnaby. *See* Bernard *and* Barnaby.

Barr, Barre A short form of Bernard and Barnard. *See* Bernard *and* Barnard.

Barret, Barrett A short form of Barnet. *See* Barnet.

Barri, Barrie Variant spellings of Barry. *See* Barry.

Barry A Welsh patronymic form of Harry, meaning "son of Harry." *See* Harry. Also, a pet form of Baruch. *See* Baruch.

Bart A pet form of Barton and Bartholomew. *See* Barton *and* Bartholomew.

Barth A variant spelling of Bart. *See* Bart.

Bartholomew From the Greek and Aramaic, meaning "son of Talmai." *See* Talmai.

Bartlet, Bartlett Variant forms of Bartholomew. *See* Bartholomew.

Barton From the Anglo-Saxon, meaning "barley town," or from the Old English, meaning "bear town." HEBREW EQUIVALENTS: Dagan, Dov, Goren. FEMININE HEBREW EQUIVALENTS: Degana, Deganit, Duba.

Baruch (בָּרוּךְ) From the Hebrew, meaning "blessed." The exact Hebrew equivalent is Baruch. FEMININE HEBREW EQUIVALENTS: Beracha, Berucha.

Barzilai (בַּרְזִילַי) From the Aramaic, meaning "man of iron." The exact Hebrew equivalent is Barzilai. FEMININE HEBREW EQUIVALENTS: Amtza, Ariel, Atzma, Gibora.

Basil From the Greek, meaning "royal, kingly." HEBREW EQUIVALENTS: Adoniya, Avimelech, Katriel, Melech. FEMININE HEBREW EQUIVALENTS: Atara, Malka, Yisr'ela.

Bava (בָּבָא) From the Aramaic, meaning "gate." The exact masculine and feminine Hebrew equivalent is Bava.

Bazak (בָּזָק) From the Hebrew, meaning "flash of light." The exact Hebrew equivalent is Bazak. FEMININE HEBREW EQUIVALENTS: Bareket, Behira, Me'ira, Nehora, Ora.

Bear From the German name Baer, meaning "bear." The exact Hebrew equivalent is Dov. FEMININE HEBREW EQUIVALENTS: Dova, Dovit, Duba.

Beau From the Latin and French, meaning "pretty, handsome." HEBREW EQUIVALENTS: Adin, Hadar, Noi, P'er, Ra'anan, Yefet. FEMININE HEBREW EQUIVALENTS: Hadura, Na'a, Nava, Nehedara, Ranana.

Beaumont From the French, meaning "beautiful mountain." HEBREW EQUIVALENTS: Adin, Aharon, Gal, Gali, Haran, Harel, Naom, P'er, Yefet. FEMININE HEBREW EQUIVALENTS: Aharona, Chermona, Hadura, Harela, Yafa, Yafit.

Beck From the Middle English and Old Norse, meaning "brook." HEBREW EQUIVALENTS: Afek, Arnon, Aviyam, Beri, Chamat, Dalfon, Dela'ya. FEMININE HEBREW EQUIVALENTS: Arona, Afeka, Bat-Yam, Miryam.

Bede From the Middle English, meaning "prayer." HEBREW EQUIVALENTS: Eflal, Elipal, Paliel, Palal, Tachan. FEMININE HEBREW EQUIVALENTS: Ateret, Atira, Tachan, Tehila.

Bedell From the Old French, meaning "messenger." The exact masculine and feminine Hebrew equivalent is Malach.

Beebe From the Anglo-Saxon, meaning "one who lives on a bee farm." HEBREW EQUIVALENTS: Bustana'i, Chaklai, Yogev, Zore'a. FEMININE HEBREW EQUIVALENTS: Davrat, Devora, Devorit, Shadmit.

Bell From the Latin and French, meaning "beautiful." HEBREW EQUIVALENTS: Adin, Hadar, Kalil, Melabev, Naveh, Nechmad, Ra'anan. FEMININE HEBREW EQUIVALENTS: Hadura, Na'ama, Na'ami, Nofiya, Yafa, Yafit, Yefefiya.

Bellamy From the Latin and French, meaning, "beautiful friend." HEBREW EQUIVALENTS: Avinoam, David, Na'ama, Ra'anan, Yafim, Yefet. FEMININE HEBREW EQUIVALENTS: Adina, Davida, Shifra, Yafit.

Belton From the French and Anglo-Saxon, meaning "beautiful town." HEBREW EQUIVALENTS: Avinoam, Chilkiya, David, Galil, Galili. FEMININE HEBREW EQUIVALENTS: Adina, Galiliya, Nachala, Nachalat, Shifra, Yafit.

Ben (בֶּן) From the Hebrew, meaning "son." The exact Hebrew equivalent is Ben. The exact feminine Hebrew equivalent is Bat.

Ben-Ami (בֶּן־עַמִי) From the Hebrew, meaning "son of my people." The exact Hebrew equivalent is Ben-Ami. The exact feminine Hebrew equivalent is Bat-Ami.

Benedict From the Latin, meaning "blessed." HEBREW EQUIVALENTS: Asher, Baruch, Berachya. FEMININE HEBREW EQUIVALENTS: Ashra, Beracha, Berucha.

Benesh (בֶּענֶעש) The Yiddish form of Benedict. *See* Benedict.

Ben-Gurion (בֶּן־גּוּרְיוֹן) From the Hebrew, meaning "son of the lion" or "son of might." The exact Hebrew equivalent is Ben-Guryon. FEMININE HEBREW EQUIVALENTS: Gavrila, Gevura, Gibora, Uza, Uziela.

Benish (בֶּעניש) A Yiddish form of Benedict. *See* Benedict.

Benjamin The Anglicized form of Binyamin. *See* Binyamin.

Bennet, Bennett. Variant English forms of the Latin Benedict. *See* Benedict.

Benor, Ben-Or (בֶּן־אוֹר) From the Hebrew, meaning "son of light." The exact Hebrew equivalent is Benor. FEMININE HEBREW EQUIVALENTS: Behira, Eliora, Liora, Ora.

Benroy From the Gaelic and French, meaning "royal mountain." HEBREW EQUIVALENTS: Aharon, Haran, Harel, Sinai. FEMININE HEBREW EQUIVALENTS: Aharona, Chermona, Harela, Horiya.

Benson Either a patronymic form, meaning "son of Ben [Benjamin]," or a form of Ben Zion. *See* Binyamin *and* Ben Zion.

Bentley From the Old English, meaning "meadows of ben [grass]." HEBREW EQUIVALENTS: Dashe, Gan, Hevel, Rotem, Yarden. FEMININE HEBREW EQUIVALENTS: Gana, Ganit, Ginat, Yardeniya.

Benton From the Old English, meaning "Ben's town." *See* Ben.

Bentzi A pet form of Ben-Tziyon and Binyamin. *See* Ben-Tziyon *and* Binyamin.

Ben-Tziyon (בֶּן־צִיוֹן) From the Hebrew, meaning "excellence" or "son of Zion." Ben Zion is a variant spelling. The exact Hebrew equivalent is Ben-Tziyon. The exact feminine Hebrew equivalent is Bat-Tziyon.

Benzecry A patronymic form, meaning "son of Zechariah." *See* Zechariah.

Benzi A pet form of Ben Zion. *See* Ben Zion.

Ben Zion A variant spelling of Ben-Tziyon. *See* Ben-Tziyon.

Ber A Yiddish name from the German name Baer, meaning "bear." HEBREW EQUIVALENTS: Dov, Dubi. FEMININE HEBREW EQUIVALENTS: Dova, Doveva, Duba, Dubit.

Berg From the German, meaning "mountain." HEBREW EQUIVALENTS: Aharon, Haran, Harel. FEMININE HEBREW EQUIVALENTS: Aharona, Harela.

Bergen From the German, meaning "one who lives on a hill or mountain." HEBREW EQUIVALENTS: Aharon, Haran, Harel. FEMININE HEBREW EQUIVALENTS: Aharona, Harela, Horiya.

Berger A variant form of Burgess. *See* Burgess. Also, a form of Bergen. *See* Bergen.

Beril (בֶּעְרִיל) A variant spelling of Beryl. *See* Beryl.

Berish (בֶּעְרִישׁ) A variant Yiddish form of Ber. *See* Ber.

Berk, Berke Variant spellings of Burk. *See* Burk.

Berkeley, Berkley, Berkly From the Anglo-Saxon, meaning "from the birch meadow." HEBREW EQUIVALENTS: Amir, Arzi, Bar-Ilan, Bros, Etzyoni, Ilan, Luz. FEMININE HEBREW EQUIVALENTS: Almuga, Alona, Arna, Ilanit, Shikma, Shikmona.

Berlin, Berlyn From the German, meaning "boundary line." HEBREW EQUIVALENTS: Efes, Galil, Galili. FEMININE HEBREW EQUIVALENTS: Galila, Gedera, Gelila, Geliliya.

Bern, Berna From the German, meaning "bear." HEBREW EQUIVALENTS: Dov, Dubi. FEMININE HEBREW EQUIVALENTS: Dova, Doveva, Dubit.

Bernard From the Old High German, meaning "bold as a bear." HEBREW EQUIVALENTS: Barzilai, Binyamin, Boaz, Dov. FEMININE HEBREW EQUIVA-LENTS: Ariel, Atzma, Duba, Dubit, Gavrila, Gibora.

Bernardo The Spanish form of Bernard. *See* Bernard.

Bernarr A variant form of Bernard. *See* Bernard.

Bernd, Berndt Variant forms of Bernard. *See* Bernard.

Bernhard, Bernhardt Variant German forms of Bernard. *See* Bernard.

Berni, Bernie Pet forms of Bernard. *See* Bernard.

Bert, Bertie Pet forms of Albert, Berthold, Bertol, and Bertram.

Berthold From the German, meaning "bright." HEBREW EQUIVALENTS: Avner, Bahir, Barak, Bezek, Me'ir, Zahir, Zerach. FEMININE HEBREW EQUIVALENTS: Bareket, Behira, Me'ira, Tzelila, Zakit, Ziva, Zivanit.

Bertin A variant form of Bertram. *See* Bertram.

Bertol, Bertold Variant forms of Berthold. *See* Berthold.

Berton A variant form of Berthold. *See* Berthold.

Bertram From the Old High German, meaning "bright, illustrious one." HEBREW EQUIVALENTS: Barak, Bazak, Gedalya, Hillel, Me'ir, Shem-Tov. FEMININE HEBREW EQUIVALENTS: Behira, Levana, Me'ira, Rivka, Shifra, Tehila.

Bertran A variant form of Bertram. *See* Bertram.

Bertrand A variant form of Bertram. *See* Bertram.

Bertrem A variant spelling of Bertram. *See* Bertram.

Berwin From the Anglo-Saxon, meaning "powerful friend." HEBREW EQUIVALENTS: Aluf, Amit, Amitan, David, Raya, Regem, Re'uel, Yadid, Yedidya. FEMININE HEBREW EQUIVALENTS: Achva, Amit, Amita, Rut, Yedida.

Beryl From the Greek, meaning "sea-green precious stone," or from the Yiddish, meaning "bear," connoting strength. HEBREW EQUIVALENTS: Barak, Boaz, Dov, Gibor, Leshem, Penini, Sapir, Yahalom, Yakar. FE-

MININE HEBREW EQUIVALENTS: Bareket, Duba, Gavrila, Gibora, Margalit, Penina.

Betzalel (בְּצַלְאֵל) From the Hebrew, meaning "shadow of God," signifying God's protection. The exact Hebrew equivalent is Betzalel. FEMININE HEBREW EQUIVALENTS: Avigdora, Shemura, Shimrit, Tzina, Ya'akova.

Beverley, Beverly From the Old English, meaning "beaver meadow" or "field." HEBREW EQUIVALENTS: Carmel, Carmeli, Yara. FEMININE HEBREW EQUIVALENTS: Carmela, Gana, Nava.

Bezalel A variant spelling of Betzalel. See Betzalel.

Bibi (בִּיבִי) A pet form of Binyamin. See Binyamin.

Bichri (בִּכְרִי) From the Hebrew, meaning "my eldest" or "youthful." The exact Hebrew equivalent is Bichri. FEMININE HEBREW EQUIVALENTS: Bakura, Bechira, Bechora.

Bildad (בִּלְדַד) From the Hebrew, meaning "Baal has loved." The exact Hebrew equivalent is Bildad. FEMININE HEBREW EQUIVALENTS: Ahuva, Davida, Rut, Yedida.

Bilga, Bilgah (בִּלְגָה) From the Hebrew, meaning "joy, cheer." The exact Hebrew equivalent is Bilga. FEMININE HEBREW EQUIVALENTS: Avigal, Aviga'yil, Gil, Gila, Gilana.

Bilgai (בִּלְגַי) From the Arabic and Aramaic meaning "joy, cheerfulness." The exact Hebrew equivalent is Bilgai. FEMININE HEBREW EQUIVALENTS: Aviga'yil, Bilga, Gila, Rina.

Bilguy A variant spelling of Bilgai. See Bilgai.

Bil, Billie, Billy, Billye Pet forms of William. See William.

Bin A pet form of Binyamin. See Binyamin.

Binyamin (בִּנְיָמִין) From the Hebrew, meaning "son of my right hand," having the connotation of strength. The exact Hebrew equivalent is Binyamin. The exact feminine Hebrew equivalent is Binyamina.

Bird From the English and Anglo-Saxon *bridd,* which by metathesis became "bird." HEBREW EQUIVALENTS: A'ya, Deror, Efron, Nesher, Paruach, Tzipor. FEMININE HEBREW EQUIVALENTS: A'ya Da'ya, Efrona, Kanarit, Tzifriya, Tzipora, Tziporit.

Birk A variant form of Barker. See Barker.

Blaine From the Old English, meaning "the source of a river." HEBREW EQUIVALENTS: Afek, Beri, Chamat, Dalfon, Yuval. FEMININE HEBREW EQUIVALENTS: Afeka, Bat-Yam, Miryam, Yaval.

Blake From the Anglo-Saxon, meaning "to whiten, to bleach." HEBREW EQUIVALENTS: Lavan, Livni. FEMININE HEBREW EQUIVALENTS: Levana, Levona, Tzechora.

Blanchard A variant form of Blake. See Blake.

Boaz (בֹּעַז) From the Hebrew, meaning "strength" or "swiftness." The exact Hebrew equivalent is Boaz. FEMININE HEBREW EQUIVALENTS: Azriela, Gavrila, Gibora, Me'uza, Tzivya, Uza, Uziela.

Bo, Bobbie, Bobby Pet forms of Robert. See Robert.

Bonesh From the Yiddish, meaning "good." HEBREW EQUIVALENTS: Bechiel, Ben-Tovim, Elituv, Litov, Metav, Tivon. FEMININE HEBREW EQUIVALENTS: Shapira, Tavit, Tova, Tovit, Yatva.

Boni From the Italian, meaning "good." *See* Boniface.

Boniface From the Latin, meaning "well-doer." HEBREW EQUIVALENTS: Ben-Tovim, Litov, Tovi, Toviel, Tov-Shilem, Tuviyahu. FEMININE HEBREW EQUIVALENTS: Tova, Tovit, Tuvit, Yatvata.

Booker From the Anglo-Saxon, meaning "beech tree." An occupational name for one who copies books, since paper for books was made from the beech tree. HEBREW EQUIVALENTS: Bar-Ilan, Bros, Elon, Eshel, Oren, Safra, Safran, Shaked, Sofer. FEMININE HEBREW EQUIVALENTS: Almuga, Ariza, Etzyona, Ilana, Shikma, Shikmona, Soferet.

Boone From the Latin and the Old French, meaning "good." HEBREW EQUIVALENTS: Ben-Tov, Ben-Tovim, Toviel, Tuvi, Tuviya. FEMININE HEBREW EQUIVALENTS: Tiva, Tova, Tovat, Tuvit, Yatva, Yatvat.

Borg From the Old Norse, meaning "castle." Also a variant form of the German name Berg, meaning "mountain." HEBREW EQUIVALENTS: Aharon, Armon, Armoni, Devir, Harel. FEMININE HEBREW EQUIVALENTS: Aharon, Armona, Armonit, Harela, Hariya.

Boris From the Russian, meaning "fight" or "warrior." HEBREW EQUIVALENTS: Ben-Cha'yil, Gera, Gibor, Mordechai. FEMININE HEBREW EQUIVALENTS: Gavrila, Gibora, Yisr'ela.

Bowen A Celtic patronymic, meaning "son [or descendant] of Owen." HEBREW EQUIVALENTS: Ben-Cha'yil, Ben-Gever, Ben-Guryon, Ben-Oni, Ben-Tziyon, Buni. FEMININE HEBREW EQUIVALENTS: Bat-Ami, Bat-Galim, Bat-Tziyon, Betuel.

Boyd From the Slavic, meaning "fighting warrior," or from the Celtic, meaning "yellow." HEBREW EQUIVALENTS: Ben-Azai, Ben-Cha'yil, Ben-Gever, Ben-Guryon, Binyamin, Boaz, Zahav. FEMININE HEBREW EQUIVALENTS: Amitza, Avicha'yil, Gavriela, Gavrila, Gevura, Gibora, Zehuva.

Brad A pet form of Braden and Bradley. *See* Braden *and* Bradley.

Braden From the Old English, meaning "broad, wide." HEBREW EQUIVALENTS: Artzi, Nof, Rechavam, Rechavya, Shetach. FEMININE HEBREW EQUIVALENTS: Artzit, Eretz, Merchava, Merchavya, Nofiya.

Bradford From the Anglo-Saxon, meaning "broad ford." HEBREW EQUIVALENTS: Arnan, Arnon, Rechavya, Yuval, Zerem. FEMININE HEBREW EQUIVALENTS: Afeka, Arnona, Arnonit, Merchavya.

Bradley From the Old English, meaning "broad lea, meadow." HEBREW EQUIVALENTS: Carmela, Ginat, Rechavam, Rechavya, Zimri. FEMININE HEBREW EQUIVALENTS: Carmela, Carmelit, Gana, Merchava, Shedema.

Brady From the Anglo-Saxon, meaning "broad island." HEBREW EQUIVALENTS: Afek, Arnon, Rechavya, Yuval, Zerem. FEMININE HEBREW EQUIVALENTS: Afeka, Arnona, Arnonit, Merchavya.

Brahm, Bram Short form of Abram. *See* Abram.

Bran From the Irish, meaning "raven." HEBREW EQUIVALENTS: Efron, Orev, Tavas, Tzipor, Yarkon. FEMININE HEBREW EQUIVALENTS: Efrona, Kanit, Senuit, Tzipora, Tziporit, Tzofit.

Branch From the Late Latin, meaning "an extension from the tree trunk." HEBREW EQUIVALENTS: Arzi, Bar-Ilan, Bros, Ilan, Oren, Tzameret. FEMININE HEBREW EQUIVALENTS: Almuga, Alona, Ariza, Etyona, Ilana, Shikma.

Brand A variant form of Bran. *See* Bran.

Brandon A variant form of Brand. *See* Brand.

Brandt A variant form of Brand. *See* Brand.

Bremel, Breml Yiddish pet forms of Avraham. *See* Avraham.

Bret, Brett From the Celtic, meaning "Breton, a native of Brittany." *See* Brit.

Brian From the Celtic and Gaelic, meaning "strength." Also, "one who is nobly born and eloquent." HEBREW EQUIVALENTS: Abir, Amarya, Amira, Barzilai, Ben-Cha'yil, Niv, Otniel, Yisrael. FEMININE HEBREW EQUIVALENTS: Abira, Amira, Doveva, Dovevet, Gavrila, Gibora, Neva, Sara, Yisr'ela.

Briand From the French, meaning "castle." HEBREW EQUIVALENTS: Armoni. FEMININE HEBREW EQUIVALENTS: Armona, Armonit.

Brit, Britt (בְּרִית) A short form of Briton. *See* Briton. An early name for Wales. Also, from the Hebrew, meaning "covenant." The exact Hebrew equivalents are Brit and Brit-El.

Brock From the Anglo-Saxon and Gaelic, meaning "badger." Also, an early name for a "grain dealer." HEBREW EQUIVALENTS: Dagan, Goren, Kela'ya, Shever. FEMININE HEBREW EQUIVALENTS: Chita, Degana, Deganit, Deganya, Kama.

Broderick A name compounded from Brad and Richard, meaning "rich, flat land." HEBREW EQUIVALENTS: Artzi, Rechavam, Rechavya, Ya'ar. FEMININE HEBREW EQUIVALENTS: Artzit, Eretz, Merchav, Merchavya, Ya'ara, Ya'arit.

Bromley From the Anglo-Saxon, meaning "meadow" or "field of brushwood." HEBREW EQUIVALENTS: Artza, Artzi, Hevel, Nir, Nirel, Padon, Ya'ar, Yanir. FEMININE HEBREW EQUIVALENTS: Artzit, Eretz, Nira, Nirit, Ya'ara, Ya'arit.

Brook, Brooke From the Old English, meaning "stream." HEBREW EQUIVALENTS: Arnon, Yaval, Yoval, Yuval, Zerem. FEMININE HEBREW EQUIVALENTS: Afeka, Arnona, Arnonit, Nadyan.

Brooks A variant form of Brook. *See* Brook.

Bruce A Scottish name of French origin, probably meaning "woods, thicket." HEBREW EQUIVALENTS: Artzi, Carmel, Carmeli, Yara. FEMININE HEBREW EQUIVALENTS: Artzit, Carmela, Carmelit, Gana, Nava.

Bruno From the Old German, meaning "brown, dark in appearance." Also, a form of the German name Brunn, meaning "fountain." HEBREW EQUIVALENTS: Arnon, Ayfai, Kush, Pinchas. FEMININE HEBREW EQUIVALENTS: Arnona, Chachila, Tzila.

Bry A short form of Bryan. *See* Bryan.

Bryan, Bryant Variant forms of Brian. *See* Brian.

Bubba   From the German, meaning "boy." HEBREW EQUIVALENTS: Bachur, Ben, Na'arai, Na'ari. FEMININE HEBREW EQUIVALENTS: Alma, Aluma, Bat, Betula, Na'ara.

Buck   From the Anglo-Saxon and German, meaning "male deer" or "he-goat." HEBREW EQUIVALENTS: A'yal, A'yalon, Ben-Tzvi, Efer, Tzevi. FEMININE HEBREW EQUIVALENTS: A'yala, A'yelet, Ofra, Re'ema, Tzivya.

Bucky   A pet form of Buck. See Buck.

Bud, Budd   From the Old English, meaning "messenger," or from the Welsh, meaning "rich, victorious." Also, a variant spelling of Bud. HEBREW EQUIVALENTS: Calev, Mevaser, Yishai. FEMININE HEBREW EQUIVALENTS: Bat-Shua, Dafna, Hadasa.

Buddy   A pet form of Budd. See Budd.

Buell   A variant spelling of the British *bul,* meaning "bull." HEBREW EQUIVALENTS: Arad, Ard, Ardi.

Buki (בָּקִי)   From the Hebrew, meaning "bottle" or "test, investigate." The exact Hebrew equivalent is Buki. The feminine Hebrew equivalent is Bakara.

Buna (בּוּנָה)   From the Hebrew, meaning "knowledge, understanding." The exact masculine and feminine Hebrew equivalent is Buna.

Buni, Bunni (בּוּנִי)   From the Hebrew, meaning "built, constructed." The exact Hebrew equivalent is Buni. FEMININE HEBREW EQUIVALENTS: Bona, Buna, Yavn'ela.

Bunim (בּוּנִים)   From the Yiddish, meaning "good." HEBREW EQUIVALENTS: Bechiel, Ben-Tov, Ben-Tovim, Tabai, Tivon, Tov-Shilem. FEMININE HEBREW EQUIVALENTS: Tiva, Tova, Tovat, Tovit, Yatva, Yatvata.

Burdette   From the Middle English, meaning "small bird." HEBREW EQUIVALENTS: Deror, Efron, Gozal, Tzipor, Yarkon. FEMININE HEBREW EQUIVALENTS: Efrona, Gozala, Salit, Silit, Tzipora.

Burgess   From the Middle English and Old French, meaning "shop-keeper," signifying a free man. HEBREW EQUIVALENTS: Avidror, Derori, Pesach, Pesachya, Rechavam. FEMININE HEBREW EQUIVALENTS: Derora, Ge'ula, Rachav.

Burk, Burke   Old English forms of the German name Burg, meaning "castle." HEBREW EQUIVALENTS: Armon, Armoni. FEMININE HEBREW EQUIVALENTS: Armona, Armonit.

Burl, Burle   From the Latin, meaning "coarse hair." Also, from the Middle English, meaning "tree knot." HEBREW EQUIVALENTS: Anuv, Esav, Isur. FEMININE HEBREW EQUIVALENTS: Dala, Delila, Nima, Rivka.

Burleigh   From the Old English, meaning "field with prickly, burr-covered plants." HEBREW EQUIVALENTS: Avgar, Ezrach, Iris, Narkis, Shalmon, Shatul, Shetel, Zore'a. FEMININE HEBREW EQUIVALENTS: Afrit, Atzmonit, Iris, Marganit, Marva, Nurita, Rakefet.

Burley   A variant spelling of Burleigh. See Burleigh.

Burr   A short form of Burleigh. See Burleigh.

Burt, Burte   Either a form of Burton (*see* Burton) or from the Anglo-Saxon, meaning "bright, clear, excellent." HEBREW EQUIVALENTS: Ben-

Tzion, Me'ir, Tuviya, Uri. FEMININE HEBREW EQUIVALENTS: Bat-Tziyon, Behira, Me'ira, Ora, Orit, Tova, Tovit.

Burton From the Old English, meaning "town on a hill." HEBREW EQUIVA-LENTS: Aharon, Chaga, Gal, Galil, Harel, Talmi, Tel-Chai, Telem. FEMI-NINE HEBREW EQUIVALENTS: Aharona, Galit, Galya, Givona, Talma, Talmit.

Bustan (בּוּסְתָּן) From the Arabic and Hebrew, meaning "garden." The exact Hebrew equivalent is Bustan. FEMININE HEBREW EQUIVALENTS: Gana, Ganit, Ganya, Ginat, Yardeniya.

Byk From the Polish, meaning "ox." HEBREW EQUIVALENTS: Arad, Ard, Ar-di, Shor.

Byrd From the Anglo-Saxon, meaning "bird." HEBREW EQUIVALENTS: De-rori, Efron, Nesher, Tzipor, Yarkon. FEMININE HEBREW EQUIVALENTS: Ef-rona, Tzipora, Tzipori, Tziporit, Tzofit.

Byron From the German, meaning "cottage," or from the Old English, meaning "bear." HEBREW EQUIVALENTS: Dov, Dubi. FEMININE HEBREW EQUIVALENTS: Dova, Dovit, Duba, Dubit.

Cal A pet form of Caleb. *See* Caleb.

Calder From the Celtic, meaning "from the stony river." HEBREW EQUIVA-LENTS: Chamat, Even, Regem, Sapir, Ye'or, Ye'ori. FEMININE HEBREW EQUIVALENTS: Afeka, Gazit, Yaval.

Cale Possibly a pet form of Caleb. *See* Caleb.

Caleb An Anglicized spelling of Kalev. *See* Kalev.

Calvert An Old English occupational name for a herdsman. HEBREW EQUIVALENTS: Eder, Edri, Maron. FEMININE HEBREW EQUIVALENTS: Eder, Merona.

Calvin From the Latin, meaning "bald." The exact Hebrew equivalent is Korach.

Camillus From the Latin, meaning "attendant" or "messenger." HEBREW EQUIVALENTS: Aharon, Azarya, Ezra, Kalev, Malachi, Ovadya, Ozer. FE-MININE HEBREW EQUIVALENTS: Aleksandra, Ozera, Sa'ada.

Capp A variant form of Chaplin. *See* Chaplin.

Carey From the Welsh or Cornish, meaning "rock island." HEBREW EQUIV-ALENTS: Almog, Avi'yam, Tzur, Tzuri, Tzuriel. FEMININE HEBREW EQUIVA-LENTS: Avniela, Miryam, Ritzpa, Tzurel, Tzuriya.

Carl A variant form of Charles. *See* Charles.

Carlton From the Old English, meaning "Carl's town." *See* Carl.

Carmel (בַּרְמֶל) From the Hebrew, meaning "vineyard" or "garden." The exact Hebrew equivalent is Carmel. FEMININE HEBREW EQUIVALENTS: Carma, Carmiya, Carmit.

Carmeli (בַּרְמְלִי) From the Hebrew, meaning "my vineyard." The exact Hebrew equivalent is Carmeli. FEMININE HEBREW EQUIVALENTS: Carmela, Carmelit, Carmiela, Gafna.

Carmen The Spanish form of Carmel. *See* Carmel.

Carmiel (בַּרְמִיאֵל) From the Hebrew, meaning "the Lord is my vineyard." The exact Hebrew equivalent is Carmiel. FEMININE HEBREW EQUIVALENTS: Carmela, Carmelit, Carmiela, Gafna, Gafnit.

Carmine The Italian form of Carmen. *See* Carmel.

Carney From the Celtic, meaning "fighter." HEBREW EQUIVALENTS: Gad, Gavriel, Gevarya, Gibor, Ish-Cha'yil, Mordechai, Nimrod, Yechezkel. FEMININE HEBREW EQUIVALENTS: Gada, Gavriela, Gibora, Tigra, Uza, Uziela, Yechezkela.

Carol, Caroll Variant forms of Charles. *See* Charles.

Carrol, Carroll Variant forms of Charles. *See* Charles.

Carol A variant form of Charles. *See* Charles.

Carr From the Scandinavian and Old Norse, meaning "marshy land." HEBREW EQUIVALENTS: Avi'yam, Beri, Dalfon. FEMININE HEBREW EQUIVALENTS: Bat-Yam, Miryam, Yaval.

Carrol, Carroll Variant spellings of Carol. *See* Carol.

Cary A variant spelling of Carey. *See* Carey.

Case From the Old French, meaning "chest, box." HEBREW EQUIVALENTS: Aran, Aron. FEMININE HEBREW EQUIVALENTS: Arona.

Casey From the Celtic, meaning "valorous." HEBREW EQUIVALENTS: Abir, Abiri, Ben-Guryon, Chason, Chutzpit, No'az, Ometz, Uzi, Uziel, Yechezkel. FEMININE HEBREW EQUIVALENTS: Avniela, No'az, Odeda, Odedya, Uza, Uzit, Yechezkela.

Cash A short form of Cassius. *See* Cassius.

Caspar From the German, meaning "imperial." HEBREW EQUIVALENTS: Achimelech, Elimelech, Katriel, Malkam, Melech. FEMININE HEBREW EQUIVALENTS: Atara, Malka, Tzefira.

Casper A variant spelling of Caspar. *See* Caspar.

Cecil From the Latin, meaning "blind." EUPHEMISTIC MASCULINE HEBREW EQUIVALENTS: Koresh, Me'ir, Shimshon, Uriel, Zerach. EUPHEMISTIC FEMININE HEBREW EQUIVALENTS: Laya, Me'ira, Noga, Ora, Zohora.

Cedric A Welsh name meaning "bountiful" or "war chief." HEBREW EQUIVALENTS: Hotir, Huna, Yishai, Yitro. FEMININE HEBREW EQUIVALENTS: Ashira, Bat-Shua, Negida, Yitra.

Cerf From the French, meaning "hart, deer." HEBREW EQUIVALENTS: A'yal, Ben-Tzevi, Efer, Efron, Ofri, Tzevi, Tzeviel. FEMININE HEBREW EQUIVALENTS: A'yala, A'yelet, Hertzela, Hertzeliya, Ofra, Re'ema, Tzeviya.

Chad From the Celtic, meaning "battle" or "warrior." HEBREW EQUIVALENTS: Ben-Cha'yil, Gad, Gidon, Ish-Cha'yil, Mordechai. FEMININE HEBREW EQUIVALENTS: Amitza, Atzma, Gavrila, Gibora.

Chag (חַג) From the Hebrew, meaning "holiday." The exact Hebrew equivalent is Chag. FEMININE HEBREW EQUIVALENTS: Chagit, Chagiga, Chagiya.

Chagai (חַגַי) From the Aramaic and Hebrew, meaning "my feast(s), festive." The exact Hebrew equivalent is Chagai. FEMININE HEBREW EQUIVALENTS: Chagiga, Chagit, Chagiya.

Chagi (חַגִּי) A variant form of Chagai. *See* Chagai. The exact Hebrew equivalent is Chagi.

Chai (חַי) From the Hebrew, meaning "life." The exact Hebrew equivalent is Chai. The exact feminine Hebrew equivalent is Cha'ya.

Chaim (חַיִּים) A variant spelling of Chayim. *See* Chayim.

Champ From the Latin *campus*, meaning "field, stadium where games are played." Also, from the Middle English and Old French, meaning "gladiator." HEBREW EQUIVALENTS: Gad, Gadiel, Gevaryahu, Gidon, Ish-Cha'yil, Mordechai, Nir, Niram. FEMININE HEBREW EQUIVALENTS: Gada, Gadit, Merav, Nira, Nirit, Tigra.

Champion A variant form of Champ. *See* Champ.

Chanan (חָנָן) A variant form of Chanina. The exact Hebrew equivalent is Chanan. *See* Chanina *and* Yochanan *for additional equivalents.*

Chancellor From the Middle English and Old French, meaning "keeper of records" or "secretary." HEBREW EQUIVALENTS: Betach, Mivtach, Mivtzar, Raz, Shalev, Shilo, Sofer. FEMININE HEBREW EQUIVALENTS: Mivtechet, Razi, Raziela, Soferet.

Chandler From the French, meaning "maker or seller of candles." HEBREW EQUIVALENTS: Aviner, Avner, Ner, Neri, Neriya, Oran, Uriel. FEMININE HEBREW EQUIVALENTS: Nehara, Nehira, Nehura, Nera, Ner-Li, Nurya.

Chanina (חֲנִינָא) From the Aramaic, meaning "gracious" or "compassionate." The exact masculine and feminine Hebrew equivalent is Chanina.

Chanoch (חֲנוֹךְ) From the Hebrew, meaning "dedicated" or "educated." The exact Hebrew equivalent is Chanoch. The exact feminine Hebrew equivalent is Chanuka.

Chapin A contracted form of the Old French, meaning "chaplain." *See* Chaplain.

Chaplin From the Middle English, meaning "chaplain." HEBREW EQUIVALENTS: Aharon, Likchi, Moran, Rav, Rabi, Yora. FEMININE HEBREW EQUIVALENTS: Aharona, Horiya, Mora, Morit, Moriya.

Chapman From the Middle English, meaning "trader." HEBREW EQUIVALENTS: Amal, Amali, Mahir. FEMININE HEBREW EQUIVALENTS: Amal, Amalya, Amel.

Charle A variant spelling of Charley or Charlie. *See* Charley.

Charles A French form of the Anglo-Saxon, meaning "manly, strong" or "full-grown." HEBREW EQUIVALENTS: Abir, Bechor, Ben-Cha'yil, Chizki, Chizkiyahu, Ish-Cha'yil, Kalev, Shamir, Sharir, Sherira, Yo'az. FEMININE HEBREW EQUIVALENTS: Abira, Amtza, Ariel, Ariela, Gavrila, Gibora, Uza, Uzit, Yechezkela.

Charley, Charlie Pet forms of Charles. *See* Charles.

Charlton A French-German name, meaning "Charles's town." *See* Charles.

Charney From the Slavic, meaning "black." HEBREW EQUIVALENTS: Adar, Cham, Chumi, Kush, Pinchas. FEMININE HEBREW EQUIVALENTS: Adara, Laila, Shechora.

Chase From the Old French and Middle English, meaning "hunt." HE-BREW EQUIVALENTS: Tzedani, Sheva'ya. The feminine Hebrew equivalent is Tzedanit.

Chauncey, Chauncy Pet forms of Chancellor. *See* Chancellor.

Chavakuk (חֲבַקּוּק) From the Assyrian, meaning "garden plant." The exact Hebrew equivalent is Chavakuk. FEMININE HEBREW EQUIVALENTS: Chelmit, Chelmonit, Gana, Ganit, Ginat, Zivanit.

Chaviv (חָבִיב) From the Hebrew, meaning "beloved." The exact Hebrew equivalent is Chaviv. The exact feminine Hebrew equivalent is Chaviva.

Chavivi (חֲבִיבִי) From the Hebrew, meaning "my beloved" or "my friend." The exact Hebrew equivalent is Chavivi. FEMININE HEBREW EQUIVALENTS: Chaviva, Chavuka, Davida, Yedida.

Chayim, Chayyim, Chayym (חַיִּים) From the Hebrew, meaning "life." The exact Hebrew equivalent is Cha'yim. The exact feminine Hebrew equivalent is Cha'ya.

Chermon (חֶרְמוֹן) From the Hebrew, meaning "consecrated, sacred." The exact Hebrew equivalent is Chermon. The exact feminine Hebrew equivalent is Chermona.

Chermoni (חֶרְמוֹנִי) A variant form of Chermon. *See* Chermon. The exact Hebrew equivalent is Chermoni.

Chester From the Latin, meaning "fortress" or "camp." HEBREW EQUIVA-LENTS: Chosa, Chupam, Shemarya, Shemaryahu, Sitri. FEMININE HEBREW EQUIVALENTS: Batzra, Efrat, Tzila, Ya'akova.

Chet A pet form of Chester. *See* Chester.

Chevy From the British, meaning "hunt, chase." The Hebrew equivalent is Tzedani. The feminine Hebrew equivalent is Tzedanit.

Chia A variant spelling of Chiya. *See* Chiya.

Chiel (חִיאֵל) From the Hebrew, meaning "God lives." A short form of Yechiel. The exact Hebrew equivalent is Chi'el. The feminine Hebrew equivalent is Yechi'ela.

Chilton From the Anglo-Saxon, meaning "town by the river." HEBREW EQUIVALENTS: Aviyam, Beri, Chamat, Ye'or, Ye'ori. FEMININE HEBREW EQUIVALENTS: Afeka, Bat-Yam, Miryam.

Chiram (חִירָם) From the Hebrew, meaning "lofty, exalted." The exact Hebrew equivalent is Chiram. FEMININE HEBREW EQUIVALENTS: Rami, Ramot, Romema, Romemya.

Chirom (חִירוֹם) A variant spelling of Chiram (Hiram). *See* Chiram.

Chiya (חִיָּא) A short form of Yechiel. *See* Yechiel.

Chizkiya, Chizkiyahu (חִזְקִיָּה/חִזְקִיָּהוּ) From the Hebrew, meaning "God is my strength." The exact Hebrew equivalent is Chizkiya. FEMININE HEBREW EQUIVALENTS: Avicha'yil, Chasina, Chasna, Uziela, Yechezkela.

Choni (חוֹנִי) From the Hebrew, meaning "gracious." Also spelled Honi. The exact Hebrew equivalent is Choni. FEMININE HEBREW EQUIVALENTS: Chana, Chanita, Chen, China.

Chovav (חוֹבָב) A variant form of Chovev. *See* Chovev. The exact Hebrew equivalent is Chovav.

Chovev (חוֹבֵב) From the Hebrew, meaning "friend" or "lover." The exact Hebrew equivalent is Chovev. FEMININE HEBREW EQUIVALENTS: Ahava, Ahavat, Ahuva, Chaviva, Chiba, Chibat-Tziyon.

Chris A pet form of Christopher. *See* Christopher.

Christopher From the Greek and Latin, meaning "Christ-bearer." The Christian patron saint of travelers. HEBREW EQUIVALENTS: Mashiach, Orach. The feminine Hebrew equivalent is Yiska.

Christy A Scottish pet form of Christopher. *See* Christopher.

Chur (חוּר) From the Akkadian, meaning "child." The exact Hebrew equivalent is Chur. FEMININE HEBREW EQUIVALENTS: Alma, Betula, Na'ara, Tze'ira.

Churi (חוּרִי) A variant form of Chur. *See* Chur. The exact Hebrew equivalent is Churi.

Cicero From the Latin, meaning "orator" or "guide." HEBREW EQUIVALENTS: Amarya, Amir, Divri, Dover, Omer. FEMININE HEBREW EQUIVALENTS: Amira, Doveva, Dovevet.

Cid A Spanish name derived from the Arabic, meaning "lord, sir." HEBREW EQUIVALENTS: Adir, Adon, Adoniya, Chirom, Yisrael. FEMININE HEBREW EQUIVALENTS: Adira, Adonit, Yisr'ela.

Cimon A variant spelling of Simon. *See* Simon.

Claiborn, Claiborne Compounded from the German and French, meaning "boundary marked by clovers." HEBREW EQUIVALENTS: Chavakuk, Dashe, Narkis, Rotem, Shatil, Shatul. FEMININE HEBREW EQUIVALENTS: Atzmoni, Chelmit, Chelmonit, Narkis, Shetula.

Clarence From the Latin, meaning "illustrious." HEBREW EQUIVALENTS: Gedalya, Hillel, Katriel, Melech, Shem-Tov. FEMININE HEBREW EQUIVALENTS: Malka, Sara, Yisr'ela.

Clark, Clarke From the Old English, meaning "clergyman, scholar, wise person." HEBREW EQUIVALENTS: Chanoch, Kalev, Kohen, Kohelet, Moran, Moriel. FEMININE HEBREW EQUIVALENTS: Bina, Buna, Morit, Moriya.

Claud, Claude From the French and Latin, meaning "lame." EUPHEMISTIC MASCULINE HEBREW EQUIVALENTS: Ben-Tzevi, Bo'az, Efer, Tzevi. EUPHEMISTIC FEMININE HEBREW EQUIVALENTS: A'yelet, Ofra, Tzivya.

Claudell A pet form of Claude. *See* Claude.

Clay From the German and Indo-European, meaning "to stick together." The Hebrew equivalent is Levi. FEMININE HEBREW EQUIVALENTS: Leviya, Shelavya.

Clayton A variant form of Clay, meaning "town built upon clay." HEBREW EQUIVALENTS: Adam, Admata, Artza. FEMININE HEBREW EQUIVALENTS: Adama, Artzit, Eretz. *See also* Clay.

Clem A pet form of Clement. *See* Clement.

Clement From the Latin, meaning "merciful" or "gracious." HEBREW EQUIVALENTS: Amichen, Aminadav, Chanan, Choni, Kalman, Rachamim, Yochanan. FEMININE HEBREW EQUIVALENTS: Adiva, Chana, Chanita, Dikla, Yochana.

Clemmons A variant form of Clement. *See* Clement.

Clemon A variant form of Clement. *See* Clement.

Cleo A variant spelling of Clio. *See* Clio.

Cleon A variant form of Clio. *See* Clio.

Cleve A pet form of Cleveland. *See* Cleveland.

Cleveland From the Old English, meaning "land near a steep waterfall." HEBREW EQUIVALENTS: Afek, Arnon, Artzi, Avi'yam, Beri, Chamat, Dalfon. FEMININE HEBREW EQUIVALENTS: Afeka, Artzit, Bat-Yam, Eretz, Miryam.

Clever From the Old English, meaning "claw, hand." HEBREW EQUIVALENTS: Chofni, Yeda'ya.

Cliff, Cliffe From the Old English, meaning "steep, bank." HEBREW EQUIVALENTS: Givon, Givton, Talmai, Telem, Tzur. FEMININE HEBREW EQUIVALENTS: Gali, Galit, Givona, Talma, Tzuriya.

Clifford An English local name meaning "ford" or "crossing near the cliff." HEBREW EQUIVALENTS: Aharon, Talmai, Telem, Tzuriel. FEMININE HEBREW EQUIVALENTS: Gali, Migdala, Timora, Ya'el.

Clifton From the Old English, meaning "town near the cliff." HEBREW EQUIVALENTS: Givon, Karmel, Tzuri, Tzuriel. FEMININE HEBREW EQUIVALENTS: Givona, Karmela, Ritzpa, Tzuriya, Yizr'ela.

Clint A pet form of Clinton. *See* Clinton.

Clinton From the Anglo-Saxon, meaning "town on a hill." HEBREW EQUIVALENTS: Aharon, Ir, Talmai, Talman, Tel, Tilon. FEMININE HEBREW EQUIVALENTS: Aharona, Gali, Galit, Givona, Talma.

Clio From the Greek, meaning "to praise, to acclaim." HEBREW EQUIVALENTS: Hila, Hilai, Hilan, Hillel, Shevach, Yehuda, Yishbach. FEMININE HEBREW EQUIVALENTS: Hila, Hilana, Hillela, Shavcha, Tehila.

Clive A variant form of Cliff. *See* Cliff.

Clovis From the Anglo-Saxon and German, meaning "clover." HEBREW EQUIVALENTS: Chavakuk, Dashe, Rotem, Shatul, Shetel, Tzemach, Zore'a. FEMININE HEBREW EQUIVALENTS: Chelmit, Chelmonit, Dalya, Gada, Marva, Rakefet, Yizr'ela.

Clyde From the Welsh, meaning "heard from afar." HEBREW EQUIVALENTS: Azanya, Shama, Shema, Shema'yahu, Shemuel, Shimi, Shimon, Ya'azanya. FEMININE HEBREW EQUIVALENTS: Kashuva, Shemuela, Shimat, Shimona.

Clydell A variant form of Clyde. *See* Clyde.

Colby From the Old English and Danish, meaning "coal town." The Hebrew equivalent is Rishpon. FEMININE HEBREW EQUIVALENTS: Rishpa, Rishpona, Ritzpa.

Cole A pet form of Colby or Coleman. *See* Colby *and* Coleman.

Coleman Either from the Latin, meaning "dove"; the Icelandic, meaning "chief"; or the Middle English, meaning "charcoal maker" or "cabbage farmer." HEBREW EQUIVALENTS: Elimelech, Katriel, Kush, Melech, Yona. FEMININE HEBREW EQUIVALENTS: Chachila, Malka, Yemima, Yonina.

Colin Usually taken as a pet form of Nicholas, meaning "victory." Or, from the Celtic, meaning "cub, whelp." Some authorities consider it a variant form of Coleman. *See* Coleman. HEBREW EQUIVALENTS: Ari, Ariel, Ben-Guryon, Gover, Kefir, Netzach, Yatzliach. FEMININE HEBREW EQUIVALENTS: Ariel, Ariela, Kefira, Levia, Nitzcha, Nitzchiya.

Colvin From the Middle English, meaning "coal miner." The Hebrew equivalent is Rishpon. FEMININE HEBREW EQUIVALENTS: Rishpa, Rishpona, Ritzpa.

Conan, Conant From the Middle English, meaning "to be able" or "to be knowledgeable." Also, from the Celtic, meaning "chief, king." HEBREW EQUIVALENTS: Chashmon, Katriel, Malkiel, Melech, Yavin. FEMININE HEBREW EQUIVALENTS: Alufa, Gevira, Nevona, Sara, Yisr'ela.

Conrad From the Old High German, meaning "able counsellor." HEBREW EQUIVALENTS: Aleksander, Chachmoni, Eliezer, Ezra, Haskel, Moran, Pekach. FEMININE HEBREW EQUIVALENTS: Aleksandra, Buna, Chochma, Milka, Tushiya.

Cooper From the Latin, meaning "one who makes barrels and containers." HEBREW EQUIVALENTS: Akiva, Akuv, Yeho'achaz. The feminine Hebrew equivalent is Akuva.

Corbet, Corbett From the Old French and the Middle English, meaning "raven." The exact Hebrew equivalent is Orev. FEMININE HEBREW EQUIVALENTS: Chagla, Da'ya, Efrona, Gozala.

Corbin A variant form of Corbet. *See* Corbet.

Cord A pet form of Cordell. *See* Cordell.

Cordell From the Latin and Old French, meaning "cord, rope." The Hebrew equivalent is Petil. The feminine Hebrew equivalent is Petila.

Corey A variant spelling of Cory. *See* Cory.

Corliss A variant form of Carl. *See* Carl.

Cornelius From the Norman-French, meaning "crow," or from the Latin, meaning "horn of the sun," a symbol of kingship and long life. HEBREW EQUIVALENTS: Amichai, Bar Yochai, Cha'yim, Katriel, Melech, Orev, Yechiel. FEMININE HEBREW EQUIVALENTS: Shekeda, Shikmona, Yechiela.

Corwin, Corwyn From the Latin, meaning "raven." The exact Hebrew equivalent is Orev. FEMININE HEBREW EQUIVALENTS: Da'ya, Efrona, Gozala.

Cory From the Latin, meaning "helmet," or from the Anglo-Saxon, meaning "chosen one." HEBREW EQUIVALENTS: Bachir, Bocher, Nivchar, Yivchar. FEMININE HEBREW EQUIVALENTS: Bara, Bechira, Bechura, Ila, Nivcheret.

Craig From the Celtic and Gaelic, meaning "from the crag [rugged, rocky mass]." HEBREW EQUIVALENTS: Avitzur, Avniel, Sela, Tzeror, Tzur, Tzuriel. FEMININE HEBREW EQUIVALENTS: Ritzpa, Tzurit, Tzuriya.

Crawford From the Old English, meaning "ford or stream where the crows flock." HEBREW EQUIVALENTS: Arnon, B'eri, Enan, Orev, Peleg, Yuval. FEMININE HEBREW EQUIVALENTS: Chasida, Dalia, Devora, Michal, Miryam, Tzipora.

Curt A pet form of Curtis. See Curtis. Kurt is a variant spelling.

Cy A pet form of Cyrus. See Cyrus.

Cyril From the Greek, meaning, "lord, lordly." HEBREW EQUIVALENTS: Avimelech, Avraham, Katriel, Nadav, Nedavya, Rosh. FEMININE HEBREW EQUIVALENTS: Alufa, Be'ula, Gevira, Malka, Nediva, Yisr'ela.

Cyrus (כּוֹרֶשׁ) From the Persian, meaning "sun, brightness." The exact Hebrew equivalent is Koresh. FEMININE HEBREW EQUIVALENTS: Chamaniya, Me'ira, Ora, Orit, Shimshona, Zaka.

Dab A variant form of David. See David.

Dabbey, Dabby A variant form of David. See David.

Dabney A variant form of David. See David.

Dael (דְּעָאֵל) From the Hebrew, meaning "knowledge of God." The exact Hebrew equivalent is Da'el. FEMININE HEBREW EQUIVALENTS: De'a, De'uela, Datiela.

Dag (דָּג) From the Danish and German, meaning "day." Also, from the Hebrew, meaning "fish." The exact Hebrew equivalent is Dag. FEMININE HEBREW EQUIVALENTS: Dagit, Dagiya, Yemuela.

Dagan (דָּגָן) From the Hebrew, meaning "grain." The exact Hebrew equivalent is Dagan. FEMININE HEBREW EQUIVALENTS: Deganit, Deganiya, Garna, Garnit.

Dagul (דָּגוּל) From the Hebrew, meaning "flag, emblem." The exact Hebrew equivalent is Dagul. FEMININE HEBREW EQUIVALENTS: Degula, Digla.

Dahn A variant spelling of Dan. See Dan.

Dahvid A variant spelling of David. See David.

Dale From the Old English and the Old Norse, meaning "valley." HEBREW EQUIVALENTS: Emek, Gai, Gechazi. The feminine Hebrew equivalent is Ga'ya.

Dalin A variant spelling of Dallin. See Dallin.

Dall A variant form of Dale. See Dale.

Dallin From the Anglo-Saxon, meaning "from the dale, valley." HEBREW EQUIVALENTS: Emek, Gai, Ge'ora, Gechazi. The feminine Hebrew equivalent is Ga'ya.

Dama (דָּמָה) From the Hebrew and Aramaic, meaning "to resemble." The exact Hebrew equivalent is Dama. FEMININE HEBREW EQUIVALENTS: Dumiya, Micha'ela, Michal.

Damon From the Latin, meaning "spirit, demon." Also, from the Danish and the Anglo-Saxon, meaning "day." HEBREW EQUIVALENTS: Aviri, Yemuel. The feminine Hebrew equivalent is Yemuela.

Dan (דָּן) From the Hebrew, meaning "judge." The exact Hebrew equivalent is Dan. FEMININE HEBREW EQUIVALENTS: Dana, Danit, Daniya, Dina.

Dana A variant form of Dan. See Dan.

Dani A variant form of Dan or Daniel. See Dan and Daniel.

Daniel (דָּנִיֵּאל) From the Hebrew, meaning "God is my judge." The exact Hebrew equivalent is Daniel. The exact feminine Hebrew equivalent is Daniela.

Danil, Danile, Danilo Variant forms of Daniel. See Daniel.

Dannie, Danny Pet forms of Daniel. See Daniel. Danilo is an Italian form.

Dar (דָּר) From the Hebrew, meaning "pearl, mother-of-pearl" or "marble." Also, from the British, meaning "oak." The exact Hebrew equivalent is Dar. FEMININE HEBREW EQUIVALENTS: Alon, Margalit, Penina, Peninit.

Daren A variant form of Darius. See Darius.

Darian, Darien Variant forms of Darius. See Darius.

Darin, Darren Variant forms of Darius. See Darius.

Darius (דָּרְיָוֶשׁ) From the Persian, meaning "king" or "rich." The Hebrew equivalent is Daryavesh. FEMININE HEBREW EQUIVALENTS: Ashira, Bat-Shua, Negida, Yitra.

Darlin From the British, meaning "grove of oak trees." HEBREW EQUIVALENTS: Alon, Armon, Ela, Elon. FEMININE HEBREW EQUIVALENTS: Alona, Ela, Elona.

Daro A variant form of Darrow. See Darrow.

Darold A variant form of Darrell and Darlin. See Darrell and Darlin.

Darom (דָּרוֹם) From the Hebrew, meaning "south." The exact Hebrew equivalent is Darom. The exact feminine Hebrew equivalent is Daroma.

Darrell From the Anglo-Saxon, meaning "dear, darling." HEBREW EQUIVALENTS: Chaviv, David, Dodi, Eldad, Yedidya. FEMININE HEBREW EQUIVALENTS: Ahuva, Davida, Doda, Yedida.

Darren From the British, meaning "small, rocky hill." HEBREW EQUIVALENTS: Aharon, Chagai, Gal, Harel, Talmai, Tel, Tilom. FEMININE HEBREW EQUIVALENTS: Aharona, Gal, Gali, Givona, Talma, Talmi.

Darrol, Darroll Variant forms of Darrell. See Darrell.

Darrow From the Old English, meaning "spear." HEBREW EQUIVALENTS: Sirya, Siryon. FEMININE HEBREW EQUIVALENTS: Chanit, Chinit, Moran, Moranit.

Darry A pet form of Darren. See Darren. Also, from the French, meaning "from Harry." See Harry.

Darryl A variant form of Darren. See Darren.

Darwin From the British and Anglo-Saxon, meaning "lover of the sea." HEBREW EQUIVALENTS: Avigal, Avi'yam, Dalfon, Dela'ya. FEMININE HEBREW EQUIVALENTS: Bat-Galim, Bat-Yam, Miryam, Yama, Yamit.

Daryl, Daryle Variant spellings of Darrell. See Darrell.

Datan (דָּתָן) From the Hebrew, meaning "law." The exact Hebrew equivalent is Datan. FEMININE HEBREW EQUIVALENTS: Dina, Nadin.

Daud The Arabic form of David. *See* David.

Dave A pet form of David. *See* David.

Davey A pet form of David. *See* David.

Davi A pet form of David. *See* David. Used also as a feminine name.

David (דָּוִד) From the Hebrew, meaning "beloved." The exact Hebrew equivalent is David. The exact feminine Hebrew equivalent is Davida.

Davie A pet form of David. *See* David.

Daviel A variant form of David. *See* David. The exact Hebrew equivalent is Daviel.

Davis A patronymic form of David, meaning "son of David." *See* David.

Davy A pet form of David. *See* David.

Davyd A variant spelling of David. *See* David.

Daw, Dawe From the Old English, meaning "doe." HEBREW EQUIVALENTS: A'yal, Efer, Efron, Ofar, Tzevi. FEMININE HEBREW EQUIVALENTS: A'yala, A'yelet, Tzivya. Also, a variant form of David. *See* David.

Dawson A patronymic form, meaning "son of David." *See* David.

Dean, Deane From the Old French, meaning "head, leader." HEBREW EQUIVALENTS: Chanoch, Rabi, Rosh, Tana. FEMININE HEBREW EQUIVALENTS: Moriel, Morit, Moriya, Rishona.

Dekel (דֶּקֶל) From the Arabic and Hebrew, meaning "palm (date) tree." The exact Hebrew equivalent is Dekel. FEMININE HEBREW EQUIVALENTS: Dikla, Diklit.

Delano From the Old French, meaning "of the night," or from the Erse, meaning "healthy, dark man." HEBREW EQUIVALENTS: Adar, Chachalya, Chumi, Kedar, Pinchas. FEMININE HEBREW EQUIVALENTS: Adara, Efa, Laila, Layli, Tzila.

Demetrius From the Greek, meaning "lover of the earth." HEBREW EQUIVALENTS: Adam, Admata, Artza, David, Regev. FEMININE HEBREW EQUIVALENTS: Adama, Ahuva, Chiba, Davida, Eretz.

Denis The French form of the Latin and Greek name Dionysius. In Greek mythology, the god of wine and revelry. HEBREW EQUIVALENTS: Anav, Efra'yim, Gefen, Karmel, Pura, Tzemach. FEMININE HEBREW EQUIVALENTS: Anava, Bikura, Gita, Gitit, Zimra.

Dennis A variant spelling of Denis. *See* Denis.

Deno An Italian form of Dean. *See* Dean.

Denys A variant spelling of Denis. *See* Denis.

Derek An English form of the Old High German name Hrodrich, meaning "famous." HEBREW EQUIVALENTS: Achimelech, Adoniya, Elrad, Katriel, Melech, Nadav. FEMININE HEBREW EQUIVALENTS: Atara, Be'ula, Gevira, Nediva, Yisr'ela.

Derel A variant form of Darlin. *See* Darlin.

Deror (דְּרוֹר) From the Hebrew, meaning "a bird [swallow]" or "free, freedom." The exact Hebrew equivalent is Deror. The exact feminine Hebrew equivalent is Derora.

Derori (דְּרוֹרִי) A variant form of Deror. The exact Hebrew equivalent is Derori. The exact feminine equivalent is Derorit.

Derorli, Deror-Li (דְּרוֹרְלִי) From the Hebrew, meaning "I am free." The exact Hebrew equivalent is Derorli. FEMININE HEBREW EQUIVALENTS: Derora, Derorit, Derorya.

Derrek, Derrick, Derrik Variant forms of Darlin. *See* Darlin.

Derry From the British, meaning "oak tree." The Hebrew equivalent is Alon. The feminine Hebrew equivalent is Alona.

Desi A pet form of Desiderio. *See* Desiderio.

Desiderio From the Latin, meaning "desire." HEBREW EQUIVALENTS: Chamadel, Chamadya, Chemdan, Chemdat, Chemdiya, Chemed, Chemdiel. FEMININE HEBREW EQUIVALENTS: Chamuda, Cheftzi-Ba, Chemda, Chemdat, Nirtza.

Desmond From the French and Latin, meaning "world" or "mankind." HEBREW EQUIVALENTS: Adam, Cheldai, Cheled, Enosh. FEMININE HEBREW EQUIVALENTS: Adama, Gavriela.

Deuel (דְּעוּאֵל) From the Hebrew, meaning "knowledge of God." The exact Hebrew equivalent is De'uel. The exact feminine Hebrew equivalent is De'uela.

Devir (דְּבִיר) From the Hebrew, meaning "innermost room" or "sanctuary." The exact Hebrew equivalent is Devir. The exact feminine equivalent is Devira.

Devlin An Irish form of David. *See* David.

Dewey A Welsh form of David. *See* David.

Diamond From the Latin and Greek, meaning "precious stone." HEBREW EQUIVALENTS: Amikar, Chamadel, Chamud, Chemed, Leshem, Shoham. FEMININE HEBREW EQUIVALENTS: Bareket, Chamuda, Kevuda, Sapirit, Yakira.

Dick, Dickey, Dickie, Dicky Pet forms of Richard. *See* Richard.

Didi (דִּידִי) From the Hebrew, meaning "beloved." A pet form of Yedidya. The exact Hebrew equivalent is Didi. FEMININE HEBREW EQUIVALENTS: Davida, Yedida.

Dimitry A variant form of Demetrius. *See* Demetrius.

Dirk An English form of the Old High German name Hrodrich, meaning "famous." HEBREW EQUIVALENTS: Hillel, Noda, Shevach, Yehalel, Yehuda, Yehudi. FEMININE HEBREW EQUIVALENTS: Degula, Hillela, Shavcha, Tehila, Yehudit, Yudit.

Divri (דִּבְרִי) From the Hebrew, meaning "orator." The exact Hebrew equivalent is Divri. FEMININE HEBREW EQUIVALENTS: Amira, Dovevet.

Dix A patronymic form of Dick, meaning "Dick's son." A pet form of Richard. *See* Richard.

Dixie A pet form of Dix. *See* Dix.

Dixon A patronymic form of Richard, meaning "Richard's [Dick's] son." *See* Richard.

Dob A variant form of Robert. *See* Robert.

Dodic, Dodick Pet forms of David. *See* David.

Dodo (דּוֹדוֹ) From the Hebrew meaning, "his beloved" or "his uncle." The exact Hebrew equivalent is Dodo. The exact feminine Hebrew equivalent is Doda.

Doeg (דֹּאֵג) From the Hebrew, meaning "anxious, concerned." The exact Hebrew equivalent is Do'eg. FEMININE HEBREW EQUIVALENTS: Letifa, Rachmiela, Ruchama, Yeruchama.

Dolph A short form of Adolph. *See* Adolph.

Dom A pet form of Dominic. *See* Dominic.

Dominic, Dominick From the Latin, meaning "pertaining to God." HEBREW EQUIVALENTS: Amiel, Daniel, De'uel, Micha'el. FEMININE HEBREW EQUIVALENTS: Daniela, Michal, Yisr'ela.

Don A pet form of Donald. *See* Donald.

Donald From the Irish, meaning "brown stranger." Also, from the Celtic and Scottish, meaning "proud ruler." HEBREW EQUIVALENTS: Adoniya, Avinadav, Gershom, Katriel, Melech, Nadav, Yisrael. FEMININE HEBREW EQUIVALENTS: Atara, Be'ula, Gevira, Laya, Malka, Yisr'ela.

Donnie, Donny Pet forms of Donald. *See* Donald.

Donniel A variant spelling of Daniel. *See* Daniel.

Dor (דּוֹר) From the Hebrew, meaning "generation." Also, a French name derived from the Latin, meaning "of gold." The exact Hebrew equivalent is Dor. The exact feminine Hebrew equivalent is Dorit.

Doran (דּוֹרָן) From the Hebrew and Greek, meaning "gift." *See* Doron. The exact Hebrew equivalent is Doran.

Dore From the Greek, meaning "gift." HEBREW EQUIVALENTS: Doran, Doron, Doroni. FEMININE HEBREW EQUIVALENTS: Dorina, Doriya, Dorona, Doronit.

Dori (דּוֹרִי) A variant form of Dor, meaning "my generation." The exact Hebrew equivalent is Dori. The exact feminine Hebrew equivalent is Dorit.

Doron (דּוֹרוֹן) From the Hebrew, meaning "gift, present." The exact Hebrew equivalent is Doron. FEMININE HEBREW EQUIVALENTS: Dorina, Doriya, Dorona, and Doronit.

Dorris The masculine form of the feminine Doris. *See* Doris.

Dotan (דּוֹתָן) From the Hebrew, meaning "law." The exact Hebrew equivalent is Dotan. FEMININE HEBREW EQUIVALENTS: Dana, Daniela, Danit.

Dothan An Anglicized form of Dotan. *See* Dotan.

Doug A pet form of Douglas. *See* Douglas.

Douglas From the Celtic, meaning "gray." Also, from the Gaelic, meaning "black stream." HEBREW EQUIVALENTS: Adar, Avi'yam, Aynan (Enan), Kedar, Peleg. FEMININE HEBREW EQUIVALENTS: Adara, Devora, Laila, Marata, Miryam, Tzila.

Dov (דּוֹב) From the Hebrew, meaning "bear." The exact Hebrew equivalent is Dov. The exact feminine Hebrew equivalent is Duba.

Dovev (דּוֹבֵב) From the Hebrew, meaning "to speak, whisper." The exact Hebrew equivalent is Dovev. FEMININE HEBREW EQUIVALENTS: Doveva, Dovevit.

Drew A pet form of Andrew. See Andrew.

Dror A variant form of Deror. See Deror.

Drori A variant spelling of Derori. See Derori.

Dru A variant spelling of Drew. See Drew.

Duane A variant form of Wayne. See Wayne.

Dubi (דּוּבִּי) From the Hebrew, meaning "my bear." The exact Hebrew equivalent is Dubi. FEMININE HEBREW EQUIVALENTS: Duba, Dubit.

Dudley From the Old English, meaning "Dodd's meadow [lea]" or "Duda's meadow." HEBREW EQUIVALENTS: Adam, Admata, Artza, Hevel, Karmeli, Regev. FEMININE HEBREW EQUIVALENTS: Adama, Gana, Karmel, Shedema, Yizr'ela.

Dudu (דּוּדוּ) A pet form of David. See David. The exact Hebrew equivalent is Dudu.

Duff From the Celtic, meaning "dark, black-faced." HEBREW EQUIVALENTS: Adar, Ashchur, Chumi, Kedar, Pinchas. FEMININE HEBREW EQUIVALENTS: Ayfa (Efa), Chachila, Laila, Tzila.

Duke From the Latin, meaning "leader." HEBREW EQUIVALENTS: Aluf, Avraham, Raba, Rav, Rava, Solel, Yisrael. FEMININE HEBREW EQUIVALENTS: Alufa, Sara, Tzameret, Yisr'ela.

Duma (דּוּמָה) From the Hebrew, meaning "silence." The exact Hebrew equivalent is Duma. The exact feminine Hebrew equivalent is Dumit.

Duncan From the Celtic, meaning "warrior with dark skin." HEBREW EQUIVALENTS: Adar, Chumi, Gavriel, Gibor, Kedar, Pinchas. FEMININE HEBREW EQUIVALENTS: Adara, Chachila, Gavriela, Gibora, Tzila.

Dunn, Dunne From the Old English, meaning "brown." HEBREW EQUIVALENTS: Chum, Chumi. FEMININE HEBREW EQUIVALENTS: Chum, Chuma, Chumit.

Dunstan From the Old English, meaning "brown, rock quarry." HEBREW EQUIVALENTS: Chum, Chumi, Etan, Even, Sela. FEMININE HEBREW EQUIVALENTS: Chum, Chumit, Etana, Ritzpa.

Dur (דּוּר) From the Hebrew, meaning "to heap, pile up" or "to circle." Also, from the Old English, meaning "wild animal, deer." The exact Hebrew equivalent is Dur. FEMININE HEBREW EQUIVALENTS: Bat-Galim, Talmit, Tzivya, Ya'el.

Durand The French form of the Latin, meaning "enduring." HEBREW EQUIVALENTS: Mishmar, Notzer, Oved, Shemaryahu, Shoter. FEMININE HEBREW EQUIVALENTS: Notera, Noteret, Shimriya, Shimrit.

Durant, Durante   Variant Italian forms of Durand. *See* Durand.

Duriel (דוּרִיאֵל)   From the Hebrew, meaning "God is my dwelling place." The exact Hebrew equivalent is Duriel. FEMININE HEBREW EQUIVALENTS: Devira, Me'ona, Shafrira, Zevula.

Durk   A variant spelling of Dirk. *See* Dirk.

Duryea   From the Latin, meaning "enduring, eternal." HEBREW EQUIVALENTS: Amiad, Netzach, Nitzchi. FEMININE HEBREW EQUIVALENTS: Chava, Cha'ya, Nitzchiya.

Dustin   A variant form of Dunstan. *See* Dunstan.

Dusty   A pet form of Dustin. *See* Dustin.

Dwight   From the Anglo-Saxon, meaning "white, fair." HEBREW EQUIVALENTS: Ben-Chur, Churi, Lavan, Levanon, Livni. FEMININE HEBREW EQUIVALENTS: Levana, Levona, Tzechora, Zahara.

Dyck   A variant spelling of Dick. *See* Dick.

Dyke, Dykes   Variant spellings of Dick and Dix. *See* Dick *and* Dix.

Dylan   From the Welsh, meaning "sea." HEBREW EQUIVALENTS: Avi'yam, Aynan (Enan), Ma'ayan, Micha, Moshe. FEMININE HEBREW EQUIVALENTS: Michal, Miryam, Rut, Tarshisha.

Earl, Earle   From the Middle English, meaning "nobleman, well-bred, intelligent." HEBREW EQUIVALENTS: Achban, Buna, Chanoch, Maskil, Navon, Yavin. FEMININE HEBREW EQUIVALENTS: Bina, Milka, Ne'ora.

Eban   A variant form of Even. *See* Even.

Ebin   A variant form of Even. *See* Even.

Ebril (עֶבְרִיל)   A Yiddish form of Abraham. *See* Abraham.

Ed   A pet form of Edward. *See* Edward.

Edan   From the Celtic, meaning "fire, flame." HEBREW EQUIVALENTS: Lapid, Nur, Nuri, Nuriel, Reshef, Uri. FEMININE HEBREW EQUIVALENTS: Avuka, Shalhevet, Urit.

Edd   A pet form of Edward. *See* Edward.

Eddie   A pet form of Edward. *See* Edward.

Eddy   From the Middle English, meaning "whirlpool" or "unresting, energetic." HEBREW EQUIVALENTS: Arnon, Yaziz, Ziva. FEMININE HEBREW EQUIVALENTS: Charutza, Tirtza, Zeriza. Also, a pet form of Edward. *See* Edward.

Eden (עֵדֶן)   From the Hebrew, meaning "delight." The exact Hebrew equivalent is Eden (Ayden). The exact feminine Hebrew equivalent is Adina.

Eder (עֵדֶר)   From the Hebrew, meaning "herd, flock." The exact masculine and feminine Hebrew equivalent is Eder.

Edgar   From the Anglo-Saxon, meaning "happy, blessed warrior." HEBREW EQUIVALENTS: Baruch, Gad, Gavriel, Gibor, Gidon, Gera, Yatzliach. FEMININE HEBREW EQUIVALENTS: Avicha'yil, Beracha, Matzliach, Gavrila, Gibora, Gila.

Edison A patronymic form, meaning "son of Ed [Edward]." *See* Edward.

Edlow From the Old English, meaning "fruitful hill." HEBREW EQUIVA-LENTS: Bar-Ilan, Efra'yim, Merom, Periel, Romem, Talmi. FEMININE HEBREW EQUIVALENTS: Gal, Givona, Pora, Porachat, Pura, Talma, Talmit.

Edmond From the Anglo-Saxon, meaning "rich, fortunate, happy warrior or protector." HEBREW EQUIVALENTS: Asher, Ashir, Gad, Gavriel, Gibor. FEMININE HEBREW EQUIVALENTS: Ashera, Ashira, Gada, Gavriela, Gibora.

Edmund A variant spelling of Edmond. *See* Edmond.

Edri (עֶדְרִי) From the Hebrew, meaning "my flock." The exact Hebrew equivalent is Edri. The feminine Hebrew equivalent is Eder.

Edric From the Anglo-Saxon, meaning "rich ruler." HEBREW EQUIVALENTS: Aluf, Ba'al, Elrad, Melech, Moshel, Yisrael. FEMININE HEBREW EQUIVA-LENTS: Alufa, Malka, Sara, Sarit, Yisr'ela.

Edsel From the Anglo-Saxon, meaning "rich, prosperous." HEBREW EQUIV-ALENTS: Ashir, Hotir, Huna, Yishai, Yitro. FEMININE HEBREW EQUIVALENTS: Ashira, Yitra.

Edson A patronymic form, meaning "son of Ed [Edward]." *See* Edward.

Edward From the Anglo-Saxon, meaning "blessed, happy guardian." HE-BREW EQUIVALENTS: Avigdor, Mishmar, Noter, Shemaryahu, Simcha, Yachdiel, Yitzchak. FEMININE HEBREW EQUIVALENTS: Efrat, Migdala, Notera, Notzeret, Shimra, Shimrit, Shimriya.

Edwin From the Anglo-Saxon, meaning "happy, blessed friend." HEBREW EQUIVALENTS: Asher, Baruch, Chovav, David, Dodi, Eldad, Medad, No'am, Yedidya. FEMININE HEBREW EQUIVALENTS: Berucha, Davida, Doda, Liba, Yedida.

Edy A variant spelling of Eddy. *See* Eddy.

Efraim A variant spelling of Efrayim. *See* Efrayim.

Efrat (אֶפְרָת) From the Hebrew, meaning "honored, distinguished." The exact masculine and feminine Hebrew equivalent is Efrat.

Efrayim (אֶפְרַיִם) From the Hebrew, meaning "fruitful." The exact Hebrew equivalent is Efra'yim. FEMININE HEBREW EQUIVALENTS: Nitza, Pora, Poriya, Tenuva, Zimra.

Efrem A variant form of Efrayim. *See* Efrayim.

Efron (עֶפְרוֹן) From the Hebrew, meaning "bird." The exact Hebrew equivalent is Efron. The exact feminine Hebrew equivalent is Efrona.

Egan From the Anglo-Saxon, meaning "formidable, strong." HEBREW EQUIVALENTS: Abir, Amotz, Aziel, Aziz, Gavriel, Gever, Gibor. FEMININE HEBREW EQUIVALENTS: Abira, Adira, Amtza, Gavriela, Gibora, Uziela, Yechezkela.

Egon A variant spelling of Egan. *See* Egan.

Egoz (אֱגוֹז) From the Hebrew, meaning "nut." The exact Hebrew equivalent is Egoz. The exact feminine Hebrew equivalent is Egoza.

Eitan (אֵיתָן) From the Hebrew, meaning "strong, firm, permanent." The exact Hebrew equivalent is Etan (Eitan). The exact feminine Hebrew equivalent is Etana.

Elad (אֶלְעָד) From the Hebrew, meaning "forever, eternal." The exact Hebrew equivalent is Elad. The exact feminine Hebrew equivalent is Elada.

Elan A variant spelling of Ilan. See Ilan. Also, from the British, meaning "young deer." HEBREW EQUIVALENTS: A'yal, A'yalon, Efer, Tzevi, Tzeviel. FEMININE HEBREW EQUIVALENTS: A'yala, A'yelet, Ofra, Re'ema, Tzivya.

Elazar (אֶלְעָזָר) From the Hebrew, meaning "God has helped." The exact Hebrew equivalent is Elazar. FEMININE HEBREW EQUIVALENTS: Azriela, Ezra, Ezr'ela, Ezriela, Milka, Sa'ada.

Elbert A variant form of Albert. See Albert.

Elbie A pet form of Elbert. See Elbert.

Eldad (אֶלְדָד) From the Hebrew, meaning "beloved of God." The exact Hebrew equivalent is Eldad. FEMININE HEBREW EQUIVALENTS: Ahava, Amita, Chaviva, Davida, Yedida.

Eldar (אֶלְדָר) From the Hebrew, meaning "habitation of God." The exact Hebrew equivalent is Eldar. FEMININE HEBREW EQUIVALENTS: Devira, Me'ona, Zevula.

Elden From the Anglo-Saxon, meaning "older." HEBREW EQUIVALENTS: Kadmiel, Kedem, Saba, Sava, Yiftach, Yishai, Zaken. FEMININE HEBREW EQUIVALENTS: Bilha, Yeshisha, Zekena.

Elder From the Old English, meaning "old, older." See Elden.

Eleazar (אֶלְעָזָר) A variant spelling of Eliezer. See Eliezer.

Elex A variant form of Alex. See Alex.

Elford From the Old English, meaning "the old river crossing." HEBREW EQUIVALENTS: Aviyam, Beri, Chamat, Dalfon, Yuval. FEMININE HEBREW EQUIVALENTS: Afeka, Bat-Yam, Miryam.

Elgin From the Old English, meaning "true nobility." HEBREW EQUIVALENTS: Adar, Adir, Adon, Aminadav, Nadav, Nedavya, Nedivi, Yisrael, Yonadav. FEMININE HEBREW EQUIVALENTS: Adina, Adira, Matrona, Nediva, Negida, Sara, Yisr'ela.

Eli (אֵלִי) From the Hebrew, meaning "ascend" or "uplift." The exact Hebrew equivalent is Eli. FEMININE HEBREW EQUIVALENTS: Aliya, Elya, Ya'el. Also, a short form of Eliyahu. See Eliyahu.

Eliad (אֶלִיעָד) From the Hebrew, meaning "my God is eternal." The exact Hebrew equivalent is Eliad. FEMININE HEBREW EQUIVALENTS: Nitzcha, Nitzchiya, Nitzchona.

Eliah A variant form of Eliyahu. See Eliyahu.

Eliahu A variant spelling of Eliyahu. See Eliyahu.

Elias The Greek form of Elijah. See Elijah.

Eliata (אֶלִיאָתָה) From the Hebrew, meaning "my God has come." The exact Hebrew equivalent is Eliata. FEMININE HEBREW EQUIVALENTS: Eliya, Imanuela, Michal, Yo'ela.

Eliav (אֶלִיאָב) From the Hebrew, meaning "my God is [my] Father." The exact Hebrew equivalent is Eliav. FEMININE HEBREW EQUIVALENTS: Avia, Aviel, Aviela, Aviya, Avuya.

Eliaz (אֱלִיעַז) From the Hebrew, meaning "my God is strong." The exact Hebrew equivalent is Eliaz. FEMININE HEBREW EQUIVALENTS: Azriela, Gamliela, Gavriela, Uziela, Yechezkela.

Elidad (אֱלִידָד) From the Hebrew, meaning "my God is a friend." The exact Hebrew equivalent is Elidad. FEMININE HEBREW EQUIVALENTS: Amit, Amita, Re'uela, Rut, Yedida.

Elie A form of Eliyahu. *See* Eliyahu.

Eliezer (אֱלִיעֶזֶר) A variant form of Elazar. From the Hebrew, meaning "my God has helped." The exact Hebrew equivalent is Eliezer. FEMININE HEBREW EQUIVALENTS: Azriela, Ezra, Ezr'ela, Ezriela.

Elihu (אֱלִהוּא) A variant form of Eliyahu. The exact Hebrew equivalent is Elihu. Akin to Eliyahu.

Elijah The Anglicized form of Eliyahu. *See* Eliyahu.

Elika A variant form of Elyakim. *See* Elyakim.

Elio A Spanish form of Elijah. *See* Elijah.

Elior (אֱלִיאוֹר) From the Hebrew, meaning "my God is light." The exact Hebrew equivalent is Elior. The exact feminine Hebrew equivalent is Eliora.

Eliot A variant form of Elijah. *See* Elijah.

Eliram (אֱלִירָם) From the Hebrew, meaning "my God is mighty." The exact Hebrew equivalent is Eliram. FEMININE HEBREW EQUIVALENTS: Adira, Amtza, Ariel, Gavriela.

Eliraz (אֱלִירָז) From the Hebrew, meaning "my God is joy." The exact Hebrew equivalent is Eliraz. FEMININE HEBREW EQUIVALENTS: Aliza, Ditza, Gila, Ronela, Ronit.

Elisha (אֱלִישָׁע) From the Hebrew, meaning "my God is salvation." The exact Hebrew equivalent is Elisha. FEMININE HEBREW EQUIVALENTS: Aleksandra, Elisheva, Milka, Moshava, Teshua, Yeshua.

Elison A variant spelling of Ellison. *See* Ellison.

Eliya A short form of Eliyahu. *See* Eliyahu.

Eliyahu (אֱלִיָהוּ) From the Hebrew, meaning "the Lord is my God." The exact Hebrew equivalent is Eliyahu. FEMININE HEBREW EQUIVALENTS: Aviela, Aviya, Elisheva, Yocheved.

Elkan (אֶלְקָאן) A Yiddish form of Elkanah. *See* Elkanah.

Elkana, Elkanah (אֶלְקָנָה) From the Hebrew, meaning "God has acquired." The exact Hebrew equivalent is Elkana. The feminine Hebrew equivalent is Be'ula.

Elkin (אֶלְקִין) A variant spelling of Elkan. *See* Elkan.

Ellery From the Old English, meaning "alder tree," connoting growth. HEBREW EQUIVALENTS: Ela, Erez, Ilan, Luz, Miklot. FEMININE HEBREW EQUIVALENTS: Ariza, Arna, Arnit, Ela, Ilana, Ilanit.

Elliot, Elliott A variant spelling of Eliot. *See* Eliot.

Ellis A variant form of Elisha. *See* Elisha.

Ellison A patronymic form, meaning "son of Elijah." *See* Elijah.

Elly A pet form of Elijah. *See* Elijah.

Elmer From the Old English, meaning "noble, famous." HEBREW EQUIVALENTS: Gedalya, Hillel, Mehalel, Mehulal, Shevach, Shimi. FEMININE HEBREW EQUIVALENTS: Devora, Hila, Hillela, Odeleya.

Elmo A variant form of Elmer. *See* Elmer.

Elmor, Elmore Variant forms of Elmer. *See* Elmer.

Elnatan (אֶלְנָתָן) From the Hebrew, meaning "gift of God." The exact Hebrew equivalent is Elnatan. The exact feminine Hebrew equivalent is Netanela.

Elrad (אֶלְרָד) From the Hebrew, meaning "God is the ruler." The exact Hebrew equivalent is Elrad. FEMININE HEBREW EQUIVALENTS: Alufa, Atara, Be'ula, Laya, Malka, Miryam, Tzefira.

Elroy From the Latin, meaning "royal, king." HEBREW EQUIVALENTS: Avimelech, Elrad, Malkiel, Malkiram, Malkitzedek. FEMININE HEBREW EQUIVALENTS: Alufa, Atara, Malka, Malkit.

Elsen A patronymic form, meaning "son of Ellis" or "son of Elias." *See* Ellis *and* Elias.

Elvin From the Anglo-Saxon, meaning "godly friend." HEBREW EQUIVALENTS: Chaviv, Chovav, David, Eldad, Yedidya. FEMININE HEBREW EQUIVALENTS: Chaviva, Davida, Doda, Liba, Rut, Yedida.

Elwyn A variant spelling of Elvin. *See* Elvin.

Ely A pet form of Eliyahu. *See* Eli.

Elyakim (אֶלְיָקִים) From the Hebrew, meaning "God will establish." The exact Hebrew equivalent is Elyakim. FEMININE HEBREW EQUIVALENTS: Mashena, Mosada, Sa'ada.

Elyakum (אֶלְיָקוּם) A variant form of Elyakim. *See* Elyakim. The exact Hebrew equivalent is Elyakum.

Emanuel (עִמָּנוּאֵל) From the Hebrew, meaning "God is with us" or "God is our protector." The exact Hebrew equivalent is Imanuel. The exact feminine Hebrew equivalent is Imanuela.

Emerson A patronymic form, meaning "son of Emery." *See* Emery.

Emery From the Old High German, meaning "rich in accomplishments" or "industrious." HEBREW EQUIVALENTS: Arnon, Mahir, Yaziz, Yeter, Yitran, Ziruz, Ziza. FEMININE HEBREW EQUIVALENTS: Amela, Amalya, Charutza, Erana, Eranit, She'ifa, Yitra, Zeriza.

Emil From the Latin, meaning "industrious." HEBREW EQUIVALENTS: Arnon, Yaziz, Ziruz, Ziza. FEMININE HEBREW EQUIVALENTS: Amela, Amalya, Charutza, Tirtza, Zeriza.

Emile A French form of Emil. *See* Emil.

Emmanuel A variant spelling of Emanuel. *See* Emanuel.

Emmet, Emmett (אֱמֶת) From the Hebrew, meaning, "truth," or from the Anglo-Saxon, meaning "ant." The exact masculine and feminine Hebrew equivalent is Emmet.

Emory A variant spelling of Emery. *See* Emery.

Ennis A short form of Denis. *See* Denis.

Enoch (חֲנוֹךְ) An Anglicized form of the Hebrew name Chanoch, meaning "educated" or "dedicated." The exact Hebrew equivalent is Chanoch. The exact feminine Hebrew equivalent is Chanukah.

Enosh (אֱנוֹשׁ) From the Hebrew, meaning "man." The exact Hebrew equivalent is Enosh. FEMININE HEBREW EQUIVALENTS: Adonit, Adoniya, Gevira.

Ephraim A variant spelling of Efrayim. See Efrayim.

Er (עֵר) From the Hebrew, meaning "awake" or "guardian." The exact Hebrew equivalent is Er. FEMININE HEBREW EQUIVALENTS: Era, Erana, Eranit.

Eran (עֵירָן) From the Hebrew, meaning "industrious" or "awake." The exact Hebrew equivalent is Eran. The exact feminine Hebrew equivalent is Erana.

Erel (אֶרְאֵל) From the Hebrew, meaning "I will see God." The exact Hebrew equivalent is Erel. The exact feminine Hebrew equivalent is Erela.

Eri (עֵרִי) From the Hebrew, meaning "my guardian." The exact Hebrew equivalent is Eri. FEMININE HEBREW EQUIVALENTS: Mishmeret, Nitzra, Notera, Notzeret, Samara, Tiri.

Eric, Erich From the Old Norse, meaning "honorable ruler," and from the Anglo-Saxon, meaning "brave king." HEBREW EQUIVALENTS: Amatzya, Avicha'yil, Chizki, Eliram, Elitzur, Gur, Guryon, Katriel, Melech, Sharir, Sherira, Yo'az. FEMININE HEBREW EQUIVALENTS: Atara, Gavrila, Gibora, Katriela, Malka, Odeda, Tzefira, Uziela, Yechezkela.

Erik A variant spelling of Eric. See Eric.

Ernest From the Old High German, meaning "resolute, earnest, sincere." HEBREW EQUIVALENTS: Amitai, Amitan, Amnon, Avishur, Konanyahu, Yashar, Yesher, Yeshurun. FEMININE HEBREW EQUIVALENTS: Amana, Amita, Berura, Tamar, Temima.

Ernie A pet form of Ernest. See Ernest.

Erno A Hungarian form of Ernest. See Ernest.

Ernst A variant form of Ernest. See Ernest.

Errol From the Latin, meaning "to wander, wanderer," having the connotation of stranger. HEBREW EQUIVALENTS: Aminad, Gershom, Golyat, Sarid, Zerubavel. FEMININE HEBREW EQUIVALENTS: Avishag, Hagar, Sarida.

Erv A variant spelling of Irv (Irving). See Irving.

Erve A short form of Herve. See Herve.

Ervin A variant form of Irvin. See Irvin.

Erwin A variant form of Ervin. See Ervin.

Eryk A variant spelling of Eric. See Eric.

Eryle A variant spelling of Errol. See Errol.

Eshel (אֵשֶׁל) From the Hebrew, meaning "[tamarisk] tree." The exact Hebrew equivalent is Eshel. FEMININE HEBREW EQUIVALENTS: Ela, Shikma, Shikmona.

Eshkol (אֶשְׁכּוֹל) From the Hebrew, meaning "cluster of grapes." The exact Hebrew equivalent is Eshkol. The exact feminine Hebrew equivalent is Eshkola.

Esmond From the Anglo-Saxon, meaning "gracious protector." HEBREW EQUIVALENTS: Betzalel, Chasun, Elitzafan, Machaseh, Magen, Shemer, Shimri, Sitri, Ya'akov. FEMININE HEBREW EQUIVALENTS: Avigdora, Chaya, Chosa, Setura, Shimra, Shimrat, Shimriya, Sitriya.

Esmund A variant spelling of Esmond. *See* Esmond.

Etan A variant spelling of Eitan. *See* Eitan.

Ethan An Anglicized spelling of Eitan. *See* Eitan.

Eugen A variant form of Eugene. *See* Eugene.

Eugene From the Greek, meaning "well-born, born lucky, one of noble descent." HEBREW EQUIVALENTS: Aminadav, Mazal, Mazal-Tov, Nadav, Yehonadav, Yoram, Yehoram, Yisrael. FEMININE HEBREW EQUIVALENTS: Malka, Mazal, Nediva, Nesicha, Yisr'ela.

Evan A Welsh form of John, meaning "gracious." Also, from the Celtic, meaning "young warrior." HEBREW EQUIVALENTS: Avi-Cha'yil, Ben-Cha'yil, Gad, Gibor, Gidon, Yochanan. FEMININE HEBREW EQUIVALENTS: Amtza, Chana, Gavrila, Gibora, Yochana.

Evander A variant form of Evan. *See* Evan.

Evans A patronymic form of Evan. *See* Evan.

Even (אֶבֶן) From the Hebrew, meaning "stone." The exact Hebrew equivalent is Even. FEMININE HEBREW EQUIVALENTS: Avna, Avniela, Gazit, Tzur-El, Tzurit, Tzuriya.

Everett, Everette From the Anglo-Saxon, meaning "boar." Also, from the Norse, meaning "warrior." HEBREW EQUIVALENTS: Avicha'yil, Ben-Cha'yil, Gad, Gera, Gidon, Mordechai, Naftali, Nimrod. FEMININE HEBREW EQUIVALENTS: Atzma, Gavrila, Gibora, Merav, Tigra.

Evril (עֶבְרִיל) A Yiddish form of Avraham. *See* Avraham.

Evron (עֶבְרוֹן) From the Hebrew, meaning "overflowing anger, fury." The exact Hebrew equivalent is Evron. The exact feminine Hebrew equivalent is Evrona.

Ewen Probably a variant form of Evan, the Welsh form of John. *See* Evan *and* John.

Eyal A variant spelling of A'yal. *See* A'yal.

Eytan A variant spelling of Eitan. *See* Eitan.

Ezekiel (יְחֶזְקֵאל) From the Hebrew, meaning "God will strengthen." The exact Hebrew equivalent is Yechezkel. The exact feminine Hebrew equivalent is Yechezkela.

Ezer (עֶזֶר/עֵזֶר) From the Hebrew, meaning "help." The exact Hebrew equivalent is Ezer. FEMININE HEBREW EQUIVALENTS: Ezra, Ezr'ela, Ezriela, Mosha'a, Sa'ada, Teshua.

Ezra (עֶזְרָה/עֶזְרָא) From the Hebrew, meaning "help." The exact masculine and feminine Hebrew equivalent is Ezra.

Ezri (עֶזְרִי) From the Hebrew, meaning "my help." The exact Hebrew equivalent is Ezri. FEMININE HEBREW EQUIVALENTS: Ezra, Ezr'ela, Ezriela, Teshua.

Fabian A variant form of Fabius. *See* Fabius.

Fabius From the Latin, meaning "bean, bean farmer." HEBREW EQUIVALENTS: Adam, Karmel, Karmeli, Yizr'el. FEMININE HEBREW EQUIVALENTS: Eretz, Karmela, Nava, Yizr'ela.

Farleigh, Fairley, Farley From the Anglo-Saxon, meaning "beautiful meadow." HEBREW EQUIVALENTS: Adam, Bustanai, Choresh, Hevel, P'er, Shadmon, Shifron. FEMININE HEBREW EQUIVALENTS: Adama, Nofi'ya, Shadmit, Shedema, Shifra.

Farrel, Farrell From the Celtic, meaning "valorous one." HEBREW EQUIVALENTS: Abir, Abiri, Chutzpit, Gibor, No'az, Uzi, Uziya. FEMININE HEBREW EQUIVALENTS: Abira, Avniela, Aziela, Gibora, No'aza, Odeda.

Feibush A variant form of Feivel. *See* Feivel.

Feivel (פִּיינְוֶעל / פִּיינְל) The Yiddish form of Phoebus, from the Latin and Greek, meaning "bright one." HEBREW EQUIVALENTS: Avner, Bahir, Barak, Bazak, Me'ir, Ziv, Zivan, Zivi. FEMININE HEBREW EQUIVALENTS: Behira, Me'ira, Ora, Tzelila, Ziva, Zivanit, Zivi, Zivit.

Feiwel A variant spelling of Feivel. *See* Feivel.

Felix From the Latin, meaning "happy, fortunate, prosperous." HEBREW EQUIVALENTS: Asher, Gad, Gadi, Gadiel, Mazal, Mazal-Tov, Osher, Oshri, Yimna, Yitzchak. FEMININE HEBREW EQUIVALENTS: Ashera, Asherit, Gadiela, Gadit, Me'usheret, Ushara, Ushriya.

Ferd, Ferde A short form of Ferdinand. *See* Ferdinand.

Ferdie A pet form of Ferd. *See* Ferd.

Ferdinand. From the German, meaning "to be bold, courageous." HEBREW EQUIVALENTS: Abir, Amtza, Amotz, Kalev, Uziel, Uziya. FEMININE HEBREW EQUIVALENTS: Abira, Amtza, Ariel, Gavrila, Gibora, Uziela.

Ferdy A pet form of Ferd. *See* Ferd.

Fergus From the Irish and Gaelic, meaning "manly." HEBREW EQUIVALENTS: Ben-Azai, Ben-Cha'yil, Ben-Gever, Ben-Guryon, Uziya, Yechezkel. FEMININE HEBREW EQUIVALENTS: Abira, Amitza, Avicha'yil, Me'uza, Nili, Uza, Uzit.

Ferrin A variant form of Ferris. *See* Ferris.

Ferris From the Latin, meaning "iron," symbolizing strength. HEBREW EQUIVALENTS: Barzilai, Ben-Azai, Ben-Cha'yil, Peled, Pildash, Yechezkel. FEMININE HEBREW EQUIVALENTS: Avniela, Chasina, Etana, Uza, Uzit, Yechezkela.

Fish From the German, meaning "fish." HEBREW EQUIVALENTS: Dag, Nun. FEMININE HEBREW EQUIVALENTS: Dagit, Dagiya.

Fishel (פִּישְׁל/פִּישֶׁעל) A Yiddish pet form of Fish. *See* Fish.

Fishke (פִישׁקֶע) A Yiddish pet form of Fish. *See* Fish.

Fishkin A Slavic form of Fish. *See* Fish.

Fishlin A pet form of Fish. *See* Fish.

Fisk, Fiske From the Scandinavian, meaning "fish." *See* Fish.

Floren, Florence, Florentz, Florenz From the Latin, meaning "blooming." HEBREW EQUIVALENTS: Atlai, Miklot, Pekach, Pekachya, Tzemach, Yigdal, Yitzmach. FEMININE HEBREW EQUIVALENTS: Atalya, Perach, Pericha, Pircha, Pirchit, Pirchiya, Porachat, Tzemicha.

Floyd A corrupt form of Lloyd. *See* Lloyd.

Forest, Forrest From the Latin, meaning "woods." HEBREW EQUIVALENTS: Karmel, Karmeli, Ya'ar, Ya'ari. FEMININE HEBREW EQUIVALENTS: Gana, Karmel, Karmela, Ya'ara, Ya'arit.

Forester An Old French occupational name, meaning "one in charge of a forest." *See* Forest.

Fox From the German, meaning "fox." The exact Hebrew equivalent is Shual. The exact feminine Hebrew equivalent is Shuala.

Fraime (פְרֵיימֶע) A Yiddish pet form of Ephraim. *See* Ephraim.

Francis From the Middle English, meaning "a free man." HEBREW EQUIVALENTS: Avideror, Cherut, Deror, Deror-Li, Pesach, Pesachya, Rechavam, Rechavya. FEMININE HEBREW EQUIVALENTS: Chufshit, Derora, Derorit, Ge'ula, Li-Deror, Rachav.

Frank A pet form of Francis and Franklin. *See* Francis *and* Franklin.

Frankie A pet form of Frank. *See* Frank.

Franklin From the Old English, meaning "freeholder," connoting ownership and independence. HEBREW EQUIVALENTS: Ba'al, Elkana, Ka'yin, Kenan, Konen, Pesach, Pesachya, Rechavam. FEMININE HEBREW EQUIVALENTS: Be'ula, Devora, Ge'ula, Rachav.

Franklyn A variant spelling of Franklin. *See* Franklin.

Franz The German form of Francis. *See* Francis.

Fred, Freddie, Freddy Pet forms of Frederick. *See* Frederick.

Frederic A variant spelling of Frederick. *See* Frederick.

Frederick From the Latin and Old High German, meaning "peaceful ruler." HEBREW EQUIVALENTS: Avshalom, Ish-Shalom, Katriel, Margo'a, Melech, Sha'anan, Shalom, Shelomo. FEMININE HEBREW EQUIVALENTS: Rivka, Sha'anana, Shelomit, Shulamit, Za'yit.

Frederic, Fredrick Variant spellings of Frederick. *See* Frederick.

Freed A variant form of Freeman. *See* Freeman.

Freeman From the Anglo-Saxon, meaning "one born free." HEBREW EQUIVALENTS: Amidror, Avidror, Cherut, Dror, Dror-Li, Pesach, Rechavya. FEMININE HEBREW EQUIVALENTS: Cherut, Cheruta, Derora, Li-Dror, Serach.

Fremont From the French, meaning "freedom mountain." HEBREW EQUIVALENTS: Aharon, Avidror, Chagai, Chagiya, Cherut, Harel, Pesachya. HEBREW EQUIVALENTS: Aharona, Cheruta, Derora, Serach, Talmi.

Frits A variant spelling of Fritz. *See* Fritz.

Fritz A German form of Frederick. *See* Frederick.

Froim, Froime (פְרוֹימֶע/פְרוֹיִים) Yiddish pet forms of Ephraim. *See* Ephraim.

From, Fromel, Frommel (פְרָאמֶעל/פְרָאם) Yiddish forms of Avraham (Abraham). *See* Abraham.

Gab A pet form of Gabriel. *See* Gabriel.

Gabai (גַבַּי/גַבָּאי) From the Hebrew, meaning "communal official." The exact Hebrew equivalent is Gabai. FEMININE HEBREW EQUIVALENTS: Alufa, Tzameret.

Gabby A pet form of Gabriel. *See* Gabriel.

Gabe A pet form of Gabriel. *See* Gabriel.

Gabi (גַבִּי) A pet form of Gabriel. *See* Gabriel.

Gabriel (גַבְרִיאֵל) From the Hebrew, meaning "God is my strength." The exact Hebrew equivalent is Gavriel. FEMININE HEBREW EQUIVALENTS: Gavrila, Gavriela.

Gad (גָד) From the Hebrew and Arabic, meaning "happy, fortunate, lucky" or "warrior." The exact Hebrew equivalent is Gad. FEMININE HEBREW EQUIVALENTS: Gada, Gadit.

Gadi, Gaddi (גַדִי) Variant forms of Gad. *See* Gad.

Gadiel (גַדִיאֵל) From the Hebrew, meaning "God is my good fortune." The exact Hebrew equivalent is Gadiel. The exact feminine Hebrew equivalent is Gadiela.

Gafni (גַפְנִי) From the Hebrew, meaning "my vineyard." The exact Hebrew equivalent is Gafni. FEMININE HEBREW EQUIVALENTS: Gafna and Gafnit.

Gai (גַי/גַיְא) From the Hebrew, meaning "valley." The exact Hebrew equivalent is Gai. The exact feminine Hebrew equivalent is Ga'ya.

Gal (גַל) From the Hebrew, meaning "wave" or "heap, mound." The exact masculine and feminine Hebrew equivalent is Gal.

Gali (גַלִי) From the Hebrew, meaning "my wave" or "my hill." *See* Gal. The exact masculine and feminine Hebrew equivalent is Gali.

Galia A variant form of Galya. *See* Galya.

Galil (גַלִיל) From the Hebrew, meaning "roll up, a rolled sheet." Also, the name of the northern part of Israel. The exact Hebrew equivalent is Galil. The exact feminine Hebrew equivalent is Gelila.

Galmud (גַלְמוּד) From the Hebrew, meaning "lonely." The exact Hebrew equivalent is Galmud.

Galya (גַלְיָה) From the Hebrew, meaning "wave of God" or "hill of God." The exact masculine and feminine Hebrew equivalent is Galya.

Gamal (גָמָל) From the Arabic and Hebrew, meaning "camel." The exact Hebrew equivalent is Gamal.

Gamaliel A variant spelling of Gamliel. *See* Gamliel.

Gamliel (גַּמְלִיאֵל) From the Hebrew, meaning "God is my reward." The exact Hebrew equivalent is Gamliel. The exact feminine Hebrew equivalent is Gamliela.

Gan (גַּן) From the Hebrew, meaning "garden." The exact Hebrew equivalent is Gan. The exact feminine Hebrew equivalent is Gana.

Gani (גַּנִּי) From the Hebrew, meaning "my garden." The exact Hebrew meaning is Gani. FEMININE HEBREW EQUIVALENTS: Gana, Ganit, Gina, Ginat.

Garden From the Old High German and Danish, meaning "enclosure, garden." HEBREW EQUIVALENTS: Gan, Gani, Gina, Ginat, Gintoy, Ginton, Yarden. FEMININE HEBREW EQUIVALENTS: Gana, Ganit, Ganya, Gina, Ginat, Yardeniya.

Gardener An occupational name. A variant form of Garden. *See* Garden.

Garfield From the Old English, meaning "promontory." HEBREW EQUIVALENTS: Adam, Artzi, Aviyam, Dalfon, Dela'ya. FEMININE HEBREW EQUIVALENTS: Adama, Artzit, Bat-Yam, Eretz, Yaval.

Garner From the Latin, meaning "granary." HEBREW EQUIVALENTS: Dagan, Goren, Idra, Shachat. FEMININE HEBREW EQUIVALENTS: Garna, Garnit, Garona.

Garnet, Garnett From the Latin, meaning "grain." Also, a precious jewel so named because of its deep red color. HEBREW EQUIVALENTS: Admon, Almog, Goren, Guni, Peruda, Zohar. FEMININE HEBREW EQUIVALENTS: Degana, Deganit, Deganya, Garnit, Gorna, Pua, Segula, Yakira.

Garon (גָּרוֹן) From the Hebrew, meaning "threshing floor [for grain]." The exact Hebrew equivalent is Garon. FEMININE HEBREW EQUIVALENTS: Garna, Garnit, Garona.

Garret, Garrett From the Old French, meaning "to watch, guard." HEBREW EQUIVALENTS: Eri, Mishmar, Nitron, Notzer, Shaked, Shemarya, Shomer. FEMININE HEBREW EQUIVALENTS: Mishmeret, Nitzra, Notera, Shakeda, Shimrit, Tzofiya.

Garth From the Old English, meaning "garden, enclosed field." HEBREW EQUIVALENTS: Gan, Gani, Ginat, Ginton. FEMININE HEBREW EQUIVALENTS: Gana, Ganit, Ganya.

Garvey From the Anglo-Saxon, meaning "spearbearer, warrior." Also, a form of Garth. *See* Garth.

Gary, Garry Variant forms of Gerard and Gerald. *See* Gerard and Gerald.

Gavan A variant spelling of Gavin. *See* Gavin.

Gavin From the Welsh, meaning "little hawk." HEBREW EQUIVALENTS: Gozal, Orev, Tzipor. FEMININE HEBREW EQUIVALENTS: Chogla, Efrona, Tzipora, Ya'en.

Gavirol (גְבִירוֹל) A Sephardic form of Gavriel. *See* Gavriel.

Gavri (גַבְרִי) A variant form of Gavriel. *See* Gavriel.

Gavriel (גַבְרִיאֵל) From the Hebrew, meaning "God is my strength." The exact Hebrew equivalent is Gavriel. The exact feminine Hebrew equivalent is Gavriela.

Gedalia, Gedaliah Variant spellings of Gedalya. *See* Gedalya.

Gedalya (גְדַלְיָה) From the Hebrew, meaning "God is great." The exact Hebrew equivalent is Gedalya. FEMININE HEBREW EQUIVALENTS: Atalya, Gedola, Gedula, Rachav.

Gedalyahu (גְדַלְיָהוּ) A variant form of Gedalya. *See* Gedalya. The exact Hebrew equivalent is Gedalyahu.

Gedi (גְדִי) From the Hebrew, meaning "goat." The exact Hebrew equivalent is Gedi. The exact feminine Hebrew equivalent is Gadya.

Gefania, Gefaniah Variant spellings of Gefanya. *See* Gefanya.

Gefanya (גְפַנְיָה) From the Hebrew, meaning "vineyard of the Lord." The exact Hebrew equivalent is Gefanya. FEMININE HEBREW EQUIVALENTS: Gafna, Gafnit, Gefen, Karmela, Soreka.

Gefen (גֶפֶן) From the Hebrew, meaning "vine." The exact masculine and feminine Hebrew equivalent is Gefen.

Gene A pet form of Eugene. *See* Eugene.

Geoff A pet form of Geoffrey. *See* Geoffrey.

Geoffrey From the Anglo-Saxon, meaning "gift of peace" or "God's peace." HEBREW EQUIVALENTS: Avshalom, Magdiel, Natan, Netanel, Netanya, Shalem, Shalom, Shelomi, Shelomo. FEMININE HEBREW EQUIVALENTS: Menucha, Migdana, Shalva, Shelomit, Shelom-Tzion, Shulamit.

George From the Greek, meaning "farmer." HEBREW EQUIVALENTS: Adam, Bustenai, Chaklai, Choresh, Ginat, Karmeli, Nota'ya, Shadinon, Yizr'el. FEMININE HEBREW EQUIVALENTS: Gana, Karmela, Nava, Shadmit, Shedema, Yizr'ela.

Gerald An Old French and German form of Gerard. *See* Gerard.

Gerard From the Anglo-Saxon, meaning "spear" or "spearbearer, warrior." HEBREW EQUIVALENTS: Gad, Gadiel, Gavriel, Gevarya, Gever, Gibor, Sirya, Siryon. FEMININE HEBREW EQUIVALENTS: Chanit, Chanita, Chinit, Gadit, Gavriela, Gibora.

Gerhard, Gerhardt, Gerhart Variant forms of Gerard. *See* Gerard.

Gerome From the Greek, meaning "holy fame" or "sacred name." HEBREW EQUIVALENTS: Ben-Shem, Chagai, Devir, Hillel, Kadish, Kalman, Shem-Tov, Shamai, Shema'ya, Shemuel. FEMININE HEBREW EQUIVALENTS: Bat-Shem, Chagit, Chagiya, Devira, Tehila, Yehudit, Zimra.

Gerre A variant spelling of Gerry. *See* Gerry.

Gerry A pet form of Gerome. *See* Gerome.

Gershom (גֵרְשׁוֹם) From the Hebrew, meaning "stranger." The exact Hebrew equivalent is Gershom. The feminine Hebrew equivalent is Gershona.

Gershon (גֵרְשׁוֹן) A variant form of Gershom. *See* Gershom. The exact Hebrew equivalent is Gershon.

Gerson A variant form of Gershon. *See* Gershon.

Getzel (גֶעצְעל/גֶעצְל) A Yiddish pet form of the German name Gottfried. *See* Gottfried.

Geva (גֶּבַע) From the Hebrew, meaning "hill." The exact Hebrew equivalent is Geva. FEMININE HEBREW EQUIVALENTS: Gal, Gali, Giva, Givona.

Gib A pet form of Gilbert. *See* Gilbert.

Gibor, Gibbor (גִּבּוֹר) From the Hebrew, meaning "strong person." The exact Hebrew equivalent is Gibor. The exact feminine Hebrew equivalent is Gibora.

Gideon A variant spelling of Gidon. *See* Gidon.

Gidi A pet form of Gidon. *See* Gidon.

Gidon (גִּדְעוֹן) From the Hebrew, meaning either "maimed" or "mighty warrior." The exact Hebrew equivalent is Gidon. The exact feminine Hebrew equivalent is Gidona.

Gidoni (גִּדְעוֹנִי) A variant form of Gidon. *See* Gidon. The exact Hebrew equivalent is Gidoni.

Gifford From the Middle English, meaning "worthy gift." HEBREW EQUIVALENTS: Avishai, Doron, Elnatan, Elzavad, Matityahu, Netanel, Yatniel. FEMININE HEBREW EQUIVALENTS: Dorona, Matana, Netanela, Netaniela, Netanya, Yehava, Zevuda.

Gil (גִּיל) From the Hebrew, meaning "joy." The exact Hebrew equivalent is Gil. The exact feminine Hebrew equivalent is Gila. Also, a pet form of Gilbert. *See* Gilbert.

Gilad (גִּלְעָד) From the Hebrew, meaning "mound [hill] of testimony." The exact Hebrew equivalent is Gilad. The exact feminine Hebrew equivalent is Gilada.

Giladi (גִּלְעָדִי) A variant form of Gilad, meaning "man from Gilad [Gilead]." *See* Gilad. The exact Hebrew equivalent is Giladi.

Gilbert From the Anglo-Saxon, meaning "light of many," "bright promise," or "sword." HEBREW EQUIVALENTS: Barak, Baraki, Eli-Or, Me'ir, Neriya, Sheraga, Shimshon, Shragai, Uri, Uriel, Zohar. FEMININE HEBREW EQUIVALENTS: Behira, Eli-Ora, Me'ira, Noga, Ora, Or-Li, Orlit, Zaka, Zohara.

Gildor (גִּלְדוֹר) From the Hebrew, meaning "generation of joy." The exact Hebrew equivalent is Gildor. FEMININE HEBREW EQUIVALENTS: Dor, Dorit, Doriya.

Giles From the Greek, meaning "goatskin," connoting a protective shield. HEBREW EQUIVALENTS: Efer, Ofri, Shaked, Shemarya, Shomer. FEMININE HEBREW EQUIVALENTS: Gadya, Mishmeret, Nitzra, Ya'ala, Ya'alat-Chen, Ya'el, Ya'ela.

Gili (גִּילִי) From the Hebrew, meaning "my joy." The exact masculine and feminine equivalent is Gili.

Gill A variant spelling of Gil. *See* Gil.

Gilli A variant spelling of Gili. *See* Gili.

Gilmore From the Celtic, meaning "valley near the sea." HEBREW EQUIVALENTS: Avigal, Aviyam, Emek, Gai, Gechazi, Livyatan. FEMININE HEBREW EQUIVALENTS: Bat-Galim, Bat-Yam, Miryam, Yama, Yamit.

Gimpel (גִּימְפֶּעל) A Yiddish form of the German Gumprecht, meaning "bright." MASCULINE HEBREW EQUIVALENTS: Me'ir, Or, Or-Cha'yim, Ori,

Oriel, Zerachya. FEMININE HEBREW EQUIVALENTS: Me'ira, Uriela, Urit, Ye'ira, Ye'ora.

Ginat (גִּינַת) From the Hebrew, meaning "garden." The exact masculine and feminine Hebrew equivalent is Ginat.

Ginson A variant spelling of Ginton. *See* Ginton.

Ginton (גִּינְתוֹן) From the Hebrew, meaning "garden, orchard." The exact Hebrew equivalent is Ginton. FEMININE HEBREW EQUIVALENTS: Gana, Ganit, Gina, Ginat.

Giora (גִּיוֹרָה/גִּיוֹרָא) From the Hebrew, meaning "strong." The exact masculine and feminine Hebrew is Giora.

Girard A variant spelling of Gerard. *See* Gerard.

Gitai (גִּיתָּאִי/גִּיתַּי) From the Aramaic, meaning "one who presses grapes." The exact Hebrew equivalent is Gitai. FEMININE HEBREW EQUIVALENTS: Gat, Gita, Gitit.

Giti (גִּיתִּי) A variant form of Gitai. *See* Gitai. The exact Hebrew equivalent is Giti.

Giva (גִּבְעָא/גִּבְעָה) From the Aramaic and Hebrew, meaning "hill." The exact masculine and feminine Hebrew equivalent is Giv'a.

Givol (גִּבְעוֹל) From the Hebrew, meaning "budding, blooming." The exact Hebrew equivalent is Givol. The exact feminine Hebew equivalent is Givola.

Givon (גִּבְעוֹן) From the Hebrew, meaning "hill, heights." The exact Hebrew equivalent is Givon. The exact feminine Hebrew equivalent is Givona.

Glen, Glenn From the Celtic, meaning "glen, secluded mountain valley." HEBREW EQUIVALENTS: Emek, Gai, Gechazi, Ge'ora, Ginton, Ya'ar, Ya'ari. FEMININE HEBREW EQUIVALENTS: Gana, Ganit, Ga'ya, Gina, Ginat, Karmiya, Ya'ara, Ya'arit.

Goddard From the Old English, meaning "good in counsel." HEBREW EQUIVALENTS: Bina, Buna, Ish-Sechel, Navon, Pele-Yo'etz, Tachkemoni, Ye'utz, Yo'etz. FEMININE HEBREW EQUIVALENTS: Chochma, Geona, Geonit, Tushiya.

Godfrey A variant form of Gottfried. *See* Gottfried.

Godwin From the Anglo-Saxon, meaning "friend of God." HEBREW EQUIVALENTS: Ahuvya, Amitai, Chovav, Chovev, Re'uel, Yedidya. FEMININE HEBREW EQUIVALENTS: Achava, Amit, Amita, Re'uela, Rut, Yedida.

Goel (גּוֹאָל) From the Hebrew, meaning "redeemer." The exact Hebrew equivalent is Go'el. FEMININE HEBREW EQUIVALENTS: Galya, Ge'ula, Go'elet, Yigalya.

Golan (גּוֹלָן) From the Hebrew, meaning "refuge." The exact Hebrew equivalent is Golan. FEMININE HEBREW EQUIVALENTS: Chosa, Luz, Sarida.

Goliath (גָּלְיָת) From the Hebrew, meaning "exiled one, stranger." The exact Hebrew equivalent is Golyat. FEMININE HEBREW EQUIVALENTS: Avishag, Hagar.

Goral (גּוֹרָל) From the Hebrew, meaning "lot, lottery" or "fate." The exact Hebrew equivalent is Goral. The exact feminine Hebrew equivalent is Gorala.

Goran From the British, meaning "cathedral." The Hebrew equivalent is Devir. The feminine Hebrew equivalent is Devira.

Gordon From the Gaelic, meaning "hero, strongman." HEBREW EQUIVALENTS: Abir, Abiri, Amitz, Atzmon, Azriel, Gavriel, Gevaram, Gevarya, Gur, Guriel, Guryon, Shamir. FEMININE HEBREW EQUIVALENTS: Abira, Azriela, Gavriela, Gavrila, Gevura, Gibora, Yechezkela.

Gore A short form of either Goran or Gordon. *See* Goran *and* Gordon.

Goren (גּוֹרֶן) From the Hebrew, meaning "threshing floor." The exact Hebrew equivalent is Goren. The exact feminine Hebrew equivalent is Garona.

Gorman From the British, meaning "member of a choir." HEBREW EQUIVALENTS: Amiron, Amishar, Liron, Meshorer, Ron, Ronel, Zimri, Zimroni. FEMININE HEBREW EQUIVALENTS: Arnit, Lirona, Mangina, Meshoreret, Ranit.

Gottfried From the German, meaning "peace of God." HEBREW EQUIVALENTS: Avshalom, Ish-Shalom, Mano'ach, Margo'a, Sha'anan, Shalom, Shelemya, Shelomi, Shilem. FEMININE HEBREW EQUIVALENTS: Achi-Shalom, Marge'a, Menucha, Sha'anana, Shalva, Shalviya, Shelomit, Shulamit.

Gozal (גּוֹזָל) From the Hebrew, meaning "young bird." The exact Hebrew equivalent is Gozal. The exact feminine Hebrew equivalent is Gozala.

Graham From the Old English, meaning "gray, dwelling place." HEBREW EQUIVALENTS: Avgar, Dur, Yeshavam, Yeshevav, Zevul, Zevulun. FEMININE HEBREW EQUIVALENTS: Lina, Me'ona, Tira, Zevula.

Granger From the Old French, meaning "farm steward." HEBREW EQUIVALENTS: Avdel, Avdi, Eved, Malachi, Ovadya, Shimshai. FEMININE HEBREW EQUIVALENTS: Adama, Ama, Shimshona.

Grant From the Old French, meaning "to grant, bequeath." HEBREW EQUIVALENTS: Avishai, Doron, Elnatan, Matan, Matanya, Matityahu, Natan, Yonatan. FEMININE HEBREW EQUIVALENTS: Matana, Migdana, Mincha, Netina, Teruma, Teshura.

Gray From the Old English, meaning "to shine." HEBREW EQUIVALENTS: Hillel, Me'ir, Yitzhar, Yizrach, Zahir, Zerach, Zerachya. FEMININE HEBREW EQUIVALENTS: Korenet, Mazhira, Me'ira, Noga, Zahara, Zahari.

Greeley, Greely Abbreviated forms of the Anglo-Saxon *greenlea*, meaning "green meadow." HEBREW EQUIVALENTS: Adam, Bustanai, Chaglai, Choresh, Shadmon, Yarkona, Yogev. FEMININE HEBREW EQUIVALENTS: Adama, Shadmit, Shedema, Yarkona.

Greg, Gregg From the Anglo-Saxon, meaning "to shine." HEBREW EQUIVALENTS: Me'ir, Yitzhar, Yizrach, Zahir, Zerach, Zerachya. FEMININE HEBREW EQUIVALENTS: Korenet, Mazhira, Me'ira, Noga, Zahara, Zehira.

Gregory From the Greek, meaning "vigilant watchman." HEBREW EQUIVALENTS: Avigdor, Ginat, Shemarya, Shemaryahu. FEMININE HEBREW EQUIVALENTS: Avigdora, Botzra, Gana, Tira, Ya'akova.

Griffin From the Welsh, meaning "strong in faith." HEBREW EQUIVALENTS: Amitai, Amnon, Buki, Heman, Yekutiel. FEMININE HEBREW EQUIVALENTS: Bitcha, Berura, Emuna, Gavrila, Gibora.

Griffith A Welsh form of Griffin. *See* Griffin.

Grover From the Anglo-Saxon, meaning "one who grows trees." HEBREW EQUIVALENTS: Alon, Amir, Arzi, Bar-Ilan, Ela, Ilan, Oren. FEMININE HEBREW EQUIVALENTS: Alona, Ariza, Arna, Artzit, Etzyona, Ilana, Shikmona.

Guni (גּוּנִי) From the Hebrew, meaning "tinge of color" or "reddish black." The exact Hebrew equivalent is Guni. FEMININE HEBREW EQUIVALENTS: Chachila, Efa, Laila, Tzila.

Gunther From the Old German, meaning "war" or "warrior." HEBREW EQUIVALENTS: Ben-Cha'yil, Chavakuk, Gad, Gera, Gibor, Gidon, Ish-Cha'yil. FEMININE HEBREW EQUIVALENTS: Amitza, Amtza, Gavrila, Gibora, Tigra.

Gur (גּוּר) From the Hebrew, meaning "young lion." The exact Hebrew equivalent is Gur. FEMININE HEBREW EQUIVALENTS: Ariel, Ariela, Gurit, Kefira, Leviya.

Gur-Ari (גּוּר־אָרִי) A variant form of Gur-Arye. *See* Gur-Arye. The exact Hebrew equivalent is Gur-Ari.

Gur-Arye, Gur-Aryeh (גּוּר־אַרְיֵה) From the Hebrew, meaning "young lion, cub." The exact Hebrew equivalent is Gur-Arye. *See* Gur *for additional equivalents.*

Guri (גּוּרִי) From the Hebrew, meaning "my young lion." The exact Hebrew equivalent is Guri. *See* Gur *for additional equivalents.*

Guria A variant spelling of Gurya. *See* Gurya.

Guriel (גּוּרִיאֵל) From the Hebrew, meaning "God is my lion" or "God is my refuge." The exact Hebrew equivalent is Guriel. FEMININE HEBREW EQUIVALENTS: Arela, Ariel, Ariela, Gurit, Kefira, Leviya.

Gurion The popular spelling of Guryon. *See* Guryon.

Gurya (גּוּרְיָה/גּוּרְיָא) An Aramaic and Hebrew form of Gur. *See* Gur. The exact Hebrew equivalent is Gurya.

Guryon (גּוּרְיוֹן) From the Hebrew, meaning "lion," signifying strength. The exact Hebrew equivalent is Guryon. *See* Gur *for additional equivalents.*

Gus A pet form of Gustavus. *See* Gustavus.

Gustaf The Swedish form of Gustavus. *See* Gustavus.

Gustav, Gustave German forms of Gustavus. *See* Gustavus.

Gustavus From the German and Swedish, meaning "the staff [weapon] of the Goths," a symbol of authority. HEBREW EQUIVALENTS: Ben-Cha'yil, Gad, Gera, Gidon, Ish-Cha'yil, Melech, Mordechai, Yisrael. FEMININE HEBREW EQUIVALENTS: Gavriela, Gavrila, Gibora, Malka, Tigra, Yisr'ela.

Guthrie From the Celtic, meaning "war serpent" or "war hero." HEBREW EQUIVALENTS: Gad, Gadi, Gavriel, Gevaryahu, Ish-Cha'yil, Mordechai, Nimrod. FEMININE HEBREW EQUIVALENTS: Gada, Gadit, Gidona, Merav, Tigra.

Guy From the Old French, meaning "a guide" or "rope [that guides]." Also, a variant spelling of Gai, meaning "valley." *See* Gai. HEBREW

EQUIVALENTS: Aluf, Chanoch, Gai, Gechazi, Petil. FEMININE HEBREW EQUIV-
ALENTS: Alufa, Petila, Rivka, Tikva, Tzefira.

Gwynn, Gwynne From the Welsh, meaning "fair, white." HEBREW EQUIVA-
LENTS: Lavon, Levanon, Malbin, Tzecharya. FEMININE HEBREW EQUIVA-
LENTS: Levana, Livna, Livnat, Malbina, Tzechira, Tzechorit.

Gyles A variant spelling of Giles. See Giles.

Habakuk, Habakkuk From the Hebrew, meaning "to embrace." Also,
an Assyrian plant-name. The exact Hebrew equivalent is Chavakuk. FE-
MININE HEBREW EQUIVALENTS: Ahuva, Kalanit, Kida, Melabevet, Yenika.

Habib a variant spelling of Chaviv. See Chaviv.

Habibi A variant spelling of Chavivi. See Chavivi.

Hada A variant form of Hadar. See Hadar.

Hadar (הָדָר/הֲדַר) From the Hebrew, meaning "beautiful, ornamented"
or "honored." The exact Hebrew equivalent is Hadar.

Hadrian From the Greek, meaning "rich." HEBREW EQUIVALENTS: Ashir,
Hotir, Huna, Yishai, Yitro. FEMININE HEBREW EQUIVALENTS: Ashira, Bat-
Shua, Yitra.

Hadriel (הַדְרִיאֵל) From the Hebrew, meaning "splendor of the Lord."
The exact Hebrew equivalent is Hadriel. FEMININE HEBREW EQUIVALENTS:
Hadara, Yifa, Yifat, Ziva, Zivi.

Hag (חַג) From the Hebrew, meaning "holiday." A variant spelling of
Chag. See Chag.

Hagai, Haggai Variant spellings of Chagai. See Chagai.

Hagi A variant spelling of Chagi. See Chagi.

Hai A variant form and spelling of Chai. See Chai.

Haim A variant spelling of Chaim. See Chaim.

Hal A pet form of Harold or Haley. See Harold *and* Haley.

Hale A pet form of Haley. See Haley.

Haley From the Old English, meaning "healthy, whole" or "holy." HE-
BREW EQUIVALENTS: Asa, Devir, Kadish, Rafa, Rafi, Refael, Yekutiel.
FEMININE HEBREW EQUIVALENTS: Refua, Rofi, Terufa.

Hallel (הַלֵּל) From the Hebrew, meaning "praise." The exact Hebrew
equivalent is Hallel. The exact feminine Hebrew equivalent is Hallela.

Halley, Hallie Variant spellings of Haley. See Haley.

Ham The Anglicized form of Cham. See Cham.

Hamilton A variant form of Hamlet and Hamlin. See Hamlet *and*
Hamlin.

Hamish A variant form of the Gaelic name Seumas, which is a form of
James. See James.

Hamlet From the Low German, meaning "enclosed area," or from the
Old German, meaning "home." HEBREW EQUIVALENTS: Betzer, Bitzaron,

Chetzrai, Chetzron, Gidron, Lotan. FEMININE HEBREW EQUIVALENTS: Efrat, Gana, Ganit, Ganya.

Hamlin From the Old English, meaning "a brook near home." HEBREW EQUIVALENTS: Arnon, Avi'yam, Beri, Chamat, Dalfon. FEMININE HEBREW EQUIVALENTS: Afeka, Arnona, Dalya, Miryam.

Hanan A variant spelling of Chanan. *See* Chanan.

Hanina A variant spelling of Chanina. *See* Chanina.

Hanoch A variant spelling of Chanoch. *See* Chanoch.

Hans A short form of the German name Johannes (John). *See* John.

Hansel A Bavarian form of Hans. *See* John.

Hansen A variant spelling of Hanson. *See* Hanson.

Hanson A Bavarian form of Hans. *See* Hans.

Harel (הַרְאֵל) From the Hebrew, meaning "mountain of God." The exact Hebrew equivalent is Harel. The exact feminine Hebrew equivalent is Harela.

Harlan From the Middle English and the Low German, meaning "hemp or flax," or from the Old English, meaning "warrior." HEBREW EQUIVALENTS: Amatzya, Ben-Cha'yil, Gavriel, Ish-Cha'yil, Gera, Gibor, Korach. FEMININE HEBREW EQUIVALENTS: Amtza, Gavriela, Gavrila, Gibora, Shalgit, Shalgiya, Tigra.

Harley From the Old English, meaning "field of plants." HEBREW EQUIVALENTS: Chavakuk, Ezrach, Narkis, Neta, Nufar, Yizr'el, Zichrini, Zoraya. FEMININE HEBREW EQUIVALENTS: Marganit, Marva, Ofrit, Rakefet, Ritma, Rotem, Zichriya.

Harlin A variant spelling of Harlan. *See* Harlan.

Harlow From the Old Norse, meaning "army leader." HEBREW EQUIVALENTS: Gad, Gadiel, Gevarya, Gevaryahu, Gever, Meron, Mordechai, Nimrod, Yisrael. FEMININE HEBREW EQUIVALENTS: Chila, Gada, Gadit, Gidona, Yisr'ela.

Harman From the Anglo-Saxon, meaning "soldier," or from the Old English, meaning "keeper of hares and deer." HEBREW EQUIVALENTS: A'yal, Mishmar, Nitron, Noter, Tzevi. FEMININE HEBREW EQUIVALENTS: A'yala, A'yelet, Shimrit, Shomera, Tzivya.

Harmon From the Greek, meaning "peace, harmony." HEBREW EQUIVALENTS: Achishalom, Avshalom, Ish-Shalom, Sha'anan, Shalom, Shelomo. FEMININE HEBREW EQUIVALENTS: Menucha, Meshulemet, Shalva, Shalviya, Shelomit, Shulamit.

Harold From the Old English, meaning "leader of the army" or "warrior." HEBREW EQUIVALENTS: Avicha'yil, Barzilai, Chizki, Chizkiyahu, Gad, Gevarya, Medan, Meron, Mordechai. FEMININE HEBREW EQUIVALENTS: Gada, Gadit, Gidona, Merav, Tigra.

Harris A patronymic form of Harry, meaning "Harry's son." *See* Harry.

Harrison A patronymic form, meaning "Harry's son." *See* Harry.

Harry From the Middle English, a variant form of Henry. *See* Henry.

Hart, Harte From the Middle English, meaning "deer, stag." HEBREW EQUIVALENTS: A'yal, Ben-Tzvi, Efer, Efron, Tzevi, Tzeviel. FEMININE HEBREW EQUIVALENTS: A'yala, A'yelet, Ofra, Re'ema, Tzivya.

Hartley From the Old English, meaning "field in which the deer roam." HEBREW EQUIVALENTS: A'yal, Ben-Tzevi, Efer, Hertzel, Tzevi. FEMININE HEBREW EQUIVALENTS: A'yala, A'yelet, Hertzela, Ofra, Tzivya.

Harvey From the Old High German, meaning "army battle." Also, from the Celtic, meaning "progressive, liberal, flourishing." HEBREW EQUIVALENTS: Gad, Gidoni, Meron, Mordechai, Pesach, Pesachya, Rechavam. FEMININE HEBREW EQUIVALENTS: Amtza, Chila, Gada, Gadit, Gidona, Merav, Tigra.

Haskel, Haskell (הַשְׂכֵּל) From the Hebrew, meaning "wise, wisdom." Also, from the Anglo-Saxon, meaning "ash tree." Also, a Yiddish form of the Hebrew name Yechezkel, meaning "God is my strength." See Yechezkel. HEBREW EQUIVALENTS: Achban, Bina, Buna, Chachmoni, Chanoch, Ish-Sechel, Navon, Utz, Yosha, Zavin. FEMININE HEBREW EQUIVALENTS: Chochma, Ge'ona, Nevona, Tushiya.

Havelock From the Anglo-Saxon, meaning "dwelling near the lake." HEBREW EQUIVALENTS: Dur, Yeshevav, Zevulun. FEMININE HEBREW EQUIVALENTS: Lina, Me'ona, Tira, Zevula.

Haviv A variant spelling of Chaviv. See Chaviv.

Hayden From the Anglo-Saxon, meaning "hay field, pasture land." HEBREW EQUIVALENTS: Bustanai, Chaklai, Choresh, Shadmon, Yagev, Zore'a. FEMININE HEBREW EQUIVALENTS: Churshit, Shadmit, Shedma.

Haym A variant spelling of Chaim. See Chaim.

Hayyim, Hayym A variant spellings of Chayim. See Chayim.

Hector From the Greek, meaning "anchor, protector." HEBREW EQUIVALENTS: Avigdor, Chetzron, Ginat, Refa'el, Sa'adya, Shemarya, Shemaryahu, Ya'akov, Yachmai. FEMININE HEBREW EQUIVALENTS: Batzra, Chasya, Chosa, Shimrit, Tira, Ya'akova.

Hed (הֵד) From the Hebrew, meaning "echo." The exact Hebrew equivalent is Hed. The feminine Hebrew equivalent is Hedya.

Hedley From the Old English, meaning "covering" or "covered meadow." HEBREW EQUIVALENTS: Betzer, Chupa, Chupam, Gidron, Shafrir. FEMININE HEBREW EQUIVALENTS: Shafrira, Talal, Talila, Tal-Li, Tzina.

Heinrich The German form of Henry. See Henry.

Helem (הֶלֶם) From the Hebrew, meaning "hammer." The exact Hebrew equivalent is Helem. The feminine Hebrew equivalent is Makabit.

Heller An Old High German form of the Latin, meaning "sun." HEBREW EQUIVALENTS: Charsom, Koresh, Shimshon. FEMININE HEBREW EQUIVALENTS: Chamaniya, Shimshona.

Heman (הֵימָן) From the Hebrew, meaning "faithful." The exact equivalent is Heman. FEMININE HEBREW EQUIVALENTS: Amana, Amanya, Emuna, Ne'emana.

Henri The French form of Henry. See Henry.

Henry From the Anglo-Saxon, meaning "ruler of the home, rich lord."

HEBREW EQUIVALENTS: Adoniya, Aluf, Avraham, Avram, Chashmon, Chashmona'i, Katriel, Malachi, Melech, Rav, Rava, Rosh, Yisrael. FEMININE HEBREW EQUIVALENTS: Alufa, Atara, Malka, Miryam, Sara, Sarit, Yisr'ela.

Herbert From the Old High German, meaning "clever, smart" or "excellent ruler." HEBREW EQUIVALENTS: Adoniya, Avraham, Haskel, Katriel, Melech, Nadav. FEMININE HEBREW EQUIVALENTS: Alufa, Atara, Malka, Sara, Sarit, Yisr'ela.

Hercules From the Greek, meaning "glory." HEBREW EQUIVALENTS: Amihod, Hadar, Hod, Hodiya, Ish-Hod. FEMININE HEBREW EQUIVALENTS: Adra, Tifara, Tiferet, Yocheved.

Herman From the Old High German, meaning "army man, soldier." HEBREW EQUIVALENTS: Gad, Gera, Gibor, Mordechai, Yariv, Yisrael. FEMININE HEBREW EQUIVALENTS: Gavriela, Gavrila, Gibora, Tigra, Yisr'ela.

Hermann A variant German spelling of Herman. *See* Herman.

Hermon The Anglicized form of Chermon. *See* Chermon.

Hermoni The Anglicized form of Chermoni. *See* Chermoni.

Hersch, Herschel Variant spellings of Hersh and Hershel. *See* Hersh *and* Hershel.

Hersh (הֶערש) From the Yiddish, meaning "deer." HEBREW EQUIVALENTS: A'yal, A'yalon, Efron, Ofer, Tzevi, Tzivyon. FEMININE HEBREW EQUIVALENTS: A'yala, A'yelet, Tzivya, Ya'ala, Ya'alit.

Hershel (הֶערשֶעל/הֶערשֶל) A pet form of Hersh. *See* Hersh.

Hertz (הֶערץ) A pet form of Hersh. *See* Hersh.

Hertzel (הֶערצֶל) A variant form spelling of Herzl. *See* Herzl.

Hertzl (הֶערצֶל) A diminutive form of Hertz. *See* Hertz.

Herz A variant spelling of Hertz. *See* Hertz.

Herzl A variant spelling of Hertzel. *See* Hertzl.

Heschel (הֶעשֶעל/הֶעשֶל) A variant form of Hershel. *See* Hershel.

Hesh (הֶעש) A Yiddish pet form of Hersh. *See* Hersh.

Heshel A variant spelling of Heschel. *See* Heschel.

Heske A pet form of Heskel. *See* Heskel.

Heskel (הֶעשקֶל/הֶעשקֶל) A variant form of Haskel. *See* Haskel.

Hesketh Probably a variant form of Hezekia. *See* Hezekia.

Heskiah A variant spelling of Hezekia. *See* Hezekia.

Hevel (הֶבֶל) From the Hebrew, meaning "breath, vapor," or from the Assyrian, meaning "son." Abel is the Anglicized form. The exact Hebrew equivalent is Hevel. FEMININE HEBREW EQUIVALENTS: Bat, Batya, Nafshiya, She'ifa.

Heywood From the Old English, meaning "hay field" or "dark forest." HEBREW EQUIVALENTS: Efa, Karmel, Kedar, Pinchas, Ya'ari. FEMININE HEBREW EQUIVALENTS: Chachila, Efa, Karmela, Laila, Tzila, Ya'ara.

Hezekia, Hezekiah Variant spellings of Chizkiya. *See* Chizkiya.

Hi A pet form for a variety of names, including Hilary, Hiram, and Hyman. High is a variant spelling.

Hiel A variant spelling of Chiel. *See* Chiel.

High From the Old English, meaning "high, a hillsite." *See* Hi.

Hila (הִילָה/הִלָא) From the Aramaic and Hebrew, meaning "praise." The exact masculine and feminine Hebrew equivalent is Hila.

Hilary From the Greek and Latin, meaning "cheerful." Also, from the Anglo-Saxon, meaning "guardian, protector." HEBREW EQUIVALENTS: Avigdor, Chasun, Shemarya, Shemaryahu, Simcha, Simchon, Yagil, Yachmai. FEMININE HEBREW EQUIVALENTS: Aviga'yil, Avigdora, Botzra, Chedva, Gila, Shimrit, Ya'akova.

Hili (הִילִי/הִלִי) A pet form of Hillel. *See* Hillel.

Hill From the Anglo-Saxon, meaning "hill, high place." HEBREW EQUIVALENTS: Aharon, Geva, Givon, Haran, Harel, Marom, Talmai, Telem. FEMININE HEBREW EQUIVALENTS: Gal, Gali, Gilada, Harela, Meroma, Talma, Talmit.

Hillard A variant form of Hill. *See* Hill.

Hillary A variant form of Hilary. *See* Hilary.

Hillel (הִלֵּל) From the Hebrew, meaning "praised, famous." The exact Hebrew equivalent is Hillel. The exact feminine Hebrew equivalent is Hillela.

Hilliard A variant form of Hill. *See* Hill.

Hiram A variant spelling of Chiram. *See* Chiram.

Hirsch A variant spelling of Hersh. *See* Hersh.

Hirsh, Hirshel Variant spellings of Hersh and Hershel. *See* Hersh *and* Hershel.

Hob A variant Middle English form of Rob and Robert. *See* Robert.

Hobart From the Danish, meaning "Bart's hill." *See* Hill.

Hobert A variant form of Hobart. *See* Hobart.

Hobs A variant form of Hob, meaning "son of Hob." *See* Hob.

Hod (הוֹד) From the Hebrew, meaning "splendor, vigor." The exact Hebrew equivalent is Hod. The exact feminine Hebrew equivalent is Hodiya.

Hodia, Hodiah Variant spellings of Hodiya. *See* Hodiya.

Hodiya (הוֹדִיָה) A biblical name derived from the Hebrew, meaning "God is my splendor." The exact masculine and feminine Hebrew equivalent is Hodiya.

Holden From the Old English *haldan*, meaning "to tend sheep." Also, from the Greek, meaning "swift horse." HEBREW EQUIVALENTS: Bo'az, Cha'yil, Maron, Sisera, Susi. FEMININE HEBREW EQUIVALENTS: Mahira, Marona.

Hollis A variant form of Haley. *See* Haley.

Holm From the Old Norse, meaning "island." HEBREW EQUIVALENTS: Afek, Aviyam, Dalfon, Itamar. FEMININE HEBREW EQUIVALENTS: Afeka, Bat-Yam, Miryam.

Holmes A variant form of Holm. *See* Holm.

Holt From the Old English and the German, meaning "wood, wooded area." HEBREW EQUIVALENTS: Ya'ar, Ya'ari. FEMININE HEBREW EQUIVALENTS: Ya'ari, Ya'arit.

Homer From the Greek and Latin, meaning "hostage, one being led," hence, one who is blind. EUPHEMISTIC HEBREW EQUIVALENTS: Koresh, Me'ir, Shimshon, Uri, Uriel, Zerach. EUPHEMISTIC FEMININE HEBREW EQUIVALENTS: Me'ira, Noga, Ora, Zahara.

Hon (הוֹן) From the Hebrew, meaning "wealth." The exact Hebrew equivalent is Hon. FEMININE HEBREW EQUIVALENTS: Ashira, Yitra.

Honi A variant spelling of Choni. *See* Choni.

Honor, Honore From the Middle English and the Latin, meaning "dignity, esteem." HEBREW EQUIVALENTS: Atzil, Efrat, Hadar, Kavud, Mokir, Nichbad, Zevulun. FEMININE HEBREW EQUIVALENTS: Atzila, Efrat, Efrata, Mechubada, Nichbada.

Hopkins A pet form of Hob and Hobs, which are pet forms of Robert. *See* Robert.

Horace From the Greek, meaning "to see, behold." HEBREW EQUIVALENTS: Achazya, Chazael, Chazon, Nevat, Re'aya, Roeh. FEMININE HEBREW EQUIVALENTS: Nevia, Ro'a, Re'uvena, Tzofi, Tzofiya, Tzofit.

Horatio The Italian form of Horace. *See* Horace.

Horton From the Latin, meaning "garden." HEBREW EQUIVALENTS: Bustan, Bustanai, Gan, Gani, Gintoi, Ginton. FEMININE HEBREW EQUIVALENTS: Gana, Ganit, Ganya, Gina, Ginat.

Hosea The Anglicized form of Hoshe'a. *See* Hoshe'a.

Hoshe'a (הוֹשֵׁעַ) From the Hebrew, meaning "salvation." The exact Hebrew equivalent is Hoshe'a (Hoshaya). FEMININE HEBREW EQUIVALENTS: Matzila, Mosha'a, Shua, Teshua, Yishma.

Howard From the Anglo-Saxon, meaning "watchman, protector." HEBREW EQUIVALENTS: Avigdor, Chetzron, Gina, Refa'el, Sa'adya. FEMININE HEBREW EQUIVALENTS: Botzra, Chasya, Chosa, Shimrit, Tira, Ya'akova.

Howe From the Anglo-Saxon, meaning "hill." HEBREW EQUIVALENTS: Aharon, Gal, Gali, Harel, Talmi. FEMININE HEBREW EQUIVALENTS: Aharona, Galit, Galya, Givona.

Howel, Howell From the Old English, meaning "well on the hill." HEBREW EQUIVALENTS: Aharon, Be'er, Be'eri, Gal, Harel, Ma'ayan. FEMININE HEBREW EQUIVALENTS: Aharona, Be'era, Be'erit, Galit, Harela.

Howie A pet form of Howard. *See* Howard.

Hubert A variant form of Herbert. *See* Herbert.

Huey A pet form of Hubert. *See* Hubert.

Hugh A pet form of Hubert. *See* Hubert.

Hugo A pet form of Hubert. *See* Hubert.

Humphrey, Humphry From the Anglo-Saxon, meaning "protector of the home," or from the Old German, meaning "man of peace." HEBREW EQUIVALENTS: Akiva, Aleksander, Machseh, Magen, Meshulam, Shalem, Shemer, Shimrai, Shemarya, Shomer, Tzelafchad, Ya'akov. FEMININE

HEBREW EQUIVALENTS: Avigdora, Chasya, Magena, Megina, Shamira, Shulamit, Ya'akova, Zehira.

Hur The Anglicized form of Chur. *See* Chur.

Hy A pet form of Hyland and Hyman. *See* Hyland *and* Hyman.

Hyland From the Anglo-Saxon, meaning "one who lives on high land." Akin to Hyman. *See* Hyman.

Hyman From the Anglo-Saxon, meaning "one who lives in a high place." HEBREW EQUIVALENTS: Aharon, Givon, Harel, Haran, Ram, Talmai, Yishpa. FEMININE HEBREW EQUIVALENTS: Gal, Gali, Gilada, Harela, Talma, Talmit.

Ian The Scottish form of John. *See* John.

Idan (עֶדָן) From the Aramaic, meaning "time, era." The exact Hebrew equivalent is Idan. FEMININE HEBREW EQUIVALENTS: Itai, Itiel, Itiya.

Idi A variant form of Ido. *See* Ido.

Ido, Iddo (עֲדוֹא/עֲדוֹ) From the Hebrew and Aramaic, meaning "to rise up [like a cloud]" or "to reckon time." The exact Hebrew equivalent is Ido. FEMININE HEBREW EQUIVALENTS: Alita, Aliya, Ya'el.

Idra (אִדְרָא) From the Aramaic, meaning "granary." The exact Hebrew equivalent is Idra. FEMININE HEBREW EQUIVALENTS: Degana, Garna, Garnit.

Igor From the Scandinavian, meaning "hero." HEBREW EQUIVALENTS: Abir, Abiri, Avigdor, Aviram, Gavri, Gavriel, Gevaram, Gever. FEMININE HEBREW EQUIVALENTS: Avigdora, Magena, Megina, Shamira, Shemura, Shimrat, Shimriya, Ya'akova.

Ike A pet form of Isaac. *See* Isaac.

Ila (עִילָא) From the Aramaic, meaning "exalted," and the Arabic, meaning "noble cause." The exact Hebrew equivalent is Ila. FEMININE HEBREW EQUIVALENTS: Ge'ona, Ge'onit, Ramit, Roma, Sara, Sarit.

Ila'i (עִילָאִי) From the Hebrew and Aramaic, meaning "superior." The exact Hebrew equivalent is Ila'i. FEMININE HEBREW EQUIVALENTS: Ram, Rama, Rami, Ramit, Romema, Romit.

Ilan (אִילָן) From the Hebrew, meaning "tree." The exact Hebrew equivalent is Ilan. The exact feminine Hebrew equivalent is Ilana.

Ili (עִילִי/עִילִי) A variant form of Ila. *See* Ila. The exact Hebrew equivalent is Ili.

Ilie A variant form of Elijah or Elisha. *See* Elijah *and* Elisha.

Ilija A variant Slavic form of Elijah. *See* Elijah.

Ilya A variant spelling of Ilija. *See* Ilija.

Imanuel, Immanuel (עִמָנוּאֵל) From the Hebrew, meaning "God is with us." The exact Hebrew equivalent is Imanuel. The exact feminine Hebrew equivalent is Imanuela.

Imri, Imrie (אִמְרִי) From the Hebrew, meaning "my utterance." The exact Hebrew equivalent is Imri. FEMININE HEBREW EQUIVALENTS: Amira, Doveva, Dovevet, Neva.

Ingmar From the Old English, meaning "meadow near the sea." HEBREW EQUIVALENTS: Avigal, Livyatan, Nir, Nirel, Sharon. FEMININE HEBREW EQUIVALENTS: Bat-Galim, Bat-Yam, Miryam, Nira, Nirit, Sharona.

Ir (עִיר) From the Hebrew, meaning "city, town." The exact Hebrew equivalent is Ir. The exact feminine Hebrew equivalent is Irit.

Ira (עִירָא) From the Hebrew and Arabic, meaning "to escape [by being swift]." The exact Hebrew equivalent is Ira. FEMININE HEBREW EQUIVALENTS: Mahira, Sarid, Tzivya.

Iran A variant form of Ira. See Ira.

Iri A variant form of Ira. See Ira.

Irvin From the Gaelic, meaning "beautiful, handsome, fair." HEBREW EQUIVALENTS: Avino'am, Chemdan, Na'aman, Ra'anan, Shapir, Shefer, Shifron, Yafeh. FEMININE HEBREW EQUIVALENTS: Achino'am, Adina, Na'ama, Ra'anana, Rivka, Yafa, Yafit.

Irvine A variant form of Irvin. See Irvin.

Irving A variant form of Irvin. See Irvin.

Irwin, Irwyn Variant spellings of Irvin. See Irvin.

Is A short form of Isaiah. See Isaiah.

Isa, Issa Short forms of Isaiah and Isaac. See Isaiah *and* Isaac.

Isaac (יִצְחָק) From the Hebrew, meaning "he will laugh." The exact Hebrew equivalent is Yitzchak. The exact feminine Hebrew equivalent is Yitzchaka.

Isador, Isadore Variant spellings of Isidor. See Isidor.

Isaiah (יְשַׁעְיָה/יְשַׁעְיָהוּ) From the Hebrew, meaning "God is salvation." HEBREW EQUIVALENTS: Yesha'ya, Yesha'yahu. FEMININE HEBREW EQUIVALENTS: Aleksandra, Milka, Teshua, Yesha, Yeshua.

Isak A variant spelling of Isaac. See Isaac.

Iser A variant spelling of Isser. See Isser.

Ishmael (יִשְׁמָעֵאל) An Anglicized form of the Hebrew name Yishmael, meaning "God will hear." The exact Hebrew equivalent is Yishmael. FEMININE HEBREW EQUIVALENTS: Shimat, Shimona, Shemuela, Shmuela.

Ish-Shalom (אִישׁ־שָׁלוֹם) From the Hebrew, meaning "man of peace." The exact Hebrew equivalent is Ish-Shalom. FEMININE HEBREW EQUIVALENTS: Achishalom, Shelomit, Shelom-Tziyon, Shulamit.

Ish-Tov (אִישׁ־טוֹב) From the Hebrew, meaning "good man." The exact Hebrew equivalent is Ish-Tov. FEMININE HEBREW EQUIVALENTS: Tova, Tovit, Tuvit, Yatva.

Isidor, Isidore From the Greek, meaning "gift of Isis," the Egyptian moon-goddess. HEBREW EQUIVALENTS: Avishai, Elnatan, Elzavad, Levanon, Matityahu, Yarchi, Yaro'ach, Yehonatan, Yerach, Yonatan. FEMININE HEBREW EQUIVALENTS: Levana, Matana, Migdana, Sahara, Zevida, Zevuda.

Isidoro The Spanish form of Isidor. See Isidor.

Ismar A variant form of Itamar. See Itamar.

Israel (יִשְׂרָאֵל) The Anglicized form of the Hebrew, meaning "prince of God" or "wrestled with God." The exact Hebrew equivalent is Yisrael. The exact feminine Hebrew equivalent is Yisr'ela.

Issachar (יִשָּׂשכָר) From the Hebrew, meaning "there is a reward." The exact Hebrew equivalent is Yisachar. FEMININE HEBREW EQUIVALENTS: Ashera, Beracha, Gamliela, Gamlielit, Gemula.

Isser (אִיסָער/אִיסֶר) A Yiddish form of Yisrael (Israel). *See* Yisrael *and* Israel.

Issi (אִיסִי) A pet form of Isser. *See* Isser.

Itai (אִיתַי) From the Hebrew, meaning "friendly, compassionate" or, literally, "God is with me." The exact masculine and feminine Hebrew equivalent is Itai.

Itamar (אִיתָמָר) From the Hebrew, meaning "island of palms." The exact Hebrew equivalent is Itamar. FEMININE HEBREW EQUIVALENTS: Tamar, Timora.

Itiel (אִיתִיאֵל) From the Hebrew, meaning "God is with me." The exact Hebrew equivalent is Itiel. FEMININE HEBREW EQUIVALENTS: Eliana, Eliezra, Eliora, Itai.

Ittai A variant spelling of Itai. *See* Itai.

Ittamar A variant spelling of Itamar. *See* Itamar.

Itzig, Itzik (אִיצִיק/אִיצִיג) Yiddish forms of Yitzchak (Isaac). *See* Yitzchak.

Ivan The Russian form of John, meaning "grace." *See* John.

Ivri (עִבְרִי) From the Hebrew, meaning "Hebrew." The exact Hebrew equivalent is Ivri. The exact feminine Hebrew equivalent is Ivriya.

Iz A pet form of Isidor. *See* Isidor.

Izzie, Izzy Pet forms of Isidor. *See* Isidor.

Jack A pet form of Jacob. *See* Jacob. A nickname for John. *See* John.

Jackie A pet form of Jack. *See* Jack.

Jackson A patronymic form, meaning "son of Jack" or "son of Jacob." *See* Jack *and* Jacob.

Jacob (יַעֲקֹב) The Anglicized form of Ya'akov. From the Hebrew, meaning "held by the heel, supplanted, or protected." The exact Hebrew equivalent is Ya'akov. The exact feminine Hebrew equivalent is Ya'akova.

Jacobo A Spanish form of Jacob. *See* Jacob.

Jacque, Jacques French forms of Jacob. *See* Jacob.

Jaime A Spanish form of Chayim. *See* Chayim.

Jaimie A pet form of James. *See* James.

Jake A pet form of Jacob. *See* Jacob.

Jakob A variant spelling of Jacob. *See* Jacob.

James The English form of the Hebrew name Jacob. *See* Jacob.

Jan A form of John. *See* John. Also, a pet form of James. *See* James.

Janus From the Latin, meaning "gate, passageway" or "opening, beginning," from which the month January takes its name. HEBREW EQUIVALENTS: Bava, Rav, Rosh, Sha'arya, She'arya. FEMININE HEBREW EQUIVALENTS: Bava, Rishona.

Japhet, Japheth Variant spellings of Yefet. *See* Yefet.

Jardine From the Anglo-Saxon and French, meaning "garden." HEBREW EQUIVALENTS: Gan, Gani, Gina, Ginat, Gintoi, Ginton. FEMININE HEBREW EQUIVALENTS: Gana, Ganit, Ganya, Gina, Yardena.

Jared A variant spelling of Yared. *See* Yared.

Jaron A variant spelling of Yaron. *See* Yaron.

Jarvis From the Old English, meaning "battle spear" or "conqueror." HEBREW EQUIVALENTS: Gavriel, Gevarya, Gidoni, Ish-Cha'yil, Sirya, Siryon. FEMININE HEBREW EQUIVALENTS: Chanit, Chanita, Chinanit, Gadit, Gavriela, Moran, Moranit.

Jascha A Russian form of James and Jacob. *See* James and Jacob.

Jason From the Greek, meaning "healer." HEBREW EQUIVALENTS: Asa, Assi, Rafa, Refa'el, Refa'ya, Refi, Ya'akov. FEMININE HEBREW EQUIVALENTS: Asa'ela, Refa'ela, Refa'ya, Refua, Rofi, Ya'akova.

Jaspar, Jasper From the Greek, meaning "precious stone." Also, from the Persian, meaning "secret." HEBREW EQUIVALENTS: Nofech, Penini, Safir, Sapir, Shoham, Shovai, Tarshish, Yahalom. FEMININE HEBREW EQUIVALENTS: Sapira, Sapirit, Yahaloma, Yahalomit, Yakira.

Jay From the Old French and Latin, referring to a bird in the crow family. Also, from the Anglo-Saxon, meaning "happy." HEBREW EQUIVALENTS: A'ya, Efron, Gil, Gila, Gozal, Orev, Simcha, Tzipor, Yarkon, Zamir. FEMININE HEBREW EQUIVALENTS: A'ya, Gozala, Kanarit, Salit, Semecha, Tzipora, Tziporit.

Jean The French form of John. *See* John.

Jed From the Arabic, meaning "hand." HEBREW EQUIVALENTS: Chofni, Yeda'ya. Also, a pet form of Jedediah. *See* Jedediah.

Jedediah A variant form of Yedidya. *See* Yedidya.

Jef, Jeff Short forms of Jeffrey and Geoffrey. *See* Jeffrey *and* Geoffrey.

Jeffers A patronymic form, meaning "son of Jeffrey." *See* Jeffrey *and* Geoffrey.

Jefferson A patronymic form, meaning "son of Jeffers." *See* Jeffers.

Jeffery, Jefferey Variant spellings of Geoffrey. *See* Geoffrey.

Jeffrey A variant spelling of Geoffrey. *See* Geoffrey.

Jeffry A variant spelling of Geoffrey. *See* Geoffrey.

Jehiel A variant spelling of Yechiel. *See* Yechiel.

Jehoiakim A variant spelling of Yehoyakim. *See* Yehoyakim.

Jekuthiel, Jekutiel Variant forms of Yekutiel. *See* Yekutiel.

Jephthah, Jephtah Variant spellings of Yiftach. *See* Yiftach.

Jerald A variant spelling of Gerald. *See* Gerald.

Jere A variant spelling of Jerry. *See* Jerry. Also, a short form of Jeremiah. *See* Jeremiah.

Jered A variant spelling of Yered. *See* Yered.

Jeremiah (יִרְמְיָהוּ/יִרְמְיָה) From the Hebrew, meaning "God will loosen [the bonds]" or "God will uplift [the spirit]." The exact Hebrew equivalent is Yirmeyahu. *See* Yirmeyahu.

Jeremias The Greek form of Jeremiah. *See* Jeremiah.

Jeremy A pet form of Jeremiah. *See* Jeremiah.

Jerold A variant spelling of Gerald. *See* Gerald.

Jerome A variant spelling of Gerome, meaning "holy person" or "sacred name." HEBREW EQUIVALENTS: Chagai, Devir, Ish-Tov, Kadish, Kadosh, Shem-Tov, Tamir, Zakai. FEMININE HEBREW EQUIVALENTS: Chagit, Chagiya, Devira.

Jerrald A variant spelling of Jerold. *See* Jerold.

Jerrold A variant spelling of Jerold. *See* Jerold.

Jerry A pet form of Jerold, Jerome, and Jeremiah. *See* Jerold, Jerome, *and* Jeremiah.

Jess A short form of Jesse. *See* Jesse.

Jesse (יִשַׁי) From the Hebrew, meaning "wealthy" or "gift." The exact Hebrew equivalent is Yishai. FEMININE HEBREW EQUIVALENTS: Ashira, Dorona, Matana, Netanela, Yitra.

Jethro (יִתְרוֹ) From the Hebrew, meaning "abundance, riches." The exact Hebrew equivalent is Yitro. The exact feminine Hebrew equivalent is Yitra.

Jim, Jimm Pet forms of James. *See* James.

Jimbo A pet form of James, probably a short form of Jimboy. *See* James.

Jimmie, Jimmy Pet forms of James. *See* James.

Joab A variant spelling of Yoav. *See* Yoav.

Job (אִיּוֹב) From the Hebrew, meaning "hated, oppressed."

Joce A variant form of Joseph. *See* Joseph.

Jochanan A variant spelling of Yochanan. *See* Yochanan.

Jody A pet form of Joseph. *See* Joseph.

Joe, Joey Pet forms of Joseph. *See* Joseph.

Joel (יוֹאֵל) From the Hebrew, meaning "God is willing." The exact Hebrew equivalent is Yo'el. The exact feminine Hebrew equivalent is Yo'ela.

Johanan A variant spelling of Yochanan. *See* Yochanan.

Johannes A Latin form of John. *See* John.

John (יְהוֹחָנָן/יוֹחָנָן) The Anglicized form of Yochanan, meaning "God is gracious." HEBREW EQUIVALENTS: Yehochanan, Yochanan. The feminine Hebrew equivalent is Yochana.

Johnnie, Johnny Pet forms of John. *See* John.

Jojo A pet form of Joseph. *See* Joseph.

Jon A pet form of John or Jonathan. *See* John *and* Jonathan.

Jona, Jonah (יוֹנָה) From the Hebrew, meaning "dove." The exact masculine and feminine Hebrew equivalent is Yona.

Jonas The Greek and Latin form of Jonah. *See* Jonah.

Jonathan (יְהוֹנָתָן/יוֹנָתָן) From the Hebrew, meaning "God has given" or "gift of God." The exact Hebrew equivalent is Yehonatan. FEMININE HEBREW EQUIVALENTS: Netanela, Netanya, Netina, Yehava.

Jonji A pet form of Jonathan. *See* Jonathan.

Jon-Jon A pet form of Jonathan. *See* Jonathan.

Jonni, Jonnie, Jonny Pet forms of Jonathan. *See* Jonathan.

Jordan The exact Hebrew form is Yarden. *See* Yarden.

Jordy A pet form of Jordan. *See* Jordan.

Jori, Jory Pet forms of Jordan. *See* Jordan.

Jose An Aramaic form of Joseph. *See* Joseph.

Joseph (יוֹסֵף) From the Hebrew, meaning "He [God] will add, increase." The exact Hebrew equivalent is Yosef. The exact feminine Hebrew equivalents are Yosefa and Yosifa.

Josephus (יוֹסִיפוּס) The Latin form of Joseph. The exact Hebrew equivalent is Yosifus. *See* Joseph *for additional equivalents.*

Josh A pet form of Joshua. *See* Joshua.

Joshua (יְהוֹשֻׁעַ) From the Hebrew, meaning "the Lord is my salvation." The exact Hebrew equivalent is Yehoshua. *See* Yehoshua *for feminine Hebrew equivalents.*

Josiah (יֹאשִׁיָּהוּ/יֹאשִׁיָּה) From the Hebrew, meaning "fire of the Lord." The exact Hebrew equivalent is Yoshiyahu. *See* Yoshiyahu *for feminine Hebrew equivalents.*

Jotham A variant spelling of Yotam. *See* Yotam.

Jud A variant spelling of Judd. *See* Judd.

Judah (יְהוּדָה) From the Hebrew, meaning "praise." The exact Hebrew equivalent is Yehuda. The exact feminine Hebrew equivalent is Yehudit.

Judas The Latin form of Judah. *See* Judah.

Judd A variant form of Judah. *See* Judah.

Judel A Yiddish form of Judah. *See* Judah.

Judson A patronymic form of Judah, meaning "Judah's [or Judd's] son." *See* Judah.

Jule, Jules Variant forms of Julian or Julius. *See* Julian *and* Julius.

Julian From the Greek, meaning "soft-haired, mossy-bearded," symbolizing youth. HEBREW EQUIVALENTS: Aviv, Avrech, Elino'ar, Irad, Iram, Zuta, Zutai. FEMININE HEBREW EQUIVALENTS: Aviva, Dala, Delila, Nima.

Julius A variant form of Julian. *See* Julian.

Junior From the Latin, meaning "young." HEBREW EQUIVALENTS: Aviv, Avrech, Bachur, Becher, Bichri, Elino'ar, Yafet, Yefet, Zutra. FEMININE HEBREW EQUIVALENTS: Aviva, Elino'ar, Gurit, Tze'ira.

Junius From the Latin, meaning "young lion." HEBREW EQUIVALENTS: Arel, Areli, Ari, Ariav, Ariel, Arye, Ben-Guryon, Gur-Arye, Kefir, Lavi. FEMININE HEBREW EQUIVALENTS: Ariel, Ariela, Gurit, Kefira, Levia.

Justin A variant form of Justus. See Justus.

Justus From the Latin, meaning "just, honest." HEBREW EQUIVALENTS: Avidan, Dan, Dani, Daniel, Da'yan, Yadin, Yadon, Yehoshafat, Yudan. FEMININE HEBREW EQUIVALENTS: Daniela, Danit, Danya.

Kadi (כַּדִי) From the Hebrew, meaning "my pitcher." The exact Hebrew equivalent is Kadi. The exact feminine Hebrew equivalent is Kadya.

Kadish, Kaddish (קָדִיש) From the Hebrew, meaning "sanctification." The exact Hebrew equivalent is Kadish. FEMININE HEBREW EQUIVALENTS: Chagit, Chagiya, Chermona, Devira, Kedosha.

Kadmiel (קַדְמִיאֵל) From the Hebrew, meaning "the Ancient One is my God." The exact Hebrew equivalent is Kadmiel. FEMININE HEBREW EQUIVALENTS: Bilha, Kadmiela, Keshisha, Yeshana.

Kadosh (קָדוֹש) From the Hebrew, meaning "holy, holy one." The exact Hebrew equivalent is Kadosh. The exact feminine Hebrew equivalent is Kedosha.

Kailil A variant form of Kalil. See Kalil.

Kal (קַל) A short form of Kalman. See Kalman.

Kalev (כָּלֵב) From the Hebrew, meaning "dog" or "heart." Also, from the Assyrian, meaning "messenger" or "priest," and from the Arabic, meaning "bold, brave." Also spelled Calev. Caleb is the Anglicized form. The exact Hebrew equivalent is Kalev. FEMININE HEBREW EQUIVALENTS: Libi, No'aza, Odeda.

Kalil (כָּלִיל) From the Greek, meaning "beautiful." Also, from the Hebrew, meaning "crown, wreath." The exact Hebrew equivalent is Kalil. The exact feminine Hebrew equivalent is Kelila.

Kalman A short form of Kalonymos. See Kalonymos.

Kalonymos, Kalonymus (קָלוֹנִימוֹס) Variant forms of the Latin name Clement, meaning "merciful" or "gracious." Also, from the Greek, meaning "beautiful name." The exact Hebrew equivalent is Kalonimos and Shem-Tov. FEMININE HEBREW EQUIVALENTS: Bat-Shem, Tova, Tovit, Yatva, Yatvata.

Kanai (קַנָאִי) From the Hebrew, meaning "zealous." The exact Hebrew equivalent is Kana'i. The feminine Hebrew equivalent is Chasida.

Kane A variant form of Keene. See Keene.

Kani (קָנִי) A pet form of Kaniel. See Kaniel.

Kaniel (קָנִיאֵל) From the Hebrew, meaning "reed [support]." Also, from the Arabic, meaning "spear." The exact Hebrew equivalent is Kaniel. The exact feminine Hebrew equivalent is Kaniela.

Kareem From the Arabic, meaning "noble, exalted." HEBREW EQUIVALENTS: Achiram, Adonikam, Atlai, Ila, Ram, Rama, Romem, Yigdal,

Yoram. FEMININE HEBREW EQUIVALENTS: Ge'ona, Ge'onit, Ramit, Romema, Romit, Romiya, Sara.

Karel A variant form of Carol. *See* Carol.

Karim A variant spelling of Kareem. *See* Kareem.

Karin (קָרִין) From the Arabic, meaning "horn." The exact Hebrew equivalent is Karin. FEMININE HEBREW EQUIVALENTS: Karnay, Karniela, Karniya, Ya'el.

Karl A variant spelling of Carl. *See* Carl.

Karmel (כַּרְמֶל) From the Hebrew, meaning "vineyard." The exact masculine and feminine Hebrew equivalent is Karmel.

Karmeli (כַּרְמְלִי) From the Hebrew, meaning "my vineyard." The exact Hebrew equivalent is Karmeli. FEMININE HEBREW EQUIVALENTS: Karmel, Karmela, Karmelit, Karmit.

Karna (קַרְנָא) From the Aramaic, meaning "horn." The exact Hebrew equivalent is Karna. FEMININE HEBREW EQUIVALENTS: Karniela, Karnit, Karniya.

Karni (קַרְנִי) From the Hebrew, meaning "my horn." The exact Hebrew equivalent is Karni. FEMININE HEBREW EQUIVALENTS: Karniela, Karnit, Karniya.

Karniel (קַרְנִיאֵל) From the Hebrew, meaning "God is my horn." The exact Hebrew equivalent is Karniel. The exact feminine Hebrew equivalent is Karniela.

Kaski (קָסְקִי) A Yiddish pet form of Yechezkel. *See* Yechezkel.

Karol, Karole Variant spellings of Carol. *See* Carol.

Kasriel A variant spelling of Katriel. *See* Katriel.

Kati (כַּתִּי) A short form of Katriel. *See* Katriel. The exact Hebrew equivalent is Kati.

Katriel (כַּתְרִיאֵל) From the Hebrew, meaning "God is my crown." The exact Hebrew equivalent is Katriel. The exact feminine Hebrew equivalents is Katriela.

Katzin (קָצִין) From the Hebrew, meaning "rich lord." The exact Hebrew equivalent is Katzin. FEMININE HEBREW EQUIVALENTS: Adira, Adonit, Yisr'ela.

Kaufman, Kaufmann From the German, meaning "buyer." *See* Yaakov.

Kay From the Greek, meaning "rejoicing," or from the Anglo-Saxon, meaning "warden of a fortified place." HEBREW EQUIVALENTS: Akiva, Avigdor, Lotan, Magen, Shemarya, Shimron, Shomer, Ya'akov. FEMININE HEBREW EQUIVALENTS: Avigdora, Magena, Marnina, Megina, Shemura, Shimrat, Tzina, Ya'akova.

Kedem (קֶדֶם) From the Hebrew, meaning "east." The exact Hebrew equivalent is Kedem. The feminine Hebrew equivalent is Kedma.

Keenan A variant form of Keene. *See* Keene.

Keene From the Old English, meaning "wise, learned," and from the German, meaning "bold." HEBREW EQUIVALENTS: Avida, Bina, Buna,

Chachmoni, Navon, No'az, Utz, Zavin. FEMININE HEBREW EQUIVALENTS: Chochma, Ge'ona, Ge'onit, No'aza, Tushiya.

Keith From the Old Gaelic, meaning "wood, woody area." HEBREW EQUIVALENTS: Adam, Ya'ar, Ya'ari, Yara. FEMININE HEBREW EQUIVALENTS: Adama, Ya'ara, Ya'arit.

Kefir (כְּפִיר) From the Hebrew, meaning "young lion cub." The exact Hebrew equivalent is Kefir. The exact feminine Hebrew equivalent is Kefira.

Kelsey A variant form of Kelson. *See* Kelson.

Kelson From the Middle Dutch, meaning "boat." The Hebrew equivalent is Sira. The feminine Hebrew equivalent is Aniya.

Kelvin, Kelwin, Kelwyn From the Anglo-Saxon, meaning "lover of ships." HEBREW EQUIVALENTS: Ahuv, Bildad, Narkis, Ohad, Ohev, Sira, Yedidya. FEMININE HEBREW EQUIVALENTS: Ahuva, Aniya, Chiba.

Ken A pet form of Kenneth. *See* Kenneth.

Kendal, Kendall From the Celtic, meaning "ruler of the valley." HEBREW EQUIVALENTS: Emek, Gai, Gechazi, Gi'ora, Katriel, Melech, Moshel, Yamlech, Yisrael. FEMININE HEBREW EQUIVALENTS: Ga'ya, Malka, Sara, Sarit, Yisr'ela.

Kendrick From the Anglo-Saxon, meaning "royal." HEBREW EQUIVALENTS: Katriel, Malkam, Malki, Malkiel, Malkiram, Melech. FEMININE HEBREW EQUIVALENTS: Alufa, Malka, Sara, Sarit, Yisr'ela.

Kene A variant spelling of Kenny. *See* Kenny.

Kenen From the Old English and German, meaning "to know." HEBREW EQUIVALENTS: Bina, Buna, Yada, Yavin. FEMININE HEBREW EQUIVALENTS: Bina, Buna, Datiela.

Kenneth From the Celtic and Scottish, meaning "beautiful, handsome." HEBREW EQUIVALENTS: Adin, Hadar, Kalil, Nechmad, Pe'er, Ra'anan, Shapir, Yafeh, Yefet. FEMININE HEBREW EQUIVALENTS: Na'a, Na'ama, Nava, Nofiya, Noya, Ra'anana, Yafa, Yafit.

Kennie A pet form of Kenneth. *See* Kenneth.

Kenny A pet form of Kenneth. *See* Kenneth.

Kent A variant form of Kenneth. *See* Kenneth.

Kerby A variant spelling of Kirby. *See* Kirby.

Kerem (כֶּרֶם) From the Hebrew, meaning "vineyard." The exact masculine and feminine Hebrew equivalent is Kerem.

Keren (קֶרֶן) From the Hebrew, meaning "horn." The exact Hebrew equivalent is Keren. FEMININE HEBREW EQUIVALENTS: Karniela, Karnit, Karniya.

Kermit From the Dutch, meaning "church." HEBREW EQUIVALENTS: Devir, Kadosh. FEMININE HEBREW EQUIVALENTS: Devira, Kedosha.

Kern From the Old Irish, meaning "band of soldiers." HEBREW EQUIVALENTS: Gad, Gadiel, Gavriel, Gevarya, Gidon, Gidoni, Meron, Mordechai, Nimrod. FEMININE HEBREW EQUIVALENTS: Gadat, Gadit, Gavrila, Gibora, Gidona, Tigra.

Kerr From the Norse, meaning "marshland." HEBREW EQUIVALENTS: Avi'-yam, Beri, Dalfon, Dela'ya. FEMININE HEBREW EQUIVALENTS: Afeka, Bat-Yam, Miryam, Yaval.

Keter (כֶּתֶר) From the Hebrew, meaning "crown." The exact Hebrew equivalent is Keter. FEMININE HEBREW EQUIVALENTS: Katriela, Kelila, Kelula, Kitra, Kitron, Tzefira.

Kevin From the Gaelic, meaning "handsome, beautiful." HEBREW EQUIVALENTS: Hadar, Kalil, Nechmad, Ne'edar, Shefer, Yafim. FEMININE HEBREW EQUIVALENTS: Hadura, Na'ama, Na'omi, Nava, Nofiya, Ra'anana.

Kibby From the British, meaning "cottage by the water." HEBREW EQUIVALENTS: Aviyam, Avgar, Betuel, Bitan, Chamat, Dalfon. FEMININE HEBREW EQUIVALENTS: Afeka, Bat-Yam, Molada, Moledet, Yaval.

Kidd From the British, meaning "strong." HEBREW EQUIVALENTS: Amitz, Az, Azai, Aziel, Chizkiya, Yechezkel, Yo'ash, Yo'az. FEMININE HEBREW EQUIVALENTS: Adira, Amitza, Avniela, Azriela, Etana, Odeda, Odedya.

Kile A variant spelling of Kyle. See Kyle.

Kin A pet form of Kingsley and Kingston. See Kingsley and Kingston.

King From the Anglo-Saxon, meaning "ruler." The exact Hebrew equivalent is Melech. The exact feminine Hebrew equivalent is Malka.

Kingsley From the Anglo-Saxon, meaning "from the king's meadow." HEBREW EQUIVALENTS: Ben-Carmi, Carmel, Gan, Gani, Ginton, Katriel, Melech, Malkam. FEMININE HEBREW EQUIVALENTS: Gana, Ginat, Katriela, Malka, Yardeniya.

Kingston From the Old English, meaning "king's town." HEBREW EQUIVALENTS: Avimelech, Elimelech, Malkam, Melech, Moshel, Yamlech, Yisrael. FEMININE HEBREW EQUIVALENTS: Malka, Malkit, Sara, Sarit, Yisr'ela.

Kinori (כִּנּוֹרִי) From the Hebrew, meaning "my lyre, my harp." The exact Hebrew equivalent is Kinori. The feminine Hebrew equivalent is Kinneret.

Kinsey From the British, meaning "royal." HEBREW EQUIVALENTS: Elrad, Melech, Moshel, Rozen, Yamlech, Yisrael. FEMININE HEBREW EQUIVALENTS: Malka, Sara, Sarit, Yisr'ela.

Kirby From the Old English and Middle English, meaning "church," and from the British, meaning "cottage by the water." HEBREW EQUIVALENTS: Avi'yam, Dalfon, Devir, Dela'ya, Kadish, Kadosh. FEMININE HEBREW EQUIVALENTS: Afeka, Bat-Yam, Devira, Kedosha, Miryam.

Kirk From the Old Norse and Old English, meaning "church." HEBREW EQUIVALENTS: Devir, Kadish, Kadosh. FEMININE HEBREW EQUIVALENTS: Devira, Kedosha.

Kitron (כִּתְרוֹן) From the Hebrew, meaning "crown." The exact masculine and feminine Hebrew equivalent is Kitron.

Kiva (קִיבָא/קִיבָה) A pet form of Akiva. See Akiva.

Kive A pet form of Akiva and Yaakov. See Akiva and Yaakov.

Kivi (קִיבִי) A pet form of Akiva and Yaakov. See Akiva and Yaakov.

Konrad A variant spelling of Conrad. See Conrad.

Koppel (קאפּעל/קאפּל)   A Yiddish form of Yaakov. *See* Yaakov.

Korach (קרח)   From the Hebrew, meaning "bald." The exact Hebrew equivalent is Korach.

Korah   A variant spelling of Korach. *See* Korach.

Kovi (קובי)   A pet form of Yaakov. *See* Yaakov.

Kurt   A pet form of Konrad. *See* Konrad.

Kus (קוּת)   A short form of Yekusiel (Yekutiel). *See* Yekutiel.

Kyle   A Gaelic form of the Old English, meaning "hill where the cattle graze." HEBREW EQUIVALENTS: Aharon, Gal, Gali, Galil, Galya, Harel, Talmai, Tel. FEMININE HEBREW EQUIVALENTS: Gal, Gali, Galit, Geva, Gilada, Talma.

Laban   A variant spelling of Lavan. *See* Lavan.

Label (לייבּעל/לייבּל)   A pet form of the Yiddish name Leib, meaning "lion." HEBREW EQUIVALENTS: Ari, Ariel, Arye, Kefir, Lavi. FEMININE HEBREW EQUIVALENTS: Ariel, Ariela, Kefira, Levia.

Lamar, Lamarr   From the Latin and French, meaning "of the sea." HEBREW EQUIVALENTS: Avi'yam, Chaifa, Shuni. FEMININE HEBREW EQUIVALENTS: Bat-Galim, Bat-Yam, Miryam, Shunit, Yama, Yamit.

Lambert   From the German and French, meaning "brightness of the land." HEBREW EQUIVALENTS: Avner, Hillel, Lapidot, Me'ir, Uri, Uriya, Yehuda. FEMININE HEBREW EQUIVALENTS: Hila, Hillela, Levana, Me'ira, Noga, Yehudit, Zahara.

Lance   From the Latin, meaning "servant, spear-carrier." HEBREW EQUIVALENTS: Avda, Avdel, Avdi, Malach, Malachi, Ovadya, Patiel, Sa'adya. FEMININE HEBREW EQUIVALENTS: Aleksandra, Ama, Ezr'ela, Imanuela, Sa'ada.

Lancelot   A variant form of Lance. *See* Lance.

Landan   From the Anglo-Saxon, meaning "open, grassy area; lawn." HEBREW EQUIVALENTS: Bustan, Dasheh, Gan, Gani, Gina, Ginton, Rotem, Yarden. FEMININE HEBREW EQUIVALENTS: Gana, Ganiya, Ginat, Yardeniya.

Landis   A variant form of Landan. *See* Landan.

Lane   From the Old English, meaning "to move ahead," hence a path. HEBREW EQUIVALENTS: Nativ, Shovav, Solel. FEMININE HEBREW EQUIVALENTS: Netiva, Selila.

Lang   From the German, meaning "long, tall." HEBREW EQUIVALENTS: Aram, Aricha, Aryoch. The feminine Hebrew equivalent is Meroma.

Lapid (לפּיד)   From the Hebrew, meaning "flame, torch." The exact Hebrew equivalent is Lapid. FEMININE HEBREW EQUIVALENTS: Avuka, Shalhevet, Uriela.

Lapidos   A variant form of Lapidot. *See* Lapidot.

Lapidot (לפּידות)   From the Hebrew, meaning "flame, torch." The exact Hebrew equivalent is Lapidot. FEMININE HEBREW EQUIVALENTS: Avuka, Bareket, Shalhevet, Uriela.

Larry A pet form of Laurence. *See* Laurence.

Lars A Swedish pet form of Laurence. *See* Laurence.

Laurence From the Latin, meaning "laurel, crown." HEBREW EQUIVA-LENTS: Atir, Kalil, Katriel, Keter, Kitron, Melech, Taga. FEMININE HEBREW EQUIVALENTS: Atara, Ateret, Atura, Katriela, Kelila, Malka.

Lavan (לָבָן) From the Hebrew, meaning "white." The exact Hebrew equivalent is Lavan. The exact feminine Hebrew equivalent is Levana.

Lavi (לָבִיא) From the Hebrew, meaning "lion." The exact Hebrew equivalent is Lavi. FEMININE HEBREW EQUIVALENTS: Ariel, Ariela, Kefira, La'yish, Levia.

Lawrence A variant spelling of Laurence. *See* Laurence.

Lazar (לַאזאר) A Yiddish form of Eliezer. *See* Eliezer. Also, a short form of Lazarus. *See* Lazarus.

Lazarus The Greek form of Elazar and Eliezer. *See* Elazar *and* Eliezer.

Lebush A variant spelling of Leibush. *See* Leibush.

Lee A pet form of Leo, Leon, Leonard, or Leslie. *See* Leonard. Also, from the Anglo-Saxon, meaning "meadow." HEBREW EQUIVALENTS: Adam, Bustenai, Carmel, Lavi, Yizr'el. FEMININE HEBREW EQUIVALENTS: Adama, Carmela, Gana, Ganit, Levia, Yizr'ela.

Leeser (לִיסָער) A Yiddish form of Eliezer. *See* Eliezer.

Leib (לֵיב) A Yiddish form of the German name Loeb, meaning "lion." HE-BREW EQUIVALENTS: Arel, Areli, Arye, Gur, Lavi, La'yish. FEMININE HEBREW EQUIVALENTS: Ariel, Ariela, Gurit, Kefira, Levia.

Leibel (לֵייבֶעל) A pet form of Leib. *See* Leib.

Leibush (לֵייבּוּש) A variant form of Leib. *See* Leib.

Leif An Old Norse form of Lief. *See* Lief.

Leigh A variant spelling of Lee. *See* Lee.

Len A pet form of Leonard. *See* Leonard.

Lenn A variant spelling of Len. *See* Len.

Lennard, Lennart Variant forms of Leonard. *See* Leonard.

Lennie A pet form of Leonard. *See* Leonard.

Leo From the Latin, meaning "lion" or "the lion's nature." *See* Leonard.

Leon The Greek form of Leo, meaning "lion." *See* Leo.

Leonard A French form of the Old High German, meaning "strong as a lion." HEBREW EQUIVALENTS: Ari, Ariel, Aryeh, Lavi, La'yish, Uzi, Uziel. FEMININE HEBREW EQUIVALENTS: Amtza, Ariela, Gavrila, Gibora, Levia.

Leopold From the Old High German and the Old English, meaning "bold, free man" and "defender of people." HEBREW EQUIVALENTS: Avigdor, Chosa, Shemarya, Shemaryahu, Ya'akov, Zimri. FEMININE HEBREW EQUIVALENTS: Avigdora, Efrat, Migdala, Shimrit, Tzila, Ya'akova.

Leor, Le-or Variant spelling of Lior. *See* Lior.

Leron, Lerone Variant spellings of Liron. *See* Liron.

LeRoy A French form of the Latin, meaning "the king, royalty." HEBREW EQUIVALENTS: Avimelech, Elimelech, Katriel, Melech, Yisrael. FEMININE HEBREW EQUIVALENTS: Atara, Katriela, Laya, Malka, Yisr'ela.

Les A pet form of Leslie and Lester. *See* Leslie *and* Lester.

Leser A variant spelling of Lesser. *See* Lesser.

Leshem (לֶשֶׁם) From the Hebrew, meaning "precious stone." The exact Hebrew equivalent is Leshem. FEMININE HEBREW EQUIVALENTS: Yahaloma, Yakira, Yekara.

Lesley A variant spelling of Leslie. *See* Leslie.

Leslie From the Anglo-Saxon, meaning "meadowlands." HEBREW EQUIVALENTS: Karmel, Karmeli, Sharon, Ya'ari. FEMININE HEBREW EQUIVALENTS: Gana, Ganit, Karmela, Sharona, Ya'ara.

Lesser (לֶעסֶר/לֶעסֶער) A Yiddish form of Eliezer. *See* Eliezer.

Lester Originally Leicester, a place-name in England. From the Latin and the Old English, meaning "camp, protected area." HEBREW EQUIVALENTS: Avigdor, Chasun, Gonen, Latan, Lot, Tzilai, Yahel. FEMININE HEBREW EQUIVALENTS: Avigdora, Chasya, Magena, Shimra, Shimrit, Tzina.

Lev (לֵב) Either from the Hebrew, meaning "heart," or from the Yiddish, meaning "lion." The exact Hebrew equivalent is Lev. FEMININE HEBREW EQUIVALENTS: Arela, Ariela, Kefira, Levia.

Levanon (לְבָנוֹן) From the Hebrew, meaning "white" or "moon, month." The exact Hebrew equivalent is Levanon. The exact feminine Hebrew equivalent is Levana.

Levi (לֵוִי) From the Hebrew, meaning "joined to" or "attendant upon." The exact Hebrew equivalent is Levi. The exact feminine Hebrew equivalent is Levia.

Levitas (לְוִיטַס) A variant form of Levi. *See* Levi.

Lew A pet form of Lewis. *See* Lewis.

Lewes A variant spelling of Lewis. *See* Lewis.

Lewi The Hawaiian form of Levi. *See* Levi.

Lewis An English form of the French name Louis. *See* Louis.

Lezer (לֶעזֶר/לֶעזֶער) A Yiddish form of Eliezer. *See* Eliezer.

Li (לִי) From the Hebrew, meaning "me" or "to me." The exact masculine and feminine Hebrew equivalent is Li.

Liba (לִיבָּא) A variant spelling of Lieber. *See* Lieber.

Lieb (לִיב) A short form of Lieber. *See* Lieber.

Lieber (לִיבֶּער) A Yiddish form of the German, meaning "beloved." Akin to Lief. *See* Lief.

Lief From the Middle English and the old English, meaning "beloved, dear." HEBREW EQUIVALENTS: Bildad, Eldad, Chavivel, David, Dodi, Yedidya. FEMININE HEBREW EQUIVALENTS: Ahuva, Chaviva, Chiba, Davida, Liba, Yedida.

Liezer (לִי-עֶזֶר/לִיעֶזֶר) A short form of Eliezer. *See* Eliezer.

Limon (לִימוֹן) From the Hebrew, meaning "lemon." The exact Hebrew equivalent is Limon.

Linc A pet form of Lincoln. *See* Lincoln.

Lincoln From the Old English and the German, meaning "lithe, flexible," referring to the trees of the linden family. Or, from the Old English and Latin, meaning "camp near the stream." HEBREW EQUIVALENTS: Aviyam, Dalfon, Dela'ya, Miklos, Oren, Peleg. FEMININE HEBREW EQUIVALENTS: Miryam, Tirza, Tzeruya, Yaval.

Lindsay A variant form of Lindsey. *See* Lindsey.

Lindsey From the Old English, meaning "linden trees near the water [sea]." HEBREW EQUIVALENTS: Aviyam, Beri, Chamat, Dalfon, Ilan, Raviv. FEMININE HEBREW EQUIVALENTS: Afeka, Bat-Yam, Ilana, Miryam, Reviva, Yaval.

Lindsy A variant spelling of Lindsey. *See* Lindsey.

Link From the Old English, meaning "enclosure." HEBREW EQUIVALENTS: Avigdor, Betzer, Bitzaron, Chetzrai, Chupa, Gidron, Lotan. FEMININE HEBREW EQUIVALENTS: Afeka, Avigdora, Efrat, Gana, Ganit, Ganya.

Lion A variant spelling of Leon. *See* Leon.

Li-On (לִי־אוֹן/לִיאוֹן) From the Hebrew, meaning "I have strength." The exact Hebrew equivalent is Li-On (Li'on). FEMININE HEBREW EQUIVALENTS: Avicha'yil, Azriela, Gavriela, Gavrila, Nili, Uziela.

Lionel A variant form of Lion. *See* Lion.

Lior, Li-Or (לִי־אוֹר/לִיאוֹר) From the Hebrew, meaning "my light" or "I see." The exact Hebrew equivalent is Lior. The exact feminine Hebrew equivalent is Liora.

Lipman, Lipmann (לִיפְּמָן/לִיפְּמָאן) A Yiddish form of the German name Liebman, meaning "lover of man." HEBREW EQUIVALENTS: Bildad, Chaviv, David, Eldad, Lipman. FEMININE HEBREW EQUIVALENTS: Ahuva, Chaviva, Davida, Liba, Yedida.

Liron, Li-Ron (לִי־רוֹן/לִירוֹן) From the Hebrew, meaning "song is mine." The exact Hebrew equivalent is Liron. The exact feminine Hebrew equivalent is Lirona.

Livni (לִבְנִי) From the Hebrew, meaning "white" or "frankincense [because of its white color]." The exact Hebrew equivalent is Livni. FEMININE HEBREW EQUIVALENTS: Levona, Livnat, Malbina.

Llewellyn From the Welsh, meaning "in the likeness of a lion." HEBREW EQUIVALENTS: Ari, Ariel, Lavi, La'yish. FEMININE HEBREW EQUIVALENTS: Ariela, Kefira, Levia.

Lloyd From the Celtic or Welsh, meaning "grey or brown" or "dark-complexioned person." HEBREW EQUIVALENTS: Adar, Kedar, Pinchas, Tziltai. FEMININE HEBREW EQUIVALENTS: Chachila, Efa, Laila, Tzila.

Loeb (לוֹיב) From the German, meaning "lion." HEBREW EQUIVALENTS: Arel, Areli, Ari, Aryeh, Lavi, La'yish. FEMININE HEBREW EQUIVALENTS: Ariel, Ariela, Kefira, Levia.

Loel A variant spelling of Lowell. *See* Lowell.

Lon, Lonnie, Lonny   Pet forms of Alphonso, from the Old German, meaning "of noble family." *See* Alphonso.

Lorence   A variant spelling of Laurence. *See* Laurence.

Lorn, Lorne   Variant forms of Laurence. *See* Laurence.

Lorry   A variant spelling of Laurie and a pet form of Laurence. *See* Laurie.

Lot (לוֹט)   From the Hebrew, meaning "envelop, protect." The exact Hebrew equivalent is Lot. FEMININE HEBREW EQUIVALENTS: Afeka, Avigdora, Efrat, Gana, Shimrit.

Lotan (לוֹטָן)   From the Hebrew, meaning "envelop, protect." The exact Hebrew equivalent is Lotan. Akin to Lot. *See* Lot *for additional equivalents.*

Lothar   From the Anglo-Saxon, meaning "renowned warrior" or "hero of the people." HEBREW EQUIVALENTS: Abir, Amitz, Ben-Cha'yil, Etan, Gad, Gidon, Ish-Cha'yil, Naftali, Yisrael.   FEMININE HEBREW EQUIVALENTS: Amtza, Avicha'yil, Avirama, Etana, Gavriela, Gavrila, Yisr'ela.

Lother   A variant spelling of Lothar. *See* Lothar.

Lothur   A variant spelling of Lothar. *See* Lothar.

Louis   From the Old French and the Old High German, meaning "famous in battle" or "refuge of the people." HEBREW EQUIVALENTS: Avicha'yil, Ben-Cha'yil, Ish-Cha'yil, La'yish, Lot, Lotan, Naftali, Shemarya, Yisrael. FEMININE HEBREW EQUIVALENTS: Gada, Gadit, Gavriela, Gavrila, Gibora, Sara, Tigra, Yisr'ela.

Lovell   A variant form of Lowell. *See* Lowell.

Lowe   A variant form of the German name Loeb. *See* Loeb.

Lowell   From the Old English, meaning "beloved." Also, from the Old English, meaning "hill." HEBREW EQUIVALENTS: Bildad, Eldad, David, Dodi, Gilad, Talmai, Talmi, Yedid, Yedidya. FEMININE HEBREW EQUIVALENTS: Ahuva, Chaviva, Davida, Liba, Talma, Yedida.

Loy   A pet form of Loyal. *See* Loyal.

Loyal   From the Old French and the Latin, meaning "faithful, true." HEBREW EQUIVALENTS: Amanya, Amitai, Amitan, Amnon, Ne'eman, Omen. FEMININE HEBREW EQUIVALENTS: Amana, Emuna, Ne'emana.

Lucas   A variant form of Lucius. *See* Lucius.

Lucian   A variant form of Lucius. *See* Lucius.

Lucius   From the Latin, meaning "light." HEBREW EQUIVALENTS: Avner, Barak, Elior, Lior, Ma'or, Me'ir, Orli, Uri, Uriya. FEMININE HEBREW EQUIVALENTS: Behira, Eliora, Liora, Liorit, Me'ira, Me'irit, Uranit.

Lucky   From the Middle English, meaning "good fortune." HEBREW EQUIVALENTS: Mazal, Mazal-Tov, Siman-Tov. FEMININE HEBREW EQUIVALENTS: Mazal, Mazala, Mazalit.

Ludwig   A German form of Louis. *See* Louis.

Luke   The English form of Lucius. *See* Lucius.

Lupo   From the Latin, meaning "wolf." The Hebrew equivalent is Ze'ev. The feminine Hebrew equivalent is Ze'eva.

Lupus A variant form of Lupo. *See* Lupo.

Luz (לוז) From the Hebrew, meaning "almond tree." The exact Hebrew equivalent is Luz. The exact feminine Hebrew equivalent is Luza.

Lyall A variant form of Lyle. *See* Lyle.

Lyell A variant form of Lyle. *See* Lyle.

Lyle A French form of the Latin, meaning "from the island." Also, a Scottish name meaning "little." HEBREW EQUIVALENTS: Arnon, Enan, Katan, Moshe, Peleg, Ze'ira. FEMININE HEBREW EQUIVALENTS: Arnona, Devora, Gali, Ketana, Mara, Miryam.

Lynn From the Old English and Welsh, meaning "cataract, lake, brook." HEBREW EQUIVALENTS: Arnon, Avi'yam, Dela'ya, Peleg, Raviv, Silon, Yuval. FEMININE HEBREW EQUIVALENTS: Arnona, Galiya, Miryam, Reviva, Silona, Silonit.

Lyon The French form of Lion. *See* Lion.

Lyonell A variant form of Lyon. *See* Lyon.

Lyron A variant spelling of Liron. *See* Liron.

Mac From the Gaelic, meaning "son of." The exact Hebrew equivalent is Ben. The exact feminine Hebrew equivalent is Bat.

Macabee, Maccabee (מַכַּבִּי) From the Hebrew, meaning "hammer." The exact Hebrew equivalent is Makabi. The exact feminine Hebrew equivalent is Makabiya.

Mace An English form of the Old French, meaning "club, hammer." *See* Macabee *for Hebrew equivalents.*

Macey A variant form of Mace. *See* Mace.

Mack A variant spelling of Mac. *See* Mac.

Mackey A variant form of Mack. *See* Mack.

Macy A variant spelling of Macey. *See* Macey.

Magen (מָגֵן) From the Hebrew, meaning "protector." The exact Hebrew equivalent is Magen. The exact feminine Hebrew equivalent is Magena.

Magnus From the Latin, meaning "great." HEBREW EQUIVALENTS: Gedalya, Gedalyahu, Gidel, Rav, Rava, Rechavya, Yigdalyahu. FEMININE HEBREW EQUIVALENTS: Atalya, Gedola, Gedula, Rachav.

Maher (מַהֵר) From the Hebrew, meaning "quick, industrious, expert." The exact Hebrew equivalent is Maher. The exact feminine Hebrew equivalent is Mehira.

Mahir (מָהִיר) From the Hebrew, meaning "quick, industrious, expert." The exact Hebrew equivalent is Mahir. The exact feminine Hebrew equivalent is Mehira.

Maimon (מַיְמוֹן) From the Arabic, meaning "luck, good fortune." The exact Hebrew equivalent is Maimon. FEMININE HEBREW EQUIVALENTS: Mazal, Mazala, Mazalit.

Maimun A variant spelling of Maimon. *See* Maimon.

Major From the Latin, meaning "great." Akin to Magnus. *See* Magnus.

Makabi A variant spelling of Macabee. *See* Macabee.

Maks A variant spelling of Max. *See* Max.

Malachai A variant spelling of Malachi. *See* Malachi.

Malachi (מַלְאָכִי) From the Hebrew, meaning "my messenger, my minister" or "my servant." The exact Hebrew equivalent is Malachi. FEMININE HEBREW EQUIVALENTS: Aleksandra, Ama, Milka, Sa'ada.

Malachy A variant form of Malachi. *See* Malachi.

Malbin (מַלְבִּין) From the Hebrew, meaning "to whiten," signifying embarrassment. The exact Hebrew equivalent is Malbin. The exact feminine Hebrew equivalent is Malbina.

Malcam A variant spelling of Malkam. *See* Malkam.

Malcolm From the Arabic, meaning "dove," or from the Gaelic, meaning "servant of St. Columba." HEBREW EQUIVALENTS: Avdi, Malachi, Ovadya, Oved, Yona. FEMININE HEBREW EQUIVALENTS: Malka, Malkit, Sa'ada, Yemima, Yonina.

Malkam (מַלְכָּם) From the Hebrew, meaning "God is their King." The exact Hebrew equivalent is Malkam. The feminine Hebrew equivalent is Malka.

Malki (מַלְכִּי) From the Hebrew, meaning "my king." The exact Hebrew equivalent is Malki. The feminine Hebrew equivalent is Malka.

Malon (מָלוֹן) From the Hebrew, meaning "lodge, inn." The exact Hebrew equivalent is Malon. FEMININE HEBREW EQUIVALENTS: Magena, Magina, Mishan, Shimra, Shimrat.

Malvin A variant spelling of Melvin. *See* Melvin.

Manashi A variant spelling of Menashi. *See* Menashi.

Manasseh An Anglicized form of Menashe. *See* Menashe.

Mandel From the Old French and the Middle Latin, meaning "almond." HEBREW EQUIVALENTS: Luz, Shaked. FEMININE HEBREW EQUIVALENTS: Luza, Shekeda.

Mandy A pet form of Manfred. *See* Manfred.

Manford From the Anglo-Saxon, meaning "small bridge over a brook." HEBREW EQUIVALENTS: Arnon, Geshur. The feminine Hebrew equivalent is Arnona.

Manfred From the German, meaning "man of peace." HEBREW EQUIVALENTS: Achishalom, Avshalom, Ish-Shalom, Shalom, Shlomo. FEMININE HEBREW EQUIVALENTS: Menucha, Meshulemet, Shlomit, Shulamit.

Mani A pet form of Emanuel, Manasseh, Manfred, and Manuel.

Manin A variant form of Mann. *See* Mann.

Manis A variant form of Mann. *See* Mann.

Manish (מאַניש) A Yiddish form of Mann. *See* Mann.

Manley, Manly From the Old English, meaning "protected field." HEBREW EQUIVALENTS: Bitzaron, Chasun, Gonen, Niram, Nirel, Shimran, Shimron. FEMININE HEBREW EQUIVALENTS: Chasya, Chosa, Churshit, Magena, Niriya, Shemura, Zehira.

Mann From the German, meaning "man." HEBREW EQUIVALENTS: Adam, Ben-Azai, Ben-Gever, Enosh, Gavriel. FEMININE HEBREW EQUIVALENTS: Adama, Gavriela. Also, a variant form of Menachem. *See* Menachem.

Mannes, Mannis (מַאנִיס/מַאנֶעס) Variant Yiddish forms of Mann. *See* Mann.

Manni A variant spelling of Mani and Manny. *See* Mani *and* Manny.

Manny, Mannye Pet forms of Emanuel, Manasseh, Manfred, and Manuel. *See* Emanuel.

Manu A pet form of Manuel. *See* Manuel.

Manuel A short form of Emanuel. *See* Emanuel.

Manus A variant form of Magnus. *See* Magnus.

Maon (מָעוֹן) From the Hebrew, meaning "dwelling." The exact Hebrew equivalent is Ma'on. The exact feminine Hebrew equivalent is Me'ona.

Maor (מָאוֹר) From the Hebrew, meaning "light." The exact Hebrew equivalent is Ma'or. The exact feminine Hebrew equivalent is Me'ora.

Maoz (מָעוֹז) From the Hebrew, meaning "strength" or "fortress." The exact Hebrew equivalent is Ma'oz. FEMININE HEBREW EQUIVALENTS: Me'-uza, Odeda, Uza, Uziela.

Mar From the Aramaic, meaning "master" or "lord." The exact Hebrew equivalent is Mar. FEMININE HEBREW EQUIVALENTS: Sara, Yisr'ela.

Marc A short form of Marcus. *See* Marcus.

Marcel A popular French pet form of Marcus. *See* Marcus.

Marcelo, Marcello Pet forms of Marcus. *See* Marcus.

March A variant form of Marcus. *See* Marcus.

Marchall A variant spelling of Marshall. *See* Marshall.

Marcos A variant form of Marcus. *See* Marcus.

Marcus From the Latin name Mars, meaning "warlike." HEBREW EQUIVALENTS: Ben-Cha'yil, Ish-Cha'yil, Gad, Gidon, Makabi, Medan, Midyan, Mordechai. FEMININE HEBREW EQUIVALENTS: Amtza, Atzma, Gavriela, Gavrila, Gibora, Yisr'ela.

Marcy A variant form of Marcus. *See* Marcus.

Marek A Polish form of Marcus. *See* Marcus.

Mari A pet form of Marius. *See* Marius.

Marin From the Latin, meaning "small harbor." HEBREW EQUIVALENTS: Moshe, Nemali, Nemalya, Nemuel, Nimli, Shuni. FEMININE HEBREW EQUIVALENTS: Chaifa, Yama, Yamit.

Mario A variant form of Marian or Marcus. *See* Marcus *and* Marian.

Maris From the Old English and French, meaning "sea, lake." HEBREW EQUIVALENTS: Avigal, Avi'yam, Livyatan, Moshe, Nemuel, Shuni. FEMININE HEBREW EQUIVALENTS: Bat-Galim, Bat-Yam, Miryam, Yama.

Marius A variant form of Marcus. *See* Marcus.

Mark A variant spelling of Marcus. *See* Marcus.

Marlin From the Latin, Old English, and French, meaning "sea." HE-BREW EQUIVALENTS: Avigal, Avi'yam, Beri, Dalfon, Moshe. FEMININE HEBREW EQUIVALENTS: Bat-Galim, Bat-Yam, Yama, Yamit.

Malkosh (מַלְקוֹשׁ) From the Hebrew, meaning "rain." The exact Hebrew equivalent is Malkosh. The exact feminine Hebrew equivalent is Mal-kosha.

Marlo A variant form of Marlin. *See* Marlin.

Marlow, Marlowe A variant form of Marlin. *See* Marlin.

Marne From the Latin, Old English, and French, meaning "sea." HEBREW EQUIVALENTS: Avigal, Avi'yam, Livyatan, Moshe. FEMININE HEBREW EQUIV-ALENTS: Bat-Galim, Bat-Yam, Miryam, Yamit.

Marnin (מַרְנִין) From the Hebrew, meaning "one who creates joy" or "one who sings." The exact Hebrew equivalent is Marnin. The exact feminine Hebrew equivalent is Marnina.

Marom (מָרוֹם) From the Hebrew, meaning "lofty, exalted." The exact Hebrew equivalent is Marom. The exact feminine Hebrew equivalent is Meroma.

Maron (מָרוֹן) From the Hebrew, meaning "flock of sheep." The exact Hebrew equivalent is Maron. The exact feminine Hebrew equivalent is Marona.

Marshal, Marshall From the Old English, meaning "one who grooms a horse, one who masters a horse" and "an officer in charge of military matters." HEBREW EQUIVALENTS: Ben-Cha'yil, Cha'yil, Ish-Cha'yil, Peresh, Rechev, Susi, Yisrael. FEMININE HEBREW EQUIVALENTS: Amtza, Gavrila, Gavriela, Gevira, Uziela, Yisr'ela.

Marshe A variant form of Marcus and Marshal. *See* Marcus *and* Marshal.

Martin A French form of the Latin name Martinus. Akin to Marcus, meanng "warlike." *See* Marcus.

Marvin From the Old English, meaning "friend of the sea" or "friendly sea." Also, from the Celtic, meaning "white sea," and from the Gaelic, meaning "mountainous area. HEBREW EQUIVALENTS: Aharon, Avi'yam, Giva, Haran, Medan, Moshe, Talmai, Talmi, Tel-Chai, Telem. FEMININE HEBREW EQUIVALENTS: Amit, Davida, Marata, Migdala, Miryam, Talma, Talmit, Ya'el.

Marwin A variant form of Marvin. *See* Marvin.

Masad (מָסָד) From the Hebrew, meaning "foundation, support." The exact Hebrew equivalent is Masad. The exact feminine Hebrew equivalent is Masada.

Mashiach (מָשִׁיחַ) From the Hebrew, meaning "Messiah, anointed one." The exact Hebrew equivalent is Mashiach. FEMININE HEBREW EQUIVALENT: Mosha'a, Yiska.

Maskil (מַשְׂכִּיל) From the Hebrew, meaning "enlightened, educated." The exact Hebrew equivalent is Maskil. The exact feminine Hebrew equivalent is Maskila.

Mason From the Anglo-Saxon, meaning "mason, worker in stone." HE-
BREW EQUIVALENTS: Elitzur, Even, Shamir, Tzeror, Tzur, Tzuriel. FEMI-
NINE HEBREW EQUIVALENTS: Gazit, Ritzpa, Tzurel, Tzuriya, Tzurit.

Mat A pet form of Matthew. *See* Matthew.

Matan (מַתָּן) From the Hebrew, meaning "gift." The exact Hebrew
equivalent is Matan. The exact feminine Hebrew equivalent is Matana.

Matania, Mataniah Variant spellings of Matanya. *See* Matanya.

Matanya, Matanyahu (מַתַּנְיָהוּ/מַתַּנְיָה) From the Hebrew, meaning "gift
of God." The exact Hebrew equivalent is Matanya. FEMININE HEBREW
EQUIVALENTS: Matana, Matat, Netanela, Netanya.

Mateo A Spanish form of Matthew. *See* Matthew.

Mati (מַתִּי) A pet form of Matanya. *See* Matanya. Also, a pet form of
Mattathias. *See* Mattathias.

Matia, Matiah Variant spellings of Matya. *See* Matya.

Matitya, Matityahu (מַתִּתְיָהוּ/מַתִּתְיָה) From the Hebrew, meaning "gift
of God." Mattathias is a Greek form. *See* Mattathias.

Matmon (מַטְמוֹן) From the Hebrew, meaning "treasure, wealth." The
exact Hebrew equivalent is Matmon. The exact feminine Hebrew equivalent is Matmona.

Matok (מָתוֹק) From the Hebrew, meaning "sweet." The exact Hebrew
equivalent is Matok. The exact feminine Hebrew equivalent is Metuka.

Matri (מַטְרִי) From the Hebrew, meaning "rain, my rain." The exact Hebrew equivalent is Matri. FEMININE HEBREW EQUIVALENTS: Malkosha,
Ravital, Reviva.

Matt A pet form of Matthew. *See* Matthew.

Mattathias (מַתִּתְיָהוּ) From the Greek, meaning "gift of God." The exact
Hebrew equivalent is Matityahu. FEMININE HEBREW EQUIVALENTS: Matana, Matat, Migdana, Mincha, Netanel, Netina, Zevida, Zevuda.

Matthew A variant form of Mattathias. *See* Mattathias.

Mattie, Matty, Mattye Pet forms of Matthew. *See* Matthew.

Maurey A pet form of Maurice. *See* Maurice.

Maurice From the Greek, Latin, and Middle English, meaning "moorish,
dark-skinned." HEBREW EQUIVALENTS: Adar, Ayfai, Cham, Kedar, Pinchas. FEMININE HEBREW EQUIVALENTS: Ayfa, Chachila, Shechora, Tzila.

Maurie A pet form of Maurice. *See* Maurice.

Maury A pet form of Maurice. *See* Maurice.

Max A short form of Maximilian. *See* Maximilian.

Maximilian From the Latin, meaning "great" or "famous." HEBREW
EQUIVALENTS: Gedalya, Gidel, Hillel, Migdal, Mehulal, Raba, Rav, Rava.
FEMININE HEBREW EQUIVALENTS: Atalya, Gedula, Migdala, Ya'el, Yehudit,
Zimra.

Maxwell An English form of Maximilian. *See* Maximilian.

Mayer A variant spelling of Meir. *See* Meir.

Maynard From the Old High German, meaning "powerful, strong," or from the Latin and the French, meaning "hand." HEBREW EQUIVALENTS: Arye, Amotz, Binyamin, Chofni, Gavriel, Yeda'ya. FEMININE HEBREW EQUIVALENTS: Amtza, Ariel, Ariela, Atzma, Gavriela, Gibora.

Mazal (מָזָל) From the Hebrew, meaning "star" or "luck." The exact masculine and feminine Hebrew equivalent is Mazal.

Mazal-Tov (מָזָל־טוֹב) From the Hebrew, meaning "good star, lucky star." The exact Hebrew equivalent is Mazal-Tov. FEMININE HEBREW EQUIVALENTS: Mazal, Mazala, Mazalit.

Medad (מֵידָד) From the Hebrew, meaning "measurement." The exact Hebrew equivalent is Medad.

Meged (מֶגֶד) From the Hebrew, meaning "goodness, sweetness, excellence." The exact Hebrew equivalent is Meged. FEMININE HEBREW EQUIVALENTS: Migda, Migdana.

Meir (מֵאִיר) From the Hebrew, meaning "one who brightens or shines." The exact Hebrew equivalent is Me'ir. The exact feminine Hebrew equivalent is Me'ira.

Meiri (מֵאִירִי) A variant form of Meir. See Meir. The exact Hebrew equivalent is Me'iri.

Mel, Mell Pet forms of Melvin. See Melvin.

Melchior A variant form of the Latin name Melchita. Derived from the Hebrew melech, meaning "king." HEBREW EQUIVALENT: Melech. FEMININE HEBREW EQUIVALENT: Malka.

Melech (מֶלֶךְ) From the Hebrew, meaning "king." The exact Hebrew equivalent is Melech. The exact feminine Hebrew equivalent is Malka.

Melton A variant form of Milton. See Milton.

Melville From the Old English, meaning "village near the mill." HEBREW EQUIVALENTS: Chetzrai, Chetzron, Goren, Ir, Kimchi. FEMININE HEBREW EQUIVALENTS: Degana, Deganiya, Keret, Kirya.

Melvin From the Celtic, meaning "leader" or "chief." Also, from the Anglo-Saxon, meaning "friendly toiler" or "famous friend." HEBREW EQUIVALENTS: Amel, Amit, David, Gedalya, Ovadya, Oved, Rav, Yehuda. FEMININE HEBREW EQUIVALENTS: Amalya, Amita, Atara, Davida, Yehudit, Yisr'ela.

Melvyn A variant spelling of Melvin. See Melvin.

Menachem (מְנַחֵם) From the Hebrew, meaning "comforter." The exact Hebrew equivalent is Menachem. The exact feminine Hebrew equivalent is Menachema or Nechama.

Menahem A variant spelling of Menachem. See Menachem.

Menashe (מְנַשֶׁה) From the Hebrew, meaning "causing to forget." The Anglicized form is Manasseh. The exact Hebrew equivalent is Menashe. FEMININE HEBREW EQUIVALENTS: Atalya, Gedola, Gedula, Rachav.

Menashi (מְנַשִׁי) A variant form of Menashe. See Menashe. The exact Hebrew equivalent is Menashi.

Mendel (מֶעְנְדְל/מֶענְדְעל) From the Middle English menden, meaning "to repair." Also, a Yiddish name derived from Menachem. See Menachem.

Mendl A variant spelling of Mendel. *See* Mendel.

Meredith From the Anglo-Saxon, meaning "sea dew" or "sea defender." Also, of Welsh origin, meaning "great chief, defender of the people." HEBREW EQUIVALENTS: Arnon, Avi'yam, Enan, Gedalya, Melech, Oved, Peleg. FEMININE HEBREW EQUIVALENTS: Atara, Malka, Mara, Marata, Miryam.

Merom (מֵרוֹם) From the Hebrew, meaning "heights." The exact Hebrew equivalent is Merom. The exact feminine Hebrew equivalent is Meroma.

Meron (מֵרוֹן) From the Hebrew, meaning "sheep." The exact Hebrew equivalent is Meron. The exact feminine Hebrew equivalent is Merona.

Merrill From the Old English, meaning "sea, pool, river." Also, from the Old English, meaning "famous." HEBREW EQUIVALENTS: Avi'yam, Beri, Gedalya, Hillel, Mehulal, Shem-Tov, Shimi, Yehuda. FEMININE HEBREW EQUIVALENTS: Afeka, Bat-Yam, Hillela, Miryam, Tehila, Yehudit.

Merton From the Anglo-Saxon, meaning "from the farm by the sea." HEBREW EQUIVALENTS: Avigal, Avi'yam, Beri, Livyatan, Peleg. FEMININE HEBREW EQUIVALENTS: Afeka, Bat-Galim, Bat-Yam, Dalya, Miryam, Yama, Yamit.

Mervin A Welsh form of Marvin. *See* Marvin.

Mervyn A variant spelling of Mervin. *See* Mervin.

Merwin, Merwyn Variant forms of Marvin. *See* Marvin.

Meshi (מֶשִׁי) From the Hebrew, meaning "silk." The exact Hebrew equivalent is Meshi.

Meyer A variant spelling of Meir. *See* Meir.

Mica, Micah Anglicized forms of Micha. *See* Micha.

Micha (מִיכָה) From the Hebrew, meaning "Who is like God?" A short form of Michael. The exact Hebrew equivalent is Micha. The exact feminine Hebrew equivalent is Michal.

Michael (מִיכָאֵל) From the Hebrew, meaning "Who is like God?" The exact Hebrew equivalent is Michael. FEMININE HEBREW EQUIVALENTS: Michaela, Michal.

Michal (מִיכַל) A short form of Michael. *See* Michael.

Michel A variant form of Michael. *See* Michael.

Mickey, Mickie, Micky Pet forms of Michael. *See* Michael.

Mika A variant spelling of Micah. *See* Michah.

Mike A pet form of Michael. *See* Michael.

Mikel A pet form of Michael. *See* Michael.

Mikhail A Russian form of Michael. *See* Michael.

Miki A pet form of Michael. *See* Michael.

Miles From the Greek and Latin, meaning "warrior, soldier," or from Old German, meaning "beloved." Used in England as a short form of Michael. HEBREW EQUIVALENTS: David, Gad, Gidon, Mordechai, Medan, Midyan, Yedidya. FEMININE HEBREW EQUIVALENTS: Ahava, Amtza,

Chaviva, Davida, Gavriela, Gavrila, Gibora, Yedida. *See* Michael *for additional equivalents.*

Milton From the Old English, meaning "mill town." HEBREW EQUIVA-LENTS: Adam, Bustenai, Chaklai, Choresh, Shadmon, Yagev, Yizr'el. FEMININE HEBREW EQUIVALENTS: Adama, Shadmit, Shedema, Yizr'ela.

Misha A Russian form of Michael. *See* Michael. Also, a pet form of Moshe. *See* Moshe.

Mishael (מִישָׁאֵל) From the Hebrew, meaning "borrowed." The exact Hebrew equivalent is Mishael. FEMININE HEBREW EQUIVALENTS: Sha'ula, Sha'ulit.

Mitch A pet form of Mitchell. *See* Mitchell.

Mitchel, Mitchell Variant forms of Michael. *See* Michael.

Mo, Moe A pet form of Morris. *See* Morris.

Moise, Moises French forms of Moses. *See* Moses.

Monroe From the Celtic, meaning "red marsh." HEBREW EQUIVALENTS: Arnon, Avi'yam, Moshe, Peleg. FEMININE HEBREW EQUIVALENTS: Arnona, Mara, Marata, Miryam.

Montague The French form of the Latin, meaning "from the pointed mountain." HEBREW EQUIVALENTS: Aharon, Amir, Gal, Gali, Haran, Harel, Marom. FEMININE HEBREW EQUIVALENTS: Aharona, Galiya, Gilada, Givona, Meroma, Talma, Talmit.

Monte A pet form of Montague and Montgomery. *See* Montague *and* Montgomery.

Montgomery The English variant of the French name Montague. *See* Montague.

Monty A variant spelling of Monte. *See* Monte.

Mordecai The Anglicized form of Mordechai. *See* Mordechai.

Mordechai (מָרְדְּכַי) From the Persian and Babylonian, meaning "warrior, warlike." The exact Hebrew equivalent is Mordechai. FEMININE HEBREW EQUIVALENTS: Amtza, Atzma, Gavriela, Gavrila, Gibora, Tigra.

Mordy A pet form of Mordechai. *See* Mordechai.

Moreg (מוֹרַג) From the Hebrew, meaning "grain thresher." The exact Hebrew equivalent is Moreg. The exact feminine Hebrew equivalent is Morega.

Morenu (מוֹרֵנוּ) From the Hebrew, meaning "our teacher." The exact Hebrew equivalent is Morenu. FEMININE HEBREW EQUIVALENTS: Moran, Morit, Moriya.

Morey A pet form of Maurice. *See* Maurice.

Morgan From the Celtic, meaning "one who lives near the sea." HEBREW EQUIVALENTS: Arnon, Avigal, Avi'yam, Chaifa, Livyatan, Shuni. FEMININE HEBREW EQUIVALENTS: Arnona, Bat-Galim, Bat-Yam, Miryam, Yama, Yamit.

Mori, Morie From the Hebrew, meaning "my teacher." Also, variant spellings of Morey. *See* Morey.

Moritz   A variant form of Maurice. *See* Maurice.

Morrey   A variant spelling of Morey. *See* Morey.

Morrie   A variant spelling of Morey. *See* Morey.

Morris   A variant form of Maurice. *See* Maurice. Also, from the Gaelic, meaning "great warrior." HEBREW EQUIVALENTS: Gad, Gadi, Gadiel, Gavriel, Madai, Medan, Meron, Mordechai. FEMININE HEBREW EQUIVALENTS: Gada, Gadit, Gavriela, Gavrila, Merav, Merona.

Morrison   A patronymic form, meaning "son of Morris." *See* Morris.

Morry   A variant spelling of Morey. *See* Morey.

Morse   A variant form of Maurice. *See* Maurice.

Mortimer   From the Anglo-French, meaning "one who lives near the sea" or "one who dwells near still water." HEBREW EQUIVALENTS: Avi'yam, Beri, Chaifa, Dalfon, Dela'ya, Moshe. FEMININE HEBREW EQUIVALENTS: Afeka, Bat-Galim, Bat-Yam, Miryam, Yamit, Yaval.

Morton   From the Old English, meaning "town near the sea" or "farm on the moor." HEBREW EQUIVALENTS: Adam, Avi'yam, Beri, Dalfon, Ma'ayan, Shadmon, Yogev, Zore'a. FEMININE HEBREW EQUIVALENTS: Adama, Afeka, Bat-Yam, Miryam, Shadmit, Silonit.

Mosad, Mossad (מוֹסָד)   From the Hebrew, meaning "establishment." The exact Hebrew equivalent is Mosad. The exact feminine Hebrew equivalent is Mosada.

Mose   A pet form of Moses. *See* Moses.

Moses   The Anglicized form of Moshe. *See* Moshe.

Mosha (מוֹשֵׁעַ)   From the Hebrew, meaning "salvation." The exact Hebrew equivalent is Mosha. The exact feminine Hebrew equivalent is Mosha'a.

Moshe (מֹשֶׁה)   From the Hebrew, meaning "drawn out [of the water]." Or, from the Egyptian, meaning "son, child." The exact Hebrew equivalent is Moshe. FEMININE HEBREW EQUIVALENTS: Dalit, Daliya, Matzila, Miryam, Mosha'a.

Moss   An English variant form of Moses. *See* Moses.

Motel (מָאטֶל/מָאטֶעל)   A Yiddish pet form of Mordechai. *See* Mordechai.

Moti, Motti (מָתִי)   Nicknames for Mordechai. *See* Mordechai. The exact Hebrew equivalent is Moti.

Moy, Moyse   Variant English forms of Moses. *See* Moses.

Muki   A pet form of Meir. *See* Meir.

Murray   From the Celtic and Welsh, meaning "sea" or "seaman." HEBREW EQUIVALENTS: Arnon, Avi'yam, Mosha, Moshe, Peleg. FEMININE HEBREW EQUIVALENTS: Arnona, Bat-Galim, Bat-Yam, Mara, Miryam, Mosha'a. Also, a variant form of Maurice. *See* Maurice.

Mychal   A variant spelling of Michael. *See* Michael.

Myer   A variant spelling of Mayer. *See* Mayer.

Myles   A variant spelling of Miles. *See* Miles.

Myron From the Greek, meaning "fragrant, sweet, pleasant." HEBREW EQUIVALENTS: Achino'am, Avino'am, Magdiel, Matok, Meged, Mehudar, Na'aman, Na'am. FEMININE HEBREW EQUIVALENTS: Achinoam, Devasha, Metuka, Na'ama, Na'amana Na'omi.

Myrton A variant spelling of Merton. *See* Merton.

Naam (נַעַם/נֶעֱם) From the Hebrew, meaning "sweet, pleasant." The exact Hebrew equivalent is Na'am. The exact feminine Hebrew equivalent is Na'omi.

Naaman (נַעֲמָן) From the Hebrew, meaning "sweet, beautiful, pleasant, good." The exact Hebrew equivalent is Na'aman. The exact feminine Hebrew equivalent is Na'amana.

Nachman (נַחְמָן) From the Hebrew, meaning "comforter." The exact Hebrew equivalent is Nachman. The exact feminine Hebrew equivalent is Nachmana.

Nachmani (נַחְמָנִי) From the Hebrew, meaning "comfort." The exact Hebrew equivalent is Nachmani. FEMININE HEBREW EQUIVALENTS: Nachmana, Nechama.

Nachum (נָחוּם) From the Hebrew, meaning "comfort." The exact Hebrew equivalent is Nachum. The exact feminine Hebrew equivalent is Nechama.

Nadav (נָדָב) From the Hebrew, meaning "generous, noble." The exact Hebrew equivalent is Nadav. The exact feminine Hebrew equivalent is Nedava.

Nadiv (נָדִיב) From the Hebrew, meaning "princely, generous." The exact Hebrew equivalent is Nadiv. FEMININE HEBREW EQUIVALENTS: Nedava, Nediva.

Naf A pet form of Naftali. *See* Naftali.

Naftali, Naftalie (נַפְתָּלִי) From the Hebrew, meaning "to wrestle" or "to be crafty." Also, from the Hebrew, meaning "likeness, comparison." The exact Hebrew equivalent is Naftali. FEMININE HEBREW EQUIVALENTS: Naftala, Naftalya.

Nagid (נָגִיד) From the Hebrew, meaning "ruler, prince." The exact Hebrew equivalent is Nagid. The exact feminine Hebrew equivalent is Negida.

Nagiv (נָגִיב) From the Hebrew, meaning "pertaining to the south." Akin to Negev. The exact Hebrew equivalent is Nagiv. FEMININE HEBREW EQUIVALENTS: Deroma, Deromit.

Nahir (נָהִיר) A variant form of Nahor. *See* Nahor. The exact Hebrew equivalent is Nahir.

Nahor (נָהוֹר) From the Aramaic, meaning "light." The exact Hebrew equivalent is Nahor. FEMININE HEBREW EQUIVALENTS: Nehara, Nehira, Nehura, Ne'ora, Noga, Nurya.

Nahum A variant spelling of Nachum. *See* Nachum.

Naim (נָעִים) From the Hebrew, meaning "pleasant." The exact Hebrew equivalent is Na'im. FEMININE HEBREW EQUIVALENTS: Na'omi, Na'ama, and Ne'ima.

Namer (נָמֵר) From the Hebrew, meaning "leopard." The exact Hebrew equivalent is Namer. The exact feminine Hebrew equivalent is Nemera.

Namir (נָמִיר) From the Hebrew, meaning "leopard." The exact Hebrew equivalent is Namir. The exact feminine Hebrew equivalent is Nemera.

Nanod (נָנוֹד) From the Hebrew, meaning "wanderer." The exact Hebrew equivalent is Nanod. FEMININE HEBREW EQUIVALENTS: Gershona, Gerusha, Giora, Hagar, Zara.

Naom (נָעֹם) A variant form of Naaman. See Naaman. The exact Hebrew equivalent is Na'om.

Naor (נָאוֹר) From the Hebrew, meaning "light" or "enlightened." The exact Hebrew equivalent is Na'or. The exact feminine Hebrew equivalent is Ne'ora.

Naphtali, Naphthali Variant spellings of Naftali. See Naftali.

Nasi (נָשִׂיא) From the Hebrew, meaning "prince, leader." The exact Hebrew equivalent is Nasi. The exact feminine Hebrew equivalent is Nesia.

Nason A variant form of Natan. See Natan.

Natan (נָתָן) From the Hebrew, meaning "gift." The exact Hebrew equivalent is Natan. The exact feminine Hebrew equivalent is Netana.

Nate A pet form of Nathan. See Nathan.

Nathan A variant spelling of Natan. See Natan.

Nathanel, Nathaniel Variant spellings of Netanel. See Netanel.

Nativ (נָתִיב) From the Hebrew, meaning "path, road." The exact Hebrew equivalent is Nativ. The exact feminine Hebrew equivalent is Netiva.

Navon (נָבוֹן) From the Hebrew, meaning "wise." The exact Hebrew equivalent is Navon. The exact feminine Hebrew equivalent is Nevona.

Neal, Neale From the Middle English and the Gaelic, meaning "champion, courageous person" or "dark-complexioned." HEBREW EQUIVALENTS: Abir, Abiri, Adar, Ayfai, Cham, Gavrila, Gibor, Kedar, Pinchas. FEMININE HEBREW EQUIVALENTS: Amtza, Ayfa, Chachila, Gavriela, No'aza, Odeda, Shechora.

Nechemia, Nechemiah Variant spellings of Nechemya. See Nechemya.

Nechemya (נְחֶמְיָה) From the Hebrew, meaning "comforted by the Lord." The exact Hebrew equivalent is Nechemya. FEMININE HEBREW EQUIVALENTS: Menachema, Nachmanit, Nachmaniya, Nechama.

Ned A pet form of Edmond and Edward. See Edmond *and* Edward.

Neddy A pet form of Edmond and Edward. See Edmond *and* Edward.

Negev (נֶגֶב) From the Hebrew, meaning "south, southerly." Akin to Nagiv. The exact Hebrew equivalent is Negev. FEMININE HEBREW EQUIVALENTS: Deroma, Deromit.

Nehemia, Nehemiah Variant spellings of Nechemya. See Nechemya.

Neil A variant spelling of Neal. See Neal.

Neilson A patronymic form of Neil, meaning "son of Neil." See Neil.

Nelson A patronymic form of Neal, meaning "son of Neal." See Neal.

Nemuel (נְמוּאֵל) From the Hebrew, meaning "ant," hence, industrious. The exact Hebrew equivalent is Nemuel. FEMININE HEBREW EQUIVALENTS: Amalya, Amela, Charutza.

Ner (נֵר) From the Hebrew, meaning "light." The exact Hebrew equivalent is Ner. The exact feminine Hebrew equivalent is Nera.

Neri (נֵרִי) From the Hebrew, meaning "my light." The exact Hebrew equivalent is Neri. FEMININE HEBREW EQUIVALENTS: Ne'ira, Ne'ora, Nera, Ner-Li, Nirel.

Nerli, Ner-Li (נֵר־לִי/נֵרְלִי) From the Hebrew, meaning "I have [a] light." The exact masculine and feminine Hebrew equivalent is Nerli.

Nes, Ness (נֵס) From the Hebrew, meaning "miracle." The exact Hebrew equivalent is Nes. FEMININE HEBREW EQUIVALENTS: Nasya, Nesya, Nisya, Pelia.

Nesher (נֶשֶׁר) From the Hebrew, meaning "eagle." The exact Hebrew equivalent is Nesher. The feminine Hebrew equivalent is Tzipora.

Netanel (נְתַנְאֵל) From the Hebrew, meaning "gift of God." The exact Hebrew equivalent is Netanel. The exact feminine Hebrew equivalent is Netanela.

Netaniel (נְתַנִיאֵל) A variant form of Netanel. *See* Netanel. The exact Hebrew equivalent is Netaniel.

Netanya (נְתַנְיָה) From the Hebrew, meaning "gift of God." Used also as a feminine name. The exact masculine and feminine Hebrew equivalent is Netanya.

Netanyahu (נְתַנְיָהוּ) A variant form of Netanya. *See* Netanya. The exact Hebrew equivalent is Netanyahu.

Nethanel A variant spelling of Netanel. *See* Netanel.

Nethaniel A variant spelling of Netanel. *See* Netanel.

Nevil, Nevile, Nevill, Neville From the French, meaning "new town." HEBREW EQUIVALENTS: Chetzron, Dur, Ir, Yeshavam, Zevul, Zevulun. FEMININE HEBREW EQUIVALENTS: Keret, Lina, Shafrira, Tira.

Newbold From the Old English, meaning "new town [beside the tree]." Akin to Newton. *See* Newton.

Newman From the Anglo-Saxon, meaning "new man." HEBREW EQUIVALENTS: Adam, Chadash. FEMININE HEBREW EQUIVALENTS: Adama, Chadasha.

Newton From the Old English, meaning "from the new farmstead" or "new town." Akin to Newbold. HEBREW EQUIVALENTS: Adam, Bustena'i, Karmel, Karmeli, Shadmon, Yizr'el. FEMININE HEBREW EQUIVALENTS: Adama, Karmela, Nava, Shadmit, Shedema, Yizr'ela.

Nicholas From the Greek, meaning "victory of the people." HEBREW EQUIVALENTS: Gavriel, Gover, Netzach, Yatzliach. FEMININE HEBREW EQUIVALENTS: Dafna, Hadasa, Nitzcha, Nitzchiya, Nitzchona.

Nicolas A variant spelling of Nicholas. *See* Nicholas.

Nidri (נִדְרִי) From the Hebrew, meaning "my oath." The exact Hebrew equivalent is Nidri. FEMININE HEBREW EQUIVALENTS: Batsheva, Elisheva, Sheva.

Niel A variant Norse form of Nicholas. *See* Nicholas.

Nike A pet form of Nicholas. *See* Nicholas.

Niles A patronymic form of Neal, meaning "son of Neal." *See* Neal.

Nili (נִילִי) An acronym of the Hebrew words "the glory (or eternity) of Israel will not lie" (I Samuel 15:29). The exact masculine and feminine Hebrew equivalent is Nili.

Nils A patronymic form of Neal, meaning "son of Neal." *See* Neal.

Nir (נִיר) From the Hebrew, meaning "to plough, to cultivate a field." The exact Hebrew equivalent is Nir. The exact feminine Hebrew equivalent is Nira.

Nirel, Nir-El (נִיר־אֵל/נִירְאֵל) From the Hebrew, meaning "cultivated field of the Lord." The exact masculine and feminine Hebrew equivalent is Nirel. FEMININE HEBREW EQUIVALENTS: Nira, Nirit.

Niria, Niriah Variant spellings of Niriya. *See* Niriya.

Niriel (נִירִיאֵל) A variant form of Nirel. *See* Nirel. The exact Hebrew equivalent is Niriel.

Niriya (נִירִיָה) From the Hebrew, meaning "cultivated field of the Lord." The exact Hebrew equivalent is Niriya. FEMININE HEBREW EQUIVALENTS: Nira, Nirit, Odera.

Nirya (נִירְיָה) A variant form of Niriya. *See* Niriya. The exact Hebrew equivalent is Nirya.

Nisan, Nissan (נִיסָן) From the Hebrew, meaning "banner, emblem" or "miracle." The exact Hebrew equivalent is Nissan. FEMININE HEBREW EQUIVALENTS: Digla, Nasya, Nesya, Peliya.

Nissi (נִסִי) A variant form of Nisim. *See* Nisim. The exact Hebrew equivalent is Nissi.

Nisim, Nissim (נִסִים) From the Hebrew, meaning "miracles." The exact Hebrew equivalent is Nisim. FEMININE HEBREW EQUIVALENTS: Nasya, Nesya, Nisya, Remazya.

Niv (נִיב) From the Aramaic and Arabic, meaning "speech, expression." The exact Hebrew equivalent is Niv. The exact feminine Hebrew equivalent is Niva.

Noach (נֹחַ) From the Hebrew, meaning "rest, quiet, peace." The exact Hebrew equivalent is No'ach. FEMININE HEBREW EQUIVALENTS: Menucha, Meshulemet, Nachat, Shelomit, Shulamit.

Noah The Anglicized form of Noach. *See* Noach.

Noam (נֹעַם) From the Hebrew, meaning "sweetness" or "friendship." The exact Hebrew equivalent is No'am. FEMININE HEBREW EQUIVALENTS: Na'ama, Na'omi.

Noaz (נוֹעָז) From the Hebrew, meaning "daring, bold." The exact Hebrew equivalent is No'az. The exact feminine Hebrew equivalent is No'aza.

Noble From the Latin, meaning "well-known, famous." HEBREW EQUIVALENTS: Hillel, Noda, Shevach, Yehuda. FEMININE HEBREW EQUIVALENTS: Degula, Hillela, Tishbacha, Yehudit.

Noda (נוֹדָע) From the Hebrew, meaning "famous, well-known." The exact Hebrew equivalent is Noda. FEMININE HEBREW EQUIVALENTS: Hillela, Tishbacha, Yehudit.

Noel An Old French form of the Latin name Natalis, meaning "to be born" or "birthday." HEBREW EQUIVALENTS: Aharon, Amiram, Amiron, Ana, Liron, Ron, Roni, Ronel, Yaron. FEMININE HEBREW EQUIVALENTS: Aharona, Lirit, Liron, Mangina, Rina, Shira, Yarona.

Nof (נוֹף) From the Hebrew, meaning "beautiful landscape." The exact Hebrew equivalent is Nof. The exact feminine Hebrew equivalent is Nofiya.

Noga (נֹגַה) From the Hebrew, meaning "light, bright." The exact masculine and feminine Hebrew equivalent is Noga.

Nolan From the Celtic, meaning "noble" or "famous." HEBREW EQUIVALENTS: Hillel, Noda, Shevach, Yehuda. FEMININE HEBREW EQUIVALENTS: Degula, Hillela, Tishbacha, Yehudit.

Noland A variant form of Nolan. *See* Nolan.

Norbert From the German, meaning "divine brightness." HEBREW EQUIVALENTS: Avner, Bahir, Barak, Me'ir, Noga, Uriel, Zerachya. FEMININE HEBREW EQUIVALENTS: Behira, Me'ira, Noga, Ora, Uriela, Zivanit.

Norman From the Anglo-Saxon, meaning "man from the north." HEBREW EQUIVALENTS: Tzefanya, Tzefanyahu. The feminine Hebrew equivalent is Tzafona.

Normann A variant spelling of Norman. *See* Norman.

Norris From the Anglo-Saxon, meaning "the dwelling place of a man from the north," or from the French-Latin, meaning "caretaker." HEBREW EQUIVALENTS: Ovadya, Oved, Tzefanya, Tzefanyahu. FEMININE HEBREW EQUIVALENTS: Magena, Tzafona.

North From the Anglo-Saxon, meaning "man from the north." HEBREW EQUIVALENTS: Tzefanya, Tzefanyahu. The feminine Hebrew equivalent is Tzafona.

Norton From the Anglo-Saxon, meaning "town in the north." HEBREW EQUIVALENTS: Avgar, Dor, Dur, Devir, Ma'on, Tzefanya, Tzefanyahu, Zevulun. FEMININE HEBREW EQUIVALENTS: Devira, Me'ona, Tzafona, Zevula.

Norwood From the Old English, meaning "woods in the north." HEBREW EQUIVALENTS: Artza, Artzi, Tzefanya, Tzefanyahu, Ya'ar, Ya'ari, Yara. FEMININE HEBREW EQUIVALENTS: Eretz, Tzafona, Ya'ara, Ya'arit.

Nosson A variant form of Natan. *See* Natan.

Noy (נוֹי) From the Hebrew, meaning "beauty." The exact Hebrew equivalent is Noy. The exact feminine Hebrew equivalent is No'ya.

Nun (נוּן) From the Hebrew, meaning "fish." The exact Hebrew equivalent is Nun. FEMININE HEBREW EQUIVALENTS: Dagit, Dagiya.

Nur (נוּר) From the Hebrew and Aramaic, meaning "fire, light." The exact Hebrew equivalent is Nur. The exact feminine Hebrew equivalent is Nura.

Nuri (נוּרִי) From the Hebrew and Aramaic, meaning "my fire, my light." The exact Hebrew equivalent is Nuri. FEMININE HEBREW EQUIVALENTS: Ne'ira, Ne'ora, Nera, Nurya.

Nuria, Nuriah Variant spellings of Nuriya. *See* Nuriya.

Nuriel (נוּרִיאֵל) From the Aramaic and Hebrew, meaning "fire of the Lord." The exact Hebrew equivalent is Nuriel. The exact feminine Hebrew equivalent is Nuriela.

Nuriya (נוּרִיָּה) From the Aramaic and Hebrew, meaning "fire of the Lord." The exact Hebrew equivalent is Nuriya. FEMININE HEBREW EQUIVALENTS: Nehira, Nehura, Ner-Li, Nura, Nurya.

Nurya (נוּרְיָה) A variant form of Nuriya. *See* Nuriya. The exact masculine and feminine Hebrew equivalent is Nurya.

Nyle A variant Irish form of Neal. *See* Neal.

Oakleigh A variant spelling of Oakley. *See* Oakley.

Oakley From the Old English, meaning "field of oak trees." HEBREW EQUIVALENTS: Alon, Elon. FEMININE HEBREW EQUIVALENTS: Alona, Elona.

Obadiah The Anglicized form of Ovadya. *See* Ovadya.

Obe A pet form of Obadiah. *See* Obadiah.

Oded (עוֹדֵד) From the Hebrew, meaning "to restore." The exact Hebrew equivalent is Oded. The exact feminine Hebrew equivalent is Odeda.

Odo From the Old German and the Old English, meaning "rich." HEBREW EQUIVALENTS: Achikar, Ashir, Etzer, Huna, Oshri, Yitro. FEMININE HEBREW EQUIVALENTS: Ashira, Batshua, Yitra.

Ofar (עוֹפָר) From the Hebrew, meaning "young deer." The exact Hebrew equivalent is Ofar. The exact feminine Hebrew equivalent is Ofra.

Ofer (עוֹפֶר) From the Hebrew, meaning "young mountain goat" or "young deer." The exact Hebrew equivalent is Ofer. The exact feminine Hebrew equivalent is Ofra.

Ofra (עָפְרָה) From the Hebrew, meaning "young mountain goat" or "young deer." The exact masculine and feminine Hebrew equivalent is Ofra.

Ofri (עָפְרִי) From the Hebrew, meaning "my goat" or "my deer." The exact Hebrew equivalent is Ofri. The exact feminine Hebrew equivalent is Ofra.

Og (עוֹג) From the Hebrew, meaning "giant." The exact Hebrew equivalent is Og. FEMININE HEBREW EQUIVALENTS: Atalya, Gedola, Rachav.

Ogen (עוֹגֵן) From the Hebrew, meaning "to imprison" or "to chain, anchor." The exact Hebrew equivalent is Ogen. The exact feminine Hebrew equivalent is Aguna.

Ohev (אוֹהֵב) From the Hebrew, meaning "lover." The exact Hebrew equivalent is Ohev. The exact feminine Hebrew equivalent is Ahuva.

Olaf From the Norse and Danish, meaning "ancestor." HEBREW EQUIVALENTS: Kadmiel, Kedem. FEMININE HEBREW EQUIVALENTS: Kadmiela, Kedma, Yeshisha.

Oleg From the Norse, meaning "holy." HEBREW EQUIVALENTS: Chaga, Devir, Kadish, Kadosh. FEMININE HEBREW EQUIVALENTS: Chagit, Chagiya, Devira, Kadisha, Kedosha.

Olin From the Old English and the Middle English, meaning "holy." HEBREW EQUIVALENTS: Chaga, Devir, Kadish, Kadosh. FEMININE HEBREW EQUIVALENTS: Chagit, Chagiya, Devira, Kadisha, Kedosha.

Oliver From the Latin, meaning "man of peace." HEBREW EQUIVALENTS: Avshalom, Manoach, No'ach, Shalom, Shelomo, Zetan. FEMININE HEBREW EQUIVALENTS: Achishalom, Marge'a, Menucha, Meshulemet, Shelomit, Shulamit.

Olivier The French form of Oliver. See Oliver.

Ollie A pet form of Oliver. See Oliver.

Omen (אוֹמֶן) From the Hebrew, meaning "faithful." The exact Hebrew equivalent is Omen (Omayn). FEMININE HEBREW EQUIVALENTS: Amana, Amanya, Ne'emana.

Omer (עוֹמֶר) From the Hebrew, meaning "sheaf." The exact Hebrew equivalent is Omer. FEMININE HEBREW EQUIVALENTS: Omrit, Umarit.

Ometz (אוֹמֶץ) From the Hebrew, meaning "strength." The exact Hebrew equivalent is Ometz. The exact feminine Hebrew equivalent is Amtza.

Omri (עָמְרִי) From the Hebrew, meaning "my sheaf." Also, from the Arabic, meaning "long life." The exact Hebrew equivalent is Omri. FEMININE HEBREW EQUIVALENTS: Chava, Cha'ya, Chiyuta, Yechiela.

Opher A variant spelling of Ofer. See Ofer.

Orde From the Latin, meaning "order," and from the Old English, meaning "beginning." HEBREW EQUIVALENTS: Rishon, Sadir, Sidra. FEMININE HEBREW EQUIVALENTS: Rishona, Sidra.

Oren (אוֹרֶן) From the Hebrew, meaning "a tree [cedar or fir]." The exact Hebrew equivalent is Oren. FEMININE HEBREW EQUIVALENTS: Arza, Ayla, Ilana, Ilanit.

Orev (עוֹרֵב) From the Hebrew, meaning "raven." The exact Hebrew equivalent is Orev (Orayv). FEMININE HEBREW EQUIVALENTS: Efrona, Gozala, Tzipora.

Ori (אוֹרִי) From the Hebrew, meaning "my light." The exact Hebrew equivalent is Ori. FEMININE HEBREW EQUIVALENTS: Or, Ora, Orali, Orli, Orlit.

Orin, Orrin Variant forms of Oren. See Oren.

Orland A variant form of Roland and Rolando by reversal of letters. See Roland.

Orlando A variant form of Orland. See Orland.

Oron (אוֹרוֹן) From the Hebrew, meaning "light." The exact Hebrew equivalent is Oron. FEMININE HEBREW EQUIVALENTS: Or, Ora, Orali, Orna, Ornina. Also, a variant form of Oren. See Oren.

Orson From the Latin, meaning "bear." HEBREW EQUIVALENTS: Dov, Dubi. FEMININE HEBREW EQUIVALENTS: Dova, Dovit, Duba.

Orval A variant form of Orville. See Orville.

Orville From the French, meaning "golden city." HEBREW EQUIVALENTS: Elifaz, Ofar, Ofir, Paz, Zahavi. FEMININE HEBREW EQUIVALENTS: Ofira, Paziya, Zehava, Zehuvit.

Osbert From the Anglo-Saxon and German, meaning "famous [bright] god." HEBREW EQUIVALENTS: Bahir, Hillel, Noda, Shevach, Yehuda, Yehudi. FEMININE HEBREW EQUIVALENTS: Behira, Degula, Hillela, Tehila, Yehudit.

Oscar From the Anglo-Saxon, meaning "divine spear" or "divine strength." Also, from the Celtic, meaning "leaping warrior." HEBREW EQUIVALENTS: Gad, Gidon, Kaniel, Mordechai, Medan, Midyan, Yisrael. FEMININE HEBREW EQUIVALENTS: Amtza, Atzma, Chanita, Chinit, Gavrila, Gibora, Yisr'ela.

Oshri (אָשְׁרִי) From the Hebrew, meaning "my good fortune." The exact Hebrew equivalent is Oshri. The exact feminine Hebrew equivalent is Oshrat.

Osman From the Anglo-Saxon, meaning "servant of God" or "protected by God." HEBREW EQUIVALENTS: Avigdor, Avimelech, Avdi, Betzalel, Eltzafan, Ovadya, Oved, Rozen, Ya'akov. FEMININE HEBREW EQUIVALENTS: Avigdora, Chosa, Magena, Setura, Shamira, Ya'akova.

Osmand A variant form of Osman. See Osman.

Osmond A variant spelling of Osmand. See Osmand.

Osmund A variant spelling of Osmond. See Osmond.

Ossie A pet form of Oscar or Oswald. See Oscar and Oswald.

Oswald From the Old English, meaning "god of the forest" or "house steward." HEBREW EQUIVALENTS: Avdi, Avimelech, Melech, Ovadya, Oved, Rozen, Ya'ar, Ya'ari. FEMININE HEBREW EQUIVALENTS: Aleksandra, Amitza, Amtza, Gavrila, Gibora, Ya'ara, Ya'arit.

Otis From the Greek, meaning "one who hears well." HEBREW EQUIVALENTS: Oz, Ozni, Shama, Shimi, Shimon, Shmuel, Yishmael. FEMININE HEBREW EQUIVALENTS: Kashuva, Shimat, Shimona, Shmuela.

Otniel (עָתְנִיאֵל) From the Hebrew, meaning "strength of God" or "God is my strength." The exact Hebrew equivalent is Otniel. FEMININE HEBREW EQUIVALENTS: Amitza, Atzmona, Etana, Nili, Odedya.

Otto From the Old High German, meaning "prosperous, wealthy." HEBREW EQUIVALENTS: Hotir, Huna, Yishai, Yitro. FEMININE HEBREW EQUIVALENTS: Bat-Shua, Matzlicha, Yitra.

Otzar (אוֹצָר) From the Hebrew, meaning "treasure." The exact Hebrew equivalent is Otzar. The exact feminine Hebrew equivalent is Otzara.

Ovadya (עֹבַדְיָה) From the Hebrew, meaning "servant of God." The exact Hebrew equivalent is Ovadya. FEMININE HEBREW EQUIVALENTS: Ama, Shimshona.

Ovadyahu (עֹבַדְיָהוּ) A variant form of Ovadya. See Ovadya. The exact Hebrew equivalent is Ovadyahu.

Owen From the Latin, meaning "well-born," or from the Welsh, meaning "young warrior." HEBREW EQUIVALENTS: Avicha'yil, Avinadav, Ben-Cha'yil, Ish-Hod, Nadav, Nadiv, Yisrael. FEMININE HEBREW EQUIVALENTS: Amtza, Gavriela, Gavrila, Malka, Nediva, Sara, Yisr'ela.

Oz (עֹז) From the Hebrew, meaning "strength." The exact Hebrew equivalent is Oz. FEMININE HEBREW EQUIVALENTS: Atzmona, Etana, Odedya, Uza, Uziela.

Ozar A variant spelling of Otzar. *See* Otzar.

Ozer (עוֹזֵר) From the Hebrew, meaning "strength" or "helper." The exact Hebrew equivalent is Ozer. FEMININE HEBREW EQUIVALENTS: Eliezra, Ezr'ela, Ozera, Uza, Uziela, Uzit.

Ozni (אָזְנִי) From the Hebrew, meaning "my ear" or "my hearing." The exact Hebrew equivalent is Ozni. FEMININE HEBREW EQUIVALENTS: Kashuva, Shimat, Shimona.

Ozzi A pet form of Oswald. *See* Oswald.

Ozri (עוֹזְרִי) From the Hebrew, meaning "my helper." The exact Hebrew equivalent is Ozri. FEMININE HEBREW EQUIVALENTS: Ezra, Ezr'ela, Ezriela.

Paddy A pet form of Patrick. *See* Patrick.

Page From the Italian, meaning "boy attendant, servant." HEBREW EQUIVALENTS: Avda, Avdel, Ovadya, Shamash, Shimshon. FEMININE HEBREW EQUIVALENTS: Ama, Shimshona.

Palmer From the Middle English, meaning "pilgrim who carries a palm leaf," as proof that he had been to the Holy Land. HEBREW EQUIVALENTS: Dekel, Dikla, Itamar, Tamar. FEMININE HEBREW EQUIVALENTS: Dikla, Diklit, Lulava, Tamar, Tamara.

Palti (פַּלְטִי) From the Hebrew, meaning "my escape, my deliverance." The exact Hebrew equivalent is Palti. FEMININE HEBREW EQUIVALENTS: Mosha'a, Sarid, Teshua, Yeshua.

Paltiel (פַּלְטִיאֵל) From the Hebrew, meaning "God is my savior." The exact Hebrew equivalent is Paltiel. FEMININE HEBREW EQUIVALENTS: Mosha'a, Shua, Teshua, Yisha.

Parker An occupational name, meaning "one who tends a park." HEBREW EQUIVALENTS: Ben-Carmi, Gan, Gani, Kerem. FEMININE HEBREW EQUIVALENTS: Carma, Carmelit, Gana, Ganit, Ganya.

Parnell A variant form of Peter. *See* Peter.

Pat A pet form of Patrick. *See* Patrick.

Patrick From the Latin, meaning "patrician, one of noble descent." HEBREW EQUIVALENTS: Avinadav, Chirom, Nadav, Yisrael. FEMININE HEBREW EQUIVALENTS: Nediva, Sara, Yisr'ela.

Paul From the Latin, meaning "small." HEBREW EQUIVALENTS: Katan, Tzuar, Vofsi, Ze'ira, Zutra. FEMININE HEBREW EQUIVALENTS: Delila, Katanya, Ketana, Ketina, Pe'uta.

Pauley A variant form of Paul. *See* Paul.

Paxton From the Latin, meaning "town of peace." HEBREW EQUIVALENTS: Avshalom, Meshulam, Shalem, Shalom, Shlomo, Yechi-Shalom. FEMININE HEBREW EQUIVALENTS: Achishalom, Menucha, Sha'anana, Shalva, Shulamit.

Payton The Scottish form of Patrick. *See* Patrick.

Paz (פָּז) From the Hebrew, meaning "gold, golden, sparkling." The exact masculine and feminine Hebrew equivalent is Paz.

Pazi (פָּזִי) From the Hebrew, meaning "my gold." The exact Hebrew equivalent is Pazi. FEMININE HEBREW EQUIVALENTS: Paz, Pazit, Paziya, Pazya.

Pedro A Spanish and Portuguese form of Peter. *See* Peter.

Pele, Peleh (פֶּלֶא) From the Hebrew, meaning "miracle." The exact Hebrew equivalent is Peleh. FEMININE HEBREW EQUIVALENTS: Peliya, Pili.

Peli (פְּלָאִי) A variant form of Pele. *See* Pele. The exact Hebrew equivalent is Peli.

Peniel (פְּנִיאֵל) A variant form of Penuel. *See* Penuel.

Penini (פְּנִינִי) From the Hebrew, meaning "pearl" or "precious stone." The exact Hebrew equivalent is Penini. FEMININE HEBREW EQUIVALENTS: Margalit, Penina, Peninit.

Penuel (פְּנוּאֵל) From the Hebrew, meaning "face of God" or "sight of God." The exact Hebrew equivalent is Penuel. FEMININE HEBREW EQUIVALENTS: Mofa'at, Nevia, Ofna, Ro'a, Shechina.

Per A Swedish form of Peter. Akin to the English Piers. *See* Peter.

Peretz (פֶּרֶץ) From the Hebrew, meaning "burst open." The exact Hebrew equivalent is Peretz. FEMININE HEBREW EQUIVALENTS: Nitza, Nitzana.

Perez A variant spelling of Peretz. *See* Peretz.

Perry The French form of Peter. *See* Peter.

Pesach (פֶּסַח) From the Hebrew, meaning "to pass over" or "to limp." The Hebrew name of the Passover (freedom) holiday. The exact Hebrew equivalent is Pesach. FEMININE HEBREW EQUIVALENTS: Derora, Derorit, Ge'ula, Li-Deror, Rachav.

Pete A pet form of Peter. *See* Peter.

Peter From the Greek and the Latin, meaning "rock." HEBREW EQUIVALENTS: Achitzur, Avitzur, Avniel, Sela, Shamir, Tzeror, Tzur, Tzuriel. FEMININE HEBREW EQUIVALENTS: Avniela, Ritzpa, Tzuriya, Tzurit.

Phelps A variant form of Philip. *See* Philip.

Philip A variant spelling of Phillip. *See* Phillip.

Phillip From the Greek, meaning "lover of horses." HEBREW EQUIVALENTS: Avicha'yil, Ben-Cha'yil, Cha'yil, Mordechai, Naftali, Peresh, Susi. FEMININE HEBREW EQUIVALENTS: Ahada, Ahava, Ahavat, Ahuva, Chiba.

Phillipe A French form of Phillip. *See* Phillip.

Phillipp A Scottish spelling of Phillip. *See* Phillip.

Philo From the Greek, meaning "loving." HEBREW EQUIVALENTS: Ahud, Ahuv, Bildad, David, Yedidya. FEMININE HEBREW EQUIVALENTS: Ahada, Ahava, Ahuva, Chiba, Davida.

Phineas The Anglicized form of Pinchas. *See* Pinchas.

Phoebus In Greek mythology, the god of light and sun. HEBREW EQUIVALENTS: Bahir, Me'ir, Shimshon, Shimshai, Uri, Uriya. FEMININE HEBREW EQUIVALENTS: Behira, Me'ira, Noga, Shimshona, Zahara.

Pierce A form of Peter, meaning "rock." *See* Peter.

Pierre A French form of Peter. *See* Peter.

Piers An English variant form of Peter. *See* Peter.

Pinchas (פִּנְחָס) From the Egyptian, meaning "Negro, dark-complexioned." Also, from the Hebrew, meaning "mouth of a snake." The exact Hebrew equivalent is Pinchas. FEMININE HEBREW EQUIVALENTS: Ayfa, Chachila, Shechora, Tzila.

Pinchos A variant spelling of Pinchas. *See* Pinchas.

Pincus A variant form of Pinchas. *See* Pinchas.

Pinhas A variant spelling of Pinchas. *See* Pinchas.

Pini (פִּינִי) A pet form of Pinchas. *See* Pinchas.

Pinkas A variant form of Pinchas. *See* Pinchas.

Pinkus A variant form of Pincus. *See* Pincus.

Pip A pet form of Philip. *See* Philip.

Placid From the Latin, meaning "to be tranquil, at peace." HEBREW EQUIVALENTS: Avshalom, Meshulam, Shalem, Shalom, Shlomo. FEMININE HEBREW EQUIVALENTS: Achishalom, Menucha, Sha'anana, Shalva, Shulamit.

Pol (פּוֹל) From the Hebrew, meaning "bean." The exact Hebrew equivalent is Pol.

Poul A variant spelling of Paul. *See* Paul.

Prentice From the Middle English, meaning "beginner, learner." HEBREW EQUIVALENTS: Chadash, Petachya, Yiftach. FEMININE HEBREW EQUIVALENTS: Chadasha, Chadusha.

Prentiss A variant spelling of Prentice. *See* Prentice.

Preston An Old English name, meaning "priest's town." HEBREW EQUIVALENTS: Devir, Kadish, Kahana, Kalev, Kohen, Yekutiel. FEMININE HEBREW EQUIVALENTS: Buna, Chaga, Chagit, Devira, Kedosha.

Price From the Middle English and Old French, meaning "price, value." HEBREW EQUIVALENTS: Machir, Michri, Yakar, Yakir. FEMININE HEBREW EQUIVALENTS: Mechora, Yakira, Yakara.

Quentin From the Latin, meaning "fifth." There are no Hebrew equivalents.

Quenton A variant spelling of Quentin. *See* Quentin.

Quincy A variant form of Quentin. *See* Quentin.

Quinn A variant form of Quentin. *See* Quentin.

Raam (רַעַם) From the Hebrew, meaning "thunder, noise." The exact Hebrew equivalent is Ra'am. The feminine Hebrew equivalent is Kolya.

Raamya (רַעַמְיָה) From the Hebrew, meaning "God's thunder." The exact Hebrew equivalent is Ra'amya. The feminine Hebrew equivalent is Kolya.

Raanan (רַעֲנָן) From the Hebrew, meaning "fresh, luxuriant, beautiful." The exact Hebrew equivalent is Ra'anan. The exact feminine Hebrew equivalent is Ra'anana.

Rabi (רַבִּי) From the Hebrew, meaning "my teacher." The exact Hebrew equivalent is Rabi. FEMININE HEBREW EQUIVALENTS: Aharona, Mora, Morit, Moriya.

Rachaman (רַחֲמָן) From the Hebrew, meaning "compassionate One [God]." The exact Hebrew equivalent is Rachaman. FEMININE HEBREW EQUIVALENTS: Rachmiela, Ruchama.

Rachamim (רַחֲמִים) From the Hebrew, meaning "compassion, mercy." The exact Hebrew equivalent is Rachamim. FEMININE HEBREW EQUIVALENTS: Rachmiela, Ruchama.

Rafa (רָפָא) From the Hebrew, meaning "heal." The exact Hebrew equivalent is Rafa. FEMININE HEBREW EQUIVALENTS: Rafya, Refa'ela, Refua, Rofi.

Rafael A Spanish form of Refael. See Refael.

Rafi (רָפִי) A pet form of Refael and its variant forms. See Refael.

Raleigh From the Old French, meaning "field of wading birds," or from the Old English, meaning "deer meadow." HEBREW EQUIVALENTS: Efer, Gozal, Karmel, Karmeli, Tzevi, Tzeviel. FEMININE HEBREW EQUIVALENTS: Gana, Gozala, Karmela, Nava, Tzevia, Tzivya.

Ralph From the Old Norse and Anglo-Saxon, meaning "courageous advice" or "fearless advisor." HEBREW EQUIVALENTS: Aleksander, Azarya, Azriel, Bina, Eliezer, Melitz, Yo'etz. FEMININE HEBREW EQUIVALENTS: Aleksandra, Buna, Ge'ona, Milka, Tushiya.

Ram (רָם) From the Hebrew, meaning "high, exalted, mighty." The exact Hebrew equivalent is Ram. The exact feminine Hebrew equivalent is Rama.

Rami (רָמִי) A variant form of Ram. The exact Hebrew equivalent is Rami. FEMININE HEBREW EQUIVALENTS: Meroma, Rama, Roma.

Ramon A Spanish form of Raymond. See Raymond.

Ramsay A variant spelling of Ramsey. See Ramsey.

Ramsey From the Old English, meaning "ram's island." HEBREW EQUIVALENTS: Itamar, Meron, Talya, Zimri. FEMININE HEBREW EQUIVALENTS: Merona, Tamar, Timora.

Ran (רָן) From the Hebrew, meaning "joy" or "song." The exact Hebrew equivalent is Ran. The exact feminine Hebrew equivalent is Ranit.

Ranan A variant spelling of Raanan. See Raanan.

Randal, Randall From the Anglo-Saxon, meaning "superior protection." HEBREW EQUIVALENTS: Avigdor, Shemarya, Shemer, Shimron, Shomer, Ya'akov, Zahir. FEMININE HEBREW EQUIVALENTS: Avigdora, Chasya, Shamira, Shimriya, Ya'akova, Zehira.

Randell A variant spelling of Randall. See Randall.

Randi A variant spelling of Randy. See Randy.

Randolph From the Anglo-Saxon, meaning "good counsel." HEBREW EQUIVALENTS: Aleksander, Azarya, Azriel, Bina, Buna, Eliezer, Navon,

Yo'etz. FEMININE HEBREW EQUIVALENTS: Aleksandra, Buna, Ge'ona, Ge'on-it, Nevona, Tushiya.

Randy A pet form of Randal or Randolph. *See* Randal *and* Randolph.

Ranen (רַנֵן) From the Hebrew, meaning "to sing, to be joyous." The exact Hebrew equivalent is Ranen. The exact feminine Hebrew equivalent is Renana.

Rani (רָנִי) From the Hebrew, meaning "my joy" or "my song." The exact Hebrew equivalent is Rani. The exact feminine Hebrew equivalent is Ranit.

Ranon (רָנוֹן) A variant form of Ranen. *See* Ranen. The exact Hebrew equivalent is Ranon. FEMININE HEBREW EQUIVALENTS: Ranit, Ranita, Ranya, Renana, Renanit.

Raoul A French form of Ralph and Randolph. *See* Ralph *and* Randolph.

Raphael A variant spelling of Refael. *See* Refael.

Raul A variant spelling of Raoul. *See* Raoul.

Rav (רַב) From the Hebrew, meaning "great" or "teacher." The exact Hebrew equivalent is Rav. FEMININE HEBREW EQUIVALENTS: Gedola, Horiya, Mora, Moran, Moriel.

Rava (רָבָא) A variant form of Rav. *See* Rav.

Raven From the Old English, meaning "raven," a bird of the crow family. The exact Hebrew equivalent is Orev. FEMININE HEBREW EQUIVALENTS: Gozala, Tzipora, Tziporit.

Ravi A variant form of Rabi. *See* Rabi.

Ravid (רָבִיד) From the Hebrew, meaning "ornament, jewelry." The exact Hebrew equivalent is Ravid. FEMININE HEBREW EQUIVALENTS: Ada, Adina, Adiya, Edna.

Raviv (רָבִיב) From the Hebrew, meaning "rain" or "dew." The exact Hebrew equivalent is Raviv. The exact feminine Hebrew equivalent is Reviva.

Ray From the Old English, meaning "stream" or from the Celtic, meaning "grace." HEBREW EQUIVALENTS: Arnon, Chanan, Chanina, Choni, Yuval, Zerem. FEMININE HEBREW EQUIVALENTS: Arnona, Arnonit, Chana, Chanita. Also, a pet form of Raymond. *See* Raymond.

Raya (רֵעַ) From the Hebrew, meaning "friend." The exact masculine and feminine Hebrew equivalent is Raya (Re'a).

Raymond From the Old French, meaning "mighty protector," or from the German, meaning "quiet, peaceful." HEBREW EQUIVALENTS: Avigdor, Gonen, Lot, Magen, Mishan, Shalom, Shelomo, Shemaryahu. FEMININE HEBREW EQUIVALENTS: Avigdora, Botzra, Efrat, Shlomit, Shulamit, Setura, Shamira, Zehira.

Raymund A variant spelling of Raymond. *See* Raymond.

Raz (רָז) From the Aramaic, meaning "secret." The exact masculine and feminine Hebrew equivalent is Raz.

Razi (רָזִי) From the Hebrew, meaning "my secret." The exact masculine and feminine Hebrew equivalent is Razi.

Raziel (רָזִיאֵל) From the Aramaic, meaning "God is my secret" or "secret of the Lord." The exact Hebrew equivalent is Raziel. The exact feminine Hebrew equivalent is Raziela.

Read, Reade From the Old English, meaning "reed." The Hebrew equivalent is Kaniel. The feminine Hebrew equivalent is Kaniela.

Redd A variant form of Read. *See* Read.

Reece A Welsh form of the Old English, meaning "stream." HEBREW EQUIVALENTS: Arnon, Yuval, Zerem. FEMININE HEBREW EQUIVALENTS: Arnona, Arnonit, Miryam.

Reed A variant spelling of Read. *See* Read.

Reese A variant spelling of Reece. *See* Reece.

Refael (רְפָאֵל) From the Hebrew, meaning "God has healed." The exact Hebrew equivalent is Refa'el. The exact feminine Hebrew equivalent is Refa'ela.

Refi (רְפִי) A pet form of Refael. *See* Refael.

Regem (רֶגֶם) From the Hebrew, meaning "to stone." Also, from the Arabic, meaning "friend." The exact Hebrew equivalent is Regem. FEMININE HEBREW EQUIVALENTS: Ahuva, Amita, Avniel, Davida, Na'ama.

Reg, Reggie Pet forms of Reginald. *See* Reginald.

Reginald From the Old High German, meaning "wise, judicious" or "powerful ruler." HEBREW EQUIVALENTS: Barzilai, Gavriel, Gibor, Katriel, Melech, Razin, Rozen, Yechezkel. FEMININE HEBREW EQUIVALENTS: Atara, Gavriela, Gevira, Gibora, Malka, Yisr'ela.

Reid A variant spelling of Read. *See* Read.

Reinhard, Reinhart Variant forms of Reynard. *See* Reynard.

Reinhold A German form of Reginald. *See* Reginald.

Remez (רֶמֶז) From the Hebrew, meaning "sign" or "signal." The exact Hebrew equivalent is Remez. The exact feminine Hebrew equivalent is Remiza.

Rene A French name from the Latin, meaning "to be reborn, renew." HEBREW EQUIVALENTS: Chadash, Cha'yim. FEMININE HEBREW EQUIVALENTS: Chadasha, Cha'ya, Techiya, Tekuma.

Renen (רֶנֶן) From the Hebrew, meaning "song." The exact Hebrew equivalent is Renen. The exact feminine Hebrew equivalent is Renana.

Rennie A pet form of Reginald. *See* Reginald.

Reo A variant form of the Old English *rae*, meaning "stream." HEBREW EQUIVALENTS: Arnan, Arnon, Mitala, Moshe, Yoval, Yuval, Zerem. FEMININE HEBREW EQUIVALENTS: Afeka, Arnona, Arnonit, Miryam.

Rephael A variant spelling of Refael. *See* Refael.

Rephi A variant spelling of Refi. *See* Refi.

Reuben, Reubin Variant forms of Reuven. *See* Reuven.

Reuel (רְעוּאֵל) From the Hebrew, meaning "friend of God." The exact Hebrew equivalent is Re'uel. The exact feminine Hebrew equivalent is Re'uela.

Re'uvain A variant spelling of Reuven. *See* Reuven.

Reuven (רְאוּבֵן) From the Hebrew, meaning "Behold, a son." The exact Hebrew equivalent is Re'uven. The exact feminine Hebrew equivalent is Re'uvena.

Rex From the Latin, meaning "king." HEBREW EQUIVALENTS: Avimelech, Elimelech, Malkam, Melech, Razin, Rozen. FEMININE HEBREW EQUIVALENTS: Atara, Malka, Malkiel, Malkit, Malchiya, Tzefira.

Reynard From the Old High German, meaning "rich in good counsel." HEBREW EQUIVALENTS: Avida, Bina, Buna, Navon, Ye'utz, Yo'etz. FEMININE HEBREW EQUIVALENTS: Buna, Ge'ona, Ge'onit, Nevona, Tushiya.

Reynold A variant French form of Reginald. *See* Reginald.

Rhett From the Old English, meaning "small stream." HEBREW EQUIVALENTS: Arnan, Arnon, Mitala, Moshe, Yoval, Yuval, Zerem. FEMININE HEBREW EQUIVALENTS: Afeka, Arnona, Arnonit, Miryam.

Ricardo, Riccardo Spanish and Italian forms of Richard. *See* Richard.

Ricci A pet form of Richard. *See* Richard.

Ricco A pet form of Richard. *See* Richard.

Rich, Richie Pet forms of Richard. *See* Richard.

Richard A French form of the Old High German Reynard, meaning "powerful, rich ruler" or "valiant rider." HEBREW EQUIVALENTS: Barzilai, Ben-Cha'yil, Ish-Cha'yil, Gavriel, Gibor, Gur, Guri, Guriel, Katriel, Peresh, Susi. FEMININE HEBREW EQUIVALENTS: Amtza, Ashira, Gavriela, Gavrila, Sara, Sarit, Yisr'ela.

Richardo A Spanish form of Richard. *See* Richard.

Rici, Ricci Pet forms of Richard. *See* Richard.

Richie A pet form of Richard. *See* Richard.

Ricki, Rickie, Ricky Pet forms of Richard. *See* Richard.

Rimon, Rimmon (רִמּוֹן) From the Hebrew, meaning "pomegranate." The exact Hebrew equivalent is Rimon. The exact feminine Hebrew equivalent is Rimona.

Rip From the Latin, meaning "river bank." HEBREW EQUIVALENTS: Arnon, Ye'or, Ye'ori. FEMININE HEBREW EQUIVALENTS: Arnona, Arnonit.

Rishon (רִאשׁוֹן) From the Hebrew, meaning "first." The exact Hebrew equivalent is Rishon. The exact feminine Hebrew equivalent is Rishona.

Rob A pet form of Robert. *See* Robert.

Robard, Robart Variant French forms of Robert. *See* Robert.

Robert From the Anglo-Saxon, meaning "bright, wise counsel." HEBREW EQUIVALENTS: Azriel, Bahir, Barak, Eliezer, Ezra, Hillel, Me'ir, Zerach. FEMININE HEBREW EQUIVALENTS: Aleksandra, Ezra, Ezr'ela, Hillela, Milka, Me'ira, Yehudit.

Robin A pet form of Robert popular in France. *See* Robert.

Robson A patronymic form, meaning "son of Rob [Robert]." *See* Robert.

Robyn A variant spelling of Robin. *See* Robin.

Rocco A pet form of Richard or Rockne. *See* Richard *and* Rockne.

Rock From the Old English, meaning "rock." A short form of Rockne. *See* Rockne.

Rockne From the Old English, meaning "rock." HEBREW EQUIVALENTS: Avniel, Sela, Shamir, Tzeror, Tzur, Tzuri, Tzuriel. FEMININE HEBREW EQUIVALENTS: Avna, Avniela, Ritzpa, Tzur-El, Tzurit.

Rockwell From the Old English, meaning "the well near the rock." HEBREW EQUIVALENTS: Arnon, Avitzur, Avniel, Even, Sela, Shamir, Tzur, Tzuriel. FEMININE HEBREW EQUIVALENTS: Arnona, Avniela, Tzurit, Tzuriya.

Rocky A pet form of Rockne and Rockwell. *See* Rockne *and* Rockwell.

Rod, Rodd From the British, meaning "open, cleared land." HEBREW EQUIVALENTS: Adam, Admata, Artza, Artzi, Regev. FEMININE HEBREW EQUIVALENTS: Adama, Artzit, Eretz. Also, a pet form of Roderick. *See* Roderick.

Roddy A pet form of Rod or Rodman. *See* Rod *and* Rodman.

Roderic, Roderick From the Old High German, meaning "famous ruler." HEBREW EQUIVALENTS: Avimelech, Gedalya, Hillel, Melech, Rosh, Yisrael. FEMININE HEBREW EQUIVALENTS: Hillela, Malka, Sara, Tzefira, Yisr'ela.

Rodger A variant spelling of Roger. *See* Roger.

Rodgers A patronymic form of Roger. *See* Roger.

Rodney From the Old English, meaning "cleared land near the water" or "one who carries a leveling rod, a surveyor." HEBREW EQUIVALENTS: Artzi, Aryoch, Beri, Dela'ya, Medad, Miklot, Silon. FEMININE HEBREW EQUIVALENTS: Artzit, Bat-Yam, Miryam, Silona, Silonit.

Roger From the Old French and the Anglo-Saxon, meaning "famous, noble warrior" or "honorable man." HEBREW EQUIVALENTS: Amitai, Avicha'yil, Efrat, Hillel, Meshar, Me'ushar, Mordechai, Nichbad, Yehuda. FEMININE HEBREW EQUIVALENTS: Efrat, Efrata, Hillela, Merav, Nichbada, Tigra, Yehudit, Yeshara.

Rohn From the Greek, meaning "rose." The exact masculine and feminine Hebrew equivalent is Vered.

Roland A French form of the Old High German, meaning "fame of the land." HEBREW EQUIVALENTS: Adam, Artza, Gedalya, Hila, Hillel, Shevach, Yehuda, Yehudi. FEMININE HEBREW EQUIVALENTS: Adama, Eretz, Hila, Hillela, Tehila, Tishbacha, Yehudit.

Rolando An Italian and Portuguese form of Roland. *See* Roland.

Rolf, Rolfe Pet forms of Rudolph. *See* Rudolph.

Rolland A variant spelling of Roland. *See* Roland.

Rollen, Rollin Variant forms of Roland. *See* Roland.

Rom (רוֹם) From the Hebrew, meaning "heights." The exact Hebrew equivalent is Rom. The exact feminine Hebrew equivalent is Roma.

Romem (רוֹמֵם) A variant form of Rom. *See* Rom. The exact Hebrew equivalent is Romem.

Romi, Romie (רוֹמִי)   From the Hebrew, meaning "heights" or "nobility." The exact Hebrew equivalent is Romi. FEMININE HEBREW EQUIVALENTS: Rama, Ramit, Roma, Romit.

Ron (רוֹן)   From the Hebrew, meaning "joy" or "song." The exact masculine and feminine Hebrew equivalent is Ron. Also, a pet form of Ronald. *See* Ronald.

Ronald   The Scottish form of Reginald. *See* Reginald.

Ronel (רוֹנְאֵל)   From the Hebrew, meaning "song of the Lord" or "joy of the Lord." The exact Hebrew equivalent is Ronel. The exact feminine Hebrew equivalent is Ronela.

Ronen (רוֹנֵן)   From the Hebrew, meaning "song" or "joy." The exact Hebrew equivalent is Ronen. The exact feminine Hebrew equivalent is Ronena.

Ronli, Ron-Li (רוֹן־לִי/רוֹנְלִי)   From the Hebrew, meaning "song is mine." The exact masculine and feminine Hebrew equivalent is Ronli.

Ronnie, Ronny   Pet forms of Ronald. *See* Ronald.

Rory   An Irish form of Roderick. *See* Roderick. Also, from the Celtic, meaning "the ruddy one." MASCULINE HEBREW EQUIVALENTS: Admon, Almog, Guni, Tzochar. FEMININE HEBREW EQUIVALENTS: Almoga, Odem, Tzachara.

Roscoe   A variant form of Ross. *See* Ross.

Ross   From the Anglo-Saxon, meaning "woods, meadows." HEBREW EQUIVALENTS: Artza, Karmel, Karmeli, Yara. FEMININE HEBREW EQUIVALENTS: Eretz, Gana, Karmela, Nava, Ya'ari.

Rowe   A short form of Rowland. *See* Rowland.

Rowland   From the Old English, meaning "rugged land." Also, a variant form of Roland. *See* Roland.

Rowle   A variant form of Ralph. *See* Ralph.

Roy   From the Old French, meaning "king." HEBREW EQUIVALENTS: Avimelech, Elimelech, Katriel, Melech, Yisrael. FEMININE HEBREW EQUIVALENTS: Atara, Gavrila, Malka, Yisr'ela.

Royal   From the Middle English and the Latin, meaning "king." HEBREW EQUIVALENTS: Avimelech, Elimelech, Katriel, Malki, Melech, Yisrael. FEMININE HEBREW EQUIVALENTS: Atara, Gavrila, Malka, Yisr'ela.

Roye   A variant spelling of Roy. *See* Roy.

Rube   A pet form of Reuben. *See* Reuben.

Ruben   A variant spelling of Reuben. *See* Reuben.

Rubens   A patronymic form of Reuben, meaning "son of Reuben." *See* Reuben.

Rubin   A variant spelling of Reuben. *See* Reuben.

Ruby   A pet form of Reuben. *See* Reuben.

Rudd   From the Anglo-Saxon, meaning "red." HEBREW EQUIVALENTS: Admon, Almog, Edom. FEMININE HEBREW EQUIVALENTS: Almoga, Odem, Tzachara.

Rudolph A variant form of Randolph and Ralph. *See* Randolph *and* Ralph.

Rueben A variant spelling of Reuben. *See* Reuben.

Ruel A variant spelling of Reuel. *See* Reuel.

Rufus From the Latin, meaning "red, red-haired." HEBREW EQUIVALENTS: Admon, Almog, Chachalya, Edom, Guni, Tzochar. FEMININE HEBREW EQUIVALENTS: Delila, Nima, Odem, Tzachara.

Rupert A variant English, French, and German form of Robert. *See* Robert.

Russ A pet form of Russell. *See* Russell.

Russel, Russell French forms of the Latin, meaning "rusty-haired." Also, from the Anglo-Saxon, meaning "horse." HEBREW EQUIVALENTS: Admon, Almog, Edom, Guni, Peresh, Susi. FEMININE HEBREW EQUIVALENTS: Avicha'yil, Delila, Nima, Odem, Pua.

Ruvane A variant spelling of Reuven. *See* Reuven.

Saad (סָעַד) From the Aramaic, meaning "support." The exact Hebrew equivalent is Sa'ad. The exact feminine Hebrew equivalent is Sa'ada.

Saadi (סַעְדִי) From the Hebrew, meaning "my support." The exact Hebrew equivalent is Sa'adi. FEMININE HEBREW EQUIVALENTS: Mosada, Sa'ada.

Saadia, Saadiah Variant spellings of Saadya. *See* Saadya.

Saadli (סַעַדְלִי) A variant form of Saadi. *See* Saadi. The exact Hebrew equivalent is Sa'adli.

Saadya (סַעַדְיָה) From the Hebrew, meaning "God is my support." The exact Hebrew equivalent is Saadya. The exact feminine Hebrew equivalent is Sa'ada.

Saba A variant form of Sava. *See* Sava.

Sabra (סַבְרָה) From the Aramaic, meaning "cactus" or "prickly pear." The exact masculine and feminine Hebrew equivalent is Sabar. Tzabar (צָבָּר) is an alternate form.

Sacha A Russian pet form of Alexander. *See* Alexander.

Sachar (שָׂכָר) A short form of Yisachar (Issachar). *See* Yisachar. The exact Hebrew equivalent is Sachar.

Sadir (סָדִיר) From the Aramaic, meaning "order." The exact Hebrew equivalent is Sadir. The exact feminine Hebrew equivalent is Sadira.

Sagi (סַגִיא) From the Aramaic and Hebrew, meaning "sufficient" or "strong, mighty." The exact Hebrew equivalent is Sagi. FEMININE HEBREW EQUIVALENTS: Amitza, Aza, Aziza, Etana, Gibora.

Sagiv (סָגִיב) From the Aramaic and Hebrew, meaning "tall, noble" or "strong, mighty." The exact Hebrew equivalent is Sagiv. The exact feminine Hebrew equivalent is Sagiva.

Sagy A variant spelling of Sagi. *See* Sagi.

Sal From the Latin, meaning "salt," or from the Old English, meaning "willow." Also, a pet form of Salvador. *See* Salvador.

Salem (שָׁלֵם) The English form of the Hebrew *shalom*, meaning "peace." The exact Hebrew equivalent is Shalem. FEMININE HEBREW EQUIVALENTS: Shlomit, Shlom-Tzion, Shulamit.

Sali (סָלִי) From the Hebrew, meaning "my basket." Also, a pet form of Yisrael, a name popular among Jews of Morocco. *See* Yisrael. The exact Hebrew equivalent is Sali. FEMININE HEBREW EQUIVALENTS: Salit, Yisr'ela.

Salil (סָלִיל) From the Hebrew, meaning "path." The exact Hebrew equivalent is Salil. The exact feminine Hebrew equivalent is Selila.

Salman A variant spelling of Salmon. *See* Salmon.

Salmon (שַׁלְמוֹן) From the Aramaic, meaning "garment," or a variant form of Solomon. HEBREW EQUIVALENTS: Salmon, Shlomo. FEMININE HEBREW EQUIVALENTS: Salma, Shelomit, Shulamit.

Salo A short form of Saloman. *See* Saloman.

Saloman, Salomon Variant forms of Solomon. *See* Solomon.

Salu (סָלוּ) From the Aramaic, meaning "basket." The exact Hebrew equivalent is Salu. The feminine Hebrew equivalent is Salit.

Salvador, Salvatore From the Latin, meaning "to be saved." HEBREW EQUIVALENTS: Elisha, Elishua, Ezra, Hoshe'a, Mosha, Moshe, Yehoshua. FEMININE HEBREW EQUIVALENTS: Mosha'a, Teshua, Yeshua.

Sam A pet form of Samuel. *See* Samuel.

Samal (סָמָל) From the Aramaic, meaning "sign, symbol." Also, from the modern Hebrew, meaning "sergeant." The exact Hebrew equivalent is Samal. FEMININE HEBREW EQUIVALENTS: Remazya, Simona.

Samm A variant spelling of Sam. *See* Sam.

Sammy A pet form of Samuel. *See* Samuel.

Sampson A variant spelling of Samson. *See* Samson.

Samson (שִׁמְשׁוֹן) From the Hebrew, meaning "sun." The exact Hebrew equivalent is Shimshon. The exact feminine Hebrew equivalent is Shimshona.

Samuel (שְׁמוּאֵל) From the Hebrew, meaning "His name is God" or "God has dedicated." The exact Hebrew equivalent is Shemuel. The exact feminine Hebrew equivalent is Shemuela.

Samy A pet form of Samuel. *See* Samuel.

Sander A short form of Alexander. *See* Alexander.

Sanders A patronymic form of Sander. *See* Sander.

Sandor A variant spelling of Sander, a pet form of Alexander. *See* Alexander.

Sandy A pet form of Alexander and Sanford. *See* Alexander.

Sanford From the Old English, meaning "sandy river crossing" or "peaceful counsel." HEBREW EQUIVALENTS: Avshalom, Palal, Shalom, Shlomo, Ye'or, Ye'ori. FEMININE HEBREW EQUIVALENTS: Aleksandra, Bina, Buna, Shulamit.

Sapir (סַפִּיר) From the Greek, meaning "precious stone." The exact Hebrew equivalent is Sapir. The exact feminine Hebrew equivalent is Sapira.

Sar (שַׂר) From the Hebrew, meaning "prince." The exact Hebrew equivalent is Sar. FEMININE HEBREW EQUIVALENTS: Sara, Yisr'ela.

Sarid (שָׂרִיד) From the Hebrew, meaning "remnant." The exact Hebrew equivalent is Sarid. The exact feminine Hebrew equivalent is Sarida.

Sasha A Russian pet form of Alexander. *See* Alexander.

Saul (שָׁאוּל) From the Hebrew, meaning "borrowed." The Anglicized form of Shaul. *See* Shaul.

Saunders A variant spelling of Sanders. *See* Sanders.

Sava (סָבָה/סָבָא) From the Aramaic, meaning "grandfather" or "old man." The exact Hebrew equivalent is Sava. The exact feminine Hebrew equivalent is Savta.

Sayer From the Old German, meaning "victory of the people." HEBREW EQUIVALENTS: Gevarya, Gover, Netzach, Shua. FEMININE HEBREW EQUIVALENTS: Nitzcha, Nitzchiya, Nitzchona.

Scott The Late Latin form for "Scotchman," meaning "tattooed one." The Hebrew equivalent is Sofer. The feminine Hebrew equivalent is Soferet.

Scottie, Scotty Pet forms of Scott. *See* Scott.

Sean A popular Gaelic form of John. *See* John.

Seff (סֶעףּ) A Yiddish form of Zev (Ze'ev) meaning "wolf." *See* Zev.

Sefi (סָפִי) A pet form of Yosef (Joseph). *See* Yosef.

Segel (סֶגֶל) From the Hebrew, meaning "treasure." The exact Hebrew equivalent is Segel. The exact feminine Hebrew equivalent is Segula.

Segev (שֶׂגֶב) From the Hebrew, meaning "glory, majesty, exalted." The exact Hebrew equivalent is Segev. FEMININE HEBREW EQUIVALENTS: Atalya, Atara, Malka, Sara.

Seguv (שְׂגוּב) From the Hebrew, meaning "exalted." The exact Hebrew equivalent is Seguv. FEMININE HEBREW EQUIVALENTS: Atalya, Atara, Malka, Sara.

Selby A variant form of Shelby. *See* Shelby.

Selden, Seldon From the Middle English, meaning "rare," connoting an article of value. HEBREW EQUIVALENTS: Avikar, Chamdiel, Chemed, Leshem, Penini, Sapira, Tarshish. FEMININE HEBREW EQUIVALENTS: Margalit, Penina, Sapira, Sapirit, Yekara.

Seled (סֶלֶד) From the Hebrew, meaning "leap for joy" or "praise." The exact Hebrew equivalent is Seled. FEMININE HEBREW EQUIVALENTS: Hillela, Sasona, Simcha, Simchit, Simchona.

Selig (סֶעלִיג) A Yiddish name, from the German and Old English, meaning "blessed, holy." HEBREW EQUIVALENTS: Asher, Baruch, Berachya, Kadosh, Mevorach. FEMININE HEBREW EQUIVALENTS: Beracha, Berucha, Kedosha, Mevorechet, Oshra.

Selwyn From the Anglo-Saxon, meaning "holy place" or "friend at court." HEBREW EQUIVALENTS: Bildad, David, Devir, Eldad, Kadish, Kadosh, Ray'i. FEMININE HEBREW EQUIVALENTS: Ahuva, Chaviva, Davida, Devira, Kedosha, Rut, Yedida.

Semel (סֶמֶל) From the Hebrew, meaning "sign, symbol." The exact equivalent is Semel. FEMININE HEBREW EQUIVALENTS: Remazya, Simona.

Sender (סָנְדָר/סֶענְדְער) A Yiddish form of Sander, a form of Alexander. See Alexander.

Senior From the Latin, meaning "elder." Shneur is a Yiddish variant form. HEBREW EQUIVALENTS: Kadmiel, Kedem, Kedma, Yeshishai, Zaken. FEMININE HEBREW EQUIVALENTS: Bilha, Kedma, Yeshana, Zekena.

Serge From the Old French and the Latin, meaning "serve." HEBREW EQUIVALENTS: Eved, Malachi, Ovadya, Oved. FEMININE HEBREW EQUIVALENTS: Ezra, Ezriela.

Seth The Anglicized form of Shet, the son of Adam. See Shet.

Seton From the Anglo-Saxon, meaning "town near the sea." HEBREW EQUIVALENTS: Avigal, Avi'yam, Livyatan, Moshe. FEMININE HEBREW EQUIVALENTS: Bat-Galim, Bat-Yam, Miryam, Yamit.

Seward From the Anglo-Saxon, meaning "defender of the sea coast." HEBREW EQUIVALENTS: Avi'yam, Moshe, Shemer, Shimri, Shemarya, Ya'akov. FEMININE HEBREW EQUIVALENTS: Bat-Galim, Bat-Yam, Miryam, Shimra, Shemura, Ya'akova.

Sewell From the Old English, meaning "well near the sea." HEBREW EQUIVALENTS: Arnon, Avi'yam, Moshe, Peleg. FEMININE HEBREW EQUIVALENTS: Arnona, Bat-Galim, Bat-Yam, Miryam.

Seymore A variant spelling of Seymour. See Seymour.

Seymour From the Old English, meaning "marshy land near the sea." HEBREW EQUIVALENTS: Arnon, Avi'yam, Dalfon, Karmel, Peleg, Yizr'el. FEMININE HEBREW EQUIVALENTS: Arnona, Karmela, Nava, Yizr'ela.

Shaanan (שַׁאֲנָן) From the Hebrew, meaning "peaceful." The exact Hebrew equivalent is Sha'anan. The exact feminine Hebrew equivalent is Sha'anana.

Shabbetai, Shabetai Variant spellings of Shabtai. See Shabtai.

Shabbtai, Shabtai (שַׁבְּתַאי/שַׁבְּתַי) From the Hebrew and Aramaic, meaning "rest, sabbath." The exact Hebrew equivalent is Shabtai. FEMININE HEBREW EQUIVALENTS: Mashen, Menucha, Nacha, Shalva.

Shabtiel (שַׁבְּתִיאֵל) A variant form of Shabtai. See Shabbtai. The exact Hebrew equivalent is Shabtiel.

Shael (שָׁאֵל) A pet form of Mishael. See Mishael.

Shai (שַׁי) From the Hebrew and Aramaic, meaning "gift." Also, a pet form of Yesha'ya (Isaiah). The exact Hebrew equivalent is Shai. FEMININE HEBREW EQUIVALENTS: Matana, Migda, Teruma, Teshura.

Shalem (שָׁלֵם) From the Hebrew, meaning "whole." The exact Hebrew equivalent is Shalem. FEMININE HEBREW EQUIVALENTS: Gimra, Gomer, Meshulemet, Shlomit, Shulamit, Temima.

Shalev (שָׁלֵו) From the Hebrew, meaning "peaceful." The exact Hebrew equivalent is Shalev. The exact feminine Hebrew equivalent is Shalva.

Shalman (שַׁלְמָן) From the Assyrian, meaning "to be complete" or "to be rewarded." The exact Hebrew equivalent is Shalman. FEMININE HEBREW EQUIVALENTS: Gomer, Meshulemet, Shlomit, Shulamit.

Shalom (שָׁלוֹם) From the Hebrew, meaning "peace." The exact Hebrew equivalent is Shalom. FEMININE HEBREW EQUIVALENTS: Meshulemet, Shelomit, Shulamit, Za'yit.

Shalum, Shallum (שָׁלוּם) From the Hebrew, meaning "whole, complete peace" or "reward." The exact Hebrew equivalent is Shalum. FEMININE HEBREW EQUIVALENTS: Gemula, Meshulemet, Shelomit, Shulamit, Za'yit.

Shalvi (שַׁלְוִי) A variant form of Shalev. See Shalev. The exact Hebrew equivalent is Shalvi. FEMININE HEBREW EQUIVALENTS: Shalva, Shalviya.

Shamir (שָׁמִיר) From the Aramaic and Hebrew, meaning "diamond" or "flint." The exact Hebrew equivalent is Shamir. FEMININE HEBREW EQUIVALENTS: Ritzpa, Tzuriel, Tzuriya, Tzurit.

Shamai, Shammai (שַׁמַּאי/שַׁמַּי) From the Hebrew and Aramaic, meaning "name." The exact Hebrew equivalent is Shamai. FEMININE HEBREW EQUIVALENTS: Shimat, Shimona, Shmuela, Tehila, Yehudit.

Shanan A variant spelling of Shaanan. See Shaanan.

Shane A variant form of Sean used prominently in Ireland. See Sean.

Shanon A variant spelling of Shanan. See Shanan.

Shapir (שָׁפִּיר) From the Aramaic, meaning "beautiful." The exact Hebrew equivalent is Shapir. FEMININE HEBREW EQUIVALENTS: Na'omi, Nava, Nofiya, Noya.

Sharp, Sharpe From the Old English, meaning "clever, perceptive." HEBREW EQUIVALENTS: Avida, Bina, Buna, Chacham, Navon. FEMININE HEBREW EQUIVALENTS: Bina, Buna, Ge'ona, Ge'onit, Nevona.

Shatil (שָׁתִיל) From the Hebrew, meaning "plant." The exact Hebrew equivalent is Shatil. The exact feminine Hebrew equivalent is Shatila.

Shatul (שָׁתוּל) A variant form of Shatil. See Shatil. The exact Hebrew equivalent is Shatul.

Shaul (שָׁאוּל) From the Hebrew, meaning "asked" or "borrowed." The Anglicized form is Saul. The exact Hebrew equivalent is Sha'ul. The exact feminine Hebrew equivalent is Sha'ula.

Shaun, Shawn Variant spellings of Sean. See Sean.

Shay A variant spelling of Shai. See Shai.

Shaya, Shaye (שַׁעְיָה) Short forms of Yesha'ya (Isaiah). See Yesha'ya. The exact Hebrew equivalent is Sha'ya.

Shea, Sheah Variant spellings of Shia. See Shia.

Shebsel, Shebsil (שֶׁעבְּתָעל/שֶׁעבְּתִיל) Variant forms of Shepsel and Shepsil. See Shepsel and Shepsil.

Shefer (שֶׁפֶר) From the Hebrew, meaning "pleasant, beautiful." The exact Hebrew equivalent is Shefer. The exact feminine Hebrew equivalent is Shifra.

Shelby From the Anglo-Saxon, meaning "sheltered town." HEBREW EQUIVALENTS: Chasun, Eltzafun, Gonen, Lot, Shemer, Shimri, Shimron, Ya'akov. FEMININE HEBREW EQUIVALENTS: Setura, Shamira, Shimriya, Sitriya, Ya'akova.

Sheldon From the Old English, meaning "shepherd's hut on a hill" or "protected hill." HEBREW EQUIVALENTS: Aharon, Avigdor, Chosa, Shemarya, Tal, Talmai. FEMININE HEBREW EQUIVALENTS: Aharona, Botzra, Migdala, Shimrit, Tira.

Sheli (שֶׁל-לִי/שֶׁלִי) From the Hebrew, meaning "mine, belonging to me." The exact Hebrew equivalent is Sheli. Also, a variant spelling of Shelley. See Shelley.

Shelley From the Old English, meaning "island of shells." HEBREW EQUIVALENTS: Avi'yam, Aynan, Deror, Peleg. FEMININE HEBREW EQUIVALENTS: Derora, Miryam, Rachel, Tzila.

Shelly A variant spelling of Shelley. See Shelley.

Shelomi A variant spelling of Shlomi. See Shlomi.

Shelomo A variant spelling of Shlomo. See Shlomo.

Shem (שֵׁם) From the Hebrew, meaning "name," connoting reputation. The exact Hebrew equivalent is Shem. FEMININE HEBREW EQUIVALENTS: Bat-Shem, Hila, Hillela, Tehila, Yehudit.

Shemaria, Shemariah Variant spellings of Shemarya. See Shemarya.

Shemarya (שְׁמַרְיָה) From the Hebrew, meaning "protection of God." The exact Hebrew equivalent is Shemarya. FEMININE HEBREW EQUIVALENTS: Shamira, Shemura, Shimra, Shimrat, Shimriya.

Shemaryahu (שְׁמַרְיָהוּ) A variant form of Shemarya. See Shemarya. The exact Hebrew equivalent is Shemaryahu.

Shemer (שֶׁמֶר) From the Hebrew, meaning "to guard, watch" or "preserve." The exact Hebrew equivalent is Shemer. FEMININE HEBREW EQUIVALENTS: Shemura, Shimra, Shimriya.

Shemuel A variant spelling of Shmuel. See Shmuel.

Shepard From the Anglo-Saxon, meaning "shepherd." HEBREW EQUIVALENTS: Meron, Ro'i, Talya, Zimri. FEMININE HEBREW EQUIVALENTS: Merona, Rachel.

Shepherd From the Old English, meaning "one who tends sheep, protector." HEBREW EQUIVALENTS: Ro'i, Shemarya, Shermaryahu, Ya'akov. FEMININE HEBREW EQUIVALENTS: Botzra, Magena, Migdala, Rachel, Ya'akova.

Shepley From the Old English, meaning "sheep meadow." HEBREW EQUIVALENTS: Hevel, Ro'i, Talya, Zimri. FEMININE HEBREW EQUIVALENTS: Merona, Rachel.

Sheppard A variant spelling of Shepherd. See Shepherd.

Shepsel, Shepsil (שֶׁעפְּסֶעל/שֶׁעפְּסִיל) From the Yiddish, meaning "sheep." See Shepherd and Shepley for equivalents.

Sheraga, Sheragai (שְׁרָגָא) From the Aramaic, meaning "light." HEBREW EQUIVALENTS: Sheraga, Sheragai. FEMININE HEBREW EQUIVALENTS: Behira, Me'ira, Nahara, Noga, Ora.

Sherira (שְׁרִירָא) From the Aramaic, meaning "strong." The exact Hebrew equivalent is Sherira. FEMININE HEBREW EQUIVALENTS: Abira, Adira, Gavriela, Uza, Uziela.

Sherman From the Old English, meaning "servant [or resident] of the shire [district]" or "one who shears [sheep]." HEBREW EQUIVALENTS: Avdi, Avdon, Malachi, Ovadya, Ro'i, Shamash, Shimshai, Shimshon. FEMININE HEBREW EQUIVALENTS: Merona, Rachel, Shimshona.

Sherry A pet form of Sherman. See Sherman.

Sherwin From the Anglo-Saxon, meaning "one who shears the wind." Also, from the Old English, meaning "shining friend." HEBREW EQUIVALENTS: Amit, Amitai, David, Hai, Me'ir, Rayi, Regem. FEMININE HEBREW EQUIVALENTS: Ahuva, Amita, Davida, Rut, Tirtza.

Sherwood From the Anglo-Saxon, meaning "forest, wooded area." HEBREW EQUIVALENTS: Karmel, Karmeli, Ya'ar, Ya'ari. FEMININE HEBREW EQUIVALENTS: Gana, Karmela, Nava, Ya'ara, Ya'arit.

Shet (שֵׁת) From the Hebrew, meaning "garment" or "appointed." Also, from the Syriac, meaning "appearance." The exact Hebrew equivalent is Shet. FEMININE HEBREW EQUIVALENTS: Mofaat, No'ada, Ofna, Salma.

Shia, Shiah (שַׁעְיָה) Short forms of Yesha'ya (Isaiah). See Yesha'ya. The exact Hebrew equivalent is Shia.

Shimi (שִׁמְעִי) From the Hebrew, meaning "my name" or "reputation." The exact Hebrew equivalent is Shimi. FEMININE HEBREW EQUIVALENTS: Bat-Shem, Shimona.

Shimmel (שִׁימְעֶל) A Yiddish form of Shimon. See Shimon.

Shimon (שִׁמְעוֹן) From the Hebrew, meaning "to hear, to be heard" or "reputation." Simon and Simeon are Anglicized forms. The exact Hebrew equivalent is Shimon. The exact feminine Hebrew equivalent is Shimona.

Shimri (שִׁמְרִי) From the Hebrew, meaning "my guard." The exact Hebrew equivalent is Shimri. FEMININE HEBREW EQUIVALENTS: Shamira, Shemura, Shimrat, Shimriya.

Shimshon (שִׁמְשׁוֹן) From the Hebrew, meaning "sun." The exact Hebrew equivalent is Shimshon. The exact feminine Hebrew equivalent is Shimshona.

Shipley A variant form of Shepley. See Shepley.

Shiron (שִׁירוֹן) From the Hebrew, meaning "song, songfest." The exact Hebrew equivalent is Shiron. FEMININE HEBREW EQUIVALENTS: Shir, Shira, Shiri, Shir-Li.

Shlomi (שְׁלוֹמִי) From the Hebrew, meaning "my peace." The exact Hebrew equivalent is Shlomi. The exact feminine Hebrew equivalent is Shlomit.

Shlomo (שְׁלֹמֹה) From the Hebrew, meaning "his peace." The exact Hebrew equivalent is Shlomo. FEMININE HEBREW EQUIVALENTS: Shlomit, Shulamit.

Shmuel (שְׁמוּאֵל) From the Hebrew, meaning "His name is God." The exact Hebrew equivalent is Shmuel. The exact feminine Hebrew equivalent is Shmuela.

Shneur (שְׁנִיאוּר)   A Yiddish form of Senior. *See* Senior.

Sholom   A variant spelling of Shalom. *See* Shalom.

Shor (שׁוֹר)   From the Hebrew, meaning "ox." The exact Hebrew equivalent is Shor.

Shoshan (שׁוֹשָׁן)   From the Hebrew, meaning "lily." The exact Hebrew equivalent is Shoshan.

Shraga (שְׁרָגָא)   A Yiddish form of Sheraga. *See* Sheraga.

Shushan (שׁוּשָׁן)   From the Hebrew, meaning "lily." The exact Hebrew equivalent is Shushan. The exact feminine Hebrew equivalent is Shoshana.

Si   A pet form of Seymour, Simon, and Simeon. *See* Seymour, Simon, *and* Simeon.

Sidney   A contracted form of Saint Denys. The original form of Denys is Dionysius, the Greek god of wine, drama, and fruitfulness. HEBREW EQUIVALENTS: Efra'yim, Gefanya, Gefen, Gitai, Karmeli, Porat, Pura. FEMININE HEBREW EQUIVALENTS: Bikura, Gat, Gitit, Nitza, Zimra.

Siegfried   From the German, meaning "victorious peace." HEBREW EQUIVALENTS: Avshalom, Netzach, Shlomo, Yatzliach. FEMININE HEBREW EQUIVALENTS: Dafna, Hadasa, Shlomit, Shulamit.

Siegmond, Siegmund   From the German, meaning "victory" and "protection." HEBREW EQUIVALENTS: Avigdor, Chosa, Shemarya, Shemaryahu, Yatzliach. FEMININE HEBREW EQUIVALENTS: Efrat, Magena, Shimrit, Tzila.

Sigi   A pet form of Sigmond. *See* Sigmond.

Sigmond, Sigmund   Variant spellings of Siegmond and Siegmund. *See* Siegmond *and* Siegmund.

Silvester   A variant spelling of Sylvester. *See* Sylvester.

Simcha (שִׂמְחָה)   From the Hebrew, meaning "joy." The exact masculine and feminine Hebrew equivalent is Simcha.

Simeon   An Anglicized form of Shimon. *See* Shimon.

Simha   A variant spelling of Simcha. *See* Simcha.

Simi, Simie, Simmie   Pet forms of Simeon and Simon. *See* Simeon *and* Simon.

Simon (שִׁמְעוֹן)   A Greek form of Shimon. *See* Shimon.

Simpson   A patronymic form, meaning "son of Simon." *See* Simon.

Sinclair   From the Latin, meaning "shining" or "sanctified." HEBREW EQUIVALENTS: Aharon, Chagai, Devir, Kadosh, Zerach, Zerachya, Ziv. FEMININE HEBREW EQUIVALENTS: Aharona, Behira, Me'ira, Noga, Zahari, Zehorit, Zoheret.

Sisi (שִׂישִׂי)   From the Hebrew, meaning "my joy." The exact Hebrew equivalent is Sisi. FEMININE HEBREW EQUIVALENTS: Alisa, Alitza, Rina, Roni, Sisa.

Sivan (סִיוָן)   The third month of the Jewish year, corresponding to May-June. In the Zodiac its sign is Gemini ("twins"). The exact Hebrew equivalent is Sivan. The exact feminine Hebrew equivalent is Sivana.

Sloan From the Celtic, meaning "warrior." HEBREW EQUIVALENTS: Gad, Gadi, Gadiel, Gavriel, Gevarya, Gibor, Ish-Cha'yil, Nimrod. FEMININE HEBREW EQUIVALENTS: Gavriela, Gavrila, Gibora, Gidona, Merav, Tigra.

Sodi (סוֹדִי) From the Hebrew, meaning "my secret." The exact Hebrew equivalent is Sodi. FEMININE HEBREW EQUIVALENTS: Eliraz, Liraz, Raz, Razi.

Sol From the Latin, meaning "sun." The exact Hebrew equivalent is Shimshon. The exact feminine Hebrew equivalent is Shimshona. Also, a pet form of Solomon. See Solomon.

Solomon (שְׁלֹמֹה) From the Hebrew, meaning "peace." The exact Hebrew equivalent is Shlomo (Shelomo). FEMININE HEBREW EQUIVALENTS: Shlomit (Shelomit), Shulamit.

Sonny A popular nickname, meaning "son" or "boy." The exact Hebrew equivalent is Ben. The exact feminine Hebrew equivalent is Bat.

Spencer From the Anglo-Saxon, meaning "steward, administrator, guardian." HEBREW EQUIVALENTS: Avdi, Avigdor, Ovadya, Oved, Shemarya, Shemaryahu. FEMININE HEBREW EQUIVALENTS: Avigdora, Efrat, Tira, Tzila, Ya'akova.

Stacey, Stacy From the Latin, meaning "firmly established." HEBREW EQUIVALENTS: Elyakim, Elyakum, Konen, Sa'adya, Yachin, Yeho'yakim. FEMININE HEBREW EQUIVALENTS: Amitza, Kana, Mashena, Sa'ada.

Stan A pet form of Stanley. See Stanley.

Stanford From the Old English, meaning "from the stone [or paved] ford." HEBREW EQUIVALENTS: Achitzur, Avitzur, Avniel, Elitzur, Shamir, Tzur. FEMININE HEBREW EQUIVALENTS: Tzur-El, Tzurit, Tzuriya.

Stanley From the Old English, meaning "from the stony field." HEBREW EQUIVALENTS: Achitzur, Avitzur, Avniel, Elitzur, Shamir, Tzur. FEMININE HEBREW EQUIVALENTS: Tzur-El, Tzurit, Tzuriya.

Stefan A variant spelling of the German Stephan. See Stephan.

Stefano An Italian form of Stefan. See Stefan.

Stephan The German form of Stephen. See Stephen.

Stephen From the Greek, meaning "crown." HEBREW EQUIVALENTS: Avimelech, Elimelech, Katriel, Kitron, Malkam, Malkiel, Malkiya, Melech. FEMININE HEBREW EQUIVALENTS: Atara, Ateret, Kelila, Kelula, Tzefira, Taga.

Stevan A variant form of Stephen. See Stephen.

Steven A variant form of Stephen. See Stephen.

Stewart From the Anglo-Saxon, meaning "guardian, keeper of the estate." HEBREW EQUIVALENTS: Avdi, Avigdor, Ovadya, Oved, Shemarya, Shemaryahu, Ya'akov. FEMININE HEBREW EQUIVALENTS: Efrat, Tira, Tzila, Ya'akova.

Stone From the Old English, meaning "stone, rock." HEBREW EQUIVALENTS: Avniel, Even, Even-Ezer, Regem, Sapir. FEMININE HEBREW EQUIVALENTS: Avna, Gazit, Tzuriya.

Stu A pet form of Stuart. See Stuart.

Stuart A variant form of Stewart. See Stewart.

Sumner From the French and Latin, meaning "one who summons a messenger." HEBREW EQUIVALENTS: Malach, Malachi, Mevaser, Mevaser-Tov. The feminine Hebrew equivalent is Malach.

Sy A pet form of Seymour and Sylvan. *See* Seymour *and* Sylvan.

Sydney A variant spelling of Sidney. *See* Sidney.

Sylvan From the Latin, meaning "forest, woods." HEBREW EQUIVALENTS: Ya'ar, Ya'ari. FEMININE HEBREW EQUIVALENTS: Ya'ara, Ya'arit.

Sylvester A variant form of Silvan. *See* Silvan.

Syshe (סִישֶׁע) From the Yiddish, meaning "sweet." Zushe, Zusye, and Zisya are variant forms. HEBREW EQUIVALENTS: Avinoam, Magdiel, Matok, Meged, Na'aman, Na'am. FEMININE HEBREW EQUIVALENTS: Achinoam, Metuka, Na'ama, Na'omi.

Tab A pet form of David. *See* David.

Tabai, Tabbai (טַבָּאי) From the Aramaic, meaning "good." The exact Hebrew equivalent is Tabai. FEMININE HEBREW EQUIVALENTS: Tova, Tovit.

Tad A pet form of Thadeus. *See* Thadeus.

Tal (טַל) From the Hebrew, meaning "dew." The exact masculine and feminine Hebrew equivalent is Tal.

Tali (טַלִי) A variant form of Tal. *See* Tal. The exact masculine and feminine Hebrew equivalent is Tali.

Tal-Shachar (טַל-שַׁחַר) From the Hebrew, meaning "morning dew." The exact Hebrew equivalent is Tal-Shachar. FEMININE HEBREW EQUIVALENTS: Tal, Talal, Tali, Talila, Talya.

Talia, Taliah Variant spellings of Talya. *See* Talya.

Talmai (תַּלְמַי) From the Aramaic, meaning "mound" or "hill." The exact Hebrew equivalent is Talmai. FEMININE HEBREW EQUIVALENTS: Talma, Talmi.

Talmi (תַּלְמִי) From the Hebrew, meaning "hill, mound." The exact masculine and feminine Hebrew equivalent is Talmi.

Talmon (טַלְמוֹן) From the Aramaic, meaning "to oppress, injure." The exact Hebrew equivalent is Talmon. FEMININE HEBREW EQUIVALENTS: Bat-Shua, Bilha.

Tal-Or (טַל-אוֹר) From the Hebrew, meaning "dew of the light [morning]." The exact masculine and feminine Hebrew equivalent is Tal-Or.

Talya (טַלְיָא) From the Aramaic, meaning "young lamb." The exact masculine and feminine Hebrew equivalent is Talya.

Tam (תָּם) From the Hebrew, meaning "complete, whole" or "honest." A nickname for Jacob (Genesis 25:27). The exact Hebrew equivalent is Tam. The exact feminine Hebrew equivalent is Temima.

Tami (תָּמִי) A variant form of Tam. *See* Tam. The exact Hebrew equivalent is Tami.

Tamir (תָּמִיר) From the Hebrew, meaning "tall, stately, like the palm tree." The exact Hebrew equivalent is Tamir. The exact feminine Hebrew equivalent is Temira.

Tamur (תָּמוּר) A variant form of Tamir. See Tamir. The exact Hebrew equivalent is Tamur.

Tanchum (תַּנְחוּם) From the Hebrew, meaning "comfort, consolation." The exact Hebrew equivalent is Tanchum. FEMININE HEBREW EQUIVALENTS: Menachema, Nachmanit, Nachmaniya, Ruchama.

Tanhum A variant spelling of Tanchum. See Tanchum.

Tate From the Old English, meaning "tenth, tithing" or "to be cheerful." HEBREW EQUIVALENTS: Agil, Chushiel, Ditz, Gil, Simcha, Yachdiel, Yagil. FEMININE HEBREW EQUIVALENTS: Aliza, Chedva, Ditza, Simcha, Simchona, Tzahala.

Tavi (טָבִי) From the Aramaic, meaning "good." The exact Hebrew equivalent is Tavi. FEMININE HEBREW EQUIVALENTS: Tova, Tovit.

Taylor Orginially a surname, from the Late Latin, meaning "to split, cut," referring specifically to one who cuts garments. HEBREW EQUIVALENTS: Bavai, Gidon, Gidoni, Salmai, Salmoni. FEMININE HEBREW EQUIVALENTS: Gitit, Giza, Kesarit, Salma.

Ted, Teddy Pet forms of Theodor. See Theodor.

Tel (תֵּל) A variant form of Telem. See Telem. The exact Hebrew equivalent is Tel.

Telem (תֶּלֶם) From the Hebrew, meaning "mound" or "furrow." Also, from the Aramaic, meaning "oppress, injure." The exact Hebrew equivalent is Telem. FEMININE HEBREW EQUIVALENTS: Talma, Talmi.

Tema, Temah (תֵּימָא) From the Hebrew and Aramaic, meaning "astonishment, wonder." The exact Hebrew equivalent is Tema. FEMININE HEBREW EQUIVALENTS: Peliya, Tama.

Teman (תֵּימָן) From the Hebrew, meaning "right side," denoting the south. (When facing east, toward Jerusalem, south is to the right). The exact Hebrew equivalent is Teman. The feminine Hebrew equivalent is Deromit.

Temani (תֵּימָנִי) A variant form of Teman. The exact Hebrew equivalent is Temani.

Tene, Teneh (טֶנֶא) From the Hebrew, meaning "basket." The exact Hebrew equivalent is Teneh. The feminine Hebrew equivalent is Salit.

Terence, Terrance, Terrence From the Latin, meaning "tender, good, gracious." HEBREW EQUIVALENTS: Chanan, Na'aman, Tuviya, Yochanan. FEMININE HEBREW EQUIVALENTS: Chana, Na'ami, Tova, Tziyona.

Terri, Terry A pet form of Terence. See Terence.

Tewel, Tewele Yiddish forms of David. See David.

Thaddeus, Thadeus From the Greek, meaning "gift of God." HEBREW EQUIVALENTS: Avi-Natan, Avishai, Hadar, Hadar-Am, Hadar-Ezer, Natan, Netanel. FEMININE HEBREW EQUIVALENTS: Doronit, Matana, Matat, Netanela, Teruma, Teshura.

Than From the Greek, meaning "death." EUPHEMISTIC HEBREW EQUIVALENTS: Chai, Cha'yim, Yechiel. EUPHEMISTIC FEMININE HEBREW EQUIVALENTS: Chava, Cha'ya.

Thane A Danish form of Than. See Than.

Theo A pet form of Theobald and Theodore. *See* Theobald *and* Theodore.

Theobald, Theobold From the Old German, meaning "brave people." HEBREW EQUIVALENTS: Abir, Abiri, Ben-Gever, Ben-Guryon, Bo'az, Calev, Gavriel, Yechezkel, Yo'ash, Yo'az. FEMININE HEBREW EQUIVALENTS: Abira, Abiri, Atzmona, Chasina, Etana, Gavriela, Uziela.

Theodor, Theodore From the Greek, meaning "divine gift." HEBREW EQUIVALENTS: Elnatan, Matanya, Matityahu, Natan, Netanel, Yehonatan, Yonatan, Yahav. FEMININE HEBREW EQUIVALENTS: Deronit, Matana, Migdana, Netina, Teshura, Zevida, Zevuda, Yahava.

Thomas (תְּאוֹם) From the Hebrew and Aramaic, meaning "twin." Also, from the Phoenician, meaning "sun god." The exact Hebrew equivalent is Te'om. FEMININE HEBREW EQUIVALENTS: Amior, Behira, Ora, Orit, Or-Li, Sivana.

Tibon, Tibbon Variant spellings of Tivon. *See* Tivon.

Tiger From the Greek, Latin, and Old French, meaning "tiger." The Hebrew equivalent is Namer. The feminine Hebrew equivalent is Nemera.

Tikva (תִּקְוָה) From the Hebrew, meaning "hope." The exact masculine and feminine Hebrew equivalent is Tikva.

Tim A pet form of Timothy. *See* Timothy.

Timo A short form of Timothy. *See* Timothy.

Timothy From the Greek, meaning "to honor [or fear] God." HEBREW EQUIVALENTS: Chatat, Hadar, Hadaram, Hadarezer, Hadur, Mechubad, Mokir, Sered. FEMININE HEBREW EQUIVALENTS: Hadura, Kevuda, Nichbada.

Timur (תִּימוּר) From the Hebrew, meaning "tall, stately" or "to rise up." The exact Hebrew equivalent is Timur. The exact feminine Hebrew equivalent is Timora.

Tip A nickname for Thomas. *See* Thomas.

Tiv (טִיב) From the Hebrew and Aramaic, meaning "good, goodness." The exact Hebrew equivalent is Tiv. The exact feminine Hebrew equivalent is Tova.

Tivon (טִבְעוֹן) From the Hebrew, meaning "natural." The exact Hebrew equivalent is Tivon. The exact feminine Hebrew equivalent is Tivona.

Tobiah A variant form of Tuviya. *See* Tuviya.

Tobias The Greek form of Tobiah. *See* Tobiah.

Tod From the Old English, meaning "thicket." Also, from the Scottish and Norse, meaning "fox." HEBREW EQUIVALENTS: Ilan, Kotz, Shu'al, Ya'ar, Ya'ari, Yara. FEMININE HEBREW EQUIVALENTS: Chochit, Ilana, Shu'ala, Ya'ara, Ya'arit.

Toda, Todah (תּוֹדָה) From the Hebrew, meaning "thanks, thankfulness." The exact masculine and feminine Hebrew equivalent is Toda.

Todd A variant spelling of Tod. *See* Tod.

Todros From the Greek, meaning "gift." Akin to Theodore. *See* Theodore.

Tolya A variant form of Anatoly (Anatol). *See* Anatol.

Tom A pet form of Thomas. *See* Thomas.

Tomer (תּוֹמֶר) A variant form of Tamar. *See* Tamar (feminine section). The exact masculine and feminine Hebrew equivalent is Tomer.

Tommy A pet form of Thomas. *See* Thomas.

Toni, Tony Pet forms of Anthony. *See* Anthony.

Tov (טוֹב) From the Hebrew, meaning "good." The exact Hebrew equivalent is Tov. The exact feminine Hebrew equivalent is Tova.

Tovi (טוֹבִי) A variant form of Tov, meaning "my good." The exact Hebrew equivalent is Tovi. *See* Tov.

Tovia, Toviah Variant spellings of Toviya. *See* Toviya.

Toviel (טוֹבִיאֵל) From the Hebrew, meaning "my God is goodness." The exact Hebrew equivalent is Toviel. FEMININE HEBREW EQUIVALENTS: Tova, Tovat, Tovit, Tuvit.

Toviya (טוֹבִיָה) From the Hebrew, meaning "goodness of God." The exact Hebrew equivalent is Toviya. FEMININE HEBREW EQUIVALENTS: Tova, Tovat, Tovit, Yatva, Yatvata.

Tracey, Tracy From the Old French, meaning "path" or "road." HEBREW EQUIVALENTS: Nativ, Shoval, Solel. FEMININE HEBREW EQUIVALENTS: Netiva, Selila.

Trygve From the British, meaning "town by the water." HEBREW EQUIVALENTS: Afek, Afik, Beri, Chamat, Dalfon, Dela'ya, Moshe. FEMININE HEBREW EQUIVALENTS: Afeka, Bat-Yam, Miryam, Yaval.

Tuvia, Tuviah Variant spellings of Tuviya. *See* Tuviya.

Tuviya (טוּבִיָה) From the Hebrew, meaning "God is good," or "the goodness of God." The exact Hebrew equivalent is Tuviya. FEMININE HEBREW EQUIVALENTS: Bat-Tziyon, Tova, Tovit, Tziyona, Yatva.

Tuviyahu (טוּבִיָהוּ) A variant form of Tuviya. *See* Tuviya. The exact Hebrew equivalent is Tuviyahu.

Tyron, Tyrone From the Greek, meaning "lord, ruler." Also, from the Latin, meaning "young soldier." HEBREW EQUIVALENTS: Avraham, Gavriel, Katriel, Malkiram, Melech, Yisrael. FEMININE HEBREW EQUIVALENTS: Atara, Be'ula, Gevira, Malka, Sara.

Tzefanya (צְפַנְיָה) From the Hebrew, meaning "God has treasured." The exact Hebrew equivalent is Tzefanya. FEMININE HEBREW EQUIVALENTS: Adiya, Otzara, Segula, Sima, Simai.

Tzefanyahu (צְפַנְיָהוּ) A variant form of Tzefanya. *See* Tzefanya. The exact Hebrew equivalent is Tzefanyahu.

Tzevi (צְבִי) From the Hebrew, meaning "deer, gazelle." The exact Hebrew equivalent is Tzevi. The feminine Hebrew equivalent is Tzivya.

Tzi (צִי) From the Hebrew, meaning "ship" or "navy." The exact Hebrew equivalent is Tzi. The feminine Hebrew equivalent is Aniya.

Tzofi (צוֹפִי) From the Hebrew, meaning "scout, guard, protector." The exact Hebrew equivalent is Tzofi. The exact feminine Hebrew equivalent is Tzofiya.

Tzvee A variant spelling of Tzevi. *See* Tzevi.

Tzvi A variant spelling of Tzevi. *See* Tzevi.

Uel A short form of Samuel. *See* Samuel.

Uri (אוּרִי) From the Hebrew, meaning "my flame" or "my light." The exact Hebrew equivalent is Uri. FEMININE HEBREW EQUIVALENTS: Uriela, Urit.

Uria, Uriah Variant spellings of Uriya. *See* Uriya.

Uriel (אוּרִיאֵל) From the Hebrew, meaning "God is my light" or "God is my flame." The exact Hebrew equivalent is Uriel. The exact feminine Hebrew equivalent is Uriela.

Uriya (אוּרִיָה) From the Hebrew, meaning "God is my flame." The exact Hebrew equivalent is Uriya. FEMININE HEBREW EQUIVALENTS: Uriela, Urit.

Uza (עֻזָא/עֻזָּה) From the Hebrew, meaning "strength." The exact masculine and feminine Hebrew equivalent is Uza.

Uzi (עֻזִּי) From the Hebrew, meaning "my strength." The exact Hebrew equivalent is Uzi. FEMININE HEBREW EQUIVALENTS: Uza, Uziela, Uzit.

Uziel (עֻזִּיאֵל) From the Hebrew, meaning "God is my strength." The exact Hebrew equivalent is Uziel. The exact feminine Hebrew equivalent is Uziela.

Uziya (עֻזִּיָה) From the Hebrew, meaning "God is my strength." The exact Hebrew equivalent is Uziya. FEMININE HEBREW EQUIVALENTS: Uza, Uziela, Uzit.

Uzza A variant spelling of Uza. *See* Uza.

Uzzi A variant spelling of Uzi. *See* Uzi.

Uzziah A variant spelling of Uziya. *See* Uziya.

Vail From the Latin, meaning "valley." HEBREW EQUIVALENTS: Gai, Gayora, Gaychazi. The feminine Hebrew equivalent is Ga'ya.

Val A French form of Vail. Also, a pet form of Valentine and Valery. *See* Valentine *and* Valery.

Vale A variant spelling of Vail. *See* Vail.

Valentine From the Latin, meaning "strong, valorous." HEBREW EQUIVALENTS: Abir, Abiri, Amotz, Gavriel, Gever, Gibor, La'yish, Uzi. FEMININE HEBREW EQUIVALENTS: Amitza, Aza, Aziza, Chasina, Gavrila, Gibora.

Vaughan, Vaughn From the Celtic, meaning "small." HEBREW EQUIVALENTS: Katan, Tzuar, Yaktan, Ze'ira, Zutra. FEMININE HEBREW EQUIVALENTS: Katanya, Ketana, Ketina, Pe'uta.

Velvel (וֶעֶלוֶועֶל) A pet form of the Yiddish Volf. *See* Volf.

Vered (וֶרֶד) From the Hebrew, meaning "rose." The exact masculine and feminine Hebrew equivalent is Vered.

Vern From the British, meaning "alder tree." Also, a pet form of Vernon. *See* Vernon.

Vernon From the Latin, meaning "belonging to spring, springtime," hence flourishing. HEBREW EQUIVALENTS: Aviv, Avivi, Mifrach, Perach, Perachya, Yarkon. FEMININE HEBREW EQUIVALENTS: Demumit, Devoranit, Pericha, Tifracha, Yarkona.

Vic, Vickie Pet forms of Victor. *See* Victor.

Victor From the Latin, meaning "victor, conqueror." HEBREW EQUIVALENTS: Gavriel, Gover, Katriel, Netzach, Yatzliach. FEMININE HEBREW EQUIVALENTS: Atara, Ateret, Dafna, Dafnit, Gevira, Hadasa.

Vida A variant form of Vitas. *See* Vitas.

Vince A pet form of Vincent. *See* Vincent.

Vincent From the Latin, meaning "victor, conqueror." HEBREW EQUIVALENTS: Gevarya, Gevaryahu, Netzach, Netziach, Nitzchi. FEMININE HEBREW EQUIVALENTS: Nitzcha, Nitzchiya, Nitzchona.

Vitas From the Latin, meaning "life." HEBREW EQUIVALENTS: Avichai, Bachya, Chai, Cha'yim, El-Chai, Yechiel, Yocha'i. FEMININE HEBREW EQUIVALENTS: Achiya, Chava, Cha'ya, Techiya, Yechiela.

Vivian, Vivien Used only occasionally as masculine names. *See* Vivian (*feminine section*).

Volf (װאָלף) A Yiddish form of Wolf. *See* Wolf.

Vyvyan A variant spelling of Vivian. *See* Vivian.

Wal A short form of Wallace and Walter. *See* Wallace *and* Walter.

Walbert From the Old English, meaning "secure fortification." HEBREW EQUIVALENTS: Eltzafan, Lot, Lotan, Magen, Tzelafchad, Ya'akov. FEMININE HEBREW EQUIVALENTS: Magena, Megina, Tzina, Ya'akova.

Walker From the Greek, meaning "to roll up," and from the Old English, meaning "to journey." HEBREW EQUIVALENTS: Aminad, Darkon, Divon, Shuach. FEMININE HEBREW EQUIVALENTS: Gershona, Gioret, Hagar.

Wallace From the Anglo-French and the Middle English, meaning "foreigner, stranger." HEBREW EQUIVALENTS: Gershom, Gershona, Giora, Golyat. FEMININE HEBREW EQUIVALENTS: Avishag, Gershona, Gerusha, Gioret, Hagar.

Wallie A pet form of Walter. *See* Walter.

Wally A pet form of Walter and Wallace. *See* Walter *and* Wallace.

Walt A short form of Walter. *See* Walter.

Walter From the Old English, meaning "woods" or "master of the woods." Also, from the Old French, meaning "army general," and the Welsh-Latin, meaning "pilgrim, stranger." HEBREW EQUIVALENTS: Chashmon, Gavriel, Gershom, Gershon, Golyat, Malkiel, Melech, Yisrael, Yoav. FEMININE HEBREW EQUIVALENTS: Avishag, Gavrila, Gerusha, Hagar, Malka, Nediva, Sara.

Ward From the Old English, meaning "to guard, guardian." HEBREW EQUIVALENTS: Natron, Noter, Shimron, Shomer, Shoter. FEMININE HEBREW EQUIVALENTS: Mishmeret, Shimra, Shimrit, Shimriya.

Warner A variant form of Warren. *See* Warren.

Warren From the Middle English and the Old French, meaning "to protect, preserve" or "enclosure, park." HEBREW EQUIVALENTS: Chapam, Gina, Karmel, Karmeli, Magen, Shemarya, Shomer. FEMININE HEBREW EQUIVALENTS: Gana, Karmela, Magena, Shamira, Shemura, Shimriya, Tira.

Wayne From the British, meaning "meadow," or from the Old English, meaning "maker of wagons." HEBREW EQUIVALENTS: Adam, Artzi, Eglon, Hevel, Sharon. FEMININE HEBREW EQUIVALENTS: Adama, Agala, Arzit, Eretz, Sharona.

Wendel, Wendell From the British, meaning "good dale or pleasant valley," or from the Old English, meaning "wanderer, stranger." HEBREW EQUIVALENTS: Gershom, Gershon, Giora, Golyat. FEMININE HEBREW EQUIVALENTS: Avishag, Gershona, Gerusha, Hagar.

Werner A variant form of Warren. *See* Warren.

Wesley From the Old English, meaning "west meadow." HEBREW EQUIVALENTS: Ma'arav, Sharon. FEMININE HEBREW EQUIVALENTS: Sharona, Yama.

Whitney From the Old English, meaning "land near the water" or "white palace." HEBREW EQUIVALENTS: Armon, Armoni, Bitan, Dalfon, Itamar, Lavan. FEMININE HEBREW EQUIVALENTS: Armona, Bat-Yam, Bira, Levana, Miryam.

Wilber, Wilbert Variant forms of Walbert. *See* Walbert.

Wilfred, Wilfrid, Wilfried From the Old English, meaning "hope for peace." HEBREW EQUIVALENTS: Sha'anan, Shabtai, Shalev, Shalom, Shlomo. FEMININE HEBREW EQUIVALENTS: Menucha, Meshulemet, Shalva, Shelomit, Shulamit.

Wilhelm The German form of William. *See* William.

Will A pet form of William. *See* William.

Willard From the Old English, meaning "yard of willow trees." HEBREW EQUIVALENTS: Almog, Alon, Ilan, Ilan-Chai, Ilan-Tov. FEMININE HEBREW EQUIVALENTS: Almona, Almuga, Ilana, Ilanit.

Willi A pet form of William. *See* William.

William A variant form of the Old French Willaume and the Old High German Willehelm, meaning "resolute protector." HEBREW EQUIVALENTS: Betzalel, Gad, Gavriel, Gibor, Katriel, Magen, Melech, Shemarya, Shimri, Ya'akov. FEMININE HEBREW EQUIVALENTS: Chasya, Chosa, Magena, Megina, Shimra, Shimriya, Ya'akova.

Willie A pet form of William. *See* William.

Willis A patronymic form, meaning "son of William." *See* William.

Willoughby From the Old English, meaning "place by the willows." Akin to Willard. *See* Willard.

Willy A pet form of William. *See* William.

Wilmar, Wilmer, Willmer From the Old English, meaning "willows near the sea." Akin to Willard. *See* Willard.

Wilt A variant form of Walt (Walter). *See* Walter.

Wilton From the Old English, meaning "from the farmstead by the spring." HEBREW EQUIVALENTS: Aviyam, Enan, Moshe, Peleg. FEMININE HEBREW EQUIVALENTS: Afeka, Derora, Marata, Miryam.

Win A short form of Winston. *See* Winston.

Winston From the Old English, meaning "victory town" or "a friend firm as a stone." HEBREW EQUIVALENTS: Achitzur, Amit, Avniel, No'am, Shamir, Tzur. FEMININE HEBREW EQUIVALENTS: Amita, Avna, Davida, Na'omi, Tirtza, Tzurit.

Winthrop From the Old English, meaning "victory at the crossroads" or "friendly village." HEBREW EQUIVALENTS: Ach, Bildad, Medad, Nitzchan, No'am, Rayi, Regem. FEMININE HEBREW EQUIVALENTS: Ahuva, Chaviva, Davida, Na'ama, Rut.

Wolf, Wolfe From the Anglo-Saxon, meaning "wolf," connoting strength. HEBREW EQUIVALENTS: Ben-Cha'yil, Binyamin, Gavriel, Yechezkel, Z'ev, Z'evi. FEMININE HEBREW EQUIVALENTS: Amtza, Ariel, Gavriela, Gavrila, Gibora.

Wood, Woods From the Anglo-Saxon, meaning "from the wooded area." HEBREW EQUIVALENTS: Adam, Artza, Ilan, Karmel, Ya'ari. FEMININE HEBREW EQUIVALENTS: Eretz, Ilana, Karmela, Yara.

Woodie A pet form of Woodrow. *See* Woodrow.

Woodrow From the Anglo-Saxon, meaning "wooded hedge." *See* Wood.

Woody A pet form of Woodrow. *See* Woodrow.

Wyn, Wynn From the British, meaning "white, fair." HEBREW EQUIVALENTS: Lavan, Levanon, Livni, Malbin, Tzachar. FEMININE HEBREW EQUIVALENTS: Livnat, Levona, Malbina, Tzechira.

Xavier From the Latin, meaning "savior," or from the Arabic, meaning "bright." HEBREW EQUIVALENTS: Bahir, Mashiach, Me'ir, Zahur, Zohar. FEMININE HEBREW EQUIVALENTS: Behira, Me'ira, Zahara, Zehira, Zehorit.

Xeno From the Greek, meaning "sign, symbol." HEBREW EQUIVALENTS: Nisan, Samal, Siman. FEMININE HEBREW EQUIVALENTS: Simana, Simona.

Yaacov A variant spelling of Yaakov. *See* Yaakov.

Yaakov (יַעֲקֹב) From the Hebrew, meaning "supplanted" or "held by the heel." Jacob is the Anglicized form. The exact Hebrew equivalent is Ya'akov. The exact feminine Hebrew equivalent is Ya'akova.

Yadid (יָדִיד) From the Hebrew, meaning "beloved, friend." The exact Hebrew equivalent is Yadid. The exact feminine Hebrew equivalent is Yedida.

Yadin (יָדִין) A variant form of Yadon. *See* Yadon. The exact Hebrew equivalent is Yadin.

Yadon (יָדוֹן) From the Hebrew, meaning "he will judge." The exact Hebrew equivalent is Yadon. FEMININE HEBREW EQUIVALENTS: Daniela, Danit, Danza, Dina, Nadin.

Yadua (יָדוּעַ) From the Hebrew, meaning "celebrity" or "that which is known." The exact Hebrew equivalent is Yadua. FEMININE HEBREW EQUIVALENTS: Bina, Buna, Yediela.

Yael (יָעֵל) From the Hebrew, meaning "mountain goat." The exact masculine and feminine Hebrew equivalent is Ya'el.

Yafet (יָפֶת) A variant form of Yefet. See Yefet. The exact Hebrew equivalent is Yafet.

Yagel A variant form of Yagil. See Yagil.

Yagil (יָגִיל) From the Hebrew, meaning "to rejoice." The exact Hebrew equivalent is Yagil. FEMININE HEBREW EQUIVALENTS: Gila, Gili, Giliya, Gilit, Ronli.

Yair (יָאִיר) From the Hebrew, meaning "to light up" or "to enlighten." The exact Hebrew equivalent is Ya'ir. FEMININE HEBREW EQUIVALENTS: Me'ira, Nurya, Uranit, Urit, Ye'ora.

Yakar (יָקָר) From the Hebrew, meaning "precious, dear, beloved, honorable." The exact Hebrew equivalent is Yakar. FEMININE HEBREW EQUIVALENTS: Yakira, Yekara, Yikrat.

Yaki (יַקִי) A pet form of Yaakov. See Yaakov.

Yakim (יָקִים) A short form of Yehoyakim (Jehoiakim). See Yehoyakim. The exact Hebrew equivalent is Yakim.

Yakir (יַקִיר) A variant form of Yakar. See Yakar. The exact Hebrew equivalent is Yakir.

Yale From the Anglo-Saxon, meaning "one who yields [pays]." HEBREW EQUIVALENTS: Efra'yim, Heman, Porat, Pura. FEMININE HEBREW EQUIVALENTS: Bikura, Porat, Poriya, Tenuva, Zimra.

Yamin (יָמִין) From the Hebrew, meaning "right, right-handed." The exact Hebrew equivalent is Yamin. The exact feminine Hebrew equivalent is Yemina.

Yancy A variant form of the Danish Jon (John). See John.

Yankel (יַאנְקֶעל) A Yiddish form of Yaakov (Jacob). See Yaakov.

Yarden (יַרְדֵן) From the Hebrew, meaning "to flow down, descend." The exact Hebrew equivalent is Yarden. The exact feminine Hebrew equivalent is Yardena.

Yardeni (יַרְדֵנִי) A variant form of Yarden. See Yarden. The exact Hebrew equivalent is Yardeni.

Yared (יָרֶד) From the Hebrew, meaning "descend, descendant." The exact Hebrew equivalent is Yared. FEMININE HEBREW EQUIVALENTS: Tzelila, Tzelilit, Yardena, Yardeniya.

Yariv (יָרִיב) From the Hebrew, meaning "he will quarrel, contend." The exact Hebrew equivalent is Yariv. The feminine Hebrew equivalent is Tigra.

Yarkon (יַרְקוֹן) From the Hebrew, meaning "green." The exact Hebrew equivalent is Yarkon. The exact feminine Hebrew equivalent is Yarkona.

Yarom (יָרוֹם) From the Hebrew, meaning "he will raise up." The exact Hebrew equivalent is Yarom. FEMININE HEBREW EQUIVALENTS: Merima, Meroma.

Yaron (יָרוֹן) From the Hebrew, meaning "he will sing, cry out." The exact Hebrew equivalent is Yaron. The exact feminine Hebrew equivalent is Yarona.

Yashar (יָשָׁר) A variant form of Yesher. *See* Yesher. The exact Hebrew equivalent is Yashar. The exact feminine Hebrew equivalent is Yeshara.

Yavin (יָבִין) From the Hebrew, meaning "one who is intelligent." The exact Hebrew equivalent is Yavin. FEMININE HEBREW EQUIVALENTS: Bina, Buna.

Yavne'el (יַבְנְאֵל) From the Hebrew, meaning "God builds." The exact Hebrew equivalent is Yavne'el. The exact feminine Hebrew equivalent is Yavne'ela.

Yavniel (יַבְנִיאֵל) A variant form of Yavne'el. *See* Yavne'el. The exact Hebrew equivalent is Yavniel.

Yaziz (יָזִיז) From the Assyrian and Hebrew, meaning "to move, to rise up" or "to be agitated, angry." The exact Hebrew equivalent is Yaziz. FEMININE HEBREW EQUIVALENTS: Evrona, Tigra.

Yechezkel (יְחֶזְקָאל) From the Hebrew, meaning "God is my strength." The exact Hebrew equivalent is Yechezkel. The exact feminine Hebrew equivalent is Yechezkela.

Yechiel (יְחִיאֵל) From the Hebrew, meaning "May God live." The exact Hebrew equivalent is Yechiel. The exact feminine Hebrew equivalent is Yechiela.

Yechieli (יְחִיאֵלִי) A variant form of Yechiel. *See* Yechiel. The exact Hebrew equivalent is Yechieli.

Yedid (יְדִיד) A variant form of Yadid. *See* Yadid.

Yedidya (יְדִידְיָה) From the Hebrew, meaning "friend of God" or "beloved of God." The exact Hebrew equivalent is Yedidya. The exact feminine Hebrew equivalent is Yedida.

Yediel (יְדִיעָאל) From the Hebrew, meaning "knowledge of the Lord." The exact Hebrew equivalent is Yediel. The exact feminine Hebrew equivalent is Yediela.

Yefet (יֶפֶת) From the Hebrew, meaning "beautiful," or from the Aramaic, meaning "abundant, spacious." The exact Hebrew equivalent is Yefet. FEMININE HEBREW EQUIVALENTS: Yafa, Yafit.

Yehiel A variant spelling of Yechiel. *See* Yechiel.

Yehieli A variant spelling of Yechieli. *See* Yechieli.

Yehonatan (יְהוֹנָתָן) From the Hebrew, meaning "God has given" or "gift of God." The exact Hebrew equivalent is Yehonatan. FEMININE HEBREW EQUIVALENTS: Dorona, Matana, Migda, Migdana, Netanela, Yehava.

Yehoram (יְהוֹרָם) From the Hebrew, meaning "God is exalted." The exact Hebrew equivalent is Yehoram. FEMININE HEBREW EQUIVALENTS: Ram, Rama, Ramit, Ramot, Sara.

Yehoshua (יְהוֹשֻׁעַ) From the Hebrew, meaning "God is salvation." The exact Hebrew equivalent is Yehoshua. FEMININE HEBREW EQUIVALENTS: Mosha'a, Shua, Teshua, Yisha.

Yehoyakim (יְהוֹיָקִים)   From the Hebrew, meaning "God will establish." The exact Hebrew equivalent is Yehoyakim. FEMININE HEBREW EQUIVALENTS: Asael, Mosada, Sa'ada.

Yehuda, Yehudah (יְהוּדָה)   From the Hebrew, meaning "praise." The exact Hebrew equivalent is Yehuda. The exact feminine Hebrew equivalent is Yehudit.

Yehudi   A variant form of Yehuda. *See* Yehuda.

Yekusiel   The Ashkenazic form of Yekutiel. *See* Yekutiel.

Yekutiel (יְקוּתִיאֵל)   From the Hebrew, meaning "God will nourish." The exact Hebrew equivalent is Yekutiel. FEMININE HEBREW EQUIVALENTS: Mashena, Mosada, Sa'ada.

Yemin (יָמִין)   From the Hebrew, meaning "right, right-handed." The exact Hebrew equivalent is Yemin. The exact feminine Hebrew equivalent is Yemina.

Yered (יֶרֶד)   From the Hebrew, meaning "descend." The exact Hebrew equivalent is Yered. FEMININE HEBREW EQUIVALENTS: Yardena, Yardeniya.

Yermi (יַרְמִי)   A pet form of Yirmeyahu (Jeremiah). *See* Yirmeya.

Yeshaya (יְשַׁעְיָה)   From the Hebrew, meaning "God is salvation." The exact Hebrew equivalent is Yesha'ya. FEMININE HEBREW EQUIVALENTS: Mosha'a, Shua, Teshua.

Yeshayahu (יְשַׁעְיָהוּ)   A variant form of Yesha'ya. *See* Yesha'ya. The exact Hebrew equivalent is Yesha'yahu.

Yesher (יֵשֶׁר)   From the Hebrew, meaning "upright, honest." The exact Hebrew equivalent is Yesher. The exact feminine Hebrew equivalent is Yeshara.

Yeshurun (יְשׁוּרוּן)   From the Hebrew, meaning "upright." The exact Hebrew equivalent is Yeshurun. FEMININE HEBREW EQUIVALENTS: Amida, Tamar, Yeshara, Zekifa, Zekufa.

Yiftach (יִפְתַּח)   From the Hebrew, meaning "he will open." The exact Hebrew equivalent is Yiftach.

Yigal (יִגְאָל)   From the Hebrew, meaning "he will redeem." The exact Hebrew equivalent is Yigal. The exact feminine Hebrew equivalent is Yigala.

Yigdal (יִגְדַל)   From the Hebrew, meaning "he will grow" or "he will be exalted." The exact Hebrew equivalent is Yigdal. FEMININE HEBREW EQUIVALENTS: Atalya, Atlit, Ge'ona, Ge'onit, Tzemicha.

Yirmeya (יִרְמְיָה)   From the Hebrew, meaning "God will raise up." The exact Hebrew equivalent is Yirmeya. FEMININE HEBREW EQUIVALENTS: Rama, Ramit, Romema, Romemiya, Sarit.

Yirmeyahu (יִרְמְיָהוּ)   A variant form of Yirmeya. *See* Yirmeya. The exact Hebrew equivalent is Yirmeyahu.

Yishai (יִשַׁי)   From the Hebrew, meaning "gift." The exact Hebrew equivalent is Yishai. FEMININE HEBREW EQUIVALENTS: Matana, Netana, Netanela, Teshura, Yehava.

Yishi (יִשְׁעִי) From the Hebrew, meaning "my deliverer, savior." The exact Hebrew equivalent is Yishi. FEMININE HEBREW EQUIVALENTS: Matzlicha, Mosha'a.

Yishmael (יִשְׁמָעֵאל) From the Hebrew, meaning "God will hear." The exact Hebrew equivalent is Yishmael. The exact feminine Hebrew equivalent is Shmuela.

Yisrael (יִשְׂרָאֵל) From the Hebrew, meaning "prince of God" or "to contend, fight." The exact Hebrew equivalent is Yisrael. The exact feminine Hebrew equivalent is Yisr'ela.

Yitzchak (יִצְחָק) From the Hebrew, meaning "he will laugh." The exact Hebrew equivalent is Yitzchak. The exact feminine Hebrew equivalent is Yitzchaka.

Yitzhak A variant spelling of Yitzchak. *See* Yitzchak.

Yizhak A variant spelling of Yitzchak. *See* Yitzchak.

Yoav (יוֹאָב) From the Hebrew, meaning "God is father" or "God is willing." The exact Hebrew equivalent is Yo'av. FEMININE HEBREW EQUIVALENTS: Avi, Aviela, Aviya, Imma.

Yochanan (יוֹחָנָן) A short form of Yehochanan. *See* Yehochanan. The exact Hebrew equivalent is Yochanan.

Yoel (יוֹאֵל) From the Hebrew, meaning "God is willing" or "the Lord is God." The exact Hebrew equivalent is Yo'el. FEMININE HEBREW EQUIVALENTS: Yo'ela, Yo'elit.

Yohanan A variant spelling of Yochanan. *See* Yochanan.

Yon (יוֹן) A variant form of Yona or Yonatan. *See* Yona *and* Yonatan.

Yona, Yonah (יוֹנָה) From the Hebrew, meaning "dove." The exact masculine and feminine Hebrew equivalent is Yona.

Yonat (יוֹנַת) A pet form of Yonatan. *See* Yonatan. The exact Hebrew equivalent is Yonat.

Yora (יוֹרָה) From the Hebrew, meaning "to teach" or "to shoot." The exact Hebrew equivalent is Yora. FEMININE HEBREW EQUIVALENTS: Moriel, Morit, Moriya.

Yoram (יוֹרָם) From the Hebrew, meaning "God is exalted." The exact Hebrew equivalent is Yoram. FEMININE HEBREW EQUIVALENTS: Atalya, Malka, Roma, Romiya, Sara.

Yoran (יוֹרָן) From the Hebrew, meaning "to sing." The exact Hebrew equivalent is Yoran. FEMININE HEBREW EQUIVALENTS: Rani, Ranit, Shira, Yarona.

Yos (יָאס) A Yiddish pet form of Yosef. *See* Yosef.

Yosef (יוֹסֵף) From the Hebrew, meaning "God will add, increase." The exact Hebrew equivalent is Yosef. The exact feminine Hebrew equivalent is Yosifa.

Yosel, Yossel (יָאסְעל) Pet forms of Yosef. *See* Yosef.

Yosi, Yossi (יָאסִי) Pet forms of Yosef. *See* Yosef.

Yotam (יוֹתָם) From the Hebrew, meaning "God is perfect." The exact Hebrew equivalent is Yotam. FEMININE HEBREW EQUIVALENTS: Ne'etzala, Ne'etzelet, Nitzalov, Nitzelet.

Yuda (יוּדָה) A variant form of Yehuda. See Yehuda.

Yudan (יוּדָן) From the Hebrew, meaning "will be judged." The exact Hebrew equivalent is Yudan. FEMININE HEBREW EQUIVALENTS: Daniela, Danya, Dina.

Yuki (יוּקִי) A pet form of Yaakov. See Yaakov.

Yuri (יוּרִי) A pet form of Uriah. See Uriah.

Zacharia, Zachariah Anglicized forms of Zecharya. See Zecharya.

Zachary A variant form of Zecharya. See Zecharya.

Zak (זַק) A pet form of Yitzchak and Zecharya. See Yitzchak and Zecharya.

Zakai, Zakkai (זַכַּי/זַכָּאי) From the Aramaic and Hebrew, meaning "pure, clean, innocent." The exact Hebrew equivalent is Zakai. The exact feminine Hebrew equivalent is Zaka.

Zalkin Yiddish pet forms of Solomon. See Solomon.

Zalki A pet form of Zalkin. See Zalkin.

Zalman, Zalmen, Zalmon Yiddish short forms of Solomon. See Solomon.

Zamir (זָמִיר) From the Hebrew, meaning "song, singing." The exact Hebrew equivalent is Zamir. FEMININE HEBREW EQUIVALENTS: Zimra and Zemira.

Zan (זָן) From the Hebrew, meaning "nourish, sustain." The exact Hebrew equivalent is Zan. FEMININE HEBREW EQUIVALENTS: Mashena, Mosada, Sa'ada.

Zander A variant spelling of Sander. See Sander.

Zane A variant form of Zan. See Zan.

Zanvil A Yiddish form of Shemuel. See Shemuel.

Zavad (זָבָד) From the Hebrew, meaning "gift, portion, dowry." The exact Hebrew equivalent is Zavad. The exact feminine Hebrew equivalent is Zevuda.

Zavdi (זַבְדִּי) A variant form of Zavad. See Zavad. The exact Hebrew equivalent is Zavdi.

Zavdiel (זַבְדִיאֵל) A variant form of Zavad. From the Hebrew, meaning "God is my gift." The exact Hebrew equivalent is Zavdiel. FEMININE HEBREW EQUIVALENTS: Matana, Migdana, Zevida, Zevuda.

Zavil (זאָוויל) A variant form of Zanvil. See Zanvil.

Zayde, Zaydeh (זֵיידֶע) From the Yiddish, meaning "grandfather." See Aviav.

Zaydel (זֵיידֶעל) A pet form of Zayde. See Zayde.

Zeb A pet form of Zebulun. See Zebulun.

Zebulon, Zebulun Variant spellings of Zevulun. *See* Zevulun.

Zecharia, Zechariah Variant spellings of Zecharya. *See* Zecharya.

Zecharya (זְבַרְיָה) From the Hebrew, meaning "memory" or "remembrance of the Lord." Zachariah is the Anglicized form. The exact Hebrew equivalent is Zecharya. FEMININE HEBREW EQUIVALENTS: Zichrini, Zichriya, Zichrona.

Zecharyahu (זְבַרְיָהוּ) A variant form of Zecharya. *See* Zecharya. The exact Hebrew equivalent is Zecharyahu.

Zedekiah (צִדְקִיָה) From the Hebrew, meaning "God is righteousness." The exact Hebrew equivalent is Tzidkiya. Tzidkiyahu (צִדְקִיָהוּ) is a variant form. FEMININE HEBREW EQUIVALENTS: Dikla, Tamar, Tzedaka, Yeshara.

Ze'ev (זְאֵב) From the Hebrew, meaning "wolf." The exact Hebrew equivalent is Ze'ev. The exact feminine Hebrew equivalent is Ze'eva.

Zefania, Zefaniah Anglicized forms of the Hebrew, meaning "God has treasured." *See* Tzefanya.

Zehavi (זְהָבִי) From the Hebrew, meaning "gold." The exact feminine Hebrew equivalent is Zehava.

Zeide, Zeideh Variant spellings of Zayde and Zaydeh. *See* Zayde *and* Zaydeh.

Zeidel A variant spelling of Zaydel. *See* Zaydel.

Zeira (זְעִירָא) From the Aramaic, meaning "small, junior." The exact Hebrew equivalent is Ze'ira. FEMININE HEBREW EQUIVALENTS: Delila, Ketana.

Zeke A pet form of Zecharia. *See* Zecharia.

Zelig (זֶעְלִיג) A variant form of Selig. *See* Selig.

Zemel (זֶעְמֶעל) From the Yiddish, meaning "bread." HEBREW EQUIVALENTS: Lachma, Lachmi, Lechem. FEMININE HEBREW EQUIVALENTS: Bat-Lechem.

Zemer (זֶמֶר) From the Hebrew, meaning "song." The exact Hebrew equivalent is Zemer. The exact feminine Hebrew equivalent is Zimra.

Zemira, Zemirah (זְמִירָה) From the Hebrew, meaning "song" or "melody." The exact Hebrew equivalent is Zemira. The exact feminine Hebrew equivalent is Zimra.

Zeno A variant spelling of Xeno. *See* Xeno.

Zeph A short form of Zephaniah. *See* Zephaniah.

Zephania, Zephaniah Variant spellings of Zefania. *See* Zefania.

Zer (זֵר) From the Hebrew, meaning "wreath" or "crown." The exact Hebrew equivalent is Zer. FEMININE HEBREW EQUIVALENTS: Atara, Ateret, Atura, Tzefira.

Zera (זֶרַע) From the Hebrew, meaning "seed." The exact Hebrew equivalent is Zera. FEMININE HEBREW EQUIVALENTS: Yizr'ela, Zerua.

Zerachya (זְרַחְיָה) From the Hebrew, meaning "light of the Lord." The exact Hebrew equivalent is Zerachya. FEMININE HEBREW EQUIVALENTS: Me'ira, Uriela, Urit, Ye'ira, Ye'ora.

Zerem (זֶרֶם) From the Hebrew, meaning "stream." The exact Hebrew equivalent is Zerem. FEMININE HEBREW EQUIVALENTS: Arnona, Arnonit.

Zero A French and Italian form of the Arabic, meaning "cipher." The Hebrew equivalent is Sofer. The feminine Hebrew equivalent is Sofera.

Zetan (זֵיתָן) From the Hebrew, meaning "olive tree." The exact Hebrew equivalent is Zetan. The exact feminine Hebrew equivalent is Zetana.

Zev A variant spelling of Ze'ev. *See* Ze'ev.

Zevadia, Zevadiah Variant spellings of Zevadya. *See* Zevadya.

Zevadya (זְבַדְיָה) From the Hebrew, meaning "God has bestowed." The exact Hebrew equivalent is Zevadya. FEMININE HEBREW EQUIVALENTS: Teshura, Yehava, Zevida, Zevuda.

Zevi (צְבִי) From the Hebrew, meaning "deer." The exact Hebrew equivalent is Tzevi. The feminine Hebrew equivalent is Tzivya.

Zeviel (צְבִיאֵל) From the Hebrew, meaning "gazelle of the Lord." The exact Hebrew equivalent is Tzeviel. The exact feminine Hebrew equivalent is Tzeviela.

Zevulun (זְבוּלֻן) From the Hebrew, meaning "to exalt" or "lofty house." The exact Hebrew equivalent is Zevulun. The exact feminine Hebrew equivalent is Zevula.

Zik (זִיק) A Yiddish pet form of Itzik (Isaac). *See* Isaac.

Zimra (זִמְרָא/זִמְרָה) From the Hebrew and Aramaic, meaning "song, tune." The exact masculine and feminine Hebrew equivalent is Zimra.

Zimran (זִמְרָן) A variant form of Zimri. *See* Zimri. The exact Hebrew equivalent is Zimran.

Zimri (זִמְרִי) From the Hebrew, meaning "mountain-sheep" or "goat." The exact Hebrew equivalent is Zimri. FEMININE HEBREW EQUIVALENTS: Chosa, Gana, Shimrit, Ya'el, Zehira.

Zindel (זִינְדְּעֶל) A variant spelling of Zundel. *See* Zundel.

Zion (צִיּוֹן) From the Hebrew, meaning "a sign" or "excellent." The exact Hebrew equivalent is Tziyon. The exact feminine Hebrew equivalent is Tziyona.

Ziv (זִיו) From the Hebrew, meaning "shine, brilliance" or "gazelle." The exact Hebrew equivalent is Ziv. The exact Hebrew equivalent is Ziva.

Zohar (זֹהַר) From the Hebrew, meaning "light, brilliance." The exact masculine and feminine Hebrew equivalent is Zohar.

Zundel (זוּנְדְּעֶל) From the Yiddish, meaning "son, sonny." *See* Ben.

Zusman, Zussmann (זוּסְמַאן) Yiddish forms of the German, meaning "sweet man." HEBREW EQUIVALENTS: Avinoam, Na'am, No'am, Yivsam. FEMININE HEBREW EQUIVALENTS: Metuka, Mirit.

Zvi A variant spelling of Zevi. *See* Zevi.

Zvulun A variant spelling of Zevulun. *See* Zevulun.

Feminine Names

Feminine Names

Abbe   A pet form of Abigail. *See* Abigail.

Abbey   A pet form of Abigail. *See* Abigail.

Abbie   A pet form of Abigail. *See* Abigail.

Abby   A variant spelling of Abbey. *See* Abbey.

Abela   From the Latin, meaning "beautiful." HEBREW EQUIVALENTS: Achino'am, Adina, Rivka, Shifra. MASCULINE HEBREW EQUIVALENTS: Adin, Avino'am, Chemdan, Hadar, Na'aman, Ra'anan, Shapir, Yefet.

Abibi   A variant spelling of Avivi. *See* Avivi.

Abibit   A variant spelling of Avivit. *See* Avivit.

Abiela, Abiella   Variant spellings of Aviela. *See* Aviela.

Abigail   The Anglicized form of Aviga'yil. *See* Aviga'yil.

Abira (אֲבִירָה)   From the Hebrew, meaning "strong." The exact Hebrew equivalent is Abira. The exact masculine Hebrew equivalent is Abir.

Abiri (אֲבִירִי)   From the Hebrew, meaning "my powerful one" or "my strength." The exact feminine and masculine Hebrew equivalent is Abiri.

Abital   A variant spelling of Avital. *See* Avital.

Ada, Adah (עָדָה)   From the Hebrew, meaning "adorned, beautiful." Also, from the Latin and German, meaning "of noble birth." The exact Hebrew equivalent is Ada. MASCULINE HEBREW EQUIVALENTS: Adin, Adir, Aminadav, Avraham, Nadav, Yisrael.

Adaline   A pet form of Adelaide. *See* Adelaide.

Adamina   A feminine pet form of Adam. *See* Adam (*masculine section*).

Adda   A variant spelling of Ada. *See* Ada.

Addie   A pet form of Adelaide. *See* Adelaide.

Adela   A variant form of Adelaide. *See* Adelaide.

Adelaide   A French form of the German name Adelheid, meaning "of noble birth." HEBREW EQUIVALENTS: Adina, Malka, Ne'edara, Nesicha, Nediva, Sara, Yisr'ela. MASCULINE HEBREW EQUIVALENTS: Adir, Adiv, Adoniya, Avraham, Ish-Hod, Nadav, Yehonadav.

Adele   A variant form of Adelaide. *See* Adelaide.

Adelia   A variant form of Adelaide. *See* Adelaide.

Adelina   A pet form of Adele and Adelaide. *See* Adelaide.

Adeline   A pet form of Adelaide. *See* Adelaide.

Adella   A variant form of Adelaide. *See* Adelaide.

Adelle   A variant form of Adelaide. *See* Adelaide.

Adena (עֲדִינָה) From the Hebrew and Greek, meaning "noble" or "delicate." The exact Hebrew equivalent is Adina. MASCULINE HEBREW EQUIVALENTS: Adiel, Adin, Adoniya, Avihud, Hadar, Nadav, Yehonadav.

Aderet (אַדֶּרֶת) From the Hebrew, meaning "a cape." The exact Hebrew equivalent is Aderet. MASCULINE HEBREW EQUIVALENTS: Salma, Shet.

Adi (עֲדִי) From the Hebrew, meaning "ornament." The exact feminine and masculine equivalent is Adi.

Adie A variant spelling of Adi. See Adi.

Adiel (עֲדִיאֵל) From the Hebrew, meaning "ornament of the Lord." The exact masculine and feminine Hebrew equivalent is Adiel.

Adiela, Adiella (עֲדִיאַלָה) A variant form of Adiel. The exact Hebrew equivalent is Adiela. See Adiel.

Adina, Adinah Variant spellings of Adena. See Adena.

Adira (אַדִירָה) From the Hebrew, meaning "mighty, strong." The exact Hebrew equivalent is Adira. The exact masculine Hebrew equivalent is Adir.

Adiva (אַדִיבָה) From the Hebrew and Arabic, meaning "gracious, pleasant." The exact Hebrew equivalent is Adiva. The exact masculine Hebrew equivalent is Adiv.

Adiya (עֲדִיָה) From the Hebrew, meaning "God's treasure, God's ornament." The exact Hebrew equivalent is Adiya. MASCULINE HEBREW EQUIVALENTS: Ada'ya, Adi, Adiel, Adin.

Adoniya (אֲדוֹנִיָה) From the Hebrew, meaning "my Lord is God." The exact feminine and masculine Hebrew equivalent is Adoniya.

Adora From the Latin, meaning "one who is adored or loved." HEBREW EQUIVALENTS: Ahada, Ahava, Ahuva, Chiba, Davida. MASCULINE HEBREW EQUIVALENTS: Ahud, Ahuv, Bildad, David, Dodai, Ehud, Yedidya.

Adorna From the Anglo-Saxon, meaning "to adorn." HEBREW EQUIVALENTS: Adiel, Adina, Hadara, Hadarit, Yeho'adan. MASCULINE HEBREW EQUIVALENTS: Adiel, Adin, Hadar, Hod, Hodiya, Me'udan.

Adria, Adrian From the Greek, meaning "rich." HEBREW EQUIVALENTS: Ashira, Bat-Shua, Negida, Yitra. MASCULINE HEBREW EQUIVALENTS: Hotir, Huna, Yishai, Yitro.

Adriana A variant form of Adrian. See Adrian.

Adriane A variant spelling of Adrian. See Adrian.

Adria(e)nne Variant spellings of Adrian. See Adrian.

Adva (אַדְוָה) From the Aramaic, meaning "wave, ripple." The exact Hebrew equivalent is Adva. MASCULINE HEBREW EQUIVALENTS: Avi-yam, Be'eri, Moshe, Raviv.

Afra A variant spelling of Ofra. See Ofra.

Agala (עֲגָלָה) From the Hebrew, meaning "wagon." The exact Hebrew equivalent is Agala. MASCULINE HEBREW EQUIVALENTS: Eglon, Tzoveva.

Agatha From the Greek, meaning "good." HEBREW EQUIVALENTS: Bat-Tziyon, Shifra, Tova, Yatva. MASCULINE HEBREW EQUIVALENTS: Achituv, Ben-Tziyon, Na'aman, Tov, Tuviya, Shapir.

Agnes From the Greek and Latin, meaning "lamb," symbolizing purity and chastity. HEBREW EQUIVALENTS: Berura, Rachel, Talya, Teli, Zaka. MASCULINE HEBREW EQUIVALENTS: Amitai, Amnon, Barur, Tzadok, Yesher.

Aharona (אַהֲרוֹנָה) A feminine form of Aharon (Aaron). *See* Aharon. The exact Hebrew equivalent is Aharona. The exact masculine Hebrew equivalent is Aharon.

Aharonit (אַהֲרוֹנִית) A feminine form of Aharon (Aaron). *See* Aharon. The exact Hebrew equivalent is Aharonit.

Ahava, Ahavah (אַהֲבָה) From the Hebrew, meaning "love." The exact feminine and masculine Hebrew equivalent is Ahava.

Ahavat (אַהֲבַת) From the Hebrew, meaning "love." The exact Hebrew equivalent is Ahavat. MASCULINE HEBREW EQUIVALENTS: Ahava, Ahuv, Ohev.

Ahavia, Ahavya (אַהֲבִיָה) Variant forms of Ahuviya. *See* Ahuviya. The exact Hebrew equivalent is Ahavya.

Ahuda, Ahudah (אֲהוּדָה) From the Hebrew, meaning "adored." The exact Hebrew equivalent is Ahuda. The exact masculine Hebrew equivalent is Ahud.

Ahuva, Ahuvah (אֲהוּבָה) From the Hebrew, meaning "beloved." The exact Hebrew equivalent is Ahuva. The exact masculine Hebrew equivalent is Ahuv.

Ahuvia, Ahuviah Variant forms of Ahuviya. *See* Ahuviya.

Ahuviya (אֲהוּבִיָה) From the Hebrew, meaning "beloved of God." The exact Hebrew equivalent is Ahuviya. MASCULINE HEBREW EQUIVALENTS: Ahava, Ahuv, Ohad, Ohev.

Aida From the Latin and Old French, meaning "to help." HEBREW EQUIVALENTS: Eliezra, Ezra, Ezr'ela, Ezriela. MASCULINE HEBREW EQUIVALENTS: Achiezer, Aviezer, Eliezer, Ezra, Ezri.

Aidel A variant spelling of Eidel. *See* Eidel.

Aileen From the Greek, meaning "light." HEBREW EQUIVALENTS: Eliora, Liora, Liorit, Me'ira, Orlit, Uriela. MASCULINE HEBREW EQUIVALENTS: Elior, Lior, Ma'or, Me'ir, Orli, Uriel, Ya'ir.

Ailene A variant spelling of Aileen. *See* Aileen.

Aimee From the French and Latin, meaning "love, friendship." HEBREW EQUIVALENTS: Ahada, Ahava, Ahavat, Chiba, Davida, Yedida. MASCULINE HEBREW EQUIVALENTS: Ahud, Bildad, David, Dodai, Ohev, Yedidya.

Alaina, Alaine Variant forms of Alan. *See* Alan (*masculine section*).

Alberta The feminine form of Albert. *See* Albert (*masculine section*).

Albertina, Albertine Pet forms of Alberta. *See* Alberta.

Alcina A pet form of Alice. *See* Alice.

Alda From the Old German, meaning "old" or "rich." HEBREW EQUIVALENTS: Ashira, Negida, Keshisha, Yitra, Zekena. MASCULINE HEBREW EQUIVALENTS: Ashir, Hotir, Huna, Nagid, Yishai, Yitro, Zaken.

Aldora From the Anglo-Saxon, meaning "noble gift." HEBREW EQUIVALENTS: Darona, Matana, Migdana, Netanela, Teruma, Zevida, Zevuda.

MASCULINE HEBREW EQUIVALENTS: Doran, Doron, Elinatan, Matan, Teruma, Teshura.

Aleeza (עֲלִיזָה) From the Hebrew, meaning "joy, joyous one." The exact Hebrew equivalent is Aliza. MASCULINE HEBREW EQUIVALENTS: Alitz, Aliz, Gilam, Marnin.

Alene A variant spelling of Allene. See Allene.

Aletta From the Latin, meaning "the winged one." HEBREW EQUIVALENTS: A'ya, Da'a, Da'ya, Senunit, Tzipora. MASCULINE HEBREW EQUIVALENTS: Orev, Gozal, Tzipor.

Alexa A variant form of Alexandra. See Alexandra.

Alexandra (אֲלֶכְּסַנְדְרָה) A feminine form of the Greek name Alexander, meaning "protector of man." The exact Hebrew equivalent is Aleksandra. The exact masculine Hebrew equivalent is Aleksander.

Alexandrina A pet form of Alexandra. See Alexandra.

Alexia A variant form of Alexandra. See Alexandra.

Alexis A variant form of Alexandra. See Alexandra.

Alfreda The feminine form of Alfred, meaning "all peace" or "wise counsellor." HEBREW EQUIVALENTS: Aleksandra, Bina, Buna, Shlomit, Shulamit. MASCULINE HEBREW EQUIVALENTS: Aleksander, Avshalom, Eflal, Shalom, Shlomo, Utz, Ye'utz.

Ali A pet form of Alice and Alison. See Alice *and* Alison.

Alice From the Middle English and the Old French, meaning "of noble birth." HEBREW EQUIVALENTS: Malka, Matana, Nediva, Netanya, Sara, Yisr'ela. MASCULINE HEBREW EQUIVALENTS: Adar, Adoniya, Elinatan, Elzavad, Netanel, Yisrael.

Alisa A variant form of Alice. See Alice.

Alison A matronymic form, meaning "son of Alice." See Alice.

Alissa A variant form of Alice. See Alice.

Alita (עֲלִיתָה) From the Hebrew, meaning "high, above" or "excellent." The exact Hebrew equivalent is Alita. MASCULINE HEBREW EQUIVALENTS: Aharon, Ben-Tziyon, Marom, Tuviya, Yatva.

Alitza, Alitzah (עֲלִיצָה) From the Hebrew, meaning "joy, happiness." The exact Hebrew equivalent is Alitza. The exact masculine Hebrew equivalent is Alitz.

Aliya, Aliyah (עֲלִיָה) From the Hebrew, meaning "to ascend, to go up." The exact Hebrew equivalent is Aliya. MASCULINE HEBREW EQUIVALENTS: Atlai, Ram, Rama, Rom, Romem.

Alix A variant form of Alexandra. See Alexandra.

Aliza, Alizah Variant spellings of Aleeza and Alitza. See Aleeza *and* Alitza.

Allegra From the Latin, meaning "cheerful." HEBREW EQUIVALENTS: Alisa, Aliza, Aviga'yil, Elza, Ronli. MASCULINE HEBREW EQUIVALENTS: Alitz, Aliz, Eletz, Eliran.

Allene A feminine form of Allen. See Allen (*masculine section*).

Ally   A variant spelling of Ali. *See* Ali.

Allyn   A feminine section of Allen. *See* Allen (*masculine section*).

Alma (עַלְמָה)   From the Hebrew, meaning "maiden." The exact Hebrew equivalent is Alma. MASCULINE HEBREW EQUIVALENTS: Elam, Cha'yim, Na'am, Na'aman.

Almana (אַלְמָנָה)   From the Hebrew, meaning "alone, lonely, widow." The exact Hebrew equivalent is Almana. The exact masculine Hebrew equivalent is Alman.

Alona (אַלּוֹנָה)   From the Hebrew, meaning "oak tree." The exact Hebrew equivalent is Alona. The exact masculine Hebrew equivalent is Alon.

Althea   From the Greek and Latin, meaning "to heal" or "healer." HEBREW EQUIVALENTS: Refua, Rofi, Terufa. MASCULINE HEBREW EQUIVALENTS: Asa, Asa'el, Marpay, Rafa, Refa'el.

Alufa (אַלּוּפָה)   From the Hebrew, meaning "leader" or "princess." The exact Hebrew equivalent is Alufa. The exact masculine Hebrew equivalent is Aluf.

Aluma, Alumah (עֲלוּמָה)   From the Hebrew, meaning "girl maiden" or "secret." The exact Hebrew equivalent is Aluma. MASCULINE HEBREW EQUIVALENTS: Bachur, Elam, Na'arai, Na'arya, Raziel.

Alumit (אֲלוּמִית)   A variant form of Aluma. *See* Aluma. The exact Hebrew equivalent is Alumit.

Alyce   A variant spelling of Alice. *See* Alice.

Alysa, Alyssa   A variant spelling of Alisa and Alissa. *See* Alisa *and* Alissa.

Alyson   A variant spelling of Allison. *See* Alison.

Amabel   Compounded from the Latin *amor,* meaning "love," and the French *belle,* meaning "beautiful." HEBREW EQUIVALENTS: Ahuva, Chaviva, Davida, Yedida. MASCULINE HEBREW EQUIVALENTS: Ahuv, Chaviv, David, Yedid.

Amal (עָמָל)   Popular as a masculine name. *See* Amal (*masculine section*).

Amalia   A variant spelling of Amalya. *See* Amalya.

Amalie   A German variant form of Amelia. *See* Amelia.

Amalya (עֲמַלְיָה)   From the Hebrew, meaning "work of the Lord." The exact Hebrew equivalent is Amalya. The exact masculine Hebrew equivalent is Amel.

Amana (אֲמָנָה)   From the Hebrew, meaning "faithful." The exact Hebrew equivalent is Amana. MASCULINE HEBREW EQUIVALENTS: Amitai, Amitan, Amnon, Heman, Ne'eman.

Amanda   From the Latin, meaning "love." HEBREW EQUIVALENTS: Ahada, Ahava, Ahuda, Chaviva, Chiba, Davida. MASCULINE HEBREW EQUIVALENTS: Ahuv, Ahuviya, Chovev, David.

Amandalina   A pet form of Amanda. *See* Amanda.

Amber   From the Old French and Arabic, meaning "amber" or "golden, brownish-yellow." HEBREW EQUIVALENTS: Ofira, Paza, Pazit, Paziya,

Zehava. MASCULINE HEBREW EQUIVALENTS: Elifaz, Ofir, Paz, Upaz, Zahavi.

Amela (עֲמֵלָה) From the Hebrew, meaning "to work." The exact Hebrew equivalent is Amela. The exact masculine Hebrew equivalent is Amel.

Amelia From the Latin, meaning "to work, to be industrious." HEBREW EQUIVALENTS: Amalya, Arnona, Tirtza, Zeriza. MASCULINE HEBREW EQUIVALENTS: Arnon, Amel, Oved, Ovadya, Yaziz.

Ami (עֲמִי) A variant spelling of Amy. See Amy. Also, from the Hebrew, meaning "my nation, my people." The exact feminine and masculine Hebrew equivalent is Ami.

Amie A variant spelling of Ami. See Ami.

Amila (עֲמִילָה) A variant form of Amela. See Amela. The exact Hebrew equivalent is Amila.

Amina (אֲמִינָה/אֲמִינָא) From the Hebrew and Arabic, meaning "trusted, faithful." The exact Hebrew equivalent is Amina. MASCULINE HEBREW EQUIVALENTS: Amitai, Amitan, Amnon, Amun.

Amira (אֲמִירָה) From the Hebrew, meaning "speech, utterance." The exact Hebrew equivalent is Amira. The exact masculine Hebrew equivalent is Amir.

Amit (אָמִית) From the Hebrew, meaning "upright, honest." The exact feminine and masculine Hebrew equivalent is Amit.

Amita (אֲמִיתָה) A variant form of Amit. See Amit. The exact Hebrew equivalent is Amita.

Amity From the Latin, meaning "love, friendship." HEBREW EQUIVALENTS: Ahava, Chiba, Davida, Yedida. MASCULINE HEBREW EQUIVALENTS: Ahud, Ahuv, Bildad, David, Ohev.

Amitza, Amitzah (אֲמִיצָה) From the Hebrew, meaning "strong, powerful." The exact Hebrew equivalent is Amitza, The exact masculine Hebrew equivalent is Amitz.

Amiza, Amizza Variant spellings of Amitza. See Amitza.

Amtza, Amtzah (אַמְצָה) From the Hebrew, meaning "strength." The exact Hebrew equivalent is Amtza. The exact masculine Hebrew equivalent is Amotz.

Amy A variant spelling of Aimee. See Aimee.

Ana A variant spelling of Anna. See Anna.

Anat (עֲנָת) From the Hebrew, meaning "to sing." The exact Hebrew equivalent is Anat. MASCULINE HEBREW EQUIVALENTS: Aharon, Aharoni, Ana'ya, Eliram, Liron, Shiron.

Anava, Anavah (עֲנָבָה) From the Hebrew, meaning "grape." The exact Hebrew equivalent is Anava. The exact equivalent is Anav.

Anchelle A feminine form of Anshel. See Anshel (*masculine section*).

Andra From the Old Norse, meaning "breath." HEBREW EQUIVALENTS: Chava, She'ifa. MASCULINE HEBREW EQUIVALENTS: Hevel, Terach.

Andrea The feminine form of the Greek name Andrew, meaning "valiant, strong, courageous." HEBREW EQUIVALENTS: Amitza, Amtza,

Aza, Etana, Odeda. MASCULINE HEBREW EQUIVALENTS: Abir, Abiri, Amotz, Datan, Otniel, Uziel.

Andye A feminine form of Andy. *See* Andy (*masculine section*).

Anett A variant spelling of Annette. *See* Annette.

Angela From the Latin, meaning "angel," or from the Greek, meaning "messenger." HEBREW EQUIVALENTS: Aharona, Erela, Malach. MASCULINE HEBREW EQUIVALENTS: Aharon, Kalev, Malachi, Mevaser-Tov.

Angelica The Latin form of Angela. *See* Angela.

Angelina A pet form of Angela. *See* Angela.

Angeline A pet form of Angela. *See* Angela.

Angelique A pet form of Angela. *See* Angela.

Angelita A pet form of Angela. *See* Angela.

Aniela, Aniella Pet forms of Ann and Annie. *See* Ann *and* Annie.

Anina (עֲנִינָא) A pet form of Anna. *See* Anna. Also, from the Aramaic, meaning "answer my prayer."

Anita A pet form of Anna. *See* Anna.

Aniya (אֳנִיָּה) From the Hebrew, meaning "boat, ship." The exact Hebrew equivalent is Oniya. The masculine Hebrew equivalent is Sira.

Ann A variant form of Anna. *See* Anna.

Anna (חַנָּה) The Greek form of the Hebrew name Chana, meaning "gracious." The exact Hebrew equivalent is Chana. MASCULINE HEBREW EQUIVALENTS: Chanan, Chonen, Chonyo, Elchanan, Yochanan.

Annabel Either a hybrid of Anna and Bela, meaning "gracious, beautiful," or a variant form of the Latin name Amabel, meaning "lovable." HEBREW EQUIVALENTS: Ahuva, Chana, Davida, Hadura, Nofiya, Tifara, Tiferet. MASCULINE HEBREW EQUIVALENTS: Ahuv, Bildad, David, Eldad, Nof, Noy.

Anabella, Annabelle Variant forms of Annabel. *See* Annabel.

Anne (חַנָּה) A French form of Hannah, meaning "gracious." *See* Hannah. Anne is a variant form. *See* Anna.

Annetta A pet form of Anna. *See* Anna.

Annette A French form of Anna. *See* Anna.

Annie A pet form of Anna. *See* Anna.

Antoinette From the Greek and Latin, meaning "of high esteem, revered." HEBREW EQUIVALENTS: Adonit, Atalya, Ahuda, Malka, Ode'le-ya, Shevach, Tishbacha. MASCULINE HEBREW EQUIVALENTS: Aminadav, Gedalya, Hillel, Mehulal, Melech.

Antonella A pet form of Anton. *See* Anton (*masculine section*).

Antoina The Italian and Swedish form of Antoinette. *See* Antoinette.

April From the Latin, meaning "to open," symbolic of springtime. HEBREW EQUIVALENTS: Aviva, Avivi, Avivit. MASCULINE HEBREW EQUIVALENTS: Aviv, Avivi.

Arabel From the German *ara*, meaning "eagle," and the Latin *bella*, meaning "beautiful." HEBREW EQUIVALENTS: Gozala, Hadura, Na'ama, Ra'anana, Yafa. MASCULINE HEBREW EQUIVALENTS: Adin, Hadar, Nechmad, Nesher.

Arabela, Arabella   Variant forms of Arabel. *See* Arabel.

Arabelle   A variant spelling of Arabel. *See* Arabel.

Ardra   From the Celtic, meaning "high, high one." HEBREW EQUIVALENTS: Aharona, Gali, Galit, Givona, Meroma, Talma. MASCULINE HEBREW EQUIVALENTS: Aharon, Amir, Givon, Marom, Talmai.

Arela, Arella (אַרְאֵלָה)   From the Hebrew, meaning "angel, messenger." The exact Hebrew equivalent is Arela. The exact masculine Hebrew equivalent is Arel.

Ari   A pet form of Ariel. *See* Ariel.

Ariana, Arianna   From the Latin, meaning "song." HEBREW EQUIVALENTS: Mangina, Liron, Ne'ima, Rina, Shira, Yarona, Zimra. MASCULINE HEBREW EQUIVALENTS: Aharon, Amiran, Ana, Yaron, Zimra, Zimran, Zemarya.

Ariel (אַרִיאֵל)   From the Hebrew, meaning "lioness of God." The exact feminine and masculine Hebrew equivalent is Ariel.

Ariela, Ariella (אַרִיאֵלָה)   Variant forms of Ariel. *See* Ariel. The exact Hebrew equivalent is Ariela.

Arielle   A variant spelling of Ariel. *See* Ariel.

Ariza (אַרִיזָה)   From the Hebrew, meaning "cedar panels" and "to package." The exact Hebrew equivalent is Ariza. MASCULINE HEBREW EQUIVALENTS: Arzi, Erez.

Arleen   A variant spelling of Arlene. *See* Arlene.

Arlene   A variant spelling of Arline. *See* Arline.

Arlett   A pet form of Arlene. *See* Arlene.

Arline   From the German, meaning "girl," and from the Celtic, meaning "pledge, oath." HEBREW EQUIVALENTS: Alma, Bat-Sheva, Betula, Elisheva, Na'ara, Tze'ira. MASCULINE HEBREW EQUIVALENTS: Moshe, Na'arai, Na'arya, Nun, Sheva.

Arlyne   A variant spelling of Arline. *See* Arline.

Armona (אַרְמוֹנָה)   From the Hebrew, meaning "castle" or "fortress." The exact Hebrew equivalent is Armona. The exact masculine Hebrew equivalent is Armon.

Armonit (אַרְמוֹנִית)   A variant form of Armona. *See* Armona. The exact Hebrew equivalent is Armonit.

Arni (אַרְנִי)   A pet form of Aharona. *See* Aharona.

Arnina (אַרְנִינָה)   A pet form of Arni. *See* Arni.

Arninit (אַרְנִינִית)   A variant form of Arni. *See* Arni.

Arnit (אַרְנִית)   A variant form of Arni. *See* Arni.

Arnolde   A feminine form of Arnold. *See* Arnold (*masculine section*).

Arnoldine   A French variant form of Arnold meaning "eagle's rule," signifying power. HEBREW EQUIVALENTS: Abira, Adira, Amitza, Etana, Odeda.

MASCULINE HEBREW EQUIVALENTS: Abir, Ariel, Atzmon, Etan, Chaltzon, Nesher, Uziel.

Arnona (אַרְנוֹנָה) From the Hebrew, meaning "roaring stream." The exact Hebrew equivalent is Arnona. The exact masculine Hebrew equivalent is Arnon.

Arnonit (אַרְנוֹנִית) A pet form of Arnona. See Arnona.

Arona (אֲרוֹנָה) A variant form of Aharona, the feminine form of Aharon (Aaron). See Aharona.

Arza (אַרְזָה) From the Hebrew, meaning "cedar panels." The exact Hebrew equivalent is Arza. MASCULINE HEBREW EQUIVALENTS: Arzi, Erez, Oren.

Arzit (אַרְזִית) A variant form of Arza. See Arza. The exact Hebrew equivalent is Arzit.

Asaela (עֲשָׂהאֵלָה) From the Hebrew, meaning "God has created." The exact Hebrew equivalent is Asa'ela. The exact masculine Hebrew equivalent is Asa'el.

Ashera (אֲשֵׁרָה) From the Hebrew, meaning "blessed, fortunate" or "idol." The exact Hebrew equivalent is Ashera. The exact masculine Hebrew equivalent is Asher.

Ashira (עֲשִׁירָה) From the Hebrew, meaning "wealthy." The exact Hebrew equivalent is Ashira. The exact masculine Hebrew equivalent is Ashir.

Ashley From the Old English, meaning "grove of ash trees." HEBREW EQUIVALENTS: Alona, Arna, Arzit, Ilana, Ilanit. MASCULINE HEBREW EQUIVALENTS: Eshel, Pardes.

Asisa (עֲסִיסָה) From the Hebrew, meaning "juicy, ripe." The exact Hebrew equivalent is Asisa. The exact masculine Hebrew equivalent is Asis.

Asisya (עֲסִיסְיָה) From the Hebrew, meaning "juice [fruit] of the Lord." A variant form of Asisa. See Asisa. The exact Hebrew equivalent is Asisya.

Asta A variant form of Astera. See Astera.

Astera, Asteria From the Persian and Greek, meaning "star." Akin to Esther. See Esther.

Atalia, Ataliah Variant spellings of Atalya. See Atalya.

Atalya (עֲתַלְיָה) From the Assyrian, meaning "to grow, to be great." Also, from the Hebrew, meaning "God is exalted." The exact feminine and masculine Hebrew equivalent is Atalya.

Atara (עֲטָרָה) From the Hebrew, meaning "crown, wreath." The exact Hebrew equivalent is Atara. MASCULINE HEBREW EQUIVALENTS: Atur, Katriel, Kitron, Melech, Tzofar.

Ateret (עֲטֶרֶת) A variant form of Atara. See Atara. The exact Hebrew equivalent is Ateret.

Athalia, Athaliah Variant spellings of Atalya. See Atalya.

Atida, Atidah (עֲתִידָה) From the Hebrew, meaning "future." The exact Hebrew equivalent is Atida. The exact masculine Hebrew equivalent is Atid.

Atira (עֲתִירָה) From the Hebrew, meaning "prayer." The exact Hebrew equivalent is Atira. The exact masculine Hebrew equivalent is Atir.

Atlit (עֲתְלִית) A variant form of Atalya. *See* Atalya. The exact Hebrew equivalent is Atlit.

Atura (עֲטוּרָה) From the Hebrew, meaning "ornamented, adorned with a crown." The exact Hebrew equivalent is Atura. The exact masculine Hebrew equivalent is Atur.

Atzila (אֲצִילָה) From the Hebrew, meaning "honorable, noble." The exact Hebrew equivalent is Atzila. The exact masculine Hebrew equivalent is Atzil.

Audrey From the Old English, meaning "noble strength." HEBREW EQUIVALENTS: Abira, Ariel, Malka, Nediva, Nesicha, Sara. MASCULINE HEBREW EQUIVALENTS: Adir, Adoniya, Adiv, Chirom, Yehonadav, Yehoram.

Audrina A pet form of Audrey. *See* Audrey.

Audris From the Old German, meaning "fortunate" or "wealthy." HEBREW EQUIVALENTS: Asher, Asherit, Ashira, Yitra. MASCULINE HEBREW EQUIVALENTS: Asher, Ashir, Oshri, Yitro.

Augusta From the Latin, meaning "revered, sacred." HEBREW EQUIVALENTS: Atalya, Berucha, Chermona, Sara. MASCULINE HEBREW EQUIVALENTS: Aviram, Chermon, Gedalya, Kadish, Yirmeyahu.

Augustina A German form of Augusta. *See* Augusta.

Augustine A French form of Augusta. *See* Augusta.

Aura From the Greek, meaning "air, atmosphere." HEBREW EQUIVALENTS: Avirit, She'ifa. MASCULINE HEBREW EQUIVALENTS: Avira, Hevel, Nafish.

Aurea A variant form of Aurelia. *See* Aurelia.

Aurelia A feminine form of the Latin name Aurelius, meaning "gold." HEBREW EQUIVALENTS: Ofira, Paza, Paziya, Pazit, Tzehuva, Zehava, Zehuvit. MASCULINE HEBREW EQUIVALENTS: Ofir, Paz, Upaz, Zahavi.

Aurora From the Latin, meaning "dawn." HEBREW EQUIVALENTS: Shachar, Shacharit, Tzefira. MASCULINE HEBREW EQUIVALENTS: Ben-Shachar, Shacharya.

Aury A pet form of Aurelia. *See* Aurelia.

Ava From the Latin, meaning "bird." Also, from the Hebrew, meaning "to desire" or "to agree." HEBREW EQUIVALENTS: A'ya, Chasida, Derora, Tzipora, Ya'en. MASCULINE HEBREW EQUIVALENTS: Gozal, Orev, Tzipor.

Aveline From the French, meaning "hazelnut." The Hebrew equivalent is Egoza. The masculine Hebrew equivalent is Egoz.

Avella A pet form of Aveline. *See* Aveline.

Avi (אָבִי) From the Assyrian and Hebrew, meaning "father." The exact feminine and masculine Hebrew equivalent is Avi.

Avia, Aviah Variant spellings of Aviya. *See* Aviya.

Aviela, Aviella (אֲבִיאֵלָה) From the Hebrew, meaning "God is my father." The exact Hebrew equivalent is Aviela. The exact masculine Hebrew equivalent is Aviel.

Avigal (אֲבִיגַל)   From the Hebrew, meaning "father of joy." The exact feminine and masculine Hebrew equivalent is Avigal.

Avigayil (אֲבִיגַיִל)   From the Hebrew, meaning "father's joy" or "my father is joy." Abigail is the popular English form. The exact Hebrew equivalent is Aviga'yil. MASCULINE HEBREW EQUIVALENTS: Abba, Abahu, Agil, Avuya, Bilgai, Elez, Gil, Gilan, Gilon, Yagil, Yitzchak.

Avigdora (אֲבִיגְדוֹרָה)   The feminine form of the masculine Avigdor. *See* Avigdor (*masculine section*). The exact Hebrew equivalent is Avigdora.

Avirit (אֲוִירִית)   From the Hebrew, meaning "air, atmosphere, spirit." The exact Hebrew equivalent is Avirit. The exact masculine Hebrew equivalent is Aviri.

Avis   An Old German name, meaning "refugee, fortress." Also, from the Latin, meaning "bird." HEBREW EQUIVALENTS: Armona, Metzada, Migdala, Tzina. MASCULINE HEBREW EQUIVALENTS: Armon, Armoni, Betzer, Bitzaron, Mivtach, Luz.

Avital (אֲבִיטַל)   From the Hebrew, meaning "father of dew," referring to God as sustainer. The exact feminine and masculine Hebrew equivalent is Avital.

Aviva, Avivah (אֲבִיבָה)   From the Hebrew, meaning "springtime," connoting youthfulness. The exact Hebrew equivalent is Aviva. The exact Hebrew equivalent is Aviv.

Avivi (אֲבִיבִי)   From the Hebrew, meaning "springlike." The exact feminine and masculine Hebrew equivalent is Avivi.

Avivia   A variant spelling of Aviviya. *See* Aviviya.

Avivit (אֲבִיבִית)   A variant form of Aviva. *See* Aviva. The exact Hebrew equivalent is Avivit.

Aviviya (אֲבִיבִיָה)   A variant form of Aviya. *See* Aviya. The exact Hebrew equivalent is Aviviya.

Aviya (אֲבִיָה)   From the Hebrew, meaning "God is my father." The exact feminine and masculine Hebrew equivalent is Aviya.

Avna (אַבְנָה)   From the Hebrew, meaning "stone, rock." The exact Hebrew equivalent is Avna. MASCULINE HEBREW EQUIVALENTS: Avniel, Even, Tzur, Tzuriel.

Avuka (אֲבוּקָה)   From the Hebrew, meaning "torch, flame." The exact Hebrew equivalent is Avuka. MASCULINE HEBREW EQUIVALENTS: Lapid, Lapidot, Nur, Nuri, Nuriya, Nuriel, Ud, Udi.

Aya, Ayah (עַיָה)   From the Hebrew, meaning "to fly swiftly." The exact feminine and masculine Hebrew equivalent is A'ya.

Ayala, Ayalah (אַיָלָה)   From the Hebrew, meaning "deer, gazelle." The exact Hebrew equivalent is A'yala. The exact masculine Hebrew equivalent is A'yal.

Ayelet (אַיֶלֶת)   From the Hebrew, meaning "deer, gazelle." The exact Hebrew equivalent is A'yelet. MASCULINE HEBREW EQUIVALENTS: A'yal, A'yalon, Tzevi, Tzivyon.

Ayla (אֵלָה)   From the Hebrew meaning "oak tree." A variant form of Ela.

The exact Hebrew equivalent is Ayla (Ela). The exact masculine Hebrew equivalent is Aylon (Elon).

Aza, Azah (עַזָה) From the Hebrew, meaning "strong, powerful." The exact Hebrew equivalent is Aza. MASCULINE HEBREW EQUIVALENTS: Az, Azai, Azan, Oz, Uzi.

Aziza, Azizah (עֲזִיזָה) From the Hebrew, meaning "strong." The exact Hebrew equivalent is Aziza. The exact masculine Hebrew equivalent is Aziz.

Bab A pet form of Barbara and Elizabeth. *See* Barbara *and* Elizabeth.

Babette A pet form of Barbara. *See* Barbara.

Babs A variant form of Bab. *See* Bab.

Baila, Baile Variant spellings of Bayla and Bayle. *See* Bayla *and* Bayle.

Bambi A pet form of the Italian name Bambalina, meaning "little doll" or "boy." HEBREW EQUIVALENTS: Aluma, Alumit, Bat-Tziyon, Buba, Riva. MASCULINE HEBREW EQUIVALENTS: Ben, Ben-Tziyon, Na'arai, Na'arya.

Bara (בָּרָה) From the Hebrew, meaning "to choose." The exact Hebrew equivalent is Bara. MASCULINE HEBREW EQUIVALENTS: Bachir, Nivchar, Yivchar.

Barbara From the Greek, meaning "strange, stranger, foreign." HEBREW EQUIVALENTS: Avishag, Hagar, Sarida. MASCULINE HEBREW EQUIVALENTS: Gershom, Gershon, Golyat, Sarid, Zerubavel.

Barbi A pet form of Barbara. *See* Barbara.

Bari A feminine form of Barry. *See* Barry *(masculine section)*.

Barrie Used primarily as masculine name. *See* Barrie *(masculine section)*.

Basha A Yiddish form of Basya (Batya) and Bas-Sheva (Bat-Sheva). *See* Batya *and* Bat-Sheva.

Bashe A variant form of Basha. *See* Basha.

Bas-Sheva (בַּת־שֶׁבַע) The Ashkenazic pronunciation of Bat-Sheva. *See* Bat-Sheva.

Basya (בַּתְיָה) The Ashkenazic form of Batya. *See* Batya.

Bathsheba (בַּת־שֶׁבַע) The Anglicized form of Bat-Sheva. *See* Bat-Sheva.

Batli (בַּת־לִי/בַּתְלִי) From the Hebrew, meaning "I have a daughter." The exact Hebrew equivalent is Batli. The exact masculine Hebrew equivalent is Benli.

Bat-Sheva, Batsheva (בַּת־שֶׁבַע) From the Hebrew, meaning "daughter of an oath." The exact Hebrew equivalent is Bat-Sheva. MASCULINE HEBREW EQUIVALENTS: Amarya, Ela, Sheva.

Bat-Shir (בַּת־שִׁיר) From the Hebrew, meaning "songbird." The exact Hebrew equivalent is Bat-Shir. MASCULINE HEBREW EQUIVALENTS: Shir, Shiron, Yashir, Zimri.

Bat-Shua, Batshua (בַּת־שׁוּעַ) A biblical variant spelling of Bat-Sheva. *See* Bat-Sheva. The exact Hebrew equivalent is Bat-Shua.

Bat-Tziyon (בַּת־צִיוֹן) From the Hebrew, meaning "daughter of Zion" or "daughter of excellence." The exact Hebrew equivalent is Bat-Tziyon. The exact masculine Hebrew equivalent is Ben-Tziyon.

Batya (בַּתְיָה) From the Hebrew, meaning "daughter of God." The exact Hebrew equivalent is Batya. MASCULINE HEBREW EQUIVALENTS: Ben-Shem, Ben-Tziyon, Binyamin.

Bat-Yam (בַּת־יָם) From the Hebrew, meaning "daughter of the sea." The exact Hebrew equivalent is Bat-Yam. MASCULINE HEBREW EQUIVALENTS: Avi'yam, Dalfon, Dela'ya.

Bayla (בֵּיילָא) A Yiddish form of the Hebrew name Bilha. *See* Bilha. Also, a Yiddish form of Bela. *See* Bela.

Bayle (בֵּיילְעַ) A variant form of Bayla. *See* Bayla.

Bea, Beah Pet forms of Beatrice. *See* Beatrice.

Beata From the Latin, meaning "blessed." A variant form of Beatrice. *See* Beatrice.

Beate A short form of Beatrice. *See* Beatrice.

Beatrice From the Latin, meaning "one who brings happiness and blessing." HEBREW EQUIVALENTS: Ashera, Ashra, Aviga'yil, Beracha, Berucha, Gila, Ronena. MASCULINE HEBREW EQUIVALENTS: Asher, Baruch, Berachya, Gadiel, Mevorach, Ranon, Ron.

Beatrix The original form of Beatrice. *See* Beatrice.

Beccie A variant spelling of Beckie. *See* Beckie.

Beckie, Becky Pet forms of Rebecca. *See* Rebecca.

Behira (בְּהִירָה) From the Hebrew, meaning "light, clear, brilliant." The exact Hebrew equivalent is Behira. The exact masculine Hebrew equivalent is Bahir.

Bela Either a form of Isabella, meaning "God's oath," or from the Hungarian, meaning "nobly bright." Also, from the Latin, meaning "beautiful one." HEBREW EQUIVALENTS: Achino'am, Bat-Sheva, Behira, Elisheva, Me'ira, Na'ama, Rivka, Shifra. MASCULINE HEBREW EQUIVALENTS: Avino'am, Bahir, Barak, Me'ir, Na'aman, Uri, Uriel, Uriya.

Belinda An Old Germanic name derived from the Latin, meaning "beautiful serpent," having the connotation of shrewdness. HEBREW EQUIVALENTS: Buna, Ge'ona, Rivka, Yafa. MASCULINE HEBREW EQUIVALENTS: Achban, Bina, Buna, Chemdan, Nachshon, Yavin, Ye'utz.

Belita A Spanish pet form of Belle. *See* Belle.

Bella A short form of Isabella. *See* Isabella.

Belle A variant form of Bella. *See* Bella.

Belva From the Latin, meaning "beautiful view." HEBREW EQUIVALENTS: Adina, Na'ama, Na'omi, Nava, Nehedara, Nofiya, Ranana. MASCULINE HEBREW EQUIVALENTS: Adin, Hadar, Naveh, Shifron, Yafeh.

Benedicta A feminine form of the Latin name Benedict, meaning "blessed." HEBREW EQUIVALENTS: Ashera, Beracha, Berucha, Beruchiya. MASCULINE HEBREW EQUIVALENTS: Asher, Baruch, Berachya, Berechya.

Benette A feminine form of Ben and Benjamin. *See* Ben *and* Benjamin (*masculine section*).

Benjamina (בִּנְיָמִינָה) A feminine form of Benjamin. *See* Benjamin (*masculine section*). The exact Hebrew equivalent is Binyamina.

Beracha (בְּרָכָה) A variant form of Bracha. *See* Bracha.

Berenice From the Greek, meaning "bringer of victory." HEBREW EQUIVALENTS: Dafna, Dafnit, Hadasa, Nitzcha, Nitzchiya. MASCULINE HEBREW EQUIVALENTS: Gavriel, Gibor, Gover, Netziach, Yatzliach.

Bernadette From the French and German, meaning "bold as a bear." HEBREW EQUIVALENTS: Dova, Doveva, Dovit, Duba. MASCULINE HEBREW EQUIVALENTS: Dov, Dubi, Kalev, No'az.

Bernadina A pet form of Bernadette. *See* Bernadette.

Bernadine A pet form of Bernadette. *See* Bernadette.

Bernette A variant form of Bernadette. *See* Bernadette.

Bernice A variant form of Berenice. *See* Berenice.

Bernine A pet form of Bernice and Bernadette. *See* Bernice *and* Bernadette.

Bernita A pet form of Berenice. *See* Berenice.

Berta A variant spelling of Bertha. *See* Bertha.

Bertha From the Anglo-Saxon, meaning "bright, beautiful, famous." HEBREW EQUIVALENTS: Behira, Hillela, Me'ira, Na'ama, Zahara, Zaka. MASCULINE HEBREW EQUIVALENTS: Avino'am, Avner, Bahir, Hillel, Me'ir, Na'aman, Ra'anan, Shevach.

Berucha (בְּרוּכָה) From the Hebrew, meaning "blessed." The exact Hebrew equivalent is Berucha. The exact masculine Hebrew equivalent is Baruch.

Beruchiya (בְּרוּכִיָה) A variant form of Beruchya. *See* Beruchya.

Beruchya (בְּרוּכִיָה) From the Hebrew, meaning "blessed of the Lord." The exact Hebrew equivalent is Beruchya. MASCULINE HEBREW EQUIVALENTS: Baruch, Berachya, Mevorach.

Berura (בְּרוּרָה) From the Hebrew, meaning "pure, clean." The exact Hebrew equivalent is Berura. The exact masculine Hebrew equivalent is Barur.

Berurit (בְּרוּרִית) A variant form of Berura. *See* Berura. The exact Hebrew equivalent is Berurit.

Beruriya (בְּרוּרִיָה) A variant form of Berura. *See* Berura. The exact Hebrew equivalent is Beruriya.

Berurya (בְּרוּרִיָה) A variant form of Berura. *See* Berura. The exact Hebrew equivalent is Berurya.

Beryl From the Greek and the Sanskrit, meaning "precious stone." Also, from the Persian and Arabic, meaning "crystal clear." HEBREW EQUIVA-

LENTS: Ada, Bahat, Berura, Margalit, Tarshisha, Yakira. MASCULINE HEBREW EQUIVALENTS: Leshem, Nofach, Sapir, Shoham, Yahalom.

Bess A popular pet form of Elizabeth. *See* Elizabeth.

Bessie A pet form of Elizabeth. *See* Elizabeth.

Bet (בַּת) From the Hebrew, meaning "daughter." A variant form of Beth. The exact Hebrew equivalent is Bat. The exact masculine Hebrew equivalent is Ben.

Beth (בַּת) A short form of Elizabeth. *See* Elizabeth. Also, a variant spelling of Bet. *See* Bet.

Bethuel (בְּתוּאֵל) The Anglicized form of Betuel. A masculine name in the Bible. The exact Hebrew equivalent is Betuel.

Betsey, Betsy Pet forms of Elizabeth. *See* Elizabeth.

Bette A pet form of Elizabeth. *See* Elizabeth.

Bettina A pet form of Elizabeth. *See* Elizabeth.

Betty, Bettye Pet forms of Elizabeth. *See* Elizabeth.

Betuel (בְּתוּאֵל) From the Hebrew, meaning "daughter of God." The exact feminine and masculine Hebrew equivalent is Betuel.

Betula, Betulah (בְּתוּלָה) From the Hebrew, meaning "maiden girl." The exact Hebrew equivalent is Betula. MASCULINE HEBREW EQUIVALENTS: Bachur, Ben, Ben-Gover, Ben-Tziyon, Na'arai.

Beula, Beulah (בְּעוּלָה) From the Hebrew, meaning "married" or "possessed." The exact Hebrew equivalent is Be'ula. MASCULINE HEBREW EQUIVALENTS: Avimelech, Ba'al, Rav, Raba, Zimri.

Beverlee A variant spelling of Beverly. *See* Beverly.

Beverley, Beverly From the Old English, meaning "beaver's meadow." HEBREW EQUIVALENTS: Gana, Carmela, Nava, Nirel. MASCULINE HEBREW EQUIVALENTS: Carmel, Carmeli, Ya'ari, Zimri.

Bilha, Bilhah (בִּלְהָה) From the Hebrew, meaning "old, weak, troubled." The exact Hebrew equivalent is Bilha. MASCULINE HEBREW EQUIVALENTS: Iyov, Kedma, Yiftach, Zaken.

Billie A feminine pet form of William. *See* William (*masculine section*). Also, a pet form of Wilhelmina. *See* Wilhelmina.

Bina (בִּינָה) From the Hebrew, meaning "understanding, intelligence, wisdom." The exact feminine and masculine Hebrew equivalent is Bina.

Binyamina (בִּנְיָמִינָה) A feminine form of Binyamin (Benjamin). *See* Binyamin (*masculine section*). The exact Hebrew equivalent is Binyamina.

Bira (בִּירָה) From the Hebrew, meaning "fortified city" or "capital." The exact Hebrew equivalent is Bira. MASCULINE HEBREW EQUIVALENTS: Armon, Armoni.

Biranit (בִּירָנִית) A variant Hebrew form of Bira. *See* Bira. The exact Hebrew equivalent is Biranit.

Bird, Birdie From the English, meaning "bird." HEBREW EQUIVALENTS: A'ya, Efrona, Gozala, Senunit, Tziparta, Tzipora. MASCULINE HEBREW EQUIVALENTS: Efron, Gozal, Orev, Tzipor.

Blair, Blaire From the Gaelic, meaning "field" or "battle." HEBREW EQUIVALENTS: Churshit, Nira, Nirit, Odera. MASCULINE HEBREW EQUIVALENTS: Nir, Niram, Nirel, Niriel, Yamir.

Blanca The Spanish form of the Old French *blanc,* meaning "white, fair," or from the Latin, meaning "pure." HEBREW EQUIVALENTS: Levana, Na'omi, Yafa, Zaka, Zahara. MASCULINE HEBREW EQUIVALENTS: Lavan, Livni, Zakai.

Blanch, Blanche Variant forms of Blanca. *See* Blanca.

Blima (בְּלִימָא) A variant form of Bluma. *See* Bluma.

Blossom From the Old English, meaning "blooming flower." HEBREW EQUIVALENTS: Nirit, Nitza, Ofrit, Perach, Pirchiya, Pirchit, Shoshana. MASCULINE HEBREW EQUIVALENTS: Efra'yim, Nitzan, Perach, Perachya, Pura, Shoshan.

Bluma (בְּלוּמָא) From the German and Yiddish, meaning "flower." *See* Blossom *for equivalents.*

Blume (בְּלוּמֶע) A variant form of Bluma. *See* Bluma.

Blythe From the Anglo-Saxon, meaning "happy." HEBREW EQUIVALENTS: Aliza, Aviga'yil, Gila, Rina. MASCULINE HEBREW EQUIVALENTS: Bilgai, Gilon, Ron, Simcha.

Bobbe A pet form of Babette, Barbara, and Roberta. *See* Barbara *and* Roberta.

Bona (בּוֹנָה) From the Hebrew, meaning "builder." The exact Hebrew equivalent is Bona. MASCULINE HEBREW EQUIVALENTS: Bena'ya, Bena'yahu, Yavniel.

Bonita A Spanish form of Bonnie. *See* Bonnie.

Bonnie, Bonny From the Latin and the French, meaning "good" or "pretty." HEBREW EQUIVALENTS: Na'ama, Na'omi, Nofiya, Tova, Yafa, Yatva. MASCULINE HEBREW EQUIVALENTS: Achituv, Ben-Tziyon, Na'aman, Shefer, Tuviya.

Bracha (בְּרָכָה) From the Hebrew, meaning "blessing." The exact Hebrew equivalent is Bracha. The exact masculine Hebrew equivalent is Baruch. Beracha is a variant spelling.

Bree A pet form of Gabriela. *See* Gabriela.

Breindel (בְּרֵיינדֶל) A pet form of the Yiddish name Bruna. *See* Bruna.

Brenda From the Celtic, meaning "dark-haired." HEBREW EQUIVALENTS: Chachila, Efa, Dala, Delila, Tzila. MASCULINE HEBREW EQUIVALENTS: Adar, Efai, Kedar, Kush, Pinchas.

Brian More popular as a masculine name. *See* Brian (*masculine section*).

Bridget From the Celtic, meaning "strong" or "lofty." HEBREW EQUIVALENTS: Abira, Adira, Amitza, Gavriela, Gavrila, Gibora, Uzit. MASCULINE HEBREW EQUIVALENTS: Abir, Abiri, Barzilai, Ben-Cha'yil, Binyamin, Gavriel, Gever, Gibor, Uziya.

Bridgit, Bridgitte Variant forms of Bridget. *See* Bridget.

Brigit, Brigitte Variant spellings of Bridget. *See* Bridget.

Brina, Brine (בְּרִינֶע/בְּרַיינָא) Variant forms of Bruna and Brune. *See* Bruna *and* Brune.

Brit, Brita Pet forms of Bridget. *See* Bridget.

Brook, Brooke From the Old English and Middle English, meaning "to break out," referring to a stream of water. HEBREW EQUIVALENTS: Arnona, Nadyan. MASCULINE HEBREW EQUIVALENTS: Arnon, Peretz.

Bruna, Brune (בְּרוּנֶע/בְּרוּנָא) Yiddish forms, from the German, meaning "brunette" or "brown." HEBREW EQUIVALENTS: Chuma, Chumit. MASCU-LINE HEBREW EQUIVALENTS: Chum, Chumi.

Bryna A variant form of Bruna. *See* Bruna.

Buba (בֻּבָּה) From the Hebrew, meaning "doll." The exact Hebrew equivalent is Buba.

Bubati (בֻּבָּתִי) From the Hebrew, meaning "my doll." The exact Hebrew equivalent is Bubati.

Buna (בּוּנָה) From the Hebrew, meaning "understanding, intelligence." The exact feminine and masculine Hebrew equivalent is Buna.

Buni, Bunie A variant form of Buna. *See* Buna. The exact Hebrew equivalent is Buni.

Bunny A nickname for Barbara and Roberta. *See* Barbara *and* Roberta.

Byrd A variant spelling of Bird. *See* Bird.

Byrdie A variant spelling of Birdie. *See* Birdie.

Caasi A pet form of Catherine. *See* Catherine.

Camilla, Camille From the Latin, meaning "servant, helper" or "virgin of unblemished character." HEBREW EQUIVALENTS: Aleksandra, Ezra, Ezr'ela, Ezriela, Sa'ada, Zaka. MASCULINE HEBREW EQUIVALENTS: Eved, Oved, Ovadyahu, Sa'adya, Zakai.

Candace From the Greek, meaning "fire-white, incandescent." Also, from the Latin, meaning "pure, unsullied." HEBREW EQUIVALENTS: Avuka, Levana, Ora, Shalva, Udiya, Urit, Zaka, Zakit. MASCULINE HEBREW EQUIVALENTS: Ami-Chai, Barur, Lavan, Nuri, Tzach, Tzachai, Ud, Uri, Zakai.

Candance A variant form of Candace. *See* Candace.

Candice A variant spelling of Candace. *See* Candace.

Candida, Candide Variant forms of Candace. *See* Candace.

Candy A pet form of Candace. *See* Candace.

Candyce A variant spelling of Candace. *See* Candace.

Cara A pet form of Caroline and Charlotte. *See* Caroline *and* Charlotte.

Caren A pet form of Catherine. *See* Catherine.

Caressa From the Latin, meaning "caring, loving." HEBREW EQUIVALENTS: Ahuva, Chiba, Davida, Latifa. MASCULINE HEBREW EQUIVALENTS: Ahuv, Bildad, David, Latif, Yedidya.

Carla, Carlana Feminine forms of Carl or Charles. Also, pet forms of Caroline. *See* Caroline.

Carlena A pet form of Caroline. *See* Caroline.

Carley A pet form of Caroline. *See* Caroline.

Carlina A pet form of Caroline. *See* Caroline.

Carlita An Italian pet form of Caroline. *See* Caroline.

Carly A variant spelling of Carley. *See* Carley.

Carma A variant form of Carmel. *See* Carmel.

Carmela (כַּרְמֶלָה) From the Hebrew, meaning "garden, orchard." The exact Hebrew equivalent is Carmela. The exact masculine Hebrew equivalent is Carmel.

Carmelit (כַּרְמְלִית) A variant form of Carmela. *See* Carmela. The exact Hebrew equivalent is Carmelit.

Carmen The Spanish form of Carmel. *See* Carmel.

Carmia A variant spelling of Carmiya. *See* Carmiya.

Carmiela (כַּרְמִיאֶלָה) A variant form of Carmiya. *See* Carmiya. The exact Hebrew equivalent is Carmiela.

Carmit (כַּרְמִית) A variant Hebrew form of Carmiya. *See* Carmiya. The exact Hebrew equivalent is Carmit.

Carmiya (כַּרְמִיָה) From the Hebrew, meaning "vineyard of the Lord." The exact Hebrew equivalent is Carmiya. MASCULINE HEBREW EQUIVALENTS: Carmi, Carmiel.

Carna (קַרְנָה) From the Aramaic, meaning "horn," symbolizing strength. The exact Hebrew equivalent is Carna. The exact masculine Hebrew equivalent is Keren.

Carni (קַרְנִי) A variant form of Carna. *See* Carna. The exact Hebrew equivalent is Carni.

Carnia A variant form of Carniya. *See* Carniya.

Carniela, Carniella (קַרְנִיאֶלָה) Variant forms of Carniya. *See* Carniya. The exact Hebrew equivalent is Carniela.

Carniya (קַרְנִיָה) From the Hebrew, meaning "horn of God." A variant form of Carna. *See* Carna. The exact Hebrew equivalent is Carniya. The exact masculine Hebrew equivalent is Carniel.

Carol From the Gaelic, meaning "melody, song." Also, a pet form of Caroline. *See* Caroline. HEBREW EQUIVALENTS: Lirona, Rani, Ranit, Rina, Shira, Tehila, Yarona. MASCULINE HEBREW EQUIVALENTS: Aharon, Amiran, Eliran, Liron, Ronen, Ronli, Shiri.

Caroline From the French, meaning "strong, virile." HEBREW EQUIVALENTS: Abira, Amtza, Aziela, Avicha'yil, Chasina, Gavriela, Gibora, Uziela. MASCULINE HEBREW EQUIVALENTS: Amitz, Cha'yil, Gavriel, Gibor, Gur, Uzi, Uziel, Yo'az.

Carolyn A variant spelling of Caroline. *See* Caroline.

Caron A variant spelling of Caren. *See* Caren.

Carren A variant spelling of Caren. *See* Caren.

Carrie A pet form of Caroline. *See* Caroline.

Carroll A variant spelling of Carol. *See* Carol.

Carry, Cary Pet forms of Caroline. *See* Caroline.

Caryl A variant spelling of Carol. *See* Carol.

Catherine From the Greek, meaning "pure, unsullied." HEBREW EQUIVA-
LENTS: Berura, Beruriya, Tehora, Zaka, Zakit, Zakiya. MASCULINE
HEBREW EQUIVALENTS: Amizakai, Barur, Tzach, Zakai.

Cathleen A variant form of Catherine. *See* Catherine.

Cathryn A variant spelling of Catherine. *See* Catherine.

Cathy A pet form of Catherine and Cathleen. *See* Catherine *and* Cathleen.

Cecelia From the Latin, meaning "blind" or "dim-sighted." EUPHEMISTIC
HEBREW EQUIVALENTS: Behira, Me'ira, Noga, Ora, Zahara. EUPHEMISTIC
MASCULINE HEBREW EQUIVALENTS: Bahir, Koresh, Me'ir, Shimshon, Uriel,
Zerach, Zerachya.

Cecil A variant form of Cecelia. *See* Cecelia.

Cecile, Cecille Variant spellings of Cecil. *See* Cecil.

Cecily A variant form of Cecilia. *See* Cecilia.

Ceil A pet form of Cecelia. *See* Cecelia.

Cele A variant spelling of Ceil. *See* Ceil.

Celeste From the Latin, meaning "heavenly." HEBREW EQUIVALENTS:
Ester, Kochava, Kochavit, Kochevet, Levana, Mazala. MASCULINE
HEBREW EQUIVALENTS: Bar-Kochva, Kochav, Mazal, Shimshon.

Celia A variant form of Cecilia. *See* Cecilia.

Cerena A variant spelling of Serena. *See* Serena.

Chagit (חָגִית) From the Aramaic, meaning "feast, festival, festive celebration." The exact Hebrew equivalent is Chagit. MASCULINE HEBREW
EQUIVALENTS: Chag, Chagai, Chagi, Chagiga.

Chagiya (חַגִיָה) From the Hebrew, meaning "God's festival." The exact
Hebrew equivalent is Chagiya. MASCULINE HEBREW EQUIVALENTS: Chagai,
Chagi, Chagiga.

Chamuda (חֲמוּדָה) From the Hebrew, meaning "desired one." The exact
Hebrew equivalent is Chamuda. The exact masculine Hebrew equivalent is Chamud.

Chana, Chanah (חַנָה) From the Hebrew, meaning "grace, gracious, mer-
ciful." Hannah is the Anglicized form. The exact Hebrew equivalent is
Chana. MASCULINE HEBREW EQUIVALENTS: Chanan, Chananel, Chanun,
Elchanan, Yochanan.

Charity From the Latin, meaning "love, affection." HEBREW EQUIVALENTS:
Ahuva, Chaviva, Davida, Tzedaka, Yedida. MASCULINE HEBREW EQUIVA-
LENTS: Bildad, Chovav, David, Tzadik, Tzadok, Yedidya.

Charlayne A variant form of Charlene. *See* Charlene.

Charleen A variant spelling of Charlene. *See* Charlene.

Charlene A variant form of Caroline, meaning "strong, valiant." HEBREW EQUIVALENTS: Aza, Aziza, Gavrila, Gibora, Uzit. MASCULINE HEBREW EQUIVALENTS: Az, Gavriel, Gevaram, Gever, Gevarya, Gibor, Uzi, Uziel.

Charlet A variant form of Charlotte. See Charlotte.

Charlot A variant spelling of Charlotte. See Charlotte.

Charlotta The Italian form of Charlotte. See Charlotte.

Charlotte The feminine of Charles, meaning "strong." HEBREW EQUIVALENTS: Azriela, Chasina, Gavriela, Uziela, Uzit. MASCULINE HEBREW EQUIVALENTS: Ben-Cha'yil, Ben-Guryon, Chaltzon, Chasin, Cheletz, Gavriel, Gur.

Chasida, Chasidah (חֲסִידָה) From the Hebrew, meaning "stork" or "righteous." The exact Hebrew equivalent is Chasida. The exact Hebrew equivalent is Chasid.

Chasina (חֲסִינָה) From the Aramaic, meaning "strong, powerful." The exact Hebrew equivalent is Chasina. The exact masculine Hebrew equivalent is Chasin.

Chasna (חַסְנָה/חַסְנָא) From the Aramaic, meaning "strong, powerful." The exact Hebrew equivalent is Chasna. MASCULINE HEBREW EQUIVALENTS: Chasin, Chason, Cheletz, Chizki, Chosen.

Chasya (חַסְיָה) From the Hebrew, meaning "protected by God." The exact Hebrew equivalent is Chasya. MASCULINE HEBREW EQUIVALENTS: Chaltzon, Chasin, Chason, Cha'yil.

Chava (חַוָה) From the Hebrew, meaning "life." The exact Hebrew equivalent is Chava. The masculine Hebrew equivalent is Cha'yim.

Chaviva (חֲבִיבָה) From the Hebrew, meaning "beloved." The exact Hebrew equivalent is Chaviva. The exact masculine Hebrew equivalent is Chaviv.

Chaya (חַיָה) From the Hebrew, meaning "alive, living." The exact Hebrew equivalent is Cha'ya. The exact masculine Hebrew equivalent is Cha'yim.

Cheftzi-Ba From the Hebrew, meaning "she is my desire." The exact Hebrew equivalent is Cheftzi-Ba. MASCULINE HEBREW EQUIVALENTS: Chamadel, Chamud, Chefetz, Chemdan, Chemed.

Chemda (חֶמְדָה) From the Hebrew, meaning "desirable, charming." The exact Hebrew equivalent is Chemda. MASCULINE HEBREW EQUIVALENTS: Chamdel, Chamadya, Chamud.

Cher, Chere Pet forms of Cheryl. See Cheryl.

Cheri, Cherie French pet forms of Cheryl. See Cheryl.

Cherlene A variant form of Charlene. See Charlene.

Cherri, Cherrie Pet forms of Cheryl. See Cheryl.

Cheryl, Cheryle From the French, meaning "dear, beloved." HEBREW EQUIVALENTS: Ahuva, Chaviva, Chiba, Davida, Yedida. MASCULINE HEBREW EQUIVALENTS: Ahuv, Bildad, Chovav, David, Eldad, Yedidya.

Chesna From the Slavic, meaning "peaceful." HEBREW EQUIVALENTS:

Meshulemet, Shlomit, Shulamit. MASCULINE HEBREW EQUIVALENTS: Ish-Shalom, Shabtai, Shalom, Shlomo.

Chita (חִיטָה/חִיטָא) From the Aramaic and Hebrew, meaning "grain, wheat." The exact Hebrew equivalent is Chita. MASCULINE HEBREW EQUIVALENTS: Dagan, Goren.

Chloe From the Greek, meaning "blooming, verdant." HEBREW EQUIVALENTS: Pora, Porachat, Poriya, Yarkona. MASCULINE HEBREW EQUIVALENTS: Ben-Ilan, Efra'yim, Pura, Yarkon.

Chloris A variant form of Chloe. *See* Chloe.

Christa A pet form of Christina. *See* Christina.

Christina A feminine form of the name Christian, from the Greek, meaning "annointed."

Chrystal Variant spellings of Crystal. *See* Crystal.

Cicely A variant from of Cecilia. *See* Ceceilia.

Cicily A variant form of Cecilia.

Cindy A pet form of Cynthia. *See* Cynthia.

Cipora A variant spelling of Tzipora. *See* Tzipora.

Ciporit A variant spelling of Tziporit. *See* Tziporit.

Cis, Ciss, Cissy Pet forms of Cecilia. *See* Cecilia.

Civia A variant spelling of Tzivya. *See* Tzivya.

Claire A French form of Clara. *See* Clara.

Clara From the Latin, meaning "clear, bright." HEBREW EQUIVALENTS: Behira, Me'ira, Noga, Ora, Zahara, Zaka. MASCULINE HEBREW EQUIVALENTS: Bahir, Barak, Koresh, Me'ir, Neriya, Shimshon, Uri, Zerachya.

Clarabella, Clarabelle Names compounded of the Latin, meaning "bright" and "beautiful." HEBREW EQUIVALENTS: Behira, Keshet, Me'ira, Ne'ora, Noga, Ora, Zakit, Zakiya. MASCULINE HEBREW EQUIVALENTS: Avner, Bahir, Barak, Na'aman, Zerach, Ziv, Zivi.

Clare A variant spelling of Claire. *See* Claire.

Clarette A variant form of Clara. *See* Clara.

Clarissa, Clarisse Italian forms of Clara. *See* Clara.

Claudette A French pet form of Claudia. *See* Claudia.

Claudia From the Latin, meaning "lame." EUPHEMISTIC HEBREW EQUIVALENTS: A'yelet, Mehira, Ofra, Tzivya. EUPHEMISTIC MASCULINE HEBREW EQUIVALENTS: Bo'az, Efer, Gidon, Maher, Mahir, Tzevi.

Claudine A French pet form of Claudia. *See* Claudia.

Clementine A French form of the Latin, meaning "merciful." HEBREW EQUIVALENTS: Chana, Chanina, Chanuna, Ruchama. MASCULINE HEBREW EQUIVALENTS: Ben-Chesed, Chanun, Rachmiel, Yerachmiel, Yerucham.

Clio From the Greek, meaning "to celebrate, glorify." HEBREW EQUIVALENTS: Adra, Chagiga, Hadara, Tifara, Tiferet, Yocheved. MASCULINE HEBREW EQUIVALENTS: Amihod, Chag, Hadar, Hod, Hodiya, Pe'er.

Cloe   A variant spelling of Chloe. *See* Chloe.

Colette   From the Latin, meaning "victorious." HEBREW EQUIVALENTS: Gavriela, Gibora, Nitzcha, Nitzchiya, Nitzchona. MASCULINE HEBREW EQUIVALENTS: Gevarya, Gevaryahu, Gover, Netzach.

Colleen   From the Irish, meaning "girl." HEBREW EQUIVALENTS: Bat, Bat-Sheva, Betula, Na'ara. MASCULINE HEBREW EQUIVALENTS: Bachur, Ben, Ben-Guryon, Ben-Tziyon, Na'arya.

Collette   A variant spelling of Colette. *See* Colette.

Connie   A pet form of Constance. *See* Constance.

Constance   From the Latin, meaning "constant, firm, faithful." HEBREW EQUIVALENTS: Bitcha, Emuna, Tama, Temima, Tikva. MASCULINE HEBREW EQUIVALENTS: Amitai, Amnon, Heman, Konanyahu, Nachon, Tikva.

Cora   From the Greek, meaning "maiden." HEBREW EQUIVALENTS: Alma, Aluma, Betula, Na'ara, Tze'ira. MASCULINE HEBREW EQUIVALENTS: Bachur, Na'arai, Na'arya.

Coral (גּוֹרְלָה)   From the Hebrew and Greek, meaning "small stone, pebble." The exact Hebrew equivalent is Gorala. The exact masculine Hebrew equivalent is Goral.

Coralee   A variant form of Coral. *See* Coral.

Coralie   A variant form of Coral. *See* Coral.

Coreen   A pet form of Cora. *See* Cora.

Coretta   A pet form of Cora. *See* Cora.

Corette   A variant form of Coretta. *See* Coretta.

Corey   From the Gaelic, meaning "ravine, enclosed place." HEBREW EQUIVALENTS: Afeka, Bik'a, Berecha, Efrat, Ganya. MASCULINE HEBREW EQUIVALENTS: Betzer, Bitzaron, Gai, Gaychazi, Gidron, Lotan.

Cori, Corie   Variant spellings of Corey. *See* Corey.

Corinna, Corinne   From the Greek, meaning "hummingbird." Also, French forms of Cora. *See* Cora.

Corita   A pet form of Cora. *See* Cora.

Corna   A pet form of Cornelia. *See* Cornelia.

Cornelia   From the Greek, meaning "cornell tree," or from the Latin, meaning "horn of the sun," symbol of royalty. HEBREW EQUIVALENTS: Ilana, Malka, Malkiela, Malkit, Molechet. MASCULINE HEBREW EQUIVALENTS: Avimelech, Elimelech, Ilan, Malkiel, Melech.

Correy   A variant spelling of Corey. *See* Corey.

Corri, Corrie   Variant spellings of Corey. *See* Corey.

Cory, Corry   Variant spellings of Corey. *See* Corey.

Courteny, Courtney   Variant forms of Corey. *See* Corey.

Crystal   From the Greek, meaning "clear glass." HEBREW EQUIVALENTS: Behira, Me'ira, Noga, Ora, Zaka, Zivit. MASCULINE HEBREW EQUIVALENTS: Bahir, Bazak, Me'iri, Noga, Zerachya.

Cybil, Cybill From the Latin, meaning "soothsayer." HEBREW EQUIVA-LENTS: Amira, Doveva, Dovevet, Niva. MASCULINE HEBREW EQUIVALENTS: Amir, Anan, Anani, Ananya, Divri, Imri, Yaniv.

Cyma From the Greek and Latin, meaning "to sprout, grow, flourish." HEBREW EQUIVALENTS: Carmel, Nitza, Shoshana, Varda. MASCULINE HEBREW EQUIVALENTS: Efra'yim, Pekach, Perachya, Tzemach.

Cyndi A pet form of Cynthia. See Cynthia.

Cynthia From the Greek, meaning "from the cynthus." In Greek, mythology, a mountain on which Artemis, goddess of the moon, was born. Hence, Cynthia came to mean "the moon personified." HEBREW EQUIVA-LENTS: Chodesh, Levana, Me'ira, Ora, Zaka. MASCULINE HEBREW EQUIVA-LENTS: Me'ir, Neriya, Sheraga, Yerach, Zerachya.

Dafna A variant spelling of Daphna. See Daphna.

Dafne A variant spelling of Daphne. See Daphne.

Dafnit (דָּפְנִית) The Hebrew form of the Greek Daphne. See Daphne. The exact Hebrew equivalent is Dafnit.

Deganya A variant spelling of Deganya. See Deganya.

Dahlia A variant spelling of Dalya. See Dalya.

Daisy Usually taken as a nickname for Margaret. See Margaret.

Dalia A variant spelling of Daliya and Dalya. See Dalya and Daliya.

Dalgia A variant spelling of Dalgiya. See Dalgiya.

Dalgiya (דַּלְגִיָּה) From the Hebrew, meaning "rope." The exact Hebrew equivalent is Dalgiya. The masculine Hebrew equivalent is Petil.

Dalit (דָּלִית) From the Hebrew, meaning "to draw water" or "bough, branch." The exact Hebrew equivalent is Dalit. MASCULINE HEBREW EQUIVALENTS: Avi'yam, Beri, Chamat, Dela'ya, Silon.

Daliya (דַּלִיָה) A variant form of Dalya. See Dalya. The exact Hebrew equivalent is Daliya.

Dalya (דַּלְיָה) From the Hebrew, meaning "branch, bough" or "to draw water." The exact Hebrew equivalent is Dalya. The exact masculine Hebrew equivalent is Dela'ya.

Dama From the Latin, meaning "lady." HEBREW EQUIVALENTS: Adiva, Gevira, Sara. MASCULINE HEBREW EQUIVALENTS: Adoniya, Adoniram, Yisrael.

Dame A variant form of Dama. See Dama.

Damita A Spanish form of Dama. See Dama.

Dana (דָּנָה) From the Latin, meaning "bright, pure as day." Also, from the Hebrew, meaning "to judge." The exact Hebrew equivalent is Dana. The exact masculine Hebrew equivalent is Dan.

Danette A pet form of Dana. See Dana.

Dania, Daniah Variant spellings of Danya. See Danya.

Daniela, Daniella (דְנִיאֵלָה) Feminine forms of the masculine Daniel, meaning "God is my judge." The exact Hebrew equivalent is Daniela. The exact masculine Hebrew equivalent is Daniel.

Daniele, Danielle Variant spellings of Daniela. *See* Daniela.

Danit (דָנִית) A variant form of Daniela. *See* Daniela. The exact Hebrew equivalent is Danit.

Danita (דָנִיתָה) A variant form of Daniela. *See* Daniela. The exact Hebrew equivalent is Danita.

Danna A variant spelling of Dana. *See* Dana.

Danya (דַנְיָה) A feminine form of Dan, meaning "judgment of the Lord." The exact Hebrew equivalent is Danya. MASCULINE HEBREW EQUIVALENTS: Dan, Daniel.

Daphna, Daphne (דַפְנָה) From the Greek, meaning "laurel" or "bay-tree," symbols of victory. The exact Hebrew equivalent is Dafna. MASCULINE HEBREW EQUIVALENTS: Gover, Netziach, Yatzliach.

Daphnit A variant spelling of Dafnit. *See* Dafnit.

Dapna A variant form of Daphne. *See* Daphne.

Darcie From the Celtic, meaning "dark." HEBREW EQUIVALENTS: Chachila, Efa, Laila, Tzila. MASCULINE HEBREW EQUIVALENTS: Adar, Ashchur, Efai, Chachalya, Pinchas.

Daria The feminine form of the Persian name Darius, meaning "wealth." *See* Darius (*masculine section*).

Darla From the Middle English, meaning "dear, loved one." HEBREW EQUIVALENTS: Ahada, Ahava, Ahuva, Chiba, Davida, Yedida. MASCULINE HEBREW EQUIVALENTS: Ahud, Ahuv, Bildad, Chovav, David, Dodai, Yedidya.

Daroma (דָרוֹמָה) From the Hebrew, meaning "south, southward." The exact Hebrew equivalent is Daroma. The exact masculine Hebrew equivalent is Darom.

Darona (דָרוֹנָה) A Hebrew form of the Greek, meaning "gift." The exact Hebrew equivalent is Darona. Akin to Dorona. The exact masculine Hebrew equivalent is Daron.

Daryl From the Old English, meaning "dear, beloved." Used also as a masculine name. HEBREW EQUIVALENTS: Ahuva, Chaviva, Davida, Dodi. MASCULINE HEBREW EQUIVALENTS: Ahuv, Chaviv, David, Dodo, Yakar, Yakir.

Dasi, Dassi (דָסִי) Pet forms of Hadassah. *See* Hadassah. The exact Hebrew equivalent is Dasi.

Dati (דָתִי) From the Hebrew, meaning "religious, observant." The exact Hebrew equivalent is Dati. The exact masculine Hebrew equivalent is Datan.

Datit (דָתִית) A variant form of Dati. *See* Dati. The exact Hebrew equivalent is Datit.

Datya (דָתְיָה) From the Hebrew, meaning "faith in God" or "law of the Lord." The exact Hebrew equivalent is Datya. MASCULINE HEBREW EQUIVALENTS: Datan, Datiel, Da'yan.

Davene A feminine form of David, meaning "beloved, friend." *See* David (*masculine section*).

Davida, Davide (דָוִידָה) Feminine forms of David. *See* David (*masculine section*). The exact Hebrew equivalent is Davida.

Davina A Scottish form of David used in the seventeenth century. *See* David (*masculine section*).

Davita A Spanish form of David. *See* David (*masculine section*).

Dayana (דַיָנָה) From the Hebrew, meaning "judge." The exact Hebrew equivalent is Da'yana. The exact masculine Hebrew equivalent is Da'yan.

Dawn, Dawne From the Old Norse and Old English, meaning "dawn." HEBREW EQUIVALENTS: Barakit, Bareket, Bat-Shachar, Tzafra, Tzafrira, Tzafririt. MASCULINE HEBREW EQUIVALENTS: Avi-Shachar, Tzafrir, Tzafriri, Tzofar.

Daya (דָיָה) The Hebrew name of a bird of prey. The exact Hebrew equivalent is Da'ya. MASCULINE HEBREW EQUIVALENTS: Gozal, Orev, Tzipor.

Dean, Deane Feminine forms of Dean. *See* Dean (*masculine section*).

Deanna, Deanne Variant forms of Diana or Dinah. *See* Diana *and* Dinah.

Debbe, Debbi, Debby Pet forms of Deborah. *See* Deborah.

Debi A pet form of Deborah. *See* Deborah.

Debora A variant spelling of Deborah. *See* Deborah.

Deborah The Anglicized form of Devora. *See* Devora.

Debra A variant form of Deborah. *See* Deborah.

Deena From the Anglo-Saxon, meaning "from the valley." Also a variant spelling of Dinah. *See* Dinah.

Deenie A pet form of Dinah. *See* Dinah.

Degania, Deganiah Variant spellings of Deganya. *See* Deganya.

Deganit (דְגָנִית) A variant form of Deganya. *See* Deganya. The exact Hebrew equivalent is Deganit.

Deganya (דְגָנְיָה) From the Hebrew, meaning "grain." The exact Hebrew equivalent is Deganya. The exact masculine Hebrew equivalent is Dagan.

Degula (דְגוּלָה) From the Hebrew, meaning "honored, famous." The exact Hebrew equivalent is Degula. MASCULINE HEBREW EQUIVALENTS: Ben-Tziyon, Dagul, Hillel, Mehalalel, Yehuda, Yehudi.

Deidra A variant spelling of Deidre. *See* Deidre.

Deidre From the Middle Irish, meaning "young girl." HEBREW EQUIVALENTS: Alma, Aluma, Betuel, Betula, Tze'ira. MASCULINE HEBREW EQUIVALENTS: Bachur, Na'arai, Na'ari, Na'arya.

Deirdre A variant form of Deidre. *See* Deidre.

Delila, Delilah (דְלִילָה) From the Hebrew, meaning "hair" or "poor." The exact Hebrew equivalent is Delila. MASCULINE HEBREW EQUIVALENTS: Esav, Micha, Se'orim.

Dell, Della, Delle Variant pet forms of Adela and Adeline. *See* Adela *and* Adeline.

Dena A variant spelling of Dinah. *See* Dinah.

Delta A Greek and Latin form of the Hebrew *dalet,* meaning "door." The Hebrew equivalent is Dalet. MASCULINE HEBREW EQUIVALENTS: Bava, Sha'arya.

Denice, Deniece, Deniese Variant spellings of Denise. *See* Denise.

Denise A feminine form of Denis, derived from Dionysius, the Greek god of wine and drama. *See* Denis (*masculine section*).

Denna From the Anglo-Saxon, meaning "valley." The Hebrew equivalent is Ga'ya. The masculine Hebrew equivalent is Gai.

Denyse A variant spelling of Denise. *See* Denise.

Derora, Derorah (דְּרוֹרָה) From the Hebrew, meaning "flowing stream" or "bird [swallow]" or "freedom, liberty." The exact Hebrew equivalent is Derora. The exact masculine Hebrew equivalent is Deror.

Deuela, Deuella (דְּעוּאֵלָה) From the Hebrew, meaning "knowledge of the Lord." The exact Hebrew equivalent is De'uela. The exact masculine Hebrew equivalent is De'uel.

Devir (דְּבִיר) From the Hebrew, meaning "sanctuary." The exact feminine and masculine Hebrew equivalent is Devir.

Devira (דְּבִירָה) A variant form of Devir. *See* Devir. The exact Hebrew equivalent is Devira.

Devora, Devorah (דְּבוֹרָה) From the Hebrew, meaning "swarm of bees" or "to speak kind words." The exact Hebrew equivalent is Devora. MASCULINE HEBREW EQUIVALENTS: Amarya, Chavila, Divri, Dovev, Imri, Niv.

Devorit (דְּבוֹרִית) A variant form of Devora. *See* Devora. The exact Hebrew equivalent is Devorit.

Devra A variant form of Devora. *See* Devora.

Di A pet form of Diana. *See* Diana.

Diana, Diane, Dianne From the Latin, meaning "bright, pure as a day." HEBREW EQUIVALENTS: Behira, Me'ira, Noga, Zaka. MASCULINE HEBREW EQUIVALENTS: Aharon, Bahir, Me'ir, Neri, Neriya, Shimshon.

Diedre A variant spelling of Deidre. *See* Deidre.

Digla (דִּגְלָה) From the Hebrew, meaning "flag." The exact Hebrew equivalent is Digla. MASCULINE HEBREW EQUIVALENTS: Dagul, Diglai.

Diglat (דִּגְלַת) A variant form of Digla. *See* Digla. The exact Hebrew equivalent is Diglat.

Dikla, Diklah (דִּקְלָה) The Aramaic form of the Hebrew, meaning "palm [date] tree." The exact Hebrew equivalent is Dikla. The exact masculine Hebrew equivalent is Dekel.

Diklit (דִּקְלִית) A variant form of Dikla. *See* Dikla. The exact Hebrew equivalent is Diklit.

Dina, Dinah (דִּינָה) From the Hebrew, meaning "judgment." The exact Hebrew equivalent is Dina. The exact masculine Hebrew equivalent is Dan.

Disa, Dissa (דִּיתָה)   Pet Yiddish forms of Yehudit (Judith). *See* Yehudit.

Ditza, Ditzah (דִּיצָה)   From the Hebrew, meaning "joy." The exact Hebrew equivalent is Ditza. The exact masculine Hebrew equivalent is Ditz.

Diza, Dizah   Variant spellings of Ditza. *See* Ditza.

Dobe   A pet form of Devora. *See* Devora.

Dobra, Dobrah (רָאבְּרָא)   Variant Yiddish forms of Deborah. *See* Deborah. Also from the Slavic, meaning "good." The exact Hebrew equivalent is Tova.

Doda, Dodah (דּוֹדָה)   From the Hebrew, meaning "friend, beloved" or "aunt." The exact Hebrew equivalent is Doda. The exact masculine Hebrew equivalent is Dod.

Dodi, Dodie (דּוֹדִי)   From the Hebrew, meaning "my friend, my beloved." The exact feminine and masculine Hebrew equivalent is Dodi.

Dodo (דּוֹדוֹ)   A pet form of Dorothy. *See* Dorothy. Also, a variant form of Doda. *See* Doda.

Dody   A variant spelling of Dodi. *See* Dodi.

Doe   From the Old English, meaning "female deer." The exact Hebrew equivalent is Tzivya. The exact masculine Hebrew equivalent is Tzevi.

Dolley   A variant spelling of Dolly. *See* Dolly.

Dollie   A variant spelling of Dolly. *See* Dolly.

Dolly   A variant form of Dorothy. *See* Dorothy.

Dolores   A Christian name, from the Latin, meaning "lady of sorrows."

Dona   A variant spelling of Donna. *See* Donna.

Donna   From the Latin and Italian, meaning "lady of nobility." HEBREW EQUIVALENTS: Adina, Adoniya, Matrona, Nagida, Ne'edara, Ne'edert. MASCULINE HEBREW EQUIVALENTS: Achinadav, Adon, Aminadav, Nadiv, Yehonadav.

Dora   A diminutive form of Dorothy. *See* Dorothy.

Doraleen, Doralene   Pet forms of Dora. *See* Dora.

Dore   A German form of Dorothea. *See* Dorothea.

Dorea   A variant form of Doris. *See* Doris.

Doreen   A pet form of Dorothy and its diminutive Dora. *See* Dorothy.

Doreet   A variant spelling of Dorit. *See* Dorit.

Dorene   A variant spelling of Doreen. *See* Doreen.

Doretha   A variant form of Dorothy. *See* Dorothy.

Doretta, Dorette   A French form of Dorothy. *See* Dorothy.

Dorina   A pet form of Dora. *See* Dora.

Doris   From the Greek, meaning "sacrificial knife." In Greek mythology, the mother of sea gods. HEBREW EQUIVALENTS: Afeka, Bat-Yam, Miryam, Reviva, Yaval. MASCULINE HEBREW EQUIVALENTS: Avi'yam, Beri, Chamat, Dalfon, Dela'ya, Raviv.

Dorit (דּוֹרִית)   From the Greek, meaning "to heap, to pile" or "dwelling place." Also, from the Hebrew, meaning "generation." The exact Hebrew equivalent is Dorit. The exact masculine Hebrew equivalent is Dor.

Dorona (דּוֹרוֹנָה) From the Greek, meaning "gift." The exact Hebrew equivalent is Dorona. The exact masculine Hebrew equivalent is Doron.

Doronit (דּוֹרוֹנִית) A variant form of Dorona. See Dorona. The exact Hebrew equivalent is Doronit.

Dorothea A variant form of Dorothy. See Dorothy.

Dorothy From the Greek, meaning "gift of God." HEBREW EQUIVALENTS: Doronit, Matana, Matat, Migdana, Mincha, Netanel, Netanya, Teruma, Zevuda. MASCULINE HEBREW EQUIVALENTS: Avishai, Doron, Doroni, Elinatan, Elnatan, Elzavad, Zavad, Zavdi.

Dorri, Dorrie Pet forms of Dorothy. See Dorothy.

Dorris A variant spelling of Doris. See Doris.

Dorrit A variant spelling of Dorit. See Dorit.

Dot, Dottie, Dotty Pet forms of Dorothy. See Dorothy.

Dovrat (דָּבְרַת) A variant form of Devora. See Devora. The exact Hebrew equivalent is Dovrat.

Duba (דֻּבָּה) From the Hebrew, meaning "bear." The exact Hebrew equivalent is Duba. The exact masculine Hebrew equivalent is Dov.

Dulcie From the Latin, meaning "charming, sweet." HEBREW EQUIVALENTS: Achino'am, Metuka, Na'ama, Na'omi. MASCULINE HEBREW EQUIVALENTS: Avino'am, Magdiel, Matok, Meged, Na'aman.

Durene From the Latin, meaning "enduring, lasting." HEBREW EQUIVALENTS: Nitzcha, Nitzchiya, Nitzchona. MASCULINE HEBREW EQUIVALENTS: Amiad, Aviad, Cheled, Elad, Netzach, Nitzchi.

Dvora, Dvorah A variant spelling of Devora. See Devora.

Dvorit A variant spelling of Devorit. See Devorit.

Dyan A variant form of Diana. See Diana.

Dyana A variant spelling of Diana. See Diana.

Earla A feminine form of Earl. See Earl (*masculine section*).

Earlene A feminine form of Earl. See Earl (*masculine section*).

Eda, Edda From the Icelandic, meaning "poet" or "songwriter." HEBREW EQUIVALENTS: Aharona, Lirit, Ne'ima, Rina, Shira, Shiri, Shir-Li, Zimra. MASCULINE HEBREW EQUIVALENTS: Aharon, Amiran, Amishar, Ana, Liron, Yaron, Zimran.

Ede A pet form of Edith. See Edith.

Edel A variant spelling of Eidel. See Eidel.

Edia, Ediah Variant spellings of Edya. See Edya.

Edie A popular Scottish pet form of Edith. See Edith.

Edina From the Anglo-Saxon, meaning "rich friend." HEBREW EQUIVA-

LENTS: Ahuva, Ashira, Bat-Shua, Chaviva, Rut, Yedida. MASCULINE HEBREW EQUIVALENTS: Ashir, Avishai, David, Tzefanya, Yedidya, Yishai.

Edita   A Spanish pet form of Edith. *See* Edith.

Edith   From the Anglo-Saxon, meaning "rich, prosperous, happy warrior." HEBREW EQUIVALENTS: Ashira, Bat-Shua, Matzlicha, Yitra. MASCULINE HEBREW EQUIVALENTS: Ashir, Etzer, Matzliach, Yatzliach, Yitro.

Edna, Ednah (עֶדְנָה)   From the Hebrew, meaning "delight, desired, adorned, voluptuous." Also, a contracted form of the Anglo-Saxon name Edwina, meaning "rich friend." HEBREW EQUIVALENTS: Amita, Ashira, Bat-Shua, Chaviva, Davida, Yedida, Yitra. MASCULINE HEBREW EQUIVALENTS: Amitai, Ashir, David, Eden, Etzer, Osher, Yedidya, Yitro.

Edya, Edyah (עֶדְיָה)   From the Hebrew, meaning "adornment of the Lord." The exact Hebrew equivalent is Edya. MASCULINE HEBREW EQUIVALENTS: Ada'ya, Adi, Adiel, Hadar, Hadur.

Edyth, Edythe   Variant spellings of Edith. *See* Edith.

Efrat (אֶפְרָת)   From the Hebrew, meaning "honored, distinguished" or "fruitful." Also, from the Aramaic, meaning "mantle, turban." The exact Hebrew equivalent is Efrat and Efrata. The exact masculine Hebrew equivalent is Efra'yim.

Efrata (אֶפְרָתָה)   A variant form of Efrat. *See* Efrat. The exact Hebrew equivalent is Efrata.

Efrona (עֶפְרוֹנָה)   From the Hebrew, meaning "bird." The exact Hebrew equivalent is Efrona. The exact masculine Hebrew equivalent is Efron.

Eidel (אײדֶל)   From the Yiddish, meaning "delicate, gentle." HEBREW EQUIVALENTS: Adina, Adiva, Anuga, Chana, Chanita, Matmona, Ruchama. MASCULINE HEBREW EQUIVALENTS: Adin, Adiv, Chananel, Mishmana, Rachamim.

Eila, Eilah (אֵלָה)   From the Hebrew, meaning "oak tree, terebinth tree." The exact masculine and feminine Hebrew equivalent is Ela (Ayla).

Eilat (אֵילַת)   From the Hebrew, meaning "gazelle" or "tree." The exact feminine and masculine Hebrew equivalent is Aylat.

Eileen   A popular Irish form of Helen. *See* Helen.

Elain, Elaine   French forms of Helen, meaning "light." *See* Helen.

Elana   A variant spelling of Ilana, meaning "tree." *See* Ilana.

Elayne   A variant spelling of Elaine. *See* Elaine.

Elberta   The feminine form of Elbert. *See* Elbert (*masculine section*).

Eldora   From the Spanish, meaning "gilded." HEBREW EQUIVALENTS: Ofira, Paz, Paza, Pazit, Zehava, Zehavit. MASCULINE HEBREW EQUIVALENTS: Elifaz, Ofar, Ofir, Zahav, Zehavi.

Ele   A pet form of Eleanor. *See* Eleanor.

Eleanor   A German form of Helen, from the Greek, meaning "light." HEBREW EQUIVALENTS: Behira, Me'ira, Nitza, Noga, Ora. MASCULINE HEBREW EQUIVALENTS: Bahir, Me'ir, Neriya, Zerachya.

Eleanora   A variant form of Eleanor. *See* Eleanor.

Eleanore A variant spelling of Eleanor. *See* Eleanor.

Elen A variant spelling of Ellen. *See* Eleanor.

Elena From the Greek, meaning "light." The Italian form of Helen. *See* Helen.

Elenor A variant spelling of Eleanor. *See* Eleanor.

Eleora A variant spelling of Eliora. *See* Eliora.

Eliana, Eliane, Elianna From the Hebrew, meaning "My God has answered." The exact Hebrew equivalent is Eliana.

Eliava, Eliavah (אֱלִיאָבָה) From the Hebrew, meaning "My God is willing." The exact Hebrew equivalent is Eliava. The exact masculine Hebrew equivalent is Eliav.

Elie (אֱלִי) A pet form of Eleanor. *See* Eleanor.

Eliezra (אֱלִיעֶזְרָה) From the Hebrew, meaning "My God is salvation." The exact Hebrew equivalent is Eliezra. The exact masculine Hebrew equivalent is Eliezer.

Elinoar (אֱלִינֹעַר) From the Hebrew, meaning "God is my youth." The exact Hebrew equivalent is Elino'ar. MASCULINE HEBREW EQUIVALENTS: Aviv, Elam, Na'arai, Na'arya.

Elin A variant spelling of Ellen. *See* Ellen.

Elinor A variant spelling of Eleanor. *See* Eleanor.

Elinora A variant spelling of Eleanora. *See* Eleanora.

Elinore A variant spelling of Eleanor. *See* Eleanor.

Eliora (אֱלִיאוֹרָה) From the Hebrew, meaning "My God is light." The exact Hebrew equivalent is Eliora. The exact masculine Hebrew equivalent is Elior.

Eliraz (אֱלִירָז) From the Hebrew, meaning "My God is my secret." The exact Hebrew equivalent is Eliraz. MASCULINE HEBREW EQUIVALENTS: Raz, Razi, Raziel.

Elisa A short form of Elisabeth. *See* Elisabeth.

Elisabeta The Hawaiian form of Elisabeth. *See* Elisabeth.

Elisabeth A variant spelling of Elizabeth. *See* Elizabeth.

Elise A pet form of Elisabeth. *See* Elisabeth.

Elisheva (אֱלִישֶׁבַע) From the Hebrew, meaning "God is my oath." Elizabeth and Elisabeth are Anglicized forms. The exact Hebrew equivalent is Elisheva. MASCULINE HEBREW EQUIVALENTS: Amarya, Ela, Sheva.

Elissa A pet form of Elisabeth. *See* Elisabeth.

Eliza A short form of Elizabeth. *See* Elizabeth.

Elizabeth (אֱלִישֶׁבַע) From the Hebrew, meaning "God's oath." The exact Hebrew equivalent is Elisheva. MASCULINE HEBREW EQUIVALENTS: Amarya, Ashbay, Ela, Sheva.

Elize A short form of Elizabeth. *See* Elizabeth.

Elka, Elke A pet form of Alice and Alexandra. *See* Alice *and* Alexandra.

Elki, Elkie Variant forms of Elka. *See* Elka.

Ella From the Old German, meaning "all," or a variant form of Eleanor. *See* Eleanor.

Ellen A short form of Eleanor. *See* Eleanor.

Ellette A pet form of Ella. *See* Ella.

Ellie A pet form of Eleanor. *See* Eleanor.

Ellin A variant spelling of Ellen. *See* Ellen.

Ellyn, Ellynne Variant spellings of Ellen. *See* Ellen.

Elma From the Greek and Latin, meaning "pleasant, fair, kind." HEBREW EQUIVALENTS: Achino'am, Adiva, Na'ama, Na'amiya, Ne'ima. MASCULINE HEBREW EQUIVALENTS: Achino'am, Adin, Na'im, Elna'am, Na'aman, No'am.

Elona (אֵלוֹנָה) From the Hebrew, meaning "oak tree." The exact Hebrew equivalent is Elona (Aylona). The exact masculine Hebrew equivalent is Elon (Aylon).

Elsa, Else German pet forms of Elizabeth. *See* Elizabeth.

Elsie A variant form of Elisabeth. *See* Elisabeth.

Elvera, Elvira From the Latin, meaning "noble truth." HEBREW EQUIVALENTS: Amita, Emet. MASCULINE HEBREW EQUIVALENTS: Amit, Amitai, Amitana.

Elvita From the Latin, meaning "noble life." HEBREW EQUIVALENTS: Achiya, Chava, Cha'ya, Yechiela. MASCULINE HEBREW EQUIVALENTS: Amichai, Bar-Yochai, Cha'yim, Yechiel.

Elyn, Elynn Variant spellings of Ellen. *See* Ellen.

Elysa, Elyse Variant forms of Elisabeth. *See* Elisabeth.

Elyssa, Elysse Variant forms of Elisabeth. *See* Elisabeth.

Elza (עֶלְזָה) A pet form of Elizabeth. *See* Elizabeth. Also, from the Hebrew, meaning "joy." The exact Hebrew equivalent is Elza. The exact masculine Hebrew equivalent is Elez.

Em A pet form of Emma. *See* Emma.

Emanuela, Emanuella (עֲמָנוּאֵלָה) Feminine forms of Emanuel, meaning "God is with us." The exact Hebrew equivalent is Imanuela. The exact masculine Hebrew equivalent is Imanuel.

Emilie From the Anglo-Saxon, meaning "flatterer." Also, a variant spelling of Emily. *See* Emily.

Emily From the Latin, meaning "industrious, ambitious." HEBREW EQUIVALENTS: Charutza, Tirtza, Zeriza. MASCULINE HEBREW EQUIVALENTS: Amel, Mahir, Meretz, Yaziz, Ziruz, Ziza.

Emma From the Anglo-Saxon, meaning "big one" or "grandmother." HEBREW EQUIVALENTS: Atalya, Ima, Gedula, Rachav. MASCULINE HEBREW EQUIVALENTS: Abba, Gedalya, Raba, Rava, Sava.

Emmie A pet form of Emma. *See* Emma.

Emuna, Emunah (אֱמוּנָה) From the Hebrew, meaning "faith, faithful." The exact Hebrew equivalent is Emuna. MASCULINE HEBREW EQUIVALENTS: Amit, Amitai, Amitan, Emet.

Ena A variant spelling of Ina. Or, a pet form of Eugenia. *See* Ina *and* Eugenia.

Enid From the Anglo-Saxon, meaning "fair," or from the Celtic, meaning "soul, life." HEBREW EQUIVALENTS: Chava, Cha'ya, Nafshiya, Techiya, Yechiela. MASCULINE HEBREW EQUIVALENTS: Amichai, Chai, Cha'yim, Yechiel, Yocha'i.

Erela (אַרְאֵלָה) From the Hebrew, meaning "angel, messenger." The exact Hebrew equivalent is Erela. The exact masculine Hebrew equivalent is Erel.

Eretz (אֶרֶץ) From the Hebrew, meaning "land, earth." The exact Hebrew equivalent is Eretz. MASCULINE HEBREW EQUIVALENTS: Artza, Artzi.

Erez A variant spelling of Eretz. *See* Eretz. Used also as a masculine name. From the Hebrew, meaning "cedar." *See* Erez (*masculine section*).

Erga From the Hebrew, meaning "yearning, hope, longing." The exact Hebrew equivalent is Erga. MASCULINE HEBREW EQUIVALENTS: Tikva, Yachil, Yachl'el.

Erica The feminine form of Eric, meaning "ever-kingly, brave, powerful." *See* Eric (*masculine section*).

Erika A variant spelling of Erica. *See* Erica.

Erin From the Irish, meaning "peace." HEBREW EQUIVALENTS: Achishalom, Menucha, Meshulemet, Shalviya, Shlomit, Shulamit. MASCULINE HEBREW EQUIVALENTS: Avishalom, Sar-Shalom, Shalem, Shalev, Shalom, Shlomo.

Erma A variant spelling of Irma. *See* Irma.

Erna From the Anglo-Saxon, meaning "retiring, shy, reserved, peaceful." HEBREW EQUIVALENTS: Achishalom, Margaya, Menucha, Sha'anana, Shalva, Shulamit. MASCULINE HEBREW EQUIVALENTS: Avishalom, Ish-Shalom, Shalev, Shalom, Shelomi, Shlomo.

Ernesta, Ernestine Feminine forms of Ernest. *See* Ernest (*masculine section*).

Essie A pet form of Esther. *See* Esther.

Esta, Estee Variant forms of Esther. *See* Esther.

Estella A Spanish form of Esther. *See* Esther.

Estelle A variant form of Esther. *See* Esther.

Ester, Esther (אֶסְתֵּר) From the Persian, meaning "star." The commonly used Hebrew equivalent is Ester, although the exact equivalent is Hadasa. *See* Hadasa. MASCULINE HEBREW EQUIVALENTS: Bar-Kochva, Kochav, Kochva, Mazal, Oran, Zik.

Esti A pet form of Esther. *See* Esther.

Etana (אִיתָנָה) From the Hebrew, meaning "strong." Also spelled Aytana. The exact Hebrew equivalent is Etana. The exact masculine Hebrew equivalent is Etan (Aytan). The Anglicized masculine form is Ethan.

Ethel From the Anglo-Saxon, meaning "noble." HEBREW EQUIVALENTS: Adina, Adira, Adoniya, Atzila, Matrona, Nediva, Sara, Yisr'ela. MASCULINE HEBREW EQUIVALENTS: Achiram, Adar, Adir, Adon, Aminadav, Nadav, Yisrael, Yonadav.

Eti A pet form of Esther. *See* Esther.

Etka (עֶטְקאָ) The Yiddish pet form of Ita and Yetta. *See* Ita *and* Yetta.

Etta A pet form of Harriet and Henrietta, meaning "mistress of the house, lord, ruler." *See* Harriet *and* Henrietta.

Etti, Etty Pet forms of Esther. *See* Esther.

Eudice A variant spelling of Eudit. *See* Eudit.

Eudit (יוּדִית) A variant form of Yehudit (Judith). *See* Yehudit.

Eudora From the Greek, meaning "good gift." HEBREW EQUIVALENTS: Dorona, Doronit, Matana, Migdana, Netanel, Netaniela. MASCULINE HEBREW EQUIVALENTS: Doran, Doron, Doroni, Elinatan, Elnatan, Natan, Netanya.

Eugenia From the Greek, meaning "well-born." HEBREW EQUIVALENTS: Adina, Adira, Malka, Nediva, Sara. MASCULINE HEBREW EQUIVALENTS: Adin, Adir, Adiv, Chirom, Nadav, Yehonadav.

Eugenie The French form of Eugenia. *See* Eugenia.

Eunice From the Greek, meaning "happy victory." HEBREW EQUIVALENTS: Dafna, Hadasa, Nitzcha, Nitzchiya. MASCULINE HEBREW EQUIVALENTS: Gevarya, Netziach, Nitzchi, Yatzliach.

Eva A variant form of Eve. *See* Eve.

Evangeline From the Greek, meaning "bearer of glad tidings, messenger." HEBREW EQUIVALENTS: Ditza, Gila, Malach, Renana, Sisa. MASCULINE HEBREW EQUIVALENTS: Malachi, Mevaser, Sason, Simcha, Yagil, Yitzchak.

Eve A Latin and German form, from the Hebrew, meaning "life." The exact Hebrew equivalent is Chava. MASCULINE HEBREW EQUIVALENTS: Chai, Cha'yim.

Evelyn A pet form of Eve. *See* Eve. Also, from the Celtic, meaning "pleasant, good." HEBREW EQUIVALENTS: Achino'am, Na'ama, Na'omi, Shifra, Tova, Yafa, Yatva. MASCULINE HEBREW EQUIVALENTS: Avinoam, Ben-Tziyon, Na'aman, No'am, Tuviya.

Evelyne A variant spelling of Evelyn. *See* Evelyn.

Evita A Spanish pet form of Eve. *See* Eve.

Evonne A pet form of Eva and Evelyn. *See* Eva *and* Evelyn. Or, a variant form of Yvonne. *See* Yvonne.

Evrona (עֶבְרוֹנָה) From the Hebrew, meaning "overflowing anger, fury." The exact Hebrew equivalent is Evrona. The exact masculine Hebrew equivalent is Evron.

Evy A variant spelling of Evie. *See* Evie.

Ezra (עֶזְרָה/עֶזְרָא) Basically a masculine name, but used in Israel as a unisex name. *See* Ezra (*masculine section*).

Ezraela, Ezraella (עֶזְרָאֵלָה) Variant forms of Ezra, meaning "God is my help." *See* Ezra. The exact Hebrew equivalent is Ezra'ela.

Ezriela, Ezriella (עֶזְרִיאֵלָה) Variant forms of Ezra, meaning "God is my help." *See* Ezra.

Fabia From the Greek, meaning "bean farmer." HEBREW EQUIVALENTS: Adama, Karmela, Nava, Yizr'ela. MASCULINE HEBREW EQUIVALENTS: Adam, Karmel, Karmeli, Yizr'el.

Fabiana A feminine form of the masculine Fabian. *See* Fabian (*masculine section*).

Faga A variant spelling of Feiga. *See* Feiga.

Faiga (פֵּיינָא) A Yiddish form of the German *Vogel*, meaning "bird." HEBREW EQUIVALENTS: A'ya, Chasida, Chogla, Efrona, Gozala, Tzipora, Tzipori. MASCULINE HEBREW EQUIVALENTS: Deror, Nesher, Efron, Gozal, Tzipor, Yarkon.

Faige (פֵּיינֶע) A variant spelling of Faiga. *See* Faiga.

Faigel (פֵּיינְגֶל) A Yiddish pet form of Faiga. *See* Faiga.

Faith From the Anglo-Saxon, meaning "unswerving trust, hope." HEBREW EQUIVALENTS: Amana, Bitcha, Emuna, Tikva, Tzipiya. MASCULINE HEBREW EQUIVALENTS: Amitai, Amnon, Buki, Heman, Ne'eman.

Falice, Falicia Variant spellings of Felice and Felicia. *See* Felice *and* Felicia.

Fani A variant spelling of Fannie. *See* Fannie.

Fania A pet form of Frances. *See* Frances.

Fannie, Fanny, Fannye Pet forms of Frances. *See* Frances.

Fanya A variant spelling of Fania. *See* Fania.

Fawn From the Latin, meaning "young deer," or from the Middle English, meaning "friendly." HEBREW EQUIVALENTS: Amita, A'yala, A'yelet, Davida, Tzivya, Yedida. MASCULINE HEBREW EQUIVALENTS: Amit, Amitai, Chaviv, Efer, David, Tzevi, Tzivyon.

Fawna A variant form of Fawn. *See* Fawn.

Fawne A variant spelling of Fawn. *See* Fawn.

Fawnia A variant form of Fawn. *See* Fawn.

Fay, Faye From the Old French, meaning "fidelity." HEBREW EQUIVALENTS: Amana, Bitcha, Emuna, Ne'emana, Tikva, Tzipiya. MASCULINE HEBREW EQUIVALENTS: Amit, Amitai, Amnon, Buki, Ne'eman.

Fayette A pet form of Fay. *See* Fay.

Feiga (פֵּיינָא) A variant form of Feige. *See* Feige.

Feige (פֵּיינֶע) From the Yiddish *feig*, meaning "fig." Also, a variant form of Feigel and Faiga, meaning "bird." *See* Faiga.

Feigel (פֵּיינְגֶל) A variant spelling of Faigel. *See* Faigel.

Felecia A variant spelling of Felicia. *See* Felicia.

Felice, Felicia From the Latin, meaning "happy, fortunate." HEBREW EQUIVALENTS: Ashera, Asherit, Gada, Mazal, Oshra, Ushriya. MASCULINE HEBREW EQUIVALENTS: Adna, Asher, Gad, Maimon, Mazal-Tov, Siman-Tov.

Feliciana A Spanish form of Felice. See Felice.

Felicite, Felicity French and Spanish forms of Felice. See Felice.

Felisa, Felise, Felisse Variant spellings of Felice. See Felice.

Fern, Ferne From the Anglo-Saxon, meaning "strong, brave." Also, a plant name. HEBREW EQUIVALENTS: Amitza, Ariel, Gavriela, Kalanit, Kana, Kida, Marganit, No'it, Neta, Netiya, Savyon. MASCULINE HEBREW EQUIVALENTS: Amotz, Gavriel, Narkis, Shatil, Tzemach, Zoraya.

Fidelia From the Latin, meaning "faithful." HEBREW EQUIVALENTS: Amana, Bitcha, Emuna, Tikva, Tzipiya. MASCULINE HEBREW EQUIVALENTS: Amitai, Amnon, Buki, Ne'eman.

Fidella A variant form of Fidelia. See Fidelia.

Fiona From the Celtic, meaning "white." The feminine and masculine Hebrew equivalent is Livna.

Flavia From the Latin, meaning "yellow-haired, blond." HEBREW EQUIVALENTS: Paz, Pazit, Paziya, Zehava, Zahuv.

Fleur A French form of the Latin, meaning "flower." See Florence.

Fleurette A pet form of Fleur. See Fleur.

Flora From the Latin, meaning "flower." See Florence.

Floreen A variant form of Florence. See Florence.

Florella A pet form of Florence. See Florence.

Floren A short form of Florence. See Florence.

Florence From the Latin, meaning "blooming, flowery, flourishing." HEBREW EQUIVALENTS: Irit, Nitza, Pericha, Pircha, Pirchiya, Pirchit, Shoshana, Yenika. MASCULINE HEBREW EQUIVALENTS: Efra'yim, Nirit, Nitzan, Pekach, Perach, Perachya, Pura, Savya, Shoshan.

Florentina A pet form of Florence. See Florence.

Floria A variant form of Flora. See Flora.

Florrie A pet form of Flora and Florence. See Flora and Florence.

Floryn A pet form of Flora and Florence. See Flora and Florence.

Flossie A pet form of Flora and Florence. See Flora and Florence.

Fradel (פֿרײַדעל) A pet form of Frayda. See Frayda.

Fran A pet form of Frances. See Frances.

Francene A pet form of Frances. See Frances.

Frances From the Anglo-Saxon, meaning "free, liberal." HEBREW EQUIVALENTS: Cheruta, Chufshit, Derora, Derorit, Ge'ula, Li-Deror, Rachav, Serach. MASCULINE HEBREW EQUIVALENTS: Amidror, Avideror, Cherut, Pesach, Pesachya, Rechavam, Rechavya.

Francesca An Italian form of Frances. See Frances.

Francine   A pet form of Frances. *See* Frances.

Frani   A pet form of Frances. *See* Frances.

Frankie   A pet form of Frances. *See* Frances.

Frayda, Frayde (פְרֵיידָא/פְרֵיידֶע)   From the Yiddish, meaning "joy." HE-BREW EQUIVALENTS: Aliza, Aviga'yil, Ditza, Gila, Gilana, Ranita, Rena-nit, Rona, Ronena, Sasona, Simchit. MASCULINE HEBREW EQUIVALENTS: Alitz, Eletz, Eliran, Gil, Gili, Marnin, Ranon, Ronen, Simchon, Sim-choni, Yagil, Yitzchak.

Freda   A variant form of Frieda. *See* Frieda.

Fredda   A pet form of Frederica and Frieda. *See* Frederica *and* Frieda.

Frederica   The feminine form of Frederick, meaning "peaceful ruler." HE-BREW EQUIVALENTS: Malka, Menucha, Sha'anana, Shalva, Shelomit, Shulamit. MASCULINE HEBREW EQUIVALENTS: Achimelech, Avshalom, Ish-Shalom, Malkam, Melech, No'ach, Shabtai, Shalom, Shelomo.

Freida, Freide   Variant forms of Frieda. *See* Frieda. Also, variant spell-ings of Frayda. *See* Frayda.

Frieda   From the Old High German, meaning "peace." HEBREW EQUIVA-LENTS: Menucha, Sha'anana, Shalva, Shlomit, Shulamit, Za'yit. MASCU-LINE HEBREW EQUIVALENTS: Avshalom, Ish-Shalom, No'ach, Shabtai, Shalev, Shalom, Shelomo.

Friedel   A pet form of Frieda. *See* Frieda.

Fritzi   A pet form of Frederica and Frieda. *See* Frederica *and* Frieda.

Fruma (פרומָא)   From the Yiddish, meaning "pious one." HEBREW EQUIVA-LENTS: Chasida, Chasuda, Tzadika. MASCULINE HEBREW EQUIVALENTS: Chasdiel, Chasid, Chisdai, Tzadik.

Frume (פרומֶע)   A variant form of Fruma. *See* Fruma.

Frumet, Frumeth   Variant forms of Frume. *See* Frume.

Gabi (גַבִּי)   A pet form of Gabriella. *See* Gabriella. The exact Hebrew equivalent is Gabi.

Gabriela, Gabriella   Anglicized feminine forms of Gavriel. *See* Gav-riela.

Gabriele, Gabrielle   Variant French forms of Gabriela and Gabriella. *See* Gabriela *and* Gabriella.

Gada (גָּדָה)   The feminine form of Gad. *See* Gad (*masculine section*). The exact Hebrew equivalent is Gada.

Gadiela, Gadiella (גְּדִיאֵלָה)   Variant forms of Gadiel. *See* Gadiel.

Gadit (גָּדִית)   A variant form of Gada. *See* Gada. The exact Hebrew equiv-alent is Gadit.

Gafna (גַּפְנָה)   The Aramaic form of Gefen. *See* Gefen. The exact Hebrew equivalent is Gafna.

Gafnit (גַּפְנִית)   A variant form of Gafna. *See* Gafna. The exact Hebrew equivalent is Gafnit.

Gail A short form of Abigail. *See* Abigail.

Gal (גָּל) From the Hebrew, meaning "mound, hill" or "wave" or "fountain, spring." The exact feminine and masculine Hebrew equivalent is Gal.

Gala A variant form of Gal. *See* Gal.

Gale A variant form of Gail. *See* Gail.

Gali (גָּלִי) A variant form of Gal. *See* Gal. The exact feminine and masculine Hebrew equivalent is Gali.

Galila (גְּלִילָה) From the Hebrew, meaning "roll up, roll away." The exact Hebrew equivalent is Galila. The exact masculine Hebrew equivalent is Galil.

Galina The Russian form of Helen. *See* Helen.

Galit (גָּלִית) A variant form of Gal. *See* Gal. The exact Hebrew equivalent is Galit.

Galiya (גַּלְיָה) A variant form of Galya. *See* Galya. The exact Hebrew equivalent is Galiya.

Galya (גַּלְיָה) From the Hebrew, meaning "hill of God." The exact Hebrew equivalent is Galya. MASCULINE HEBREW EQUIVALENTS: Gal, Gilad.

Gamliela (גַּמְלִיאֵלָה) A feminine form of Gamliel. *See* Gamliel (*masculine section*). The exact Hebrew equivalent is Gamliela.

Gana (גַּנָּה) From the Hebrew, meaning "garden." The exact Hebrew equivalent is Gana. MASCULINE HEBREW EQUIVALENTS: Ginat, Ginton.

Gania A variant spelling of Ganya. *See* Ganya.

Ganit (גַּנִּית) A variant form of Gana. *See* Gana. The exact Hebrew equivalent is Ganit.

Ganya (גַּנְיָה) From the Hebrew, meaning "garden of the Lord." The exact Hebrew equivalent is Ganya. MASCULINE HEBREW EQUIVALENTS: Gan, Gani, Ginton.

Garnit (גַּרְנִית) From the Hebrew, meaning "granary." The exact Hebrew equivalent is Garnit. MASCULINE HEBREW EQUIVALENTS: Dagan, Goren.

Garret, Garrett Used primarily as a masculine name. *See* Garret (*masculine section*).

Gavi (גַּבִּי) A pet form of Gavriela. *See* Gavriela. The exact Hebrew equivalent is Gavi.

Gavriela, Gavriella (גַּבְרִיאֵלָה) From the Hebrew, meaning "heroine." The exact Hebrew equivalent is Gavriela. The exact masculine Hebrew equivalent is Gavriel.

Gavrila (גַּבְרִילָה) Variant forms of Gavriela. *See* Gavriela. The exact Hebrew equivalent is Gavrila.

Gay From the Anglo-Saxon, meaning "gay, merry." HEBREW EQUIVALENTS: Aviga'yil, Gila, Giliya, Gilit, Renana, Rina, Simcha. MASCULINE HEBREW EQUIVALENTS: Bilgai, Gil, Gilam, Gilan, Simcha, Yitzchak.

Gayle A variant spelling of Gail. *See* Gail.

Gayora (גִּיאוֹרָה) From the Hebrew, meaning "valley of light." The exact Hebrew equivalent is Gayora. MASCULINE HEBREW EQUIVALENTS: Elior, Lior, Me'ir, Ori, Uriya.

Gazella From the Latin, meaning "gazelle, deer." HEBREW EQUIVALENTS: A'yala, A'yelet, Tzivya. MASCULINE HEBREW EQUIVALENTS: A'yal, A'yalon, Tzevi.

Gazit (גָּזִית) From the Hebrew, meaning "hewn stone." The exact Hebrew equivalent is Gazit. MASCULINE HEBREW EQUIVALENTS: Elitzur, Even, Even-Ezer, Tzuriya.

Geela, Geelah Variant spellings of Gila. See Gila.

Gefen, Geffen (גֶּפֶן) From the Hebrew, meaning "vine." The exact feminine and masculine equivalent is Gefen.

Gemma From the Latin, meaning "swelling bud" or "precious stone." HEBREW EQUIVALENTS: Bareket, Chemda, Sapirit, Yahaloma, Yahalomit, Yakira. MASCULINE HEBREW EQUIVALENTS: Avikar, Penini, Sapir, Yahalom, Yakar.

Gena, Gene Variant spellings of Gina. See Gina.

Genevieve From the Celtic, meaning "white wave." HEBREW EQUIVALENTS: Bat-Galim, Levana, Miryam, Yama, Zahara. MASCULINE HEBREW EQUIVALENTS: Avigal, Lavan, Livni, Moshe, Peleg.

Georgeanne A hybrid of George and Anne. See George (*masculine section*) *and* Anne.

Georgette A pet form of Georgia. See Georgia.

Georgia From the Greek, meaning "husbandman, farmer." HEBREW EQUIVALENTS: Adama, Eretz, Gana, Karmela, Nava, Shedma, Yizr'ela. MASCULINE HEBREW EQUIVALENTS: Adam, Karmel, Shadmon, Yizr'el.

Georgiana A variant form of Georgeanne. See Georgeanne.

Georgina, Georgine Pet forms of Georgia. See Georgia.

Geraldene, Geraldine From the Old High German, meaning "spear-wielder, warrior." HEBREW EQUIVALENTS: Chanit, Chanita, Gavrila, Gibora, Tigra, Yisr'ela. MASCULINE HEBREW EQUIVALENTS: Gad, Gera, Gidon, Naftali, Yisrael.

Geralyn A hybrid of Geraldine and Lynn. See Geraldine *and* Lynn.

Gerda From the Old High German, meaning "protected one." HEBREW EQUIVALENTS: Gana, Magena, Migdala, Shimrit, Tzina. MASCULINE HEBREW EQUIVALENTS: Magen, Sa'adya, Shemarya, Zimri.

Gerrie, Gerry Pet forms of Geraldine and Gerardine. See Geraldine *and* Gerardine.

Gershona (גֵּרְשׁוֹנָה) The feminine form of Gershon. See Gershon (*masculine section*). The exact Hebrew equivalent is Gershona.

Gertrude From the Old High German, meaning "battlemaid" or "adored warrior." HEBREW EQUIVALENTS: Gada, Gavrila, Gibora, Tigra, Yisr'ela. MASCULINE HEBREW EQUIVALENTS: Gad, Gera, Gevarya, Gidon, Naftali, Yisrael.

Geula, Geulah (גְּאוּלָה) From the Hebrew, meaning "redemption." The exact Hebrew equivalent is Ge'ula. MASCULINE HEBREW EQUIVALENTS: Ge'alya, Go'el, Yiga'el.

Gevira, Gevirah (גְּבִירָה)   From the Hebrew, meaning "lady" or "queen." The exact Hebrew equivalent is Gevira. MASCULINE HEBREW EQUIVALENTS: Adiv, Adoniya, Gavra, Gever, Melech.

Gevura, Gevurah (גְּבוּרָה)   From the Hebrew, meaning "strength." The exact Hebrew equivalent is Gevura. MASCULINE HEBREW EQUIVALENTS: Aviaz, Avicha'yil, Gavriel, Gever, Gibor, Uzi.

Ghila   A variant spelling of Gila. See Gila.

Ghity, Ghitty   Pet forms of Gitel. See Gitel.

Gibora, Giborah (גְּבוֹרָה)   From the Hebrew, meaning "strong, heroine." The exact Hebrew equivalent is Gibora. The exact masculine Hebrew equivalent is Gibor.

Gidona (גִּרְעוֹנָה)   The feminine form of Gidon. See Gidon (*masculine section*). The exact Hebrew equivalent is Gidona.

Gila, Gilah (גִּילָה)   From the Hebrew, meaning "joy." The exact Hebrew equivalent is Gila. The exact masculine Hebrew equivalent is Gil.

Gilada, Giladah (גִּלְעָדָה)   From the Hebrew, meaning "[the] hill is [my] witness" or "Joy is forever." The exact Hebrew equivalent is Gilada. The exact masculine Hebrew equivalent is Gilad.

Gilana, Gilanah (גִּילָנָה)   From the Hebrew, meaning "joy" or "stage of life." A variant form of Gila. See Gila. The exact Hebrew spelling of Gilana.

Gilat (גִּילַת)   A variant form of Gilana. See Gilana. The exact Hebrew equivalent is Gilat.

Gilberta   The feminine form of Gilbert. See Gilbert (*masculine section*).

Gilda   From the Celtic, meaning "servant of God," or from the Old English, meaning "coated with gold." HEBREW EQUIVALENTS: Aleksandra, Mashena, Sa'ada, Shimshona, Zehava. MASCULINE HEBREW EQUIVALENTS: Avda, Avdel, Avdi, Eved, Ovadya, Shimshon, Zehavi.

Gili (גִּילִי)   From the Hebrew, meaning "my joy." The exact feminine and masculine Hebrew equivalent is Gili.

Gilit (גִּילִית)   A variant form of Gilana. See Gilana. The exact Hebrew equivalent is Gilit.

Gill   From the Old English, meaning "girl." HEBREW EQUIVALENTS: Alma, Betula, Na'ara, Tze'ira. MASCULINE HEBREW EQUIVALENTS: Ben, Ben-Tziyon, Na'arai, Na'arya.

Gilla   A variant spelling of Gill. See Gill.

Gillian   A variant form of the Latin name Juliana, the feminine form of Julian. See Julian (*masculine section*).

Gina (גִּינָה)   From the Hebrew, meaning "garden." The exact feminine and masculine Hebrew equivalent is Gina.

Ginat (גִּינַת)   A variant form of Gina. See Gina. The exact Hebrew equivalent is Ginat.

Ginger   A pet form of Virginia. See Virginia.

Gisa   From the Anglo-Saxon, meaning "gift." HEBREW EQUIVALENTS: Dorona, Matana, Migdana, Mincha, Netanela. MASCULINE HEBREW EQUIVALENTS: Elnatan, Matityahu, Natan, Netanel, Yishai.

Gisela, Gisella   From the Anglo-Saxon, meaning "the bright hope of the people" or "sword." HEBREW EQUIVALENTS: Behira, Me'ira, Noga, Ora, Zahara, Zakit. MASCULINE HEBREW EQUIVALENTS: Uri, Uriel, Zakai, Zerach, Zerachya.

Giselle   A variant form of Gisela. See Gisela.

Gita (גִיתָה)   A variant form of Gitit. See Gitit. The exact Hebrew equivalent is Gita. See also Gitel.

Gitel, Gitele, Gittel (גִיטֶל)   From the Yiddish, meaning "good." The exact Hebrew equivalent is Tova. MASCULINE HEBREW EQUIVALENTS: Achituv, Amituv, Ben-Tziyon, Tabai, Tuviya, Tziyon.

Gitit (גִיתִית)   From the Hebrew, meaning "wine press." The exact Hebrew equivalent is Gitit. The masculine Hebrew equivalent is Gitai.

Gittie, Gitty   Pet forms of Gitel. See Gitel.

Giva, Givah (גִבְעָה)   From the Hebrew, meaning "hill, high place." The exact feminine and masculine Hebrew equivalent is Giva.

Givona (גִבְעוֹנָה)   A variant form of Giva. See Giva. The exact Hebrew equivalent is Givona.

Giza (גִיזָה)   From the Hebrew, meaning "cut stone." The exact Hebrew equivalent is Giza. MASCULINE HEBREW EQUIVALENTS: Bavai, Elitzur, Even, Gidon, Gidoni.

Gizela   A variant spelling of Gisela. See Gisela.

Gladys   A Welsh form of the Latin name Claudia, meaning "lame." Also, from the Celtic, meaning "brilliant, splendid." HEBREW EQUIVALENTS: Behira, Me'ira, Noga, Ora, Tzelili, Zahara. MASCULINE HEBREW EQUIVALENTS: Bahir, Me'ir, Shimshon, Zerach, Zerachya, Zohar.

Gladyce   A variant spelling of Gladys.

Glenda   A variant form of Glendora or Glenna. See Glendora and Glenna.

Glendora   A hybrid of Glenna and Dora. See Glenna and Dora.

Glenna   The feminine form of Glenn. See Glenn (masculine section).

Glikel (גְלִיקֶעל)   A pet form of Gluke. See Gluke.

Glora   A variant form of Gloria. See Gloria.

Gloria   From the Latin, meaning "glory, glorious." HEBREW EQUIVALENTS: Ahuda, Devora, Hillela, Tehila, Yehudit, Yocheved, Zimra. MASCULINE HEBREW EQUIVALENTS: Ahud, Gedalya, Hadar, Hillel, Shevach, Yehuda.

Gloriana   A variant form of Gloria. See Gloria.

Glory   A variant form of Gloria. See Gloria.

Gloryette   A pet form of Glory. See Glory.

Gluke (גְלוּקֶע)   From the German and Yiddish, meaning "luck, good fortune." The exact feminine and masculine Hebrew equivalent is Mazal.

Glynda   A variant form of Glenda. See Glenda.

Glynis, Glynnis From the British, meaning "glen, narrow valley." The Hebrew equivalent is Ga'ya. MASCULINE HEBREW EQUIVALENTS: Emek, Gai, Ge'ora, Gechazi.

Golda (גּוֹלְדָה/גּוֹלְדָא) A popular Yiddish name, from the Old English and German, meaning "gold, golden." HEBREW EQUIVALENTS: Delila, Ofira, Paza, Pazit, Zehava, Zehavit, Zehuva. MASCULINE HEBREW EQUIVALENTS: Elifaz, Ofir, Paz, Upaz, Zahav, Zehavi.

Goldie, Goldy Pet forms of Golda. See Golda.

Gomer (גָּמַר) From the Hebrew, meaning "to finish, complete." The exact feminine and masculine Hebrew equivalent is Gomer.

Gorala (גּוֹרָלָה) From the Hebrew, meaning "lot, lottery." The exact Hebrew equivalent is Gorala. The exact masculine Hebrew equivalent is Goral.

Gozala (גּוֹזָלָה) From the Hebrew, meaning "young bird." The exact Hebrew equivalent is Gozala. The exact masculine Hebrew equivalent is Gozal.

Grace From the Latin, meaning "grace." HEBREW EQUIVALENTS: Chana, Chanita, Chanya, Dikla, Tamar, Yochana. MASCULINE HEBREW EQUIVALENTS: Elchanan, Chanina, Chanan, Itamar, Yochanan.

Graciela A variant form of Grace. See Grace.

Greer From the Greek and Latin, meaning "guard, guardian." HEBREW EQUIVALENTS: Mishmeret, Nitzra, Notera, Noteret, Shimra, Shimrit. MASCULINE HEBREW EQUIVALENTS: Eri, Gonen, Mishmar, Natron, Noter, Shemarya, Shomer.

Greta A Swedish pet form of Margaret. See Margaret.

Gretchen A German pet form of Margaret. See Margaret.

Gretel A variant form of Gretchen. See Gretchen.

Gurit (גּוּרִית) From the Hebrew, meaning "young lion." The exact Hebrew equivalent is Gurit. The exact masculine Hebrew equivalent is Gur.

Gussie, Gussy Popular pet forms of Augusta. See Augusta.

Gustine A variant form of Augusta. See Augusta.

Gwen From the Welsh, meaning "white, fair" or "beautiful, blessed." HEBREW EQUIVALENTS: Achino'am, Berucha, Na'ama, Na'omi, Levana, Yafa, Yafit. MASCULINE HEBREW EQUIVALENTS: Avino'am, Baruch, Lavan, Livni, Na'aman, Yafeh.

Gwenn, Gwenne Variant spellings of Gwen. See Gwen.

Gwyn, Gwynn, Gwynne Variant forms of Gwen. See Gwen.

Hada A pet form of Hadasa. See Hadasa.

Hadar (הָדָר) From the Hebrew, meaning "ornamented, beautiful, honored." The exact feminine and masculine Hebrew equivalent is Hadar.

Hadara (הֲדָרָה) A variant form of Hadar. *See* Hadar. The exact Hebrew equivalent is Hadara.

Hadarit (הֲדָרִית) A variant form of Hadar. *See* Hadar. The exact Hebrew equivalent is Hadarit.

Hadas (הֲדַס) A short form of Hadasa. *See* Hadasa. The exact Hebrew equivalent is Hadas.

Hadasa, Hadassa, Hadassah (הֲדַסָה) From the Hebrew, meaning "myrtle tree," a symbol of victory. The exact Hebrew equivalent is Hadasa. The exact masculine Hebrew equivalent is Hadas.

Hadura (הֲדוּרָה) From the Hebrew, meaning "ornamented, beautiful." The exact Hebrew equivalent is Hadura. The exact masculine Hebrew equivalent is Hadur.

Hagar From the Hebrew, meaning "emigration, forsaken, stranger." The exact Hebrew equivalent is Hagar. MASCULINE HEBREW EQUIVALENTS: Gershom, Gershon, Golyat, Sarid.

Hagia, Haggiah Variant spellings of Chagiya. *See* Chagiya.

Hagit A variant spelling of Chagit. *See* Chagit.

Hallela (הַלְלָה) From the Hebrew, meaning "praise." The exact Hebrew equivalent is Hallela. The exact masculine Hebrew equivalent is Hillel.

Haley From the Norse, meaning "hero." HEBREW EQUIVALENTS: Abiram, Gavriela, Gavrila, Gibora, Yisr'ela. MASCULINE HEBREW EQUIVALENTS: Abir, Abiri, Aviram, Gavri, Gavriel, Gever, Gibor, Yisrael.

Halie A variant spelling of Haley. *See* Haley.

Halina From the Hawaiian, meaning "resemblance." Also, a Polish form of Helen. *See* Helen.

Hallie, Hally Variant spellings of Haley. *See* Haley.

Hana A variant spelling of Chana. *See* Chana.

Hania A variant spelling of Chaniya. *See* Chaniya.

Hanina A variant spelling of Chanina. *See* Chanina.

Hanit A variant spelling of Chanit. *See* Chanit.

Hanita A variant spelling of Chanita. *See* Chanita.

Haniya A variant spelling of Chaniya. *See* Chaniya.

Hanna, Hannah Variant spellings of Hana. *See* Hana.

Happy A modern English name, meaning "joyful." HEBREW EQUIVALENTS: Aliza, Aviga'yil, Ditza, Gila, Gilit, Ronena, Simchit, Simchona. MASCULINE HEBREW EQUIVALENTS: Aliz, Eletz, Eliran, Gili, Marnin, Rani, Sisi, Yitzchak, Yitzhal.

Harela (הַרְאֵלָה) The feminine form of Harel. *See* Harel (*masculine section*). The exact Hebrew equivalent is Harela.

Harmony From the Greek, meaning "unity, peace." HEBREW EQUIVALENTS: Achishalom, Margaya, Shlomit, Shulamit, Temima, Tumi. MASCULINE HEBREW EQUIVALENTS: Avshalom, Chever, Chevron, Kalil, Meshulam, Shalom, Shelomo.

Harriet, Harriette From the Old English, meaning "mistress of the house, ruler, lord." HEBREW EQUIVALENTS: Adonit, Alufa, Malka, Sara, Sarit, Yisr'ela. MASCULINE HEBREW EQUIVALENTS: Adon, Adoniya, Aluf, Ba'al, Melech, Moshel, Sar, Yisrael.

Hasida A variant spelling of Chasida. See Chasida.

Hasina A variant spelling of Chasina. See Chasina.

Hasna A variant spelling of Chasna. See Chasna.

Hasya A variant spelling of Chasya. See Chasya.

Hava A variant spelling of Chava. See Chava.

Haviva A variant spelling of Chaviva. See Chaviva.

Haya A variant spelling of Chaya. See Chaya.

Hazel From the Old English, meaning "hazel tree," connoting protection and authority. HEBREW EQUIVALENTS: Magena, Shimrit, Tzila, Ya'akova. MASCULINE HEBREW EQUIVALENTS: Asaf, Chetzron, Lot, Tachan, Ya'akov.

Hazelbelle A hybrid of Hazel and Belle. See Hazel and Belle.

Heather From the Anglo-Saxon, meaning "heath, plant, shrub." HEBREW EQUIVALENTS: Ketzia, Marva, Neta, Neti'a, Rechana, Shetila, Shetula. MASCULINE HEBREW EQUIVALENTS: Narkis, Shatil, Shatul, Tzemach, Zoraya.

Hedda From the German, meaning "strife, warfare." HEBREW EQUIVALENTS: Amtza, Gavriela, Gavrila, Gibora, Tigra. MASCULINE HEBREW EQUIVALENTS: Avicha'yil, Ben-Cha'yil, Naftali, Yisrael.

Hedva, Hedvah Variant spellings of Chedva. See Chedva.

Hedy, Heddy Pet forms of Hedda, Hester, and Esther. See Hedda, Hester, and Esther.

Hedya (הֶדְיָה) From the Hebrew, meaning "echo [voice] of the Lord." The exact Hebrew equivalent is Hedya. MASCULINE HEBREW EQUIVALENTS: Amarya, Divri, Imri.

Hefziba, Hefzibah Anglicized forms of Chefzi-Ba. See Chefzi-Ba.

Heidi Probably a variant form of Hester and Esther. See Esther.

Helaine A variant form of Helen. See Helen.

Helen From the Greek, meaning "light." HEBREW EQUIVALENTS: Amior, Behira, Me'ira, Nahara, Nehira, Ora, Orit, Orli, Tzefira, Ye'ira, Zahara. MASCULINE HEBREW EQUIVALENTS: Achiner, Barak, Barkai, Me'ir, Nahir, Neriya, Or, Ori, Uri, Zerachya.

Helena A variant form of Helen. See Helen.

Helene The French form of Helen. See Helen.

Heleni A variant form of Helene. See Helene.

Helenmae A combination of Helen and Mae. See Helen and Mae.

Heline The Hawaiian form of Helen. See Helen.

Hella A variant form of Helen. See Helen.

Hemda A variant spelling of Chemda. See Chemda.

Hen   A variant spelling of Chen. *See* Chen.

Henda, Hende (הֶענדֶע/הֶענדָא)   Variant Yiddish forms of Hene. *See* Hene.

Hendel (הֶנדֶל)   A Yiddish pet form of Chana. *See* Chana.

Hene, Heneh (הֶענֶע)   Yiddish pet forms of Chana. *See* Chana.

Henia (הֶעניָא)   A Yiddish pet form of Henrietta. *See* Henrietta.

Henna (הֶענָא)   A Yiddish form of Hannah. *See* Hannah.

Henrietta, Henriette   Variant forms of Harriet. *See* Harriet.

Henya (הֶעניָא)   A Yiddish pet form of Henrietta. *See* Henrietta.

Hephziba, Hephzibah   Variant spellings of Hefziba. *See* Hefziba.

Hepzi, Hepzia   Pet forms of Hephziba. *See* Hephziba.

Hepziba, Hepzibah   Variant forms of Hefziba. *See* Hefziba.

Herma   From the Latin, meaning "stone pillar, signpost." HEBREW EQUIVALENTS: Gal, Gilada, Giva, Givat. MASCULINE HEBREW EQUIVALENTS: Gal, Gali, Gilad, Talmai.

Hermine   A variant form of Hermione. *See* Hermione.

Hermione   In Greek mythology, the messenger and servant of gods. HEBREW EQUIVALENTS: Aharona, Malach, Shimshona. MASCULINE HEBREW EQUIVALENTS: Avda, Malachi, Ovadya, Shimshon.

Hermona   A feminine form of Hermon. *See* Hermon (*masculine section*).

Hertzela (הֶרצֶלָה)   The feminine form of Herzl. *See* Herzl (*masculine section*). The exact Hebrew equivalent is Hertzela.

Hertzliya (הֶרצֶליָה)   A variant form of Hertzela. *See* Hertzela. The exact Hebrew equivalent is Hertzliya.

Herzlia, Herzliah   Variant spellings of Hertzliya. *See* Hertzliya.

Hester   The Latin form of Esther. *See* Esther.

Hesther   A variant form of Hester. *See* Hester.

Hetta   A pet form of Harriet. *See* Harriet.

Hetty   A pet form of Harriet. *See* Harriet.

Hila, Hilah (הִילָה)   From the Hebrew, meaning "praise." The exact Hebrew equivalent is Hila. The exact masculine Hebrew equivalent is Hillel.

Hilaire   The French form of Hilary. *See* Hilary.

Hilana (הִלָנָה)   A variant form of Hila. *See* Hila. The exact Hebrew equivalent is Hilana.

Hilary, Hillary   From the Greek and the Latin, meaning "cheerful." HEBREW EQUIVALENTS: Aviga'yil, Elza, Gil, Gilana, Gilit, Giliya, Ronena, Roniya, Simchona. MASCULINE HEBREW EQUIVALENTS: Aliz, Bilgai, Gilad, Gilon, Marnin, Ranon, Roni, Simcha, Yitzchak.

Hilda, Hilde   Short forms of Hildegard. *See* Hildegard.

Hildegard, Hildegarde, Hildergarde   From the German, meaning "warrior, battlemaid." HEBREW EQUIVALENTS: Alma, Amtza, Gavriela, Gavrila, Gibora, Tigra. MASCULINE HEBREW EQUIVALENTS: Amotz, Gavriel, Gibor, Mordechai, Medan, Naftali, Yisrael.

Hildi, Hildy Pet forms of Hildegard. *See* Hildegard.

Hili A pet form of Hilda and Hillela. *See* Hilda *and* Hillela.

Hilla, Hillah Variant spellings of Hila. *See* Hila.

Hillary A variant spelling of Hilary. *See* Hilary.

Hillela (הִלְלָה) The feminine form of Hillel, meaning "praise." The exact Hebrew equivalent is Hillela. The exact masculine Hebrew equivalent is Hillel.

Hilma Probably a variant form of Wilhelmina. *See* Wilhelmina.

Hinda (הִינְדָא) From the German and Yiddish, meaning "hind, deer." HE-BREW EQUIVALENTS: A'yala, A'yelet, Ofra, Re'ema, Tzivya. MASCULINE HEBREW EQUIVALENTS: A'yal, Ben-Tzevi, Efer, Ofar, Tzevi, Tzevi-El.

Hindel, Hindelle (הִינְדְל) Yiddish pet forms of Hinda. *See* Hinda.

Hindi, Hindie (הִינְדִי) Pet forms of Hinda. *See* Hinda.

Hode, Hodeh (הָאדֶע) Yiddish forms of Hadasah. *See* Hadasah.

Hodel (הָאדְל) A Yiddish pet form of Hadasah. *See* Hadasah.

Hodi (הָאדִי) A Yiddish form of Hadasah. *See* Hadasah.

Hodia, Hodiah Variant spellings of Hodiya. *See* Hodiya.

Hodiya (הוֹדִיָה) From the Hebrew, meaning "praise the Lord." The exact feminine and masculine Hebrew equivalent is Hodiya.

Holiday From the Anglo-Saxon, meaning "festive day, holiday." HEBREW EQUIVALENTS: Chagiya, Chagit, Kedosha, Simcha. MASCULINE HEBREW EQUIVALENTS: Chag, Chagai, Chagi, Simcha, Yom-Tov.

Holis A variant spelling of Hollace. *See* Hollace.

Hollace A variant form of Haley. *See* Haley.

Holli A variant spelling of Holly. *See* Holly.

Hollis A variant spelling of Hollace. *See* Hollace.

Holly, Hollye From the Anglo-Saxon, meaning "holy." HEBREW EQUIVA-LENTS: Devira, Chagit, Chagiya, Kedosha. MASCULINE HEBREW EQUIVA-LENTS: Devir, Kadish, Kadosh, Yom-Tov.

Honey From the Anglo-Saxon, meaning "honey." The exact feminine and masculine Hebrew equivalent is Devash.

Honor From the Latin, meaning "glory" or "respect." HEBREW EQUIVA-LENTS: Adra, Hodiya, Tifara, Tiferet, Yocheved. MASCULINE HEBREW EQUIVALENTS: Amihod, Hadar, Hod, Nehedar, Pe'er.

Honora A variant form of Honor. *See* Honor.

Honorine A pet form of Honor. *See* Honor.

Hope From the Anglo-Saxon, meaning "trust, faith." HEBREW EQUIVA-LENTS: Bitcha, Emuna, Erga, Tochelet, Tzipiya. MASCULINE HEBREW EQUIVALENTS: Amit, Amitai, Amnon, Ne'eman, Yachil.

Horia, Horiah Variant spellings of Horiya. *See* Horiya.

Horiya, Horiyah (הוֹרִיָה) From the Hebrew, meaning "teaching of the Lord." The exact Hebrew equivalent is Horiya. MASCULINE HEBREW EQUIV-ALENTS: Aharon, Moran, Mori, Moriel, Yora.

Hortense From the Latin, meaning "gardener." HEBREW EQUIVALENTS: Adama, Gana, Karmela, Nava. MASCULINE HEBREW EQUIVALENTS: Adam, Ginat, Karmel, Karmeli.

Hude, Hudes (הוּדֶעס/הוּדְרֶע) Yiddish forms of Hadasah. *See* Hadasah. Also used as nicknames for Yehudit. *See* Yehudit.

Hudel (הוּדְל) A pet form of Hude. *See* Hude.

Hulda, Huldah Variant spellings of Chulda. *See* Chulda.

Ida From the Old English, meaning "fortunate warrior," or from the Old Norse, meaning "industrious." Also, from the Greek, meaning "happy." HEBREW EQUIVALENTS: Aliza, Aviga'yil, Charutza, Ditza, Gila, Semecha, Simcha, Zeriza. MASCULINE HEBREW EQUIVALENTS: Amel, Simcha, Yachdiel, Yagil, Yitzchak, Ziruz.

Idalee A combination of Ida and Lee. *See* Ida *and* Lee.

Idel, Idelle Pet forms of Ida. *See* Ida.

Idena A hybrid name of Ida and Dena (Dinah). *See* Ida *and* Dena.

Idette A pet form of Ida. *See* Ida.

Idit (אִידִית) A Yiddish form of the Hebrew name Yehudit (Judith). *See* Yehudit.

Idra (אִדְרָא/אִדְרָה) From the Aramaic, meaning "bone of a fish" or "fig tree," a symbol of scholarship. The exact Hebrew equivalent is Idra. MASCULINE HEBREW EQUIVALENTS: Aluf, Divla'yim, Moriel, Yora, Yorai.

Idria A variant spelling of Idriya. *See* Idriya.

Idrit (אִדְרִית) A variant form of Idriya. *See* Idriya. The exact Hebrew equivalent is Idrit.

Idriya (אִדְרִיָה) From the Hebrew, meaning "duck." The exact Hebrew equivalent is Idriya. The masculine Hebrew equivalent is Barvaz.

Ila A variant form of Ilit. *See* Ilit.

Ilana (אִילָנָה) From the Hebrew, meaning "tree." The exact Hebrew equivalent is Ilana. The exact masculine Hebrew equivalent is Ilan.

Ilanit (אִילָנִית) A variant form of Ilana. *See* Ilana. The exact Hebrew equivalent is Ilanit.

Ilene A variant spelling of Eileen. *See* Eileen.

Ilisa, Ilise Variant forms of Elisabeth. *See* Elisabeth.

Ilit (עִלִית) From the Aramaic, meaning "uppermost, superlative." The exact Hebrew equivalent is Ilit. MASCULINE HEBREW EQUIVALENTS: Adif, Ula.

Ilita (עִלִיתָה) A variant form of Ilit. *See* Ilit. The exact Hebrew equivalent is Ilita.

Ilsa, Ilse Variant forms of Elisabeth. *See* Elisabeth.

Ilyse A variant form of Elisabeth. *See* Elisabeth.

Ima A variant spelling of Imma. *See* Imma.

Imma (אִמָּא) From the Hebrew, meaning "mother." The exact Hebrew equivalent is Imma. The exact masculine Hebrew equivalent is Abba.

Imogen, Imogene From the Latin, meaning "image, likeness." HEBREW EQUIVALENTS: Michal, Micha'ela. MASCULINE HEBREW EQUIVALENTS: Micha, Micha'el.

Ina From the Latin, meaning "mother." The exact Hebrew equivalent is Imma. The exact masculine Hebrew equivalent is Abba.

Inez From the Greek and Portuguese, meaning "pure." HEBREW EQUIVALENTS: Penuya, Zaka, Zakit, Zakiya. MASCULINE HEBREW EQUIVALENTS: Amizakai, Tzach, Tzachai, Zakai.

Inga, Inge From the Old English, meaning "meadow." HEBREW EQUIVALENTS: Gana, Ganit, Sharona, Yardena, Yardeniya. MASCULINE HEBREW EQUIVALENTS: Gani, Ginton, Sharon, Yarden.

Inger A variant form of Inga. See Inga.

Ingrid From the Old English, meaning "Ing's ride." In Norse mythology, Ing is the god of fertility and peace. HEBREW EQUIVALENTS: Pora, Poriya, Shlomit, Shulamit. MASCULINE HEBREW EQUIVALENTS: Efra'yim, Pura, Shalom, Shlomi, Shlomo.

Iora From the Latin, meaning "gold." HEBREW EQUIVALENTS: Ofira, Paz, Paza, Zehava, Zehuvit. MASCULINE HEBREW EQUIVALENTS: Elifaz, Ofar, Ofir, Paz, Pazi, Zehavi.

Irena A Polish form of Irene. See Irene.

Irene From the Greek, meaning "peace." HEBREW EQUIVALENTS: Margaya, Rivka, Sha'anana, Shlomit, Shulamit. MASCULINE HEBREW EQUIVALENTS: Avshalom, Sha'anan, Shalom, Shelomo, Shelomya, Shlomiel.

Irenee A variant form of Irene. See Irene.

Irina A variant form of Irena. See Irena.

Iris In Greek mythology, the goddess of the rainbow. From the Latin, meaning "faith, hope." HEBREW EQUIVALENTS: Amana, Bitcha, Emuna, Keshet, Tzipiya. MASCULINE HEBREW EQUIVALENTS: Amitai, Amnon, Ne'eman, Yachil.

Irit (עִירִית) From the Hebrew, meaning "animal fodder." The exact Hebrew equivalent is Irit. MASCULINE HEBREW EQUIVALENTS: Garnit, Goren, Shachat.

Irma From the Anglo-Saxon, meaning "noble maid." HEBREW EQUIVALENTS: Alma, Batya, Na'ara, Nediva. MASCULINE HEBREW EQUIVALENTS: Adoniya, Aminadav, Avihud, Nadav, Yisrael.

Isa A pet form of Isabel, used chiefly in Scotland. See Isabel.

Isaaca (יִצְחָקָה) The feminine form of Issac, meaning "laughter." See Isaac (*masculine section*). The exact Hebrew equivalent is Yitzchaka.

Isabel, Isabele, Isabella, Isabelle Variant forms of Elisabeth, meaning "God's oath." See Elisabeth.

Isadora, Isidora Feminine forms of the masculine Isadore. See Isadore (*masculine section*).

Isobel A variant Scottish spelling of Isabel. See Isabel.

Israela A variant spelling of Yisraela. *See* Yisraela.

Israelit A variant spelling of Yisraela. *See* Yisraela.

Ita (אִיטָא) From the Celtic, meaning "thirsty." Also, a corrupt Yiddish form of Yehudit (Judith). *See* Yehudit. Also, a variant form of Yetta. *See* Yetta.

Iti (אִתִּי) From the Hebrew, meaning "with me." The exact Hebrew equivalent is Iti. MASCULINE HEBREW EQUIVALENTS: Itai, Itiel.

Itia A variant spelling of Itiya. *See* Itiya.

Itiya (אִיתִיָה) From the Hebrew, meaning "God is with me." The exact Hebrew equivalent is Itiya. MASCULINE HEBREW EQUIVALENTS: Itai, Itiel.

Itta A variant spelling of Ita. *See* Ita.

Itti A variant spelling of Itti. *See* Iti.

Ivana, Ivanna Feminine forms of Ivan, the Russian form of John. *See* John (*masculine section*).

Ivette A variant spelling of Yvette. *See* Yvette.

Ivria, Ivriah Variant spellings of Ivriya. *See* Ivriya.

Ivrit (עִבְרִית) From the Hebrew, meaning "Hebrew [language]." The exact Hebrew equivalent is Ivrit. The masculine Hebrew equivalent is Ivri.

Ivrita A variant form of Ivrit. *See* Ivrit.

Ivriya (עִבְרִיָה) The feminine form of Ivri, meaning "Hebrew." The exact Hebrew equivalent is Ivriya. The exact Hebrew equivalent is Ivri.

Ivy From the Middle English, meaning "vine." HEBREW EQUIVALENTS: Gafna, Gafnit, Gefen, Karmel, Karmela, Soreka. MASCULINE HEBREW EQUIVALENTS: Carmel, Gafni, Gefen, Kerem, Pardes.

Jackee A pet form of Jacoba and Jacqueline. *See* Jacob *and* Jacqueline.

Jacklyn, Jaclyn, Jaclynn Variant forms of Jacqueline. *See* Jacqueline.

Jacoba (יַעֲקֹבָה) The feminine form of Jacob, meaning "supplant" or "protect." *See* Jacob (*masculine section*). The exact Hebrew equivalent is Ya'akova. The exact masculine Hebrew equivalents are Ya'akov and Ya'akova.

Jacqueline A French form of Jacoba. *See* Jacoba.

Jacquelyn, Jacquelynne Variant spellings of Jacqueline. *See* Jacqueline.

Jael (יָעֵל) From the Hebrew, meaning "mountain goat" or "to ascend." The exact feminine and masculine Hebrew equivalent is Ya'el.

Jaen A variant spelling of Yaen. *See* Yaen.

Jaffa A variant spelling of Yafa. *See* Yafa.

Jafit A variant spelling of Yafit. *See* Yafit.

Jaime, Jaimee, Jaimie Feminine forms of James, derived from Jacob, meaning "to supplant" or "to protect." The exact Hebrew equivalent is Ya'akova. The exact masculine Hebrew equivalent is Ya'akov.

Jamie A variant spelling of Jaime. *See* Jaime.

Jan A pet form of Janice or Jeanette. *See* Janice *and* Jeanette.

Jane A variant English form of Johanna. *See* Johanna. Also, a feminine form of John. *See* John (*masculine section*).

Janet An English and Scottish form of Johanna. *See* Johanna.

Janetta An English form of Johanna. *See* Johanna.

Janette A variant spelling of Janet. *See* Janet.

Jani A pet form of Jane. *See* Jane.

Janice A variant form of Jane. *See* Jane.

Janie A pet form of Jane. *See* Jane.

Janiece A variant spelling of Janice. *See* Janice.

Janina, Janine Pet forms of Jane. *See* Jane.

Janis A variant spelling of Janice. *See* Janice.

Janita A Spanish pet form of Jane. *See* Jane.

Janna A pet form of Johanna. *See* Johanna.

Jardena A variant spelling of Yardena. *See* Yardena.

Jardenia A variant spelling of Yardeniya. *See* Yardeniya.

Jasmina (יַסְמִינָה) A variant form of Jasmine. *See* Jasmine. The exact Hebrew equivalent is Yasmina.

Jasmine (יַסְמִין) A Persian flower-name, usually referring to a flower in the olive family. The exact Hebrew equivalent is Yasmin. MASCULINE HEBREW EQUIVALENTS: Za'yit, Zefan.

Jean, Jeane Scottish forms of Johanna. *See* Johanna.

Jeanetta A variant form of Jeanette. *See* Jeanette.

Jeanette A French form of Johanna. *See* Johanna.

Jeanice A variant form of Jean. *See* Jean.

Jeanie A pet form of Jean. *See* Jean.

Jeanine A pet form of Jean. *See* Jean.

Jeanne A French form of Johanna. *See* Johanna.

Jeannette A variant spelling of Jeanette. *See* Jeanette.

Jeannine A variant spelling of Jeanine. *See* Jeanine.

Jedida, Jedidah Variant spellings of Yedida. *See* Yedida.

Jehane, Jehanne French forms of Johanna. *See* Johanna.

Jemima A variant spelling of Yemima. *See* Yemima.

Jemina A variant spelling of Yemina. *See* Yemina.

Jen A short form of Jeanette. *See* Jeanette. Also, a pet form of Jennifer.

Jenat A variant form of Jeanette. *See* Jeanette.

Jene A variant spelling of Jean. *See* Jean.

Jenerette A pet form of Jane. *See* Jane.

Jenine A pet form of Jane. *See* Jane.

Jenna A variant form of Jeanette. *See* Jeanette.

Jennie A pet form of Jean, Jeanette, and Jennifer. *See* Jean, Jeanette *and* Jennifer.

Jennifer From the Welsh, meaning "friend of peace." HEBREW EQUIVA-LENTS: Achishalom, Menucha, Sha'anana, Shalviya, Shelomit, Shula-mit. MASCULINE HEBREW EQUIVALENTS: Avshalom, Ish-Shalom, Meshu-lam, Shalom, Shelomo, Shlomi.

Jennilee A name created by combining Jennifer and Lee. *See* Jennifer *and* Lee.

Jenny An English and Scottish pet form of Johanna. *See* Johanna.

Jeralyn A variant spelling of Geralyn. *See* Geralyn.

Jeri, Jerri Pet forms of Geraldene. *See* Geraldene.

Jerriann A name created by combining Jerri and Ann. *See* Jerry (*masculine section*) *and* Ann.

Jerrilyn A name created by combining Jerri and Lyn. *See* Jerry (*masculine section*) *and* Lyn.

Jessica A variant form of Jessie. *See* Jessie.

Jessie A Scottish form of Johanna. *See* Johanna. Also, a feminine form of Jesse. *See* Jesse (*masculine section*).

Jethra (יִתְרָה) A feminine form of Jethro, meaning "abundance, riches." *See* Jethro (*masculine section*). The exact Hebrew equivalent is Yitra.

Jewel, Jewell From the Old French, meaning "joy." HEBREW EQUIVA-LENTS: Aliza, Ditza, Gila, Rina. MASCULINE HEBREW EQUIVALENTS: Simcha, Yachdiel, Yagil, Yitzchak.

Jill A variant spelling of Gill. *See* Gill.

Joan A variant form of Johanna. *See* Johanna.

Joann, Jo Ann Short forms of Joanna. *See* Joanna.

Joanna A short form of Johanna. *See* Johanna.

Joanne A variant spelling of Joann. *See* Joann.

Jo-Anne A hybrid name compounded of Jo (Josephine) and Ann(e). *See* Josephine *and* Ann(e).

Jocelin, Joceline German forms of the Hebrew Jacoba, the feminine form of Jacob, meaning "supplant" or "protect." The exact Hebrew equivalent is Ya'akova. The exact masculine Hebrew equivalent is Ya'akov.

Jocelyn, Jocelyne Variant spellings of Jocelin. *See* Jocelin.

Jodette A French form of Jodi or Jocelin. *See* Jodi *and* Jocelin.

Jodi, Jodie, Jody Pet forms of Judith. *See* Judith. Also, pet forms of Josephine. *See* Josephine.

Joela, Joella (יוֹאָלָה) Feminine forms of Joel, meaning "God is willing." The exact Hebrew equivalent is Yo'ela. The exact masculine Hebrew equivalent is Yo'el.

Joelle A variant form of Joela. *See* Joela.

Joellen A variant form of Joelynn. *See* Joelynn.

Joelynn A hybrid form of Joela and Lynn. *See* Joela *and* Lynn.

Joette A pet form from the masculine Joseph. *See* Joseph (*masculine section*).

Johan, Johanna, Johanne German and English forms of the Hebrew masculine name Yochanan, meaning "God is gracious." The exact masculine Hebrew equivalent is Yochanan.

Johanne A variant form of Johanna. *See* Johanna.

Johnna A variant form of Johanna. *See* Johanna.

Joice A variant spelling of Joyce. *See* Joyce.

Jolanda A variant spelling of Yolande. *See* Yolande.

Jolene A pet form of Jolie. *See* Jolie.

Joletta A pet form of Jolie. *See* Jolie.

Jolie From the French, meaning "high spirits, good humor, pleasant." HEBREW EQUIVALENTS: Achino'am, Adina, Adiva, Na'ama, Na'omi, Na'amiya, Ne'ima. MASCULINE HEBREW EQUIVALENTS: Achino'am, Adin, Adiv, Na'aman, No'am.

Joliet A variant form of Jolie or Juliet. *See* Jolie *and* Juliet.

Jonina A variant spelling of Yonina. *See* Yonina.

Jonit, Jonita Variant spellings of Yonit and Yonita. *See* Yonit.

Jordana, Jordena Feminine forms of Jordan. *See* Jordan (*masculine section*).

Jordi, Jordie Pet forms of Jordana. *See* Jordana.

Joscelin An Old French form of Jocelin. *See* Jocelin.

Joscelind A variant form of Jocelin. *See* Jocelin.

Josefa, Josepha Variant spellings of Yosifa. *See* Yosifa.

Josephine A feminine French form of Joseph. *See* Joseph (*masculine section*).

Josetta, Josette Pet forms of Jocelyn and Josephine. *See* Jocelyn *and* Josephine.

Joslyn A variant spelling of Jocelyn. *See* Jocelyn.

Jovita A Spanish pet form of Joy. *See* Joy.

Joy A short form of Joyce. *See* Joyce.

Joya A variant form of Joy. *See* Joy.

Joyce From the Latin, meaning "jovial, merry." HEBREW EQUIVALENTS: Avigal, Aviga'yil, Gila, Gilit, Giliya, Ronela, Ronena, Yitzchaka. MASCULINE HEBREW EQUIVALENTS: Gil, Gildad, Gili, Marnin, Ranen, Ranon, Yagil, Yitzchak.

Judi, Judie Pet forms of Judith. *See* Judith.

Judith An Anglicized form of Yehudit. *See* Yehudit.

Judy A pet form of Judith. *See* Judith.

Jule A variant form of Julia. *See* Julia.

Julee A variant spelling of Julie. *See* Julie.

Juleen A variant form of Julia. *See* Julia.

Jules A variant form of Julia. *See* Julia.

Julia From the Greek, meaning "soft-haired," symbolizing youth. HE-
BREW EQUIVALENTS: Alma, Aviva, Delila, Nima, Tze'ira, Yenika, Zilpa.
MASCULINE HEBREW EQUIVALENTS: Aviv, Elam, Se'orim, Yefet.

Julian, Juliana Variant forms of Julia. *See* Julia.

Julie A pet form of Julia. *See* Julia.

Julienne The French form of Julia. *See* Julia.

Juliet A French pet form of Julia. *See* Julia.

Julieta A pet form of Julia. *See* Julia.

Juliette A French pet form of Julia. *See* Julia.

June From the Latin, meaning "ever youthful." HEBREW EQUIVALENTS:
Aviva, Avivi, Avivit, Tze'ira, Yenika. MASCULINE HEBREW EQUIVALENTS:
Aviv, Avrech, Elino'ar, Zuta, Zutra.

Justina, Justine Feminine forms of Justin. *See* Justin (*masculine
section*).

Kadia A variant spelling of Kadiya. *See* Kadiya.

Kadisha (קַדִישָׁה) From the Hebrew, meaning "holy." The exact equivalent is Kadisha. The exact masculine Hebrew equivalent is Kadish.

Kadiya (כַּדִיָה) From the Hebrew, meaning "pitcher." The exact Hebrew
equivalent is Kadiya. The exact masculine Hebrew equivalent is Kadi.

Kadya A variant form of Kadiya. *See* Kadiya.

Kaethe A variant form of Kathy. *See* Kathy.

Kaile, Kaille Variant forms of Kelila. *See* Kelila.

Kalanit (כַּלָנִית) A cup-shaped plant with colorful flowers, grown in
Israel. The exact Hebrew equivalent is Kalanit. MASCULINE HEBREW
EQUIVALENTS: Chavakuk, Shatil, Tzemach.

Kaley A variant form of Kelly. *See* Kelly.

Kalia A variant form of Kelila. *See* Kelila.

Kara A pet form of Katherine. *See* Katherine.

Karen A Danish form of Katherine. *See* Katherine.

Kari A variant spelling of Carrie. *See* Carrie.

Karin A variant spelling of Karen. *See* Karen.

Karla A feminine form of Karl. *See* Karl (*masculine section*).

Karleen A pet form of Karla. *See* Karla.

Karlene A pet form of Karla. *See* Karla.

Karma A variant spelling of Carma. *See* Carma.

Karmel A variant spelling of Carmel. *See* Carmel.

Karmela A variant spelling of Carmela. *See* Carmela.

Karmeli A variant spelling of Carmeli. *See* Carmeli.

Karmelit A variant spelling of Carmelit. *See* Carmelit.

Karmit A variant spelling of Carmit. *See* Carmit.

Karmiya A variant spelling of Carmia. *See* Carmia.

Karna A variant spelling of Carna. *See* Carna.

Karni A variant spelling of Carni. *See* Carni.

Karnia A variant spelling of Carnia. *See* Carnia.

Karniela, Karniella Variant spellings of Carniela. *See* Carniela.

Karnit A variant spelling of Carnit. *See* Carnit.

Karol, Karole Variant spellings of Carol. *See* Carol.

Karolina The Polish form of Karolyn. *See* Karolyn.

Karolyn A variant spelling of Carolyn and Caroline. *See* Caroline.

Karon A variant spelling of Karen. *See* Karen.

Karyl A variant spelling of Carol. *See* Carol.

Karyn A variant spelling of Karen. *See* Karen.

Kaspit (כַּסְפִּית) From the Hebrew, meaning "silver." The exact Hebrew equivalent is Kaspit. MASCULINE HEBREW EQUIVALENTS: Kaspi, Kesef.

Katania, Kataniya (קְטַנְיָה) From the Hebrew, meaning "small." The exact Hebrew equivalent is Kataniya. The exact masculine Hebrew equivalent is Katan.

Kate A pet form of Katherine. *See* Katherine.

Katharine A variant spelling of Katherine. *See* Katherine.

Kathe A pet form of Katherine. *See* Katherine.

Katherine From the Greek, meaning "pure, unsullied." Catherine is the more popular spelling. HEBREW EQUIVALENTS: Berura, Penuya, Zaka, Zakiya, Zakit. MASCULINE HEBREW EQUIVALENTS: Amizakai, Barur, Tzach, Tzachai, Zakai.

Kathie A pet form of Katherine. *See* Katherine.

Kathleen A variant spelling of Cathleen. *See* Cathleen.

Kathryn A variant spelling of Katherine. *See* Katherine.

Kathy A pet form of Katherine. *See* Katherine.

Kati, Katie Pet forms of Katherine. *See* Katherine.

Katrina, Katrine Variant forms of Katherine. *See* Katherine.

Katy A pet form of Katherine. *See* Katherine.

Kay From the Greek, meaning "rejoice." *See* Joyce. Also, a form of Katherine. *See* Katherine.

Kayla, Kayle (קיילָא/קיילֶע) Variant forms of Kelila. Or, a Yiddish form of Celia. *See* Kelila *and* Celia.

Kedma (קַדְמָה) From the Hebrew, meaning "east, eastward." The exact feminine and masculine Hebrew equivalent is Kedma.

Kefira (כְּפִירָה) From the Hebrew, meaning "young lioness." The exact Hebrew equivalent is Kefira. The exact masculine Hebrew equivalent is Kefir.

Kelila (כְּלִילָה) From the Hebrew, meaning "crown" or "laurels." The exact Hebrew equivalent is Kelila. MASCULINE HEBREW EQUIVALENTS: Kalil, Kalul.

Kelula (כְּלוּלָה) A variant form of Kelila. See Kelila. The exact Hebrew equivalent is Kelula.

Kenna From the Old Norse, meaning "to have knowledge." HEBREW EQUIVALENTS: Buna, Chochma, Ge'ona. MASCULINE HEBREW EQUIVALENTS: Bina, Buna, Navon, Yediel.

Kerem (כֶּרֶם) From the Hebrew, meaning "vineyard." The exact feminine and masculine Hebrew equivalent is Kerem.

Keren, Keryn (קֶרֶן) From the Hebrew, meaning "horn." The exact feminine and masculine Hebrew equivalent is Keren.

Keret (קֶרֶת) From the Hebrew, meaning "city, settlement." The exact Hebrew equivalent is Keret. MASCULINE HEBREW EQUIVALENTS: Dur, Devir, Zevul, Zevulun.

Keshet (קֶשֶׁת) From the Hebrew, meaning "bow, rainbow." The exact Hebrew equivalent is Keshet. MASCULINE HEBREW EQUIVALENTS: Raviv, Tal.

Keshisha (קְשִׁישָׁה) From the Hebrew, meaning "old, elder." The exact Hebrew equivalent is Keshisha. MASCULINE HEBREW EQUIVALENTS: Yashish, Yeshishai, Zaken.

Ketaniya (קְטַנִיָה) A variant form of Kataniya. See Kataniya. The exact Hebrew equivalent is Ketaniya.

Ketifa (קְטִיפָה) From the Hebrew and Arabic, meaning "to pluck [fruit]." The exact Hebrew equivalent is Ketifa. MASCULINE HEBREW EQUIVALENTS: Achazya, Gidon, Kotz.

Ketana (קְטַנָה) From the Hebrew, meaning "small." The exact Hebrew equivalent is Ketana. The exact masculine Hebrew equivalent is Katan.

Ketina (קְטִינָא/קְטִינָה) From the Aramaic, meaning "minor" or "small child." The exact Hebrew equivalent is Ketina. The exact masculine Hebrew equivalent is Katan.

Ketzia, Ketziah (קְצִיעָה) From the Hebrew, meaning "a powdered, fragrant, cinnamon-like bark." The exact Hebrew equivalent is Ketzia. The masculine Hebrew equivalent is Bosem.

Kevuda (כְּבוּדָה) From the Hebrew, meaning "precious" or "respected." The exact Hebrew equivalent is Kevuda. The exact masculine Hebrew equivalent is Kavud.

Kezi A pet form of Ketzia. See Ketzia.

Kezia, Keziah Variant spellings of Ketzia. See Ketzia.

Kezzi, Kezzie, Kezzy Pet forms of Ketzia. See Ketzia.

Kim A pet form of Kimberly. See Kimberly.

Kimberley, Kimberly From "kimberlite," a type of rock formation containing diamonds. HEBREW EQUIVALENTS: Yahaloma, Yahalomit. The masculine Hebrew equivalent is Yahalom.

Kinneret (כִּנֶּרֶת) Probably from the Hebrew, meaning "harp." The exact Hebrew equivalent is Kinneret. The masculine Hebrew equivalent is Kinori.

Kirsten From the Old English, meaning "stone, church." HEBREW EQUIVALENTS: Devira, Gazit. MASCULINE HEBREW EQUIVALENTS: Devir, Even-Ezer.

Kit A pet form of Katherine. See Katherine.

Kitra (כִּתְרָה/כִּתְרָא) From the Aramaic, meaning "crown." The exact Hebrew equivalent is Kitra. The masculine Hebrew equivalent is Kitron.

Kitrit (כִּתְרִית) A variant form of Kitra. See Kitra. The exact Hebrew equivalent is Kitrit.

Kitron (כִּתְרוֹן) From the Hebrew, meaning "crown." The exact feminine and masculine Hebrew equivalent is Kitron.

Kitty A pet form of Katherine. See Katherine.

Klara A variant spelling of Clara. See Clara.

Kosbi A variant spelling of Kozvi. See Kozvi.

Kozvi (כָּזְבִּי) From the Hebrew, meaning "lie, falsehood." The exact Hebrew equivalent is Kosvi. The masculine Hebrew equivalent is Mirma.

Kochava (כּוֹכָבָה) From the Hebrew, meaning "star." The exact Hebrew equivalent is Kochava. The exact masculine Hebrew equivalent is Kochav.

Kochavit (כּוֹכָבִית) A variant form of Kochava. See Kochava.

Koranit (קוֹרָנִית) From the Hebrew, meaning "thistle." The exact Hebrew equivalent is Koranit. The masculine Hebrew equivalent is Kotz.

Korenet (קוֹרֶנֶת) From the Hebrew, meaning "to shine, emit rays." The exact Hebrew equivalent is Korenet. MASCULINE HEBREW EQUIVALENTS: Karin, Karni, Karniel.

Kori A variant spelling of Corey. See Corey.

Krayna, Krayne (קְרײַנֶע/קְרײַנָא) Variant forms of Kreine. See Kreine.

Kreindel (קְרײַנְדֶעל) A pet form of Kreine. See Kreine.

Kreine (קְרײַנֶע) A Yiddish form of the German *Krone,* meaning "crown." HEBREW EQUIVALENTS: Atara, Ateret, Atura, Kelila, Kelula, Kitra. MASCULINE HEBREW EQUIVALENTS: Atur, Eter, Kalul, Katriel, Keter, Kitron.

Kryna A variant spelling of Kreine. See Kreine.

Kyla, Kyle (קײַלָע/קײַלָא) Variant forms of Kelila. See Kelila.

Laeh A variant spelling of Leah. See Leah.

Laila A variant spelling of Leila. See Leila.

Laili, Lailie Variant spellings of Leili and Leilie. See Leili.

Lana From the Latin, meaning "woolly." The Hebrew equivalent is Tzameret. The masculine equivalent is Tzemari.

Lani From the Hawaiian, meaning "sky, heaven." HEBREW EQUIVALENTS: Meroma, Rama, Ramit, Romema, Romiya, Ruma. MASCULINE HEBREW EQUIVALENTS: Marom, Merom, Ram, Rami, Romem.

Lara A variant spelling of Laura. *See* Laura.

Laraine, Larainne From the Latin, meaning "sea bird." HEBREW EQUIVALENTS: A'ya, Da'a, Da'ya, Tziparta, Tzipora, Tziporiya. MASCULINE HEBREW EQUIVALENTS: Gozal, Tzipor.

Laris, Larisa, Larissa From the Latin, meaning "cheerful." HEBREW EQUIVALENTS: Aviga'yil, Elza, Gila, Gilana, Giliya, Gilit, Rina. MASCULINE HEBREW EQUIVALENTS: Aliz, Gilon, Eliran, Elez, Yagil.

Lavina A variant form of Lavinia. *See* Lavinia.

Lavinia From the Latin, meaning "woman of Rome," symbolizing sophistication. HEBREW EQUIVALENTS: Adoniya, Bina, Buna, Sara. MASCULINE HEBREW EQUIVALENTS: Ga'on, Navon, Zavin.

Lark From the Old English, meaning "old" or "large." Also, a name applied to a large family of songbirds. HEBREW EQUIVALENTS: A'ya, Da'a, Da'ya, Tzipora, Tziporiya, Zekena. MASCULINE HEBREW EQUIVALENTS: Gozal, Tzipor, Zaken.

Laura A variant form of the masculine Laurel, meaning "laurel," a symbol of victory. HEBREW EQUIVALENTS: Atara, Dafna, Gavriela, Hadasa, Tzefira. MASCULINE HEBREW EQUIVALENTS: Gavriel, Gever, Gover, Netziach, Yatzliach.

Lauraine A variant form of Laura. *See* Laura.

Laure A variant form of Laura. *See* Laura.

Laurel A variant form of Laura. *See* Laura.

Lauren A variant form of Laura. *See* Laura.

Lauretta, Laurette Pet forms of Laura. *See* Laura.

Lauri, Laurie Pet forms of Laura. *See* Laura.

Laurice A variant form of Laurel. *See* Laurel.

Laverne From the Latin and French, meaning "spring, springlike" or "verdant." HEBREW EQUIVALENTS: Aviva, Avivi, Silona, Silonit, Yarkona. MASCULINE HEBREW EQUIVALENTS: Aviv, Avivi, Silon, Yarkon.

Laya (לֵאָה) The Hebrew form of Leah. *See* Leah. The exact Hebrew equivalent is Laya.

Laylie A variant spelling of Leili. *See* Leili.

Lea (לֵאָה) A French form of Leah. *See* Leah.

Leah (לֵאָה) From the Hebrew, meaning "to be weary." The exact Hebrew equivalent is Laya. The masculine Hebrew equivalent is Do'eg.

Leanne A name created by combining Leah and Anne. *See* Leah *and* Anne.

Leanor, Leanore Variant forms of Eleanor. *See* Eleanor.

Leatrice A name created by combining Leah and Beatrice. *See* Leah *and* Beatrice.

Lee From the Anglo-Saxon, meaning "field, meadow." HEBREW EQUIVALENTS: Chursha, Nira, Nirit, Sharona. MASCULINE HEBREW EQUIVALENTS: Carmel, Hevel, Sharon. Also, a pet form of Leah. *See* Leah.

Leeba A variant spelling of Liba. *See* Liba.

Leesa, Leeza Variant spellings of Lisa. *See* Lisa.

Leila, Leilah (לַיְלָה) From the Arabic and Hebrew, meaning "night" or "dark, oriental beauty." The exact Hebrew equivalent is Laila. MASCULINE HEBREW EQUIVALENTS: Adar, Ashchur, Kalil, Nechmad, Ra'anan, Yefet.

Leilani From the Hawaiian, meaning "heavenly flower." HEBREW EQUIVALENTS: Chelmit, Chelmonit, Kalanit, Shoshana, Yasmin. MASCULINE HEBREW EQUIVALENTS: Admon, Nitzan, Perach, Shoshan, Yasmin.

Leili, Leilie A variant form of Leila. *See* Leila.

Lela From the Anglo-Saxon, meaning "loyal, faithful." HEBREW EQUIVALENTS: Amnona, Bitcha, Emuna, Tikva. MASCULINE HEBREW EQUIVALENTS: Amitai, Amnon, Buki, Heman.

Leland From the Old English, meaning "meadowland." HEBREW EQUIVALENTS: Gana, Ganit, Ganya, Gina, Sharona, Yardeniya. MASCULINE HEBREW EQUIVALENTS: Bustenai, Gan, Ginton, Sharon, Yarden.

Lelani A variant spelling of Leilani. *See* Leilani.

Lelia A variant form of Lela. *See* Lela.

Lena (לִינָה) A pet form of Eleanor, Helen, and Magdalene. *See* Eleanor, Helen, *and* Magdalene. Also, from the Hebrew, meaning "lodging, dwelling place," and from the Old English, meaning "farm." The exact Hebrew equivalent is Lina. MASCULINE HEBREW EQUIVALENTS: Dur, Malon, Zevul, Zevulun.

Lennie A pet form of Eleanor. *See* Eleanor.

Lenora, Lenore Pet forms of Eleanor. *See* Eleanor.

Leola From the Anglo-Saxon, meaning "deer," connoting swiftness. HEBREW EQUIVALENTS: A'yelet, Ofra, Tzivya, Ya'ala, Ya'alit. MASCULINE HEBREW EQUIVALENTS: Bo'az, Efer, Tzevi, Tzeviel, Tzivyon.

Leona From the Greek, meaning "lion-like," connoting strength. HEBREW EQUIVALENTS: Amtza, Ariel, Ariela, Gavrila, Gibora, Kefira, Levia. MASCULINE HEBREW EQUIVALENTS: Ari, Ariel, Aryeh, Avicha'yil, Gavriel, Lavi, La'yish.

Leonia A variant spelling of Leona. *See* Leona.

Leonie A pet form of Leona. *See* Leona.

Leonora, Leonore Variant forms of Eleanor. *See* Eleanor.

Leontine, Leontyne From the Latin, meaning "lion-like." HEBREW EQUIVALENTS: Ariel, Ariela, Gurit, Kefira, Levia. MASCULINE HEBREW EQUIVALENTS: Arel, Ari, Ariel, Gur, Gur-Aryeh, Lavi.

Leora A variant spelling of Liora. *See* Liora.

Leorit A variant spelling of Liorit. *See* Liorit.

Leron A variant spelling of Liron. *See* Liron.

Lerone A variant spelling of Leron. *See* Leron.

Lesley, Leslie From the Anglo-Saxon, meaning "meadowland." HEBREW EQUIVALENTS: Gana, Karmela, Nava, Sharona, Yardeniya. MASCULINE HEBREW EQUIVALENTS: Gan, Ginton, Karmeli, Ya'ari, Yarden.

Leta Probably a form of Elizabeth. *See* Elizabeth.

Letifa, Letipha (לְטִיפָה) From the Hebrew, meaning "caress." The exact Hebrew equivalent is Letifa. The exact masculine Hebrew equivalent is Latif.

Letitia From the Latin, meaning "joy." HEBREW EQUIVALENTS: Aliza, Elza, Gila, Gilana, Liron, Ronli. MASCULINE HEBREW EQUIVALENTS: Agil, Eliran, Eles, Elez, Gilon, Yachdiel, Yitzchak.

Lettie, Letty Pet forms of Elizabeth. *See* Elizabeth.

Leuma (לְאוּמָה) From the Hebrew, meaning "nation." The exact Hebrew equivalent is Le'uma. The exact masculine Hebrew equivalent is Le'umi.

Leumi (לְאוּמִי) From the Hebrew, meaning "nation, national." The exact feminine and masculine Hebrew equivalent is Le'umi.

Levana (לְבָנָה) From the Hebrew, meaning "white" or "moon." The exact Hebrew equivalent is Levana. The exact masculine Hebrew equivalent is Lavan.

Levani (לְבָנִי) From the Fijian, meaning "anointed with oil." Also, a variant form of Levana. *See* Levana. The exact Hebrew equivalent is Levani. MASCULINE HEBREW EQUIVALENTS: Lavan, Levana, Mashiach, Yitzhar.

Levia, Leviah (לְבִיאָה) From the Hebrew, meaning "lioness of the Lord." The exact Hebrew equivalent is Levia. The exact masculine Hebrew equivalent is Lavi.

Levina From the Middle English, meaning "to shine." HEBREW EQUIVALENTS: Hillela, Korenet, Levana, Me'ira, Yahaloma, Yahalomit, Zohar. MASCULINE HEBREW EQUIVALENTS: Hillel, Me'ir, Yizrach, Zarchi, Zerach, Zivi, Zohar.

Leviva (לְבִיבָה) From the Hebrew, meaning "pancake." The exact Hebrew equivalent is Leviva.

Levona (לְבוֹנָה) From the Hebrew, meaning "frankincense," so called because of its white color. The exact Hebrew equivalent is Levona. The exact masculine Hebrew equivalent is Lavan.

Leya A variant spelling of Leah. *See* Leah.

Leyla A variant spelling of Leila. *See* Leila.

Li (לִי) From the Hebrew, meaning "to me." *See* Lee.

Lia, Liah Variant spellings of Leah. *See* Leah.

Liba (לִיבָּא) A variant Yiddish form of Libe. *See* Libe.

Libbie, Libby Diminutive forms of Elizabeth. *See* Elizabeth.

Libe (לִיבֶּע) A Yiddish form of the German *liebe,* meaning "loved one, dear one." Also, from the Hebrew *lev,* meaning "heart." HEBREW EQUIVALENTS: Ahava, Chaviva, Chiba, Davida. MASCULINE HEBREW EQUIVALENTS: Chaviv, David, Ehud, Yakar, Yakir.

Liberty From the Latin, meaning "freedom." HEBREW EQUIVALENTS: Chafshiya, Cheruta, Derora, Li-Dror. MASCULINE HEBREW EQUIVALENTS: Cherut, Deror, Rechavam, Rechavya.

Libi (לִבִּי) A variant form of Liba. *See* Liba.

Libke, Libkeh (לִיבְּקֶע) Yiddish pet forms of Libe. *See* Libe.

Lieba (לִיבָּא) A variant Yiddish form of Liebe. *See* Liebe.

Liebe (לִיבֶּע) A variant spelling of Libe. *See* Libe.

Lila, Lilac, Lilah (לִילָךְ) Flower names of Persian origin. The exact Hebrew equivalent is Lilach. MASCULINE HEBREW EQUIVALENTS: Efra'yim, Pekach, Perachya, Tzemach.

Lili, Lilia Variant forms of Lilian. *See* Lilian.

Lilian From the Greek and Latin, meaning "lily." HEBREW EQUIVALENTS: Chavatzelet, Nitza, Shoshan, Shoshana. MASCULINE HEBREW EQUIVALENTS: Efra'yim, Pekach, Perachya, Sheva, Shoshan, Shushan.

Lilibet A pet form of Elizabeth. *See* Elizabeth.

Lilita A pet form of Lilian. *See* Lilian.

Lilli A pet form of Lillian. *See* Lillian.

Lillian A variant spelling of Lilian. *See* Lilian.

Lilo (לִי־לוֹ/לִילוֹ) From the Hebrew, meaning "to be generous." HEBREW EQUIVALENTS: Nedavya, Nediva. MASCULINE HEBREW EQUIVALENTS: Nadav, Nadiv, Nedavya.

Lilly A pet form of Lillian. *See* Lillian.

Lily A pet form of Lilian. *See* Lilian.

Lilyan A variant spelling of Lilian. *See* Lilian.

Lilybeth A hybrid name of Lily (Lilian) and Beth (Elizabeth). *See* Lilian *and* Elizabeth.

Lina A pet form of Caroline and Adelina. *See* Caroline *and* Adelina. Also, a variant spelling of Lena. *See* Lena.

Linda From the Latin and Spanish, meaning "handsome, pretty," or from the Anglo-Saxon, meaning "lovely or gentle maid." HEBREW EQUIVALENTS: Alma, Na'ama, Na'omi, Tova, Yafa. MASCULINE HEBREW EQUIVALENTS: Binyamin, Chemdan, Moshe, Na'arai, Nun.

Linn, Linne From the Welsh, meaning "waterfall, lake." HEBREW EQUIVALENTS: Arnona, Ashdoda, Derora, Marata, Miryam, Silona, Silonit. MASCULINE HEBREW EQUIVALENTS: Arnon, Avi'yam, Enan, Eshed, Moshe, Peleg, Silon.

Linnet From the Latin, meaning "flaxen or golden-haired." HEBREW EQUIVALENTS: Paziya, Pazit, Tzehuva, Zehuva. MASCULINE HEBREW EQUIVALENTS: Elifaz, Paz, Zahavi.

Lior (לי־אור/ליאור) From the Hebrew, meaning "I have light." The exact feminine and masculine Hebrew equivalent is Lior.

Liora (לי־אורה/ליאורה) From the Hebrew, meaning "Light is mine." The exact Hebrew equivalent is Liora. The exact masculine Hebrew equivalent is Lior.

Liorit (ליאורית) A variant form of Liora. See Liora. Liorit is the exact Hebrew equivalent.

Lipke, Lipkeh (ליפקע) Variant forms of the Yiddish Libke. See Libke.

Lirit (לירית) A Hebrew form of the Greek, meaning "lyrical, musical, poetic." The exact Hebrew equivalent is Lirit. MASCULINE HEBREW EQUIVALENTS: Amiram, Liron, Yaron, Zemarya, Zimran.

Liron (לי־רון/לירון) From the Hebrew, meaning "Song is mine." The exact feminine and masculine Hebrew equivalent is Liron.

Lirona (לירונה) A variant form of Liron. See Liron.

Lirone A variant spelling of Liron. See Liron.

Lisa A pet form of Elizabeth. See Elizabeth.

Lital (ליטל) From the Hebrew, meaning "Dew [rain] is mine." The exact Hebrew equivalent is Lital. MASCULINE HEBREW EQUIVALENTS: Tal, Tal-Or, Tal-Shachar.

Livana A variant spelling of Levana. See Levana.

Livia A short form of Olivia. See Olivia.

Liviya A variant form of Levia. See Levia.

Livna (לבנה) From the Hebrew, meaning "white." The exact Hebrew equivalent is Livna. The exact masculine Hebrew equivalent is Lavan.

Livnat (לבנת) A variant form of Livna. See Livna. The exact Hebrew equivalent is Livnat.

Livya (לויה) From the Hebrew, meaning "crown." The exact Hebrew equivalent is Livya. MASCULINE HEBREW EQUIVALENTS: Kalil, Katriel, Keter, Kitron, Taga.

Liza A pet form of Elizabeth. See Elizabeth.

Lizbeth A pet form of Elizabeth. See Elizabeth.

Lize A variant spelling of Liza. See Liza.

Lizette A pet form of Elizabeth. See Elizabeth.

Lizzie, Lizzy Pet forms of Elizabeth. See Elizabeth.

Lois From the Greek, meaning "good, desirable." HEBREW EQUIVALENTS: Bat-Tziyon, Shifra, Tova, Yatva. MASCULINE HEBREW EQUIVALENTS: Ben-Tziyon, Na'am, Na'aman, Tuviya.

Lola A pet form of the Italian Carlotta. See Carlotta.

Lora From the Latin, meaning "she who weeps, sorrowful," or from the Old High German, meaning "famous warrior." HEBREW EQUIVALENTS: Bat-Shua, Mara, Marata, Miryam, Tzara. MASCULINE HEBREW EQUIVALENTS: Amos, Ben-Oni, Iyov, Onan.

Loraine A variant form of Lora. See Lora.

Loran, Lorann Hybrid forms of Laura and Ann. *See* Laura *and* Ann.

Loree A variant spelling of Laurie. *See* Laurie.

Lorelei From the German, meaning "melody, song." HEBREW EQUIVALENTS: Lirit, Rina, Shira, Tehila. MASCULINE HEBREW EQUIVALENTS: Aharon, Ana, Liron, Yaron, Zemer.

Loren From the Latin, meaning "crowned with laurel," connoting victory. HEBREW EQUIVALENTS: Dafna, Hadasa, Kelila, Kelula, Livya, Taga. MASCULINE HEBREW EQUIVALENTS: Katriel, Kitron, Netziach, Yatzliach.

Loretta, Lorette From the Anglo-Saxon, meaning "ignorant." EUPHEMISTIC HEBREW EQUIVALENTS: Bina, Buna, Da'at, Datiela, Milka. EUPHEMISTIC MASCULINE HEBREW EQUIVALENTS: Achban, Bina, Bun, Datan, Chanoch, Yavin, Yosha.

Lori A pet form of Lora. *See* Lora.

Lorna From the Anglo-Saxon, meaning "lost, forlorn, forsaken." HEBREW EQUIVALENTS: Azuva, Hagar, Sarida. MASCULINE HEBREW EQUIVALENTS: Gershom, Gershon, Sarid, Yisma.

Lorraine A variant spelling of Loraine. *See* Loraine.

Lorri A pet form of Laura. *See* Laura.

Lorrin A variant form of Lora. *See* Lora.

Loryn A variant form of Lora. *See* Lora.

Lotta, Lotte Pet forms of Charlotte. *See* Charlotte.

Lottie A pet form of Charlotte. *See* Charlotte.

Louisa From the Anglo-Saxon, meaning "refuge of the people, warrior-prince." HEBREW EQUIVALENTS: Gavriela, Gavrila, Sara, Tigra, Yisr'ela. MASCULINE HEBREW EQUIVALENTS: Avicha'yil, La'yish, Naftali, Shemar-yahu.

Louise A French form of Louisa. *See* Louisa.

Loura A variant spelling of Laura. *See* Laura.

Luan, Luann, Luanne Hybrid forms of Laura and Ann. *See* Laura *and* Ann.

Luba (לוּבָּא) A variant Yiddish form of Liba. *See* Liba.

Lucette A pet form of Lucille. *See* Lucile.

Luci A pet form of Lucile. *See* Lucile.

Lucia A diminutive form of Lucile. *See* Lucile.

Lucette A pet form of Lucile. *See* Lucile.

Luci A pet form of Lucile. *See* Lucile.

Lucia A diminutive form of Lucile. *See* Lucile.

Lucie A pet form of Lucile. *See* Lucile.

Lucile, Lucille From the Latin, meaning "light" or "daybreak." HEBREW EQUIVALENTS: Behira, Me'ira, Liora, Nahara, Ora. MASCULINE HEBREW EQUIVALENTS: Me'ir, Lapidos, Lior, Uriel, Zerachya.

Lucinda An English form of Lucia. *See* Lucia.

Lucy   An English form of Lucia. *See* Lucia.

Luella   A hybrid of Louise and Ella. *See* Louise *and* Ella.

Luisa   An Italian and Spanish form of Louise. *See* Louise.

Luise   A variant French form of Louise. *See* Louise.

Lula   A pet form of Louise. *See* Louise.

Lulu   A pet form of Louise. *See* Louise.

Luna   From the Latin, meaning "moon" or "shining one." The exact Hebrew equivalent is Levana. MASCULINE HEBREW EQUIVALENTS: Elior, Lavan, Lior, Me'ir, Shraga, Shragai, Uri.

Lunetta, Lunette   Pet forms of Luna. *See* Luna.

Lupita   From the Latin, meaning "wolf." The Hebrew equivalent is Alma. MASCULINE HEBREW EQUIVALENTS: Ze'ev, Zev.

Lyda   A Greek place-name, meaning "maiden from Lydia." HEBREW EQUIVALENTS: Alma, Bat-Tziyon, Na'ara, Riva, Tze'ira. MASCULINE HEBREW EQUIVALENTS: Ben, Binyamin, Re'uven.

Lydia   A variant form of Lyda. *See* Lyda.

Lyn   A variant spelling of Linn. *See* Linn.

Lynette   A pet form of Lyn. *See* Lyn.

Lynn, Lynne   Variant spellings of Linn. *See* Linn.

Lys   A pet form of Elisabeth. *See* Elisabeth.

Mabel   From the Latin, meaning "my beautiful one," or from the Old Irish, meaning "merry." HEBREW EQUIVALENTS: Achino'am, Avicha'yil, Gila, Na'omi, Shifra. MASCULINE HEBREW EQUIVALENTS: Avino'am, Chemdan, Na'am, Na'aman, Simcha, Yagil.

Mabella, Mabelle   Variant forms of Mabel. *See* Mabel.

Mable   A variant spelling of Mabel. *See* Mabel.

Madelaine   A variant form of Magdalene. *See* Magdalene.

Madeleine, Madeline   French forms of Magdalene. *See* Magdalene.

Madelon   A variant form of Magdalene. *See* Magdalene.

Madelyn   A variant form of Magdalene. *See* Magdalene.

Madge   A pet form of Margaret. *See* Margaret.

Mady   A pet form of Madge or Magdalene. *See* Madge *and* Magdalene.

Mae   A variant form of Mary and a variant spelling of May. *See* Mary *and* May.

Mag   A pet form of Margaret or Magdalene. *See* Margaret *and* Magdalene.

Magda   A pet form of Magdalene. *See* Magdalene.

Migdala   From the Hebrew, meaning "tower." The exact Hebrew equivalent is Migdala. The exact masculine Hebrew equivalent is Migdal.

Magdalen   A variant spelling of Magdalene. *See* Magdalene.

Magdalene A Greek form of the Hebrew *migdal,* meaning "high tower." The exact Hebrew equivalent is Migdala. The exact masculine Hebrew equivalent is Migdal.

Magdaline A variant spelling of Magdalene. *See* Magdalene.

Magena (מָגֵנָה) From the Hebrew, meaning "covering" or "protector." The exact Hebrew equivalent is Magena. The exact masculine Hebrew equivalent is Magen.

Maggie A pet form of Margaret. *See* Margaret.

Magina (מָגִינָה) A variant form of Magena. *See* Magena. Magina is the exact Hebrew equivalent.

Magna From the Latin, meaning "great." HEBREW EQUIVALENTS: Atalya, Gedola, Gedula, Rachav. MASCULINE HEBREW EQUIVALENTS: Gadol, Gedalya, Gedula.

Magnolia From Modern Latin, meaning "the big laurel tree," a symbol of victory. HEBREW EQUIVALENTS: Dafna, Hadasa. MASCULINE HEBREW EQUIVALENTS: Hadas, Matzliach, Netziach, Yatzliach.

Mahira A variant spelling of Mehira. *See* Mehira.

Maia In Roman mythology, goddess of the earth and growth. *See* May.

Maida, Maide From the Anglo-Saxon, meaning "maiden." HEBREW EQUIVALENTS: Alma, Na'ara, Riva, Tze'ira. MASCULINE HEBREW EQUIVALENTS: Bachur, Na'arai, Na'arya.

Maire An Irish form of Mary. *See* Mary.

Maisie From the British, meaning "field." Also, a Scottish pet form of Margaret. *See* Margaret.

Maital A variant spelling of Meital. *See* Meital.

Maksima (מַקְסִימָה) From the Hebrew, meaning "diviner, performer of miracles." The exact Hebrew equivalent is Maksima. The exact masculine Hebrew equivalent is Maksim.

Malbina (מַלְבִּינָה) From the Hebrew, meaning "to whiten" or "embarrass." The exact masculine Hebrew equivalent is Malbina. The exact masculine Hebrew equivalent is Malbin.

Malia The Hawaiian form of Mary. *See* Mary.

Malinda A variant spelling of Melinda. *See* Melinda.

Malka, Malkah (מַלְכָּה) From the Hebrew, meaning "queen." The exact Hebrew equivalent is Malka. The exact masculine Hebrew equivalent is Melech.

Malkia, Malkiah Variant spellings of Malkiya. *See* Malkiya.

Malkit (מַלְכִּית) From the Hebrew, meaning "queen, queenly." The exact Hebrew equivalent is Malkit. The exact masculine Hebrew equivalent is Melech.

Malkiya (מַלְכִּיָה) From the Hebrew, meaning "God is my king." The exact Hebrew equivalent is Malkiya. The exact masculine Hebrew equivalent is Melech.

Malvina A variant spelling of Melvina. *See* Melvina.

Mamie A pet form of Mary. *See* Mary.

Mana (מְנָה) From the Hebrew, meaning "share, portion, gift." The exact Hebrew equivalent is Mana. MASCULINE HEBREW EQUIVALENTS: Matan, Matanya, Natan.

Manda A pet form of Amanda. *See* Amanda.

Mandy A pet form of Amanda. *See* Amanda.

Manette A pet form of Marion. *See* Marion.

Mangena A variant spelling of Mangina. *See* Mangina.

Mangina (מַנְגִּינָה) From the Hebrew, meaning "song, melody." The exact Hebrew equivalent is Mangina. MASCULINE HEBREW EQUIVALENTS: Zamir, Zemarya, Zemer, Zimra, Zimran.

Manuela A Spanish feminine form of Manuel. *See* Manuel (*masculine section*).

Mara, Marah (מָרָה) From the Hebrew, meaning "bitter, bitterness." The exact Hebrew equivalent is Mara. MASCULINE HEBREW EQUIVALENTS: Merari, Mera'ya.

Maralee A hybrid form of Mara and Lee. *See* Mara *and* Lee.

Maralyn A variant spelling of Marilyn. *See* Marilyn.

Marata (מָרָתָה) The Aramaic form of Mara. *See* Mara. The exact Hebrew equivalent is Marata.

Marcella From the Latin, meaning "brave, martial" or "hammer." HEBREW EQUIVALENTS: Amtza, Gada, Gavriela, Gavrila, Tigra. MASCULINE HEBREW EQUIVALENTS: Gad, Gera, Makabi, Medan, Mordechai, Naftali.

Marcelyn A variant form of Marcella. *See* Marcella.

Marcia A variant form of Marcella. *See* Marcella.

Marcie A variant form of Marcia. *See* Marcia.

Marcilen A variant form of Marcella. *See* Marcella.

Marcy A variant form of Marcia. *See* Marcia.

Mardi A pet form of Martha. *See* Martha.

Maree A variant spelling of Marie. *See* Marie.

Mareea A variant spelling of Maria. *See* Maria.

Maren, Marena From the Latin, meaning "sea." HEBREW EQUIVALENTS: Bat-Galim, Bat-Yam, Miryam, Yama. MASCULINE HEBREW EQUIVALENTS: Avigal, Avi'yam, Moshe, Livyatan.

Marenda A variant form of Miranda. *See* Miranda.

Margalit (מַרְגָּלִית) A Hebrew form of the Greek *margarit*, meaning "pearl." The exact Hebrew equivalent is Margalit. MASCULINE HEBREW EQUIVALENTS: Dar, Penini, Tarshish.

Margalita (מַרְגָּלִיתָה) A variant form of Margalit. *See* Margalit. The exact Hebrew equivalent is Margalita.

Marganit (מַרְגָּנִית) A plant with blue, gold, and red flowers, common in Israel. The exact Hebrew equivalent is Marganit. MASCULINE HEBREW EQUIVALENTS: Chavakuk, Neti'a, Shatil, Shatul.

Margaret From the Greek, meaning "pearl" or "child of light." HEBREW EQUIVALENTS: Levana, Margalit, Me'ira, Penina, Peninit. MASCULINE HEBREW EQUIVALENTS: Dar, Me'ir, Penini, Tarshish.

Margarete A German form of Margaret. *See* Margaret.

Margaretta A Spanish pet form of Margaret. *See* Margaret.

Margarita A Spanish form of Margaret. *See* Margaret.

Marge A pet form of Margaret. *See* Margaret.

Margene A variant form of Margaret. *See* Margaret.

Margerie A variant spelling of Margery. *See* Margery.

Margery A variant form of Margaret. *See* Margaret.

Marget A pet form of Margaret. *See* Margaret.

Margie A pet form of Margaret. *See* Margaret.

Margo A variant form of Margaret. *See* Margaret.

Margy A pet form of Margaret. *See* Margaret.

Mari A variant spelling of Mary. *See* Mary.

Maria A variant spelling of Mary. *See* Mary.

Mariah A variant spelling of Maria. *See* Maria.

Mariamne An early form of Mary. *See* Mary.

Marian, Mariane, Marianne Variant hybrid forms of Mary and Ann. *See* Mary *and* Ann.

Maribel A variant form of Mary, meaning "beautiful Mary." *See* Mary.

Marie The French and Old German form of Mary. *See* Mary.

Mariel A Dutch form of Mary. *See* Mary.

Mariele A variant form of Mary. *See* Mary.

Marien, Marienne Variant forms of Marion. *See* Marion.

Marietta An Italian pet form of Mary. *See* Mary.

Mariette A French pet form of Mary. *See* Mary.

Marilyn, Marilynn Variant forms of Mary, meaning "Mary's line, descendants of Mary." *See* Mary.

Marina, Marinna From the Latin, meaning "sea." HEBREW EQUIVALENTS: Bat-Galim, Bat-Yam, Miryam, Yama, Yamit. MASCULINE HEBREW EQUIVALENTS: Avi'yam, Moshe, Livyatan.

Marion A pet form of the French name Marie. Also, a variant form of Mary. *See* Mary.

Maris, Marisa, Marise From the Latin, meaning "sea." HEBREW EQUIVALENTS: Bat-Galim, Bat-Yam, Miryam, Yama, Yamit. MASCULINE HEBREW EQUIVALENTS: Avi'yam, Moshe, Peleg.

Marissa A variant spelling of Marisa. *See* Marisa.

Marita A pet form of Martha. *See* Martha.

Marjorie, Marjory Variant spellings of Margery, popular in Scotland. *See* Margery.

Malca A variant spelling of Malka. *See* Malka.

Marlee A pet form of Marleen. *See* Marleen.

Marleen A Slavic form of Magdalene. *See* Magdalene.

Marlena A variant form of Marleen. *See* Marleen.

Marlene A variant form of Marleen. *See* Marleen.

Marli, Marlie A pet form of Marleen. *See* Marleen.

Marlo A variant form of Marleen. *See* Marleen.

Marlyn, Marlynn Contracted forms of Marilyn. *See* Marilyn.

Marna, Marne A variant form of Marina. *See* Marina.

Marni A pet form of Marina. *See* Marina.

Marnina (מַרְנִינָה) From the Hebrew, meaning "rejoice." The exact Hebrew equivalent is Marnina. The exact masculine Hebrew equivalent is Marnin.

Marona (מְרוֹנָה) From the Hebrew, meaning "flock of sheep." The exact Hebrew equivalent is Marona. The exact masculine Hebrew equivalent is Maron.

Marsha, Marshe Variant spellings of Marcia. *See* Marcia.

Marta A variant form of Martha. *See* Martha.

Martelle A French feminine form of Martin. *See* Martin (*masculine section*).

Martha (מָרְתָה) From the Aramaic, meaning "sorrowful" or "mistress." The exact Hebrew equivalent is Marata. MASCULINE HEBREW EQUIVALENTS: Avimelech, Amos, Ben-Oni, Iyov, Malkam, Melech, Merari, Mera'yot.

Marthe A French form of Martha. *See* Martha.

Marti A pet form of Martina. *See* Martina.

Martina, Martine Feminine forms of Martin. *See* Martin (*masculine section*).

Marva (מַרְוָה) From the Hebrew, referring to a plant of the mint family. The exact Hebrew equivalent is Marva. MASCULINE HEBREW EQUIVALENTS: Narkis, Neta, Neti'a, Tzemach.

Marvel, Marvella From the Middle English and the Latin, meaning "to wonder, admire." HEBREW EQUIVALENTS: Maksima, Nasya, Nesya, Peliya, Tama. MASCULINE HEBREW EQUIVALENTS: Nes, Nisan, Nisim, Peleh, Tema.

Mary The Greek form of Miryam (Miriam), from the Hebrew, meaning "sea of bitterness." The exact Hebrew equivalent is Miryam. MASCULINE HEBREW EQUIVALENTS: Arnon, Avi'yam, Enan, Moshe, Peleg.

Marya A Russian and Polish form of Mary. *See* Mary.

Maryanne A hybrid of Mary and Anne. *See* Mary *and* Anne.

Maryashe (מַרְיאַשֶׁע) A Yiddish form of Miriam. *See* Miriam.

Marylin, Maryline Variant spellings of Marilyn. *See* Marilyn.

Masada, Massada (מְסָדָה) From the Hebrew, meaning "foundation, support." The exact Hebrew equivalent is Masada. MASCULINE HEBREW EQUIVALENTS: Sa'ad, Sa'adya, Sa'id.

Matana (מַתָּנָה) From the Hebrew, meaning "gift." The exact Hebrew equivalent is Matana. The exact masculine Hebrew equivalent is Matan.

Matat (מַתָּת) From the Hebrew, meaning "gift." The exact feminine and masculine Hebrew equivalent is Matat. Also, a short form of Matityahu. *See* Matityahu.

Mathilda, Mathilde From the Old High German and Anglo-Saxon, meaning "powerful in battle" or "battlemaid." HEBREW EQUIVALENTS: Alma, Gada, Gavriela, Gavrila, Gibora, Sara, Tigra. MASCULINE HEBREW EQUIVALENTS: Gad, Gavriel, Makabi, Medan, Midyan, Mordechai, Naftali, Yisrael.

Matilda A variant spelling of Mathilda. *See* Mathilda.

Matti, Mattie Pet forms of Mathilda. *See* Mathilda.

Matty, Mattye Pet forms of Mathilda. *See* Mathilda.

Matya (מַתְיָה) A Yiddish pet form of Mathilda. *See* Mathilda.

Maud, Maude French pet forms of Mathilda. *See* Mathilda.

Maura A form of Mary commonly used in Ireland. *See* Mary. Also, from the Celtic, meaning "dark." HEBREW EQUIVALENTS: Chachila, Efa, Miryam, Tzila. MASCULINE HEBREW EQUIVALENTS: Adar, Efar, Kedar, Pinchas.

Maureen, Maurine Variant forms of Maura. *See* Maura.

Mavis A bird-name that evolved in France from an Old English word meaning "song thrush." HEBREW EQUIVALENTS: Derora, Efrona, Gozala, Tziparta, Tzipora. MASCULINE HEBREW EQUIVALENTS: Deror, Efron, Gozal, Orev, Tzipor.

Maxa A feminine form of Max. *See* Max.

Maxene A variant spelling of Maxine. *See* Maxine.

Maxima A variant spelling of Maksima. *See* Maksima.

Maxime A feminine form of Maximilian. *See* Maximilian (*masculine section*).

Maxine A variant form of Maxime. *See* Maxime.

May A pet form of Mary and Margaret. *See* Mary *and* Margaret. Also, a month of the year connoting spring, youth, growth. HEBREW EQUIVALENTS: Alma, Na'ara, Nitza, Pirchit, Shoshana. MASCULINE HEBREW EQUIVALENTS: Efra'yim, Elam, Gedalya, Perachya.

Maya A variant spelling of Maia. *See* Maia.

Mazal (מַזָל) From the Hebrew, meaning "star," connoting good luck. The exact feminine and masculine Hebrew equivalent is Mazal.

Mazala (מַזָלָה) A variant form of Mazal. *See* Mazal. The exact Hebrew equivalent is Mazala.

Mazalit (מַזָלִית) A variant form of Mazal. *See* Mazal. The exact Hebrew equivalent is Mazalit.

Mazhira (מַזְהִירָה) From the Hebrew, meaning "shining." The exact Hebrew equivalent is Mazhira. MASCULINE HEBREW EQUIVALENTS: Me'ir, Yitzhar, Zerach, Zerachya, Zohar.

Meg A pet form of Margaret. *See* Margaret.

Megan A Welsh form of Margaret. *See* Margaret.

Mehira (מְהִירָה) From the Hebrew, meaning "swift, energetic." The exact Hebrew equivalent is Mehira. The exact masculine Hebrew equivalent is Mahir.

Meira (מְאִירָה) From the Hebrew, meaning "light." The exact Hebrew equivalent is Me'ira. The exact masculine Hebrew equivalent is Me'ir.

Meirit (מְאִירִית) A variant form of Meiri. *See* Meiri. The exact Hebrew equivalent is Me'irit.

Meirona (מֵרוֹנָה) From the Aramaic, meaning "sheep," or from the Hebrew, meaning "troops, soldiers." The exact Hebrew equivalent is Meirona (Mayrona). The exact masculine Hebrew equivalent is Meiron (Mayron).

Meital (מֵיטַל) From the Hebrew, meaning "dew drops." The exact Hebrew equivalent is Meital (Maytal). MASCULINE HEBREW EQUIVALENTS: Tal, Tali, Tal-Or.

Melanie From the Greek, meaning "black, dark." HEBREW EQUIVALENTS: Adara, Chachila, Efa, Tzila. MASCULINE HEBREW EQUIVALENTS: Adar, Efai, Kedar, Pinchas.

Melba A variant feminine form of Melvin. *See* Melvin (*masculine section*). A variant form of Melva.

Melina From the Greek, meaning "song." HEBREW EQUIVALENTS: Mangena, Mangina, Ranita, Ronit, Shira. MASCULINE HEBREW EQUIVALENTS: Amiran, Liron, Shir, Shiron, Zemer, Zimri.

Melinda From the Greek and Old English, meaning "gentle." HEBREW EQUIVALENTS: Adiva, Nediva, Na'ama, Na'omi, Rachel. MASCULINE HEBREW EQUIVALENTS: Adiv, Na'aman, Nadiv, Yehonadav.

Melissa, Melisse From the Greek, meaning "bee, honey." HEBREW EQUIVALENTS: Devasha, Devora, Metuka, Mirit, Na'ama, Na'omi. MASCULINE HEBREW EQUIVALENTS: Avino'am, Matok, Meged, Na'aman.

Melody From the Greek, meaning "melody, song." HEBREW EQUIVALENTS: Mangena, Mangina, Ranita, Ronit, Shira, Shir-Li, Yarona. MASCULINE HEBREW EQUIVALENTS: Amiran, Amishar, Liron, Shir, Shiron, Zemer, Zimri.

Melva A feminine form of Melvin. *See* Melvin (*masculine section*).

Melveen, Melvene Feminine forms of Melvin. *See* Melvin (*masculine section*).

Melvina A feminine form of Melvin. *See* Melvin (*masculine section*).

Menora, Menorah (מְנוֹרָה) From the Hebrew, meaning "candelabrum." The exact Hebrew equivalent is Menora. MASCULINE HEBREW EQUIVALENTS: Me'ir, Nahor, Nahur, Nuri, Nuriel, Nuriya.

Mercedes From the Latin, meaning "mercy, pity." HEBREW EQUIVALENTS: Nechama, Ruchama. MASCULINE HEBREW EQUIVALENTS: Chanin, Rachaman, Rachmiel.

Meredith From the Old Celtic, meaning "protector of the sea." HEBREW EQUIVALENTS: Botzra, Chasya, Chosa, Magena, Migdala. MASCULINE

HEBREW EQUIVALENTS: Magen, Mivtach, Mivtachyahu, Lotan, Shemaryahu.

Meri (מְרִי) From the Hebrew, meaning "rebellious, bitterness." The exact Hebrew equivalent is Meri. MASCULINE HEBREW EQUIVALENTS: Mardut, Mordechai, Nimrod.

Merideth A variant spelling of Meredith. See Meredith.

Merie A variant spelling of Meri. See Meri.

Merla A variant form of Merle. See Merle.

Merle From the Latin and the French, meaning "bird," specifically a blackbird. HEBREW EQUIVALENTS: Adara, Chogla, Da'a, Da'ya, Gozala, Tzipora. MASCULINE HEBREW EQUIVALENTS: Adar, Gozal, Orev, Tzipor.

Merlin From the Old High German, meaning "falcon." Akin to Merle. See Merle *for equivalents.*

Meroma (מְרוֹמָה) From the Hebrew, meaning "elevated, high, noble." The exact Hebrew equivalent is Meroma. The exact masculine Hebrew equivalent is Marom.

Merona A variant spelling of Meirona. See Meirona.

Merrie From the Anglo-Saxon, meaning "joyous, pleasant." HEBREW EQUIVALENTS: Aliza, Aviga'yil, Gilana, Marnina, Renana, Rina, Semecha, Simcha, Simchona, Sos. MASCULINE HEBREW EQUIVALENTS: Avigal, Bilga, Gil, Gil-Li, Marnin, Masos, Simcha, Sisa, Sisi.

Merrielle A pet form of Merrie. See Merrie.

Merril, Merrill Variant forms of Merle and Muriel. See Merle *and* Muriel.

Merry A variant spelling of Merrie. See Merrie.

Merryl A variant spelling of Meryl. See Meryl.

Merta A variant form of Marta (Martha). See Martha.

Meryl, Meryle Variant spellings of Merril. See Merril.

Metuka (מְתוּקָה) From the Hebrew, meaning "sweet." The exact Hebrew equivalent is Metuka. The exact masculine Hebrew equivalent is Matok.

Mia (מִיָה) A short form of Michaela. See Michaela. The exact Hebrew equivalent is Miya.

Mica A short form of Michal. See Michal.

Michael Used occasionally as a feminine name. See Michael (*masculine section*).

Micha (מִיכָה) A short form of Michal. See Michal.

Michaela (מִיכָאֶלָה) The feminine form of Michael. See Michael (*masculine section*). The exact Hebrew equivalent is Michaela.

Michaelann A hybrid of Michael and Ann. See Michael *and* Ann.

Michaele A feminine form of Michael. See Michael (*masculine section*).

Michal (מִיכָל) A contracted form of Michael, meaning "Who is like God?" The exact Hebrew equivalent is Michal. The exact masculine Hebrew equivalent is Micha'el.

Michalina A pet form of Michal. *See* Michal.

Michel, Michele, Michelle Variant French forms of Michal. *See* Michal.

Micke, Mickey, Micki Pet forms of Michal. *See* Michal.

Midge A variant form of Madge. *See* Madge.

Migda (מִגְדָּה) From the Hebrew, meaning "choice thing, gift" or "excellent." The exact Hebrew equivalent is Migda. MASCULINE HEBREW EQUIVALENTS: Matan, Matanya, Matityahu, Yehonatan, Zevid, Zevuda.

Migdala (מִגְדָּלָה) From the Hebrew, meaning "fortress, tower." The exact Hebrew equivalent is Migdala. The exact masculine Hebrew equivalent is Migdal.

Migdana (מִגְדָּנָה) From the Hebrew, meaning "gift." The exact Hebrew equivalent is Migdana. MASCULINE HEBREW EQUIVALENTS: Magdiel, Meged, Natan, Netanel.

Mignon From the French, meaning "delicate, graceful, petite." HEBREW EQUIVALENTS: Adina, Adiva, Chana, Chanita, Dovev, Yochana. MASCULINE HEBREW EQUIVALENTS: Amichen, Chana, Chanan, Chonen, Yochanan.

Mildred From the Anglo-Saxon, meaning "gentle of speech" or "gentle counselor." HEBREW EQUIVALENTS: Amira, Bina, Buna, Devora, Milka, Niva. MASCULINE HEBREW EQUIVALENTS: Achban, Chachmon, Chachmoni, Dovev, Omer, Utz, Yavin, Yosha.

Mili (מִילִי) From the Hebrew, meaning "Who is for me?" or an Hebraized form of Millie. *See* Millie. The exact Hebrew equivalent is Mili.

Milka (מִלְכָּה) From the Hebrew, meaning "divine" or "queen." Akin to Malka. The exact Hebrew equivalent is Milka. The exact masculine Hebrew equivalent is Melech.

Millicent From the Latin, meaning "sweet singer," or from the Old French and Old High German, meaning "work" or "strength." HEBREW EQUIVALENTS: Aharona, Amal, Amalya, Amela, Amtza, Gavriela, Gavrila, Gibora, Rina, Shira, Tehila. MASCULINE HEBREW EQUIVALENTS: Aharon, Amatzya, Ana, Avram, Binyamin, Dovev, Gavriel, Gibor, Oved, Ovadya.

Millie, Milly Pet forms of Mildred and Millicent. *See* Mildred *and* Millicent.

Mim A pet form of Miryam. *See* Miryam.

Mimi A pet form of Miryam. *See* Miryam.

Mina A variant spelling of Minna. *See* Minna.

Minda (מִינְדָּא) A Yiddish form of Minna. *See* Minna.

Mindel (מִינְדְּעל) A Yiddish pet form of Minda. *See* Minda.

Mindi A variant spelling of Mindy. *See* Mindy.

Mindy A pet form of Melinda and Mildred. *See* Melinda *and* Mildred.

Minerva The Roman goddess of wisdom. HEBREW EQUIVALENTS: Bina, Buna, Milka. MASCULINE HEBREW EQUIVALENTS: Chachmon, Chachmoni, Gaon, Utz, Yavin, Yosha.

Minette A French pet form of Mary. *See* Mary.

Minna A pet form of Wilhelmina. *See* Wilhelmina.

Minnie, Minny Pet forms of Minna, Miriam, and Wilhelmina. *See* Minna, Miriam, *and* Wilhelmina.

Minta From the Greek, meaning "mint [an aromatic leaf]." HEBREW EQUIVALENTS: Ketzia, Tzeruya. MASCULINE HEBREW EQUIVALENTS: Mivsam, Yivsam.

Mira (מִירָה) A pet form of Miryam. *See* Miryam.

Miranda From the Latin, meaning "wonderful" or "adored one." HEBREW EQUIVALENTS: Achsa, Adina, Adva, Hadara, Hadarit, Mechubada, Sara. MASCULINE HEBREW EQUIVALENTS: Adiel, Hadar, Hod, Hodiya, Mechubad, Me'udan, Yehoyadan.

Mirel, Mirele (מִירְעֶל/מִירְל) Yiddish pet forms of Miryam. *See* Miryam.

Miri A short form of Mirit and Miryam. *See* Mirit *and* Miryam.

Miriam The Anglicized spelling of Miryam. *See* Miryam.

Miril (מִירִיל) A Yiddish pet form of Miryam. *See* Miryam.

Mirit (מִירִית) From the Hebrew, meaning "sweet wine." The exact Hebrew equivalent is Mirit. MASCULINE HEBREW EQUIVALENTS: Gafni, Gefanya, Gefen. Also, a variant form of Mira. *See* Mira.

Mirra A variant spelling of Mira. *See* Mira.

Miryam (מִרְיָם) From the Hebrew, meaning "sea of bitterness, sorrow," or from the Chaldaic, meaning "mistress of the sea." The exact Hebrew equivalent is Miryam. MASCULINE HEBREW EQUIVALENTS: Arnon, Avi'yam, Enan, Melech, Moshe, Peleg, Silon.

Miryom A variant spelling of Miryam. *See* Miryam.

Missie A modern American name, meaning "young girl." HEBREW EQUIVALENTS: Bat, Bat-Sheva, Batya, Na'ara. MASCULINE HEBREW EQUIVALENTS: Ben, Ben-Tziyon, Na'arai, Na'ari, Na'arya.

Mitzi A pet form of Mary. *See* Mary.

Mitzpa, Mitzpah (מִצְפָּה) From the Hebrew, meaning "tower." The exact Hebrew equivalent is Mitzpa. MASCULINE HEBREW EQUIVALENTS: Armon, Armoni, Chaza'ya, Chozai, Migdal.

Mizpa, Mizpah Variant spellings of Mitzpa. *See* Mitzpa.

Mollie, Molly, Mollye Pet forms of Mary, Millicent, *and* Miriam. *See* Mary, Millicent, *and* Miriam.

Mona From the Irish, meaning "noble, pure." HEBREW EQUIVALENTS: Adina, Malka, Milka, Rachel, Zaka. MASCULINE HEBREW EQUIVALENTS: Adin, Adon, Malka, Palal, Zakai.

Monica A variant form of Mona. *See* Mona.

Monique A French form of Mona. *See* Mona.

Moraga (מוֹרָגָה) The feminine form of Moreg. *See* Moreg (*masculine section*). The exact Hebrew equivalent is Moraga.

Moran (מוֹרָן) From the Hebrew, meaning "teacher." The exact feminine and masculine Hebrew equivalent is Moran.

Morasha (מוֹרָשָׁה) From the Hebrew, meaning "legacy." The exact

Hebrew equivalent is Morasha. The exact masculine Hebrew equivalent is Morash.

Morena A variant form of Maura. *See* Maura.

Morgan From the Welsh, meaning "sea dweller." HEBREW EQUIVALENTS: Bat-Galim, Bat-Yam, Miryam, Yamit. MASCULINE HEBREW EQUIVALENTS: Avigal, Avi'yam, Moshe, Peleg.

Moria, Moriah Variant spellings of Moriya. *See* Moriya.

Moriel (מוֹרִיאֵל) From the Hebrew, meaning "God is my teacher." The exact feminine and masculine Hebrew equivalent is Moriel.

Morine A variant form of Maureen. *See* Maureen.

Morit (מוֹרִית) From the Hebrew, meaning "teacher." The exact Hebrew equivalent is Morit. MASCULINE HEBREW EQUIVALENTS: Chanoch, Likchi, Moran, Moriel, Yora.

Moriya (מוֹרִיָה) From the Hebrew, meaning "teacher." The exact Hebrew equivalent is Moriya. MASCULINE HEBREW EQUIVALENTS: Chanoch, Likchi, Moriel, Rabi, Yora.

Morna From the Middle English and German, meaning "morning," or from the Celtic, meaning "gentle, beloved." HEBREW EQUIVALENTS: Bat-Shachar, Davida, Yakira, Yekara, Yedida. MASCULINE HEBREW EQUIVALENTS: Ahuv, Ben-Shachar, Chavivel, David, Nadiv, Shachar, Yakar, Yakir.

Morrisa, Morrissa The feminine form of Morris. *See* Morris (*masculine section*).

Muriel From the Irish, meaning "bright sea," or from the Middle English, meaning "merry." HEBREW EQUIVALENTS: Aliza, Gila, Gilana, Giliya, Marnina, Mazal, Renana, Semecha, Silona. MASCULINE HEBREW EQUIVALENTS: Aliz, Elez, Marnin, Mazal-Tov, Sason, Silon, Simcha, Yachdiel, Yitzchak.

Myra From the Greek and Arabic, meaning "myrrh," connoting bitterness. Also, from the Celtic, meaning "gentle, beloved." HEBREW EQUIVALENTS: Mor, Talmor. MASCULINE HEBREW EQUIVALENTS: Mara, Marata.

Myrel A variant spelling of Mirel. *See* Mirel.

Myriam A variant spelling of Miryam. *See* Miryam.

Myrna A variant form of Myra. *See* Myra.

Myrtle From the Persian, meaning "myrtle tree," a symbol of victory. The feminine and masculine Hebrew equivalent is Hadas. *See also* Hadasa.

Naama, Naamah (נַעֲמָה) From the Hebrew, meaning "pleasant, beautiful." The exact Hebrew equivalent is Na'ama. The exact masculine Hebrew equivalent is Na'aman.

Naamana (נַעֲמָנָה) From the Hebrew, meaning "pleasant." The exact Hebrew equivalent is Na'amana. The exact masculine Hebrew equivalent is Na'aman.

Naami (נָעֳמִי) A variant form of Naomi. *See* Naomi. The exact Hebrew equivalent is Na'omi.

Naamia, Naamiah Variant spellings of Naamiya. *See* Naamiya.

Naamit (נָעֳמִית) From the Hebrew, meaning "an ostrich-like bird." The exact Hebrew equivalent is Na'amit. MASCULINE HEBREW EQUIVALENTS: Gozal, Tzipor.

Naamiya (נָעֳמִיָה) From the Hebrew, meaning "pleasant, sweet." A variant form of Na'ama. *See* Na'ama. The exact Hebrew equivalent is Na'amiya.

Nada From the Slavic, meaning "hope." HEBREW EQUIVALENTS: Bitcha, Emuna, Mivtachya, Mivtechet, Tikva, Tzipiya. MASCULINE HEBREW EQUIVALENTS: Amit, Amitai, Amitan, Amon, Mivtach, Mivtachya, Yachil.

Nadia A variant form of Nada. *See* Nada.

Nadine A French form of Nada. *See* Nada.

Nadya (נַדְיָה) A Hebrew form of Nada, used in Israel. *See* Nada. The exact Hebrew equivalent is Nadya.

Nafshiya (נַפְשִׁיָה) From the Hebrew, meaning "soul" or "friendship." The exact Hebrew equivalent is Nafshiya. MASCULINE HEBREW EQUIVALENTS: Nafish, Nefesh.

Naftala (נִפְתָּלָה) From the Hebrew, meaning "to wrestle." The exact Hebrew equivalent is Naftala. The exact masculine Hebrew equivalent is Naftali.

Nagida (נְגִידָה) From the Hebrew, meaning "noble, prosperous person." The exact Hebrew equivalent is Nagida. The exact masculine Hebrew equivalent is Nagid.

Nahara (נַהֲרָה) From the Hebrew and Aramaic, meaning "light." The exact Hebrew equivalent is Nahara. MASCULINE HEBREW EQUIVALENTS: Nahir, Nahor, Nahur, Nehorai, Nerli, Noga.

Nan, Nana Pet forms of Nancy. *See* Nancy.

Nancy A pet form of Hannah. *See* Hannah.

Nanette A pet form of Anna and Hannah. *See* Anna *and* Hannah.

Nanine A variant pet form of Nanette. *See* Nanette.

Nanna A pet form of Hannah. *See* Hannah.

Naoma A variant form of Naomi. *See* Naomi.

Naomi (נָעֳמִי) From the Hebrew, meaning "beautiful, pleasant, delightful." The exact Hebrew equivalent is Na'omi. MASCULINE HEBREW EQUIVALENTS: Na'am, Na'im, Na'aman, No'am.

Natalie A French and German form of the Latin, meaning "to be born, to be alive." HEBREW EQUIVALENTS: Chava, Cha'ya, Techiya. MASCULINE HEBREW EQUIVALENTS: Chai, Cha'yim, Chiya, Nafshiya, Yechiel.

Natania, Nataniah Variant spellings of Natanya. *See* Natanya.

Nataniela, Nataniella, Natanielle Variant feminine forms of Netaniela. *See* Netaniela.

Natanya (נְתַנְיָה) The feminine form of Natan (Nathan). Also, a variant form of Netanya. *See* Netanya. The exact Hebrew equivalent is Natanya.

Nava, Navah (נָוָה/נָאוָה) From the Hebrew, meaning "beautiful, pleasant." The exact Hebrew equivalent is Nava. The exact masculine Hebrew equivalent is Naveh.

Navit (נָוִית) A variant form of Nava. *See* Nava. The exact Hebrew equivalent is Navit.

Neala A feminine form of Neal. *See* Neal (*masculine section*).

Nechama (נֶחָמָה) From the Hebrew, meaning "comfort." The exact Hebrew equivalent is Nechama. The exact masculine Hebrew equivalent is Nachum.

Nedavia, Nedaviah Variant spellings of Nedavya. *See* Nedavya.

Nedavya (נְדַבְיָה) From the Hebrew, meaning "generosity of the Lord." The exact feminine and masculine Hebrew equivalent is Nedavya.

Nediva (נְדִיבָה) From the Hebrew, meaning "noble, generous." The exact Hebrew equivalent is Nediva. The exact masculine Hebrew equivalent is Nadiv.

Neena A variant spelling of Nina. *See* Nina.

Negida (נְגִידָה) A variant form of Nagida. *See* Nagida. The exact Hebrew equivalent is Negida.

Negina (נְגִינָה) From the Hebrew, meaning "song, melody." The exact Hebrew equivalent is Negina. MASCULINE HEBREW EQUIVALENTS: Avishar, Amiran, Amiron, Amishar, Ronen, Shiron, Zemer, Zemarya.

Nehama A variant spelling of Nechama. *See* Nechama.

Nehara (נְהָרָה) A variant form of Nahara. *See* Nahara. The exact Hebrew equivalent is Nehara.

Nehira (נְהִירָה) A variant form of Nehora. *See* Nehora. The exact Hebrew equivalent is Nehira.

Nehora (נְהוֹרָה/נְהוֹרָא) From the Aramaic, meaning "light." The exact Hebrew equivalent is Nehora. The exact masculine Hebrew equivalent is Nahor.

Nehura (נְהוּרָה) A variant form of Nehora. *See* Nehora. The exact Hebrew equivalent is Nehura.

Ne'ima (נְעִימָה) From the Hebrew, meaning "pleasant one." The exact Hebrew equivalent is Ne'ima. The exact masculine Hebrew equivalent is Na'im.

Nell, Nella Pet forms of Eleanor and Helen. *See* Eleanor *and* Helen.

Nellie A pet form of Eleanor. *See* Eleanor.

Nelly A pet form of Eleanor. *See* Eleanor.

Nema A variant spelling of Nima. *See* Nima.

Neora (נְאוֹרָה) From the Aramaic and Hebrew, meaning "light" or "shine." The exact Hebrew equivalent is Ne'ora. The exact masculine Hebrew equivalent is Na'or.

Nerya (נֵרִיָה) From the Hebrew, meaning "light of the Lord." The exact

Hebrew equivalent is Nerya. MASCULINE HEBREW EQUIVALENTS: Ner, Neri, Neriya, Nerli.

Nessa From the Old Norse, meaning "promontory, headland.' Also, a short form of Vanessa. See Vanessa. HEBREW EQUIVALENTS: Artzit, Eretz. MASCULINE HEBREW EQUIVALENTS: Adam, Artza, Artzi.

Nessia A variant spelling of Nesya. See Nesya.

Nessie A Welsh pet form of Agnes. See Agnes.

Nesya (נְסִיָה) From the Hebrew, meaning "miracle of God." The exact Hebrew equivalent is Nesya. MASCULINE HEBREW EQUIVALENTS: Nes, Nisan, Nisi, Nisim.

Neta (נֶטַע) From the Hebrew, meaning "plant, shrub." The exact feminine and masculine Hebrew equivalent is Neta.

Netana (נְתַנָה) From the Hebrew, meaning "gift." The exact Hebrew equivalent is Netana. The exact masculine Hebrew equivalent is Natan.

Netania, Netaniah Variant spellings of Netanya. See Netanya.

Netaniela, Netaniella (נְתַנִיאָלָה) From the Hebrew, meaning "the gift of God." Variant forms of Netanya. See Netanya. The exact Hebrew equivalent is Netaniela.

Netanya (נְתַנְיָה) From the Hebrew, meaning "gift of God." The exact feminine and masculine Hebrew equivalent is Netanya.

Netiva (נְתִיבָה) From the Hebrew, meaning "path." The exact Hebrew equivalent is Netiva. The exact masculine Hebrew equivalent is Nativ.

Netta A variant spelling of Neta. See Neta.

Netti A variant spelling of Neti. See Neti.

Nettie, Netty Pet forms of Antoinette and Annette. See Annette and Antoinette.

Neva From the Spanish, meaning "snow," or from the Old English, meaning "new." HEBREW EQUIVALENTS: Chadasha, Shalgit, Shilgiya, Talga. The masculine Hebrew equivalent is Chadash.

Nicci An Italian form of the Latin, meaning "victory." HEBREW EQUIVALENTS: Nitzcha, Nitzchiya, Nitzchona. MASCULINE HEBREW EQUIVALENTS: Gevarya, Netzach, Netziach, Nitzchi.

Nichelle A variant form of Nicci. See Nicci.

Nicola, Nicole Italian and French feminine forms of Nicholas. See Nicholas (masculine section).

Nicolette A pet form of Nicola. See Nicola.

Nicolle A variant spelling of Nicole. See Nicole.

Nili (נִילִי) Used most commonly as a masculine name. See masculine section.

Nilit (נִילִית) A variant form of Nili. See Nili. The exact Hebrew equivalent is Nilit.

Nima (נִימָה) From the Hebrew, meaning "picture, portrait, appearance." The exact Hebrew equivalent is Nima. The masculine Hebrew equivalent is Nevat.

Nina A French and Russian pet form of Nanine, which is a form of Anne. *See* Anne.

Ninette A variant form of Nanette. *See* Nanette.

Nirel (נִירְאֵל) From the Hebrew, meaning "uncultivated field" or "light of God." The exact feminine and masculine Hebrew equivalent is Nirel.

Nirit (נִירִית) An annual plant with yellow flowers, found in Israel. The exact Hebrew equivalent is Nirit. Also related to Nirel. *See* Nirel.

Nirtza (נִרְצָה) From the Hebrew, meaning "desirable." The exact Hebrew equivalent is Nirtza. MASCULINE HEBREW EQUIVALENTS: Chamadel, Chemdan, Nachman, Ratzon, Retzin.

Nisa, Nissa (נִסָה) From the Hebrew, meaning "to test." The exact Hebrew equivalent is Nisa. MASCULINE HEBREW EQUIVALENTS: Nes, Nisi, Nisim.

Nita (נִטְעָה) From the Hebrew, meaning "to plant." The exact Hebrew equivalent is Nit'a. MASCULINE HEBREW EQUIVALENTS: Neta, Neti'a, Nitai.

Nitza, Nitzah (נִיצָה) From the Hebrew, meaning "bud of a flower." The exact feminine and masculine Hebrew equivalent is Nitza.

Nitzana (נִיצָנָה) A variant form of Nitza. *See* Nitza. The exact Hebrew equivalent is Nitzana.

Nitzanit (נִיצָנִית) A variant form of Nitza. *See* Nitza. The exact Hebrew equivalent is Nitzanit.

Nitzra (נִצְרָה) From the Hebrew, meaning "guard." The exact Hebrew equivalent is Nitzra. The exact masculine Hebrew equivalent is Notzer.

Niva (נִיבָה) From the Hebrew, meaning "speech." The exact Hebrew equivalent is Niva. The exact masculine Hebrew equivalent is Niv.

Noelle A feminine form of Noel. *See* Noel (*masculine section*).

Noemi A variant form of Naomi. *See* Naomi.

Nofiya (נוֹפִיָה) From the Hebrew, meaning "beautiful landscape." The exact Hebrew equivalent is Nofiya. The exact masculine Hebrew equivalent is Nof.

Noga (נוֹגָה) From the Hebrew, meaning "morning light, brightness." The exact feminine and masculine Hebrew equivalent is Noga.

Nola From the Celtic, meaning "famous." HEBREW EQUIVALENTS: Degula, Hillela, Odeh'le'ya. MASCULINE HEBREW EQUIVALENTS: Hillel, Noda, Shevach, Yehalal, Yehuda.

Nomi A variant spelling of Naomi. *See* Naomi.

Nophia A variant spelling of Nofia. *See* Nofia.

Nora, Norah From the Latin, meaning "honor, respect." HEBREW EQUIVALENTS: Atalya, Efrata, Hadura, Kevuda, Nediva, Nichbada. MASCULINE HEBREW EQUIVALENTS: Avinadav, Hadar, Hadur, Nadav, Yehoram, Yirmeyahu.

Noreen A variant Irish form of Nora. *See* Nora.

Norene A variant spelling of Noreen. *See* Noreen.

Nori A pet form of Noreen. *See* Noreen.

Norma From the Latin, meaning "exact to the pattern, normal, peaceful." HEBREW EQUIVALENTS: Margaya, Menucha, Meshulemet, Sha'anana, Shalva, Shelomit. MASCULINE HEBREW EQUIVALENTS: Marg'oa, Sha'anan, Shalom, Shelomi, Shelomo.

Norrie A pet form of Nora. *See* Nora.

Novela, Novella From the Latin, meaning "new, unusual." HEBREW EQUIVALENTS: Chadasha, Rishona. MASCULINE HEBREW EQUIVALENTS: Chadash, Rishon.

Noya (נוֹיָה) From the Hebrew, meaning "beautiful, ornamented." The exact Hebrew equivalent is No'ya. The exact masculine Hebrew equivalent is Noi.

Nura (נוּרָה/נוּרָא) From the Aramaic, meaning "light, bright." The exact Hebrew equivalent is Nura. The exact masculine Hebrew equivalent is Nur.

Nuriah A variant spelling of Nuriya. *See* Nuriya.

Nurit (נוּרִית) A plant with bright red and yellow flowers, common in Israel. A variant form of Nura. *See* Nura. The exact Hebrew equivalent is Nurit.

Nurita (נוּרִיתָה) A variant form of Nurit. *See* Nurit. The exact Hebrew equivalent is Nurita.

Nuriya (נוּרִיָה) From the Hebrew, meaning "light of the Lord." The exact Hebrew equivalent is Nuriya. MASCULINE HEBREW EQUIVALENTS: Neriya, Neriyahu, Uriya, Uriyahu.

Oda, Odah From the Greek, meaning "song, ode." HEBREW EQUIVALENTS: Negina, Ne'ima, Shira, Zemira, Zimra. MASCULINE HEBREW EQUIVALENTS: Zamir, Zemarya, Zemer, Zimran, Zimri.

Odeda (עוֹדְדָה) From the Hebrew, meaning "strong, courageous." The exact Hebrew equivalent is Odeda. The exact masculine Hebrew equivalent is Oded.

Odedia A variant form of Odeda. *See* Odeda.

Odeh (אוֹדֶה) From the Hebrew, meaning "I will praise." The exact Hebrew equivalent is Odeh. MASCULINE HEBREW EQUIVALENTS: Hillel, Yehalel, Yehuda.

Odele From the Greek, meaning "ode, melody." HEBREW EQUIVALENTS: Negina, Shira, Zemira, Zimrat. MASCULINE HEBREW EQUIVALENTS: Zamir, Zemer, Zimri, Zimroni.

Odeleya (אוֹדְלִיָה) From the Hebrew, meaning "I will praise God." The exact Hebrew equivalent is Odeh'le'ya. MASCULINE HEBREW EQUIVALENTS: Hillel, Yehalel, Yehuda.

Odelia A variant spelling of Odeleya. *See* Odeleya.

Odell A variant spelling of Odele. *See* Odele.

Odera (עוֹדְרָה) From the Hebrew, meaning "plough." The exact Hebrew equivalent is Odera. MASCULINE HEBREW EQUIVALENTS: Nirel, Nirya, Niv, Padon, Yanir.

Odetta A pet form of Odele. *See* Odele.

Odette A variant form of Odetta. *See* Odetta.

Odiya (אוֹדִיָה) From the Hebrew, meaning "song of praise to God." The exact Hebrew equivalent is Odiya. MASCULINE HEBREW EQUIVALENTS: Hillel, Yehuda.

Ofira (אוֹפִירָה) From the Hebrew, meaning "gold." The exact Hebrew equivalent is Ofira. The exact masculine Hebrew equivalent is Ofir.

Ofna (אָפְנָה) From the Aramaic, meaning "appearance." The exact Hebrew equivalent is Ofna. MASCULINE HEBREW EQUIVALENTS: Nevat, Peniel, Penuel, Yefuneh.

Ofnat (אָפְנַת) From the Hebrew, meaning "wheel." The exact Hebrew equivalent is Ofnat. MASCULINE HEBREW EQUIVALENTS: Galal, Galil.

Ofniya (אָפְנִיָה) A variant form of Ofna. *See* Ofna. The exact Hebrew equivalent is Ofniya.

Ofra (עָפְרָה) From the Hebrew, meaning "young mountain goat" or "young deer." The exact Hebrew equivalent is Ofra. The exact masculine Hebrew equivalent is Efer.

Ofrat (עָפְרַת) A variant form of Ofra. *See* Ofra. The exact Hebrew equivalent is Ofrat.

Ofrit (עָפְרִית) A variant form of Ofra. *See* Ofra. The exact Hebrew equivalent is Ofrit.

Ola, Olah (עוֹלָה) From the Hebrew, meaning "immigrant." Also, from the Old Norse, meaning "ancestor." The exact Hebrew equivalent is Ola. The masculine Hebrew equivalent is Oleh.

Olga From the Russian and Old Norse, meaning "holy" or "peace." HEBREW EQUIVALENTS: Chagit, Chagiya, Devira, Kedosha. MASCULINE HEBREW EQUIVALENTS: Chaga, Devir, Kadosh, Zakai.

Olive From the Latin, meaning "olive," symbol of peace. HEBREW EQUIVALENTS: Za'yit, Zayta, Zaytana. MASCULINE HEBREW EQUIVALENTS: Za'yit, Zaytan.

Oliva A variant form of Olive. *See* Olive.

Olympia From the Greek Olympus, the mountain on which the gods resided. HEBREW EQUIVALENTS: Bat-El, Betu'el, Ode'le'ya, Odiya. MASCULINE HEBREW EQUIVALENTS: Aviel, Betu'el, Elasa, Itiel.

Oona A variant form of the Latin name Una, meaning "the one." The Hebrew equivalent is Rishona. The masculine Hebrew equivalent is Rosh.

Ophelia From the Greek, meaning "serpent" or "to help." HEBREW EQUIVALENTS: Eli'ezra, Ezra'ela, Ozera, Sa'ada. MASCULINE HEBREW EQUIVALENTS: Ezra, Ezri, Nachash, Nachshon, Sa'adya.

Ophira A variant spelling of Ofira. *See* Ofira.

Ophnat A variant spelling of Ofnat. *See* Ofnat.

Ophra A variant spelling of Ofra. *See* Ofra.

Ophrat A variant spelling of Ofrat. *See* Ofrat.

Opra, Oprah Variant forms of Ofra. *See* Ofra.

Ora, Orah (אוֹרָה) From the Hebrew, meaning "light." Also, from the Latin, meaning "gold." The exact Hebrew equivalent is Ora. The exact masculine Hebrew equivalent is Or.

Oralee, Orali (אוֹרָה־לִי/אוֹרָלִי) From the Hebrew, meaning "my light." The exact Hebrew equivalent is Orali. The exact masculine Hebrew equivalent is Orli.

Oriel From the Old French and the Latin, meaning "gold." HEBREW EQUIVALENTS: Ofira, Paz, Paza, Pazit, Zehava. MASCULINE HEBREW EQUIVALENTS: Ofir, Pazi, Zehavi.

Orit (אוֹרִית) A variant form of Ora. *See* Ora. The exact Hebrew equivalent is Orit.

Orlanda A variant form of the masculine Orlando. *See* Orlando.

Or-Li, Orli (אוֹר־לִי/אוֹרְלִי) From the Hebrew, meaning "Light is mine." The exact feminine and masculine Hebrew equivalent is Orli.

Orlit (אוֹרְלִית) A variant form of Or-Li. *See* Or-Li. The exact Hebrew equivalent is Orlit.

Orly A variant spelling of Orli. *See* Orli.

Orna (אוֹר־נָא/אוֹרְנָה) From the Hebrew, meaning "Let there be light" or "pine tree." The exact Hebrew equivalent is Orna. MASCULINE HEBREW EQUIVALENTS: Or, Oren, Oron.

Orni (אוֹרְנִי) From the Hebrew, meaning "pine tree." The exact Hebrew equivalent is Orni. The exact masculine Hebrew equivalent is Oren.

Ornina (אוֹרְנִינָה) A variant form of Orni. *See* Orni. The exact Hebrew equivalent is Ornina.

Ornit (אוֹרְנִית) A variant form of Orni. *See* Orni. The exact Hebrew equivalent is Ornit.

Paloma A Spanish name from the Latin, meaning "dove." The exact feminine and masculine Hebrew equivalent is Yona.

Pam A diminutive form of Pamela. *See* Pamela.

Pamela From the Greek and the Anglo-Saxon, meaning "loved one, sweet one." HEBREW EQUIVALENTS: Ahuva, Chiba, Davida, Metuka, Mirit, Na'ama, Na'omi. MASCULINE HEBREW EQUIVALENTS: Ahuv, Bildad, David, Magdiel, Matok, No'am.

Pansy An English flower-name. Also, from the French, meaning "to think." HEBREW EQUIVALENTS: Perach, Pericha, Pircha, Pirchit, Pirchiya. MASCULINE HEBREW EQUIVALENTS: Parchi, Perach, Perachya, Pirchai.

Pat A pet form of Patricia. *See* Patricia.

Patience From the Latin, meaning "to suffer, persevere, endure." HEBREW EQUIVALENTS: Nitzcha, Nitzchiya, Nitzchona. MASCULINE HEBREW EQUIVALENTS: Amiad, Aviad, Elad, Nitzchi.

Patrice A variant form of Patricia. *See* Patricia.

Patricia The feminine form of Patrick. *See* Patrick (*masculine section*).

Patsy A pet form of Patricia. *See* Patricia.

Patti, Pattie, Patty Pet forms of Patricia. *See* Patricia.

Paula From the Greek, meaning "small." HEBREW EQUIVALENTS: Delila, Ketana. MASCULINE HEBREW EQUIVALENTS: Katan, Tzuar, Vofsi, Ze'era.

Prudence A variant spelling of Pauline. *See* Pauline.

Paulette A French pet form of Paula. *See* Paula.

Paulina, Pauline Paulina is the Spanish form of the French Pauline. *See* Paul (*masculine section*).

Paz (פָּז) From the Hebrew, meaning "gold." The exact feminine and masculine Hebrew equivalent is Paz.

Paza (פָּזָה) A variant form of Paz. *See* Paz. The exact Hebrew equivalent is Paza.

Pazit (פָּזִית) A variant form of Paz. *See* Paz. The exact Hebrew equivalent is Pazit.

Paziya (פָּזִיָה) A variant form of Pazya. *See* Pazya. The exact Hebrew equivalent is Paziya.

Pazya (פָּזִיָה) From the Hebrew, meaning "God's gold." The exact Hebrew equivalent is Pazya. MASCULINE HEBREW EQUIVALENTS: Paz, Pazi, Upaz, Zehavi.

Pearl From the Latin and Middle English, meaning "pearl." HEBREW EQUIVALENTS: Margalit, Penina, Segula, Tzefira. MASCULINE HEBREW EQUIVALENTS: Penini, Shoham, Shovai, Yakar.

Peg, Peggie, Peggy Pet forms of Margaret and Pearl. *See* Margaret *and* Pearl.

Pelia, Peliah (פְּלִיאָה) From the Hebrew, meaning "wonder, miracle." The exact Hebrew equivalent is Pelia. MASCULINE HEBREW EQUIVALENTS: Pela'ya, Peleh, Peli.

Penelope From the Greek, meaning "worker in cloth" or "silent worker." HEBREW EQUIVALENTS: Amal, Amalya, Charutza, Zeriza. MASCULINE HEBREW EQUIVALENTS: Amel, Basha, Ovádya, Oved.

Penina (פְּנִינָה) From the Hebrew, meaning "coral" or "pearl." The exact Hebrew equivalent is Penina. The exact masculine Hebrew equivalent is Penini.

Penini (פְּנִינִי) A variant form of Penina. *See* Penina. The exact feminine and masculine Hebrew equivalent is Penini.

Peninia A variant spelling of Peniniya. *See* Peniniya.

Peninit (פְּנִינִית) From the Hebrew, meaning "pearly." The exact Hebrew equivalent is Peninit. The exact masculine Hebrew equivalent is Penini.

Peniniya (פְּנִינִיָה) From the Hebrew, meaning "hen, fowl." The exact Hebrew equivalent is Peniniya. MASCULINE HEBREW EQUIVALENTS: Gozal, Tzipor.

Penney, Pennie, Penny Pet forms of Penelope. *See* Penelope.

Peninah A variant spelling of Penina. *See* Penina.

Pepita A Spanish pet form of Josephine. *See* Josephine.

Peri (פְּרִי) From the Hebrew, meaning "fruit." The exact Hebrew equivalent is Peri (P'ri). MASCULINE HEBREW EQUIVALENTS: Periel, Porat, Poriel.

Perl A Yiddish form of Pearl. See Pearl.

Peshe (פֶּעשֶׁע) A Yiddish form of Bashe. See Bashe.

Pessel (פֶּעסֶל/פֶּעסֶל) A Yiddish form of Bashe. See Bashe.

Petra A feminine form of Peter. See Peter (masculine section).

Phebe A variant spelling of Phoebe. See Phoebe.

Philippa From the Greek, meaning "lover of horses." The feminine form of Philip. See Philip (masculine section).

Phoebe From the Greek, meaning "bright, shining one." HEBREW EQUIVALENTS: Behira, Me'ira, Ora, Orit, Orli, Tzefira. MASCULINE HEBREW EQUIVALENTS: Avner, Barak, Me'ir, Shimshon, Ya'ir.

Phylicia A variant spelling of Felicia. See Felicia.

Phylis A variant spelling of Phyllis. See Phyllis.

Phyllis From the Greek, meaning "little leaf, green bough." HEBREW EQUIVALENTS: Nitza, Shoshana, Varda, Yenika. MASCULINE HEBREW EQUIVALENTS: Chavakuk, Efra'yim, Pekach, Pura.

Pia From the Latin, meaning "pious." The exact Hebrew equivalent is Chasida. The exact masculine Hebrew equivalent is Chasid.

Pier A feminine form of Pierre, the French form of Peter. See Peter (masculine section).

Pita (פִּיתָה) From the Hebrew, meaning "bread." The exact Hebrew equivalent is Pita. MASCULINE HEBREW EQUIVALENTS: Lachma, Lachmi, Lechem.

Piuta A variant form of Piyuta. See Piyuta.

Piyuta (פִּיוּטָה) A Hebrew form of the Greek, meaning "poet, poetry." The exact Hebrew equivalent is Piyuta. The exact masculine Hebrew equivalent is Piyut.

Poda (פּוּדָה) From the Hebrew, meaning "redeemed." The exact Hebrew equivalent is Poda. MASCULINE HEBREW EQUIVALENTS: Peda'el, Pedat, Pedatzur, Peda'ya.

Pola The Italian form of Pula (a seaport in Yugoslavia), meaning "rain." HEBREW EQUIVALENTS: Malkosha, Lital, Ravital, Reviva. MASCULINE HEBREW EQUIVALENTS: Dalfon, Geshem, Malkosh, Matri, Raviv.

Polly A variant form of Molly, which was at one time a popular form of Mary. See Miryam.

Pora (פּוֹרָה) From the Hebrew, meaning 'fruitful." The exact Hebrew equivalent is Pora. MASCULINE HEBREW EQUIVALENTS: Poriel, Pura.

Porat (פּוֹרָת) A variant form of Pora. See Pora. The exact Hebrew equivalent is Porat.

Poria, Poriah Variant spellings of Poriya. See Poriya.

Poriya (פּוֹרִיָה) A variant form of Pora. See Pora. The exact Hebrew equivalent is Poriya.

Portia From the Latin, meaning "hog." There are no Hebrew equivalents.

Priscilla From the Latin, meaning "ancient, old." HEBREW EQUIVALENTS: Bilha, Keshisha, Yeshana, Yeshisha, Zekena. MASCULINE HEBREW EQUIVALENTS: Kadmiel, Kedem, Kedma, Yashish, Zaken.

Prudence From the Latin, meaning "prudent, wise." HEBREW EQUIVALENTS: Bina, Buna, Chochma, Tushiya. MASCULINE HEBREW EQUIVALENTS: Chacham, Haskel, Navon.

Prue A pet form of Prudence. *See* Prudence.

Pua, Puah (פּוּעָה) From the Hebrew, meaning "to groan, cry out." The exact Hebrew equivalent is Pua.

Queena, Queene Variant forms of Queenie. *See* Queenie.

Queenie A nickname for Regina, from the Latin, meaning "queen." The Hebrew equivalent is Malka. The masculine Hebrew equivalent is Melech.

Raanana (רַעֲנָנָה) From the Hebrew, meaning "fresh, luscious, beautiful." The exact Hebrew equivalent is Ra'anana. The exact masculine Hebrew equivalent is Ra'anan.

Rachel, Rachaele Variant spellings of Rachel. *See* Rachel.

Rachel (רָחֵל) From the Hebrew, meaning "ewe," a symbol of purity and gentility. The exact Hebrew equivalent is Rachel. MASCULINE HEBREW EQUIVALENTS: Adin, Adiv, Ra'anan, Talya, Zakai, Zimri.

Rachela (רָחֵלָה) A variant form of Rachel. *See* Rachel. The exact Hebrew equivalent is Rachel.

Rachelle A variant spelling of Rachel. *See* Rachel.

Rae A pet form of Rachel. *See* Rachel.

Rafaela, Rafaele Variant spellings of Refaela. *See* Refaela.

Rafia A variant spelling of Rafya. *See* Rafya.

Rafya (רִפְיָה) From the Hebrew, meaning "the healing of the Lord." The exact Hebrew equivalent is Rafya. The exact masculine Hebrew equivalent is Refa'el.

Rahel A variant spelling of Rachel. *See* Rachel.

Raina, Raine (רֵיינֶע/רֵיינָא) From the Latin, meaning "to rule." Akin to Regina. *See* Regina. Also, from the Yiddish, meaning "clean, pure." *See* Rayna.

Raisa (רֵייסָא) From the Yiddish, meaning "rose." The exact Hebrew equivalent is Shoshana. The exact masculine Hebrew equivalent is Shoshan.

Raise (רֵייסֶע) A variant form of Raisa. *See* Raisa.

Raisel (רֵייסֶעל) A pet form of Raise. *See* Raise.

Raissa, Raisse Variant spellings of Raisa. *See* Raisa.

Raize (רייזע)   A variant form of Raise. *See* Raise.

Raizel (רייזעל/רייזל)   A pet form of Raize. *See* Raize.

Raizi   A pet form of Raizel. *See* Raizel.

Rama (רָמָה)   From the Hebrew, meaning "lofty, exalted." The exact feminine and masculine Hebrew equivalent is Rama.

Rami (רָמִי)   A variant form of Rama. *See* Rama. The exact Hebrew equivalent is Rami.

Ramit (רָמִית)   A variant form of Rama. *See* Rama. The exact Hebrew equivalent is Ramit.

Ramona   A short form of Raymonda, meaning "peace" or "protection." HEBREW EQUIVALENTS: Botzra, Efrat, Shelomit, Shulamit, Tira. MASCULINE HEBREW EQUIVALENTS: Avigdor, Shalom, Shelomo, Shemaryahu.

Ramot (רָמוֹת)   A variant form of Rama. *See* Rama. The exact Hebrew equivalent is Ramot.

Rana   A variant spelling of Raina. *See* Raina.

Ranana   A variant spelling of Raanana. *See* Raanana.

Randi, Randy   Feminine pet forms of Randolph. *See* Randolph (*masculine section*).

Rani (רָנִי)   From the Hebrew, meaning "my song." The exact Hebrew equivalent is Rani. MASCULINE HEBREW EQUIVALENTS: Ron, Ronen, Roni, Ronli.

Ranit (רָנִית)   From the Hebrew, meaning "joy" or "song." The exact Hebrew equivalent is Ranit. MASCULINE HEBREW EQUIVALENTS: Ron, Roni, Ronli.

Ranita (רָנִיתָה)   A variant form of Ranit. *See* Ranit. The exact Hebrew equivalent is Ranita.

Ranny   A pet form of Frances. *See* Frances.

Ranya (רַנְיָה)   From the Hebrew, meaning "song of the Lord." The exact Hebrew equivalent is Ranya. The exact masculine Hebrew equivalent is Zemarya.

Raoul   A variant form of Randolph and Jack. *See* Randolph *and* Jack (*masculine section*).

Raphaela   A variant spelling of Refaela. *See* Refaela.

Raquel   A variant Spanish form of Rachel. *See* Rachel.

Raviva (רָבִיבָה)   A variant form of Reviva. *See* Reviva. The exact Hebrew equivalent is Raviva.

Ravital (רָבִיטַל)   From the Hebrew, meaning "abundance of dew." The exact Hebrew equivalent is Ravital. MASCULINE HEBREW EQUIVALENTS: Raviv, Tal, Tali.

Ray, Raye   Pet forms of Rachel. *See* Rachel. Also, from the Celtic, meaning "grace, gracious." *See* Grace.

Raya (רֵעַ)   From the Hebrew, meaning "friend." The exact feminine and masculine Hebrew equivalent is Raya.

Rayna (רֵיינָא)   A Yiddish form of Catherine meaning "pure, clean." HE-

BREW EQUIVALENTS: Berura, Me'ira, Penuya, Zaka, Zakiya, Zakit. MASCU-
LINE HEBREW EQUIVALENTS: Amizakai, Barur, Me'ir, Tzach, Zakai.

Rayne (רײַנע)   A variant form of Rayna. *See* Rayna.

Rayzel (רײַזעל/רײַזל)   A pet form of Raize. *See* Raize.

Raz (רָז)   From the Aramaic, meaning "secret." The exact feminine and
masculine Hebrew equivalent is Raz.

Razi (רָזִי)   From the Hebrew, meaning "my secret." The exact feminine
and masculine Hebrew equivalent is Razi.

Razia, Raziah   Variant spellings of Raziya. *See* Raziya.

Raziela, Raziella (רָזִיאֵלָה)   From the Hebrew, meaning "God is my secret." The exact Hebrew equivalent is Razi'ela. The exact masculine
Hebrew equivalent is Razi'el.

Razil   A variant spelling of Raisel. *See* Raisel.

Razilee   A variant spelling of Razili. *See* Razili.

Razili (רָזִילִי)   From the Aramaic and Hebrew, meaning "my secret." The
exact Hebrew equivalent is Razili. MASCULINE HEBREW EQUIVALENTS: Raz,
Razi, Raziel.

Razina (רָזִינָה)   An Hebraized form of Rosina. *See* Rosina. The exact Hebrew equivalent is Razina.

Raziya (רָזִיָה)   From the Hebrew, meaning "secret of the Lord." The exact
Hebrew equivalent is Raziya. The masculine Hebrew equivalent is
Raziel.

Reba (רִיבָה)   A pet form of Rebecca. *See also* Riva. The exact Hebrew
equivalent is Riba.

Rebecca (רִבְקָה)   From the Hebrew, meaning "to tie, bind." Fattened
animals were tied before being slaughtered, hence the secondary meaning of "voluptuous, beautiful, desirable." The exact Hebrew equivalent
is Rivka. MASCULINE HEBREW EQUIVALENTS: Chemdan, Na'aman, Ra'anan,
Yo'el.

Reda   A variant form of Rita. *See* Rita.

Reena   A variant spelling of Rina. *See* Rina.

Reeta   A variant spelling of Rita. *See* Rita.

Refaela (רְפָאֵלָה)   From the Hebrew, meaning "God has healed." The
exact Hebrew equivalent is Refa'ela. The exact masculine Hebrew
equivalent is Refa'el.

Regan   A variant form of Regina. *See* Regina.

Regina   From the Latin, meaning "to rule," or from the Anglo-Saxon,
meaning "pure." HEBREW EQUIVALENTS: Atara, Berura, Malka, Sara,
Tzefira, Zakit. MASCULINE HEBREW EQUIVALENTS: Avraham, Elimelech,
Katriel, Yisrael.

Reina, Reine   Variant spellings of Rayna. *See* Rayna.

Reita   A variant spelling of Rita. *See* Rita.

Reitha   A variant spelling of Reatha. *See* Reatha.

Reizel   A variant spelling of Raisel. *See* Raisel.

Reizl A variant spelling of Raisel. *See* Raisel.

Remiza (רְמִיזָה) From the Hebrew, meaning "sign, signal." The exact Hebrew equivalent is Remiza. The exact masculine Hebrew equivalent is Remez.

Rena, Renah Short forms of Regina or Serena. *See* Regina *and* Serena. Also, variant spellings of Rina. *See* Rina.

Renana (רְנָנָה) From the Hebrew, meaning "joy" or "song." The exact Hebrew equivalent is Renana. MASCULINE HEBREW EQUIVALENTS: Ranen, Ranon, Ron, Roni, Ronli.

Renanit (רְנָנִית) A variant form of Renana. *See* Renana. The exact Hebrew equivalent is Renanit.

Renata From the Latin, meaning "to be born again." HEBREW EQUIVALENTS: Chava, Cha'ya, Techiya. MASCULINE HEBREW EQUIVALENTS: Cha'yim, Chiya, Yechiel.

Rene, Renee French forms of Renata. *See* Renata.

Renette A French pet form of Rene. *See* Rene.

Renina (רְנִינָה) A variant form of Renana. *See* Renana. The exact Hebrew equivalent is Renina.

Renita A Spanish pet form of Rene. *See* Rene.

Rephaela A variant spelling of Refaela. *See* Refaela.

Resa A pet form of Theresa. *See* Theresa.

Reubena A variant spelling of Reuvena. *See* Reuvena.

Reuvat (רְאוּבַת) A feminine form of Reuven, meaning "Behold, a son!" The exact Hebrew equivalent is Re'uvat. The masculine Hebrew equivalent is Re'uven.

Reuvena (רְאוּבֶנָה) A feminine form of Reuven (Reuben), meaning "Behold, a son!" The exact Hebrew equivalent is Re'uvena. The exact masculine Hebrew equivalent is Re'uven.

Reva (רִיבָה) A pet form of Rebecca. *See* Rebecca. The exact Hebrew equivalent is Riva.

Reviva (רְבִיבָה) From the Hebrew, meaning "dew" or "rain." The exact Hebrew equivalent is Reviva. The exact masculine Hebrew equivalent is Raviv.

Rexana The feminine form of Rex, meaning "king." HEBREW EQUIVALENTS: Atara, Malka, Tzefira. MASCULINE HEBREW EQUIVALENTS: Avimelech, Elimelech, Katriel, Melech.

Reyna A variant spelling of Rayna. *See* Rayna.

Rhea From the Greek, meaning "protector of cities." HEBREW EQUIVALENTS: Avigdora, Magena, Shimrit, Tzila. MASCULINE HEBREW EQUIVALENTS: Avigdor, Chetzron, Shemaryahu, Sisri.

Rheta A variant spelling of Rita. *See* Rita. Also, from the Greek, meaning "one who speaks well." HEBREW EQUIVALENTS: Amira, Devora, Niva. MASCULINE HEBREW EQUIVALENTS: Amaryahu, Imri, Niv.

Rhoda From the Greek, meaning "rose." The exact feminine and masculine Hebrew equivalent is Vered.

Rhode A variant form of Rhoda. *See* Rhoda.

Rhona A hybrid of Rose and Anna. *See* Rose *and* Anna.

Rhonda From the Celtic, meaning "powerful river." HEBREW EQUIVALENTS: Afeka, Arnona, Bat-Yam, Miryam, Yaval. MASCULINE HEBREW EQUIVALENTS: Arnon, Avi'yam, Ye'or, Ye'ori.

Rica A pet form of Ricarda. *See* Ricarda.

Ricarda A feminine Italian form of Ricardo (Richard). *See* Richard (*masculine section*).

Richarda A feminine form of Richard. *See* Richard (*masculine section*).

Ricka, Ricki Pet forms of Patricia, Rebecca, Ricarda, and Roberta. *See* Patricia, Rebecca, Ricarda, *and* Roberta.

Rickma (רִקְמָה) From the Hebrew, meaning "woven product." The exact Hebrew equivalent is Rikma. The exact masculine Hebrew equivalent is Rekem.

Ricky A variant spelling of Ricki. *See* Ricki.

Rifka (רִיפְקָא) A Yiddish form of Rivka. *See* Rivka.

Rifke (רִיפְקֶע) A Yiddish form of Rivka. *See* Rivka.

Riki, Rikki Pet forms of Erica. *See* Erica.

Rikma A variant spelling of Rickma. *See* Rickma.

Rimon (רִמוֹן) From the Hebrew, meaning "pomegranate." The exact feminine and masculine Hebrew equivalent is Rimon.

Rimona (רִמוֹנָה) The feminine form of Rimon. *See* Rimon. The exact Hebrew equivalent is Rimona.

Rina (רִנָּה) From the Hebrew, meaning "joy." The exact Hebrew equivalent is Rina. MASCULINE HEBREW EQUIVALENTS: Ranen, Rani, Ron, Ronel, Ronli.

Risa A pet form of Theresa. *See* Theresa.

Rishona (רִאשׁוֹנָה) From the Hebrew, meaning "first." The exact Hebrew equivalent is Rishona. The exact masculine Hebrew equivalent is Rishon.

Rita From the Sanskrit, meaning "brave" or "honest." HEBREW EQUIVALENTS: Abira, Amtza, Azriela, Gavriela, Gibora, Uziela. MASCULINE HEBREW EQUIVALENTS: Abir, Adir, Amnon, Aviram, Azriel, Gavriel. Also, a short form of Marguerita. *See* Marguerita.

Riva From the Old French, meaning "coastline, shore." Also, a pet form of Rivka. *See* Rivka.

Rivi (רִיבִי) A pet form of Rivka. *See* Rivka. The exact Hebrew equivalent is Rivi.

Rivka, Rivkah (רִבְקָה) From the Hebrew, meaning "to bind." Rebecca is the Anglicized form. *See* Rebecca.

Rivke (רִבְקֶע) A Yiddish form of Rivka. *See* Rivka.

Roanna, Roanna A hybrid of Rose and Ann. *See* Rose *and* Ann.

Robbi, Robbie Pet forms of Roberta. *See* Roberta.

Roberta   The feminine form of Robert. *See* Robert (*masculine section*).

Robertina   A pet form of Robert. *See* Robert.

Robin, Robyn   Pet forms of Roberta. *See* Roberta.

Rochel (רָאחֶעל/רָאחְל)   A Yiddish form of Rachel. *See* Rachel.

Rochelle   From the Old French, meaning "small rock." HEBREW EQUIVALENTS: Avniela, Ritzpa, Salit, Tzurit, Tzuriya. MASCULINE HEBREW EQUIVALENTS: Achitzur, Avitzur, Tzeror, Tzur, Tzuri.

Rolanda   A feminine form of Roland. *See* Roland (*masculine section*).

Roma (רוּמָה)   From the Hebrew, meaning "heights, lofty, exalted." The exact Hebrew equivalent is Roma. The exact masculine Hebrew equivalent is Rom.

Romema (רוּמֵמָה)   From the Hebrew, meaning "heights, lofty, exalted." The exact Hebrew equivalent is Romema. The exact masculine Hebrew equivalent is Romem.

Romia   A variant spelling of Romiya. *See* Romiya.

Romit (רוּמִית)   A variant form of Roma. *See* Roma. The exact Hebrew equivalent is Romit.

Romiya (רוּמִיָה)   A variant spelling of Romema. *See* Romema. The exact Hebrew equivalent is Romiya.

Ron (רוֹן)   From the Hebrew, meaning "song" or "joy." The exact feminine and masculine Hebrew equivalent is Ron.

Rona   From the Gaelic, meaning "seal," or from the Hebrew, meaning "joy." The exact Hebrew equivalent is Rona. The exact masculine Hebrew equivalent is Ron.

Ronalda   A feminine form of Ronald. *See* Ronald (*masculine section*).

Ronela, Ronella (רוֹנְאֵלָה)   Variant forms of Ron. *See* Ron. The exact Hebrew equivalent is Ronela.

Roni (רוֹנִי)   A variant form of Ron. *See* Ron. The exact feminine and masculine Hebrew equivalent is Roni.

Ronia   A variant spelling of Roniya. *See* Roniya.

Ronili (רוֹנִי־לִי/רוֹנִילִי)   From the Hebrew, meaning "Joy is mine." The exact Hebrew equivalent is Ronili. MASCULINE HEBREW EQUIVALENTS: Roni, Ronli.

Roniya (רוֹנִיָה)   A variant form of Ron, meaning "joy of the Lord." The exact Hebrew equivalent is Roniya. MASCULINE HEBREW EQUIVALENTS: Ron, Roni.

Ronli (רוֹן־לִי/רוֹנְלִי)   A variant form of Ron, meaning "Joy is mine." The exact feminine and masculine Hebrew equivalent is Ronli.

Ronne, Ronni, Ronnie   Feminine pet forms of Ronald. *See* Ronald (*masculine section*).

Ronnit   A variant spelling of Ronit. *See* Ronit.

Ronny   A variant spelling of Ronnie. *See* Ronnie.

Ronya (רוֹנְיָה)   From the Hebrew, meaning "song of God." A variant form of Roniya. *See* Roniya. The exact Hebrew equivalent is Ronya.

Rori, Rory Irish feminine forms of Roderick and Robert. *See* Roderick *and* Robert (*masculine section*).

Rose A popular Italian form of Rose. *See* Rose.

Rosabel From the Latin and French, meaning "beautiful rose." *See* Rose.

Rosalie A variant French pet form of Rose. *See* Rose.

Rosalind A pet form of Rose. *See* Rose.

Rosalinda A Spanish form of Rosalind. *See* Rosalind.

Rosaline A variant form of Rosalind. *See* Rosalind.

Rosalyn A variant form of Rosalind. *See* Rosalind.

Rosanne A hybrid form of Rose and Anne. *See* Rose *and* Anne.

Rose The English form of the Latin Rosa, meaning "rose." The feminine and masculine Hebrew equivalent is Vered.

Roselotte A combination of Rose and Lotte. *See* Rose *and* Lotte.

Roselyn A variant form of Rosalind. *See* Rosalind.

Rosemary A hybrid form of Rose and Mary. *See* Rose *and* Mary.

Rosetta An Italian pet form of Rose. *See* Rose.

Rosette A French pet form of Rose. *See* Rose.

Rosi, Rosie Pet forms of Rose. *See* Rose.

Rosina, Rosine Pet forms of Rose. *See* Rose.

Rosita A pet form of Rose. *See* Rose.

Roslyn A variant spelling of Rosalyn. *See* Rosalyn.

Rotem (רֹתֶם) From the Hebrew, meaning "to bind." Also, a plant common to southern Israel. The exact feminine and masculine Hebrew equivalent is Rotem.

Rowena From the Old English, meaning "rugged land," and from the Celtic, meaning "flowery white hair." HEBREW EQUIVALENTS: Artzit, Dala, Delila, Eretz, Levana, Nima. MASCULINE HEBREW EQUIVALENTS: Artza, Artzi, Esav, Lavan.

Roxane, Roxanna, Roxanne From the Persian, meaning "dawn, brilliant light." HEBREW EQUIVALENTS: Barakit, Bat-Shachar, Shacharit, Tzafra, Tzafrira, Tzef'ira. MASCULINE HEBREW EQUIVALENTS: Avishachar, Ben-Shachar, Shecharya, Tzafrir.

Roxie A variant spelling of Roxy. *See* Roxy.

Roxine A variant form of Roxanne. *See* Roxanne.

Roxy A pet form of Roxanne. *See* Roxanne.

Roz A pet form of Rosalyn. *See* Rosalyn.

Rozelin A variant spelling of Rosaline. *See* Rosaline.

Rozella A hybrid form of Rose and Ella. *See* Rose *and* Ella.

Rozina A variant spelling of Rosina. *See* Rosina.

Ruby From the Latin and French, meaning "a precious reddish stone." HEBREW EQUIVALENTS: Bareket, Margalit, Penina, Sapira, Segula, Tzefira, Yekara. MASCULINE HEBREW EQUIVALENTS: Avikar, Sapir, Shoham, Shovai, Yakar.

Rudelle From the Old High German, meaning "famous one." HEBREW EQUIVALENTS: Hillela, Tehila, Ya'el, Yehudit, Zimra. MASCULINE HEBREW EQUIVALENTS: Hillel, Shevach, Shimi, Yehuda, Yishbach.

Rue From the Old High German, meaning "fame." A variant form of Rudelle. *See* Rudelle.

Rula From the Middle English and the Latin, meaning "ruler." HEBREW EQUIVALENTS: Alufa, Malka, Sara, Sarit, Yisr'ela. MASCULINE HEBREW EQUIVALENTS: Aluf, Elrad, Melech, Rozen, Sar, Yisrael.

Rut The Hebraized form of Ruth. *See* Ruth.

Ruth (רוּת) From the Syriac and Hebrew, meaning "friendship." The exact Hebrew equivalent is Rut. MASCULINE HEBREW EQUIVALENTS: Amit, Amitai, David, Ray'a, Ray'i, Regem, Re'uel.

Ruthanna A hybrid of Ruth and Anna. *See* Ruth *and* Anna.

Ruti (רוּתִי) A pet form of Rut. *See* Rut. The exact Hebrew equivalent is Ruti.

Saada (סַעֲדָה) From the Hebrew, meaning "support, help." The exact Hebrew equivalent is Sa'ada. The exact masculine Hebrew equivalent is Sa'adya.

Sabaria A variant spelling of Tzabaria. *See* Tzabaria.

Saba (סָבָה/סָבָא) From the Hebrew and Aramaic, meaning "old, aged." The exact feminine and masculine Hebrew equivalent is Saba.

Sabra (צַבְּרָה) From the Hebrew, meaning "thorny cactus." The exact feminine and masculine Hebrew equivalent is Tzabara.

Sabrina A pet form of Sabra. *See* Sabra.

Sacha A pet form of Alexandra, popular in Russia. *See* Alexandra.

Sadi A modern spelling of Sadie. *See* Sadie.

Sadie A pet form of Sarah. *See* Sarah.

Sadira (סָדִירָה) From the Arabic and Hebrew, meaning "organized, regulated." The exact Hebrew equivalent is Sadira. The exact masculine Hebrew equivalent is Sadir.

Sady, Sadye Variant spellings of Sadie. *See* Sadie.

Sahara (סַהֲרָה) From the Hebrew, meaning "moon." The exact Hebrew equivalent is Sahara. MASCULINE HEBREW EQUIVALENTS: Chodesh, Yerach.

Salida From the Old German, meaning "happiness, joy." HEBREW EQUIVALENTS: Sasona, Semecha, Simcha, Simchit, Simchona. MASCULINE HEBREW EQUIVALENTS: Sason, Simcha, Simchon, Simchoni.

Salit (סַלְעִית) From the Hebrew, meaning "rock, rocky." The exact Hebrew equivalent is Salit. MASCULINE HEBREW EQUIVALENTS: Even, Even-Ezer, Regem, Sapir.

Sallie, Sally Variant forms of Sarah. *See* Sarah.

Salome (שְׁלוֹמִית) From the Hebrew, meaning "peaceful." The exact

Hebrew equivalent is Shelomit (Shlomit). The exact masculine Hebrew equivalent is Shelomo (Shlomo).

Samantha From the Aramaic, meaning "listener." Akin to Samuela. *See* Samuela.

Samara (שׁוֹמְרוֹנָה) From the Latin, meaning "seed of the elm," and from the Hebrew, meaning "guardian." The Hebrew equivalent is Shomrona. The masculine Hebrew equivalent is Shomron.

Sammy, Sammye A pet form of Samuela and Samantha. *See* Samuela *and* Samantha.

Samuela (שְׁמוּאֵלָה) The feminine form of Samuel. *See* Samuel (*masculine section*). The exact Hebrew form is Shemuela (Shmuela).

Sandi A pet form of Sandra. *See* Sandra.

Sandra A pet form of Alexandra. *See* Alexandra.

Sandy A pet form of Sandra. *See* Sandra.

Sapir (סַפִּיר) From the Hebrew, meaning "sapphire." The exact feminine and masculine Hebrew equivalent is Sapir.

Sapira (סַפִּירָה) A variant form of Sapir. *See* Sapir. The exact Hebrew equivalent is Sapira.

Sapirit (סַפִּירִית) A variant form of Sapir. *See* Sapir. The exact Hebrew equivalent is Sapirit.

Sara, Sarah (שָׂרָה) From the Hebrew, meaning "noble" or "princess." The exact Hebrew equivalent is Sara. MASCULINE HEBREW EQUIVALENTS: Adon, Aluf, Avihud, Avraham, Chiram, Chirom, Nadav, Yisrael.

Sarai (שָׂרַי) The original biblical form of Sara. *See* Sara.

Sarali (שָׂרָלִי) A pet form of Sara. *See* Sara. The exact Hebrew equivalent is Sarali.

Saran, Sarann, Saranne Hybrid forms of Sarah and Ann. *See* Sarah *and* Ann.

Sareli A variant spelling of Sarali. *See* Sarali. Also, a variant form of Yisrael (Israel). *See* Yisrael (*masculine section*).

Sarene A variant form of Sara. *See* Sara.

Sarida (שָׂרִידָה) From the Hebrew, meaning "refugee, leftover." The exact Hebrew equivalent is Sarida. The exact masculine Hebrew equivalent is Sarid.

Saretta, Sarette Pet forms of Sara. *See* Sara.

Sari A variant spelling of Sarai. *See* Sarai.

Sarina, Sarine Variant forms of Sara. *See* Sara.

Sarit (שָׂרִית) A variant form of Sara. *See* Sara. The exact Hebrew equivalent is Sarit.

Sarita (שָׂרִיתָה) A variant form of Sara. *See* Sara. The exact Hebrew equivalent is Sarita.

Saryl (שָׂרִיל) A variant Yiddish form of Sara. *See* Sara.

Saundra A variant spelling of Sandra. *See* Sandra.

Savrina (סַבְרִינָה)   A variant form of Sabra. *See* Sabra. The exact Hebrew equivalent is Savrina.

Savta (סָבְתָּא/סָבְתָה)   From the Aramaic, meaning "grandmother." The exact Hebrew equivalent is Savta. The exact masculine Hebrew equivalent is Saba.

Scarlet, Scarlett   From the Middle English, meaning "red, ruby-colored." HEBREW EQUIVALENTS: Admon, Almoga, Odem, Tzachara. MASCULINE HEBREW EQUIVALENTS: Admon, Almog, Edom, Tzachar.

Schifra   A variant spelling of Shifra. *See* Shifra.

Seema   From the Greek, meaning "sprout." Akin to Cyma. HEBREW EQUIVALENTS: Nitza, Pircha, Pirchiya, Shoshana, Tifracha. MASCULINE HEBREW EQUIVALENTS: Efra'yim, Nitzan, Savyon, Shoshan, Tzemach.

Segula (סְגוּלָה)   From the Hebrew, meaning "treasure" or "precious." The exact Hebrew equivalent is Segula. The exact masculine Hebrew equivalent is Segel.

Sela (סֶלַע)   From the Greek and Hebrew, meaning "rock." The exact feminine and masculine Hebrew equivalent is Sela.

Selda, Selde   From the Anglo-Saxon, meaning "precious, rare." Also, from the Middle English, meaning "booth, hut." HEBREW EQUIVALENTS: Ada, Chamuda, Sapira, Segula, Yekara. MASCULINE HEBREW EQUIVALENTS: Bahat, Leshem, Nofach, Sapir, Yahalom, Yakir.

Selena, Selene   From the Greek, meaning "moon." HEBREW EQUIVALENTS: Chodesh, Levana, Sahara. MASCULINE HEBREW EQUIVALENTS: Levanon, Yarchi, Yaro'ach, Yerach.

Selila (סְלִילָה)   From the Hebrew, meaning "path." The exact Hebrew equivalent is Selila. The exact masculine Hebrew equivalent is Salil.

Selima, Selimah   Arabic feminine forms of Solomon, meaning "peace." *See* Solomon (*masculine section*).

Selina   A variant spelling of Selena. *See* Selena.

Selma   From the Celtic, meaning "fair." HEBREW EQUIVALENTS: Levana, Na'ama, Na'omi, Ra'anana. MASCULINE HEBREW EQUIVALENTS: Lavan, Livni, Ra'anan.

Sema   A variant spelling of Seema. *See* Seema.

Serena   From the Latin, meaning "peaceful" or "cheerful." HEBREW EQUIVALENTS: Achishalom, Aliza, Sha'anana, Shalviya, Shlomit, Shlom-Tziyon, Simcha, Shulamit. MASCULINE HEBREW EQUIVALENTS: Aliz, Shalom, Shelomo, Yechi-Shalom.

Serita   A variant spelling of Sarita. *See* Sarita.

Severina   From the Latin, meaning "friendly, friendship." HEBREW EQUIVALENTS: Achava, Amit, Amita, Re'uela, Rut, Yedida. MASCULINE HEBREW EQUIVALENTS: Amit, Amitai, Amiti, Chovev, David, Dodi, Yedidya.

Shaina (שֵׁיינָא)   A variant form of Sheine. *See* Sheine.

Shaindel (שֵׁיינְדֶעל/שֵׁיינְדְל)   A pet form of Shaine. *See* Shaine.

Shaine (שֵׁיינֶע)   From the Yiddish, meaning "beautiful." Akin to Sheina. *See* Sheina for equivalents.

Shalva, Shalvah (שַׁלְוָה) From the Hebrew, meaning "peace, tranquility." The exact Hebrew equivalent is Shalva. The exact masculine Hebrew equivalent is Shalev.

Shamira (שְׁמִירָה) From the Hebrew, meaning "guard, protector." The exact Hebrew equivalent is Shamira. The exact masculine Hebrew equivalent is Shamir.

Shana A variant spelling of Shaina. See Shaina. Also, a nickname for Shoshana. See Shoshana.

Shane A variant spelling of Shaine. See Shaine.

Shani, Shanie (שֵׁינִי) Pet forms of Shaine. See Shaine.

Shannen A variant spelling of Shannon. See Shannon.

Shannon A feminine form of Sean. See Sean (*masculine section*).

Shareen A variant form of Sharon. See Sharon.

Sharelle A variant form of Sharon. See Sharon.

Shari A pet form of Sharon. See Sharon.

Sharin A variant spelling of Sharon. See Sharon.

Sharleen A variant spelling of Charlene. See Charlene.

Sharlene A variant spelling of Charlene. See Charlene.

Sharon (שָׁרוֹן) From the Hebrew, meaning "a plain." An area of ancient Palestine extending from Mount Carmel south to Jaffa, where roses grew in abundance. The exact feminine and masculine Hebrew equivalent is Sharon.

Sharona (שָׁרוֹנָה) A variant form of Sharon. See Sharon. The exact Hebrew equivalent is Sharona.

Sharoni (שָׁרוֹנִי) A variant form of Sharon. See Sharon. The exact Hebrew equivalent is Sharoni.

Sharonit (שָׁרוֹנִית) A variant form of Sharon. See Sharon. The exact Hebrew equivalent is Sharonit.

Sharyn A variant spelling of Sharon. See Sharon.

Shaula (שָׁאוּלָה) A feminine form of Shaul (Saul). See Shaul (*masculine section*). The exact Hebrew equivalent is Sha'ula.

Shaulit (שָׁאוּלִית) A variant form of Shaula. See Shaula.

Shayna A variant spelling of Sheina. See Sheina.

Shayndel A variant spelling of Shaindel. See Shaindel.

Shayne A variant spelling of Shaine. See Shaine.

Sheba The Anglicized form of Sheva. See Sheva.

Sheena A Gaelic form of Jane. See Jane.

Sheila, Sheilah Variant forms of Cecelia and Celia. See Cecelia.

Sheina (שֵׁינָא) From the Yiddish, meaning "beautiful." HEBREW EQUIVALENTS: Na'a, Na'ama, Na'omi, Nava, Nofiya, Noya, Yafa, Yafit. MASCULINE HEBREW EQUIVALENTS: Adin, Hadar, Nechmad, Noi, Ra'anan, Shapir, Yafeh.

Sheindel (שֵׁינְגְּרֶעל/שֵׁינְגְּדֶל) A pet form of Sheina. See Sheina.

Shelby From the Anglo-Saxon, meaning "sheltered town." Used primarily as a masculine name. *See* Shelby (*masculine section*).

Sheli (שֶׁלִי) A variant form of Shelley. *See* Shelley. Also, from the Hebrew, meaning "mine." The exact Hebrew equivalent is Sheli.

Shelia A variant spelling of Sheliya. *See* Sheliya.

Sheliya, Sheli-Ya (שְׁלִי־יָה/שֶׁלִיָה) From the Hebrew, meaning "Mine is God's." The exact Hebrew equivalent is Sheliya. MASCULINE HEBREW EQUIVALENTS: Eliya, Eliyahu, Hosha'ya, Ya'el.

Shelley, Shelly Irish pet forms of Cecelia. *See* Cecelia.

Shelomit A variant spelling of Shlomit. *See* Shlomit.

Shemuela A variant spelling of Shmuela. *See* Shmuela.

Sheree A variant form of Cheryl. *See* Cheryl.

Sherelle, Sherrelle A variant spelling of Cheryl. *See* Cheryl.

Sherelyn A pet form of Sherry. *See* Sherry.

Sheri A variant spelling of Cheri. *See* Cheri.

Sherry A variant form of Caesarina, the feminine form of the Latin Caesar, meaning "king." Hence, Sherry means "queen." The Hebrew equivalent is Malka. The masculine Hebrew equivalent is Melech.

Sheryl A variant form of Sherry. *See* Sherry.

Sheva (שֶׁבַע) From the Hebrew, meaning "oath." The exact feminine and masculine Hebrew equivalent is Sheva.

Shifra, Shifrah (שִׁפְרָה) From the Hebrew, meaning "good, handsome, beautiful" or from the Aramaic, meaning "trumpet." The exact Hebrew equivalent is Shifra. The exact masculine Hebrew equivalent is Shefer.

Shimra (שִׁמְרָה) From the Hebrew, meaning "guarded, protected." The exact Hebrew equivalent is Shimra. MASCULINE HEBREW EQUIVALENTS: Shemer, Shimri, Shemarya.

Shimrat (שִׁמְרָת) From the Aramaic, meaning "protected, guarded." The exact Hebrew equivalent is Shimrat. MASCULINE HEBREW EQUIVALENTS: Shemer, Shimri, Shemaryahu.

Shimrit (שִׁמְרִית) From the Hebrew, meaning "guarded, protected." The exact Hebrew equivalent is Shimrit. MASCULINE HEBREW EQUIVALENTS: Shemer, Shimri, Shemarya.

Shimriya (שִׁמְרִיָה) From the Hebrew, meaning "God is my protector." The exact Hebrew equivalent is Shimriya. MASCULINE HEBREW EQUIVALENTS: Shemer, Shimri, Shemarya, Shemaryahu.

Shimshona (שִׁמְשׁוֹנָה) The feminine form of Shimshon (Samson). *See* Samson (*masculine section*). The exact Hebrew equivalent is Shimshona.

Shiphra A variant spelling of Shifra. *See* Shifra.

Shira, Shirah (שִׁירָה) From the Hebrew, meaning "song." The exact Hebrew equivalent is Shira. MASCULINE HEBREW EQUIVALENTS: Shir, Shiron, Yashir.

Shirel (שִׁירָאֵל) From the Hebrew, meaning "God's song." The exact

Hebrew equivalent is Shirel. MASCULINE HEBREW EQUIVALENTS: Avishar, Shir, Shiron, Yashir.

Shirl A pet form of Shirley. *See* Shirley.

Shirlee, Shir-Lee Variant spellings of Shirli. *See* Shirli. Also, variant spellings of Shirley. *See* Shirley.

Shirley From the Old English, meaning "from the white meadow." HEBREW EQUIVALENTS: Gana, Ganit, Gina, Ginat, Sharona, Yardeniya. MASCULINE HEBREW EQUIVALENTS: Bustan, Gan, Gani, Sharon, Yarden.

Shirli, Shir-Li (שִׁיר־לִי/שִׁירְלִי) From the Hebrew, meaning "Song is mine." The exact Hebrew equivalent is Shirli. MASCULINE HEBREW EQUIVALENTS: Shir, Shiron, Yashir, Zimra, Zimri, Zimroni.

Shirra A variant spelling of Shira. *See* Shira.

Shlomit (שְׁלוֹמִית) From the Hebrew, meaning "peaceful." The exact Hebrew equivalent is Shlomit (Shelomit). The exact masculine Hebrew equivalent is Shlomo (Shelomo).

Shmuela (שְׁמוּאֵלָה) The feminine form of Shmuel (Samuel). *See* Shmuel *(masculine section)*. The exact Hebrew equivalent is Shmu'ela.

Shona (שׁוֹנָא) A variant form of Sheina. *See* Sheina.

Shoni, Shonie (שׁוֹנִי) Variant forms of Sheina. *See* Sheina.

Shoshan (שׁוֹשָׁן) From the Hebrew, meaning "lily," or from the Egyptian and Coptic, meaning "lotus." The exact feminine and masculine Hebrew equivalent is Shoshan.

Shoshana, Shoshanah (שׁוֹשַׁנָה) Variant forms of Shoshan. *See* Shoshan. The exact Hebrew equivalent is Shoshana.

Shprintza, Shprintze (שְׁפְּרִינְצָא/שְׁפְּרִינְצֶע) Yiddish forms from the Esperanto, meaning "hope." *See* Hope.

Shuala (שׁוּעָלָה) From the Hebrew, meaning "fox." The exact Hebrew equivalent is Shu'ala. The exact masculine Hebrew equivalent is Shu'al.

Shula (שׁוּלָה) A pet form of Shulamit. *See* Shulamit. The exact Hebrew equivalent is Shula.

Shulamit (שׁוּלַמִית) From the Hebrew, meaning "peace, peaceful." The exact Hebrew equivalent is Shulamit. The exact masculine Hebrew equivalent is Shlomo.

Shuli, Shuly (שׁוּלִי) Pet forms of Shulamit. *See* Shulamit. The exact Hebrew equivalent is Shuli.

Sibyl From the Greek, meaning "counsel of God." Also, from the Old Italian, meaning "wise old woman." HEBREW EQUIVALENTS: Bina, Buna, Milka. MASCULINE HEBREW EQUIVALENTS: Achban, Chachmoni, Utz, Yosha.

Sidra (סִדְרָה) From the Latin, meaning "starlike." Also, from the Hebrew, meaning "order, sequence." The exact feminine and masculine Hebrew equivalent is Sidra.

Sigal (סְגֵל) From the Hebrew, meaning "treasure." The exact Hebrew equivalent is Sigal. The exact masculine Hebrew equivalent is Segel.

Sigalia A variant spelling of Sigaliya. *See* Sigaliya.

Sigalit (סִגָלִית) A variant form of Sigal. *See* Sigal. The exact Hebrew equivalent is Sigalit.

Sigaliya (סִגָלִיָה) A variant form of Sigal. *See* Sigal. The exact Hebrew equivalent is Sigaliya.

Siglia A variant spelling of Sigaliya. *See* Sigaliya.

Siglit (סִגְלִית) A variant form of Sigal. *See* Sigal. The exact Hebrew equivalent is Siglit.

Signora From the Latin, meaning "woman, lady." HEBREW EQUIVALENTS: Aluf, Gevira. MASCULINE HEBREW EQUIVALENTS: Adon, Adoniya, Aluf.

Silona (סִילוֹנָה) From the Greek and Hebrew, meaning "water conduit, stream." The exact Hebrew equivalent is Silona. The exact masculine Hebrew equivalent is Silon.

Silonit (סִילוֹנִית) A variant form of Silona. *See* Silona. The exact Hebrew equivalent is Silonit.

Silva A variant form of Sylvia. *See* Sylvia.

Silvia A variant spelling of Sylvia. *See* Sylvia.

Sima (סִימָה) From the Aramaic, meaning "treasure." The exact feminine and masculine Hebrew equivalent is Sima.

Simajean A hybrid of Sima and Jean. *See* Sima *and* Jean.

Simcha (שִׂמְחָה) From the Hebrew, meaning "joy." The exact feminine and masculine Hebrew equivalent is Simcha.

Simchit (שִׂמְחִית) A variant form of Simcha. *See* Simcha. The exact Hebrew equivalent is Simchit.

Simchona (שִׂמְחוֹנָה) A variant form of Simcha. *See* Simcha.

Simeona A variant spelling of Simona. *See* Simona.

Simona (שִׁמְעוֹנָה) A feminine form of Simon. *See* Simon (*masculine section*). The exact Hebrew equivalent is Shimona.

Simone A French form of Simon. *See* Simon (*masculine section*).

Sindy A fanciful spelling of Cindy. *See* Cindy.

Siona (צִיוֹנָה) A variant spelling of Tziyona. *See* Tziyona.

Sirel (סִירְל) A Yiddish form of Sara. *See* Sara.

Sirena A variant spelling of Serena. *See* Serena.

Sirke (שִׁירְקֶע/סִירְקֶע) A Yiddish pet form of Sara. *See* Sara.

Sisel (סִיסְל) From the Yiddish, meaning "sweet." HEBREW EQUIVALENTS: Metuka, Mirit. MASCULINE HEBREW EQUIVALENTS: Matok, Na'im, Yivsam.

Sisi A pet form of Cecilia. *See* Cecilia.

Sisley A variant spelling of Cicely. *See* Cicely.

Sissie, Sissy Variant spellings of Sisi. *See* Sisi.

Sivana (סִינָנָה) A variant form of the masculine Sivan. *See* Sivan (*masculine section*). The exact Hebrew equivalent is Sivana.

Sivia, Sivya (צְבִיָה) Variant forms of Tzivya. *See* Tzivya.

Soferet (סוֹפֶרֶת) From the Hebrew, meaning "scribe." The exact Hebrew equivalent is Soferet. The exact masculine Hebrew equivalent is Sofer.

Sondra A variant spelling of Sandra. *See* Sandra.

Sonia A variant form of Sophia. *See* Sophia.

Sonja, Sonya Slavic forms of Sonia. *See* Sonia.

Sophia From the Greek, meaning "wisdom, wise one." HEBREW EQUIVALENTS: Bina, Buna, Chochma, Milka, Tushiya. MASCULINE HEBREW EQUIVALENTS: Achban, Chachmoni, Chanoch, Haskel, Utz, Yosha.

Sophie A French form of Sophia. *See* Sophia.

Sorale (שָׂרַאלֶע) A Yiddish pet form of Sarah. *See* Sarah.

Sorali, Soralie (שָׂרַאלִי) Yiddish pet forms of Sarah. *See* Sarah.

Soreka (שׂוֹרֵקָה) From the Hebrew, meaning "vine." The exact Hebrew equivalent is Soreka. MASCULINE HEBREW EQUIVALENTS: Gafni, Gefen, Karmiel, Kerem.

Sorka, Sorke (שָׂרְקֶע/שָׂרְקָא) A Yiddish pet form of Sara. *See* Sara.

Soroli A variant spelling of Sorali. *See* Sorali.

Stacey, Stacy Irish forms of the Greek name Anastasia, meaning "resurrection, revival." HEBREW EQUIVALENTS: Chava, Cha'ya, Yechiela. MASCULINE HEBREW EQUIVALENTS: Amichai, Bar-Yochai, Chai, Cha'yim.

Stacia, Stacie Variant pet forms of Anastasia. *See* Anastasia.

Star From the Old English, meaning "star." The exact Hebrew equivalent is Ester. MASCULINE HEBREW EQUIVALENTS: Bar-Kochva, Kochav.

Staria A variant form of Star. *See* Star.

Starletta A pet form of Star. *See* Star.

Starr A variant spelling of Star. *See* Star.

Stefana, Stefania Feminine forms of Stephen. *See* Stephen (*masculine section*).

Stefanie, Stefenie Feminine forms of Stephen. *See* Stephen (*masculine section*).

Steffi A pet form of Stefanie. *See* Stefanie.

Stella From the Latin, meaning "star." The exact Hebrew equivalent is Ester. MASCULINE HEBREW EQUIVALENTS: Bar-Kochva, Kochav.

Stephane A variant spelling of Stephanie. *See* Stephanie.

Stephania, Stephanie, Stephenie Feminine forms of Stephen. *See* Stephen (*masculine section*).

Stevana, Stevena Feminine forms of Steven. *See* Steven (*masculine section*).

Su, Sue Pet forms of Susan. *See* Susan.

Suellen A hybrid of Sue (Susan) and Ellen. *See* Susan *and* Ellen.

Sultana From the Arabic, meaning "ruler" or "victorious." HEBREW EQUIVALENTS: Malka, Nitzcha, Nitzchiya, Nitzchona. MASCULINE HEBREW EQUIVALENTS: Melech, Netzach, Nitzchan, Nitzchi.

Suri (שׂוּרִי) A variant form of Sara. *See* Sara.

Surilee (שׂוּרִילִי) A hybrid form of Suri and Lee. *See* Suri *and* Lee.

Susan (שׁוֹשָׁנָה/שׁוֹשָׁן) From the Hebrew, meaning "lily." HEBREW EQUIVA-LENTS: Shoshan, Shoshana. The masculine Hebrew equivalent is Shoshan.

Susanna, Susannah Variant forms of Susan. *See* Susan.

Susanne A variant form of Susan. *See* Susan.

Susette A pet form of Susan. *See* Susan.

Susi, Susie, Susy Pet forms of Susan. *See* Susan.

Suzanne A variant form of Susan. *See* Susan.

Suzette A French form of Susan. *See* Susan.

Suzy A pet form of Susan. *See* Susan.

Sybil, Sybille Variant spellings of Sibyl. *See* Sibyl.

Sybyl, Sybyle Variant spellings of Sibyl. *See* Sibyl.

Syd, Sydel, Sydelle Variant pet forms of Sydney. *See* Sydney.

Sydney A feminine form of the masculine Sidney. *See* Sidney (*masculine section*).

Sylvia From the Latin, meaning "forest" or "one who dwells in the woods." HEBREW EQUIVALENTS: Gana, Karmela, Nava, Ya'ara, Ya'arit. MASCULINE HEBREW EQUIVALENTS: Karmel, Karmeli, Ya'ar, Ya'ari.

Sylvie A Norwegian form of Sylvia. *See* Sylvia.

Syma A variant spelling of Cyma, Seema, and Sima. *See* Cyma, Seema, *and* Sima.

Tabita, Tabitha From the Akkadian, meaning "goat." A variant form of Tevet, the tenth month in the Hebrew calendar. Its zodiac symbol is a goat. HEBREW EQUIVALENTS: Gadya, Ya'ala, Ya'alit, Ya'el. MASCULINE HEBREW EQUIVALENTS: Efer, Ofer, Ofra, Ofri, Terach.

Taffy The Welsh form of Vida, a variant form of David. *See* David (*masculine section*).

Taga (תַּגָּה) From the Aramaic and Arabic, meaning "crown." The exact Hebrew equivalent is Taga. MASCULINE HEBREW EQUIVALENTS: Katriel, Keter, Kitron, Melech.

Tal (טַל) From the Hebrew, meaning "dew." The exact feminine and masculine Hebrew equivalent is Tal.

Tali (טַלִי) From the Hebrew, meaning "my dew." The exact feminine and masculine Hebrew equivalent is Tali.

Talia A variant spelling of Talya. *See* Talya.

Talie A variant spelling of Tali. *See* Tali.

Talma (תַּלְמָה) From the Hebrew, meaning "mound, hill." The exact Hebrew equivalent is Talma. MASCULINE HEBREW EQUIVALENTS: Geva, Harel, Talmai, Telem.

Talmit (תַּלְמִית) A variant form of Talma. *See* Talma. The exact Hebrew equivalent is Talmit.

Talmor (תַּלְמוֹר) From the Hebrew, meaning "heaped" or "sprinkled with myrrh, perfumed." The exact Hebrew equivalent is Talmor. MASCULINE HEBREW EQUIVALENTS: Mivsam, Mor, Raychan, Yivsam.

Talor, Tal-Or (טַל־אוֹר/טַלְאוֹר) From the Hebrew, meaning "morning dew." The exact feminine and masculine Hebrew equivalent is Tal-Or.

Talora, Tal-Ora (טַל־אוֹרָה/טַלְאוֹרָה) A variant form of Tal-Or. *See* Tal-Or. The exact Hebrew equivalent is Tal-Ora.

Talya (טַלְיָה) From the Hebrew, meaning "dew." The exact feminine and masculine Hebrew equivalent is Talya.

Tama, Tamah (תַּמָּה) From the Hebrew, meaning "wonder, surprise" or "whole, complete." The exact Hebrew equivalent is Tama. The exact masculine Hebrew equivalent is Tam.

Tamar (תָּמָר) From the Hebrew, meaning "palm tree" or "upright, righteous, graceful." The exact feminine and masculine Hebrew equivalent is Tamar.

Tamara, Tamarah (תָּמָרָה) From the East Indian, meaning "spice." HEBREW EQUIVALENTS: Bosemet, Ketziya, Levona, Nirdit, Tamar, Tamara. MASCULINE HEBREW EQUIVALENTS: Mivsam, Mor, Nardimon. Also, a variant form of Tamar. *See* Tamar.

Tami, Tammy Feminine forms of Thomas. *See* Thomas (*masculine section*).

Tania A variant spelling of Tanya. *See* Tanya.

Tanya From the Russian, meaning "fairy queen." HEBREW EQUIVALENTS: Malka, Malkiela, Malkit. MASCULINE HEBREW EQUIVALENTS: Avimelech, Melech.

Tara (טָרָה) From the French and Aramaic, referring to a unit of measurement. Also, from the Aramaic, meaning "throw" or "carry." The Hebrew equivalent is Tara. MASCULINE HEBREW EQUIVALENTS: Aryoch, Nasi, Yora.

Tari (טָרִי) From the Hebrew, meaning "fresh, ripe, new." The exact feminine and masculine Hebrew equivalent is Tari.

Taryn A variant form of Tara. *See* Tara.

Tate From the Anglo-Saxon, meaning "to be cheerful." HEBREW EQUIVALENTS: Aliza, Ditza, Gila, Rina, Rona, Roniya, Tzahala. MASCULINE HEBREW EQUIVALENTS: Simcha, Simchoni, Tzahal, Yachdiel, Yitzchak.

Tauba, Taube Yiddish forms of the German, meaning "dove." HEBREW EQUIVALENTS: Avi-Yona, Yemima, Yona, Yonina, Yonita. MASCULINE HEBREW EQUIVALENTS: Tor, Yona.

Tavi A variant form of the masculine name David. *See* David (*masculine section*).

Tavita A pet form of Tavi. *See* Tavi.

Taylor Used most often as a masculine name. *See* Taylor (*masculine section*).

Techiya (תְּחִיָה) From the Hebrew, meaning "life, revival." The exact Hebrew equivalent is Techiya. MASCULINE HEBREW EQUIVALENTS: Chai, Cha'yim, Yechiel.

Tehila, Tehilla (תְּהִילָה) From the Hebrew, meaning "praise, song of praise." The exact Hebrew equivalent is Tehila (T'hila). MASCULINE HEBREW EQUIVALENTS: Hila, Hillel, Mehulal, Shevach, Yehuda.

Tehiya A variant spelling of Techiya. See Techiya.

Tehora (טְהוֹרָה) From the Hebrew, meaning "pure, clean." The exact Hebrew equivalent is Tehora. MASCULINE HEBREW EQUIVALENTS: Zach, Zakai.

Teli (טְלִי) From the Aramaic and Hebrew, meaning "lamb." The exact Hebrew equivalent is Teli (T'li). The masculine Hebrew equivalent is Talya.

Tema (טֶעמָא) A Yiddish form of Tamar. See Tamar.

Temara (תְּמָרָה) A variant form of Tamar. See Tamar. The exact Hebrew equivalent is Temara.

Temima (תְּמִימָה) From the Hebrew, meaning "whole, honest." The exact Hebrew equivalent is Temima. The exact masculine Hebrew equivalent is Tam.

Temira (תְּמִירָה) From the Hebrew, meaning "tall, stately." The exact Hebrew equivalent is Temira. The exact masculine Hebrew equivalent is Tamir.

Temma A variant spelling of Tema. See Tema.

Teresa The Spanish and Italian form of Theresa. See Theresa.

Teri A pet form of Theresa. See Theresa.

Teriya (טְרִיָה) A variant form of Tari. See Tari. The exact Hebrew equivalent is Teriya.

Terry A pet form of Theresa. See Theresa.

Teruma, Terumah (תְּרוּמָה) From the Hebrew, meaning "offering, gift." The exact feminine and masculine Hebrew equivalent is Teruma.

Teshura, Teshurah (תְּשׁוּרָה) From the Hebrew, meaning "gift." The exact feminine and masculine Hebrew equivalent is Teshura.

Tetty A pet form of Elizabeth. See Elizabeth.

Tevita A Fijian form of Davida. See Davida.

Thalia From the Greek, meaning "luxurious, flourishing." HEBREW EQUIVALENTS: Ashera, Pircha, Pirchit, Tara, Teriya. MASCULINE HEBREW EQUIVALENTS: Efra'yim, Nitzan, Perach, Pura, Tara.

Thea A short form of Althea. See Althea.

Thelma From the Greek, meaning "nursing, infant," connoting youthfulness. HEBREW EQUIVALENTS: Alma, Aviva, Shetila, Tze'ira, Yenika, Zilpa. MASCULINE HEBREW EQUIVALENTS: Aviv, Bichri, Elam, Katan.

Theodora The feminine form of Theodore. See Theodore.

Theora A short form of Theodora. See Theodora.

Theresa, Therese From the Greek, meaning "harvester, farmer." HE-

BREW EQUIVALENTS: Gana, Karmela, Nava, Yardena, Yizr'ela. MASCULINE HEBREW EQUIVALENTS: Adam, Karmel, Karmeli, Yizr'el.

Tifara (תִּפְאָרָה) From the Hebrew, meaning "beauty" or "glory." The exact Hebrew equivalent is Tifara. MASCULINE HEBREW EQUIVALENTS: Hadar, Hod, Hodiya, Ne'edar.

Tiferet (תִּפְאֶרֶת) A variant form of Tifara. See Tifara. The exact Hebrew equivalent is Tiferet.

Tiffany From the Latin, meaning "three, the trinity." Also, from the Greek, meaning "manifestation of God." The exact Hebrew equivalent is Shelosha. The masculine Hebrew-Aramaic equivalent is Telat.

Tikva (תִּקְוָה) From the Hebrew, meaning "hope." The exact feminine and masculine Hebrew equivalent is Tikva.

Tilda A pet form of Mathilda. See Mathilda.

Tilla A variant form of Tillie. See Tillie.

Tillamae A hybrid of Tilla and Mae. See Tilla and Mae.

Tillie, Tilly Pet forms of Mathilda. See Mathilda. Also, from the Latin, meaning "graceful linden tree." HEBREW EQUIVALENTS: Hadasa, Ilana, Tirza. MASCULINE HEBREW EQUIVALENTS: Ela, Miklot, Oren.

Timi A pet form of Timora. See Timora.

Timora (תִּימוֹרָה) From the Hebrew, meaning "tall," like the palm tree. The exact Hebrew equivalent is Timora. MASCULINE HEBREW EQUIVALENTS: Itamar, Tamir.

Timura (תִּימוּרָה) A variant form of Timora. See Timora. The exact Hebrew equivalent is Timura.

Tina A pet form of names such as Christina and Bettina. See Christina and Bettina.

Tira (טִירָה) From the Syriac, meaning "sheepfold," or from the Hebrew, meaning "enclosure, encampment." The exact Hebrew equivalent is Tira. MASCULINE HEBREW EQUIVALENTS: Akiva, Chosa, Lot, Tachan, Ya'akov.

Tiri (טִירִי) A variant form of Tira. See Tira. The exact Hebrew equivalent is Tiri.

Tirtza, Tirtzah (תִּרְצָה) From the Hebrew, meaning "agreeable, willing." The exact Hebrew equivalent is Tirtza. MASCULINE HEBREW EQUIVALENTS: Yishva, Yishvi.

Tirza, Tirzah (תִּרְזָה) From the Hebrew, meaning "cypress tree." The exact Hebrew equivalent is Tirza. The masculine Hebrew equivalent is Bros.

Tisha A pet form of Patricia. See Patricia.

Tita A variant form of Titania. See Titania.

Titania From the Greek, meaning "great one." HEBREW EQUIVALENTS: Atalya, Gedola, Gedula, Rachav. MASCULINE HEBREW EQUIVALENTS: Gadol, Gedalya, Gidel, Raba, Rav, Rechavya.

Tiva (טִיבָה) From the Hebrew, meaning "good." The exact Hebrew equivalent is Tiva. MASCULINE HEBREW EQUIVALENTS: Tov, Toviya, Tuviya.

Tivona (טִבְעוֹנָה) From the Hebrew, meaning "lover of nature." The exact Hebrew equivalent is Tivona. The exact masculine Hebrew equivalent is Tivon.

Tivoni (טִבְעוֹנִי) A variant form of Tivona. See Tivona. The exact Hebrew equivalent is Tivoni.

Toba A variant spelling of Tova. See Tova. Akin to the masculine Tobias.

Tobelle A pet form of Toba. See Toba.

Tobey A variant form of Toba. See Toba.

Tobi A variant spelling of Toby. See Toby.

Tobit A variant spelling of Tovit. See Tovit.

Toby A pet form of Toba. See Toba.

Toda, Todah (תּוֹדָה) From the Hebrew, meaning "thanks, thank you." The exact feminine and masculine Hebrew equivalent is Toda.

Toiba, Toibe (טוֹיבָּא/טוֹיבֶּע) From the Yiddish, meaning "dove." The exact feminine and masculine Hebrew equivalent is Yona.

Toni A pet form of Antoinette. See Antoinette.

Tonia A variant form of Toni. See Toni.

Tonise A variant form of Toni. See Toni.

Tony A variant spelling of Toni. See Toni.

Topaza From the Greek, referring to a yellow variety of sapphire. The exact Hebrew equivalent is Sapira. The exact masculine Hebrew equivalent is Sapir.

Tora, Torah (תּוֹרָה) From the Hebrew, meaning "teaching" or "law." The exact Hebrew equivalent is Tora. MASCULINE HEBREW EQUIVALENTS: Datan, Datiel, Moran.

Tori (תּוֹרִי) From the Hebrew, meaning "my turtledove." The exact Hebrew equivalent is Tori. The exact masculine Hebrew equivalent is Yona. Also, a variant form of Tora. See Tora.

Tory A pet form of Victoria. See Victoria.

Totie A variant form of Dottie, a pet form of Dorothy. See Dorothy.

Tova, Tovah (טוֹבָה) From the Hebrew, meaning "good." The exact Hebrew equivalent is Tova. The exact masculine Hebrew equivalent is Tov.

Tovat (טוֹבַת) A variant form of Tova. See Tova. The exact Hebrew equivalent is Tovat.

Tovit (טוֹבִית) From the Hebrew, meaning "good." The exact Hebrew equivalent is Tovit. MASCULINE HEBREW EQUIVALENTS: Tov, Tovi, Tuviya.

Tracey, Traci Variant spellings of Tracy. See Tracy.

Tracy From the Anglo-Saxon, meaning "brave." Also, a pet form of Theresa. See Theresa. HEBREW EQUIVALENTS: Abira, Abiri, Gavriela, Gavrila, Gibora, Uziela, Uzit. MASCULINE HEBREW EQUIVALENTS: Gavriel, Gever, Gevaryahu, Gibor, Kalev.

Trella A short form of Estella, the Spanish form of Esther. See Esther.

Tricia A pet form of Patricia. *See* Patricia.

Trina A short form of Katrina. *See* Katrina.

Trish, Trisha Pet forms of Patricia. *See* Patricia.

Trix, Trixie, Trixy Pet forms of Beatrice and Beatrix. *See* Beatrice *and* Beatrix.

Truda, Trude Pet forms of Gertrude. *See* Gertrude.

Tumi (תְּמִי) From the Hebrew, meaning "whole, complete." The exact Hebrew equivalent is Tumi. The exact masculine Hebrew equivalent is Tam.

Tuvit (טוּבִית) A variant form of Tova. *See* Tova. The exact Hebrew equivalent is Tuvit.

Tyna, Tyne From the British, meaning "river." HEBREW EQUIVALENTS: Arnona, Bat-Yam, Dalya, Miryam. MASCULINE HEBREW EQUIVALENTS: Arnon, Ye'or, Ye'ori.

Tzabara (צַבָּרָה) From the Arabic, meaning "cactus." The exact Hebrew equivalent is Tzabar.

Tzabaria A variant spelling of Tzabariya. *See* Tzabariya.

Tzabariya (צַבָּרִיָה) A variant form of Tzabara. *See* Tzabara. The exact Hebrew equivalent is Tzabariya.

Tzeviya (צְבִיָה) A variant form of Tzivya. *See* Tzivya. The exact Hebrew equivalent is Tzeviya.

Tziona A variant spelling of Tziyona. *See* Tziyona.

Tzipi (צִפִּי) A pet form of Tzipora. *See* Tzipora. The exact Hebrew equivalent is Tzipi.

Tzipiya (צִפִּיָה) From the Hebrew, meaning "hope." The exact Hebrew equivalent is Tzipiya. The masculine Hebrew equivalent is Tikva.

Tzipora, Tziporah (צִפּוֹרָה) From the Hebrew, meaning "bird." The exact Hebrew equivalent is Tzipora. The exact masculine Hebrew equivalent is Tzipor.

Tzipori (צִפּוֹרִי) From the Hebrew, meaning "my bird." The exact Hebrew equivalent is Tzipori. The exact masculine Hebrew equivalent is Tzipor.

Tziporit (צִפּוֹרִית) A variant form of Tzipora. *See* Tzipora. The exact Hebrew equivalent is Tziporit. The masculine Hebrew equivalent is Tzipor.

Tziril A Yiddish form of Sara. *See* Sara.

Tzivya (צִבְיָה) From the Hebrew, meaning "deer, gazelle." The exact Hebrew equivalent is Tzivya. The exact masculine Hebrew equivalent is Tzevi (Tz'vi).

Tziyona (צִיּוֹנָה) From the Hebrew, meaning "excellent." The exact Hebrew equivalent is Tziyona. The exact masculine Hebrew equivalent is Tziyon.

Tziyonit (צִיּוֹנִית) A variant form of Tziyona. *See* Tziyona. The exact Hebrew equivalent is Tziyonit.

Tzofiya (צוֹפִיָה) From the Hebrew, meaning "watcher, guardian, scout." The exact Hebrew equivalent is Tzofiya. The exact masculine Hebrew equivalent is Tzofi.

Tzivya (צִבְיָה) A variant spelling of Tzeviya. See Tzeviya.

Unita From the Latin, meaning "one, united." The feminine and masculine Hebrew equivalent is Achava (Achva).

Uranit (אוּרָנִית) From the Hebrew, meaning "light." The exact Hebrew equivalent is Uranit. The exact masculine Hebrew equivalent is Ur.

Uriela, Uriella (אוּרִיאָלָה) From the Hebrew, meaning "light [flame] of the Lord." The exact Hebrew equivalent is Uriela. The exact masculine Hebrew equivalent is Uriel.

Urit (אוּרִית) From the Hebrew, meaning "light" or "fire." The exact Hebrew equivalent is Urit. The exact masculine Hebrew equivalent is Ur.

Ursala From the Latin, meaning "a she-bear." The exact Hebrew equivalent is Duba. MASCULINE HEBREW EQUIVALENTS: Dov, Dubi.

Uza, Uzza (עֻזָה) From the Hebrew, meaning "strength." The exact feminine and masculine Hebrew equivalent is Uza.

Uziela, Uziella (עֻזִיאָלָה) From the Hebrew, meaning "My strength is the Lord." The exact Hebrew equivalent is Uzi'ela. The exact masculine Hebrew equivalent is Uzi'el.

Uzit (עֻזִית) From the Hebrew, meaning "strength." The exact Hebrew equivalent is Uzit. The exact masculine Hebrew equivalent is Uzi.

Val A pet form of Valerie. See Valerie.

Valeria, Valerie Variant forms of the Latin, meaning "to be strong." HEBREW EQUIVALENTS: Amtza, Ariel, Gavriela, Gavrila, Gibora. MASCULINE HEBREW EQUIVALENTS: Ari, Avicha'yil, Barzilai, Gavriel, Gever, Gover.

Vana, Vanna Pet forms of Vanessa. See Vanessa.

Vanessa From the Middle English, meaning "to fan, to agitate with a fan," an old method of winnowing grain. HEBREW EQUIVALENTS: Chita, Deganya, Garnit. MASCULINE HEBREW EQUIVALENTS: Dagan, Goren, Kimchi.

Varda (וַרְדָה) From the Hebrew, meaning "rose." The exact Hebrew equivalent is Varda. The exact masculine Hebrew equivalent is Vered.

Vardia A variant spelling of Vardiya. See Vardiya.

Vardina (וַרְדִינָה) A variant form of Varda. See Varda. The exact Hebrew equivalent is Vardina.

Vardit (וַרְדִית) A variant form of Varda. See Varda. The exact Hebrew equivalent is Vardit.

Vardiya (וַרְדִיָה) A variant form of Varda. See Varda. The exact Hebrew equivalent is Vardiya.

Veda From the Sanskrit, meaning "sacred understanding." HEBREW EQUIVALENTS: Bina, Buna, Tushiya. MASCULINE HEBREW EQUIVALENTS: Achban, Chanoch, Haskel, Yavin, Yosha.

Valentina The feminine form of Valentine. *See* Valentine (*masculine section*).

Velma A pet form of Wilhelmina. *See* Wilhelmina.

Ventura From the Spanish, meaning "good fortune." HEBREW EQUIVALENTS: Ashera, Asherit, Gadiela, Gadit, Mazal, Mazala, Mazalit. MASCULINE HEBREW EQUIVALENTS: Asher, Ashri, Gad, Maimon, Mazal, Mazal-Tov.

Venus From the Latin, meaning "to love." In Greek mythology, the goddess of love and beauty. HEBREW EQUIVALENTS: Ahada, Ahava, Ahuva, Chaviva, Chiba, Davida. MASCULINE HEBREW EQUIVALENTS: Ahud, Ahuv, Bildad, Ehud, Yedida.

Vera From the Latin, meaning "truth." Also, from the Russian, meaning "faith." HEBREW EQUIVALENTS: Amita, Amnona, Emet. MASCULINE HEBREW EQUIVALENTS: Amit, Amitai, Amnon.

Vered (וֶרֶד) From the Hebrew, meaning "rose." The exact feminine and masculine Hebrew equivalent is Vered.

Verena, Verina From the Latin, meaning "one who venerates God" or "sacred wisdom." HEBREW EQUIVALENTS: Bina, Buna, Devora, Tehila, Tushiya, Yehudit. MASCULINE HEBREW EQUIVALENTS: Achban, Gedalya, Haskel, Hodiya, Yehuda.

Verita From the Latin, meaning "truth." HEBREW EQUIVALENTS: Amita, Amnona, Emet. MASCULINE HEBREW EQUIVALENTS: Amit, Amitai, Amnon, Emet.

Verity A variant form of Verita. *See* Verita.

Verna, Verne From the Latin, meaning "springlike" or "to grow green." The exact Hebrew equivalent is Yarkona. The exact masculine Hebrew equivalent is Yarkon.

Veronica A variant form of Berenice, meaning "bringer of victory," or from the Latin, meaning "truthful, faithful." HEBREW EQUIVALENTS: Amnona, Bitcha, Emet, Emuna, Tikva. MASCULINE HEBREW EQUIVALENTS: Amnon, Gover, Matzliach, Netziach, Yatzliach.

Vesta, Vestal In Roman mythology, the goddess of fire and purification. HEBREW EQUIVALENTS: Avuka, Shalhevet, Uriel, Zaka, Zakit. MASCULINE HEBREW EQUIVALENTS: Lahav, Lapid, Shedayur, Uri, Uriel, Zakai.

Vi A pet form of Violet and Victoria. *See* Violet *and* Victoria.

Vici, Vicki, Vicky Variant pet forms of Victoria. *See* Victoria.

Victoria From the Latin, meaning "victorious." HEBREW EQUIVALENTS: Dafna, Hadasa, Nitzcha, Nitzchit. MASCULINE HEBREW EQUIVALENTS: Gover, Matzliach, Netziach, Yatzliach.

Victorina, Victorine Pet forms of Victoria. *See* Victoria.

Vida A pet form of Davida. *See* Davida.

Vikki, Vikkie, Vikky Pet forms of Victoria. *See* Victoria.

Viola A Middle English flower-name, from the Latin, meaning "violet."

HEBREW EQUIVALENTS: Nitza, Shoshana, Varda. MASCULINE HEBREW EQUIVA-
LENTS: Efra'yim, Pekach, Perachya, Pura.

Violet A variant form of Viola. *See* Viola.

Virginia From the Latin, meaning "virgin, pure" or "maiden." HEBREW
EQUIVALENTS: Berura, Betula, Dikla, Rachel, Tamar, Zaka. MASCULINE HE-
BREW EQUIVALENTS: Amitai, Amnon, Itamar, Yesher, Yeshurun, Zakai.

Vita From the Latin, meaning "life, animated." HEBREW EQUIVALENTS:
Chava, Cha'ya, Techiya. MASCULINE HEBREW EQUIVALENTS: Amichai,
Cha'yim, Chiya, Yechiel.

Vittoria The feminine form of Victor. *See* Victor (*masculine section*).

Viveca An Italian pet form of the Latin Vivus. *See* Vivi.

Vivi From the Latin, meaning "alive." HEBREW EQUIVALENTS: Chava,
Cha'ya, Techiya. MASCULINE HEBREW EQUIVALENTS: Amichai, Cha'yim,
Chiya, Yechiel.

Vivian, Viviana, Vivianna Variant forms of Vivi. *See* Vivi.

Vivien, Vivienne French forms of Vivian. *See* Vivian.

Vyvyan A variant spelling of Vivian. *See* Vivian.

Walda From the Old High German, meaning "to rule." HEBREW EQUIVA-
LENTS: Atara, Malka, Sara. MASCULINE HEBREW EQUIVALENTS: Elrad, Malkiel, Melech, Yisrael.

Wanda From the Old Norse, meaning "young tree," or from the Anglo-
Saxon, meaning "wanderer." HEBREW EQUIVALENTS: Avishag, Hagar. MAS-
CULINE HEBREW EQUIVALENTS: Gershom, Gershon, Golyat, Yagli.

Wende, Wendey, Wendi, Wendy Pet forms of Genevieve, Gwendaline,
and Winnifred. *See* Genevieve, Gwendaline, *and* Winnifred.

Wilhelmina The English and Dutch form of Wilhelm (the German form
of William), meaning "warrior" or "ruler." *See* William (*masculine section*).

Willa A pet form of Wilhelmina. *See* Wilhelmina.

Willene A pet form of Wilhelmina. *See* Wilhelmina.

Wilma A pet form of Wilhelmina. *See* Wilhelmina.

Winifred From the Anglo-Saxon, meaning "friend of peace." HEBREW
EQUIVALENTS: Menucha, Meshulemet, Shelomit, Shulamit. MASCULINE
HEBREW EQUIVALENTS: Achishalom, Amishalom. Avshalom, Shalom,
Shalum.

Wynette A variant form of Wynna. *See* Wynna.

Winnie A pet form of Winifred. *See* Winifred.

Wynna, Wynne Pet forms of Gwendaline. *See* Gwendaline. Also, pet
forms of Winifred. *See* Winifred.

Xena From the Greek, meaning "great" or "stranger." HEBREW EQUIVA-
LENTS: Atalya, Avishag, Gedola, Gedula. MASCULINE HEBREW EQUIVALENTS:
Gadol, Gedalya, Gidel, Rav, Rava.

Yaakova (יַעְקְבָה) From the Hebrew, meaning "to supplant." Akin to Yaakov. Used as a feminine and masculine form. The exact Hebrew equivalent is Ya'akova.

Yaala (יַעְלָה) A variant form of Yael. *See* Yael. The exact feminine and masculine Hebrew equivalent is Ya'ala.

Yaalat (יַעְלָת) A variant form of Yael. *See* Yael. The exact Hebrew equivalent is Ya'alat.

Yaalit (יַעְלִית) A variant form of Yael. *See* Yael. The exact Hebrew equivalent is Ya'alit.

Yaanit (יַעֲנִית) A variant form of Yaen. *See* Yaen. The exact Hebrew equivalent is Ya'anit.

Yaara (יַעֲרָה) From the Hebrew, meaning "forest." The exact Hebrew equivalent is Ya'ara. The exact masculine Hebrew equivalent is Ya'ar.

Yaarit (יַעֲרִית) From the Hebrew, meaning "pertaining to the forest." The exact Hebrew equivalent is Ya'arit. The exact masculine Hebrew equivalent is Ya'ar.

Yael (יָעֵל) From the Hebrew, meaning "to ascend" or "mountain goat." The exact feminine and masculine Hebrew equivalent is Ya'el.

Yaela, Yaella (יָעֵלָה) Variant forms of Yael. *See* Yael. The exact Hebrew equivalent is Ya'ela.

Yaen (יָעֵן) From the Hebrew, meaning "ostrich." The exact Hebrew equivalent is Ya'en. MASCULINE HEBREW EQUIVALENTS: Gozal, Tzipor.

Yafa, Yaffa (יָפָה) From the Assyrian and the Hebrew, meaning "beautiful." The exact Hebrew equivalent is Yafa. The exact masculine Hebrew equivalent is Yafeh.

Yafit (יָפִית) A variant form of Yafa. *See* Yafa. The exact Hebrew equivalent is Yafit.

Yaira (יָאִירָה) From the Hebrew, meaning "to enlighten." The exact Hebrew equivalent is Ya'ira. The exact masculine Hebrew equivalent is Ya'ir.

Yakira (יַקִירָה) From the Hebrew, meaning "valuable, precious." The exact Hebrew equivalent is Yakira. The exact masculine Hebrew equivalent is Yakir.

Yama (יָמָה) From the Hebrew, meaning "toward the sea" or "westward." The exact Hebrew equivalent is Yama. MASCULINE HEBREW EQUIVALENTS: Avigal, Avi'yam, Ma'arav.

Yamit (יָמִית) From the Hebrew, meaning "pertaining to the sea." The exact Hebrew equivalent is Yamit. MASCULINE HEBREW EQUIVALENTS: Avigal, Avi'yam.

Yara A variant spelling of Yaara. *See* Yaara.

Yardena (יַרְדְּנָה) The feminine form of Yarden (Jordan). *See* Yarden (*masculine section*).

Yardenia A variant spelling of Yardeniya. *See* Yardeniya.

Yardeniya (יַרְדְּנִיָה) From the Hebrew, meaning "garden of the Lord."

The exact Hebrew equivalent is Yardeniya. The exact masculine Hebrew equivalent is Yarden.

Yarkona (יַרְקוֹנָה)   The feminine form of Yarkon, meaning "green." The exact Hebrew equivalent is Yarkona. The exact masculine Hebrew equivalent is Yarkon.

Yarona (יָרוֹנָה)   From the Hebrew, meaning "sing." The exact Hebrew equivalent is Yarona. The exact masculine Hebrew equivalent is Yaron.

Yatva (יָטְבָה)   From the Hebrew, meaning "good." The exact Hebrew equivalent is Yatva. MASCULINE HEBREW EQUIVALENTS: Tov, Tovi.

Yechiela (יְחִיאָלָה)   From the Hebrew, meaning "May God live." The exact Hebrew equivalent is Yechiela. The exact masculine Hebrew equivalent is Yechiel.

Yedida, Yedidah (יְדִידָה)   From the Hebrew, meaning "friend" or "beloved." The exact Hebrew equivalent is Yedida. The exact masculine Hebrew equivalent is Yedidya.

Yedidia, Yedidiah   Variant spellings of Yedidya. *See* Yedidya.

Yedidela (יְדִידְאָלָה)   From the Hebrew, meaning "friend of God" or "beloved of God." The exact Hebrew equivalent is Yedidela. The exact masculine Hebrew equivalent is Yedidya.

Yehiela   A variant spelling of Yechiela. *See* Yechiela.

✗ **Yehudit** (יְהוּדִית)   From the Hebrew, meaning "praise." The exact Hebrew equivalent is Yehudit (Judith). The exact masculine Hebrew equivalent is Yehuda (Judah).

Yeira, Yeirah (יְאִירָה)   From the Hebrew, meaning "light." The exact Hebrew equivalent is Ye'ira. The exact masculine Hebrew equivalent is Ya'ir.

Yekara, Yekarah (יְקָרָה)   Variant forms of Yakira. *See* Yakira. The exact Hebrew equivalent is Yekara.

Yemima (יְמִימָה)   Possibly from the Arabic, meaning "dove." The exact Hebrew equivalent is Yemima. The exact masculine Hebrew equivalent is Yona.

Yemina (יְמִינָה)   From the Hebrew, meaning "right hand," signifying strength. The exact Hebrew equivalent is Yemina. The exact masculine Hebrew equivalent is Yamin.

Yeshisha (יְשִׁישָׁה)   From the Hebrew, meaning "old." The exact Hebrew equivalent is Yeshisha. The exact masculine Hebrew equivalent is Yashish.

Yetta   A pet form of Henrietta. *See* Henrietta.

Yifat (יִפְעָת)   From the Ugaritic and Akkadian, meaning "beauty." The exact Hebrew equivalent is Yifat. The exact feminine Hebrew equivalent is Yafeh.

Yigala (יִגְאָלָה)   From the Hebrew, meaning "to redeem." The exact Hebrew equivalent is Yigala. The exact masculine Hebrew equivalent is Yigal.

Yimna (יִמְנָה) From the Hebrew and Arabic, meaning "right side," signifying good fortune. The exact feminine and masculine Hebrew equivalent is Yimna.

Yisraela (יִשְׂרָאֵלָה) The feminine form of Yisrael. *See* Yisrael (*masculine section*).

Yisr'ela (יִשְׂרְאֵלָה) A variant form of Yisraela. *See* Yisraela. The exact Hebrew equivalent is Yisr'ela. The exact masculine Hebrew equivalent is Yisrael.

Yitra (יִתְרָה) From the Hebrew, meaning "wealth, riches." The exact Hebrew equivalent is Yitra. The exact masculine Hebrew equivalent is Yitro.

Yitta (יִיטָא) A Yiddish form of Yetta. *See* Yetta.

Yitti (יִיטִי) A Yiddish form of Yetta. *See* Yetta.

Yoanna (יוֹעֲנָה) From the Hebrew, meaning "God has answered." The exact Hebrew equivalent is Yo'ana. MASCULINE HEBREW EQUIVALENTS: Yehoshua, Yesha'ya, Yo'ezer.

Yochana (יוֹחָנָה) From the Hebrew, meaning "God is gracious." The exact Hebrew equivalent is Yochana. The exact masculine Hebrew equivalent is Yochanan.

Yochebed A variant spelling of Yocheved. *See* Yocheved.

Yocheved (יוֹכֶבֶד) From the Hebrew, meaning "God's glory." The exact Hebrew equivalent is Yocheved. MASCULINE HEBREW EQUIVALENTS: Hod, Hodiya, Nehedar, Pe'er.

Yoela (יוֹאֵלָה) From the Hebrew, meaning "God is willing." The exact Hebrew equivalent is Yo'ela. The exact masculine Hebrew equivalent is Yo'el.

Yoelit (יוֹאֵלִית) A variant form of Yoela. *See* Yoela. The exact Hebrew equivalent is Yo'elit.

Yolanda, Yolande Possibly a form of the Old French name Violante, a derivative of Viola. *See* Viola. Also, from the Latin, meaning "modest, shy." HEBREW EQUIVALENTS: Anava, Anuva. MASCULINE HEBREW EQUIVALENTS: Anav, Anuv.

Yona, Yonah (יוֹנָה) From the Hebrew, meaning "dove." The exact feminine and masculine Hebrew equivalent is Yona.

Yonat (יוֹנַת) A variant form of Yona. *See* Yona. The exact Hebrew equivalent is Yonat.

Yonata (יוֹנָתָה) A variant form of Yona. *See* Yona. The exact Hebrew equivalent is Yonata.

Yonati (יוֹנָתִי) From the Hebrew, meaning "my dove." The exact Hebrew equivalent is Yonati. The exact masculine Hebrew equivalent is Yona.

Yonina (יוֹנִינָה) A variant form of Yona. *See* Yona. The exact Hebrew equivalent is Yonina.

Yonit (יוֹנִית) A variant form of Yona. *See* Yona. The exact Hebrew equivalent is Yonit.

Yonita (יוֹנִיתָה) A variant form of Yona. *See* Yona. The **exact Hebrew** equivalent is Yonita.

Yosefa, Yosepha (יוֹסָפָה) A variant form of Yosifa. *See* Yosifa. The exact Hebrew equivalent is Yosefa.

Yosifa (יוֹסִיפָה) A feminine form of Yosef (Joseph). *See* Yosef *and* **Joseph** (*masculine section*). The exact Hebrew equivalent is Yosifa.

Yudi (יוּדִי) A pet form of Yehudit. *See* Yehudit. The **exact Hebrew equiva**lent is Yudi.

Yudit (יוּדִית) A short form of Yehudit. *See* Yehudit. The **exact Hebrew** equivalent is Yudit.

Yvette A feminine form of Yves. *See* Yves (*masculine section*). Also, **a** Welsh form of Evan. *See* Evan (*masculine section*).

Yvonne A French form of Yves. *See* Yves (*masculine section*).

Zahara (זָהֲרָה) From the Hebrew, meaning "to shine." The **exact Hebrew** equivalent is Zahara. The exact masculine Hebrew equivalent is Zohar.

Zahari (זָהֲרִי) A variant form of Zahara. *See* Zahara. The **exact Hebrew** equivalent is Zahari.

Zaharit (זָהֲרִית) A variant form of Zahara. *See* Zahara. The exact **He**brew equivalent is Zaharit.

Zahava (זָהָבָה) A variant spelling of Zehava. *See* Zehava. The exact **He**brew equivalent is Zahava.

Zahavi (זָהֲבִי) A variant form of Zahava. *See* Zahava. The **exact Hebrew** equivalent is Zahavi.

Zaka, Zakah (זַכָּה) From the Hebrew, meaning "bright, pure, clear." The exact Hebrew equivalent is Zaka. The exact masculine Hebrew equivalent is Zakai.

Zakit (זַכִּית) A variant form of Zaka. *See* Zaka. The exact Hebrew equivalent is Zakit.

Zandra A variant form of Sandra. *See* Sandra.

Zara, Zarah (זָרָה) Variant forms of Sarah. *See* Sarah.

Zariza, Zarizah (זָרִיזָה) Variant forms of Zeriza. *See* Zeriza. The exact Hebrew equivalent is Zariza.

Zayit (זַיִת) From the Hebrew, meaning "olive." The exact feminine **and** masculine Hebrew equivalent is Za'yit.

Ze'eva (זְאֵבָה) From the Hebrew, meaning "wolf." The exact Hebrew equivalent is Ze'eva (Ze'ayva). The exact masculine Hebrew equivalent is Ze'ev (Ze'ayv).

Zehara (זְהָרָה) From the Hebrew, meaning "light, brightness." The exact Hebrew equivalent is Zehara. The exact masculine Hebrew equivalent is Zohar.

Zehari (זְהָרִי) A variant form of Zohar. *See* Zohar. The exact Hebrew equivalent is Zehari.

Zehava (זְהָבָה) From the Hebrew, meaning "gold, golden." The exact Hebrew equivalent is Zehava. The exact masculine Hebrew equivalent is Zehavi.

Zehavi (זְהָבִי) A variant form of Zehava. See Zehava. The exact feminine and masculine Hebrew equivalent is Zehavi.

Zehavit (זְהָבִית) A variant form of Zehava. See Zehava. The exact Hebrew equivalent is Zehavit.

Zehira (זְהִירָה) From the Hebrew, meaning "guarded, careful, cautious." The exact Hebrew equivalent is Zehira. The exact masculine Hebrew equivalent is Zahir.

Zehorit (זְהוֹרִית) A variant form of Zehara. See Zehara. The exact Hebrew equivalent is Zehorit.

Zehuva (זְהוּבָה) From the Hebrew, meaning "gilded." The exact Hebrew equivalent is Zehuva. The exact masculine Hebrew equivalent is Zehavi.

Zehuvit (זְהוּבִית) A variant form of Zehava. See Zehava. The exact Hebrew equivalent is Zehuvit.

Zeira (זְעִירָה) From the Aramaic, meaning "small." The exact Hebrew equivalent is Ze'ira. The exact masculine Hebrew equivalent is Ze'ayra.

Zeita (זַיְתָה) An Aramaic variant form of Zayit. See Zayit. The exact Hebrew equivalent is Zayta.

Zeitana (זַיְתָנָה) A variant form of Zeita. See Zeita. The exact Hebrew equivalent is Zeitana (Zaytana).

Zelda A variant spelling of Selda. See Selda.

Zemira (זְמִירָה) From the Hebrew, meaning "song, melody." The exact feminine and masculine Hebrew equivalent is Zemira.

Zemora, Zemorah (זְמוֹרָה) From the Hebrew, meaning "branch, twig." The exact Hebrew equivalent is Zemora. The exact masculine Hebrew equivalent is Zamir.

Zena A variant spelling of Xena. See Xena.

Zeriza (זְרִיזָה) From the Hebrew, meaning "energetic, industrious." The exact Hebrew equivalent is Zeriza. The exact masculine Hebrew equivalent is Zariz.

Zeta A variant form of Zeita. See Zeita.

Zetana A variant spelling of Zeitana. See Zeitana.

Zetta A variant spelling of Zeta. See Zeta.

Zeva A variant spelling of Ze'eva. See Ze'eva.

Zevida (זְבִידָה) From the Hebrew, meaning "gift." The exact feminine and masculine Hebrew equivalent is Zevida.

Zevuda (זְבוּדָה) A variant form of Zevida. See Zevida. The exact Hebrew equivalent is Zevuda.

Zevula (זְבוּלָה) From the Hebrew, meaning "dwelling place" or "palace." The exact Hebrew equivalent is Zevula. The exact masculine Hebrew equivalent is Zevul.

Zila, Zilla (צִילָה) From the Hebrew, meaning "shadow." The exact Hebrew equivalent is Tzila. The exact masculine Hebrew equivalent is Tziltai.

Zimra (זִמְרָה) From the Hebrew, meaning "choice fruit" or "song of praise." The exact feminine and masculine Hebrew equivalent is Zimra.

Zimrat (זִמְרָת) A variant form of Zimra. *See* Zimra. The exact Hebrew equivalent is Zimrat.

Zimria, Zimriah Variant spellings of Zimriya. *See* Zimriya.

Zimriya (זִמְרִיָה) From the Hebrew, meaning "songfest" or "the Lord is my song." The exact Hebrew equivalent is Zimriya. The exact masculine Hebrew equivalent is Zemer.

Ziona (צִיוֹנָה) A variant spelling of Tziyona. *See* Tziyona. The exact Hebrew equivalent is Tziyona.

Zipora, Zippora (צְפוֹרָה) Variant spellings of Tzipora. *See* Tzipora.

Zipori (צְפוֹרִי) A variant spelling of Tzipori. *See* Tzipori.

Zira (זִירָה) From the Hebrew, meaning "arena." The exact Hebrew equivalent is Zira. MASCULINE HEBREW EQUIVALENTS: Mo'adya, No'ad, No'adya.

Zita A pet form of Theresa. *See* Theresa.

Ziva (זִיוָה) From the Hebrew, meaning "brightness, brilliance, splendor." The exact Hebrew equivalent is Ziva. The exact masculine Hebrew equivalent is Ziv.

Zivit (זִיוִית) A variant form of Ziva. *See* Ziva. The exact Hebrew equivalent is Zivit.

Zlata (זְלַאטָא) A Polish-Yiddish form of Golda. *See* Golda.

Zlate (זְלַאטֶע) A variant form of Zlata. *See* Zlata.

Zoe From the Greek, meaning "life." HEBREW EQUIVALENTS: Chava, Cha'ya, Yechiela. MASCULINE HEBREW EQUIVALENTS: Chai, Cha'yim, Yechiel.

Zofi A variant spelling of Tzofi. *See* Tzofi.

Zohar (זוֹהַר) From the Hebrew, meaning "light, brilliance." The exact feminine and masculine Hebrew equivalent is Zohar.

Zoheret (זוֹהֶרֶת) A variant form of Zohar. *See* Zohar. The exact Hebrew equivalent is Zoheret.

Zonya A variant spelling of Sonya. *See* Sonya.

Zophia A variant spelling of Sophia. *See* Sophia.

Zora (זָרָה) A variant form of Zara. *See* Zara.

Zvia (צְבִיָה) A variant spelling of Tzeviya. *See* Tzeviya.

Unisex Hebrew Names

Abira	Bahat	Eilat	Lavi
Abiri	Bava	Ela	Levana
Achava	Be'era	Elat	Le'umi
Achinoam	Bela	Emmet	Li
Achishalom	Beracha	Ezra	Lior
Adi	Betuel		Liron
Adiel	Bilga	Gabi	Livna
Adoniya	Bina	Gal	
Ahava	Buna	Gali	Maayan
Amal		Geula	Malach
Amanya	Carmel	Gedula	Malka
Ami	Chagiya	Gefen	Malkiel
Amior	Chana	Gili	Malkiya
Amit	Chanina	Gina	Matat
Amitza	Chashuva	Ginat	Mazal
Anat	Chavatzinya	Giora	Menucha
Anav	Chavila	Giva	Michal
Ari	Chaviva	Gomer	Mor
Ariel	Chen	Gover	Moran
Asna	Chuba		Moriel
Atalya	Chumi	Hadar	
Avi	Chupa	Hadas	Nedavya
Avicha'yil		Hila	Neora
Aviem	Devash	Hodiya	Nerli
Avigal	Devir		Neta
Avital	Dikla	Inbal	Netana
Aviya	Dodi	Itai	Nili
A'ya	Dor		Nirel
Ayla	Doron	Karni	Nitza
Aylat		Kedma	Noam
Azgad	Eder	Kerem	Noga
	Efa	Keren	
	Efrat	Kitron	Ofra

241

Omri
Orli

Paz
Penini
Perach

Rama
Raya
Raz
Razi
Rimon
Rina
Rotem
Ron
Roni
Ronli

Saba
Sabra

Sapir
Sarid
Savta
Sela
Sharon
Sheva
Shilo
Shir
Shlomit
Shoshan
Shuni
Sidra
Sima
Simcha
Sivan

Tal
Tali
Tal-Or

Talmi
Talya
Tamar
Tamir
Tari
Tavi
Teruma
Teshura
Tikva
Timna
Toda
Tomer
Tzivya
Tzipor
Tzofi

Uza

Vered

Yaakova
Yaala
Yael
Yaen
Yara
Yarden
Yedidya
Yimna
Yoela
Yona

Za'yit
Zehavi
Zemira
Zevida
Zimra
Zohar

Popular Yiddish Names

This Appendix should prove helpful to those seeking a Hebrew equivalent for a particular Yiddish name. Names marked
with an asterisk (*) are defined in the body of the work.

Masculine Names

Aberlin, Abrasha, Abrashen   Forms of Abraham.
Abrashke   A pet form of Abrasha.
Alter*
Anshel, Anshil, Anshl   Forms of Asher.
Arki   A pet form of Aharon (Aaron).
Avril   A form of Avraham (Abraham).
Avrom*
Avrum   A form of Avram (Abram).
Avrumel, Avrumke, Avrumtchick   Pet forms of Avrum.

Benesh*
Benish*
Ber*
Bonesh*
Berel*
Bremel   A pet form of Abraham.
Breml*
Bunim*

Chaika, Chaikeh   Forms of Chayim.
Chaikel, Chaiki   Pet forms of Chaika.
Chaskel   A pet form of Yechezkel (Ezekiel).
Chatzkel   A pet form of Yechezkel (Ezekiel).
Chuna, Chuneh   Forms of Nachum (Nahum).

Dadyeh A form of David.
Dov-Ber*
Dudel A form of David.
Dudu A pet form of David.
Dudya, Dudyeh Forms of David.
DuvidlA pet form of David.

Eisig, Eisik, Eizik Forms of Isaac.
Elkan, Elkin Forms of Elkana.
Elya, Elyeh Forms of Eliyahu (Elijah).
Evreml A pet form of Avram.
Evromel, Evromele Pet forms of Avrum.

Feibush*
Feivel*
Fishel*
Fishke*
Froma A form of Ephraim.
Fromel A pet form of Froma.
Froyim A form of Ephraim.
Froyimke A pet form of Froyim.

Gadil A form of Gedalya (Gedaliah).
Gavrel, Gavril Forms of Gavriel (Gabriel).
Gavrilke A pet form of Gavril.
Gedil, Gidil Forms of Gedalya (Gedaliah).
Getz*
Getzel*
Gimpel*

Haskel A form of Yechezkel (Ezekiel).
Henach, Henech Forms of Chanoch (Enoch).
Hersh*
Hershel*
Hershele*
Hertz*
Hertzel*
Hertzl*
Hesh*
Heskel*
Hirsh*
Hirshl*
Hudel, Hudya Forms of Yehuda (Judah).

Ichal, Ichel Forms of Yechiel.
Idil A form of Yehuda (Judah).

Ilya, Ilyash   Forms of Eliyahu (Elijah).
Isser   A form of Yisrael (Israel).
Isserel   A pet form of Isser.
Itsche, Itz   Pet forms of Yitzchak (Isaac).
Itzig, Itzik   Forms of Yitzchak (Isaac).

Kapel   A form of Yaakov (Jacob).
Kaski   A pet form of Yechezkel (Ezekiel).
Kasril   A form of Kasriel (Katriel).
Kasrileke   A pet form of Kasril.
Kiva, Kiveh   Short forms of Akiva (Akiba).
Koppel   A form of Yaakov (Jacob).
Keskel, Keskil   Forms of Yechezkel (Ezekiel).

Label*
Lazer*
Leeser   A form of Eliezer.
Leib*
Leibush*
Lesser*
Lev*
Lieber*
Lipman*
Loeb*

Maimon*
Maisel   A form of Mordecai.
Mani   A pet form of Mann.
Manish   A form of Menachem.
Mann   A short form of Menachem.
Mannes, Mannis, Manshel   Forms of Menachem.
Mata, Matza, Meisel   Forms of Mordecai.
Mendel, Mendl   Forms of Menachem.
Menka, Menke, Menla, Menlin   Pet forms of Mendel.
Menshel, Menshl   Forms of Menachem.
Moishe   A form of Moshe (Moses).
Mordcheh   A form of Mordecai.
Moshke   A pet form of Moshe (Moses).
Motel, Motke   Pet forms of Mordecai.
Motta, Motti, Mudel   Forms of Mordecai.
Muel   A short form of Shemuel (Samuel).
Muki   A form of Meir.
Muta, Muteh   Forms of Mordecai.
Mutka, Mutke   Pet forms of Muta.

Nachmanke, Nechil   Pet forms of Nachman.
Nosson, Nuta, Nuteh   Forms of Natan (Nathan).

Oren, Orlik, Oron   Forms of Aaron.

Pina, Pineh   Forms of Pinchas (Phineas).
Pineleh, Pini   Pet forms of Pineh.
Pinkeh   A pet form of Pincus.
Pinya   A pet form of Pineh.
Pinyeh   A form of Pinya.

Rubel, Rubele, Ruvenka   Pet forms of Reuven (Reuben).
Ruva   A form of Reuven (Reuben).

Seff*
Sekel, Sekl   Forms of Isaac.
Selig*
Shabsi   A form of Shebsil.
Shapsi   A form of Shepsil.
Shatz*
Shatzi*
Sha'ya, Sha'yeh   Forms of Yesha'ya (Isaiah).
Shebsil*
Sheki   A form of Shmelke.
Shepsil*
Shimi, Shimmel   Pet forms of Shimon (Simeon).
Shloimeh   A form of Shlomo (Solomon).
Shloimkeh   A pet form of Shloimeh.
Shmelke   A form of Shmuel (Samuel).
Shmerel   A form of Shemarya.
Shmiel, Shmul   Forms of Shmuel (Samuel).
Shmulka, Shmulkeh   Pet forms of Shmul.
Shneur*
Shraga*
Shrageh   A form of Shraga.
Siff   A form of Seff.
Sishe   A form of Syshe.
Srol   A form of Yisrael (Israel).
Sroleh, Sroli   Pet forms of Srol.
Susha   A form of Syshe.
Syshe*

Tanel   A form of Netanel (Nathaniel).
Tebel, Tebla, Teibel, Teivel   Forms of David.
Tuli   A form of Naftali.

Uda, Udeh   Forms of Yehuda (Judah).
Udel   A pet form of Udeh.

Velvel*
Velvil, Velvl   Forms of Velvel.
Vigder, Vigdor   Forms of Avigdor.
Volf*

Yachna, Yachneh   Forms of Yochanan (Johanan).
Yaki   A pet form of Yaakov (Jacob).
Yank   A form of Yaakov (Jacob).
Yankel   A pet form of Yank.
Yantsha   A form of John.
Yekel, Yekl   Forms of Yaakov (Jacob).
Yidel   A pet form of Yudi.
Yitz   A short form of Yitzchak (Isaac).
Yoshe, Yoshka, Yoshkeh   Forms of Yehoshua (Joshua).
Yoska, Yoske, Yoss   Forms of Yosef (Joseph).
Yossel, Yossi   Pet forms of Yoss.
Yudel   A pet form of Yehuda (Judah).
Yudi   A form of Yehuda (Judah).
Yuki   A pet form of Yekutiel.

Zak   A form of Isaac.
Zalki   A pet form of Zalkin.
Zalkin   A form of Zalman (Solomon).
Zalman, Zalmen   Forms of Solomon.
Zanvil   A form of Shmuel (Samuel).
Zavil   A form of either Zanvil or Saul.
Zaydel*
Zeff   A form of Zev.
Zeidel*
Zek   A form of Isaac.
Zekil   A pet form of Zek.
Zelig*
Zemel*
Zev*
Ziff   A form of Zev.
Zik   A short form of Isaac.
Zissa, Zisseh, Ziskin   Forms of Syshe.
Zundel*
Zushe, Zussa, Zusseh, Zussel, Zussman   Forms of Syshe.

Feminine Names

Aidel*
Alteh The feminine form of Alter.
Alterkeh A pet form of Alteh.

Basha, Bashe, Basyeh Forms of Basya (Batya).
Bayla*
Bayle*
Baylke A pet form of Bayle.
Blima A form of Bluma.
Blimeh A form of Blume.
Blimele A pet form of Blimeh.
Bluma*
Blumele A pet form of Blume.
Breina A form of Brina.
Breindel A pet form of Brina.
Breine A form of Brine.
Brina*
Brine*
Bruna*
Brune*

Chani A form of Chana (Hannah).
Chiyena A form of Chaya.
Chuma A form of Nechama.

Daba, Dabe Pet forms of Dabra.
Dabra, Dabre Forms of Devora (Deborah).
Davrush, Davrusha, Davrushe Forms of Devora (Deborah).
Devashka, Devashke, Devosya Pet forms of Devora (Deborah).
Dissa A pet form of Hadassah.
Dobra, Dubsha, Dubshe Forms of Devora (Deborah). Also, from the Slavic, meaning "good."
Dusha, Dushe Forms of Devora (Deborah). Also, from the Slavic, meaning "soul."

Eidel*
Elka*
Elke*
Etka, Etke   Pet forms of Ita.

Faiga*
Faige*
Faigel*
Feige*
Feigel*
Foigl   A form of Feigel.
Frayda*
Frayde*
Fraydel, Fraydl   Pet forms of Frayde.
Freidel   A variant form of Fraydel.
Freidl   A variant form of Fraydl.
Frima   A variant form of Fruma.
Frime   A variant form of Frume.
Fruma*
Frume*

Gendel   A form of Hendel.
Ginendel   A form of Gendel.
Gita*
Giteh   A form of Gita.
Gitel*
Gitele*
Gitil   A form of Gitel.
Glicke   A form of Glicke.
Glikel   A pet form of Glicke.
Glucke*
Glukel   A pet form of Glucke.

Hadaseh, Handas   Forms of Hadassah.
Henda*
Hende*
Hendel*
Heneh*
Henia*
Henna*
Henye   A form of Hannah.
Hindal*
Hindel*
Hodel   A form of Hadassah.
Hodi   A pet form of Hodel.
Hudel   A form of Hadassah.
Hudi   A pet form of Hudel.

Ideh   A form of Yehudit.
Idele   A pet form of Ideh.
Idit   A form of Yehudit.
Ita, Itta   Forms of Yehudit.
Iti, Itti   Pet forms of Ita and Itta.
Itka   A pet form of Ita.

Kayla*
Kayle*
Krayna*
Krayne*
Kreina*
Kreindel*
Krindel   A form of Kreindel.
Kruna   A form of Kreina.
Kryna*

Liba*
Libe*
Libka   A pet form of Liba.
Libke*   A pet form of Libe.
Luba*
Lubeh   A form of Luba.

Mariasha, Mariashe   Forms of Miryam (Miriam).
Maryasha*
Matza*
Merel, Meril   Forms of Miryam (Miriam).
Michla   A form of Michal.
Michlel   A pet form of Michla.
Minda*
Mindel*
Mirel*   A pet form of Miryam (Miriam).
Miri   A short form of Miril.
Miril   A pet form of Miryam (Miriam).

Necha, Neche   Forms of Nechama.
Nechel, Necheleh   Pet forms of Neche.
Nechuma   A form of Nechama.

Perel   A form of Perl.
Perele   A pet form of Perl.
Peril   A form of Perl.
Perl*
Pesha   A form of Basha (Batya).
Peshe*
Pessel   A form of Peshe.

Pessil A form of Pessel.
Pesye A form of Peshe.

Raina*
Raine*
Raisa*
Raise*
Raisel*
Rayna*
Rayne*
Raysa A form of Raisa.
Rayse A form of Raise.
Rayte A form of Raise.
Raytza A form of Raisa.
Rayza A form of Raisa.
Rayze A form of Raise.
Rayzel*
Rayzi*
Reina*
Reine*
Reizl*
Reyna*
Rifka*
Rifke*
Rivkeh A form of Rivka (Rebecca).
Rochel A form of Rachel.
Rochele A pet form of Rochel.
Roiza A form of Raisa.
Roizeh A form of Raise.
Ruchel A form of Rachel.
Ruchele, Rula Pet forms of Ruchel.
Ruskeh A form of Rachel.

Sirel*
Siril A form of Sarah.
Sirka A pet form of Sarah.
Sirke*
Sirkil A pet form of Sara.
Sisel*
Sorale*
Sorali*
Sorele, Soreli Pet forms of Sarah.
Sorka*
Sorke*
Sotoli*
Sura, Surel Forms of Sarah.
Surele, Sureli Pet forms of Sarah.

Suri   A form of Sarah.
Susya   A form of Sisel.

Tema, Teme   Forms of Tamar.
Toiba*
Toibe*
Trana, Trayne, Treina   Forms of Esther.
Treindel   A pet form of Treina.
Tzaitel, Tzertel, Tzeitel   Forms of Sarah.
Tzerin   A form of Esther.
Tzertel, Tzirel   Forms of Sarah.
Tzipa, Tzipe   A form of Tzipora.
Tzipi   A pet form of Tzipora.
Tziril*

Yidel, Yita, Yite   Forms of Yehudit.
Yotti*
Yudis   A form of Yehudis (Yehudit).
Yuta   A form of Yehudit.
Yute   A form of Yehudit.
Yutka   A pet form of Yuta.
Yutke   A pet form of Yute.

Zisel   A form of Sisel.
Zisele   A pet form of Zisel.
Zlata*
Zlate*
Zlota   A form of Zlata.
Zlote   A form of Zlota.
Zusa   A form of Zisel.

The following is a comprehensive listing of Hebrew names that have been used by Jews for more than 3,500 years—from biblical times to the present. Many are obsolete but are nevertheless included because they are part of the record.

Masculine Names

אֲבִישׁוּר	אֲבִימָן	אֲבִידוֹר	אָב
אֲבִי־שַׁחַר	אֲבִימַעַץ	אַבִידָן	אַבָּא
אֲבִישַׁחַר	אָבִין	אַבִידַע	אַבָּא־יוּדָן
אֲבִישַׁי	אֲבִינָא	אֲבִידְרוֹר	אַבְגַּר
אֲבִישָׁלוֹם	אֲבִינָדָב	אֲבִיָּה	אַבְדִימָא
אֲבִישָׁמָע	אֲבִי־נָעִים	אֲבִיָּהוּ	אַבְדִימֵי
אֲבִישָׁר	אֲבִינָעִים	אֲבִיהוּא	אַבְדִימִי
אֲבִישָׁר	אֲבִינֹעַם	אֲבִיוֹסֵף	אַבְדָן
אֲבִיתַּגָּר	אֲבִינָתָן	אֲבִיזֶמֶר	אַבָּהוּ
אֶבְיָתָר	אֲבִיסָמָךְ	אֲבִי־חַי	אַבוּהַ
אֶבֶן	אֲבִיסָף	אֲבִיחַיִל	אַבוּיָה
אַבְנִיאֵל	אֲבִיעַד	אֲבִי־חֵן	אַבוּנָא
אֶבֶן־עֶזֶר	אֲבִיעַז	אֲבִיחֵן	אַבְטַלְיוֹן
אִבְצָן	אֲבִיעֶזֶר	אֲבִי־טוֹב	אָבִי
אַבְרָהָם	אֲבִיעֶזְרִי	אֲבִיטוֹב	אָבִי
אַבְרוֹן	אֲבִיעָם	אֲבִיטוֹל	אֲבִיאָב
אַבְרִיאֵל	אֲבִיצֶדֶק	אֲבִי־טַל	אֲבִיאוֹר
אַבְרֵךְ	אֲבִיצוּר	אֲבִיטַל	אֲבִיאוּר
אַבְרָם	אֲבִיקָם	אַבַּיֵי	אֲבִיאֵל
אַבְשִׁי	אֲבִיקָר	אָבִים	אֲבִיאָסָף
אַבְשָׁל	אַבִּיר	אֲבִימָאֵל	אָבִיב
אַבְשָׁלוֹם	אַבִּירִי	אֲבִימֵי	אֲבִיגַל
אָגָא	אֲבִירָם	אֲבִימִי	אֲבִיגְדוֹר
אַגַּאי	אֲבִישׁוּעַ	אֲבִימֶלֶךְ	אֲבִידָב

אֶגְאָל	אֲדֹנִירָם	אוֹלָם	אוֹשֶׁר
אֱגוֹז	אַדָר	אוֹמֶן	אוֹשְׁרִי
אָגוּר	אִדְרוֹן	אוֹמֶץ	אֶזְבַּי
אָגִיל	אַדְרִיאֵל	אוֹמָר	אָזְנִי
אָגֵל	אַדְרָם	אוֹנָם	אֲזַנְיָה
אַגְמוֹן	אַהֲבָה	אוֹנָן	אֲזַנְיָהוּ
אֹגֶן	אֵהֹד	אוּפָז	אֶזְרָח
אַגְנוֹן	אָהוּב	אוֹפִיר	אֶזְרָחִי
אַגְרוֹן	אֲהוּבִיָה	אוֹפֶר	אָח
אֶגְרוֹן	אֲהוּבִיָה	אוֹצָר	אַחָא
אַגְרוֹן	אֲהוּבְעָם	אוּר	אַחְאָב
אַדָא	אָהוּד	אוּר	אֲחַאי
אַדְבְּאֵל	אֵהוּד	אוֹרֵג	אַחְבָּן
אֲדַד	אֹהֶל	אוֹרְגָד	אֵחוּד
אדו	אָהֳלִי	אוֹרוֹן	אַחְוָה
אָדוֹן	אָהֳלִאָב	אוֹר־חַיִּים	אַחֲוָה
אֲדוֹנִיָה	אַהֲרֹן	אוֹר־טַל	אֲחוּזָם
אֲדוֹנִים	אוּאֵל	אוּרִי	אֲחוֹחַ
אֲדוֹנִי־צֶדֶק	אוֹבִיל	אוּרִי	אֲחוֹמַי
אָצוּק	אוֹגֶן	אוּרִיאֵל	אָחָז
אדו	אוּד	אוּרִיָה	אֲחֻזַת
אֲדוֹרָם	אוּדִי	אוּרִיָהוּ	אֲחַזַי
אַדִי	אוּדִיאֵל	אוּרִיּוֹן	אַחְזִי
אָדִיב	אוֹהֵב	אוּרִין	אַחַזְיָה
אַדִיר	אוֹהֵד	אוּרִין	אֲחַזְיָהוּ
אַדְלְיָא	אֹהַד	אוֹר־יֵשׁ	אֲחֻזָם
אָדָם	אוּזִי	אוֹר־מַלְכִּי	אֲחֻזַת
אַדְמוֹן	אוּזָל	אוֹרָן	אָחִי
אַדְמָתָא	אֱוִי	אוֹרֶן	אָחִי
אַדְנִיָה	אֲוִירָא	אוֹר־צִיּוֹן	אָחִי
אֲדֹנִיָהוּ	אֲוִירִי	אוֹשְׁיָא	אֲחִיאָב
אֲדֹנִיקָם	אוּכַל	אוֹשַׁעְיָא	אֲחִיאָם

אֲחִיאָם	אֲחִירַע	אִיסִי	אֵלִי
אֲחִיאָסָף	אֲחִישׁוּר	אִיעֶזֶר	אֱלִיאָב
אֲחִי-דוֹד	אֲחִישַׁחַר	אִיקָא	אֱלִיאוֹר
אֲחִידוֹד	אֲחִישִׁי	אִינָר	אֱלִיאֵל
אֲחִידָן	אֲחִישָׁלוֹם	אִישׁ-בַּעַל	אֶלְיָאסָף
אֲחִידָע	אֲחִישָׁר	אִישׁ-בֹּשֶׁת	אֶלְיָאתָה
אֲחִיָה	אֲחִישַׁר	אִישׁ-הוֹד	אֶלְיגָּאַל
אֲחִיָּהוּ	אֲחִיתֹפֶל	אִישׁ-חַיִל	אֶלִיגוֹאֵל
אֲחִיהוּד	אַחְלָב	אִישׁ-טוֹב	אַלְיְגַע
אָחִיו	אַחְלַי	אִישׁ-שֵׂכֶל	אֶלְיָדָד
אֲחִיחוּד	אַחְלַי	אִישׁ-שָׁלוֹם	אֶלְיָדָע
אֲחִיטוּב	אַחֵר	אִיתַּאי	אֵלִיָּה
אֲחִילוּד	אַהֲרוֹן	אִיתִּי	אֵלִיָּהוּ
אֲחִימוֹת	אַחְרַח	אִיתִי	אֱלִיהוּא
אֲחִימֶלֶךְ	אַחְרַחֵל	אִיתִיאֵל	אֱלִיהוּד
אֲחִימָן	אַחְשָׁלוֹם	אֵיתָם	אֱלִיחַי
אֲחִימַעַץ	אֲחַשְׁתָּרִי	אִיתָמָר	אֱלִיחֹרֶף
אֲחִין	אַטְמוֹן	אֵיתָן	אֱלִיטוּב
אֲחִינָא	אָטֵר	אֵלָא	אֱלִי-יָדָע
אֲחִינָדָב	אִיבוּ	אֶלְדָּד	אֱלִימוֹר
אֲחִינֹעַ	אַיָּה	אֶלְדָּעָה	אֱלִימֶלֶךְ
אֲחִינֹעַם	אִיּוֹב	אֶלְגָּבִישׁ	אֶלְיָנַעַר
אֲחִינֵר	אִי-כָבוֹד	אַלְדְּמַע	אֶלְיָנָתָן
אֲחִיסָמָךְ	אַיִל	אֶלְדָּר	אֶלְיָסָף
אֲחִיעֶזֶר	אַיָל	אֵלָה	אֱלִיעַד
אֲחִיעָם	אַיָל	אֱלוּל	אֱלִיעָד
אֲחִיפֶלֶט	אַיָּלוֹן	אַלּוֹן	אֱלִיעֶז
אֲחִיצֶדֶק	אַיָּלוֹן	אַלּוֹן	אֱלִיעֶזֶר
אֲחִיצוּר	אִילָן	אַלּוּף	אֱלִיעֵינַי
אֲחִיקָם	אַיִיר	אֶלְזָבָד	אֱלִיעָם
אֲחִיקַר	אִיִּירִי	אֶלְחַי	אֱלִיפַז
אֲחִירָם	אִיסוּר	אֶלְחָנָן	אֱלִיפָל

אָסִיף	אַמִינוֹן	אֶלְעָא	אֱלִיפְלֵהוּ
אַסִיר	אַמִיץ	אֶלְעָאי	אֱלִיפֶלֶט
אַסְנָה	אַמִיצָה	אֶלְעָד	אֱלִיצוּר
אָסָף	אַמִיצִיָה	אֶלְעָדָה	אֱלִיצֶדֶק
אֵפוֹד	אָמִיר	אֶלְעוּזִי	אֱלִיצָו
אַפִּיחַ	אֲמִישַׁי	אֶלְעוּזַי	אֱלִיצוּר
אַפַּיִם	אֲמִיתַּי	אֶלְעָזָר	אֱלִיצָפָן
אָפִיק	אֲמִיתָּן	אֶלְעֶזְרִי	אֱלִיקָא
אֶפְלָל	אֹמֶן	אֶלְעָל	אֶלְיָקוּם
אֶפֶס	אַמְנוֹן	אֶלְעָמִי	אֶלְיָקִים
אַפֵק	אֲמַנְיָה	אֶלְעָשָׂא	אֱלִירַז
אֶפְרַיִם	אֹמֶץ	אֶלְעָשָׂה	אֱלִירָם
אֶפְרָת	אַמְצִי	אָלָף	אֱלִירָן
אֶצְבּוֹן	אֲמַצְיָה	אֶלְפַּעַל	אֶלְיָשׁוּב
אָצִיל	אֲמַצְיָהוּ	אֶלְצֶדֶק	אֱלִישׁוּעַ
אָצֵל	אֹמֶר	אֶלְצָפָן	אֶלְיָשִׁיב
אֲצַלְיָה	אָמַר	אֶלְקוֹשׁ	אֶלְיָשִׁיב
אֲצַלְיָהוּ	אִמְרָה	אֶלְקָיִם	אֱלִישָׁמָע
אֹצֶם	אִמְרִי	אֶלְקָנָה	אֱלִישָׁע
אֵצֶר	אֲמַרְיָה	אֶלְרֹעִי	אֱלִישָׁפָט
אַרְא	אֲמַרְיָהוּ	אֶלְרָד	אֶלְיָתָה
אַרְאֵל	אַמְרָם	אֶלְרָם	אֲלֶכְּסַנְדֶּר
אַרְאֵל	אַמְרָפֶל	אֶלְרָן	אֲלֶכְּסַנְדְּרִי
אַרְאֵלִי	אֱמֶת	אַל־תּוּגָה	אַלְמָגוֹר
אַרְבֵּל	אֲמִתַּי	אַלְתֵּר	אַלְמוֹג
אַרְבַּע	אַמְתָּן	אָמוֹן	אַלְמוֹדָד
אַרְגָּמָן	אֱנוֹשׁ	אָמוֹן	אַלְמוֹן
אֶרֶד	אַנְטִיגְנוֹס	אָמוֹץ	אַלְמָן
אַרְדּוֹן	אֲנִיעָם	אַמִּי	אֶלְנָדָב
אַרְדִּי	אָסָא	אַמִּי	אֶלְנַעַם
אֲרוֹד	אַסִי	אֲמִימַר	אֶלְנָקָם
אֲרוֹדִי	אַסְיָה	אָמִין	אֶלְנָתָן

אַרְנָנָה	אַשְׁבֵּעַ	בַּג־בַּג	בָּטְנִית
אֶרֶז	אֶשְׁבַּעַל	בִּגְוַי	בִּיבִי
אַרְזָא	אֶשֶׁד	בְּדַד	בִּיבַי
אַרְזוֹן	אַשּׁוּר	בְּדָיָה	בֵּינָר
אַרְזִי	אֶשְׁחָד	בְּדֹלַח	בִּילוּ
אֶרֶז־יִשְׂרָאֵל	אַשְׁחוּר	בְּדָן	בִּילְק
אָרַח	אֲשִׁי	בִּדְקַר	בִּינָה
אֲרִי	אַשִׁי	בַּהַט	בִּינִי
אֲרִיאָב	אַשְׁיָה	בָּהִיר	בֵּית־אֵל
אֲרִיאֵל	אַשְׁיָן	בּוּגִי	בַּיְתּוֹס
אָרִיג	אֶשְׁכּוֹל	בּוּז	בִּיתָן
אַרְיֵה	אַשְׁכְּנַז	בּוּזִי	בְּכוֹר
אַרְיוֹךְ	אֵשֶׁל	בּוֹחֵר	בְּכוֹרַת
אֲרִיכָא	אָשֵׁר	בּוּטָא	בְּכִיאֵל
אָרִיק	אֲשֵׂרָאֵל	בָּנִי	בְּכִיר
אֲרָם	אֲשְׂרָאֵלָה	בּוֹסְטָן	בֶּכֶר
אַרְמוֹן	אָשְׂרִי	בּוֹסְתָּן	בִּכְרוּ
אַרְמוֹנִי	אַשְׂרִיאֵל	בּוֹסְתָּנַאי	בִּכְרִי
אַרְמָן	אֶשְׁתּוֹן	בּוּנָה	בִּלְגָּה
אַרְמְנִי	אֶתְאֵל	בּוּנִי	בִּלְגַּי
אָרָן	אִתַּי	בּוֹעַז	בִּלְדָּד
אָרָן	אִתַּי	בּוּקִי	בִּלְהָן
אַרְנוֹן	אֲתִיאֵל	בְּזוּקָה	בֶּלַע
אַרְנוֹנִי	אָתְנִי	בָּזָק	בַּלְפוּר
אָרְנָן	אַתַּנְיָה	בֶּזֶק	בָּלָק
אַרְנָן	אֶתְנָן	בָּחוּר	בִּמְהָל
אַרְפַּכְשַׁד		בַּחְיָא	בִּלְשָׁן
אַרְצָא	בְּאֵרָא	בְּחִיאֵל	בֵּן
אַרְצִי	בְּאֵרָה	בְּחַיַי	בֵּן
אָשׁ	בְּאֵרִי	בָּחִיר	בֶּן־אָבִי
אַשְׁבֵּל	בָּבָא	בַּחַן	בֶּן־אוֹנִי
אַשְׁבָּן	בֵּבַי	בֶּטַח	בֶּן־אוֹר

בַּרְקוֹס	בְּקִי	בְּנְלִי	בֶּן־בָּרוּךְ
בָּרֶקֶת	בְּקִנְיָה	בִּנְעָא	בֶּן־גּוּרְיוֹן
בַּר־תַּלְמַי	בְּקִנְיָהוּ	בֶּן־עַד	בֶּן־גֶּבֶר
בְּשׁוֹר	בַּר	בִּנְעָד	בֶּן־דֶּקֶר
בִּשְׁלָם	בְּרָאיָה	בֶּן־עַזַּאי	בֶּן־הֲדַד
בֹּשֶׂם	בַּר־אִילָן	בֶּן־עֶזֶר	בֶּן־הֶלֶם
בְּתוּאֵל	בַּרְגִיל	בֶּן־עֶזְרָא	בְּנוֹ
בְּתִירָא	בֶּרֶד	בֶּן־עֶזְרָה	בְּנוּי
	בָּרוּךְ	בֶּן־עַמִּי	בֶּן־זוֹחַת
גְּאוּאֵל	בְּרוּכְאֵל	בֶּן־עָשׂוֹר	בֶּן־חוּר
גְּאוּלָה	בְּרוּקָה	בֶּן־צְבִי	בֶּן־חַיִל
גָּאוֹן	בְּרוֹר	בִּנְצִי	בֶּן־חֵן
גְּאַלְיָה	בָּרוּר	בֶּן־צִיּוֹן	בֶּן־חָנָן
גַּבַּאי	בְּרוֹשׁ	בֶּן־שַׁחַר	בֶּן־חֶסֶד
גִבּוֹר	בַּרְזִילַי	בֶּן־שֵׁם	בֶּן־טוֹב
גַּבַּי	בֵּרִי	בְּסוֹדְיָה	בֶּן־טוֹבִים
גַּבִּי	בַּר־יוֹחָאִי	בֶּסִי	בְּנִי
גְּבִינִי	בַּר־יוֹחַאי	בְּסִתְּנַאי	בָּנִי
גַּבְרוֹל	בָּרִיחַ	בֹּעַז	בְּנִי
גְּבִירוֹל	בְּרִיעָה	בַּעַל	בְּנָיָה
גֶּבַע	בְּרִית	בַּעֲנָא	בְּנָיָהוּ
גִּבְעָא	בְּרִית־אֵל	בַּעֲנָה	בֶּן־יוֹסִיפָה
גִּבְעָה	בַּר־כּוֹכְבָא	בַּעֲשֵׂע	בֶּן־יַחְדּוֹ
גִּבְעוֹל	בַּרְכְאֵל	בַּעֲשֵׂיָה	בֶּן־יַחֲזִיאֵל
גִּבְעוֹן	בְּרָכָה	בֶּצִי	בִּנְיָמִין
גֶּבֶר	בְּרַכְיָה	בְּצַלְאֵל	בִּנְיָמִין־זְאֵב
גִּבָּר	בֶּרֶכְיָה	בַּצְלוּת	בְּנִינוּ
גַּבְרָא	בֶּרֶכְיָהוּ	בֶּצֶר	בֶּן־יִשַׁי
גַּבְרִי	בַּרְעָם	בִּצָּרוֹן	בֶּן־כּוֹזִיבָא
גַּבְרִיאֵל	בַּרְעָמִי	בַּקְבּוּק	בֶּן־כּוֹסִיבָה
גַּבְרִיָה	בָּרָק	בַּקְבּוּקְיָה	בֶּן־כַּרְמִי
גַּבְרִיָהוּ	בַּרְקַאי	בַּקְבָּר	בֶּן־לִי

גָּמוּל	גִּיל־דּוֹר	גּוּר־אַרְיֵה	גַּבְרְעָם
גָּמָל	גִּילְדּוֹר	גּוּרִי	גִּבְּתוֹן
גַּמְלָא	גִּילוֹן	גּוּרְיָא	גָּד
גְּמַלָּא	גִּיל־לִי	גּוּרִיאֵל	גַּדָּא
גְּמַלִּי	גִּילִי	גּוּרְיָה	גָּדוֹל
גַּמְלִיאֵל	גִּילָן	גּוּרְיוֹן	גְּדוּלָה
גֶּמֶר	גִּיל־עַד	גּוּרֶן	גְּדוֹר
גְּמַרְיָה	גִּילְעָד	גַּזֵּז	גְּדִי
גְּמַרְיָהוּ	גִּלְעָדִי	גָּזֵז	גָּדִי
גַּעַל	גִּיל־עָם	גּוֹרָל	גַּדִּי
גַּעְתָּם	גִּילְעָם	גּוֹרֶן	גַּדְרִיאֵל
גֶּפֶן	גִּינַת	גַּזָּה	גָּדִיל
גַּפְנִי	גִּינְתּוֹי	גַּזָּם	גָּדִישׁ
גַּפְנְיָה	גִּישָׁן	גְּחַזִי	גְּדֵל
גֵּרָא	גִּיתִּי	נַחַם	גְּדַלָה
גֶּרֶב	גִּיתַּאי	נַחַר	גְּדַלְיָה
גֶּרְדִי	גִּיתִּי	גַּי	גְּדַלְיָהוּ
גָּרוֹן	גַּל	גַּי	גְּדַלְתִּי
גֵּרִי	גִּלְבּוֹעַ	גַּיְא	גִּדְעוֹן
גֵּרְיוֹן	גִּלְבַּע	גַּיְא	גִּדְעוֹנִי
גֹּרֶן	גַּלִּי	גִּיבּוֹר	גַּדְרוֹן
גֵּרְשׁוֹם	גַּלְיָה	גִּידַל	גּוֹאֵל
גֵּרְשׁוֹן	גָּלִיל	גִּידֵל	גּוֹבֶר
גְּשׁוּר	גְּלִילִי	גִּידִי	גּוֹג
גֶּשֶׁם	גְּלֵלַי	גִּיּוֹר	גּוֹדְגְּדָא
גֹּשֶׁן	גָּלְיַת	גְּיוֹרָא	גּוֹזָל
גִּתַּאי	גָּלָל	גְּיוֹרָה	גּוֹזָן
גִּתִּי	גַּלְמוּד	גִּיחוֹן	גּוֹלָן
גִּתִּי	גִּלְעָד	גֵּיחֲזִי	גּוֹנִי
גֶּתֶר	גִּלְעָדִי	גִּיל	גּוֹנֵן
	נָמַד	גִּיל־אוֹן	גּוּר
דָּאַג	גַּמְדָּא	גִּילַאי	גּוּר־אַרְי

הֶדֶר	דַּפִּי	דורון	דֹב
הַדְרִיאֵל	דַּפְנָא	דורוני	דְּבִּי
הַדְלָם	דֶּקֶל	דורי	דְּבִיר
הֲדַרְעֶזֶר	דִּקְלָה	דוריאל	דִּבְלַיִם
הֲדַרְעָם	דֶּקֶר	דורן	דִּבְרִי
הוֹד	דַּר	דותן	דְּבַשׁ
הוֹדַוְיָה	דַּרְדַּע	דיבון	דָּג
הוֹדַוְיָהוּ	דָּרוֹם	דברי	דָּגוּל
הוֹדִיָה	דְּרוֹמָא	דידי	דַּגְיָה
הוֹהָם	דְּרוֹמָה	דימון	דְּגְלַאי
הוֹלִי	דְּרוֹר	דימֵי	דִּגְלִי
הוֹמָם	דְּרוֹרִי	דימִי	דִּגְלִי
הוֹן	דְּרוֹר-לִי	דַּיָן	דָּגָן
הוֹנָא	דְּרוֹרְלִי	דינאי	דֹּדָן
הוֹרְדוֹס	דָּרְיָוֶשׁ	דיפת	דּוֹאֵג
הוֹרְקְנוֹס	דַּרְקוֹן	דיץ	דּוֹב
הוֹשָׁמָע	דֶּשֶׁא	דישון	דּוֹבֶב
הוֹשֵׁעַ	דָּתִיאֵל	דישָׁן	דּוּבִּי
הוֹשַׁעְיָא	דָּתָן	דְּלָיָה	דָּוִד
הוֹשַׁעְיָה		דְּלָיָהוּ	דוד
הוֹתִיר	הֵא-הֵא	דַּלְפוֹן	דודו
הֵידָד	הַאי	דָּמָא	דודו
הִילָה	הֶבֶל	דָּמָה	דּוּדִי
הִילִי	הַגְרִי	דמי	דוֹדִי
הֵימָם	הֵד	דָּן	דּוֹלֶב
הֵימָן	הֲדַד	דָּנִי	דוֹלְפִין
הֵלָא	הָדוּר	דָּנִיאֵל	דּוּמָה
הֵלַאי	הַדּוֹרָם	דָּנִי-עָם	דּוֹנֶשׁ
הֵלָה	הֲדִי	דָּנִיעָם	דּוֹסָא
הֵלִי	הֲדַס	דַּעֲאֵל	דּוֹסְתַּאי
הַלֵּל	הֲדַר	דְּעוּאֵל	דּוּר
הָלֵּל	הָדָר	דְלִפִּי	דּוֹר

זֶמֶר	זִיו	זָבוּד	הֶלֶם
זֶמֶר	זִיוַאי	זְבוּל	הֶלֶם
זִמְרָא	זִיוִי	זְבוּלוּן	הֶלָן
זִמְרָה	זִיו-לִי	זְבוּלָן	הָמָן
זִמְרִי	זִיוְלִי	זֶבַח	הַמְנוּנָא
זְמַרְיָה	זִינָן	זַבְחֲיָה	הִצִילָיָהוּ
זִמְרָן	זִיזָא	זַבַּי	הִצְלָיָהוּ
זַן	זִיזָה	זְבִיד	הַקָנָה
זַעֲנָן	זִיכְרוֹנִי	זְבִידָא	הַרְאֵל
זְעֵירָא	זִינָא	זְבִינָא	הַרְדוֹף
זְעֵירָא	זִיע	זָהֲבִי	הָרוּם
זְעֵירִי	זֵירָא	זְהָבִי	הָרָן
זִפְרוֹן	זִירוּז	זָהוֹב	הֶרְצֵל
זַק	זַיִת	זָהוּר	הַשְׂכֵּל
זָקוּף	זֵיתָן	זָהִיר	הָשֵׁם
זָקִיף	זַן	זֶה-לִי	
זָקֵן	זַכַּאי	זָהָם	נָפְסִי
זָר	זַכִּי	זֹהַר	וֶרֶד
זְרוּבָּבֶל	זַכִּי	זָהֲרִי	נַרְדִי
זֶרַח	זַכַּי	זַהֲרִיָה	נַרְדִימוֹן
זַרְחִי	זֶכֶר	זוֹהַר	נַרְדִינוֹן
זַרְחִיָה	זִכְרוֹנִי	זוֹחַת	
זָרִיז	זִכְרִי	זוּטָא	זְאֵב
זֶרֶם	זְכַרְיָה	זוּטַאי	זְאֵבִי
זְרִיקָא	זְכַרְיָהוּ	זוּטָה	זְאֵב-יוֹסֵף
זֶרַע	זְכַרִינִי	זוּטִי	זְאָרִי
זַרְעִי	זֶלִי	זוּטְרָא	זָבָד
זַתָּם	זִמָה	זוּמָא	זָבוּד
זֶתֶר	זְמִינָא	זוּמֵר	זַבְדִי
	זָמִיר	זוֹרֵחַ	זַבְדִיאֵל
חֹבָב	זְמִירָה	זוֹרֵעַ	זְבַדְיָה
חַבָּה		זָזָא	זְבַדְיָהוּ

חָלוּץ	חֲזַקְאֵל	חֹוזַי	חֲבִי
חֲלוּצְאֵל	חִזְקִי	חֲוִילָה	חָבִיב
חָלִיל	חִזְקִיָּה	חוּל	חֲבִיבְאֵל
חַלִיפָא	חִזְקִיָּהוּ	חוּם	חֲבִיבָה
חֶלֶם	חָטוּשׁ	חוּמִי	חֲבִיבִי
חַלָמִישׁ	חֲטִיטָא	חוֹנִי	חֲבִיבְיָה
חֵלֹן	חָטִיל	חוּנְיָא	חֲבִיבְיָה
חַלְפָן	חֲטִיפָא	חוֹנִיּוֹ	חֲבִיבְעָם
חַלְפוֹן	חֹטֶר	חוֹנֵן	חֲבָיָה
חֲלַפְתָּא	חַי	חוֹסָה	חֶבְיוֹן
חֶלֶץ	חִיָּא	חוּפָם	חַבַצְגִנְיָה
חַלְצוֹן	חִיאֵל	חוֹצְפִּית	חַבַקּוּק
חֵלֶק	חַיִּים	חוּר	חֶבֶר
חֶלְקִי	חַיִל	חוֹרֵב	חֶבְרוֹן
חִלְקִנָה	חֵילִי	חוֹרִי	חַג
חִלְקִיָּהוּ	חִילָק	חוֹרִי	חַגָּא
חָם	חַיְפָּה	חוֹרִי	חַגַּאי
חָמָא	חִירָה	חוֹרֵם	חָגָב
חֶמֶד	חִירוֹם	חוּשִׁי	חֲגָבָה
חֲמַדְאֵל	חִירָם	חוּשִׁיאֵל	חַגִּי
חֶמְדָּד	חִירָם	חוּשִׁים	חַגִּי
חֲמַדְיאֵל	חַכִינַאי	חוּשָׁם	חֲגִיגָה
חֶמְדִּיאֵל	חֲכַלְיָה	חוּשִׁיעָם	חַגִּיָּה
חֲמַדְיָה	חָכָם	חוֹתָם	חֶדֶד
חֶמְדָּן	חַכְמוֹן	חֲזָאֵל	חֶדְוִי
חֶמְדַּת	חַכְמוֹנִי	חָזוֹ	חַדְלַי
חַמּוּאֵל	חֵלֶב	חָזוֹן	חָדָשׁ
חָמוּד	חֶלְבּוֹ	חֲזִי	חוֹבֵב
חֲמוּדְאֵל	חֶלֶד	חֲזִיאֵל	חוֹבָב
חָמוּל	חֶלְדַּי	חֲזָיָה	חוּג
חָמִי	חֵלוֹן	חֶזְיוֹן	חוֹגִי
חֶמְיָה	חָלוּף	חֲזִיר	חוֹדֶשׁ

טַבְיוֹמָא	חַרְחַרְיָה	חֲסַדְאֵל	חַמְרָן
טַבְלָא	חַרְחַס	חֲסַדִיאֵל	חֲמָת
טַבְלִי	חָרִים	חֲסַדְיָה	חֵן
טְבַלְיָהוּ	חָרִיף	חֹסָה	חֵן־מֶלֶךְ
טִבְעוֹן	חֶרְמוֹן	חָסוּד	חָנָא
טַבָּעוֹת	חֶרְמוֹנִי	חָסוּן	חֲנָדָד
טַבְרְמוֹן	חַרְסוֹם	חָסוֹן	חָנָה
טָדִי	חָרֶף	חֲסִיאֵל	חֲנוֹךְ
טוֹב	חֶרֶשׁ	חָסִיד	חָנוּן
טוֹבִי	חֹרֶשׁ	חָסִין	חָנוּן
טוֹבִיאֵל	חֲשַׁבְיָה	חִסְמָא	חֲנִיאֵל
טוֹבִיָּה	חֲשַׁבְיָהוּ	חֹסֶן	חֲנִינָה
טוֹבִיָּה	חֲשַׁבַּדָּנָא	חַסְרָה	חֲנִילַאי
טוֹבִיָּהוּ	חֲשַׁבְנָה	חֻפָּה	חֲנִינַאי
טוֹבִים	חֲשַׁבְנְיָה	חֻפִּים	חֲנִיתָה
טוֹבִי־שָׁלֵם	חַרְגֹּפֶר	חָפְנִי	חֲנֻכָּה
טוֹב־לִי	חַרְשָׁא	חֵפֶץ	חֵן־לִי
טוֹבְלִי	חָשׁוּב	חֵפֶר	חֶגְלִי
טוֹב־שָׁלֵם	חֲשׁוּבָה	חֹפֶשׁ	חֲנַמְאֵל
טוֹבְשָׁלֵם	חֲשׁוּפָא	חָצָב	חָנָן
טִיב	חָשֻׁם	חֲצְפִית	חָנָן
טִיל	חַשְׁמוֹן	חֶצְרוֹן	חַנָּא
טוֹדְרוֹס	חַשְׁמוֹנַאי	חֶצְרַי	חֲנַנְאֵל
טַל	חַשְׁמוֹנָאי	חֶצְרִי	חֲנַנִי
טַל־אוֹר	חֲתַת	חֲקוּפָא	חֲנַנִי
טַלְאוֹר		חֲקְלַאי	חֲנַנְיָה
טַל־שַׁחַר	טַבַּאי	חַרְבוֹנָה	חֲנַנְיָהוּ
טַלְשַׁחַר	טָבְאַל	חָרוּם	חֲנָתוֹן
טַלּוֹר	טֶבַח	חֲרוּמַף	חִנָּתוֹן
טַלִי	טָבִי	חָרוּץ	חֶסֶד
טַלְיָא	טָבִי	חֵרוּת	חִסְדָּא
טֶלֶם	טָבִיב	חַרְחוּר	חִסְדַּאי

יוֹזָבָד	יְהוֹיָדָע	יָגִיל	טַלְמוֹן
יוֹזָכָר	יְהוֹיָכִין	יָגֵל	טָמִיר
יוֹחָא	יְהוֹיָקִים	יָגְלִי	טֶנֶא
יוֹחָאִי	יְהוֹיָרִיב	יִדְבַּש	טָרִי
יוֹחַאִי	יְהוּכַל	יָדוֹ	טַרְפוֹן
יוֹחָנָן	יְהוֹנָדָב	יָדוֹן	
יוֹיָדָע	יְהוֹנָתָן	יָדוּעַ	יָאֶה
יוֹיָכִין	יְהוֹסֵף	יְדוּתוּן	יָאוּש
יוֹיָקִים	יְהוֹעַדָה	יַדִּי	יַאֲזַנְיָה
יוֹיָרִיב	יְהוֹצָדָק	יְדִיאֵל	יַאֲזַנְיָהוּ
יוּבַל	יְהוֹרָם	יָדִיד	יָאִיר
יוֹם־טוֹב	יְהוֹשֻׁעַ	יְדִיד	יאשִׁיָה
יוֹן	יְהוֹשָׁפָט	יְדִידְיָה	יאשִׁיָהוּ
יוֹנָדָב	יַהֵל	יְדִידְיָהוּ	יְאָתְרַי
יוֹנָה	יַהֲלוֹם	יְדָיָה	יְבוֹרָךְ
יוֹנִי	יַהֲלִי	יָדִין	יִבְחָר
יוֹנַת	יַהֲלִי	יְדִיאֵל	יָבִין
יוֹנָתָן	יְהַלֶלְאֵל	יְדִיעֲאֵל	יָבֵל
יוּסְטוֹס	יַהֲלֹם	יְדִיעֵל	יַבְנְאֵל
יוֹסִי	יוֹאָב	יִדְלָף	יַבְנִיאֵל
יוֹסִי	יוֹאָח	יָדַע	יִבְנְיָה
יוֹסִיאֵל	יוֹאָחָז	יַדְעִיָה	יְבָרֶךְ
יוֹסִיפָאֵל	יוֹאֵל	יְהָב	יְבֶרֶכְיָה
יוֹסִיפוֹס	יוֹאָש	יָהֵב	יְבֶרֶכְיָהוּ
יוֹסֵף	יוֹב	יַהְדַּי	יָבֵש
יוֹסִיפְיָה	יוֹבָב	יֵהוּא	יִבְשָׂם
יוֹעֶאלָה	יוּבַל	יְהוֹאָחָז	יִגְאָל
יוֹעֵד	יוֹבֵל	יְהוֹאָש	יִגְאָל
יוֹעֵז	יוּבֵל	יְהוּדָה	יָגֵב
יוֹעֶזֶר	יוֹגֵב	יְהוּדִי	יִגְדָּל
יוֹעֵץ	יוֹדָה	יְהוֹזָבָד	יִגְדַּלְיָה
יוֹעֵש	יוֹדָן	יְהוֹחָנָן	יִגְדַּלְיָהוּ

יָעִיר	יָמִין	יְחִדְיָהוּ	יוֹצָדָק
יָעִישׁ	יָמִין	יָחוֹן	יוּקִי
יַעְבָּן	יָמִיר	יַחֲזִיאֵל	יוֹקִים
יַעַל	יִמְלָה	יְחֶזְקֵאל	יוֹרָה
יָעֵל	יַמְלֵךְ	יְחִזְקִיָּה	יוֹרָה
יַעֲלָא	יִמְנָה	יְחִזְקִיָּהוּ	יוֹרִי
יַעֲלָה	יִמְנָע	יְחִיָּא	יוּרִי
יַעְלָם	יִמְרָה	יְחִיאָב	יוֹרָם
יַעַן	יַנְאִי	יְחִיאָח	יוֹרָן
יַעֲנִי	יָנוּב	יְחִיאֵל	יוֹשֵׁב־חֶסֶד
יַעֲקֹב	יָנוּחַ	יְחִיאֵלִי	יוֹשִׁיבְיָה
יַעֲקֹבָה	יָנוֹן	יָחִיד	יוֹשָׁה
יַעֲקָן	יָנוֹן	יְחִיָּה	יוֹשַׁוְיָה
יַעַר	יָנִיב	יְחִיֶּה	יוֹשָׁפָט
יַעְרָה	יָנִין	יָחִיל	יוֹשֵׁר
יַעֲרִי	יָנִיר	יְחִיעָם	יוֹתָם
יַעֲרֶשְׁיָה	יִנְעָם	יְחִי־שָׁלוֹם	יִזְהָר
יַעֲשַׂי	יִסְמַכְיָה	יָחֵל	יְזִיאֵל
יַעֲשִׂיאֵל	יִסְמַכְיָהוּ	יַחְלְאֵל	יִזִּיָּה
יִפְדְיָה	יַסְמִין	יַחְלְאֵלִי	יָזִיז
יָפֶה	יַעְבֵּץ	יַחְמַי	יִזְלִיאָה
יָפִים	יֶעְדוֹ	יָחָן	יְזַנְיָה
יָפִיעַ	יְעוּאֵל	יַחְצְאֵל	יָזֶר
יַפְלֵט	יָעוֹז	יַחַת	יִזְרַח
יִפְנֶה	יָעוּץ	יָטְבָה	יִזְרַחְיָה
יִפְרָח	יְעוּשׁ	יִטּוּר	יִזְרַחְיָהוּ
יִפְרְחְעָם	יַעֲזוּר	יָכִין	יִזְרְאֵל
יֶפֶת	יָעִישׁ	יְכָנְיָה	יִזְרְעֵאל
יֶפֶת	יַעֲזִיאֵל	יְכָנְיָהוּ	יִזְרְעֵאל
יִפְתָּח	יַעֲזִיָּהוּ	יָלוֹן	יַחַד
יִפְתַּח־אֵל	יַעֲזֵר	יָלוֹן	יַחְדּוֹ
יִצְהָל	יְעִיאֵל	יְמוּאֵל	יַחְדִּיאֵל

יְשָׁרוּן	יֵשׁוּעַ	יָרוֹם	יִצְהָר
יִשָּׂשׂכָר	יְשׁוּעָה	יָרוֹן	יִצְחָק
יִתְמָה	יְשׁוּרוּן	יְרוּשָׁלַיִם	יַצִּיב
יַתְנִיאֵל	יִשְׁחָק	יֶרַח	יִצְלָח
יֶתֶר	יִשַׁי	יַרְחָם	יַצְלִיחַ
יִתְרָא	יָשִׁיב	יְרַחְמְאֵל	יִצְמָח
יִתְרָה	יְשִׁיָה	יְרַחְמִיאֵל	יֵצֶר
יִתְרוֹ	יְשִׁיָהוּ	יַרְחָע	יִצְרִי
יִתְרָן	יְשִׁימִיאֵל	יְרִיאֵל	יֶקֶה
יִתְרְעָם	יָשִׁיר	יָרִיב	יָקוֹם
יְתֵת	יָשִׁישׁ	יִרְיָה	יְקוּתִיאֵל
	יָשִׁישׁ	יִרְיָהוּ	יַקִּי
כָּבוֹד	יְשִׁישַׁי	יַרְכִינַאי	יָקְטָן
כַּדּוּר	יִשְׁמָא	יְרֵמַי	יָקִים
כַּדּוּרִי	יִשְׁמָעֵאל	יְרֵמִי	יַקִּיר
כַּדִּי	יִשְׁמַעְיָה	יִרְמְיָה	יָקְמְיָה
בֹּהֶן	יִשְׁמַעְיָהוּ	יִרְמְיָהוּ	יָקְמְעָם
כָּהֲנָא	יִשְׁמְרִי	יְרִימוֹת	יָקָר
כַּהֲנָא	יָשֵׁן	יַרְקוֹן	יָקְשָׁן
כּוֹכָב	יֶשַׁע	יְשָׁבְאָב	יִרְאִיָה
כּוֹכְבָא	יִשְׁעִי	יָשָׁבְב	יָרֵב
כּוֹנֵן	יְשַׁעְיָה	יִשְׁבָּח	יְרֻבַּעַל
כּוֹנַנְיָה	יְשַׁעְיָהוּ	יֶשְׁבְּעָם	יָרָבְעָם
כּוֹנַנְיָהוּ	יִשְׁעָם	יִשְׁבְּעָם	יָרֵד
כּוֹרֶשׁ	יִשְׁפָּה	יִשְׁבָּק	יֶרֶד
כּוּשׁ	יִשְׁפָּן	יֶשְׁבְּקָשָׁה	יַרְדֵן
כּוּשִׁי	יָשָׁר	יֵשׁוּ	יַרְדְּנִי
כְּלְאָב	יֶשֶׁר	יֵשׁוּ	יַרְדֵּן־לִי
כָּלֵב	יֶשֶׁר	יָשׁוּב	יְרוּבַּעַל
כְּלוּב	יִשְׂרָאֵל	יִשְׁנָה	יָרוֹחַ
כְּלוּבַי	יִשְׂרָאֵל	יְשׁוֹחָיָה	יְרוּחָם
כְּלוּהוּ	יִשְׂרָאֵלָה	יִשְׁוִי	יָרוֹם

בָּלוּל	לְאוּמִי	לָטִיף	לָקִישׁ
בָּל־חוֹזֶה	לָאוֹר	לִי	לֶשֶׁם
בִּלְיוֹן	לָאוֹר	לִי־אָב	
בָּלִיל	לָאֵל	לִיאָב	מָאוֹר
בַּלִיפָה	לֹא־עַמִי	לִי־אוֹן	מֵאִיר
בִּלְבֹּל	לֵב	לִיאוֹן	מְאִירִי
בִּלָל	לָבִיא	לִי־אוֹר	מָאנִי
בִּמְהָם	לָבָן	לִיאוֹר	מְאַשֵּׁר
בִּמְהָן	לִבְנֶה	לֵיב	מְבוֹרָךְ
בָּמוֹס	לְבָנָה	לִי־הוּא	מְבוֹרָר
בִּנָיָהוּ	לְבָנוֹן	לִיהוּא	מִבְחָר
בִּנְנִי	לִבְנִי	לִי־טוֹב	מִבְטָח
בִּנְנִיָה	לִבְנַת	לִיטוֹב	מִבְטַחְיָה
בִּנְנִיָהוּ	לִבְנָתִי	לִימוֹן	מִבְטַחְיָהוּ
בִּנְעַן	לַהַב	לִי־נִוִי	מִבְנֵי
בִּנְעֲנָה	לַהַד	לִינוִי	מִבְצָר
בִּסְלוֹן	לַהַט	לִי־עַד	מְבֹרָךְ
בְּפִיר	לוֹד	לִיעַד	מִבְשָׂם
בְּרוּב	לוֹד	לִי־עֶזֶר	מְבַשֵּׂר
בַּרְכֹּס	לוּז	לִיעֶזֶר	מְבַשֵּׂר־טוֹב
כֶּרֶם	לוֹחֵשׁ	לִי־רוֹן	מַגְבִּיעָשׁ
בַּרְמִי	לוֹט	לִירוֹן	מַגְבִּישׁ
בַּרְמִיאֵל	לוֹטָם	לִירָז	מֶגֶד
בַּרְמֶל	לוֹטָם	לַיִשׁ	מַגְדִּיאֵל
בַּרְמְלִי	לוֹטָן	לְמוּאֵל	מִגְדָּל
בַּרְמְלִי	לֵוִי	לֶמֶךְ	מָגוֹג
בְּרָן	לוִיטַס	לֶמֶךְ	מַגָּל
כֶּשֶׂד	לִוְיָתָן	לַעְדָּה	מָגֵן
בַּתִּי	לוֹתָם	לַעְדָן	מָגֵן
כֶּתֶר	לַחְמָא	לַפִּיד	מָגֵן־דְּרוֹר
בִּתְרוֹן	לַחְמִי	לַפִּידוֹת	מִדָּן
בַּתְרִיאֵל	לַחַן	לִקְחִי	מָדַי

מַלְכִּי	מַיְמוֹן	מוֹשֵׁעַ	מִדְיָן
מַלְכִּיאֵל	מִנְיָמִין	מֹזֶה	מְהָדָר
מַלְכִּיָּה	מֵירוֹן	מַזָּל	מְהַדֵּר
מַלְכִּיָּהוּ	מֵישָׁא	מַזָּל-טוֹב	מְהֵטַבְאֵל
מַלְכִּיצֶדֶק	מִישָׁאֵל	מְחוּיָאֵל	מָהִיר
מַלְכִּי-רָם	מֵישַׁךְ	מָחוֹל	מְהֻלָּל
מַלְכִּירָם	מֵישָׁע	מְחוֹנָן	מַהֲלַלְאֵל
מַלְכִּישׁוּעַ	מֵישָׁע	מְחוֹגֵן	מֹהַר
מַלְכָּם	מֵישָׁר	מָחִיר	מָהֵר
מְלֵלַי	מִכְבָּד	מַחְלוֹן	מַהֲרִי
מַמְרֵא	מַכְבִּי	מַחְלִי	מַהֲרִי
מָנָה	מַכְבְּנַי	מַחְמוּד	מְהַרְשַׁע
מָנוֹחַ	מְכוּבָּד	מַחְסֶה	מוֹאָב
מְנוּחָה	מָכִי	מַחְסֵיָה	מוֹלָדָה
מְנַחֵם	מָכִיר	מַחַת	מוֹלִיד
מְנַחַת	מִכְלוֹל	מַטִּי	מוּמִי
מָנִי	מִכְלָל	מֵטִיב	מוּסָד
מִנְיוֹמֵי	מִכְמָן	מַטְמוֹן	מוֹעַדְיָה
מִנְיוֹמִי	מַכְנַדְבַּי	מַטְרִי	מוֹצָא
מִנְיָמִין	מִכְרִי	מִיאָשָׁה	מוּקִי
מְנַשֶּׁה	מַלְאָךְ	מֵידָד	מוּקִיר
מְנַשִׁי	מַלְאָכִי	מֵי-זָהָב	מוֹר
מְנַשְׁיָא	מְלַבֵּב	מְיָחָל	מוֹרַג
מַסָּד	מַלְבִּין	מְיֻחָס	מוֹרַג
מִסְפָּר	מַלּוּךְ	מֵיטָב	מוֹרִי
מִסְפֶּרֶת	מַלּוּכִי	מֵיטִיב	מוֹרִיאֵל
מַעֲדַי	מָלוֹן	מִיכָאֵל	מוֹרָן
מַעֲדְיָה	מַלּוֹתִי	מִיכָה	מוֹרֵנוּ
מְעָדָן	מְלַטְיָה	מִיכוֹן	מוֹרָשׁ
מְעוֹדַד	מֵלִיץ	מִיכָיָה	מוֹשִׁי
מָעוֹז	מֶלֶךְ	מִיכָיְהוּ	מוֹשִׁיעַ
מָעוֹזְיָה	מַלְכָּה	מִיכָל	מוֹשֵׁל

נֶאֱדָר	מַשְׂכִּיל	מֵרוֹם	מָעוֹן
נָאָה	מְשֻׁלָּם	מֵרוֹן	מְעוֹנוֹתַי
נָאוָה	מְשֻׁלָּם	מָרוֹן	מַעַזְיָה
נָאוֹר	מִשְׁלֵמוֹת	מֶרִי	מַעַזְיָהוּ
נָאוֹרַאי	מְשֶׁלֶמְיָה	מְרִיב־בַּעַל	מְעַטָּר
נָאוֹרָה	מְשֶׁלֶמְיָהוּ	מִרְיָה	מָעַי
נָאוֹת	מִשְׁמַנָּה	מֵרָיוֹן	מַעְיָן
נֶאֱמָן	מִשְׁמָע	מְרָיוֹת	מַעְיָן
נֶאֱצָל	מִשְׁמָר	מְרֵימָר	מַעֲכָה
נְבוֹ	מִשְׁעָם	מְרֵימוֹת	מַעַץ
נָבוֹן	מַשְׁעֵן	מָרִינוֹס	מַעֲרָב
נָבוֹת	מִשְׁעָן	מִרְמָה	מַעֲשַׂי
נֹבַח	מָתוֹן	מַרְנִין	מַעֲשֵׂיָה
נִבְחָר	מָתוֹק	מַרְפֵּא	מַעֲשֵׂיָהוּ
נָבֵט	מְתוּשָׁאֵל	מֶרֶץ	מְפִיבֹשֶׁת
נְבָיוֹת	מְתוּשֶׁלַח	מְרָרִי	מֻפִּים
נָבָל	מַתַּי	מָרֵשָׁה	מִפְרָח
נֶגֶב	מָתַי	מָשׁ	מִצְהָל
נָגִיב	מַתְיָא	מַשָּׂא	מַצְלִיחַ
נָגִיד	מַתְיָה	מִשְׁאָלִי	מִצְרַיִם
נָדָב	מַתָּן	מִשְׁבָּח	מִקְלוֹת
נְדַבְיָה	מַתָּנָה	מִשְׁבָּח	מִקְנֵיָהוּ
נָדִיב	מַתֶּנָה	משׁה	מַקְסִים
נְדִיבִי	מַתְּנִי	מְשׁוֹכָב	מֹר
נָדִיר	מַתְּנִי	מְשׁוּבָח	מַר
נִדְרִי	מַתַּנְיָה	מְשֻׁלָּם	מֶרַב
נֶהְדָּר	מַתַּנְיָהוּ	מְשׁוֹרֵר	מַרְגּוֹעַ
נָהוֹר	מַתְּנָן	מָשׁוֹשׁ	מַרְגִּיעַ
נָהוּר	מַתָּת	מְשֵׁזַבְאֵל	מֶרֶד
נְהוֹרַאי	מַתָּתָה	מֶשִׁי	מַרְדּוּת
נָהִיר	מַתִּתְיָה	מָשִׁיחַ	מָרְדְּכַי
נוֹגַהּ	מַתִּתְיָהוּ	מֶשֶׁךְ	מָרוֹם

נִצְחַי	נְמוּאֵל	נְחֶמְיָה	נוֹדֵע
נִצְחָן	נָמִיר	נַחְמָן	נוֹחָה
נִצָּן	נִמְלִי	נַחֲמָנִי	נוֹחָם
נֵצֶר	נָמֵר	גֵחָן	נוֹטֵעַ
נַקְדִּימוֹן	נִמְרוֹד	נַחֲרִי	נוֹטֵר
נְקוֹדָא	נֶמֶשׁ	נָחָשׁ	נוִי
נְקָנוֹר	נִמְשִׁי	נַחְשׁוֹן	נוּן
נֵר	נָנוֹד	נַחַת	נוֹעָד
נֵרְד	נַנוֹס	נְטִיעַ	נוֹעַדְיָה
נַרְדִּימוֹן	נַנָס	גֶטַע	נוֹעָז
נֵרִי	נֵס	נִטְרוֹן	נוֹעָם
גֵרְיָה	נְסִי	נַטְרוֹן	נוֹף
גֵרְיָהוּ	נְסִיָה	נַטְרוֹנַאי	נוֹפָר
נֵר-לִי	נְסִים	נִיב	נוֹצָר
נֵרְלִי	נָעוֹם	נִיבֵי	נוֹצֵר
נַרְקִיס	נָעִים	נִיבִי	נוּר
נָשִׂיא	נַעַם	גִילִי	נוּרִי
נֶשֶׁר	נָעַם	נִין	נוּרִיאֵל
נִתַּאי	נֹעַם	נִיסָן	נוּרִיָה
נָתִיב	נַעֲמָן	נִיצָה	נוּרִיָה
נָתָן	נַעֲרִי	נִיצָן	נֹחַ
נְתַן-מֶלֶךְ	נַעֲרִי	נִיקְנוֹר	נַחְבִּי
נְתַנְאֵל	נַעֲרִיָה	נִיר	נַחוּם
נְתַנִיאֵל	נְעַרְיָה	נִירְאֵל	נַחוּם
נְתַנְיָה	נַף	נִירִיאֵל	נְחוּנְיָא
נְתַנְיָהוּ	נֶפֶג	נִירִיָה	נְחוּנְיָה
	נָפִישׁ	נִירִיָה	נָחוֹר
סָבָא	נֹפֶךְ	נִירְעָם	נַחֲלִיאֵל
סַבָּא	נֶפֶשׁ	נִכְבָּד	נַחַם
סַבְיוֹן	נַפְתָּלִי	נֶכֶס	נֶחְמָד
סָבִינְעַם	גֶצַח	נָכוֹן	נַחְמִי
סְבִירָם	נִצְחִי	נִלְבָּב	נַחְמִיאֵל

עֵדוֹ	סָעִיד	סִירְיוֹן	סַבְכַּי
עַדוֹא	סַעַר	סִיסְרָא	סַבְרָה
עַדִי	סַף	סַלָּא	סַגִּי
עַדִּי	סְפֵּי	סֶלֶד	סַגִּיא
עֲדִיאֵל	סֶפִי	סַלּוּ	סָגִּיב
עֲדָיָה	סַפִּיר	סָלוּא	סֶגֶל
עֲדָיָהוּ	סַפְרָא	סַלּוּא	סָדִיר
עֵדֶן	סֹפֶרֶת	סַלַּח	סִדְרָה
עֲדִינָא	סֶרֶד	סַלִּי	סוֹדִי
עֲדִינָה	סָרִיג	סַלַּי	סוּחַ
עֲדִינוֹ	סִתָו	סָלִיל	סוֹטַי
עָדִיף	סִתְרִי	סֶלַע	סוּלִי
עַדְלַי	סִתְרִיאֵל	סָמִיר	סוֹלֵל
עֵדֶן		סְמַכְיָה	סוֹמֵךְ
עֶדֶן	עָב	סְמַכְיָהוּ	סוֹמְכוּס
עֶדֶן	עֶבֶד	סֶמֶל	סוּסִי
עַדְנָא	עַבְדָּא	סַמֶל	סוֹעֵד
עַדְנָה	עַבְדָּאֵל	סָמֶל	סוֹפֵר
עַדְנִי	עַבְדּוֹן	סְמַלְיוֹן	סְחוֹרָה
עֵדֶר	עַבְדִּי	סְנָאָה	סִינָן
עֶדֶר	עַבְדִּיאֵל	סִנְדֶּר	סִיחַ
עֶדְרִי	עֲבַדְיָה	סְנֶה	סִילוֹן
עַדְרִיאֵל	עֲבַדְיָהוּ	סְנֶה	סִימַאי
עוֹבֵד	עֶבֶד־מֶלֶךְ	סֶנֶה	סִימָה
עוֹבֵד	עֶבֶד־נְגוֹ	סְנוּאָה	סִימוֹן
עוֹבֵד־אֱדוֹם	עֵבֶר	סְנַפִּיר	סִימָן־טוֹב
עוֹבַדְיָה	עֶבְרוֹן	סִסְמַי	סִינַי
עוֹבַדְיָהוּ	עִבְרִי	סִסְמַי	סִיסִי
עוּבָל	עֶגְלוֹן	סַעַד	סִיעָה
עוֹג	עֵגֶן	סַעֲדִי	סִירָא
עוֹגֶן	עֲדָאֵל	סְעַדְיָה	סִירָה
עוֹדֵד	עֵרָד	סַעֲדְלִי	סִירְיָה

עַמּוּד	עֵינִי	עָזִי	עוּדִי
עָמוֹס	עֵינָן	עָזִי	עוּז
עָמוֹק	עֵיפָה	עֻזָּא	עֹז
עַמִּי	עֵיפִי	עֲזִיאֵל	עוּזָה
עֲמִיאוֹר	עִיר	עֻזִּיאֵל	עוּזִי
עֲמִיאֵל	עִירָא	עֲזִיָה	עוּזִיָה
עֲמִיאָסָף	עִירָד	עֲזִיָּהוּ	עוֹז־צִיוֹן
עֲמִידוֹר	עִירוּ	עֲזִיז	עוֹזֵר
עֲמִידָן	עִירוֹן	עֲזִיזָא	עוֹזְרִי
עֲמִידָר	עִירִי	עֲזִיאֵל	עוּלָא
עֲמִידְרוֹר	עִירָם	עַזְמָוֶת	עוּלָה
עֲמִיהוֹד	עִירָן	עַזָּן	עוֹמֶר
עֲמִיהוּד	עִירָן	עֹז־צִיוֹן	עוֹנִי
עֲמִיזָבָד	עַכְבּוֹר	עֶזֶר	עוֹפֶר
עֲמִיזַּי	עָכָן	עֵזֶר	עוֹפֶר
עֲמִיחוּר	עָכְרָן	עֶזְרָא	עוּץ
עֲמִיחַי	עֵלָא	עֲזַרְאֵל	עוֹצֶב
עֲמִיחֵן	עֵלָא	עֲזַרְאֵל	עוּקְבָא
עֲמִיטוּב	עֶלְאִי	עֶזְרָה	עוֹרֵב
עֲמִיטַל	עַלְבּוֹן	עֶזְרִי	עוּתַי
עֲמִינָד	עַלְוָה	עֲזַרְיאֵל	עַז
עֲמִינָדָב	עַלְוָן	עֲזַרְיָה	עֹז
עֲמִיעַד	עֶלֶז	עֲזַרְיָהוּ	עָז
עֲמִיעַז	עֲלִי	עֲזַרְיָקָם	עַזָּא
עֲמִיעֶזֶר	עָלִיז	עָטוּר	עֲזַאי
עֲמִיצֶדֶק	עַלְיָן	עָטִיר	עֲזְבּוּק
עֲמִיצוּר	עָלִיס	עֶטֶר	עֲזְגָּד
עֲמִיקָם	עָלִיץ	עֵיבָל	עַזָּה
עֲמִיקַר	עַלֶּמֶת	עִידָן	עֲזוּז
עָמִיר	עֶלֶס	עִילִי	עֲזָז
עֲמִירוֹן	עֶלֶץ	עִילַי	עֲזַוְיָה
עֲמִירָם	עַמְדִיאֵל	עֵילָם	עֲזַוְיָהוּ

עֲמִירָן	עֲנַנְיָה	עַרְמוֹנִי	פֻּנָה
עֲמִירָן	עֹנֶר	עֹרֶן	פּוּט
עֲמִישָׁב	עֲנָת	עֹרֶן	פּוּטִיאֵל
עֲמִישַׁי	עֲנָתוֹתִיָה	עֲשָׂהאֵל	פּוֹטִיפַר
עֲמִישׁוּעַ	עָסִיס	עֵשָׂו	פּוֹטִיפֶרַע
עֲמִישַׁדַּי	עֹפֶר	עָשׂוֹר	פּוּל
עֲמִישָׁלוֹם	עֹפֶר	עָשְׁנָת	פּוּל
עֲמִישָׁר	עָפְרָה	עֲשִׂיאֵל	פּוּרָה
עָמִית	עֶפְרוֹן	עֲשָׂיָה	פּוּרִיאֵל
עָמָל	עָפְרִי	עָשִׁיר	פּוּרָת
עָמָל	עֵצֶב	עֵשֶׂק	פּוּת
עַמְלִי	עֲצְבוֹנִית	עֹשֶׂר	פּוּתַי
עִמָּנוּאֵל	עֶצְיוֹן	עַתַּי	פָּז
עֲמַסְיָה	עֶצְיוֹנִי	עָתִיד	פָּזִי
עֵמֶק	עֹצֶם	עֲתָיָה	פַּטִּישׁ
עֹמֶר	עַצְמוֹן	עָתִיר	פִּיוּט
עַמְרוֹן	עֵץ־שָׁקֵד	עַתְלַי	פִּיכוֹל
עָמְרִי	עֲקַבְאֵל	עֲתַלְיָה	פִּינוֹן
עַמְרָם	עֲקַבְיָא	עָתְנִי	פִּינְחָס
עֲמָשָׂא	עֲקַבְיָה	עֲתְנִיאֵל	פִּיתוֹן
עֲמָשַׂי	עָקוּב	עָתָר	פְּלָא
עֲמַשְׂסִי	עֲקִיבָא	עֲתָר	פְּלָאִי
עָנָב	עֵקֶר		פְּלָאיָה
עַנְבִי	עֶקְרוֹן	פְּגִעִיאֵל	פֶּלֶג
עֲנָבֵּל	עֶקֶשׁ	פְּדַהְאֵל	פֶּלֶד
עַנְבָּר	עֲקַשְׁיָא	פְּדָהצוּר	פְּלָדָשׁ
עָנָה	עֵר	פְּדוֹן	פַּלּוּא
עָנוּב	עַרְבֵּל	פְּדָיָה	פִּלְחָא
עֲנִי	עֲרָד	פְּדָיָהוּ	פֶּלֶט
עֲנָיָה	עֵרִי	פְּדָיוּם	פַּלְטוּי
עָנָן	עֶרֶך	פְּדָת	פַּלְטִי
עֲנָנִי	עַרְמוֹן	פּוּאָה	פַּלְטִי

פַּלְטִיאֵל	פָּרוּחַ	צַדְקִיאֵל	צִיוֹן
פְּלַטְיָה	פֶּרַח	צִדְקִיָה	צִיץ
פְּלָיָה	פִּרְחִי	צִדְקִיָהוּ	צַף
פָּלָל	פְּרַחְיָה	צָהוֹב	צָבָאי
פְּלַלְיָה	פְּרָטָא	צָהַל	צַלְאֵל
פֶּלֶת	פְּרִיאֵל	צַהֲלוֹן	צָלוּל
פְּנוּאֵל	פְּרִידָא	צֹהַר	צָלָח
פִּנְחָס	פְּרִיצָהַר	צוֹבֶבָה	צָלִי
פְּנִיאֵל	פְּרַנְק	צוֹעַר	צָלִיל
פְּנִין	פְּרַנְס	צוּף	צַלְמוֹן
פְּנִינִי	פַּרְעֹש	צוֹפַח	צַלְמֻנָע
פֶּסַח	פַּרְפַּר	צוֹפִי	צֶלֶף
פָּסַח	פֶּרֶץ	צוֹפִי	צְלָפְחָד
פְּסַחְיָא	פֶּרֶש	צוֹפַר	צֵלֶק
פְּסַחְיָה	פֹּרָת	צוּר	צְלָתַי
פִּסְפָּה	פַּשְׁחוּר	צוּרִי	צֶמֶד
פָּסָק	פְּתוּאֵל	צוּרִיאֵל	צֶמַח
פְּעַלְתַי	פְּתַחְיָה	צוּרִיָה	צָמִיר
פַּעֲרַי		צוּרִיָה	צִמְרִי
פַּפָּא	צָאֵל	צוּרִישַׁדַי	צַמֶּרֶת
פַּפוֹס	צֹבֵבָה	צַח	צְפוֹ
פַּפּוֹס	צְבִי	צָחִי	צָפוֹן
פַּפִּי	צְבִיָא	צַחַי	צִפּוֹר
פַּצָאֵל	צְבִיָה	צֶחִי	צְפִי
פֶּקַח	צְבִיאֵל	צַחַר	צְפַי
פְּקַחְיָה	צְבִיאֵלִי	צַחַר	צְפִי
פְּקַחְיָהוּ	צִבְיוֹן	צְחַרְיָה	צִפְיוֹן
פֶּקַע	צְבִילִי	צִי	צְפַנְיָה
פִּרְאָם	צַבָּר	צִיבָא	צְפַנְיָהוּ
פַּרְדֵס	צָדוֹק	צִיחָא	צַפַּר
פֶּרָה	צַדִּיק	צִידוֹן	צַפְרִית
פְּרוֹדָה	צֶדֶק	צֵידָנִי	צַפְרִיר

צַפְרִירִי	קִיבָה	קָרַח	רֶגֶב
צַפְרִית	קִיבִּי	קָרְחָה	רָגִיב
צְרוֹר	קַיָּם	קָרִיב	רֶגֶם
צְרִי	קִימִי	קָרִין	רֶגֶם־מֶלֶךְ
צָרֶת	קַיִן	קֶרֶן	רַדִי
	קֵינָן	קַרְנָא	רְדִיפָה
קְבִי	קִישׁ	קֶרֶן־אוֹר	רוֹאֶה
קָדוֹשׁ	קִישׁוֹן	קַרְנִי	רוֹאִי
קַדִּישׁ	קִישׁוֹנִי	קַרְנִיאֵל	רָוֶה
קֶדֶם	קִישִׁי	קַשְׁתִּי	רוֹזֵן
קַדְמָה	קַל		רוֹם
קַדְמִיאֵל	קָלוֹנִימוּס	רֹאֶה	רוֹמִי
קֵדָר	קָלוֹנִימוּס	רְאוּבֵן	רוֹמֵם
קֹהֶלֶת	קָלִי	רְאוּדוֹר	רוֹמַמְתִּי־עֶזֶר
קְהָת	קְלָיָה	רֹאִי	רוֹן
קוּבָּה	קְלִיטָא	רְאָיָה	רוֹנְאֵל
קוֹבִּי	קַלְמִי	רְאָם	רוֹנִי
קוֹבִי	קַלְמָן	רָאָם	רֹנִי
קוֹהֶלֶת	קְמוּאֵל	רֹאשׁ	רוֹנִיאֵל
קוֹלְיָה	קְמוּי	רִאשׁוֹן	רוֹנְיָה
קוֹלְיָה	קָמוֹם	רַב	רוֹנֵן
קוֹמֵם	קִמְחִי	רָבָא	רוֹנְלִי
קוֹץ	קַנַּאי	רַבָּא	רוֹן־לִי
קוֹרֵא	קְנַז	רַבִּי	רוֹעִי
קוֹרַח	קְנִי	רָבִיב	רוֹתֶם
קוֹרֵן	קְנִי	רָבִיד	רוֹתֵם
קוּשָׁיָהוּ	קְנִיאֵל	רַבִּין	רָז
קוּת	קַפַּאי	רָבִינָא	רָזוֹן
קוּתִּי	קַפְרָא	רָבִיעַ	רָזִי
קוּתִיאֵל	קָצִיר	רַבְלִי	רָזִיאֵל
קְטִינָא	קַרְאֵל	רַבָּן	רְחַבְיָה
קָטָן	קָרֵחַ	רֶבַע	רְחַבְיָהוּ

רְחַבְעָם	רָנִי	שָׁאוּל	שְׁנָא
רְחוֹב	רַגֵּן	שָׁאֵל	שׁוּבָאֵל
רַחוּם	רֶגֶן	שְׁאַלְתִּיאֵל	שׁוֹבָב
רָחוּם	רֵע	שַׁאֲנָן	שׁוֹבַי
רָחוּם	רְעוּ	שְׁאָר־יָשׁוּב	שׁוֹבָל
רְחוּמִי	רְעוּאֵל	שְׁבָא	שׁוֹבָךְ
רַחִים	רֵעִי	שְׁבוּ	שׁוֹבֵק
רַחַם	רֵעִי	שְׁבוּאֵל	שׁוּחַ
רַחֲמִיאֵל	רְעֵלְיָה	שֶׁבַח	שׁוּחַ
רַחֲמִים	רַעַם	שִׁבִי	שׁוּחָה
רַחֲמָן	רַעְמָא	שְׁבֵי	שׁוּחָם
רִיבַּי	רַעְמָה	שְׁבָיָה	שׁוֹטֵר
רֵיחָן	רַעַמְיָה	שְׁבָיָה	שׁוּמָה
רִימוֹן	רַעֲנָן	שָׁבִיט	שׁוֹמֵר
רֶכֶב	רָפָא	שְׁבְנָא	שׁוּנִי
רֶכֶב	רָפָה	שְׁבַנְיָה	שׁוּעַ
רָם	רְפָאֵל	שֶׁבַע	שׁוּעָל
רַמְאוֹן	רָפוּא	שֶׁבֶר	שׁוֹפֵט
רָמוֹן	רֶפַח	שַׁבָּת	שׁוּפָם
רִמּוֹן	רְפִי	שַׁבְּתַאי	שׁוֹפָר
רֶמֶז	רָפִי	שַׁבְּתַי	שׁוֹר
רִמְזִי	רְפָיָה	שַׁבְּתִיאֵל	שׁוּר
רָמִי	רַפְרָם	שָׂגֵא	שׁוּרִי
רָמִי	רָץ	שֶׂגֶב	שַׁוְשָׁא
רָמֵי	רָצוֹן	שָׂגָה	שׁוֹשָׁן
רָמְיָה	רִצְיָא	שָׂגוּב	שׁוּשָׁן
רְמַלְיָה	רְצִין	שַׂגִּיא	שׁוּתֶלַח
רְמַלְיָהוּ	רֶקַח	שַׂגִּיב	שָׁחוֹר
רָן	רֶקֶם	שְׂדֵיאוּר	שַׁחַץ
רֹן	רֶשֶׁף	שַׂדְמוֹן	שַׁחֲפִית
רָנָה	רֹתֶם	שַׂדְמִי	שַׁחַר
רָנוֹן		שֹׁהַם	שְׁחַרְיָה

שַׁחֲרַיִם	שָׁלוּ	שְׁלַתִּיאֵל	שַׂמְלָה
שַׁחַת	שָׁלְוִי	שֵׁם	שִׂמְלָה
שֶׁטַח	שָׁלוֹם	שַׁמָּא	שֶׁמַע
שִׁטְרֵי	שָׁלוֹם	שַׁמַּי	שָׁמָע
שַׁי	שְׁלוֹמִי	שִׁמְאָה	שִׁמְעָא
שִׁיאוֹל	שְׁלוֹמִיאֵל	שְׁמָאֵבֶר	שִׁמְעָה
שִׁיאוֹן	שְׁלוֹמִית	שַׁמְגַּר	שִׁמְעוֹן
שִׁיאֵל	שָׁלוֹן	שֶׁמֶד	שִׁמְעִי
שִׁיזָא	שֶׁלַח	שַׁמָּה	שְׁמַעְיָה
שִׁיזָף	שִׁלְחִי	שָׁמָּה	שְׁמַעְיָהוּ
שִׁיחַ	שַׁל־לִי	שַׂמְהוּת	שֶׁמֶר
שִׁילָא	שְׁלִי	שְׁמוּאֵל	שֹׁמֵר
שִׁילֹה	שִׁלְיָא	שָׁמוּעַ	שֹׁמְרוֹן
שִׁימוֹן	שָׁלֵם	שָׁמוּר	שִׁמְרִי
שִׁימִי	שָׁלֵם	שִׂמְחָה	שִׁמְרִי
שִׁיר	שָׁלֵם	שִׂמְחַאי	שְׁמַרְיָה
שִׁירוֹן	שַׁלְמָא	שִׁמְחוֹן	שְׁמַרְיָהוּ
שִׁירְיָן	שַׁלְמָה	שִׁמְחוֹנִי	שְׁמַרְעָם
שִׁירָן	שְׁלֹמֹה	שָׁמוֹת	שְׁמָרָת
שִׁישָׁא	שַׁלְמוֹן	שֶׁמַח	שֶׁמֶשׁ
שִׁישִׁי	שַׁלְמוֹן	שִׂמְחָה	שִׁמְשׁוֹן
שְׁכָיָה	שַׁלְמוֹנִי	שִׁמְחוֹן	שִׁמְשַׁי
שְׁכֶם	שְׁלָמוֹת	שִׁמְחוֹנִי	שַׁמְשְׁרַי
שֶׁכֶם	שַׁלְמִי	שִׁמְחַי	שַׁנְאַצֶר
שַׁכְנָא	שֶׁלְמִי	שֶׁם־טוֹב	שֶׁנְהָב
שְׁבַנְיָה	שַׁלְמִיָּה	שְׁמִי	שֶׁנְהָר
שְׁבַנְיָהוּ	שְׁלֶמְיָה	שַׁמַּי	שָׁנִי
שֵׂכָר	שְׁלֶמְיָהוּ	שְׁמִידָע	שֵׁנִי
שִׂכְרִי	שַׁלְמָן	שָׁמִיר	שַׁן
שַׁלְדוֹן	שֶׁלֶף	שְׁמִירָמוֹת	שִׁיעָה
שֵׁלָה	שָׁלֹשׁ	שַׂמְלַאי	שַׁעְיָה
שַׁלְהֶב	שְׁלֹשָׁה	שַׂמְלַאי	שֵׂעִיר

שַׁעַף	שָׂרַי	תִּדְהָר	תֵּל
שַׁעַר	שַׂרִיאֵל	תַּדְמוֹר	תֶּלַח
שְׁעַרְיָה	שָׂרִיג	תִּדְעָל	תֵּל-חַי
שְׁעָרִים	שָׂרִיד	תּוּבַל	תֶּלֶם
שָׁפָט	שְׂרָיָה	תּוּבַל-קַיִן	תַּלְמִי
שְׁפַטְיָה	שְׂרָיָה	תּוֹגַרְמָה	תַּלְמַי
שְׁפַטְיָהוּ	שְׂרָיָהוּ	תּוֹדָה	תְּלַת
שִׁפְטָן	שִׁרְיוֹן	תוֹדוֹס	תֹּם
שְׁפוֹ	שִׂרְיָן	תּוֹדוֹס	תָּם
שְׁפוּפָם	שָׂרִיר	תּוֹדְרוּס	תַּמּוּז
שְׁפוּפָן	שְׂרִירָא	תּוֹחַ	תֶּמַח
שְׁפִי	שְׂרָלִי	תּוֹלָע	תָּמָח
שֻׁפִּים	שָׂרָף	תּוֹם	תְּמוּר
שְׁפִיפוֹן	שָׂרָר	תּוֹמֶר	תָּמוּר
שַׁפִּיר	שֶׁרֶשׁ	תּוֹרָן	תָּמִי
שַׁפִּירָא	שַׂר-שָׁלוֹם	תֹּחוּ	תָּמִיר
שְׁפָם	שָׁשׁוֹן	תְּחִינָה	תִּמְנָע
שָׁפָן	שֵׁשִׁי	תַּחְכְּמוֹנִי	תֹּמֶר
שֶׁפַע	שָׁשַׁי	תַּחְלִיפָא	תַּנָּא
שִׁפְעִי	שֵׁשָׁן	תַּחַן	תַּנְחוּם
שֶׁפֶר	שֵׁשַׁךְ	תְּחִנָּה	תַּנְחוּמָא
שִׁפְרוֹן	שָׁשָׁק	תַּחַשׁ	תַּנְחֶמֶת
שַׁפְרִיר	שֵׁשֶׁת	תַּחַת	תַּפּוּחַ
שָׁקֵד	שֵׁת	תִּילוֹן	תִּקְנָה
שִׁקְמוֹן	שָׁתוּל	תֵּימָא	תִּרַדְיוֹן
שָׁקְמוֹן	שָׁתִיל	תִּימוֹר	תֶּרַח
שַׁקְמוֹן	שְׁתִיל	תֵּימָן	תִּרְחֲנָא
שַׂרְאֶצֶר	שֶׁתֶל	תֵּימָנִי	תִּרְיָא
שֶׁרֶבְיָה		תִּימְנִי	תֹּרֶן
שְׁרַגָאִי	תְּאוֹם	תִּירוֹשׁ	תַּרְשִׁישׁ
שָׂרוּג	תָּבוֹר	תִּירְיָא	תִּשְׁבִּי
שָׂרוֹן	תָּגָא	תִּירָס	תֵּשֶׁר
שָׂרוֹנִי	תַּדַאי		

Feminine Names

אוֹרָנָה	אַהֲרוֹנָה	אֲדוֹנִיָּה	אֲבוּקָה
אוֹרְנִי	אַהֲרוֹנִית	אֲדוֹנִית	אַבְטַלְיָה
אוֹרְנִיָּה	אַהֲרֹנָה	אֲדוּקָה	אָבִי
אוֹרְנִינָה	אוֹדֶה	אֲדִיבָה	אֲבִיאֵלָה
אוֹרְנִית	אוֹדָה	אֲדִירָה	אֲבִיבָה
אוֹרְנִית	אוֹדִיָּה	אַרְמָה	אֲבִיבִי
אוּשָׁה	אַוָּה	אִדְרָא	אֲבִיבִיָּה
אוּשָׁרָה	אוֹדֶלְיָה	אִדְרָה	אֲבִיבִית
אוּשָׁרָה	אַוִירִית	אַדְרָה	אֲבִיגְדוֹרָה
אוּשְׁרִיָּה	אוּמָה	אִדְרָה	אֲבִיגִיל
אוּשֶׁרֶת	אוּמְרִית	אִדְרִיָּה	אֲבִיגַל
אַחֲנָה	אוֹנִית	אִדְרִית	אֲבִנָה
אֲחוּזָה	אוֹפִירָה	אַדֶּרֶת	אֲבִיחַיִל
אֲחוּזַת	אוֹפֶר	אַהֲבָה	אֲבִי־חֵן
אֲחֻזַת	אוֹפְנַת	אַהֲבַת	אֲבִיחֵן
אֲחִינֹעַם	אוֹצָרָה	אֹהַד	אֲבִי־יוֹנָה
אֲחִישָׁלוֹם	אוֹרְגְּדָה	אַהֲדָה	אֲבִיטַל
אִידִית	אוֹרָה	אֲהוּבָה	אֲבִימָה
אַיָּה	אוֹרָה־לִי	אֲהוּבִיָּה	אַבִּירָה
אִיזֶבֶל	אוֹרִיאֵלָה	אֲהוּבִיָּה	אַבִּירִי
אַיֶּלָה	אוֹרִינָא	אֲהוּדָה	אֲבִירָמָה
אַיָּלָה	אוֹרִית	אָהֳלָה	אֲבִישַׁג
אִילוֹנָה	אוֹרִית	אֹהֱלָה	אַבְנָה
אִילוֹנָה	אוֹר־לִי	אָהֳלִיאָב	אַבְנִיאֵלָה
אִילָנָה	אוֹרְלִי	אָהֳלִיבָה	אַבְרָהָמִית
אִילָנִית	אוֹרְלִי	אָהֳלִיבָמָה	אַבְרָמִית
אֵילַת	אוֹרְלְיָה	אָהֳלִיָּה	אֲגוּזָה
אַיֶּלֶת	אוֹרְלִית	אָהֳלִית	אַדְנָה

אַיֶּלֶת-הַשַּׁחַר	אֱלִישֶׁבַע	אֶסְתֵּר	אַרְנוֹנִית
אִילִית	אֵלִית	אַסְתֵּרָה	אֹרְנִי
אִילָנִית	אַלֶכְּסַנְדְּרָה	אַסְתֵּרִיָה	אָרְנִינָה
אֶל-עַמָּה	אַלְמָגָה	אֶסְתֵּרְלָה	אַרְנִינָה
אִירָה	אַלְמוּגָה	אַפְנָה	אַרְנִינִית
אִירִיס	אַלְמָנָה	אָפְנִיָה	אָרְנִינִית
אִירִית	אֶלְעַמָה	אָפְנַת	אָרְנִית
אִיתִיָה	אִמָּא	אַפֵּקָה	אֹרְנַת
אֵיתָנָה	אִמָּא-מִרְיָם	אַפְרוֹדִית	אָרְנַת
אַלְדָּמַע	אִמָּא-שָׁלוֹם	אֶפְרָת	אֶרֶץ
אֵלָה	אָמָה	אֶפְרָתָה	אֶשְׁכּוֹלָה
אֲלוּלָה	אָמָה	אֲצִילָה	אֶשְׁכּוֹלִית
אֲלוּמָה	אֱמוּנָה	אַרְאֵלָה	אֶשֶׁלֶת
אַלוֹנָה	אֲמִינָה	אֶרְאֵלָה	אַשְׁנָה
אַלוֹנָה	אֲמִינְתָּה	אַרְבֵּל	אַשְׁרָה
אַלוּפָה	אֲמִיצָה	אַרְבָּעָה	אֲשֵׁרָה
אֶלִי	אֲמִיצִיָה	אַרְדָּה	אַשֵׁרָה
אֱלִיאָבָה	אֲמִירָה	אַרְדּוֹנָה	אֲשְׂרִיאֵלָה
אֱלִיאוֹרָה	אָמִית	אָרוֹנָה	אַשְׂרִיָה
אֶלִיָה	אֲמִיתָה	אֲרוּסָה	אַשְׂרִית
אֶלִיָה	אַמָּנָה	אַרְזָה	אֲשֵׁרִית
אֶלִיָה	אָמְנָה	אַרְזָה	אָשְׂרַת
אֶלִיָה	אֲמַנְיָה	אַרְזִית	אַתִּי
אֱלִימָה	אַמְצָה	אַרִיאֵל	אַתִּי
אֱלִינוֹעַ	אֱמֶת	אֲרִיאֵלָה	אִתִּיאֵל
אֱלִינוֹעַר	אֲנִיָה	אַרִיזָה	אִתִּיָה
אֱלִינַעַר	אָסְפָה	אַרְמוֹנָה	אִתִּיל
אֱלִימוֹר	אַסְיָה	אַרְמוֹנִית	אֶתְנָה
אֱלִיעֶזְרָא	אַסִירָה	אַרְמְנָה	אֶתְרוֹגָה
אֱלִיעֶזְרָה	אַסְנָה	אַרְמְנִית	
אֱלִיעֲנָה	אָסְנַת	אַרְנָה	בְּאֵרָה
אֱלִירָז	אַסְפִּירָה	אַרְנוֹנָה	בְּאֵרִית

בְּכָא	בָּצְרָה	בַּת־גִּיוֹרָא	גַּבִּי
בְּכָה	בִּקְעָה	בַּת־גַּלִים	גַּבִּי
בְּבָּה	בַּקְרָה	בְּתוּאֵל	גְּבִירָה
בְּבְתִי	בָּרָה	בְּתוּלָה	גַּבִּית
בַּהַט	בְּרוּכָה	בַּת־חֵן	גִּבְעָה
בְּהִירָה	בְּרוּכִיָה	בַּתְיָא	גִּבְעוֹלָה
בּוֹנָה	בְּרוּכְיָה	בַּתְיָה	גִּבְעוֹנָה
בּוֹנָה	בְּרוּכַת	בִּתְיָה	גִּבְעוֹנִית
בּוֹנִי	בֵּרוֹנִיקָה	בַּת־יָם	גַּבְרִיאֵלָה
בּוֹסְמַת	בְּרוּרָה	בַּת־כּוֹכָב	גַּבְרִיֵלָה
בּוֹשְׂמֶת	בְּרוּרִיָה	בַּת־כּוֹכְבָא	גַּבַּת
בְּחוּרָה	בְּרוּרִיָה	בְּתִירָא	גָּדָה
בְּחִירָה	בְּרוּרִית	בַּתְלִי	גְּדוּלָה
בִּטְחָה	בְּרוֹשָׁה	בַּת־עָם	גַּדְיאֵל
בִּינָה	בְּרָכָה	בַּת־עַמִי	גַּדְיאֵלָה
בִּירָה	בְּרָכָה	בַּת־צִיוֹן	גַּדְיָה
בִּירְיָה	בַּרְקָאִית	בַּת־שֶׁבַע	גַּדִּית
בִּירָנִית	בָּרְקִית	בַּת־שׁוּעַ	גִּדְעוֹנָה
בֵּית־אֵל	בָּרֶקֶת	בַּת־שַׁחַר	גְּדֵרָה
בִּיתָנְיָה	בָּרָקַת	בַּת־שִׁיר	גוֹאֵלֶת
בְּכוּרָה	בְּשׂוֹרָה	בַּת־שֵׁם	גוֹבֵּר
בְּכוֹרָה	בְּשׂוֹרָה	בַּת־שֶׁמֶשׁ	גוֹזָלָה
בְּכוּרָה	בֹּשֶׂם		גּוֹלְדָה
בְּכוֹרַת	בָּשְׂמָה	גְּאוּלָה	גּוֹלְדָה־מְאִירָה
בְּכִירָה	בָּשְׂמַת	גְּאוֹנָה	גּוֹלְדִי
בִּלְהָה	בַּת	גְּאוֹנִית	גּוֹלָה
בַּלְפוּרָה	בַּת	גְּאִית	גּוֹמֶר
בַּלְפוּרִיָה	בַּת־אֵל	גְּאָלָה	גּוּרִית
בִּנְיָמִינָה	בַּתְאֵל	גְּאַלְיָה	גּוּרְלָה
בְּסוֹדִיָה	בַּתְאֵלָה	גְּאַלְיָה	גִּזָה
בְּעוּלָה	בַּתְאֵלִי	גְּבוֹרָה	גְּזִית
בְּעֵרָא	בַּת־אַרְצִי	גְּבוּרָה	גַּחֲלִילִית

דַּלְגָּנִיָה	דְּגָלָה	גֹּמֶר	גִּיאוֹרָה
דַּלָה	דִּגְלַת	גִּמְרָה	גִּיוֹרָה
דַּלְיָה	דָּגְמַת	גַּנָּה	גִּיוֹרֶת
דֶּלְיָה	דְּגָנָה	גַּנָּה	גִּיזָה
דְּלִילָה	דְּגָנִיָה	גַּנּוֹת	גִּיל
דָּלִית	דְּגַנְיָה	גַּנְיָה	גִּילָה
דֶּלֶת	דְּגָנִית	גַּנִּית	גִּילִי
דְּמוּמִית	דּוּבָּה	גֶּפֶן	גִּילְיָה
דָּנָה	דּוּבֶּת	גַּפְנָה	גִּילִית
דָּנִיאֵלָה	דּוּבָּה	גַּפְנִית	גִּילָנָה
דָּנְיָה	דּוֹדָה	גְּרוֹנָה	גִּילַת
דַּנְיָה	דּוֹדִי	גְּרוּשָׁה	גִּינָה
דָּנִית	דּוּמִיָה	גָּרְנָה	גִּינוֹסָרָה
דָּנִיתָה	דּוּמִית	גַּרְנִית	גִּינַת
דַּסִּי	דּוֹנָה	גֵּרְשׁוֹנָה	גִּיתָּה
דֵּעָה	דּוֹנְיָה	גַּת	גִּיתִּית
דְּעוּאֵלָה	דּוֹר	גִּתָּה	גַּל
דַּעַת	דּוֹרוֹנָה	גִּתִּית	גַּלָה
דַּפְנָה	דּוֹרוֹנִית		גָּלוּתָה
דַּפְנִית	דּוֹרִיָה	דָּאָה	גַּלִי
דְּקֵלָה	דּוֹרְיָה	דָּבָּה	גַּלְיָה
דְּקֵלִית	דִּיבוֹנָה	דְּבוֹרָה	גַּלְיָה
דַּר	דִּידְיָה	דְּבוֹרִית	גָּלִילָה
דָּרוֹמָה	דַּיָה	דְּבוֹרָנִית	גָּלִילָה
דְּרוֹמִית	דִּימוֹנָה	דָּבִיר	גְּלִילְיָה
דָּרוֹנָה	דַּיָנָה	דְּבִירָה	גַּלִינָה
דָּרוֹנִית	דִּינָה	דָּבְלָה	גַּלִית
דְּרוֹר	דִּינְיָה	דִּבְלָתָה	גְּלַלְיָה
דְּרוֹרָה	דִּינָר	דָּבְרַת	גִּלְעָדָה
דְּרוֹרְיָה	דִּיפַת	דְּבָשׁ	גְּמוּלָה
דְּרוֹרִיָה	דִּיצָה	דְּבָשָׁה	גַּמְלִיאֵלָה
דְּרוֹרִית	דִּיקְלָה	דְּגוּלָה	גַּמְלִיאֵלִית

זִמְרָה	זוֹהַר	הֶרְצֵלִיָּה	דַּרְלִי
זִמְרִיָה	זוֹהֲרָה	הֲרָרִית	דָּתִי
זִמְרַת	זוֹהֶרֶת		דַּתִּיאֵלָה
זְעֵירָא	זוּטִית	וֶרֶד	דַּתִּיָה
זְעֵירָה	זוֹנְיָה	וַרְדָּה	דָּתִית
זְפִירָה	זוֹנָה	וַרְדִּיָה	
זִפְרָה	זוֹרַחַת	וַרְדִּינָה	הָגָר
זִפְרוֹנָה	זָזָה	וַרְדִּית	הֵדָה
זְקוּפָה	זִינָה	נַשְׁתִּי	הַדּוּרָה
זְקִיפָה	זִיוִית		הֶדְיָה
זְקֵנָה	זִיוָנִית	זְאֵבָה	הֶדְיָה
זָרָה	זִיזָה	זְכוּדָה	הֶדְיָה
זְרוּבָּבְלָה	זִיזִי	זְכוּלָה	הֲדַס
זְרוּעָה	זִיכְרוֹנִי	זְבִידָה	הֲדַסָּה
זְרִיזָה	זִינָה	זָהָבָה	הָדָר
זָרִיזָה	זִיע	זְהָבָה	הֲדָרָה
זַרְעִית	זִירָה	זָהֲבִי	הֲדָרִית
	זַיִת	זֶהָבִי	הוֹדִיָּה
חִבָּה	זַיִת	זְהָבִית	הוֹרִיָּה
חֲבוּבָה	זֵיתָה	זְהָבִית	הִילָה
חֲבוּקָה	זֵיתָנָה	זְהוּבָה	הִילִי
חֲבִיבָה	זַכָּה	זְהוּבִית	הֵלָה
חֲבַצֶּלֶת	זַכּוּת	זְהוּבִית	הֵלִית
חֲבַצְנָנָה	זַכִּיָה	זְהוֹרִית	הֵלֵלָה
חֲבַצֶּלֶת־הַשָּׁרוֹן	זַכִּית	זְהִירָה	הֵלֵלָה
חִבַּת־צִיּוֹן	זִכְרוֹנָה	זֹהַר	הֵלְנָה
חֲגִיגָה	זִכְרוֹנִי	זָהֲרָה	הֵנוּמָה
חַגִּיָה	זִכְרִיָּה	זָהֲרָה	הַנָּצָה
חַגִּית	זִכְרִינִי	זָהֲרִי	הַצְלָחָה
חֲגָלָה	זִלְפָּה	זְהָרִי	הַרְאֵלָה
חֶדְוָה	זְמוֹרָה	זַהֲרִירָה	הַרְדַּפְנָה
חֲדוּשָׁה	זְמִירָה	זָהֲרִית	הֵרְצֵלָה

טַל	חַסְנָא	חֶלְמוֹנִית	חֲדָשָׁה
טַל־אוֹר	חַסְנָה	חֶלְמִית	חַנָּה
טַלְאוֹר	חֶפְצִי	חֶלְקַת	חוֹחִית
טַל־אוֹרָה	חֶפְצִי־בָּה	חֶמְדָה	חוּלְדָה
טַלְאוֹרָה	חֶפְצִיבָּה	חֶמְדַת	חוּלָה
טְלִי	חֶפְצִיָה	חֶמְדִיָה	חוּמָה
טַלִי	חָפְשִׁיָה	חָמָה	חוּמִי
טַלְיָא	חֲצרוֹנָה	חֲמוּדָה	חוּמִית
טַלְיָה	חֲרוּצָה	חֲמוּטַל	חוֹסָה
טַלִילָה	חֵרוּת	חֲמִיטַל	חוֹפְשִׁית
טַלִיתָה	חֵרוּתָה	חֲמָמָה	חוּשִׁים
טָלַל	חֲרִיצָה	חֶמְלָה	חוּרְשִׁית
טַל־לִי	חֶרְמוֹנָה	חֲמָנְיָה	חֲזוֹנָה
טַלְלִי	חַרְצִית	חֵן	חִזְקִית
טְלָלִית	חֲשׁוּבָה	חַנָּה	חִטָּא
טַלְמוֹנָה	חַשְׁמוֹנָה	חַנָּה	חִטָּה
טַלְמוֹנִית	חַשְׁמוֹנִית	חֲנוּכָּה	חַיָּה
טַלְמוֹר		חֲנוּנָה	חִיוּת
טְמִירָה	טָבְאֵלָה	חָנִי	חִיוּתָא
טְעִימָה	טְבִיתָא	חַנְיָה	חִיוּתָה
טִבְעוֹנָה	טִבְעוֹנָה	חַגְיָה	חַיֵּי־שָׂרָה
טָפַת	טִבְעוֹנִי	חַגְיָה	חַיִּימָה
טָרָה	טְהוֹרָה	חֲנִינָא	חִילָה
טְרוּדָה	טוֹבָה	חֲנִית	חֵיפָה
טָרִי	טוֹבִית	חֲנִית	חַיָתִי
טְרִיָה	טוֹבִית	חֲנִיתָא	חֲכִילָה
	טוֹבַת	חֲנִיתָה	חָכְמָה
יָאָה	טִיבָה	חֲנִית	חָכְמַת
יְאוֹרָה	טִילָה	חֲסוּדָה	חֶלְאָה
יָאִירָה	טִילִיָה	חֲסִידָה	חֶלְדָה
יְאִירָה	טִירָה	חַסְיָה	חֲלוּצָה
יַבְנְאֵלָה	טִירִי	חֲסִינָה	חֲלִי־לָה

יִשְׁעָה	יַעֲרָה	יוֹנָתִי	יְגַאֵלָה
יִשְׂרָאֵלָה	יַעְרָה	יוֹסִיפָה	יְגָאֵלָה
יִשְׂרָאֵלָה	יַעְרִי	יוֹסִיפִיָה	יְגָאֵלָה
יִשְׂרְאֵלִית	יַעֲרִית	יוֹסֵפָה	יְדִידְאֵלָה
יִשְׂרְאֵלִית	יָפָה	יוֹסִיפֶנָה	יְדִידָה
יִשְׂרָה	יְפֵהְפִיָה	יִזְרְעָאלָה	יְדִידְיָה
יִשְׂרַת	יָפוּ	יְחֶזְקֵאלָה	יָהָבָה
יִתְרָה	יָפִית	יְחִיאֵלָה	יְהָבָה
	יִפְעָה	יָטְבָה	יְהוּדִית
כְּבוּדָה	יִפְעַת	יָטְבַת	יְהוֹעָדֶן
כַּבִּירָה	יִצְחָקָה	יָטְבָתָה	יְהוֹשֶׁבַע
כַּדְיָה	יִקְהָת	יַלְתָּא	יְהוֹשַׁבְעַת
כַּדְיָה	יַקִּנְתּוֹן	יָמָה	יָהֵל
כּוֹכָבָה	יַקִּירָה	יְמוּאֵלָה	יָהֲלָה
כּוֹכָבִית	יְקָרָה	יְמִימָה	יַהֲלוֹמָה
כּוֹכֶבֶת	יִקְרַת	יְמִינָה	יַהֲלוֹמִית
כָּזְבִּי	יַרְדֵן	יָמִית	יָהֲלִי
כְּלוּלָה	יַרְדֵנָה	יִמְנָה	יַהֲלַי
כְּלִילָה	יַרְדְנִיָה	יָנוֹחָה	יוֹאֵלָה
כְּלִילַת	יְרוּחָמָה	יִסְכָּה	יוֹאֵלִית
כַּלָּנִית	יָרוֹנָה	יַסְמִין	יוֹבְלָה
כַּנָּה	יְרוּשָׁא	יַסְמִינָה	יוּדִי
כַּנְּרָה	יְרוּשָׁה	יְנִיקָה	יוֹדְפַת
כַּנָּרִית	יְרוּשָׁלַיִם	יָעֵל	יוֹחָנָה
כַּנֶּרֶת	יְרִיעוֹת	יַעֲלָה	יוֹחָנִי
כַּסְפִּית	יַרְקוֹנָה	יַעֲלָה	יוֹכֶבֶד
כְּפִירָה	יִשְׁוָה	יַעֲלָה	יוֹנָה
כֶּרֶם	יְשׁוּעָה	יַעֲלִית	יוֹנִינָה
כַּרְמָה	יְשִׁיבָה	יַעֲלִית	יוֹנִית
כַּרְמִיאֵלָה	יְשִׁישָׁה	יָעֵן	יוֹנִיתָה
כַּרְמִיָה	יִשְׁנָה	יַעֲנִית	יוֹנַת
כַּרְמִיל	יֶשַׁע	יַעֲקֹבָה	יוֹנָתָה

מְהִירָה	לִינוּר	לֵוִיָה	כַּרְמִית
מַהִירָה	לִינִית	לֵוִיָה	כַּרְמֶל
מוֹלָדָה	לִיעַד	לַחַן	כַּרְמֶלָה
מוֹלֶדֶת	לִיפַז	לָטִיפָה	כַּרְמְלִי
מוֹלֶכֶת	לִירוֹן	לוּלְבָה	כַּרְמְלִי
מוֹפַעַת	לִירוֹנָה	לִי	כַּרְמֶלִית
מוֹר	לִירָז	לִי-אוֹר	כַּרְמָנְיָה
מוֹרַג	לִירִית	לִיאוֹר	כִּתְרָא
מוֹרַגָּה	לִירָן	לִי-אוֹרָה	כִּתְרָה
מוֹרָגָּה	לַיְשׁ	לִיאוֹרָה	כִּתְרוֹן
מוֹרִיאֵל	לִיתָג	לִיאוֹרִית	כַּתְרִיאֵל
מוֹרִיָה	לָלִיב	לִי-אַת	כִּתְרִית
מוֹרִית		לִיאַת	
מוֹרָן	מְאוֹנָה	לִידוֹן	לֵאָה
מוֹרָשָׁה	מְאוֹרָה	לִי-דְרוֹר	לְאוּמָה
מוּשִׁית	מְאוּרֶשֶׁת	לִידְרוֹר	לְאוּמִי
מוּשִׁית	מְאִירָה	לִי-הִיא	לְאָמָה
מוֹשָׁעָה	מֵאִירָה	לִיהִיא	לֹא-רֻחָמָה
מַזְהִירָה	מְאִירִי	לִיָה	לִבָּה
מַזָל	מְאִירִית	לִי-טַל	לְבוֹנָה
מַזָלָה	מְבוֹרֶכֶת	לִיטַל	לִבִּי
מַזָלִית	מִבְטַחְיָה	לִילָה	לָבִיא
מְחוֹלָה	מִבְטַחַת	לַיְלָה	לְבִיאָה
מַחְלָה	מְבֹרֶכֶת	לִילוּ	לְבִיבָה
מַחֲלַת	מְבַשֶּׂרֶת	לִי-לוּ	לִבְנָה
מַטְמוֹנָה	מִגְדָּה	לֵילִי	לִבְנִי
מַטְעַמָה	מִגְדָּלָה	לִילִית	לִבְנַת
מַטְרוֹנָה	מִגְדָּנָה	לִילֶךְ	לִבְנַת
מַטְרִי	מָגִינָה	לִימוֹר	לִבְנַת
מִיָה	מָגְנָה	לִימוּר	לְבָתִי
מִיָה	מָגְנָה	לִינָה	לוּזָה
מְיוּחֶלֶת	מְדִינָה	לִינוּ	לֵוִיָה

מַשְׂכִּילָה	מַקְסִימָה	מַלְקוֹשָׁה	מֵיטַל
מַשְׂכִּית	מֹר	מַנְגִּינָה	מִיטַל
מְשֻׁלֶּמֶת	מֵרַב	מַנְגְּנָה	מִיטַלְיָה
מְשֻׁלֶּמֶת	מַרְגִּית	מַנְגֶּנָה	מִיכָאֵל
מִשְׁמֶרֶת	מַרְגָּלִית	מָנָה	מִיכָאֵלָה
מַשְׂאֵנָה	מַרְגָּלִיתָה	מְנוּחָה	מִיכָה
מְתוּקָה	מַרְגָּנִית	מְנוֹרָה	מִיכָיָהוּ
מַתְכֹּנֶת	מַרְגָּנִיתָה	מִנְחָה	מִיכַל
מַתָּנָה	מַרְגֵּעָה	מָנַחַת	מִיכַלָה
מִתְעַלָה	מַרְדוּת	מְנַחֵמָה	מִילְכָּה
מַתָּת	מָרָה	מְנַחֶמְיָה	מֵילֶת
מַתָּתָה	מְרוֹמָה	מַסָּדָה	מִים
	מְרוֹנָה	מַסְיָה	מִימִי
נָאָה	מְרוֹנָה	מַסְעוֹדָה	מֵיפַעַת
נֶאֱדָרָה	מֶרְחָבָה	מְעוּזָה	מֵירוֹנָה
נֶאֱדֶרֶת	מֶרְחַבְיָה	מְעוֹנָה	מִירִי
נָאנָה	מֶרִי	מַעְיָן	מִירִית
נָאוִית	מָרִי	מַעֲיָן	מַכְּבִּית
נְאוֹרָה	מִרְיָם	מַעֲיָנָה	מִכְבָּדָה
נָאוֹת	מְרִימָה	מַעֲכָה	מְכוּבָּדָה
נְאִירָה	מָרִית	מַעֲנִית	מְכוֹרָה
נֶאֱמָנָה	מָרִיַת	מֶפַעַת	מַלְאָךְ
נֶאֱמֶנֶת	מַרְנִינָה	מִפְרָחָה	מְלֵאַת
נֶאֱצָלָה	מִרְצָה	מִפְרַחַת	מַלְבֶּבֶת
נֶאֱצֶלֶת	מָרְתָה	מִצְדָה	מַלְבִּינָה
נְבוֹנָה	מִשְׁאָלָה	מִצְהָלָה	מַלְיָה
נִבְחָרָה	מַשְׂאֵת	מַצְהֶלֶת	מְלִיצָה
נִבְחֶרֶת	מִשְׁבָּחָה	מִצוּדָה	מַלְכָּה
נֶבֶט	מְשֻׁבַּחַת	מַצִּילָה	מִלְכָּה
נְבִיאָה	מַשׂוֹאָה	מַצְלִיחָה	מַלְכִּיאֵל
נֶגְבָּה	מְשׁוֹרֶרֶת	מִצְפָּה	מַלְכִּיָה
נֹגַה	מַשְׂכִּיָה	מַקֵּדָה	מַלְכִּית

נְעִימָה	נֶטַע	נוֹעַ	נְגוֹהָה
נֹעַם	נֶטְעִי	נוֹעֲדָה	נָגִידָה
נַעֲמָה	נִטְעָה	נוֹעָה	נְגִידָה
נָעֳמִי	נִיבָה	נוֹעֶזָה	נְגִיהָה
נַעֲמִיָה	נִיגָה	נוֹפִיָה	נְגִינָה
נָעֳמִית	נִיטַע	נוֹפִיָה	גְדְבָה
נַעֲמָנָה	נִילִי	נוֹפֶר	נְדְבִיָה
נַעֲרָה	נִילִית	נוֹפְרִית	נַדְיָה
נַפְשִׁיָה	נִימָה	נוֹצֶרֶת	נַדִין
נַפְתָּלָה	נִינָה	נוֹרָא	נְדִירָה
נַפְתַּלְיָה	נִיסָנָה	נוּרִיאֵלָה	נֶדֶן
נִצָה	נִיסָנִית	נוּרָה	נְדָרָה
נִצְחָה	נִיצָה	נוּרִיָה	נֶהְדָרָה
נִצְחוֹנָה	נִיצָנָה	נוּרִיָה	נֶהְדָרָה
נִצְחִיָה	נִיצָנִית	נוּרִית	נְהוֹרָא
נִצְחִית	נִירְאֵל	נוּרִיתָה	נְהוֹרָה
נִצָּנָה	נִירָה	גְזִירָה	נְהוֹרָה
נִצָּנִיָה	נִירִיָה	גְזִירִיָה	נְהוֹרִית
נִצָּנִית	נִירִית	גִזְרִיָה	נְהִירָה
נִצָרָה	נְכְבָּדָה	נָחָה	נְהִירָה
גִרְדָה	נְכוֹחָה	נֶחָה	נְהָרָה
נַרְדִי	נְכוֹנָה	נַחוּמָה	נָהָרָה
נֵרְדִי	נִלְבָּבָה	נַחֲלָה	נוֹאִית
נֵרָה	נִלְבֶּבֶת	נַחֲלַת	נוֹגַה
נֵרִיָה	נְמֵרָה	נֶחָמָה	נוֹגַהַת
נֵר-לִי	נִסָה	נַחְמִי	נוֹדַלְיָה
נֵרְלִי	נִסְיָה	נֶחְמָנָה	נָנָה
נִרְצָה	נִסְיָה	נַחֲמָנִיָה	נוֹחָה
נַרְקִיס	נַסְיָה	נַחֲמָנִית	נוֹטֵרָה
נַרְקִיסָה	נְסִיכָה	נְחַשְׁתָּא	נוֹטֶרֶת
נְשִׂיאָה	נֹעָה	נַחַת	נוֹנְיָה
נְשָׁמָה	נְעִילָה	נְטִיעָה	נָוִית

עֲדִית	סַפָּה	סוֹפֶרֶת	נְשֻׁמְיָה
עֶדְנָה	סְפַח	סוֹרֶקָה	נָתִי
עֵדֶר	סַפִּיר	סִיגְלָה	נְתִיבָה
עֶדְרִי	סַפִּירָה	סִיגְלְיָה	נְתִינָה
עוֹגְנִיָה	סַפִּירִית	סִיגְלִית	נְתַנְאֵלָה
עוֹגְנִיָה	סֶרַח	סִידוֹנָה	נְתַנָה
עוֹדְדָה	סָרִינָה	סִידוֹנִיָה	נְתַנְיאֵלָה
עוֹדַדְיָה	סְתָו	סִינָן	נְתַנְיָה
עוֹדְרָה	סְתָוִי	סִינָנָה	נָתַנְיָה
עוֹזֵבָה	סְתָוִית	סִילוֹנָה	
עוּזִיאֵלָה	סְתוּרָה	סִילוֹנִית	סַבְיוֹן
עוֹזֶרָה	סִתְרִיָה	סִימוֹנָה	סַבְיוֹנָה
עוּלָא		סֶלָה	סְבִירָה
עוֹלָה	עִבְרוֹנָה	סַלְחָה	סַבְלָנוּת
עוֹמֵר	עִבְרִיָה	סַלְחָן	סַבְרָה
עוֹמְרִית	עִבְרִית	סְלִילָה	סַבְתָּא
עוֹפְרָה	עִבְרִיתָה	סֶלַע	סַבְתָּה
עוּפָרָה	עַבְרוֹנָה	סְלָעוֹת	סְגוּלָה
עוֹפֶרֶת	עֲגוּנָה	סַלְעִית	סְגוּרָה
עוֹפְרִית	עֲגֻלָה	סְמָדַר	סַגִּיבָה
עוֹפֶרֶת	עֲגֻלָה	סְמִירָה	סְגָל
עֹז	עֲדָאֵל	סִינַאיָה	סְגֻלָה
עַזָה	עָדָה	סְנָאִית	סְגֻלָה
עַזָה	עֲדִי	סַנָה	סְגֻלְיָה
עֲזוּבָה	עֲדִיאֵל	סְנוּנִית	סְגָלְיָה
עֲזִיאֵלָה	עֲדִיאֵלָה	סִינָנְיָה	סְגֻלִית
עֲזִיאֵלָה	עֲדִיָה	סֻנְסַנָה	סְדִירָה
עֲזִיזָה	עֲדִיָה	סַסְגוֹנָא	סְדָרָה
עֲזִיעַז	עֲדִיָּה	סַסְגּוֹנִי	סְדְרָה
עֶזְרָא	עֲדִינָה	סַסְגוֹנִית	סַהֲרָא
עֶזְרָאֵלָה	עֲדִיפָה	סָעֲדָה	סַהֲרָה
עֶזְרָאֵלָה	עֲדִית	סְעוּדָה	סוֹפִיָה

עֲשׂוּרָה	עֲנוּבָה	עָלִית	עֶזְרָה
עֲשִׂירָה	עֲנוּגָה	עֲלִיתָא	עֶזְרִיאֵלָה
עֶשְׂרוֹנִית	עֲנָנָה	עַלְמָה	עַזְרִיאֵלָה
עֶשְׂרַנִית	עֲנוּלָה	עַלֶמֶת	עֲטוּרָה
עֲתִידָה	עֲנוּפָה	עֶלְסָה	עֲטִיָה
עֲתָיָה	עֲנִינָא	עֶלְצָה	עֲטִירָה
עֲתִירָה	עֲנֵינָא	עֲמוּמָה	עֲטָרָה
עָתְנָה	עֲנָפָה	עַמִי	עֲטֶרֶת
עֲתַלְיָה	עֲנָת	עַמִּי	עֵיבָל
עַתְלִית	עֲסִיסָה	עַמִיאוֹר	עִידִית
עֲטָרָה	עֲסִיסְיָה	עַמִיאֵלָה	עַיָה
עֲטֶרֶת	עָפָה	עֲמִידָה	עֲיָנָה
	עָפְרָה	עֲמִיָה	עִילִית
פְּאֵרָה	עָפְרָה	עֲמִיָה	עֵינִיָה
פְּאֵר־לִי	עֶפְרוֹנָה	עֲמִילָה	עֵינַת
פְּאֶרְלִי	עָפְרִית	עֲמִירָה	עֵיפָה
פְּדוּיָה	עָפְרַת	עָמִית	עִירָא
פְּדוּת	עֶצְיוֹנָה	עֲמִיתָא	עִירִית
פּוּדָה	עָצְמָה	עָמָל	עַבְסָה
פּוּעָה	עַצְמוֹנָה	עֲמֵלָה	עָלָה
פּוֹרַחַת	עַצְמוֹנִי	עֲמֵלָה	עֻלָה
פּוּרִיאֵל	עֲרָבָה	עֲמַלְיָה	עַלְוָה
פּוּרִיָה	עֲרָבָה	עִמְנוּאֵלָה	עֲלוּמָה
פּוֹרָת	עֶרְגָה	עֹמֶר	עֲלוּמִית
פָּז	עֵרָה	עָמְרָה	עֶלְוָה
פַּזָה	עַרְמוֹנָה	עָמְרִי	עֲלִיָה
פַּזְיָה	עַרְמוֹנִית	עָמְרִית	עֲלִיזָה
פַּזְיָה	עֶרְנָה	עֵנָב	עֲלִינָא
פַּזִית	עֶרְנוּת	עֵנָב	עֲלִינָה
פִּטְדָה	עֶרְנִית	עֲנָבָה	עֲלִיסָה
פִּיָה	עָרְפָּה	עֲנָבֵל	עֲלִיתָה
פִּיּוּטָה	עֲשָׂהאֵלָה	עֲנֻגָה	עֲלִיצָה

קֶדְמָה	צְמִיחָה	צֶהֱלָה	פִּירְחָתָ
קַדְמִיאֵלָה	צֶמֶרֶת	צְהוּבָה	פִּירְחִיָּה
קוֹלִיָּה	צְעָדָה	צוּבָה	פִּיתָּה
קוֹרָנִית	צְעִירָה	צוּפִי	פְּלָאִי
קוֹרֶנֶת	צָפוֹנָה	צוּפִיָּה	פְּלָאִית
קְטוּרָה	צָפוֹר	צוּפִית	פְּלִיאָה
קְטִינָא	צִפּוֹרָה	צוּקִית	פְּנוּוָּה
קְטִינָה	צִפּוֹרִי	צוּר־אֵל	פְּנִינָה
קְטִיפָה	צִפּוֹרִית	צוּרִיָּה	פְּנִינָה
קְטַנָּה	צִפֹּרֶן	צוּרִית	פְּנִינִיָה
קְטַנְיָה	צִפֹּרֶת	צֶחָה	פְּנִינִיוֹת
קְטַנְיָה	צִפִּי	צְחוֹרָה	פַּסְיָה
קָמָה	צִפִּיָּה	צְחוֹרִית	פְּעוּטָה
קַנִיאֵלָה	צְפִירָה	צְחִירָה	פְּעִילָה
קָנִית	צָפְנַת	צַחִית	פֶּרַח
קֶסֶם	צַפְרָא	צֵידָנִית	פִּרְחָה
קֵסָרִית	צַפְרָה	צִידוֹנִיָּה	פִּרְחִיָּה
קְצִיָּה	צִפְרָה	צִיּוֹנָה	פִּרְחִית
קְצִיעָה	צִפרוֹנָה	צִיּוֹנִית	פְּרִי
קְרִיָּה	צִפְרִיָּה	צִיּוּרִי	פֶּרִי
קָרִין	צַפְרִירָה	צִילָה	פְּרִיחָה
קֶרֶן	צַפְרִירִית	צִילִי	פְּרִי־לִי
קֶרֶן־אוֹר	צִפָּרְתָּא	צִינָה	פְּרִילִי
קֶרֶן־הַפוּךְ	צִפָּרְתָּה	צְלָה	
קַרְנָא	צָרָה	צְלָחָה	צְאֵלִית
קַרְנָה	צְרוּיָה	צְלִי	צְבִיאֵלָה
קַרְנִי	צְרוּעָה	צְלִיל	צְבִיָּה
קַרְנִיאֵלָה	צְרִילִי	צְלִילָה	צְבִיָּה
קַרְנִיָּה		צְלִילִי	צִבְרָה
קַרְנִי־יָעֵל	קָדָה	צְלִילִית	צַבְרִית
קַרְנִינָה	קְדוֹשָׁה	צְלֶלְפּוֹנִי	צַדִּיקָה
קַרְנִית	קְדִישָׁה	צִמְחוֹנָה	צְדָקָה

רְנַת	רָחֵלִי	רוּמִיָה	קֶרֶת
רְנַתְיָה	רְחֵלִי	רוּמִית	קַשּׁוּבָה
רֶץ	רָחָמָה	רוּמְמָה	קְשִׁישָׁה
רְעוּאֵלָה	רַחְמוֹנָה	רוּמֵמָה	קֶשֶׁת
רְעוּמָה	רַחְמִיאֵלָה	רוּמֶמְיָה	
רַעְיָה	רִיבָּה	רוּמְמִית	רָאָה
רַעֲנַנָּה	רִיבָּה	רוֹן	רְאוּאֵל
רְפָאיָה	רִיבִּי	רוֹנְאֵלָה	רְאוּבֵנָה
רְפָאֵלָה	רֵיחָנָה	רוֹנָה	רְאוּבַת
רְפוּאָה	רִימוֹן	רוֹנִי	רְאוּמָה
רֻפִּי	רִימוֹנָה	רוֹנְגִיָה	רָאוּמִי
רַפְיָה	רִינָה	רוֹנְיָה	רָאֵמָה
רִצְפָּה	רִינַת	רוֹנִית	רְאֵמָה
רְקוּדָה	רִינַתְיָה	רוֹן־לִי	רִאשׁוֹנָה
רִקְמָה	רָמָה	רוֹנְלִי	רִבּוֹנָה
רַקֶּפֶת	רִמּוֹן	רוֹנְלִילִי	רְבִיבָה
רִשְׁפָּה	רָמוֹת	רוֹנֶנָּה	רִבְיָה
רִשְׁפוֹנָה	רְמַזְיָה	רוֹקַחַת	רַבִּיטַל
רֹתֶם	רָמִי	רוּת	רַבִּינָא
רֶתֶם	רְמִיזָה	רוֹתֶם	רְבִינָא
רִתְמָה	רְמַזְיָה	רוֹתֶם	רָבִית
	רָמְזִיָה	רוּתִי	רֶבַע
	רְמִזְיָה	רָז	רִבְקָה
שָׁאֲגָה		רְזִיאֵלָה	רוּחָמָה
שָׁאוּלָה	רִנָּה	רָזְיָה	רְנָנָה
שָׁאוּלִית	רִנָּה	רָזְלִי	רְוִיטַל
שְׁאִיפָה	רָנִי	רְזִינָה	רָוִית
שְׁאָנָה	רַגְיָה	רָזְלִי	רוֹם
שַׁאֲנַנָּה	רְנִינָה	רָחָב	רוּמָה
שְׁאֵרָה	רָנִית	רֶחָה	רוּמָה
שִׁבּוֹלֶת	רָנִיתָה	רָחֵל	רוֹמִיָה
שִׁבְחָה	רְנָנָה	רָחֵלָה	רוֹמִיָה
שְׁבִיבִיָה	רְנָנִית		

שָׂרָאֵלִי	שְׁלָמָה	שַׁחֲרִית	שְׁבִיבִיָה
שַׂרְבִּיטָה	שַׁלְמוֹנָה	שַׁחֲרִיתָה	שִׁבְמָה
שָׂרָה	שְׁלֻמִּית	שַׁחַת	שִׁבֹּלֶת
שָׂרָה	שַׁלְצִיּוֹן	שְׁטָה	שֶׁבַע
שָׂרוֹן	שְׁמוּאֵלָה	שְׁאוֹנָה	שַׂגִּיבָה
שָׂרוֹנָה	שְׁמוּרָה	שֶׁיָּה	שַׂגִּית
שָׂרוֹנִי	שִׂמְחָה	שִׁילֹה	שַׂדְמָה
שָׂרוֹנִית	שְׂמֵחָה	שִׁיר	שַׂדְמִית
שֶׂרַח	שִׂמְחוֹנָה	שִׁירְאֵל	שִׂדְרָה
שָׂרִי	שִׂמְחִית	שִׁירָה	שׁוּלָה
שָׂרִיד	שְׂמִירָה	שִׁירִי	שׁוּלִית
שְׂרִידָה	שְׂמָמִית	שִׁיר-לִי	שׁוּלַמִּית
שַׂרְיָה	שִׁמְעוֹנָה	שִׁירְלִי	שׁוֹמֵרָה
שְׂרִיטָה	שִׁמְעָת	שְׁכִינָה	שׁוֹמְרוֹנָה
שָׂרִית	שִׁמְרָה	שְׁכִינָה	שׁוֹמְרִיָה
שְׂרִיתָה	שִׁמְרִיָה	שְׁלֶבִיָה	שׁוֹמְרִית
שַׂרִינָה	שִׁמְרִית	שְׁלָגָּה	שׁוּנִי
שְׁשׁוֹנָה	שִׁמְרָת	שַׁלְגִּיָה	שׁוּנִית
שְׁתוּלָה	שִׁמְשׁוֹנָה	שַׁלְגִּיָה	שׁוּנַמִּית
שְׁתִיָּה	שְׁנוּנִית	שַׁלְגִּית	שׁוּעַ
שְׁתִילָה	שָׁנִי	שַׁלְהֶבֶת	שׁוּעָא
	שְׁנִירָה	שֶׁלָּנָה	שׁוּעָלָה
תְּאוֹרָה	שַׁפִּירָא	שַׁלְוִיָּה	שׁוּרָה
תָּאִיר	שַׁפִּירָה	שְׁלוֹמָה	שׁוֹרֵקָה
תְּאֵנָה	שִׁפְעָה	שְׁלוֹמִית	שׁוֹשׁ
תְּבוּנָה	שִׁפְרָה	שְׁלוֹם-צִיּוֹן	שׁוֹשָׁן
תְּבוֹרָה	שַׁפְרִירָה	שְׁלוֹמְצִיּוֹן	שׁוֹשַׁנָּה
תַּגָּה	שְׁקֵדָה	שְׁלוֹשָׁה	שׁוֹתֵלָה
תִּגְרָה	שְׁקֵדִיָה	שְׁלִי-יָה	שׁוֹתֶלֶת
תָּהֵל	שְׁקוּפָה	שְׁלִיָּה	שְׁחוֹרָה
תְּהִילָה	שִׁקְמָה	שֶׁל-לִי	שַׁחַף
תְּהִלָּה	שִׁקְמוֹנָה	שֶׁלִּי	שַׁחַר

תִּפְרַחַת	תְּמִירָה	תִּירִי	תּוֹדָה
תִּקְנָה	תִּמְנָה	תְּכוּלָה	תּוֹחֶלֶת
תְּקוּמָה	תִּמְנָע	תְּכוֹנָה	תּוֹמִי
תְּרוּמָה	תָּמָר	תְּכֵלָה	תּוֹמֶר
תְּרוּפָה	תֹּמֶר	תַּלְמָה	תּוֹרָה
תִּרְזָה	תָּמְרָה	תַּלְמוֹר	תּוֹרִי
תִּרְיָה	תְּמָרָה	תַּלְמִית	תּוּשִׁיָה
תִּרְצָה	תְּנוּבָה	תְּלַת	תְּחִיָּה
תַּרְשִׁישָׁה	תָּנִיר	תַּמָּה	תְּחִיָּה־יְהוּדִית
תִּשְׁבָּחָה	תִּפְאָרָה	תְּמוּרָה	תַּחַן
תְּשׁוּבָה	תִּפְאֶרֶת	תְּמוֹרָה	תְּחִנָּה
תְּשׁוּעָה	תַּפּוּחַ	תָּמִי	תִּימוֹרָה
תְּשׁוּרָה	תַּפּוּחָה	תָּמִי	תִּימוּרָה
תֶּשֶׁר	תִּפְלָה	תְּמִימָה	תֵּימָנָה
	תִּפְרָחָה	תָּמִיר	תִּירוֹשׁ

Index of
Transliterated Hebrew Names

Masculine Names

Chadash, 88, 96, 99, 203, 205
Chag, 147, 149, 173
Chaga, 27, 92, 96, 206
Chagai, 28, 35, 48, 51, 66, 110, 147, 173
Chagi, 29, 147, 173
Chagiga, 11, 147, 149
Chagiya, 48
Chaglai, 54
Chai, 29, 113, 117, 160, 161, 201, 224, 227, 239
Chaifa, 17, 85
Chaklai, 20, 51, 58, 84
Chaltzon, 137, 148
Cham, 29, 81, 87
Chamadel, 37, 148, 204
Chamadya, 148
Chamat, 20, 23, 27, 30, 32, 42, 57, 71, 75, 115, 151, 155
Chamdel, 148
Chamdiel, 105
Chamud, 37, 147, 148
Chana, 198
Chanan, 29, 31, 98, 113, 135, 147, 169, 198
Chananel, 147, 157
Chanin, 196
Chanina, 29, 98, 169
Chanoch, 29, 31, 36, 40, 45, 56, 58, 189, 200, 224, 232
Chanun, 147, 149
Chapam, 118
Charsom, 58
Chasdiel, 164
Chashmon, 33, 59, 117
Chashmona'i, 59
Chasid, 148, 164, 209
Chasin, 148
Chason, 28, 148
Chasun, 46, 60, 74, 78, 108
Chatat, 114
Chavakuk, 30, 31, 32, 55, 56, 57, 180, 192, 209
Chavila, 154
Chaviv, 8, 30, 35, 44, 75, 133, 148, 152, 162
Chaviv-Am, 8
Chavivel, 74, 200
Chay'il, 60, 80, 95, 146
Cha'yim, 18, 30, 33, 99, 113, 117, 133, 148, 159, 160, 161, 201, 213, 224, 227, 233, 239
Chazael, 61
Chaza'ya, 199
Chazon, 61
Cheza'ya, 199
Chefetz, 148
Cheletz, 148
Cheldai, 37
Cheled, 37, 129, 156

Chemadya, 37
Chemdan, 37, 63, 141, 148, 190, 204, 212
Chemdiel, 37
Chemdiya, 37
Chemed, 37, 105, 148
Chermon, 30, 138
Cherut, 48, 163
Chetzrai, 57, 75, 82
Chetzron, 7, 57, 58, 61, 82, 88, 171, 213
Chever, 170
Chevron, 170
Chi'el, 8, 30
Chilkiya, 20
Chiram, 30, 218
Chirom, 4, 7, 31, 94, 138, 161, 218
Chisdai, 164
Chiya, 201, 213
Chizki, 29, 45, 57, 148
Chizkiya, 30, 71
Chizkiyahu, 29, 57
Chodesh, 217
Chofni, 32, 65, 82
Chonen, 135, 198
Choni, 30, 31, 98
Chonyo, 135
Choresh, 47, 51, 54, 58, 84
Chosa, 30, 108, 110
Chosen, 148
Chovav, 31, 41, 44, 53, 147, 148, 152
Chovev, 31, 53, 133, 219
Chozai, 199
Chum, 39, 145
Chumi, 29, 36, 39, 145
Chupa, 58, 75
Chupam, 30, 58
Chur, 30,
Churi, 31, 40
Chushiel, 113
Chutzpit, 28, 47

Da'el, 34
Dag, 47
Dagan, 20, 25, 34, 50, 149, 153, 231
Dagul, 153, 154
Dalfon, 20, 23, 28, 32, 35, 42, 50, 57, 60, 71, 75, 80, 85, 115, 118, 141, 155, 209
Dama, 34
Dan, 35, 68, 151, 152, 154
Dani, 68
Daniel, 35, 38, 68, 152
Dar, 35, 192, 193
Darkon, 8, 117
Darom, 35, 152
Daron, 152
Daryavesh, 35
Dashe, 21, 31, 32
Dasheh, 72

Enan, 34, 40, 77, 83, 119, 194, 199
Enosh, 37, 45, 79
Er, 45
Eran, 45
Erel, 45, 160
Erez, 43, 136, 137
Eri, 45, 50, 169
Esau, 26
Esav, 153, 216
Esh, 12
Eshel, 14, 24, 45, 137
Eshkol, 46
Etan, 39, 41, 76, 137, 160
Ethan, 160
Etzer, 91, 157
Etzyoni, 14, 22
Eved, 54, 106, 145, 167
Even, 27, 39, 46, 81, 101, 111, 139, 166, 168, 217
Even-Ezer, 111, 166, 183, 217
Evron, 46, 161
Ezra, 3, 27, 33, 46, 100, 104, 131, 206
Ezrach, 26, 57
Ezri, 47, 131, 206

Gabai, 49
Gacham, 12
Gad, 6, 12, 13, 28, 29, 40, 41, 46, 47, 49, 51, 55, 57, 58, 59, 70, 76, 79, 83, 85, 93, 111, 118, 163, 166, 192, 195
Gadi, 13, 47, 55, 85, 111
Gadiel, 12, 29, 47, 49, 51, 57, 70, 85, 111, 141
Gadol, 191
Gafni, 176, 199
Gai, 34, 49, 52, 53, 56, 70, 84, 116, 150, 154, 169
Gal, 7, 12, 20, 27, 35, 41, 49, 61, 72, 165, 171
Galal, 206
Gali, 7, 20, 32, 49, 61, 72, 84, 172
Galil, 20, 22, 27, 49, 72, 165, 206
Galili, 20, 22
Galmud, 49
Galya, 49, 72
Gamal, 49
Gamliel, 50
Gan, 21, 50, 61, 65, 71, 72, 94, 185, 186
Gani, 49, 50, 61, 65, 71, 72, 94, 165, 175
Ga'on, 198
Garnit, 175
Garon, 50
Gavra, 167
Gavri, 62, 170
Gavriel, 10, 11, 12, 13, 28, 39, 40, 41, 49, 50, 51, 54, 55, 57, 62, 65,

70, 79, 82, 85, 88, 99, 100, 111, 114, 115, 116, 117, 118, 119, 142, 144, 146, 148, 163, 165, 167, 170, 172, 184, 185, 195, 198, 214
Gavrila, 87
Gavora, 116
Gaychazi, 116, 150
Gechazi, 34, 52, 53, 56, 70, 169
Gedalya, 11, 31, 44, 51, 77, 81, 82, 83, 101, 135, 138, 159, 168, 191, 195
Gedalyahu, 51, 77
Gedi, 51
Gedula, 191
Gefanya, 51, 110, 199
Gefen, 36, 51, 110, 176, 199
Gemaryahu, 29
Ge'ora, 52, 53, 169
Gera, 24, 40, 46, 55, 57, 59, 166, 192
Gershom, 45, 51, 117, 118, 140, 170, 189
Gershon, 51, 118, 140, 170, 189
Gershona, 117
Gershur, 78
Geshem, 209
Geva, 52, 60
Gevaram, 54, 62, 148
Gevarya, 12, 28, 51, 54, 57, 65, 70, 105, 111, 117, 148, 150, 161, 166, 203
Gevaryahu, 55, 57, 117, 150
Gever, 10, 13, 41, 51, 57, 62, 116, 148, 167, 169, 170, 184, 231
Gibor, 6, 10, 13, 22, 24, 28, 39, 40, 41, 46, 47, 51, 52, 55, 57, 59, 87, 99, 100, 111, 116, 118, 142, 144, 146, 148, 167, 170, 172, 198
Gidel, 77, 81
Gidon, 12, 28, 29, 40, 46, 52, 55, 70, 75, 79, 83, 93, 113, 149, 166, 168, 182
Gidoni, 12, 52, 58, 65, 70, 113, 168
Gidron, 58, 75, 150
Gil, 65, 113, 139, 164, 167, 179, 197
Gila, 65, 179
Gilad, 52, 76, 165, 167, 172
Giladi, 52
Gilam, 132, 165
Gilan, 139
Gildor, 52
Gili, 52, 164, 170, 179
Gil-Li, 197
Gilon, 139, 144, 184, 186
Gina, 50, 65, 72, 118, 167
Ginat, 24, 50, 51, 53, 54, 58, 65, 165, 173
Gintoi, 61, 65
Ginton, 50, 53, 61, 65, 71, 72, 165, 175, 185, 186
Gi'ora, 53, 70, 117, 118

Katzin, 69
Kavud, 61, 182
Ka'yin, 4, 48
Kedar, 36, 39, 59, 75, 81, 87, 144, 195
Kedem, 5, 7, 10, 42, 69, 91, 106, 210
Kedma, 5, 10, 106, 143, 181, 210
Kefir, 33, 68, 70, 72, 182
Kelaya, 25
Kenan, 4, 48
Kerem, 70, 94, 176, 182
Keren, 70, 146, 182
Kesef, 181
Keter, 71, 73, 183, 188
Kimchi, 82
Kinori, 183
Kish, 11
Kishoni, 11
Kitron, 71, 73, 111, 137, 183, 188, 189
Kochav, 147, 160, 183
Kochva, 160
Kohen, 31, 96
Kohelet, 31
Konanyahu, 45, 150
Konen, 48, 111
Korach, 27, 57
Koresh, 28, 34, 58, 61, 147, 149
Kotz, 114, 182, 183
Kush, 25, 29, 33, 144

Lachma, 125, 209
Lachmi, 125, 209
Lahav, 12
Lapid, 40, 139
Lapidos, 189
Lapidot, 72, 139
Latan, 74
Latif, 145, 186
Lavan, 4, 5, 7, 23, 40, 118, 119, 144, 145, 166, 169, 186, 188, 190, 216
Lavi, 68, 72, 73, 75, 185, 186
Lavon, 56
La'yish, 73, 75, 76, 116, 185, 189
Lechem, 125, 209
Lemu'el, 10
Leshem, 22, 37, 74, 105, 143
Le'umi, 186
Lev, 74
Levana, 186
Levanon, 5, 40, 56, 63, 74, 119
Levi, 31, 74
Likchi, 29, 200
Li-On, 75
Lior, 75, 76, 131, 166, 188, 189, 190
Lipman, 75
Liron, 19, 54, 75, 90, 134, 146, 156, 188, 189, 196
Litor, 24
Livna, 5, 188

Livni, 5, 7, 23, 40, 75, 119, 144, 166, 169
Livyatan, 52, 63, 79, 80, 84, 106, 192, 193
Lot, 74, 76, 98, 108, 117, 171,
Lotan, 11, 57, 69, 75, 76, 117, 150, 197
Luz, 22, 43, 53, 77, 78, 139

Ma'ayan, 40, 61, 85
Ma'arav, 118, 232
Macheseh, 46
Machir, 96
Machseh, 61
Machseya, 11, 61
Madai, 85
Magdiel, 51, 86, 112, 156, 198, 207
Magen, 46, 61, 69, 117, 118, 166, 191, 197
Mahari, 117, 118
Maher, 77, 159
Mahir, 29, 44, 149, 159, 196
Maimon, 77, 163, 232
Makabi, 77, 79, 192, 232
Maksim, 191
Malach, 11, 20, 72, 112, 172
Malachi, 11, 27, 54, 59, 72, 78, 106, 109, 112, 135, 161, 172
Malbin, 56, 78, 119, 191
Malka, 199
Malkam, 28, 70, 71, 78, 100, 111, 164, 194, 199
Malki, 70, 78, 102
Malkiel, 33, 44, 70, 111, 117, 150
Malkiram, 44, 70, 115
Malkitzedek, 44
Malkiya, 111
Malkosh, 209
Malon, 78, 185
Mano'ach, 54, 92
Ma'on, 7, 12, 74, 140
Ma'or, 76, 79, 131
Mara, 97, 197, 200
Marata, 97, 197, 200
Mardut, 197
Margia, 202, 205
Margo'a, 48, 54, 205
Marnin, 132, 164, 170, 172, 179, 194, 197, 200
Marom, 11, 60, 84, 132, 184, 197
Maron, 27, 60, 194
Marpan, 194, 203
Marpay, 133
Marpe, 133
Mashiach, 31, 119
Maskil, 40, 80
Masos, 197
Masya, 197, 202
Matan, 8, 54, 132, 192, 195, 198
Matanya, 54, 81, 114, 192, 198

Feminine Names

Abira, 1, 10, 13, 29, 41, 47, 54, 109, 114, 129, 136, 138, 144, 146, 214, 229
Abiram, 170
Abiri, 1, 114, 129, 229
Achava, 5, 8, 53, 219, 231
Achino'am, 4, 17, 63, 86, 112, 129, 156, 159, 161, 169, 179, 190
Achishalom, 54, 63, 92, 96, 170, 178, 219
Achiya, 16, 18, 117, 159
Achsa, 199
Achuza, 4
Achva, 13, 22
Ada, 2, 98, 143, 219
Adama, 2, 31, 36, 37, 39, 47, 50, 54, 70, 73, 79, 84, 85, 88, 101, 118, 162, 166, 174
Adara, 2, 3, 29, 36, 39, 196, 197
Ada'ya, 2
Aderet, 130
Adi, 2, 130
Adiel, 130
Adiela, 2, 130
Adiella, 2
Adifa, 2, 11
Adina, 2, 3, 4, 5, 17, 20, 40, 42, 63, 98, 129, 130, 141, 155, 157, 161, 179, 198, 199
Adira, 2, 3, 4, 5, 25, 31, 41, 42, 43, 69, 71, 109, 130, 136, 144, 161
Adiva, 2, 16, 32, 130, 151, 157, 159, 179, 196, 198
Adiya, 98, 115, 130
Admon, 219
Adonit, 31, 45, 69, 135, 171
Adoniya, 3, 4, 5, 46, 155, 184
Adra, 59, 149, 173
Adva, 130, 199
Afeka, 3, 20, 23, 24, 25, 27, 30, 32, 42, 57, 60, 71, 75, 76, 83, 85, 99, 100, 115, 119, 150, 155, 214
Afrit, 26
Agala, 118, 130
Aguna, 91
Ahada, 8, 95, 130, 131, 152, 232
Aharona, 4, 7, 12, 20, 21, 24, 27, 29, 32, 35, 48, 61, 84, 90, 97, 108, 110, 131, 135, 136, 156, 172, 194, 198, 214, 217, 227, 229
Aharonit, 131
Ahava, 4, 8, 31, 42, 83, 95, 130, 131, 133, 134, 152, 232

Ahavat, 8, 31, 95, 131
Ahavya, 131
Ahuda, 31, 131, 133, 135, 168
Ahuva, 8, 23, 35, 36, 70, 74, 75, 76, 91, 95, 99, 106, 109, 119, 130, 133, 135, 145, 147, 148, 152, 157, 207, 232
Ahuyiva, 131
Ahuyva, 8, 55
Akuva, 33
Aleksandra, 3, 5, 27, 33, 43, 63, 72, 78, 93, 97, 98, 100, 104, 132, 145, 167
Alisa, 6, 110, 132
Alita, 62, 132
Alitza, 110, 132
Aliya, 42, 61, 132
Aliza, 3, 6, 43, 113, 132, 144, 164, 170, 174, 178, 186, 197, 200, 219
Alma, 26, 31, 133, 136, 150, 153, 167, 172, 175, 180, 190, 191, 195, 227
Almana, 7, 133
Almoga, 3, 7, 102, 219
Almona, 118
Almuga, 22, 24, 25, 118
Alona, 2, 4, 5, 7, 14, 19, 22, 25, 35, 55, 91, 133, 137
Alufa, 5, 7, 11, 33, 34, 39, 41, 44, 49, 56, 59, 70, 133, 171, 217, 223
Aluma, 26, 133, 140, 150, 153
Alumit, 140
Alya, 7
Ama, 54, 72, 78, 93, 94
Amal, 29, 198, 208
Amalya, 29, 44, 82, 88, 133, 134, 198, 208
Amana, 10, 45, 58, 76, 92, 133, 162, 163, 175
Amanya, 10, 58, 92
Amela, 134, 198
Ami, 134
Amida, 122
Amieta, 9
Amila, 134
Amina, 9, 10, 134
Amior, 9, 114, 171
Amiora, 9
Amira, 9, 19, 25, 31, 37, 62, 134, 151, 198, 213
Amit, 5, 8, 9, 13, 22, 43, 53, 80, 219
Amita, 5, 9, 13, 22, 42, 43, 45, 53, 82, 99, 109, 119, 134, 157, 159, 162, 219, 232

Chanina, 16, 29, 149
Chanit, 35, 51, 65, 166
Chanita, 30, 32, 51, 66, 93, 98, 157, 166, 169, 198
Chaniya, 16
Chanuka, 8, 29
Chanukah, 45
Chanuna, 149
Chanya, 16, 169
Charutza, 40, 44, 88, 159, 173, 208
Chasida, 9, 34, 138, 148, 162, 164, 208
Chasina, 30, 47, 114, 116, 146, 148
Chasna, 30, 148
Chasya, 3, 58, 61, 74, 78, 97, 118, 148, 196
Chava, 10, 16, 18, 40, 92, 113, 117, 134, 148, 159, 160, 161, 201, 213, 224, 233, 239
Chaviva, 8, 19, 30, 31, 42, 44, 74, 75, 76, 84, 106, 119, 133, 147, 148, 152, 157, 232
Chavuka, 30
Cha'ya, 8, 10, 16, 18, 29, 30, 40, 46, 92, 99, 113, 117, 148, 159, 160, 201, 213, 224, 233, 239
Cha'yuta, 8, 16, 18
Chazona, 10
Chedva, 60, 113
Chefti-Ba, 37, 148
Chelmit, 29, 32, 185
Chelmonit, 29, 32, 185
Chemda, 37, 148, 166
Chemdat, 37
Chen, 30
Chenya, 16
Chermona, 7, 20, 21, 30, 68, 138
Chermoni, 30
Cherut, 48
Cheruta, 48, 163
Chiba, 8, 31, 36, 70, 74, 95, 130, 131, 133, 134, 145, 148, 152, 207, 232
Chibat-Tziyon, 31
Chila, 57, 58
China, 30
Chinanit, 65
Chinit, 35, 51, 93
Chita, 25, 149, 231
Chiyuta, 8, 92
Chochit, 114
Chochma, 4, 33, 53, 58, 70, 182, 210, 224
Chodesh, 151, 219
Chogla, 50, 162, 197
Chosa, 3, 46, 53, 58, 61, 73, 78, 93, 118, 126, 196, 228
Chufshit, 48, 163
Chum, 39
Chuma, 39, 145
Chumit, 39, 145

Chursha, 185
Churshit, 58, 78, 144

Da'a, 132, 184, 197
Da'at, 4, 16, 189
Dafna, 26, 88, 110, 117, 142, 152, 161, 184, 189, 191, 232
Dafnit, 117, 142, 151
Dagit, 34, 47, 90
Dagiya, 34, 47, 90
Dala, 26, 67, 144, 216
Dalet, 154
Dalgiya, 151
Dalia, 34
Dalit, 85, 151
Daliya, 85
Dalya, 32, 57, 83, 151, 230
Dana, 9, 16, 35, 38, 151
Daniela, 16, 35, 38, 68, 119, 124, 152
Danit, 9, 16, 35, 38, 68, 119, 152
Danita, 16, 152
Daniya, 35
Danya, 16, 68, 124, 152
Danza, 119
Daroma, 152
Darona, 131, 152
Dati, 152
Datiela, 16, 34, 70, 189
Datit, 152
Datya, 152
Davida, 8, 19, 20, 23, 30, 35, 36, 37, 41, 44, 74, 75, 76, 80, 82, 84, 95, 99, 106, 109, 119, 130, 131, 133, 134, 135, 145, 147, 148, 152, 153, 157, 162, 200, 207, 232
Davrat, 20
Day'a, 184
Da'ya, 3, 6, 17, 23, 33, 132, 153, 197
Da'yam, 153
De'a, 4, 16, 34
Degana, 20, 25, 50, 62, 82
Deganit, 20, 25, 34, 50, 153
Deganiya, 34, 82
Deganya, 25, 50, 153, 231
Degula, 11, 34, 37, 89, 90, 93, 153, 204
Delila, 26, 67, 94, 103, 125, 153, 169, 180, 208, 216
Demumit, 117
Deroma, 86, 87
Deromit, 86, 87, 113
Deronit, 114
Derora, 9, 16, 26, 37, 48, 95, 108, 119, 138, 163, 195
Derorit, 9, 16, 37, 48, 95, 163
Deroriya, 9, 16, 37
De'uela, 16, 34, 154
Devasha, 86, 196
Devash, 173
Devira, 11, 12, 37, 40, 42, 51, 54,

Bibliography

Ames, Winthrop. *What Shall We Name the Baby?* New York: Simon & Schuster, 1935.

Bardsley, Charles. *English Surnames*. London: Chatto & Windus, 1884.

––––––. *Curiosities of Puritan Nomenclature*. London: 1897.

––––––. *The Romance of the London Directory*. London: 1879.

Baring, Gould S. *Family Names and Their Story*. London: 1932.

Barr, George. *Who's Who in the Bible*. New York: Jonathan David Publishers, 1975.

Blackie, C. *Dictionary of Place Names*. London: John Murray, 1887.

Bowman, William D. *The Story of Surnames*. London: 1932.

Burnham, S. M. *Our Names*. Boston: A. I. Bradley Co., 1900.

Burton, Dorothy. *A New Treasury of Names for the Baby*. New York: Prentice Hall, 1961.

Brown, Driver & Briggs. *Hebrew and English Lexicon of the Old Testament*. New York: Houghton Mifflin Co., 1907.

Dobrinsky, Herbert C. *A Treasury of Sephardic Laws and Customs*. New York: Ktav/Yeshiva University, 1986.

Edmunds, F. *Traces of History in the Names of Places*. London: Longmans, Green and Co., 1872.

Fisher, Henry W. *Girls' Names*. New York: Fisher's Foreign Letters, Publishers, 1910.

Grussi, A. M. *Chats on Christian Names*. Boston: The Stratford Co. 1925.

Kolatch, Alfred J. *The Complete Dictionary of English and Hebrew First Names*. New York: Jonathan David, 1984.

––––––. *The Name Dictionary*. New York: Jonathan David, 1967.

––––––. *Names for Boys and Girls*. New York: Jonathan David, 1968.

––––––. *Names for Pets*. New York: Jonathan David, 1971.

––––––. *These Are the Names*. New York: Jonathan David, 1948.

––––––. *Who's Who in the Talmud*. New York: Jonathan David, 1964.

Lambert, E., and Pei, M. *Our Names*. New York: Lothrop, 1962.

Latham, Edward. *Dictionary of Names, Nicknames, and Surnames*. London: 1904.

Loughead, F. *Dictionary of Given Names*. Glendale, California: Arthur Clark, 1966.

Moody, Sophy. *What Is Your Name?* London: Richard Bentley, 1863.

Mordacque, L. H. *History of the Names of Men, Nations and Places*. Vol. I (1862), Vol. II (1964). London: John Russel Smith, Publisher.

Palmer, G., and Lloyd, N., *Exploring Names*. London: Oldham Books, 1964.

Sleigh, L., and Johnson, C. *The Book of Boys*. New York: Thomas Y. Crowell, 1962.

_____. *The Book of Girls*. New York: Thomas Y. Crowell, 1962.

Smith, Elsdon. *American Surnames*. New York: Chilton, 1970.

_____. *Naming Your Baby*. New York: Chilton, 1970.

Stewart, George R. *American Place-Names*. New York: Oxford, 1970.

Swan, H. *Girls' Christian Names*. London.

Taggart, Jean. *Pet Names*. New York: Scarecrow Press, 1962.

Wagner, Leopold. *Names and Their Meaning*. London: T. Fisher Unwin, 1893.

_____. *More About Names*. London: T. Fisher Unwin, 1893.

Weekley, Ernest. *Surnames*. London: John Murray, second edition, 1927.

Wells, Evelyn. *What to Name the Baby*. New York: Doubleday, 1946.

_____. *A Treasury of Names*. New York: Duell, Sloan & Pearce, 1946.

Withycombe, E. G. *The Oxford Dictionary of English Christian Names*. New York: Oxford University Press, 1945.

Yonge, Charlotte M. *History of Christian Names*. London: MacMillan (1884).

About the Author

ALFRED J. KOLATCH, a graduate of the Teachers' Institute of Yeshiva University and its College of Liberal Arts, was ordained by the Jewish Theological Seminary of America, which subsequently awarded him the Doctor of Divinity degree, *honoris causa*. From 1941 to 1948 he served as rabbi of congregations in Columbia, South Carolina, and Kew Gardens, New York, and as a chaplain in the United States Army. In 1948 he founded Jonathan David Publishers, of which he has been president and editor-in-chief since its inception.

Among Rabbi Kolatch's published works are the best-selling *Jewish Book of Why* and its sequel, *The Second Jewish Book of Why*. Other popular works include *This Is the Torah, Jewish Information Quiz Book, Who's Who in the Talmud,* and *The Family Seder.*

Several of the author's books deal with nomenclature. These include *These Are the Names, The Name Dictionary,* and *The Complete Dictionary of English and Hebrew First Names.*

In addition to his scholarly work, Rabbi Kolatch is interested in the work of the military chaplaincy and has served as president of the Association of Jewish Chaplains of the Armed Forces and as vice-president of the interdenominational Military Chaplains Association of the United States.